EDUCATION
FOR A
NEW JAPAN

By

ROBERT KING HALL

NEW HAVEN
YALE UNIVERSITY PRESS
LONDON · GEOFFREY CUMBERLEGE · OXFORD UNIVERSITY PRESS
1949

PREFACE

THERE has probably occurred no educational experiment in modern times—with the possible exception of that of the Soviet Union—which is so vast, so important, and so fraught with danger to our civilization as that of the effort to re-educate the Japanese people following the second World War. Justification of the importance of a study such as that attempted in *Education for a New Japan* is therefore clearly unnecessary. But the very vastness, the very complexity, of the problem, together with the consequences which may follow an improper analysis and an unwise policy decision resulting from that analysis, make desirable some description of the materials available, the research techniques used, and the author's adequacy as an observer.

This study was begun in August 1940 during some raids on clandestine propaganda schools in the Japanese colonies in the Alta-Paulista of the state of São Paulo in southern Brazil. It was continued during the period of the author's service in the Navy, first as a student at the Naval School of Military Government and Administration at Columbia University, next as Assistant Academic Director of the Naval School of Military Government at Princeton University, then as Chief of the Education Section of the Planning Staff for the Occupation of Japan at CASA in Monterey, California, and finally as Chief of the Education Sub-Section, Educational Reorganization Officer, and Language Simplification Officer, of CI&E, GHQ, SCAP in the military occupation of Japan until the latter part of 1946. The book was written while the writer was a Guggenheim Fellow in 1947 following his release from active duty in the Navy, at his home in Castine, Maine, and at the School for Asiatic Studies in New York. His projected return to Japan in civilian capacity to check the accuracy of certain portions of the final manuscript was prohibited by the War Department, so that the final preparation of the manuscript had to be made in the United States. This was done in New York while the writer was employed in his regular capacity as a professor of comparative education at Teachers College, Columbia University.

The author is still an officer in the United States Naval Reserve on inactive duty, and although the Department of State, Department of the Army, and Department of the Navy have indicated that they have no objection to the publishing of the material in this study, it may perhaps be well to emphasize that "the opinions expressed herein are those of the author and do not necessarily reflect the views of the Navy Department."

A word should be said about certain passages which may sound rather more than familiar to the reader who has explored the literature on the Japanese Occupation. Rudyard KIPLING in his well-known posthumously published autobiography, *Something of Myself for My Friends Known and Unknown*, tells how he narrowly escaped publishing an original story based on an experience related by a chance acquaintance in Canada, when months later he happened to pick up an ancient magazine in a dentist's office in a little town in New England and found the story in all its detail. Any writer who must base his text upon interviews gathered in a military occupation or taken from the literary and official documents of an Oriental people must count himself fortunate if he does not unknowingly suffer some similar fall from grace. One must check and re-check his work —and after that have faith and take some small comfort from Brander MATTHEWS' famous essay on "The Ethics of Plagiarism" in which he recalls that even "the man who plants cabbages imitates too."

A different sort of danger lurks in the official sources of the Occupation Authorities. Before the Capitulation of Japan the author prepared a draft manuscript of a plan for re-opening the schools in the event they were closed upon invasion. In due course of time the uncontested occupation of Japan took place, the schools which had in fact been closed by the Japanese were re-opened, and on 1 November 1945 the author was instructed to prepare a detailed report on the educational accomplishments of the Occupation—and given 24 hours to complete this rather considerable task. A mere change of tense in the opening page of the draft plan provided a suitable background paragraph to start the report, which became the "7 November 1945 Basic Education Report." Directly or indirectly it has been the basis of all published evaluations of the educational control during the Occupation since that time. It was copied verbatim into the volume *Education in Japan* prepared on 15 February 1946 by the officers of CI&E, GHQ, SCAP to be used in briefing the United States Education Mission to Japan. From there it was quoted without an indication of source by the 3 April 1946 issue of *Maptalk* (Vol. V, No. 20) published in the Pacific. It was, apparently, an expressive and concise statement and next was copied with virtually no change into the first edition of *Documents and State Papers* (Vol. I, No. 1) of the United States Department of State, for April 1948. Back in Tokyo the Education Division of the Headquarters of the Supreme Commander for the Allied Powers wrote it—without quotes—into the text of the two-volume study, *Education in the New Japan*, published May 1948.

Now the use of this quote in the present volume presents a problem. Perhaps one should recall the famous dictum of MOLIÈRE who wrote in 1671, "*Je reprends mon bien où je le trouve*" (I take back my property wherever I find it). Yet it is almost impossible for the original author to re-word the passage sufficiently to conceal his style, and if he simply uses it directly it may easily be mistaken for a deliberate and unprincipled copy of what is assumed to be an original published work of another writer. In the particular instance cited, the author adopted the somewhat tortuous and quixotic expedient of citing not his own original work but the earliest known published copy of his work—the *Maptalk* paragraph of 3 April 1946.

The existence of such known episodes in which official sources have quoted without credit a source which happens to be known leaves one with the rather helpless feeling that there may be many unrecognized quotations of other writers which have crept into the manuscript from undocumented official sources, staff notes, military reports, and staff studies. If any person suspects that he sees in the pages of this work lines which he himself has written, let him be a little charitable to a fellow worker who has struggled with official reports. And to these unknown contributors the author extends his sincerest appreciation and apology.

It will be perfectly obvious to any careful reader that many of the instances reported in the third person are in fact personal experiences of the author. Why was such a cumbersome style and obvious subterfuge adopted? A very large amount of the material used in the preparation of this manuscript was originally classified as Top Secret, Secret, or Confidential. Any document which quotes even a portion of such a classified document takes on the same classification and extends that classification to all the other information, however innocuous, which is included in the quoting or secondary document. It is obvious that such a system—justifiable, perhaps, in war—becomes in time incredibly complicated and in peacetime utterly absurd. A single example will suffice. A staff study on the romanization of the Japanese language was once classified Confidential. A year and a half after Surrender this document was still so classified, even though every point contained within it had been widely discussed in the Japanese newspapers. The process of declassifying material is a very long and complicated one and the Office of the Secretary of Defense finally solved the problem by making a blanket declassification of all materials outside certain proscribed fields, such as atomic energy. In the meantime, however, the author had secured declassification and permission to use certain official materials upon a written promise that his own personal participation would not be revealed. He has never been released from these promises and the style of the present volume is dictated in part by this obligation.

The problem of documentation of material is always troublesome. The most important source of information is, of course, the firsthand evidence of a participant. A major portion of this work is composed of such firsthand evidence. Next to this in importance is the primary evidence of Japanese sources and unpublished official studies, which it was felt did not lend themselves to extensive documentation for an English reading audience. The inclusion of such Japanese documentation would have overemphasized certain parts and produced an unnecessarily unwieldy manuscript. In certain highly technical fields, such as the section on Japanese religious philosophy, a wide use was made of standard secondary sources in Japanese and English. Where such sources were directly quoted, the documentation is given in the body of the text. Where they were merely synthesized into a background pattern or where nonquotable official sources were used, there has been no attempt to provide exhaustive documentation. Such secondary sources were checked with both SCAP staff studies and wherever possible with Japanese primary sources—as, for example, with the religious authorities of the several sects in the case of the philosophies mentioned above. In addition each part which was clearly in the field of a noted Occidental specialist has been referred to such an authority for correction and criticism and a detailed appreciation of the help of these advisers is included in this preface.

A few comments on the styling of the manuscript may be useful. A modified Hepburn System of romanization has been used in presenting Japanese words, with the exception of a few proper names and titles of works written in romanized Japanese, which are given in the Japan System because that form is preferred by the individuals concerned. The Wade-Giles System of romanized Chinese has been adopted, and standard modern Turkish is used. Japanese names are presented in the Japanese order, which generally means with the family name first. As an aid to the reader unfamiliar with the several national practices involved, the name by which an individual would normally be indexed—in most cases the family name—is presented in capital letters, as for example, Itō Hirobumi. Where a family name has been adopted in English as a part of a tied phrase—as in "Tokugawa era," for example—the name is not capitalized. The names of Japanese mythological gods, for example, *Amaterasu Ōmikami*, are presented in italics. Japanese words are given in italics and with the lengthening mark over vowels as in the Modified Hepburn System. Certain Japanese place names that are so familiar to the English reading public that Anglicized forms exist have been presented without italics or the lengthening marks in the Anglicized form—as, for example, in Tokyo, Kyoto, Kobe, Yokohama, Osaka, Hokkaido, and Kyushu. Certain Japanese words whose patriotic, geographical, or religious significance is such that the corresponding word in English would be capitalized—as in *Bushidō*, *Shintō*, and *Shūshin*—are capitalized even though the original Japanese has no such typographical indication. Some words which have come to be current in modern English—like "Shinto" and "Shogun"—are presented interchangeably in their Japanese and their Anglicized forms.

The terms "Defeat," "Surrender," "Occupation," and "Headquarters," where used as proper nouns referring to episodes of the Occupation and the second World War, are capitalized. The names of books, magazines, and newspapers are italicized, and where the title of an article is given in a language other than English it is followed in parentheses by an English translation. Dates are given in the military form—"2 October 1945," for example—and unless otherwise indicated refer to local time. Dates are given in the standard Christian (Gregorian) calendar system, with B.C. and A.D. indicated wherever possible confusion might occur. Where Japanese dates are available from the original sources these have been adopted, otherwise the date as given in KUROITA Katsumi's *Kokushi Kenkyū Nempyō* (Tokyo, Iwanami, 1936)—a standard Japanese chronology—is used. All quoted materials are exact copies with no editing to make spelling and punctuation consistent with the body of the text.

Certainly the most pleasant task of any writer is that of acknowledging the assistance which others have rendered in the preparation of his work. In such assistance the present writer has been singularly fortunate. The study was made possible through the generous support of the John Simon Guggenheim Memorial Foundation, and in a very large measure has resulted from the encouragement of the Foundation's Secretary General, Dr. Henry Allen MOE. The author is particularly indebted to Dr. Isaac L. KANDEL, Professor Emeritus of Comparative Education at Teachers College, Columbia University; to Dr. George S. COUNTS, Professor of Education at Teachers College, Columbia University, and noted authority on Russian education; to Dr. William Clark TROW, Professor of Educational Psychology at the University of Michigan; to Dr. Robert ULICH, Professor of Comparative Education at Harvard University; and to Dr. Alfred CROFTS, Professor of Oriental History at the University of Denver, for reading and criticizing the outline. Professors KANDEL, COUNTS, and TROW were members of the United States Education Mission to Japan, and Professor CROFTS was Officer in Charge of Japanese Universities during the first year of the Occupation. Professors TROW and CROFTS also read the manuscript for accuracy and style.

Dr. Daniel Clarence HOLTOM, the noted Shinto authority, read the section on mythology and Shinto for accuracy and made many helpful suggestions. Dr. August Karl REISCHAUER, Visiting Lecturer on

History of Religions at Union Theological Seminary and noted scholar in the field of Japanese Buddhism, has read the section on Buddhism and suggested certain changes. Dr. Charles W. IGLEHART, Professor of Missions at Union Theological Seminary and adviser to the Headquarters of the Supreme Commander for the Allied Powers on Religions, has read the section on religious history and Christianity for accuracy of content and analysis. Dr. Ernest JACKH, former Chancellor of the Berlin *Hochshule für Politik* and lifelong friend of Mustafa KEMAL Atatürk, has read and criticized the section on Turkey. Miss Yildez SERTEL, Turkish graduate student at Teachers College, Columbia University, has checked the Turkish language section. Mr. Francis Hung CHOU, assistant to Yang Ch'u James YEN in the Mass Education Movement in China, has read and criticized the section on China. Mr. Ichiro SHIRATO, Lecturer on Japanese at Columbia University and holder of the highest administrative certificates in prewar Japanese education, has read each draft of the manuscript, has made extremely valuable suggestions on the sections dealing with the Japanese writing system and the present system of education, and has checked all proper names, Japanese words, and Japanese dates.

The writer is indebted to his friends and colleagues in military service for an immense amount of assistance in gathering, filing, and translating material. To two of these companions he is particularly indebted. Lt. John ASHMEAD, Jr., USNR, and Lt. Arthur R. DORNHEIM, USNR, successively served as the author's Japanese language officer and assisted in a very great measure in the preparation of the section on the writing system. Two Department of State translators, Mr. Akira George YOSHIDA and Mr. Howard M. IMAZEKI, contributed markedly by preparing translations of a considerable number of Japanese textbooks which were later used in this analysis. Mr. John Owen GAUNTLETT, a British subject residing in Tokyo and a Professor of Linguistics at Waseda and Keio Universities, served as translator and research assistant in the collection of material on educational organization, finances, and the writing system. The writer is particularly indebted to Mr. GAUNTLETT for checking certain factual material necessary to the final manuscript, after the author had left Japan.

No study of the type of *Education for a New Japan* could possibly have been completed without the sympathetic cooperation of a large number of Japanese scholars, educational officials, and teachers. For obvious reasons it seems unwise to mention by name those who assisted the author during his official tenure. But it is with genuine gratitude that the writer mentions the assistance which has been rendered him via correspondence since his departure from Japan on the part of Mr. KAJI Shinzō, Professor at Tokyo (formerly Tokyo Imperial)

University and Secretary to the first three Ministers of Education following Surrender.

The author is indebted to Mr. Howard P. LINTON and his staff at the East Asiatic Library of Columbia University; to Mr. Robert H. HAYNES and his staff at Harvard University Library; and to Mr. L. Felix RANLETT and his staff at the Bangor Public Library, who secured rare documents and books, checked difficult Chinese and Japanese names, and put their full research facilities at the disposal of the study.

Finally, the author is indebted to his secretary, Miss Florence MILLER, for preparation of the manuscript, reading proof, and preparation of the index; and to the staff of the Yale University Press for copy editing and advice on the preparation of the final manuscript.

ROBERT KING HALL

Teachers College
Columbia University
1 January 1949

ACKNOWLEDGMENTS

I am grateful to the following publishers for permission to quote at some length from the designated works published by them, as follows:

George Allen and Unwin, Ltd. (London):

E. STEINILBER-OBERLIN and MATSUO Kuni's *The Buddhist Sects of Japan*

The American School Publishing Corporation:

Education for International Security

Asia (magazine):

Willard PRICE, February 1946

The Atlantic Monthly:

John ASHMEAD, Jr., "A Modern Language for Japan," January 1947, Vol. 179, No. 1

The University of Chicago Press:

Henry Elisha ALLEN, *The Turkish Transformation;* D. C. HOLTOM, *The Political Philosophy of Modern Shinto*

The Clarendon Press (Oxford):

Sir George SANSOM, *Historical Grammar of Japanese*

Collier's:

Fleet Admiral William A. HALSEY, USN, "A Plan for Japan," 28 April 1945

Doubleday & Co., Inc.:

Wilfrid FLEISHER, *What to Do with Japan*

Foreign Affairs:

C. Burnell OLDS, "Education for Conquest: The Japanese Way," October 1942

Harvard University Press:

John Owen GAUNTLETT and Robert King HALL, *Kokutai no Hongi* (manuscript)

Journal of the Royal Society of Arts (London):

Baron SUYEMATSU Kencho, "The Ethics of Japan," Vol. 53, No. 2729, March 10, 1905, reprinted in the *Smithsonian Institution Annual Report* for the year ending June 30, 1905

Kegan Paul, Trench, Trubner & Co., Ltd. (London):

ANESAKI Masahara, *History of Japanese Religion;* D. C. HOLTOM, *The National Faith of Japan: A Study of Modern Shintō*

J. B. Lippincott Company:

J. Ingram BRYAN, *Japan from Within,* published by Frederick A. Stokes Company, New York, and with permission from Ernest Benn Ltd., London; John Harrington GUBBINS, *The Making of Modern Japan,* and with permission from Seeley, Service & Co, Ltd., London

John Murray (London):

Basil Hall CHAMBERLAIN, *Things Japanese,* published by Kegan Paul, Trench, Trubner & Co., Ltd., London; Baron KIKUCHI Dairoku, *Japanese Education;* Count ŌKUMA Shigenobu, *Fifty Years of New Japan,* published by Smith, Elder & Co., London

National Education Association of the United States:

Educational Policies Commission, *Education and the People's Peace*

New York Times:

Burton CRANE, "Making Japanese Easy," 24 March 1946; articles in the issue of 18 March 1947

Oxford University Press:

William C. JOHNSTONE, *The Future of Japan,* issued under the auspices of the American Council, Institute of Pacific Relations

Philadelphia Record:

Editorial, "Basic Japanese," 16 January 1946

Fleming H. Revell Company:

Otis CARY, *A History of Christianity in Japan*

Reynal & Hitchcock, Inc.:

Otto D. TOLISCHUS, *Tokyo Record*

School and Society:

Ernest W. CLEMENT, "Educational Trends in Japan," 8 February 1930

In addition I am indebted to the following agencies of the United States Government for permission to use official published materials and the unpublished materials which were gathered by myself and associates while serving in an official capacity with the Occupation Forces in Japan:

The Department of State

The War Department

The Navy Department

The Civil Information and Education Section, General Headquarters, Supreme Commander for the Allied Powers (Tokyo, Japan)

I am also indebted to Japanese sources, both official and private, for the very considerable number of documents which are directly quoted or are used as basic references. Because these materials are not protected by copyright law and because disclosure of some of the sources might prove needlessly embarrassing, I have omitted a detailed list.

CONTENTS

I

ASHES OR OPPORTUNITY

The Problem of Survival

FOLLOWING Capitulation Japan lay numbed and prostrated, a defeated and an occupied nation. Her former leaders stood at bar, waiting the judgment of the civilized world, or passed, despised, into unknown eternity. Her people were bewildered, shamed, remorseful, and hesitant. After years of listening to authority they were at a loss when they had to accept the rights and responsibilities of self-direction. Old patterns of life lay shattered and discredited. The rubble of her ruined cities was more than matched by the chaos in the hearts of her people. The very standards by which in the past they judged the values of life, were doubted. Truth was no longer truth, right no longer right. And over all hung the grim reality of defeat, total colossal defeat.

Japan must survive. A nation of 80 million people does not physically die. During the first two years of the Occupation Japan was tried and proved her capacity for physical life. Families were homeless and they built shacks of sheet iron salvaged from the ruins. They were starving and they produced a little more and ate a little less. Her industry was destroyed, and she built consumer goods in farm and shop and kitchen. Her people were scattered, and in ships loaned by the Occupying Forces, they were brought home from all the islands and the continents of the Pacific. She met and overcame the ultimate disaster to her fishing fleets and villages in the great earthquake of December 1946. Japan has proved her capacity for physical survival, but in physical life alone there may be cultural death.

Cultural survival may be bought in many forms. In the months of the Occupation Japan met adversity with poise and bore her shame with dignity. She entered the period of her penance with humility and met the demands of the Occupation with apparent sincerity and co-operation. But this was only the beginning. Will she seek survival in a patched and makeshift repair of her traditional institutions? Will she seek survival in nominal compliance until time and apathy and other interests have blunted the demands of her conquerors? Or will she seek to turn this catastrophe to her lasting advantage and become a new Japan with an honored place in the community of nations?

Japan may choose the ashes of her failure or the opportunity of a renaissance. This is her great decision.

The Legacy of Defeat

Damage to the Material System. At 0904 Tokyo time on 2 September 1945, on board the U.S.S. *Missouri* lying in Tokyo Bay, Japan unconditionally surrendered to the Allied Powers of the United States, the United Kingdom, China, the Union of Soviet Socialist Republics, Canada, Australia, New Zealand, the Netherlands, and France. At that moment virtually all educational activity in Japan was at a standstill. In its first report to the Supreme Commander for the Allied Powers, the Civil Information and Education Section of his Headquarters stated: ". . . capitulation found 18,000,000 students idle, 4,000 schools destroyed, and only 20% of the necessary textbooks available."

These were startling figures, and they have since been frequently quoted, but they do not adequately represent the staggering problem which faced both the Japanese educational authorities and the Occupation Forces.

There were two kinds of war damage to the material system of education in Japan: one was pure destruction of school properties, personnel, and equipment; the other was loss of efficiency in those that survive.

Sometime between the signing of the Surrender documents in Tokyo Bay and the establishment of operating headquarters for the Allied Powers in the city of Tokyo—the establishment of Information Dissemination Section, United States Army Forces, Pacific (USAFPAC) on 10 September 1945 may be taken as a convenient date—the *Mombushō* (Japanese Ministry of Education) conducted a rough physical school survey which indicated that 4,059 school buildings had been destroyed by bombing and that approximately 39,053 buildings were usable. If prewar figures are to be credited, there must have occurred an attrition of nearly 5,000 additional schools during the period of the war for reasons other than direct destruction by bombing. Institutions of higher learning, because of their location in cities which were the chief targets for bombing, were harder hit than elementary and secondary schools. However, because most universities and colleges were multibuilding in construction, partial damage was not so paralyzing as in the case of the lower schools. In an article, "Military School Buildings to Be Used by Universities Destroyed in Air Raids," in the 3 November 1945 issue of *Mainichi*, it is stated that: "According to the investigation by the Education Office of 400 universities and colleges under its direct supervision, more than 160 or about one-third have been reduced to ashes."

During the first three months of the Occupation there were almost daily visitors to the Headquarters of the Occupation Forces requesting that some provision be made to secure buildings and equipment for schools destroyed in the war. Others wanted official intervention to secure school properties which had been confiscated during the war or which had been diverted to such noneducational purposes as the billeting of troops after Surrender. The bombed and gutted ruins of schools in the Tokyo and Yokohama area, officially estimated more than 80% destroyed, which before the war included nearly one half of all institutions of higher learning, stood a constant reminder of the seriousness of the situation.

It was decided that a sight survey of school damage was necessary if intelligent allocation of existing facilities was to be made. The Japanese Ministry of Education was asked to conduct such a survey and was assisted in preparing the bases for the collection of statistics. The findings of the Urban Area Surveys for Civil Affairs Officers, prepared in September 1945 at the Civil Affairs Staging Area (CASA), Presidio of Monterey, Calif., and covering eleven major municipal areas of Japan, were made available to the interested officials of that Ministry. Characteristically, these studies were gratefully accepted but were not used. During the months of December 1945 and January 1946 the survey was conducted by local Japanese educational officials and reported to the Ministry.

It had, of course, been obvious that a mere enumeration of war-damaged buildings in the aggregate was well-nigh valueless. One school in Tokyo might have had a seating capacity thirty times that of a school in Hokkaido. A perfectly preserved building, standing isolated among ruins, might have no practical value as a school. The death or evacuation of school-age population in a locality might have more than kept pace with the destruction of seating capacity in the available schools. The essential thing to be measured was clearly the availability of school facilities to the existing school-age population. This involved questions of residential damage; of transportation damage; of the seating capacity and degree of damage within existing schools; of the availability of teachers; of the changes in location and composition by age groups of the general population; of the availability of facilities for school utilization beyond normal capacity—by such devices as the platoon system, night classes, and work-study rotation. All such details would have to be studied, not on a national basis, but on a local basis so small as to be bounded by the normal walking distance of children, considered approximately five kilometers in Japan.

The final report was superficially impressive. But to the impartial foreign observer two elements stood out: the statistics were so inaccurate as to be virtually of no value; and the central educational authority of Japan, the Ministry of Education, in the first five months of the Occupation had failed to secure even the data upon which to base a reasonable solution to the problem of war-damaged schools. Local officials, parents, teachers, and even the students were themselves solving the problem as it arose, locality by locality.

The second of the two kinds of war damage to the material system is seen in the loss of educational efficiency which was evident in the condition of the student, the teacher, the textbook, and the physical structure of the schools.

The Japanese student at the end of the war was not efficient. He was tired, hungry, cold, often sick, dispirited. In the first year of the Occupation the food shortage loomed very large in his life. A few headlines quoted from a single Tokyo newspaper, the *Nippon Times,* could be matched in nearly every newspaper of the nation.

Schools forced to close: Hunger keeps students away from classes in Iwate—24 October 1945.

Students can't study with empty stomachs—31 October 1945.

Food lack hits students: Class work suspended due to rise of absentees
—1 November 1945.

Student labor plan set: Foodstuff production is keypoint of program
—14 November 1945.

Students suffering from poor health—13 February 1945.

Food dearth forces closure of schools: Principals can close down institutions at their own discretion—22 May 1946.

University students sell precious books to buy food: Attendance at classes thin—27 May 1946.

Hachioji school boys pay tuition in kind to keep teachers from closing classes—8 June 1946.

Schools to advance summer vacation: All institutions above middle course affected due to food shortage—8 June 1946.

Students will help fight food lack—14 June 1946.

School kids' lunch poor: Most mothers can give children very little, survey shows—26 June 1946.

To any observer in the schools of Japan during the first year of the Occupation, the story behind these headlines was tragic. Physical exercise and sports were cut to a minimum to conserve energy and to decrease needed consumption of foodstuffs. The hard-packed playing fields and schoolyards were laboriously converted into inefficient gardens to increase production. Shorter classes, suspension of afternoon sessions, a five-day rather than the six-day school week, extended vacation, even complete suspension of all studies, were officially sanctioned remedies for the situation. The time thus saved was presumed to be used in food-buying forays into the country or in work in the fields. Too often it was spent resting at home trying to regain energy needed to attend the next classes, or in antisocial activities trying to supplement the inadequate official ration. A member of the United States Education Mission to Japan, after watching a basketball game in a middle school in Kyoto, remarked that it was the first time he had seen boys playing in utter silence. One of the accompanying officers of the Occupation Forces pointed out that it was probably the first time he had seen boys playing a vigorous sport while badly undernourished, and directed the coach to stop the demonstration. Few students died of starvation in the first months after Capitulation, but few if any were able to study effectively. An article, "The Summer Vacation Must Not Be Wasted," in the 12 July 1946 issue of the *Nippon Times*, said in part:

In war years . . . the competent authorities drastically cut the students' vacation, and, taking advantage of the time saved in this way, forced the students to engage in labor service. Not only during summer vacations, but also, for a good part of their school terms, the students were compelled to work in factories and farms toward the end of the war. This naturally caused a lowering of the educational standards of the students. However, the war ended months ago, and now it is necessary for them to make every effort to make up for the fall in the level of their scholarship.

Nonetheless, the prevailing acute food shortage prevents them from concentrating on their studies. Increasing numbers of primary school children attend school without lunch, with the result that many schools have found it unavoidable to give lessons only in the morning. Some universities and colleges also took unusually long vacations last winter. Even after a new school term began, professors freely took holidays on week-days to go on food purchasing trips. Such being the situation, most professors and students have been unable to settle down to their studies, but keep worrying themselves about the food problem.

The Japanese teacher at the end of the war was not efficient. He too was tired, hungry, cold, sick, and dispirited. For him too absenteeism was very high. He had to face an even more complex situation than did the student. He faced a searching official inquiry into his past actions, statements, and affiliations. This was not "thought control" but the "Purge." He knew that if he failed to pass he would be barred forever from his profession. He had a family and had to find them food and shelter. In badly bombed areas this frequently necessitated his living two or three hours distant from his work. Each day's commuting demanded twice this time, standing in the cold, erratic streetcars that had survived the raids. He had to go on periodic food-buying expeditions when the ration system broke down or proved utterly inadequate. His salary, set by law, had long since been lost in the spiral of inflation, and his life's savings were rapidly being spent trying to secure the necessities of life, often only purchasable through non-legal and exorbitant channels. In an article, "Nation's Teachers

Uniting to Fight for a Square Deal," published in the 30 May 1946 issue of the *Nippon Times*, INAGAKI Masanobu, lecturer for the *Zen Nippon Kyōiku Kumiai* (All-Japan Teachers' Union) wrote:

All in the teaching profession are hard up these days of inflation when one must pay at least ¥40 for one kan (3.75 kilograms) of sweet potatoes, for the regular monthly salaries for primary school teachers average only ¥93 and that for university professors ¥200. At Yokosuka, we hear that many teachers are obliged to do additional work in their struggle to keep the wolf from the door. Some are doing fatigue duty for the occupation forces and some have set up cheap eating booths, while others have taken to the business of selling wheat-gluten of their own making, clubbing together for the purpose. Many are, in the meantime, leaving the teaching profession altogether for a more lucrative occupation. As things stand, the prospects are, indeed, decidedly gloomy for teachers.

Some were leaving the profession. A waitress in an officers' mess could get a salary of from 250 yen to 400 yen per month at the old official exchange rate of 15 to 1; a place to sleep; and two meals per day of Occupation food. The monthly salary of a university professor, the equal of the black-market price of a carton of American cigarettes, was less than attractive. Six months later the black-market price for a carton of cigarettes equaled five months' salary for the same professors. Those who could translate English found ready official or private employment at several times the rate they could expect from teaching. Japanese translators in the Education Section of Occupation Headquarters for example received 1,000 yen and up at the old exchange rate, but after the 50 to 1 rate was adopted suffered severely because no realistic readjustment of salaries was made. After two years of Occupation the real exchange rate was somewhere between 200 and 300 to 1. After three years of Occupation the official exchange rate was 270 to 1 and the real rate was nearer 600 to 1. But teaching in Japan, as in every other civilized nation, is a mode of life rather than merely a form of work. Despite the attendant hardships the majority of Japanese teachers have remained and probably will continue to remain in their profession. Their efficiency, however, cannot be expected to be high.

Educational efficiency was likewise lowered by the conditions of the Japanese textbooks at the end of the war. The official

Ministry of Education estimate of the number of textbooks available was set at 20% of the number needed. This figure, while startling, did not tell all the story.

Pre-Surrender textbooks in Japan were almost universally the private property of students, so few of them remained available to the schools. They were printed on a very poor quality of paper, so few survived for repeated use. Bombing had effectively stopped the printing of the normal replacements. Japanese teachers had been systematically indoctrinated in teaching mechanically from the official textbook, and presumably would be at a complete loss without them as a guide. On such bases both an official estimate of the number "needed" and the number "available" may have been fairly accurate. But even in the 20% presumed to have survived, the majority had suffered a form of war damage which largely destroyed their usefulness. They had become obsolete.

The physical structure of the schools surviving at the end of the war likewise contributed to the inefficiency of the educational system. Much of their equipment was destroyed or had become obsolete with the necessary changes in curriculum. Electrical circuits were inadequate and had deteriorated so that schools could operate only in daylight hours. They were cold, with the buildings stripped of kitchen and heating equipment, ostensibly to be used as metal scrap in the war industry. Windowpanes were broken. Toilet facilities, showers, swimming pools, and drinking fountains were broken or disconnected and could not be repaired. All laboratory facilities, libraries, and technical equipment had suffered severe war damage. Radio education had been a prewar source of pride to Japan as one of the most highly developed mass-education media in the world. After Surrender it was disorganized, limping, ineffective. In December 1941 there were 25,860 registered elementary schools in Japan. In an official survey 22,980 of these were contacted, of which 21,770 reported that they had radios and 5,583 reported that they had complete public address systems with outlets in all classrooms. The Ministry of Education, as a result of a survey conducted in December, estimated that on 1 January 1946 only 8,225, or slightly more than a third of the elementary schools, were able to make effective use of their radio equipment. The sets survived but could not be repaired, mainly because of the unavailability of vacuum tubes.

Damage to Prestige. The second of the great areas of war damage affecting the educational system of Japan, was that of damage to prestige. Japan has been proud of her educational system. The position of the teacher and the scholar has traditionally been equal to that of high diplomatic officials, and has carried something of the personal reverence accorded on the Asiatic continent to Chinese scholars. On 14 March 1868, Emperor MEIJI in offering the famous *Charter Oath of Five Principles*, put education very high in the list of Japanese interests: "Wisdom and ability should be sought after in all quarters of the world for the purpose of firmly establishing the foundations of the Empire." (One of several official *Mombushō* trans.)

The present Emperor, HIROHITO, on 3 April 1934 spoke to 35,000 elementary schoolteachers assembled before the Imperial Palace to honor the birth of the Crown Prince:

The prosperity of the Empire to be attained through the promotion of the national morality depends fundamentally upon elementary education. Those who are concerned with this branch of education, therefore, should exert themselves to the utmost, striving day and night for its improvement and furtherance.

In an article, "Exit Thought Control," which appeared in the 3 April 1946 issue of *Maptalk*, an official publication of General Headquarters, United States Army Forces, Pacific, the statement was made:

The new [post-Meiji] educational system became the glory of Japan. At the beginning of World War II it included 16 million students, 400,000 teachers, 50,000 schools, and an estimated budget of 600 million yen. Its importance in the life of Japan can be judged by the fact that the budget was larger than that of the Japanese Army and Navy combined until 1932, that 37 percent of the nation's population was included in the elementary schools and pre-school level, and that 99.6 percent adult literacy was claimed.

It was inevitable that with defeat there should come a critical and sometimes cynical reappraisal of the whole social structure which had produced the seeds of defeat and the terrible misery of the people. In this re-examination of old institutions and beliefs, education was not spared.

The masses of the Japanese people followed a pattern which could almost have been predicted on a trend graph. First there was bewilderment, followed by dismay. Japan was occupied!

For the first time in 2,600 years a foreign enemy controlled the holy soil! People waited in fear for the horrible fate that their war propaganda had promised if capture should come.

As the evidence of their leaders' actions became public knowledge through the war crimes trials and through the emancipation of a radio and press which for nearly two decades had been directed by the same leaders, there came a deep shame. People had to believe and yet could hardly bring themselves to believe the authenticated stories of treachery, atrocity, and utter cruelty. They began to understand a little the deep hatreds which the world had built up against them during their military isolation.

This shame was accompanied or closely followed by a growing doubt of all the long-established institutions. The divinity of the Emperor and the mythological creation of Japan were doubted. All the old legends of Japan's invincibility, the strength of the national spirit, the divine protection in time of stress, the racial and national superiority, seemed somewhat hollow to people who had survived the fire raids of 9 March and 25 May 1945. The stacks of confiscated swords seemed pathetic and faintly ridiculous.

The old traditions of blind loyalty to superiors, of quasi-religious respect for authority and all its instruments—the Imperial rescripts and the official pronouncements from the Ministries—seemed almost a mockery. The leaders had been caught in bald-faced lies; they had brought suffering such as Japan had never known; they were prisoners standing in an enemy dock or were puppets dancing to strings held by the Occupation Forces.

Defeat itself, failure, seemed both the greatest crime which they had committed and the ultimate retort to any explanation or defense of their past actions. Here and there a voice would be raised urging that the country go slowly, some of the older and more conservative people argued faintly for moderation and a thoughtful appraisal of the vast changes that were coming into the national life. But the mass of people swung to a blind acceptance of foreign opposites. Often the reasons were trivial: a common soldier had been polite to an old lady on a streetcar; the occupation troops gave candy to the children; a GI had stopped and helped the owner of a stalled truck. But underlying the thinking of nearly all the people was the argument that if their system was wrong and had been defeated, then the foreign system, which had won the war, must be right.

Japan embarked on a wave of admiration for and almost frenetic imitation of foreign ways within a few weeks after the beginning of the Occupation. It was reminiscent of the similar indiscriminate discarding of the old and adoption of the new that occurred during the first 20 years of the Meiji Restoration. And as the passing months began to bring contact with some of the imperfections of the Occupying Powers, there began the inevitable disillusionment and reappraisal. This is the great moment of danger in the democratizing process. This is the period during which a sort of delayed war damage can work irreparable harm. This is the situation which will face Japanese education for years to come.

There is no need to pause long in an inventory of the elements of damage to prestige. A systematic spot censorship of the mails, a press analysis, and a public opinion sampling during the first year of the Occupation gave statistical evidence. But the trends are too familiar to any thinking Japanese or foreign observer who lived through those months to require much by way of proof of their existence. A few examples, presented more as illustrations than as evidence, will suffice.

On 15 August 1945, the recorded voice of the Emperor came over all radios of the Japanese Empire:

To our good and loyal subjects:

After pondering deeply the general trends of the world and the actual conditions obtaining in Our Empire today, We have decided to effect a settlement of the present situation by resorting to an extraordinary measure.

We have ordered Our Government to communicate to the Governments of the United States, Great Britain, China, and the Soviet Union that Our Empire accepts the provisions of their Joint Declaration.

To strive for the common prosperity and happiness of all nations as well as the security and well-being of Our subjects is the solemn obligation which has been handed down by Our Imperial Ancestors and which We lay close to the heart.

(Translation in *Nippon Times*, 15 August 1945.)

The people were bewildered. Did it mean that the Allied Powers had surrendered to Japan? In Nagano Prefecture there were public demonstrations in the streets in celebration of the "victory." Then came the official explanation of the Imperial Rescript, in terms which the common people could understand. They were stunned. In an article "Village in Wartime," appearing in the *Nippon Times* of 11 February 1946, there is a poignant recollection of that hour:

At last the Emperor spoke. The villagers thought he was urging them to greater effort to final victory. But what could they do down on the ground while their opponent was far up in the sky? Then the Emperor's words were translated into words within their vocabulary. Tears that had flowed freely down their cheeks on hearing for the first time their revered Emperor's voice dried up. Simple folk, obedient folk, these villagers. To be changed from victor to vanquished was certainly a disgrace but their new masters would speak a foreign language. They would not be able to understand their orders and if they did not obey these orders would they not be harried and beaten? So they had been told by their now fallen masters. They were without guidance. They were stunned. They waited, helpless.

The bitter disillusionment of many people in Japan after the revelations of the first weeks of the Occupation, began to be felt in "letters to the Editor," letters to the Occupation Forces, the speeches of political radicals, mass meetings, strikes. The following opening paragraph from an anonymous document delivered by messenger to the General Headquarters of the Supreme Commander for the Allied Powers (SCAP) on 30 November 1945, will serve as an illustration:

The United States of America has become not only the greatest country in the world within less than two hundred years since its establishment, but also the best nation which defends, creates and preserves whatever is best for the attainment of happiness of mankind, and which represents the most laudable main current of human civilization in the world. While Japan in spite of her speaking boastingly as an unique nation in the world with the longest unbroken line of succession of one dynasty as her ruler, she has so far contributed almost nothing for the uplifting of mankind whether it is in philosophy, in science, in literature or in mechanical invention. Nay, she has lately become one of the most heinous nations in the world by pursuing ruthlessly her war of aggression which has brought about at the end nothing but her own defeat and willingness to accept the unconditional surrender imposed by the Allied forces. As a result she has lost not only all her territories she had acquired legitimately or illegitimately since her Restoration in 1868, but also several millions of lives of people, and the countless amount of wealth. At present, her land area practically remains stationary since she was established by the first emperor Jimmu some 2600 years ago, while her present standard of living is reduced as a result of her unsuccessful war of aggression, to a degree which is no better than the living conditions of savages in primitive societies of Central Africa or the Polynesian Islands. But it is nothing compared to the losses suffered by the Chinese and other powers on account of her reckless war of aggression. The Japanese must feel a guilty conscience.

Nothing was exempted from criticism in the new-found freedom of speech. A wave of student strikes swept the country. Beginning in Tokyo early in October 1945 with the simultaneous strikes of the Mito Higher School and the Ueno Girls Higher School, the movement rapidly spread to all parts of Japan: Chiba Higher School, Yasuhara Prefectural Middle School in Fukushima, Yamanashi Prefectural Agriculture and Forestry School, Shimane Prefectural Agricultural and Forestry School, Yoichi Middle School of Hokkaido, Akita Normal School, Maebashi Middle School of Gumma, Kiso Middle School of Nagano, Otaru Technical School in Hokkaido, Kodama Agricultural School. By the end of October serious educators in Japan were becoming increasingly worried by the apparent discard of all that was old by the somewhat irresponsible students. The *Constitution*, the Emperor System, the place of women in society, the guilt of war leaders, the basic human freedoms, the inadequacy of the written language, the incompetence of the government, the feudalism of the *zaibatsu* (family economic combines), the failure of the military forces, the absurdity of the mythological origins of the nation—everything was discussed. Everything of the past was criticized. The traditional was doubted. Frequently it was neither clear to the students nor to the public exactly whom they were striking against. Their demands were for vague and generalized "improvements in conditions" or for the removal of an unpopular official.

MIYAUCHI Yosaburō, speaking on the 18 December 1945 radio program "The Teachers' Hour" from Radio Tokyo, stated in an officially sanctioned address, "The Recent Changes in Juvenile Thoughts":

The last war, being a great war risking the fate of our nation, children also seemed to have deep and intense concerns for it. From the beginning to the end of the war children had believed the victory on our side and [had] tried their best, as juveniles. For instance, they lived in the evacuation group apart from their parents; they worked hard for the production of food with the farmers' children; they tried hard to drill [and build up] their physical strength [despite] a shortage of food. They did everything for the sake of our ultimate victory.

But on the 15th of August, our defeat was reported all of a sudden. The children who had been only used to hear great war results and had simply believed them, . . . could not make out at first what had happened. Gradually coming to know that ours had not been . . . victory but defeat, they came to think that militarists and high officials of the Government [were] liars. Recently they began to understand [that] the United States possesses more aircraft, ships, richer resources of gasoline and other substances, besides more advanced scientific technique. They came to realize our defeat was not caused by a mere chance. . . .

As to the actual causes for the defeat, they think as follows: Japan had scanty aircraft; the atomic bomb appeared; the Soviet Union stood against us; the German Reich had surrendered; we had inferior scientific standards as compared to the Americans; we had a shortage of food and other substances; our people [were not] unified; the militarists monopolized . . . policies. The conclusion was that children came to know our national fighting power was much inferior to that of America. (*Mombushō* trans.)

A foreign observer may perhaps be excused for accepting such attributed reasoning on the part of children with a certain mild skepticism. It rather closely follows the pattern of adult, and official, reasoning which began long before the final military defeat of Japan. We might recall, for example, a passage in Vol. I of the *Kōtōka Kokugo Tokuhon* ("Reader for the Boys Upper Elementary School") published 15 May 1944 by the Ministry of Education:

The present war is a complete, all-out effort. Do not separate the economy from War—it is the most important thing in military power. To win the war we must have strong armaments. We have to have supplies. We must make all Greater East Asia a self-sufficient unit. The Japanese economic power must be the greatest in the world— this is the objective.

*   *   *

Our nation never worried about supply during the Sino-Japanese War, the Russo-Japanese War, the First World War or the Manchurian Incident. However, this time in the Battle of Greater East Asia we must think carefully. To win the war we must win with supplies, and hence more production of supplies is urgent. After the China Incident the younger generation was mobilized, leaving arsenals with a shortage of manpower. To overcome this shortage, preservation of existing supplies is most important. In the First World War Germany won the battles but lost the war. The main reason was the shortage of supplies. The maintenance of supplies is the same as the maintenance of ammunition.

* * *

The study of science is very important, as science is the basic element of living. Up to now the study of science has been just memory work, with no actual application of the scientific laws studied. Though they have been interested in science, the Japanese have not investigated the field thoroughly. To improve science in Japan, more students have to study it. In the Battle of Greater East Asia, the fighting of a scientific battle is the greater task—hence, Japan must improve her science or the battle will be lost.

But even if one may smile a little at the survival of this thought pattern, and its somewhat naïve presentation as the discovery of children after the Surrender, the mass of evidence of this type of thinking on the part of educated adults points to a serious problem. It makes three characteristics of the process of war damage through disillusionment and loss of prestige stand out clearly. Vocal Japan was indulging in an orgy of mutual recrimination for the defeat. Official Japan was attempting to guide the thoughts of the awakening public away from too embarrassing or dangerous channels. And educated Japan still thought of defeat in terms of technological and material inferiority, rather than as the inevitable outcome of a spiritual deterioration which made Japan unfit to be a member of the community of nations.

The first of these characteristics may be illustrated with a quotation of a part of the editorial, "Freedom of Speech," which appeared in the 12 November 1945 edition of the *Nippon Times*:

Both the daily and the periodical press are full of charges and countercharges concerning the so-called responsibility for the war. The zaibatsu are charging the military [with] the responsibility; the military blame the zaibatsu, the government bureaucrats, and even the people; and the government bureaucrats try to excuse themselves by saying that they were coerced by the military. Each group is busy shifting the blame on to the shoulder of the others. The nationalists, who were quick to change their sign-board, are trying to masquerade as democrats, while the chauvinistic commentators are shouting themselves hoarse trying to convince everyone that they are completely peace-loving. The press organs themselves are vying with each other in exposing the zaibatsu and the military.

The second of these characteristics, that of official guidance of the public's thoughts, is so natural in Japan that its absence, rather than its presence, would have been the occasion for comment. The leaders of Japan after Surrender were men who were conditioned in the society that had been prewar Japan. Even the liberals found it impossible to think completely objectively. The mass of documentary evidence of the slanting of official pronouncements, of coloring of official reports, and of deliberate editorializing in official news, is virtually limitless. Often it was quite sincere and even unconscious. To expect a Japanese to think objectively about the Emperor System, for example, is about as realistic as to expect a color-blind person to enjoy a sunset. The elements upon which to make an impartial judgment simply were not permitted to exist in prewar Japan. Perhaps a reference to an investigation conducted by KODAMA Kyūjyū, Principal of the Myojo Middle School, and reported in his lecture, "The Recent Transformation of the Students' Thoughts," on "The Teachers' Hour," Radio Tokyo, 20 December 1945, will make this clear:

Mr. KODAMA asked 362 fourth-year students, belonging to three different middle schools, the following question: "What do you think of the various discussions now going on relating to our national structure?"

The students answered in writing, and without signing their papers. These were then classified into three groups: those that favored the maintenance of the Emperor System; those that approved of a democratic political structure under the Emperor; and those who wished to abolish the Emperor System altogether. Mr. KODAMA reported his findings over the Ministry of Education sponsored radio program, as follows:

. . . 92% or [nearly] every one of them says in fiery excitement, "What a terrible thing for us, the children of Tenno, as Japanese subjects to dare to think of having no Emperor, the father of the nation. Where the Tenno is, the Japanese nation can have its existence. Not considering the history from the beginning of our nation, it was the Emperor who laid down the final decision that we could be exempted from the fathomless damage which might have befallen us with a single mis-step. Without him, our nation would have gone to ruin. He saved the nation and the people. It is ungrateful indeed to think of the abolishment of the Emperor system." They are furious (indignant). But great attention should be paid to the fact that there exist 6 students—if only 6—who dare to approve of the abolishment and one to attribute war responsibility to the Emperor. It may be the influence of the newspaper and radio, but [it] shows the grave transformation of the thoughts of middle-school boys, and the teachers should pay due consideration to it.

There certainly are the advantages in the age of free thoughts and expressions, but there may appear absurd selfish opinions. We must let the students have sound thoughts not to be stirred or affected blindly by others' views, as no one knows what kind of thoughts may come out. To do it, let them fully understand the relation of the Emperor and the subject in Japan, as it is quoted: "Loyalty between the lord and the subjects, affection between the father and the son." The fact [that] we are father and son of one nation, one great family, should be thoroughly brought home to their minds and then we can ask them whether we may slight our parents or not. They will be very grateful to the Emperor and never again will slight him. (*Mombushō* trans.)

It should be noted that Mr. KODAMA, at least at that time, was considered politically acceptable and was regarded by the Occupation Authorities as a Japanese sincerely working for the aims of the Occupation. His address was read, approved, and permitted to be broadcast on an officially sponsored radio program. It represents, of course, a survival of the traditional "thought control" policy of the Japanese.

The concept of "thought control" is so contrary to all Anglo-Saxon tradition—or was until the "loyalty checks" of public officials were begun following the second World War—and is so repugnant to the average American, that it is a little difficult to reconcile with a nation apparently wholeheartedly working for universal education. The *Nippon Times* on 16 December 1945 in an article entitled "66,000 Were Nabbed by 'Thought Police,'" briefly reviews the history of the modern Japanese control.

In order to prevent the bolshevization of Japan, the Peace Preservation Law was enforced in April, 1925, with the object of controlling the thought movement, namely, the organization of a society aiming to revolutionize the national structure and other Communist movements connected with it, as well as those which debase the dignity of the Ise Grand Shrines and Imperial Family in denying the national polity.

An extraordinary Imperial ordinance in 1928 slightly revised the original act and between that date and the Surrender, the Japanese officially admit arrest and trial of approximately 66,000 persons charged with subversive thoughts. On 10 March 1941 the Peace Preservation Law (*Chian Iji Hō*), No. 54 of 1941, was promulgated, revising and intensifying the original act. This together with the Protection and Surveillance Law for Thought Offense (*Shisō Han Hogo Kansatsu Hō*), Law No. 29 of 29 May 1936 and the numerous supporting and interpreting ordinances were among the first targets of the Occupation Authorities, and were formally abrogated by the so-called "Japanese Bill of Rights," SCAP Directive of 4 October 1945. Article 1 of Law No. 54 established the death penalty or life imprisonment, not commutable to less than seven years, for organizing any association with the object of changing the "national polity" or "national entity" (*kokutai*), and subsequent paragraphs extended severe penalties to any who in any way had contact with such movements.

If such an offense were limited to treason, in the Occidental sense, the penalties might not have seemed excessive, but three factors combined to make the law viciously oppressive to individual rights. The concept of "national polity" was integrally linked with the militaristic and ultranationalistic aspirations of Japan's military dictators and overlaid with all the mystical semireligious philosophy of State Shinto. All levels of the Japanese Government from the Bureau of Thought Control (*Shisō Kyoku*) in the Ministry of Education to the *tonari-gumi* (local block system of government) were turned into a massive espionage machine to check on the "thoughts" of each individual. And Articles 18, 22, 23, 28, 33, and 39, respectively, permitted any procurator or police officer to arrest and to imprison a suspected person in any police station without trial for a period of two months, and specifically denied all appeal after trial, denied bail and provisional release, and provided that the court might indefinitely hold in "preventive detention" any person who had already completed his sentence if a procurator requested it.

Sixty-six thousand Japanese, by official admission, paid the penalty for this law. A single case will illustrate the almost fantastic lengths to which the law was pushed in the attempt to stamp out liberalism. For over 70 years there has been a well-supported and dignified movement in Japan to replace the cumbersome Chinese characters in the writing system with some immensely simpler and more efficient phonetic system, such as the *kana* (Japan's phonetic syllabary) or *romaji* (roman letters). It has been supported by princes, members of the Imperial Cabinet, peers, and by some of the most responsible of Japanese professional and industrial leaders. The conservative clique, however, felt that if phonetic writing were adopted, the "sacred characters" used by the Emperor in such historic documents as the *Divine Oracle*, the *Imperial Rescript on Education*, and the *Imperial Rescript Addressed to Youth* would be altered, an act of lese majesty, hence an attack on the "national polity," and a crime punishable under the Peace Preservation Law. This was not a theoretical violation of a dead issue on the statute books. Scores were arrested for nothing worse than membership in a linguistic society advocating such a change. SAITŌ Hidekatsu, Editor in Chief of the *Moji To Gengo* ("Writing and Language") and the *Latinigo* (an Esperanto magazine), was arrested in the autumn of 1938 and died in prison the following year while still awaiting trial, charged with advocating language reform. HIRAI Masao, author of *Kokugo Kokuji Mondai* ("Problems of the National Language"), and a member of the *Nippon Romaji Kai* (Japanese Romanization Society) was arrested on 5 June 1939, held without trial or formal charge in a police station till the following June, then transferred to a prison and held till December 1940 when he was released on bail. In January 1941 he was tried by Chief Judge IIZUKA Toshio, and sentenced to two years' penal servitude for advocating romanization of the writing system. He was given a suspended sentence for three years.

Mr. KODAMA's radio address was not an isolated example of the survival of this pernicious doctrine. The final paragraph of the *Nippon Times* article of 16 October 1945 illustrates how completely the Japanese failed to realize that it is the abrogation of a fundamental personal liberty and not a mere misuse of an acceptable law that really characterizes "thought control." "However, in recent years, the Peace Preservation Law was improperly used to trample down the people's rights and to apply strong pressure upon public thought, thus departing from the primary object of preventing the spread of bolshevism."

The last of these characteristics of war damage through loss of prestige and through disillusionment, that of underestimating the character of defeat, is equally widespread. The overwhelming physical superiority of the Occupation Forces was so apparent that it was a temptation to look no further for an explanation of the national disaster. There was even a kind of masochistic pleasure and pride in being defeated by so powerful an enemy. From the children who flocked around jeeps, fingering and gasping over the soldiers' gear, to the intellectual trying to account for the unbelievable collapse of all that Japan had believed impregnable, there was an almost worshipful admiration of the American war machine. It is true that it was an incredibly powerful machine, one that even the most sophisticated could well find astonishing, though Japan never saw more than small token forces hardly indicative of the monster in reserve. It was the product of the greatest scientific and industrial machine the world has yet known. But the very respect the Japanese paid American power was dangerous and destructive. It continued their adulation of force above all human rights. It blinded them to the moral implications of their defeat. It built another hierarchy of authority which could be respectfully worshiped, which could be obeyed, and which inevitably must demonstrate that it was short of perfection.

A quotation from the text of a radio address which Mr. B. KIDO was scheduled to make on Radio Tokyo, 17 November 1945, on the officially sponsored program, "The Teachers' Hour," is significant. Significant also is the fact that the Occupation Authorities did not permit the broadcast. "In the Greater Asian War a country of spiritual principles was beaten by one of scientific principles. So in the strife of life, both during the war, and after, the powerlessness of education based on spiritual principles has also actually been proved in maintaining morality, social or private." (*Mombushō* trans.)

Moral aspects of defeat are always difficult to assess, and here are doubly so since the Japanese have traditionally subscribed to an ethical code quite different and in some elements repugnant to most Western and Christian nations. But until the masses of the Japanese people recognize that the Allied victory was not a simple triumph of science over ethics but rather the triumph of a higher moral concept over a more primitive and less acceptable one, Japan will continue to count this form of rationalization a great area of war damage. It will be a barrier to the rebuilding of a new Japan.

Damage to Minds. The third of the great areas of war damage affecting the educational system of Japan is that of damage to minds. Reference is not here made to those unfortunates who, under stress of bombing, have developed neurotic symptoms— although there are undoubtedly many—but rather to the less intense but more widespread phenomena of normal minds which have been harmfully influenced by their war experiences.

War itself is a school, and no one who survives can ever quite forget some of the lessons. Among Japan's millions there are many who have learned lessons that leave them warped, antisocial, ill adjusted. No survey has yet been attempted, and it is doubtful if any could be devised which would give more than the roughest estimate of the magnitude of this damage. The fact that it is widespread may be accepted. Beyond this it would be well to consider it only qualitatively rather than quantitatively. Fear, hatred, deceit, despair, nearly every undesirable characteristic of human personality is found exaggerated. The man who had been shiftless in peace, refined his techniques of evasion until the emotional exhortations of the militarists for increased production became a mockery. A week before the fire raids of 25 May 1945, residents of Tokyo were still procrastinating on digging air-raid shelters. University students, exempted from compulsory military service because of their studies, put in time as workmen in the shipyards, and vitiated the work-study plan by organized slowdowns and malingering.

Any plan for social reconstruction of Japan must take into account the entire list of these war-accentuated antisocial characteristics. A certain restricted number of them, however, compose a recurring pattern of particular importance to the educator. Among students there are fear, hatred, ignorance, indifference, and fatigue. Among teachers and educational officials there are apprehension, guile, apathy, bewilderment, and relief.

Examples could be multiplied endlessly. The following illustrations are taken from the notes of a naval officer serving as Chief of the Education Sub-Section, Civil Information and Education Section, GHQ, SCAP, during the first months of the Occupation.

Fear: K— is seven years old, the daughter of an educated middle-class woman and a university student who was conscripted and sent to China to serve under Lt. Gen. TANI Hisao just in time to participate in the Rape of Nanking begun 12 December 1937. The child has no recollection of her father, and identifies the term with a picture kept in the *kamidana* (god-shelf) of the mother's room. No word has been received from the father since the latter part of 1944 when a letter was posted from Takao, Formosa, indicating that he thought he was being sent to the Burma Front. His death is tacitly accepted, the mother works and lives with K— in her own father's house. K— is very intelligent, extremely spoiled by her grandparents, small for her age but not apparently suffering from any dietary disease. Twice during the war the house in which she was living was burned in raids, once she was evacuated from Tokyo to Kofu for several months. She experienced the fire raids of 9 March and 25 May 1945. She seems completely normal until she hears a siren or fire alarm, which she connects with the fire raids. When this happens, even at a distance which makes the sound very faint, she stops her most boisterous play, begins to moan, and whimper, starts to tremble uncontrollably, becomes increasingly hysterical until she is screaming and twitching. The attacks sometimes last more than an hour.

Hatred: H— is seventeen years old; the third son of a wealthy industrialist who died of natural causes shortly before the war; is a first-year *kōtō gakkō* (Higher School) student; and is suffering badly from malnutrition. His oldest brother was drowned in the Inland Sea when his ship hit a mine. His sister's fiancé was killed in the Philippines. His second brother was injured seriously in a raid on the factory where he worked. His city home in Tokyo was destroyed and he evacuated to Hiratsuka with his mother and sister. During a raid there, the house burned and they took refuge in the rice fields. His mother lying beside him had her leg severed at the thigh by a small incendiary bomb. H— was unable to stop the blood with a tourniquet, held the stump with his hands for hours till daybreak, carried his mother to the next town to a Navy aid station where she died of shock, bleeding, and inattention on the following night. Nine months later he still experiences nightmares in which he sees the blood oozing between his fingers. He swore to kill as many Americans as he could, deliberately planned an underground resistance despite the Imperial Rescript of 2 September 1945. He was deterred from this plan by being rescued, together with his sister, from a blizzard in the mountains south of Fuji by two enlisted men from Atsugi Air Base. Presumably he felt gratitude.

Ignorance: M— is twenty-two years old, a second-year student at Waseda University, near the top of his class academically, an excellent skiier, athletic, very serious, and ambitious. His home is in Sapporo, Hokkaido, where his father, a metallurgical engineer, and his mother and brothers live. One brother was jailed for liberal tendencies by the thought police just before the war. The family is Christian, and has always been somewhat sceptical of the mythological elements in early Japanese history. M— reads German with ease and has studied English autodidactically throughout the war. Although he does not speak it, he has performed a remarkable feat in memorizing the five thousand words in a pocket dictionary. M— should, by all the standards of other countries, be a very well read and informed student, and should be a desirable type of young citizen. On the contrary, he cannot remember back far enough to recall an uncensored press, radio, or forum, nor can he recall school classes where the students were not under surveillance for "dangerous thoughts." He simply has never heard of great events in the past ten years which are the common knowledge of even the most indifferent student in a Western University. He is attempting the almost impossible task of being an intelligent citizen and reflective student without the background information and thinking habits that are necessary. He realizes his own ignorance and sops up facts indiscriminately from any source, but he does not have the power of critical or selective learning. He is singularly suspicious and distrustful.

Fatigue: C— is nineteen years old, a former English teacher in a private school, daughter of an impoverished younger son of a wealthy family. She lived in England as a child, speaks excellent English, is able to type *romaji* (Japanese in roman letters) and English by the touch system. Because of the food shortage and the breakdown of the distribution system she had to make two trips per week to the country, with a three-hour train ride in badly deteriorated, unheated cars without seats, then a two-hour walk to a farm owned by her family. She carried a 65-pound pack (⅔ her weight) on her return. When the school was closed for lack of students, due in turn to lack of food, she got a job with the Occupation Forces as a typist. She works an eight-hour day, spends three and a half additional hours on streetcars getting to and from work, walks a mile through ruins to reach the carline. She attempted to eat the bread made from Kyoto experimental flour (contents: clay, sawdust, ground beetles, rice sweepings) but could not tolerate it. One day, climbing the stairs to her office after going without breakfast, she fainted. Since then she has occasionally been given, illegally and posing as a Nisei, a ride home or a full meal at one of the

Occupation messes by some officer with more compassion than caution.

Apprehension: Professor T— is white haired, frail, shy, a member of the Faculty of — Imperial University. He is widely travelled, has received academic honors abroad, has published both in Japanese and in European languages. His command of English is faultless. He has always been considered a liberal, was outspokenly critical of some of the policies of the pre-war Japanese Government. His intellectual standing together with the high rank of his family have given him both prestige and a sort of diplomatic immunity from the chauvinists. Entirely loyal to Japan during the war, he nevertheless recognized some of the militaristic excesses, and after surrender mildly welcomed the impact of Western civilization on Japanese society. In due course he was invited to assist in the preparation of certain documents relative to the then proposed purge of public officials. He realized that one of the proposed categories applied to himself. He once had published what then seemed an entirely innocuous and scholarly appraisal of Japan's position in the political economy of Greater East Asia. Intellectually, he still could not deny the position he had taken. Does he dare remain silent in the hope that the article will not be remembered? Does his sense of honor require him to confess to a guilt which he honestly feels is only a technical infraction? Should he quietly resign? T— has presented his own case as if it were a hypothetical one to the officer working on the papers with the suggestion that policy in such cases should be clarified. Presumably he does not know that the officer is fully aware of the article and has quite reasonably discounted its importance.

Guile: Assistant Professor K— is in early middle age, is ambitious, a member of the Faculty of — Imperial University. He is related by marriage to influential Japanese both in political and in intellectual circles. His personal position in war-time and pre-war Japan was not marked by public recognition. He is considered promising but not yet an accomplished scholar. He once studied in the United States and speaks heavily accented but accurate English. Shortly after Surrender he presented himself at Headquarters, apparently with the sincere desire to help the Occupation Authorities and Japan through his knowledge of the two languages and the psychologies of the two countries. There was not then, nor has there been since, any question of personal financial gain. Almost immediately he was able to assist the Occupation Authorities to a considerable degree through his technical knowledge and professional contacts in connection with a very important proposed directive. He became the unofficial but very obvious "go-between." He was overnight projected into a position in daily contact with the leading figures on both sides of the Occupation. Because of his apparent "indispensability" to the Occupation Authorities, he was accorded a deference by the Japanese that he had never known before. The staff study preparatory to the directive was completed and the directive issued in about two months. Prof. K—'s importance should presumably have then subsided to the level of a competent interpreter. To the detriment of his health and his classes, however, he has continued in almost daily contact with Headquarters. No job is too small and no errand too unimportant. He "arranges," with tact and despite unbelievable difficulties, meetings which a single phone call from Headquarters would have accomplished. Motives are dangerous to assign, but it is possible that he may have found that the Occupation is a convenient instrument for his own advancement.

Apathy: O— is a functionary in the Ministry of Education. He is a graduate of the Tokyo Imperial University, has been employed in one capacity or another in the Ministry for more than ten years. When, in 1938, he was transferred to the Compilation Section of the Bureau of Textbooks he purchased a new uniform in honor of the occasion, began taking books home to study the technical aspects of his work. Gradually it was forced upon him that it was in fact compilation and not authorship which was wanted. Building with old bricks, the preparation of textbooks in the form of a scrapbook of sanctioned material had been customary since September 1871, when the Bureau for the Compilation of Textbooks was first founded. At first he included the poems and legends which he remembered from his childhood. Some, though he did not know it, had been imported into Japan when Dr. David MURRAY came from the United States to act as Superintendent of Education in 1873. Some of these had in turn been exported from Europe and introduced to American schools fifty years earlier. Why change? If the stories had appeared in prior Japanese textbooks they were presumably acceptable for proposed ones. Occasionally, O— inserted a lesson on the War in China or Duty to the Emperor which had come down with a note from higher authority. He felt sure of himself when he had one of these notes. He even felt a quiet thrill at thus helping the war effort. Then came Pearl Harbor, stricter rationing, members of his own family on foreign duty, casualty notices, the stream of simulated ashes supplied by the government to families of dead whose bodies would never return to Japan. He read the newspapers with their notices of victories. He felt humble at his job. He copied into the manuscript for the next *Kōtōka Kokugo Tokuhon (Boys Upper Elementary School Reader)*: "We the people are always praying for the development of the Japanese Empire. To complete this mission we must take away obstacles and defend the

Empire. If a person does not defend the Empire, he is not a Japanese."
(Vol. I, 15 May 1944.) Air raids, harsher rationing, longer commuting, cold, the Emperor's *Surrender Rescript*, the arrival of the Occupation Forces. . . . The *Joshi Kōtō Shihan Gakkō* (Woman's
Higher Normal School), to which the bureau had been evacuated,
was dirty, cold, harder to reach from his home. He had before him,
one day, a page of instructions from the Ministry, entitled "Concrete
Examples of the Revision of Textbooks." He read the list of things to
be deleted: "The account of the *Tokubetsu Kōgeki-Tai* (Special Attack Corps) in the lesson entitled 'Doing Away with Childish
Thoughts.' " An American Naval officer attached to Headquarters
happened to come into the room. O— hardly bothered to look up. The
olive drab uniform which he had bought so happily back in 1938 was
dirty and threadbare. There was no charcoal for the *hibachi*. The last
of that week's ration of rice was in his *bentō*. He picked up a pen,
dipped it in red ink, and neatly deleted the Special Attack Corps.

Bewilderment: O— is the founder of a famous private school in Kanagawa Prefecture. Author of more than fifty works on the theory of
education, he is personally acquainted with the educational systems
of the United States, Europe, and the South Asiatic countries. His
very advanced (for Japan) educational ideas have involved him in
both academic and political difficulties, once occasioning his imprisonment. The merits of these old controversies are not at bar and seem
today to be less than unimportant. Despite these troubles, however, he
has always managed to retain a large and very loyal following of
teachers, who find in his educational writings an inspiration lacking in
the official pronouncements of the Ministries and Prefectural departments. He is the editor of an educational journal which has a wide
circulation among teachers throughout Japan. After the publication
of SCAP's Basic Educational Policy Directive, AG 350 (22 Oct 45) CIE,
he became convinced that the average teacher, far from being assisted,
had actually been confused by Occupational policy statements. He
felt that the teachers had been so accustomed to official "interpretations" of all policy statements, that they would certainly be at a loss
at the prospect of implementing what appeared superficially to be
vague generalities. To test his ideas he announced that there would be
a three-day teachers' conference held at his school during the following month to discuss the meaning and the implications of the SCAP
directive. He planned three main subjects for discussion on the
agenda:

1. What is meant by "militarism" and "ultra-nationalism"?
2. How can "democracy" be taught in the classroom?

3. How should the teacher treat "freedom of speech" in the schools?

This was an unofficial, unsponsored, unpublicized conference. Those who attended did so freely and for the sole purpose of trying to make themselves better teachers. They came by whatever transportation they could arrange, made the trip at their own expense, provided their own food. They could expect neither official recognition nor financial recompense. When the meeting was called to order, however, more than 800 teachers were present, some having come from as far as Kyushu. These 800 are a measure of Japan's bewilderment.

Relief: K— is a man in his late thirties, formerly an Assistant Professor in a commercial university in Osaka, at present holding a minor post as an educational official. He is married, has three small children, must live on his salary. He has always been an idealist, has felt keenly the necessity of a lasting peace in the Pacific and international understanding between Japan and the West. He resigned his university post to offer his services to the Government for any work designed to promote understanding between Japan and the United States, in the year before Pearl Harbor. During the war he was humiliated and mistreated, though not openly persecuted, because he still placed his faith in peace rather than war. For his family's sake he went into virtual retirement and worked in the country. He took no active part in Japan's war effort. He was completely loyal to Japan, but for four years was wracked between his sense of patriotic duty and his deep conviction that Japan had committed a great wrong in resorting to war. He lost virtually everything he owned in the fire raids. After the close of hostilities he lost his infant son because of the inadequacies of war-devastated hospital facilities. When surrender came he again offered his services and became the confidential secretary to one of the most important national political figures. With the changes in Ministries he was relegated to an obscure and relatively unimportant post neither adequate in salary nor commensurate with his abilities. But he obviously feels only a profound relief that the war is over and a hope that Japan may spiritually survive.

These people, then, these children, students, teachers, and officials, are the elements with which Japan must be rebuilt. There is an old military maxim, "Do the best you can with what you have." Japan, in our lifetime, will be what these people make it.

Inventory of Salvage

It would be a serious error to consider that defeat had left only educational destruction. The very fact that war damage exists presupposes the existence of something worth salvaging which has been damaged.

There are many elements of salvage in the postwar Japanese educational system. There are more than 39,000 schools with their equipment. There is a working educational structure—administrative, supervisory, and financial—which has been tested for 70 years. There is a profound faith in the importance of education and a tradition of schools as the mechanism for this education. There is a tremendous backlog of educated and partially educated people who contribute daily to the cultural wealth of the nation. There is an enormous body of students who not only acquiesce but actively demand their education. There is a correspondingly enormous body of teachers, of varying degrees of experience and ability, who enjoy the position of dignity and influence accorded the scholar in all Oriental communities. There is a large cultural heritage in literature, science, customs. Perhaps the most valuable asset to be salvaged is a peculiar attitude of mind which enables a Japanese to rise above adversity. The very driving force which makes him sort the salvage from the ruins of his home becomes the most valuable of all his salvage.

Not every Japanese would agree with the assumption that Japanese moral courage has survived the defeat. In a paper, "Education for Democracy," presented to the United States Education Mission to Japan during its stay in Tokyo, IMAMURA Shōichi states:

. . . reforms and new legislations are merely machineries, and their effect[s] depend largely upon the mind of the people who handle them. We can buy a new pump, but as long as the water in the well is not clean, it will not do much good for us. So is the women's vote or the new labor union bills; as long as the minds of the Japanese women and the laborers remain as they are, we cannot accomplish true democracy in Japan. . . .

Education in [the] ordinary sense deals largely with [the] superficial sphere of the mind; that is the sphere of consciousness. But consciousness in itself is the mere outcome of the fundamental emotion. Man, [in the] last analysis, is an emotional being rather than intellectual. His intellect, his views of life, and even his character are built in accord with his emotion. . . . [I find that "Fear" is the controlling, basic and universal emotion of the Japanese. Every walk of the Japanese life is built on this single and primitive emotion of fear.

He fears another man. He fears his superiors. Women fear man. They are always afraid that someone may hurt him or her. He is on guard day and night vigilantly, that nobody should steal from him, and that nobody should fool him.

Jealousy, which is [the] twin brother of fear, is another outstanding emotion of the Japanese. Jealousy and fear make the Japanese very exclusive . . . and hard to cooperate with each other. Of course any man can not be entirely free from fear and jealousy, but the case of the Japanese is an extreme one. These emotions naturally lead to mutual distrust and their life task is, therefore, to defend them from these fears. No wonder that the motto of these fear stricken Japanese is "defense first." They built thick walls around their lodgings. They hide everything they have. They keep secret what they know, think, and feel. Indeed, to keep secret is considered . . . an important virtue of the Japanese.]

Japanese moral courage, its will to survive, stems from many roots. It is in part a product of the mythology of primitive Shinto, the nihilist philosophy of Japanese Buddhism, and the ethical code of Confucianism. It is in part an expression of *Bushidō*, Japan's Way of the Warrior. It is a product of a people who have met and resolutely overcome countless disasters: the typhoon, earthquake and fire, and civil strife and war, and now defeat. It is a product of a people who for centuries were held in feudal bondage, whose life is stratified in social and economic classes.

If Japan is to survive merely in a minimum sense, as a militarily impotent nation destined to a future political insignificance and economic inferiority to its Asiatic neighbors, the will to survive will have little importance or even desirability in the eyes of a supervising foreign power. If, however, Japan is to be permitted to aspire to reassuming its position of dignity and influence, if it is to be encouraged to hope and work for spiritual survival, then this spirit becomes of paramount importance. And the minds and character of the Japanese, which are to direct this force, become the focus of any plan for the educational rehabilitation of the nation.

One of the remarkable evidences of the peculiar ethical nature of the second World War and its immediate aftermath was the intense preoccupation which the enemies of Japan showed in the problem of salvaging Japanese minds. An article entitled "A Plan for Japan" by Fleet Adm. William A. HALSEY, USN, which was published in the 28 April 1945 issue of *Collier's*, is significant. Admiral HALSEY's reputation lies in other fields than diplomacy, education, and psychology, yet even at a time when he bore a considerable responsibility for the crucial naval war in the Pacific, he flatly stated that education was the only hope for lasting peace. He wrote:

Both the Nazi youth and the Japanese youth have been trained for years in savagery. They have known practically nothing else since childhood, so it's entirely possible we may not be able to reform that element at all. *We can, however, work on the rising generation in both countries, and even if that involves a long range, ironbound program, we'll find it is strictly one of self-protection, our only insurance that our sons—and daughters—will not be immersed in another war ten or twenty years from now.*

Wilfrid FLEISHER, in his book, *What To Do with Japan* (New York, Doubleday & Co., 1945), which was cited in the 16 April 1945 issue of *Life*, wrote:

An important and urgent problem will be that of re-education in Japan. The Japanese educational system is in reality a photographic process. It consists in making an official negative and turning out millions of prints of it. Students answer questions in unison and do their thinking in unison because it is actually done for them on high.

In bringing about a reform of the education system, it will be necessary, in the first place, to provide it with a new negative with which to fashion the minds of Japan's youth. This should make it clear that Japan's mission is not one of divine conquest, but of taking a law-abiding place in the society of nations where she may, after a period of penance, be admitted. Japan's defeat should deflate the glorification of the past and of imperial virtues. The Japanese must be taught that aggression does not pay and that peace can bring them greater rewards than war.

William C. JOHNSTONE, in his volume, *The Future of Japan* (Oxford University Press, 1945), again stakes the future of Japan on the possibility of re-educating the people. He says on p. 144:

Changing Japan from a warlike to a peaceful nation, in the final analysis will involve the re-education of the whole nation. The Japanese have been taught to believe in their absolute superiority to other peoples and their unquestioned right to dominate Asia. They have been taught that their Emperor is divine and that they are endowed as a race with special and superhuman attributes not found in any other nations. They must undergo a process of re-education in which they learn to appreciate the ideas and culture of their neighbors. They must be given the opportunity to test their own ideas against those of other peoples, to measure their customs and traditions by the standards of other civilizations, and to subject their ancient myths and legends to the investigations of historical scholarship. . . . Such re-education is essential to a peaceful Japan in the future and it is basically a task that the Japanese must undertake themselves.

The United States Education Mission to Japan, in its *Report* submitted to the Supreme Commander for the Allied Powers on 30 March 1946, stated:

We . . . believe that there is an unmeasured potential for freedom and for individual and social growth in every human being.

Our greatest hope, however, is in the children. Sustaining, as they do, the weight of the future, they must not be pressed down by the heritage of a heavy past. We would, therefore, not only stop wrong teaching but also, as far as possible, equalize their opportunities, providing teachers and schools to inform their minds without hardening their hearts.

The official United States Department of State Publication No. 2671, *Occupation of Japan: Policy and Progress*, states on p. 33:

The Potsdam conferees recognized the primary importance of education as a means of establishing and strengthening democratic tendencies among the Japanese people. Only a democratically educated Japanese people would be able to stimulate and defend political progress and build a frame of mind conducive to peaceful cooperation with other nations.

Three elements stand out clearly in these statements and in the many others of which these are typical examples. The first is a faith in the potentialities of the youth of the defeated nation. The second is a faith in education as a process by which this youth may be molded into the instruments for the rehabilitation of the nation. The third is an implicit recognition of the moral rights and international desirability of a Japanese renaissance. If Americans, from the military leaders writing to the general public during the heat of a war to the educational and political leaders forging the official policy of the United States in the subsequent peace, can have this faith, then surely the Japanese must equally be able to believe.

What do the Japanese say? The Ministry of Education, in its *Guide to New Education in Japan*, published in May 1946, p. 9, says:

> . . . the responsibility of the war should be borne by the Japanese nation and they must apologize most humbly to the world for the sins they have committed.
>
> Apologizing for misbehaviour does not end by merely saying that they are sorry, or passively carrying out the demands of the Allied Powers because there is no alternative. On the contrary, they must show by their conduct that the establishment of a new Japan can only be accomplished by fulfilling voluntarily, of their own accord, the obligations stated in the Potsdam Declaration or any other directives issued by the Allied Powers. Defeat is undoubtedly bitter but if this opportunity is taken to eradicate our weakness, to correct our mistakes, and to start building a new Japan, hardship and shame may be transfigured to joy and honour. This is the task that is awaiting the Japanese people.

If it may be assumed, then, that Japan is to seek its rebirth through education, the raw material for this educational transformation becomes of importance. Evaluations of personality and national characteristics made during or following a war are dangerous. Even the American who has demonstrated a truly remarkable faith in the potential future of the defeated enemy, cannot divorce himself entirely from the physical and psychological context of his nationality and victory. The Japanese can neither erase his cultural heritage nor forget defeat. Such evaluations are like diagnoses conducted when both the doctor and the patient are temporary sufferers from severe shock. Perhaps this factor can be decreased if the national characteristics which appeared to be present before the war are examined. Continuing the metaphor, one must study the "medical history" of the patient.

But war hysteria is not the only stumbling block for those attempting to classify the national characteristics of the Japanese. Categorizing a people is almost inevitably an oversimplification. Japan is not a nation of people cringing with fear and wretched with jealousy. It is not a nation made up solely of nearsighted, undernourished fanatics attempting to die for the Emperor. Nor is it a nation of identical photographic prints taken from the official negative. Prewar Japan was a country where democracy was not completely unknown. Not all Japanese were sadists, criminals, militarists, and psychopathic ultranationalists. In postwar Japan they were not all lovers of freedom, democracy, and the Occupation Forces. There were and are Japanese who disapproved of the Emperor System, who denied the historical accuracy of the mythological elements in the origin of the country, and who recognized and disapproved of feudalistic practices in the social structure. It is true that many of these types existed in Japan—enough of them to form easily identifiable patterns which could be seized upon by the enemy propagandist to support his argument.

Japan is in reality a nation of eighty million individuals, each with his own strengths and own weaknesses. These individuals, both collectively and singly, are not static. The *kamikaze* pilot of 1945 could be the fellowship student to the conquering country in 1948, and hold both positions with complete sincerity. The very foundation of the theory of democratic education rests upon recognition of the essential worth of the individual. It is a denial of his complete subordination to either collective society or the political state. If education for the new Japan is to "strengthen the democratic tendencies" of the people, it would indeed be incongruous to begin this process by denying them the very individualism which this education is designed to strengthen. One should begin, then, by a frank recognition that each person is an individual and must have an educational development tailor made to fit him individually. As the "national characteristics" of the Japanese are listed as assets in the salvage from the war, it should be done with the full knowledge that what one is listing are fairly widespread identifiable patterns, possibly entirely inapplicable in any individual case.

The fundamental psychological endowment of the Japanese, known as *Yamato damashii,* is one of the most thoroughly explored subjects in Japanese religious and philosophical literature. A typical analysis was made by Tanaka Yoshitō, lecturer on Shinto at Tokyo Imperial University, in his volume *Shintō Hongi,* translated by Dr. D. C. Holtom in his definitive study, *The Political Philosophy of Modern Shintō* (University of Chicago Press, 1922):

(1). An intellectual nature capacitating for orderliness and unification (*Chitsujo teki tōitsu teki shisō*).

(2). A vivacious and practical (lit. "this-worldly") emotional nature (*Kaikatsu teki gensei teki kanjō*).

(3). A disposition toward development and expansion (*Hatten teki bōchō teki seikaku*).

The widow and friends of Dr. NITOBE Inazo in 1936 published in Tokyo a volume, *Lectures on Japan*, which Dr. NITOBE had delivered during his ninth trip to the United States shortly before his death. He had been speaking as a semi-official representative of the Japanese Government and as Japanese Delegate to the Canadian Council of the Institute of Pacific Relations. One lecture was entitled, "National Characteristics of the Japanese People." Perhaps this lecture may be taken as a self-appraisal of thinking Japanese before the sanity of the nation was engulfed in the wave of political assassinations, social unrest, military control, and the hysteria of the war with China. Dr. NITOBE mentioned 12 characteristics which he contended were peculiarly shown by his people. The qualities of loyalty, a sense of duty and responsibility, a cheerful view of life's pathos, a love of and contact with nature, and a realistic psychology are ones which are self-explanatory, and which are commonly recognizable patterns in Japanese society. With regard to the last of these, a realistic psychology, many might at first take issue. William C. JOHNSTONE, for example, in his book, *The Future of Japan*, p. 135, says: "Retreat into the theatrical, mystical world of ancient beliefs, religious rituals, festivals, and superstitions is a major method of making the hard realities of life bearable for the mass of the people."

Yet in the sense in which Dr. NITOBE meant "realistic" it is perhaps acceptable. He said: "We stick to realities. Our energies are directed to the solution of practical questions as they present themselves from day to day."

The other seven of Dr. NITOBE's dozen characteristics of the Japanese people are both more controversial and of more fundamental importance in planning for the re-education of Japan.

Patriotism. . . . the Japanese loves his country as he loves its ancestress, the Sun Goddess, namely, with awe and reverence. Patriotism with us is well-nigh a religion, and for that very reason is exposed to the same danger of hypocrisy, professional patriotism or bigotry, zeal beyond reason. (P. 307.)

National Unity. . . . We may regard this sense as a biological necessity of the aggregation of men occupying a small and isolated habitat. For centuries they lived by themselves; but this alone would never have fostered the consciousness of unity, especially as they are so mixed in race. Only the sense of insecurity from outside can unite a nation. . . . Whenever a foreign attack, be it by sword or by the pen, is made on our country, its people forget the differences that in ordinary times exist among them and unite in defense of it. . . . Most certainly in union there is strength, and in collectivity, power. But in mere unity there is no individual initiative, which is the source of all progress, and in enforcing unity the canaille is apt to show intolerance to the best and highest of their own compatriots. There is unreasoned and blind unity in a mob, and a whole nation can turn into a mob, unless the wise saying of Confucius is heeded, that one subject who "disputes," i.e. disagrees with his Sovereign, may save the nation, and a single voice raised against a mob may deliver a country from ruin. (Pp. 310–311.)

National Continuity. If our people are not individualistically as fully developed as many a Western race, they have evolved a sense of national personality that few nations have. The sentiment of unity is one indication of this, that of continuity is another. Symbolized by the ruling house, the nation has kept up its continuity for twenty centuries. . . . I am not arguing whether continuous rule by a single family is the highest political ideal or not. A government is not a theory. It is too serious an institution to be experimented with. It is an empirical product, varying in time and space. . . . The fact that the Japanese Ruling House has been in the enjoyment of its prestige, unbroken since its beginning, is the best argument that it is the right state form for Japan and its past is the guarantee for its future. (P. 313.)

Self-Abnegation. Be the ultimate object national unity or continuity, patriotism or loyalty, the immediate demand made on an individual in society is the surrender of himself to the general good, the absorption of a small *ego* in the great entity of the nation. This perhaps comes to the Japanese more easily than to the Westerner because of the long training to look upon self as only part of a larger whole. Both Buddhism and Shinto have taught this simple lesson. Impersonality has been their philosophy and depersonalization has been their moral teaching. (Pp. 313–314.)

Sense of Honor. Largely owing to the teaching of old Bushido ethics, there is developed among us a keen sense of honor, which oft-times transcends the limit of prudence and becomes quixotic. It also, not infrequently, deteriorates into mere sensitiveness or takes upon itself the form of quick annoyance at supposed insult. At times, too, it warps into rigid formalism. Nonetheless, it is a quality far to be preferred to callousness to shame. (P. 315.)

Sentimentality. The race is nervous, sensitive, emotional, quick to take offense, responsive to congenial spirit, unforgetful of wrong or of kindness. While, therefore, injustice rankles in their breast, an act of kindness is harbored deep in their bosom and gratitude is a marked trait of our people. (P. 317.)

Talent for Detail. . . . the Japanese are adept in the observation of minutiae and this talent is shown in their scrupulous attention to detail—whether this refers to government functions or to artistic works or to scientific research or literary productions. . . . The reputation which our men have won in science has not been in large generalization but in painstaking research work. They are great in little things. May they not be little in great things! (P. 319.)

It would be interesting to know just what the Japanese militarists and ultranationalists who were in political ascendency in the crucial war years from 1937 to 1945 considered were the outstanding characteristics of the Japanese people. It is probably impossible to know what truly was in their minds, since every public utterance was inevitably calculated propaganda. Perhaps, however, a very brief glance at their propaganda may be of value. It will at least indicate what are those characteristics which they hoped to foster. Fortunately, at least for this purpose, there exists a little volume by HASAGAWA Nyogekan entitled *Japanese National Character*, Tourist Library No. 40, which was published in 1942 by the official Board of Tourist Industry. In a typical Japanese method of presentation it attempts to describe the Japanese national character in terms of its manifestations in mythology, history, national structure, customs, art, and literature. The analysis is also characteristically vague and poorly organized, leaving the reader with a feeling that he had almost grasped some revelation of great importance but was quite unable to say just what that important idea had been. A few concrete statements, however, stand out and are pertinent:

The most essential feature of Japanese civilization is "restraint." (P. 21.)

. . . moderation and tolerance, fostered by physical and social conditions in ancient Japan, are important from the point of view that they have pervaded the national character of Japan for more than twenty centuries, weaving a continuous thread in the warp and woof of this nation's history. (P. 20.)

. . . a counter-balancing of conservatism and progressiveness operating in the same period colored the character of Japanese history with moderation, safety, and steadiness. And broadly viewed, the national character of Japan is a reflection of the character of her history. (P. 42.)

The Japanese character . . . is permeated by an element of concreteness rather than of abstraction, of practicality rather than theoretic speculation. (P. 45.)

This . . . is certainly symbolic of the distinguishing features of the Japanese character. Art is combined with wisdom and force. One might readily accept that a combination of brain power and physical force as essential to national life was known to the ancients, but what is peculiarly Japanese is the noteworthy addition of art to complete the trinity. . . . Even warfare cannot be called "Japanese" if there is lacking a happy combination of the beauty of the fighting spirit, the beauty of behavior, and the beauty of weapons. Victory won without these requisites to perfect fighting is called *kitanai* (not esthetic). (Pp. 61–62.)

Such statements did not seem absurd to a Japanese in 1942. It was propaganda and propaganda rarely seems absurd to the person for whom it was designed. Official writings of this period argued the superiority of "Japanese intuition" over "Western arguing and reason"; based their claims on almost dreamlike interpretations of ancient and mythological writings; and explained away the factual evidence and expert foreign opinion with such statements as:

[Westerners have] . . . an unfortunate non-comprehension of the legal and moral qualities vested in the Japanese State and its ruler. This error is partly due to the inability to grasp instinctively, through a lack of intuitive power in which the Orientals excel the Occidentals, the deep-lying significance of a historical phenomena. (*Ibid.*, p. 69.)

How has defeat changed the national characteristics of the Japanese? Can a Japanese today strip himself of the mysticism and rationalizations of wartime and prewar propaganda? It is easier to indicate the beliefs that have been proven false than to build up an outline of those that have survived. The Ministry of Education, in its official *Guide to New Education in Japan,* attempts to catalog the characteristics which are lacking. Under the heading, "How Did Japan Come To Be in the Condition She Is Today?," five basic reasons are advanced. Each of these is an avowed "defect or shortcoming":

1. *Japan is not yet sufficiently modernized.* In some things she has taken in modern civilization and is leading a progressive life, but on the other hand there are modes of life which are old and which would be called feudalistic. . . . Since the Meiji Restoration, Japan has been eagerly adopting and imbibing Western civilization, by which she has tried to be modernized. But it was principally the materialistic side of Western civilization, or rather, we had only learned its outward appearance and had not sufficiently grasped its underlying spirit or its substance. . . . In this way the modernization of Japan was only half-measure. . . .

2. *The Japanese Nation does not sufficiently respect Humility, Character, nor Individuality.* . . . Humility is the nature, the ability, the desires and the like qualities with which man is endowed. . . . Character is the qualification of being a human being, meaning "value," and it is built by consolidating, by his own free will, and using the various qualities which a human possesses. . . . Individuality is a nature peculiar only to that particular person. All men possess the quality of humanity and must be equally respected as an individual. The manner in which that humanity reveals itself differs according to each person. This is individuality.

* * *

3. *The Japanese lack critical spirit and are prone to obey authority blindly.* One of the attributes of the Japanese people is that those higher in rank have always loved and guided those below them, while those in inferior ranks respected and served those above them, from which the virtues of loyalty and filial duty generated. But they must be voluntarily based upon his or her own free will. When those above forced submission by authority and those below submitted blindly without exercising critical judgment, then those virtues became feudalistic demerits and not virtues.

* * *

4. *The Japanese people are scientifically backward and have a poor sense of logic.* A people who are inclined to obey authority blindly and do not possess the ability to exercise judgment are people who do not have the ability to think logically. Their scientific abilities are limited by their poor sense of logic. Japan has a number of prominent

scientists but scientifically the people as a whole are still below standard.

* * *

5. *The Japanese are self-satisfied and narrow-minded.* Those who are unable to discard feudalistic feelings take an arrogant and egoistic attitude toward those below them who are blindly obedient to their superiors. Such people do not have the magnanimity to accept people who have different opinions and beliefs. . . . Such self-satisfied attitude has led to unjustified superiority complex of the Japanese people as a whole. The belief that the Emperor was a god personified and that he was better than any other sovereign; that the Japanese race was a special race created by God; that Japan was a divine country, immortal forever; all these ideas are what would be termed as a national superiority complex. And finally under the disguise of a beautiful term "eight corners under one roof" (meaning brotherhood) [*hakkō ichi-u*], she tried to extend her authority and power over other nations. (*Mombushō* trans., pp. 3–8.)

On 1 September 1945 CINCPAC-CINCPOA, the highest Allied Naval command in the Pacific, published its Bulletin No. 209–45, *Guide to Japan*. This summary of Japanese geography, history, economy, and culture had been prepared in anticipation of Japan's capitulation as an orientation aid for American naval officers and enlisted men who were to enter Japan as a part of the Occupation Forces. It was compiled by competent workers, and, with the exception of a few easily discernible propaganda passages for military reasons, it is based on the dispassionate investigations and writings of recognized authorities on Japanese culture. In summing up what might be expected of "Fukuda-san," the mythical Japanese common man, it states that this average citizen is governed by six basic ideas: unity, compromise, indirection, patience, persistence, and ruthlessness. An appraisal of each of these alleged characteristics in the light of the experience of the Occupation may be revealing.

Unity among Japanese is a characteristic so obvious that no foreigner could overlook it. The Japanese citizen is seldom if ever an individualist. He is a member of a group—a family, clan, business, government, military force, or nation. He is bound by an intricate pattern of loyalties and duties, stemming from the five relationships of Confucianism, which demand filial piety, obedience, and loyalty to all those who are his superiors in whatever group is concerned.

Compromise is the nearly inevitable corollary of the Japanese characteristic of unity. Since the group is the basic unit, all fundamental decisions are made by groups. Officials are flanked by their assistants, who are consulted before every answer. Problems are debated and solutions reached by committee action. No individual makes an important decision for himself, whether it be on national military strategy, local political action, or such an intimate personal problem as marriage. The individual must compromise his personal views to the decision of the whole. There is no minority report in Japan. When a compromise has been reached the group presents it as a unanimous decision. The literature of Japan is filled with stories based on the conflict between *giri* (duty to society) and *ninjō* (personal desire). *Giri* inevitably wins out in such a conflict.

Indirection is a quality which the Westerner finds maddening in his relations with the Japanese. His direct question is met by what appears to him to be evasion and delay. All matters of any importance are arranged through an intermediary or "go-between." It is virtually impossible to fix responsibility or to recognize individual achievement. Bulletin No. 209–45 states:

Indirection . . . results from language difficulties and the fact that Japanese practice rarely squares with their principles. The language is not designed for precise speech. As a result it is difficult even for two Japanese to agree on a common meaning. For a westerner and a Japanese to set down in a treaty, for example, words which mean the same thing to both is almost impossible.

Because Japanese principles seem to mean certain things to us does not necessarily mean that they have the same significance to the Japanese. Consequently in western eyes the Japanese always seems to be acting indirectly and not in accordance with his declared intentions. This has, for Fukuda-san, no suggestion of hypocrisy. (P. 57.)

Patience and persistence are among the most obvious and striking characteristics of the Japanese, and are a constant source of surprise and wonder to foreigners. The raising of forests as agricultural crops that are planted, tended for two-score years, and harvested; the construction of the intricate irrigation and hydraulic systems, epitomized in the famous folk story of the "Tunneling of Ao"; the craftsman in carved lacquer who begins an

object of art knowing that his grandson will have to complete it—
these qualities are rarely found in Western civilizations.

Ruthlessness is perhaps the most controversial of the national
characteristics. Bulletin No. 209–45 summarizes: ". . . nothing
must prevent his achievement of his aim and in its accomplishment
he is prepared to be completely ruthless, free from any hindering
feelings of pity, gentleness, or kindness." (P. 57.)

Ruthlessness is present, and in unstinted quantities, as any active
participant in the war can testify. The Rape of Nanking, the
Death March of Bataan, the Prison Camp of Santo Tomás, the
abandoning of garrisons on by-passed islands to starvation, the
kamikaze attacks at Okinawa, the hysterical *banzai* charges—are
monuments to the cruelty, sadism, and ruthlessness of the Japanese. How can these historical facts be reconciled with the nation
which has been eulogized in "Madam Butterfly"? Are these the
same people who weep like children at the most preposterous
pseudo tragedy in the motion pictures? Are these the people who
love their children, delight in the delicate ceremonies of *cha-no-yu*
(the tea cult), the posturing in the *odori* (traditional dance), and
the spectacles of the *kabuki* (traditional review)? Are these the
people who hike for miles over the mountains to obtain a particularly lovely view of Mount Fuji or a valley pink with *sakura*
(Japanese cherry)? Are these the people who before the war devoured tons of so-called "modern literature" of about the intellectual level and saccharine sentimentality of the American "soap
opera" and woman's magazine?

Is it possible to reconcile in a single people all the characteristics
which have been claimed for the Japanese?

He is a man burning with religious zeal, yet tolerant of all religions. He is a man known as the "shrewd Yankee of the Orient,"
clever in business, realistic in his social life, practical in his thinking, yet he is one who is so immersed in the mythical dreamlike
world of ancient mythology that he is willing to surrender his
individual rights and even give his life for it. He is a man who wor-
ships restraint, practices self-effacement, idealizes simplicity, yet
he is hysterical, brutal, and fanatic in the battlefield. He is the
international symbol for courtesy and spends much of his life in
the practice of the highly formalized social niceties, yet he ranks
himself with the gods and treats his inferiors with disdain, contempt, or condescension. He is a man who has copied and occa-

sionally surpassed every civilization with which he has come in contact, yet has failed to acquire or even to sense the great motivating ideals which made possible these civilizations. He is cruel, repressed, frustrated, sentimental, blindly loyal, painstaking, artistic, formal, conservative. He is a child fumbling with the controls of a giant machine. He is an adolescent keyed to the breaking point in his *Sturm und Drang*. He is a man emerging from his feudalism into a world where a mistake can destroy him. And he found himself after Defeat living for the first time in more than 2,000 years in a country dominated by a foreign power.

Military Occupation

The Duration of the Occupation. The military Occupation of Japan could only be temporary. Government by directive was a necessity after the capitulation of the Japanese military commanders in August 1945, but by its inherent nature such government could only be a palliative and not a cure for the basic political and social ills of the occupied country.

General of the Armies Douglas MacArthur, as Supreme Commander for the Allied Powers (SCAP) on 17 March 1947, after a year and a half of Occupation, granted his first formal press conference since his retreat to Australia early in the war. Speaking at the Tokyo Correspondents' Club he advocated an immediate peace treaty and the withdrawal of foreign military forces from Japan. Although no official record of this momentous statement exists, the following excerpts from the notes of an Associated Press correspondent, as reproduced in the *New York Times* of 18 March 1947, are considered to be essentially accurate:

Our occupation job here can be defined as falling roughly into three phases—military, political and economic.

The military purpose, which is to insure that Japan will follow the ways of peace and never again be a menace has been, I think, accomplished. We have demobilized troops, demilitarized the country, torn down military installations. Psychologically, I believe success has been equally propitious. Japan today understands as thoroughly as any nation that war does not pay. Her spiritual revolution has been probably the greatest the world has ever known.

The political phase is approaching such completion as is possible under occupation. We have changed the laws, standards and ideals of this country from the feudalistic ideals of the past into the concept of what is the greatest thing in life, next to spiritual beauty—dignity of man. We have made them think nations exist for the welfare of those who compose them instead of the reverse. . . .

Democracy is a relative thing. It's a question of the degree of freedom you have. If you believe in the Anglo-Saxon idea you will believe this will stay here. If you are a cynic or believe in totalitarianism you may doubt it is here to stay. I believe sincerely and absolutely that it is here to stay.

I don't by that mean to say this thing called democracy has been accomplished. The process of democratization is one of continual flux. It takes years. But in so far as you can lay down the framework it is already accomplished. There is little more except to watch, control and guide.

The third phase is economic. Japan is still economically blockaded by the Allied powers. Economic warfare along those lines still is as bitter here as when the guns were firing. And now strangulation is worse because we have returned millions of repatriates from abroad.

No weapon, not even the atom bomb, is as deadly in its final effect as economic warfare. The atom bomb kills by the thousands, starvation by the millions.

Japan was thoroughly exhausted. All she had left was men. She was living on stockpiles and our blockade, after the fall of the Philippines, kept materials from coming in. Now they are scraping the bottom of the stockpiles.

Each little family had its stockpile—of clothing and heirlooms. Now these are being sold to keep men alive.

Even under the strictest rationing, Japan is not producing enough to satisfy her needs. The difference must be filled by the Allies. If we keep this economic blockade up, more and more we will have to support this country. It is an expensive luxury. But we will pay for it or let people die by the millions.

. . . But this [the economic phase] is not a phase that occupation can settle. We can only enforce economic strangulation.

The immediate and outraged protests which appeared in the world press and the stiffly noncommittal denials which were issued by the several governments of the Allied Powers indicated that there was little likelihood of this policy being immediately implemented. But the soundness of General MacArthur's statement could be attested to by a very considerable proportion of the responsible officials of the Occupation, whose strategic positions permitted them to know in detail the technical difficulties and yet whose military duties require them to remain silent. On 27 June 1947 General MacArthur repeated his recommendations to a visiting group of newspaper editors and publishers, and on 19 August 1947 the Department of State of the United States announced that it had asked the nations represented on the Far Eastern Commission to join in drafting a peace treaty.

Two fundamental conclusions affecting the educational rehabilitation of Japan may be drawn from General MacArthur's statement. The first is that Japan as a nation could not survive economically, or culturally, under a prolonged military occupation. The second is that the very military commanders who were most intimately connected with the defeat and surrender of Japan, and who presumably would be most hesitant to permit a "soft peace" or a hasty withdrawal of military controls, recognized that a military occupation force could accomplish the punitive but was powerless to compel the developmental or growth factors in a defeated nation's renaissance.

The story of this gradual re-education of the Occupation leaders is at times sordid, at times pathetic, and occasionally inspiring. The bitterly revengeful attitude which was sometimes apparent in the first weeks of the Occupation may be summed up with verbatim quotations of two high ranking military officers, whose identity will for obvious reasons be undisclosed.

One said: "If I had my way I'd kill all seventy million of the yellow bellied bastards." Japan had approximately seventy-two million people in the home islands until repatriation and war babies increased this number to about eighty millions by the end of 1946.

The other said: "What if they do starve? I could watch a Jap kid die of starvation and go back to my quarters and eat a good dinner and not even give it a thought."

The early economic commissions, and in particular the first mission headed by Ambassador Edwin A. Pauley in November 1945, recommended reparations policies and destruction of industrial potential which could only bring complete economic collapse. The record of staff meetings in the various special technical sections of the General Headquarters of the Supreme Commander for the Allied Powers is confidential and probably will never be released in its entirety. Some of the most pertinent history is entirely unrecorded. But the frequently bitter disagreements over basic economic and social policies for Japan could not be kept entirely hidden. Adamantly opposed to the destructively tough policies of some of the career military officers were a large number of able technical experts either serving as civilian employees or as reserve officers in the Army and Navy. These scientists and professional people were handicapped by lack of adequate rank or any opportunity to present their detailed investigations to the public. They frequently watched in silence the discard of their recommendations as a result of a "command decision" or saw their technical reports ignored or distorted. It was a peculiar commentary on the psychology of war that among the most vehement advocates of the "tough policy" were the officers and civilians who came to Japan with an immediate record of service in the relative security of continental United States. There was on occasion apparent an attitude of regret that they had arrived in the theater too late to vent their feelings in a physical way. It is to the lasting credit of the Supreme Commander and the more judicial members of his staff that by a year and a half after Surrender the exaggeratedly vindictive policies, reminiscent of those of the "carpetbaggers" of the Reconstruction, had been flatly rejected.

Japan simply could not feed herself upon the sole production of her four main islands. If Japan was to exist, other than as the indigent dependent of some foreign power, presumably the United States, it had to be permitted to rebuild its industrial capacity, to conduct international trade, and to import food. General MacArthur continued in his press conference of 17 March 1947:

We do not allow Japan to trade. She has got to be allowed to trade with the world. Japan is only permitted a barter system through the bottleneck of SCAP. We've got to take it out of the hands of the Government and put it in the hands of private traders.

Eighty million people need 20,000,000 tons of food (annually). Seventeen million tons are produced here. . . . There is no way I can see within the appreciable future that these people can get enough food from indigenous products. . . .

If reparations are cut too deeply, the United States will have to support Japan because we have undertaken major burdens of the occupation.

Willard Price, with an extensive first-hand knowledge of the Japanese Empire and its economics, writing in the February 1946 issue of *Asia*, stated:

. . . overpopulation or underpopulation does not depend upon the number of people to the square mile, but upon the productive facilities and power of these people. It depends also upon their access to food supplies, as New York has access to near-by agricultural states and to foreign lands, and as Japan should have access to agricultural Asia. Japan must also have freedom in her foreign trade. With these provisos, a factory Japan can support a population of from 80,000,000 to 100,000,000 on an unprecedented level of well-being without necessity of resort to plots of territorial aggression.

The incalculable importance of the nation's economic future to the educational system of Japan need hardly be amplified. Japan following Defeat faced years of fighting for her economic survival. Even the maintenance of her existing level of education was contingent upon this survival. If she was to aspire to the educational and social reforms which were proposed under the Occupation, Japan had to secure a revived economy of generous proportions. High on the list of requirements for this economic self-sufficiency, and equally for political self-direction, was the necessity for withdrawal of stringent Occupational controls.

Japan early faced the problem of determining her future policy in view of two contingencies—a short- or a long-term Occupation. If the Occupation were to be a lengthy one, each of the reforms advocated by the Allied Powers would have to be carefully evaluated and selectively adopted. For there could be no presumption of later evasion, noncompliance, or reversal of policy and the economic and educational commitments would be continuing. But if it were to be a brief one, any reform advanced by the Allied Powers might well be accepted without hesitation in the knowledge that such acquiescence was temporary and would involve only nonrecurring commitments. There can be no certain knowledge of which of these two possibilities appeared most probable to the Japanese, though their evident desire to have the protection of an American garrison force for some years to come would indicate that the long-term Occupation was preferred. One thing appears certain. The Japanese authorities were well aware that a military occupation can force a people to do things, but that it is powerless to force them to believe things. As long as the Allied Powers presented their ideology in the form of military directives, the Japanese authorities needed to have little fear of losing control over the dissemination of ideas. An army cannot teach democracy.

The Organization of the Occupation. One of the truisms which came to be recognized in the disillusionment of the years between the two great wars was that it is possible to win military victory and still be defeated. The peace must also be won. Early in the second World War, while the Allied Armies in the field were still at best holding their own and on occasion were suffering humiliating defeat, there were started both military and naval schools to train officers to serve in the occupations which were anticipated following victory. In the past half century there has been ample practical experimentation in various forms of occupational technique.

The officers charged with planning for the eventual occupation of Japan had nearly two-score well-documented records of actual military occupations representing approximately a dozen clearly recognizable techniques. Four basic types were thoroughly explored and considered: a geographical division of territory under separate command of the several Allied Powers, as in the Rhineland Occupation after the first World War and the Occupation of Germany after the second World War; a unified command over the entire nation exercised by an Allied Control Council, similar to that organization used in the Occupation of Sicily and Italy during the progress of the second World War; a decentralized control by unit field commanders or garrison forces, usually considered the only practical form of military government in the first or combat phase of an occupation but also used by the Japanese in the war with China in 1937–45 and in their occupation of Korea in 1906–7 following the Russo-Japanese War; and a centralized control of a unified geographical territory by a General Headquarters composed of either military or civil governors, similar to the German Occupation of Belgium in 1914–15.

The actual organization adopted in the Occupation of Japan did not follow any of these forms exactly but most nearly paralleled the last. It was in fact an evolutionary organization passing through a number of distinct phases: decentralized control until about 10 September 1945 when the first special staff sections were established in General Headquarters, United States Army Forces, Pacific (GHQ, USAFPAC); centralization of policy controls after 2

October 1945 with the establishment of the special staff sections of General Headquarters, Supreme Commander for the Allied Powers (GHQ, SCAP); unification of field command and inspection under the Eighth Army after the withdrawal of the Sixth Army during January 1946; extreme consolidation of controls in GHQ, SCAP, during the first half of 1946; increasing transferal of technical controls to civilian employees following July 1946; and attempted decentralization of inspection and enforcement duties initiated at different times by different staff sections but begun about January 1947 in education. In order to minimize unimportant details a single typical organization will be described. The organization of the Occupation Forces and of the Imperial Japanese Government at the time of the United States Education Mission to Japan, March 1946, has been selected.

At the apex of both systems of government was one towering figure, General of the Armies Douglas MacArthur. Standing just below him over the Japanese system, and in very pale replica of his powers and personality, was the Emperor of Japan, Hirohito, formerly spiritual leader and currently political chief of some 80 million Japanese. The Occupation was singularly free from the confusing histrionics of powerful and flamboyant personalities. It was rare indeed when anyone lower in the military command than a staff section chief was mentioned by name in public notices, and in those isolated cases it was usually a dignified recognition of credit in some technical investigation. Even staff section chiefs and the members of the personal staff of the Supreme Commander worked in comparative anonymity. In part this was the calculated policy of the Army Public Relations Office which credited to General MacArthur all the multitude of actions and decisions for which in the aggregate he had to take responsibility. But it was equally caused by the fact that General MacArthur was in fact as well as title the Supreme Commander for the Allied Powers. He and he alone spoke officially for them. And the Emperor and the Emperor alone spoke officially for the Imperial Japanese Government—although after the new *Constitution* became effective on 3 May 1947 his position became largely titulary and legal authority passed to the Diet and the Cabinet. From this have arisen a myth and a tradition.

The myth at one time reached such proportions as to attract official Occupation attention and is noted by Dr. Ernest R. Hil-

GARD of the United States Education Mission to Japan in his article, "The Enigma of Japanese Friendliness" in the fall, 1946, issue of *The Public Opinion Quarterly*. This myth holds that General MacArthur is not a foreigner but a true Japanese, born in the mountains of a distant prefecture and accorded his position as a divine subject of the Sun-Goddess *Amaterasu Ōmikami*. Traced to its origin this myth is believed to have originated in the attempt to explain the unprecedented indignity of the Emperor calling upon a foreign general on the occasion of his first official meeting with General MacArthur. The photograph of the General, dressed informally in sun-tan shirt and trousers and towering over the formally attired Emperor, was widely circulated in Japan and caused amazement, bewilderment, and finally a frantic rationalization.

The tradition, however, had a more complex explanation. Each sunny day, and occasionally even in the penetrating cold of a Tokyo winter, there assembled in front of the *Dai Ichi* Building, Headquarters of the Supreme Commander, a crowd of curious, worshipful, silent Japanese. They sometimes blocked the broad avenue that runs in front of the Emperor's palace grounds. They were there to catch a glimpse of General MacArthur as he left the building on his way to lunch. Was it just idle curiosity to see the man who commanded the forces that killed their husband or brother or son? The comments that one heard in the crowds that drifted away after the General had driven off would indicate that it was something much more fundamental. The Japanese had been accustomed to submission to authority. Their own leaders had been discredited and this foreign officer provided the essential superior force. Their fear of the invader had turned to dependency. The ascetic remoteness and grave dignity of the Supreme Commander, his unquestioned domination of all Occupation policy, his world renown as a military commander, combined to make him a suitable master. Around him were growing Japanese legends of infallibility. When mistakes were made, and as the Occupation progressed and decisions became increasingly complex, mistakes were not infrequent, they were excused on the same grounds as were those of the Emperor. An adviser had misled him. The crowds that gathered daily at the *Dai Ichi* Building were there to pay respect, not to stare. If this demonstration was quietly encouraged by Occupational sources, it is perhaps understandable.

Awe of the Supreme Commander was not without value in the control of a defeated people.

In one feature at least the myth and the tradition recognize an essential element of the Occupation's organization. The decisions of the Supreme Commander, and of the Emperor within his restricted sphere, were necessarily based on the advice of subordinates. At the time of the United States Education Mission there were nearly 14,000 persons attached to GHQ, SCAP. Of this impressive total probably 500 were officers who in one way or another directly influenced the making and interpretation of official Occupational policy. In the Education Division of CI&E, GHQ, SCAP, alone there were 19 officers or civilians holding comparable civil service ratings who directly affected basic policy. Each of these was in turn dependent upon the technical researches or translations of an indeterminate number of American and Japanese employees who collected, analyzed, and reported on data pertinent to whatever study was under consideration. When these section chiefs, and division chiefs, and sub-section chiefs, and officers, and researchists, and statisticians, and translators were wise and conscientious, the Supreme Commander was wise. When they were not, he could be no better than the composite of his sources of information. The Supreme Commander for the Allied Powers was not an individual. He was a symbol. He was the complex of the minds, and experience, and abilities of his subordinates.

The official organization of GHQ, SCAP, took place on 2 October 1945. Prior to that day the Occupation was directed by the Advanced Echelon of GHQ, USAFPAC, the Army command which had directed the successful military campaigns leading to victory in the Pacific. In the interval just preceding Capitulation and just following the initial occupation of Japan there took place a quiet behind-the-scenes struggle to determine the position of Military Government relative to the traditional General Staff sections of this military command.

Three forms of organization had recent military precedent and were supported by various military groups. Military Government could be a completely distinct agency, having its own Military Governor and holding cognizance over all political, economic, and social problems in the Occupation. Since it would be in no way subordinate to the military forces which would garrison the country, such a government demanded an extensive field organization with both technical and command channels, trained personnel, and housekeeping units located in even the smallest political subdivision, the town or village. The Germans had used this form of administration with comparative success in their Occupation of France in the second World War. It was opposed openly by career military officers on the grounds of duplication of services and lack of economy in personnel, and secretly on the grounds that it would usurp much of their position of command in the Occupation. It was advocated by many of the technically trained civil affairs officers, most of whom were reservists without career aspirations in the military service, on the grounds that only people trained for government service could adequately direct so complex a government organization. As an alternative to this, many of the civil affairs officers favored the creation of a Fifth General Staff Section (G-5) holding parity with the traditional four in an Army GHQ. This had been attempted by General of the Armies Dwight D. EISENHOWER, in the organization of GHQ, SHAEF, in preparation for the invasion of Western Europe. A certain number of career officers in both Army and Navy felt that the functions of government could be undertaken by the existing organization of the four General Staff sections in an Army Headquarters, or by the staff of the Commander of a Naval Fleet in their respective jurisdictions. In retrospect it seems incredible that for months, while these divergent views were being reconciled, the thousands of trained civil affairs officers were put in the humiliating position of having to apologize for their assignment, training, and existence as a military unit.

At the time of Capitulation there was at the Civil Affairs Staging Area (CASA), the Presidio of Monterey in California, and in the various Army Civil Affairs Training Schools (CATS), a large body of trained officers, either organized into military government teams or serving on planning staffs. A tentative plan for the military government of Japan was nearly completed. An advanced echelon from the CASA planning staff had been established in Manila, charged with revising these plans, advising the Army staff on technical problems of government, and preparing to move into Japan with the combat troops. This group was known as "Military Government" and its function and authority were still undecided after Advance GHQ, USAFPAC, had been moved from Manila to Tokyo. This unit, in common with practically all military government units which had served in other theaters and in the islands of the Pacific, was commanded by career combat officers who with few exceptions had no training, experience, or interest in civil affairs. Many considered it a disastrous setback in their professional careers.

The "Initial Post-Surrender Policy for Japan" prepared by the State-War-Navy Co-ordinating Committee (SWNCC) and radioed to General MACARTHUR on 29 August 1945 said in part:

In view of the present character of Japanese society and the desire of the United States to attain its objectives with a minimum commitment of its forces and resources, the Supreme Commander will exercise his authority through Japanese governmental machinery and agencies, including the Emperor, to the extent that this satisfactorily furthers United States objectives. . . . The policy is to use the existing form of Government in Japan, not to support it.

General MACARTHUR and his Chief of Staff, Lt. Gen. Richard K. SUTHERLAND, did not long delay in deciding what should be done with the anomalous civil affairs unit.

The trained military government officers were released to other duty and the section itself subsided into moribund inaction. Many of the most able specialist officers, long dismayed by the obvious lack of top leadership in their branch of the service, requested transfers to other staffs. They constituted the nucleus of trained personnel which made the outstanding record conceded to the Occupation in its first year. The "Military Government," subsequently renamed the Government Section and under new leadership, performed excellently as a special staff section in directing the rewriting of the *Constitution*, reorganization of local governments, and the direction of both Diet and Cabinet.

Three features characterize the type of governmental organization which was created by General MACARTHUR's General Orders of 2 October 1945. Only the Supreme Commander for the Allied Powers could have direct official contact with the Imperial Japanese Government. Military Government was reduced to the advisory services of a series of special staff sections attached to the General Headquarters and located in Tokyo. And Japanese channels of command, together with Japanese officials and existing organizations, were utilized to implement policy enunciated in the official directives from SCAP to the Imperial Japanese Government. In practice this concept was considerably modified.

The General Order No. 1 of 2 October 1945, which abolished
the interim military government in Japan and replaced it with
SCAP, established an Office of the General Procurement Agent and
a series of special staff sections. The Economic and Scientific,
Natural Resources, Government, Public Health and Welfare,
Civil Communications, Civil Information and Education, and
Legal Sections are self-explanatory. By March 1946 there had
been added a Civil Property Custodian to administer the holdings
of enemy and friendly nationals; a section on Statistics and Reports to assemble, edit, and publish pertinent data and reports on
the Occupation; a Civil Intelligence Section charged with civil
public safety and investigation of Japanese compliance with SCAP
directives; an Office of Civilian Personnel to handle the program
of replacing military personnel with civilian employees in the
Occupation Forces; and an International Prosecution Section,
which assumed a portion of the former duties of the Legal Section
in "preparing for trial and prosecuting cases involving crimes resulting from planning, initiation, or participation in a war of aggression or in violation of international agreements." These special
staffs were supplemented by the four General Staff sections directing the military garrison forces and providing certain housekeeping functions to all Occupation personnel; the Adjutant General;
the Public Relations Officer; the General Accounting Section;
and the Secretary, General Staff. All of these latter served primarily as administrative departments within the General Headquarters and were not directly concerned with the Japanese civil
government.

Mention should be made of the somewhat anomalous position
of a series of international advisory boards. As a result of an invitation issued on 21 August 1945 by the United States there was
established in Washington a Far Eastern Advisory Commission
(FEAC) which was charged with making recommendations on
"policies, principles and standards" and on procedural steps for
ensuring the compliance of Japan with the provisions of surrender.
It was specifically barred from making recommendations on military operations and territorial adjustments. Australia, Great Britain, Canada, China, France, India, the Netherlands, New Zealand,
and the Philippine Commonwealth joined the United States on
the Commission but the USSR declined. On 27 December 1945 at
the conclusion of the Moscow Conference of Foreign Ministers

it was announced that FEAC would be replaced by a Far Eastern Commission (FEC) located in Washington and an Allied Council for Japan (ACJ) located in Tokyo. When FEC convened on 26 February 1946 the USSR was represented. FEC retained the original functions of FEAC with the addition that it was charged with review, on the request of any member, of any directive issued by SCAP. It was bound to recognize and respect existing control machinery in Japan including the military chain of command from the United States Government to SCAP and the Supreme Commander's command of Occupation Forces. For months the actual influence of these bodies on the Occupation was little more than their exercising the threat of unfavorable publicity, a position so humiliating that at least one of the members of ACJ is reported to have openly advocated dissolution of the Council. But gradually the influence of FEC grew until on 11 July 1947 it issued the basic policy which was to govern the conduct of the Occupation until a peace treaty was signed.

Of the 12 special staff sections which existed at the time of the United States Education Mission to Japan in March 1946 the Civil Information and Education Section alone had direct jurisdiction over educational matters concerning the civil population of Japan. General Order No. 4 of 2 October 1945, which established this section, stated that its primary duty was to advise the Supreme Commander on policies relating to public information, education, religion, and "other sociological problems" of Japan and Korea. Stripped of the traditional military phraseology, such as "to effect the accomplishment of the information and educational objectives . . . ," this basic order charged the section with three responsibilities: to recommend; to maintain liaison; and to prepare plans and matériel. The section was to make recommendation with regard to policy on the civil liberties and democratic reorientation; with regard to the establishment of information programs designed to inform the Japanese of their war guilt and of Occupational plans and policies; with regard to the establishment of public opinion surveys; and with regard to the demilitarization of the educational system, and the introduction of democratized education. It was directed to maintain liaison with the pertinent Japanese Ministries; with press, radio, motion pictures, and other information media; with educational institutions; and with religious, political, professional, and commercial organizations, to ensure their understanding and co-operation with enunciated Occupation policies. Finally, the section was expected to direct the preparation of plans, materials, and programs necessary to implement the information and education policies of the Occupation. With the addition of jurisdiction over the protection, preservation, salvage, and disposition of works of art and antiquity and objects classed as national treasures, as directed in General Order No. 27 of 3 June 1946, the original duties, functions, and authority established on 2 October 1945 were continued.

The internal organization of the Civil Information and Education Section (CI&E) changed repeatedly in its brief history. Some were mere paper reorganizations with shuffling of the boxes on an organization chart, a pastime which continues to fascinate a certain type of military mind. Some were administrative devices—the creation of positions for deserving senior officers, or the removal of able subordinates from the stultifying control of a too conservative senior, and, on occasion, the reverse. Some were necessary reorganizations to consolidate overlapping efforts of various divisions, as in the creation of a central Analysis and Research Division and the establishment of a central translators' pool.

The March 1946 organization of CI&E was typical. Headed by a Chief and Assistant Chief, the section was serviced by an Administrative Section which handled routine military housekeeping functions with the exception of billeting and messing. Six divisions operated under the direct supervision of the Chief of Section: Analysis and Research; Cultural Resources (sometimes called Arts and Monuments); Religions; Education; Planning and Special Projects (which included the highly important subsection on labor unions); and Information Dissemination. The Analysis and Research Division was divided into two sub-sections: Media Analysis which scanned, evaluated, and reported on all Japanese information channels; and Research and Information which collected data, conducted research, and prepared materials and reports requested by the other sections in CI&E. The Information Dissemination Division was divided into four main subsections: Press and Publications which served also as Public Relations Office and censored all Japanese publications; Motion Pictures and Theater; Radio; and the Reference Library supplying American books to the Japanese public in the Tokyo area.

The two divisions which directly controlled educational matters were the Division of Religions which was charged with separation of Church and State involving the removal of Shinto influences from all public educational institutions, one of the major operations of the Occupation, and the Education Division which was in direct liaison with the Ministry of Education and was held responsible for all policy affecting education. What has been noted with regard to reorganizations within CI&E was at least equally true of the Education Division. It was reorganized so many times, and apparently for so many motives, that a continuing pattern is difficult to discern. In broad oversimplification it may be said to have fluctuated between an organization paralleling the educational institutions of the Japanese system and an organization reflecting the various educational services which the Occupation desired incorporated in the Japanese system.

The March 1946 organization of the Education Division, CI&E, included a Chief, assisted by an executive officer and aided by a number of advisers, and three sub-sections: Plans and Policies, Operations, and Administration. The advisers to the Chief of the Division were composed largely of Japanese or European nationals with long residence in Japan and a presumed technical knowledge of the educational system. From time to time this group was supplemented by United States citizens with extended prewar Japanese residence—the "Old Japan Hands."

The Administration Sub-Section included translators, interpreters, Japanese nationals serving as "examiners" or proofreaders and as technical advisers on matters involving materials in the Japanese language, and a variety of clerks, stenographers, and typists in both English and Japanese. The Operations Sub-Section included specialist officers and their assistants for each of the types of Japanese educational institution (elementary school, boys middle school, girls middle school, continuation and vocational school, higher school, higher technical school, normal schools, and university). In addition there was a liaison officer who was responsible for all liaison with subordinate military units in the Occupation Forces and a series of field liaison officers, the majority of whom were trained language officers in Japanese with some military intelligence service, who made spot inspections and conducted investigations of serious foci of resistance involving education. The third sub-section, Plans and Policies, included specialist officers and their assistants in Educational Reorganization, Language Simplification, Textbooks and Curricula, "Female Education" (including the vital work on granting women equality in political and educational matters), "Male Education" (an intriguing puzzle even to the members of the staff, and a position never filled), Teacher Training, Continuation and Vocational Education, and Miscellaneous Media (including visual education, radio, the press, and other mass media).

As originally conceived this organization was intended to satisfy the requirements of the 2 October 1945 activating order with the Operations Sub-Section performing the liaison function and the Plans and Policies Sub-Section performing the policy recommendation function. In order to secure the best available technical advice in education, without relinquishing the positive control which the military staff officers did not care to lose, it was planned to provide a civilian adviser for each of the major sub-divisions of the Plans and Policies Sub-Section. These civilian advisers were supposed to provide disinterested and highly professional technical advice and to be directly responsible only to the Chief of the Education Division. A number of practical considerations combined to frustrate the full realization of this plan. Many of the key military officers, being reservists with extended prior service, were released from service, causing a constant change in personnel. First communications were slow, then authorized tables of staff size were cut, then incentive salaries were reduced. There was never an adequately sized staff. As a result advisers found they were put to work and required to perform routine duties alike with the other officers. The insistence that civilian technical experts be given a simulated rank or civil service rating inferior to that of the military officer serving as chief of a section or division, frequently a lieutenant colonel, removed any monetary or prestige incentive for educators of established position in the United States. Civilians without military background on occasion were resentful of the military authority which was imposed on their work. By the end of the first year of the Occupation it was evident that a position in education in the Occupation could not be considered a professional advancement for educators of the caliber that was needed.

Brief excerpts from the letters of two officers, both professional educators in civilian life, written on their termination of service with the Educational Division, are not without interest. Their identity is withheld for obvious reasons.

One wrote:

Education progresses slowly even yet. I know that Japan has taken a back seat in world news. That was true even last summer. . . . Education and the CI&E are too scared to say their soul is their own. That is not particularly new, however. Sometimes I become very disgusted with the whole business.

The other wrote:

At the time I left . . . was pretty disgusted with the whole mincing attitude and about half ready to tell them they could take the job and . . . if they didn't intend it to *be* a job.

The whole Education Division was confronted with difficulties about the time I left. As far as concrete planning in any field goes, I can't see that they are any further along than . . . [a year ago]. The Japanese are showing increasing signs of balking when it comes down to the dirty work of making actual changes. The famous old phrase of having "the *Mombushō* [Ministry of Education] emasculate itself" isn't working out so well. The boys over there, when the knife comes into actual view, show a singular reluctance toward the idea of emasculation. They've taken the phrase "freedom of education" to their bosoms, but figure it should mean that the Ministry of Education is free to run it as it sees fit. This year has afforded a classic example of the Japanese tactic of yielding to the enemy—but just so far. . . .

To paraphrase T. S. Eliot, our show is dying with a whimper.

One of the standing jokes among military government officers returned to lecture at the Civil Affairs Training Schools after foreign duty during the war was that the most desirable duty in military government was that of an education officer because you could always be assured of a fine rating on inspection if you just had the children stand at attention and sing "America" or "The Star Spangled Banner" for any "visiting brass." The following quotation from a GHQ Special News Service Bulletin, sent early in 1947 from Tokyo to the members of the former United States Education Mission to Japan, defies comment:

. . . the Seisho primary school in the city of Kyoto was visited by Lt. Gen. Robert L. Eichelberger, Commanding General Eighth Army, and a party of American educators recently. The general was visibly impressed when he heard a group of fourth grade boys singing an English song at the top of their lungs.

The Organization of the Japanese Government. It was inevitable that basic reorganizations of the Japanese political structure should occupy the Allied Powers after Surrender. The Japanese Government was an obvious and vulnerable target for the punitive action of the Occupation Forces. By 17 March 1947 General MacArthur was able to announce that in his opinion the political reform was rapidly approaching such completion as was possible under occupation. He felt that in so far as democracy could be forced on Japan from the outside there was little more that could be accomplished. The new *Constitution* was completed and was to be put into use on 3 May 1947. The higher political offices had been purged. The first Diet to be completely re-elected and re-organized under the Occupation was soon to convene. The governmental organization of Japan had completed its first major change since 11 February 1889, when Emperor MUTSUHITO, later known as Emperor MEIJI, gave the *Constitution* and a series of supplementary laws to the nation.

The Constitutional Government which developed during the Meiji Restoration was a direct outgrowth of a Commission of Administrative Reform headed by Prince ITŌ Hirobumi after his return from Germany in 1884. ITŌ Miyoji, KANEKO Kentarō, and INOUE Tsuyoshi were the first assistants of Prince ITŌ in drafting the *Constitution* and General Prince YAMAGATA, a close personal friend of Prince ITŌ, became the powerful unofficial adviser. The commission was attached to the Imperial Household as the Privy Council and after May 1888 met with Emperor MEIJI and his advisers, IWAKURA Tomomi and SANJŌ Sanetomo, in completing the final draft. It is generally conceded that the German governmental organization, epitomized by the political philosophy of Chancellor BISMARCK, became the basic model. Prince ITŌ had known BISMARCK during his European visit and was most impressed by his unification of the German states. The final product was a mixture of German constitutional authority and French law and bureau organization, both of which were systems which could be imposed from the top by authority and did not require the slow growth, and loss of central control, which characterized a decentralized democracy. The half century before the second World War saw only minor modifications and no basic changes in the structure then conceived.

The Emperor was a triune leader of the Japanese. He was the

spiritual, or more properly in Shinto philosophy, the ritualistic head of the Japanese nation. He was the chief executive, occupying the post of Commander in Chief of the Army and Navy, alone holding authority to determine their organization and peacetime strength, to declare war, make peace, conclude treaties, and declare a state of siege (comparable to a state of national emergency in Occidental nations). And he was the chief legislative power, with sole authority to sanction, promulgate, and execute laws and ordinances, to convoke, open, close, and adjourn the Diet, and to issue Imperial ordinances in place of law. Under a powerful and determined Emperor, the position could become that of a dictator or an absolutist monarch. Under a weak or indifferent Emperor, the position could become a figurehead for powerful cliques which were able to control his actions. Two of these cliques, the *zaibatsu* or family economic combines, and the *gumbatsu* or militarists, were primarily responsible for the policy of Japan after the assassination of Prime Minister INUKAI Tsuyoshi on 15 May 1932.

The prewar Japanese National Government (*Nippon Seifu*) was organized along three vertical channels: a series of administrative and executive offices and agencies known as the extraconstitutional bodies; the Constitutional Assembly or Imperial Diet (*Teikoku Gikai*); and the Imperial Cabinet (*Naikaku*) with its subordinate executive Ministries and the Privy Council (*Sūmitsu-in*). The functions of these agencies have fluctuated between executive and legislative in their sixty-year history. Those which are executive in nature have been both administrative and advisory. In retrospect what was outwardly a constitutional monarchy appears to have been in reality a military oligarchy. The Emperor proved to be the pawn, perhaps at times willingly, of the officer class operating through the centralized authority of the Imperial Cabinet and various advisory groups.

The most important of the extraconstitutional bodies is the Imperial Conference (*Gozen Kaigi*) convened in times of great political or military crisis to determine fundamental national policy. Although precedent for such conferences to advise the Emperor and *Shōgun* had existed for centuries, the first recognized Imperial Conference after the granting of the 1889 *Constitution* occurred on 27 June 1894 to determine the policy to be followed in light of the invasion of Korea by a Chinese Army. Slightly more than a dozen such conferences have occurred in the intervening years, each occasioned by some extremely grave crisis, each attended by military leaders, nobles, Ministers, and private advisers of the Emperor upon his personal invitation, and each resulting in a statement of policy sanctioned by the Emperor and indicating "complete agreement" of all government bodies.

The military services were represented by two official, but extraconstitutional bodies: the Board of Marshals and Fleet Admirals (*Gensui-fu*); and the Supreme War Council (*Gunji Sangi-in*). The former was founded in 1898 but soon became more honorary than political. The latter was founded informally in 1887 and was granted official status by Imperial Ordinance No. 294 of 1903. It included the marshals and fleet admirals of the former body together with the General Staff and Naval Staff and certain high-ranking officers appointed personally by the Emperor. It was charged with basic military policy. Both these organizations have, of course, been disbanded with the demobilization of all military organizations in compliance with the terms of surrender.

Two advisory political groups have played a remarkable part in Japanese modern history. They are the Elder Statesmen (*Genrō*) and the Principal Subjects (*Jūshin*). The first of these was an informal group of gifted advisers to the Emperor MEIJI who helped establish domestic and foreign policy and who traditionally chose the successive Prime Ministers. Since its importance derived from the personal ability and influence of its members rather than from the importance of an official position, and since it was a self-perpetuating organization and the last of the *Genrō*, Prince SAIONJI Kimmochi, appointed by Imperial Ordinance in December 1926, expressed a desire that the institution end with himself, the group has passed into tradition. The Principal Subjects, however, may well be the successor to this earlier group. On three occasions (15 May 1932 when Prime Minister INUKAI was assassinated; 3 July 1934 to recommend Admiral OKADA as successor to Prime Minister SAITŌ; and 26 February 1936 on the occasion of the rebellion of young army officers) Prince SAIONJI called together a group of outstanding public figures, which he referred to as Principal Subjects to distinguish them from the Elder Statesmen, to assist in naming new heads of the Cabinet. Since those meetings the *Jūshin* have largely taken over the old functions of the *Genrō*.

Among official offices considered extraconstitutional in character were those of the Lord Keeper of the Privy Seal (*Naidaijin*) and the Minister of the Imperial Household (*Kunai Daijin*). The former acted as a personal adviser to the Emperor, who directly appointed the statesman for a limited tenure. Since this official handled all bills and ordinances which required Imperial sanction the post was not without importance. It was formally abolished on 24 November 1945 with the routine work being assumed by the Grand Chamberlain, the Minister of the Imperial Household, and the President of the Privy Council, and with the advisory functions being abolished entirely.

Paralleling the extraconstitutional bodies in function, but being specifically provided for in both the old *Constitution* (Article LXXII) and the new *Constitution* (Article XC), is the Board of Audit (*Kaikei Kensa-in*). Its authority stems from the Law of Audit No. 15, 10 May 1889, which establishes it on a semi-autonomous basis responsible directly to the Emperor independent of both the Diet and the Ministries of State. It is required to audit all national accounts, supervise the expenditure of public monies, and report annually to the Emperor. Under the new *Constitution* this annual report shall be made to the Diet.

The second of the three vertical administrative channels is the Imperial Diet (*Teikoku Gikai*). It was divided into two houses: the House of Peers (*Kizoku-in*); and the House of Representatives (*Shūgi-in*). Although ostensibly granted broad powers the Diet had until the period of the Occupation been stripped of most of its power by a series of calculated political devices which relegated it to a position of executive power subordinate to the Emperor. It was not a legislative body as conceived of in Occidental government. This was vitally changed with the adoption of the new *Constitution* which states in Article XLI: "The Diet shall be the highest organ of State power, and shall be the sole law-making organ of the State." (United States State Department trans.)

The House of Peers in the past was composed of members of the Imperial Family; princes and marquises; certain counts, viscounts, and barons elected by the members of their respective Court orders; a number of persons personally appointed by the Emperor for meritorious service to the nation; and a small number (about 16%) elected popularly from major taxpayers, who then required Imperial sanction for seating. The House of Peers was governed by the *Constitution* and the "Imperial Ordinance for the House of Peers" (*Kizoku-in Rei*) which could only be amended by that body. Articles XLII, XLIII, and XLIV of the new *Constitution* replace the House of Peers with a House of Councilors (*Sangi-in*) composed of elected members, representative of the people, and with all discrimination because of race, creed, sex, social status, or family origin specifically forbidden. Whereas the old House of Peers could only be adjourned even though the House of Representatives could be dissolved, under the new *Constitution*, Article LIV, the House of Councilors must also be closed, except in grave national emergencies when action can be taken but with the stipulation that measures must remain provisional until the House of Representatives approves them.

The old House of Representatives was composed of representatives of 119 electoral districts, each district electing 3 to 5 members to make a total membership of 466 seats divided into 352 rural and 112 urban. Male subjects 30 years of age and over were eligible for office and males 25 years of age and over held the right to vote, with the exception of certain class exclusions such as heads of noble families, indigents, quasi-incompetents, officers on active military service, etc. Election was governed by the 1925 Law of Elections which has been revised under the Occupation in line with the provisions of the new *Constitution*. Whereas the old House of Representatives was without real legislative power, serving more as a public opinion sounding board and as a manipulated rubber-stamp for Cabinet decisions, under the provisions of Articles LIX and LX of the new *Constitution* the House of Representatives is given new dignity and power. Among basic powers is final decision (in the event of a disagreement with the House of Councilors) over the National Budget or conclusion of a treaty, and the right to override a House of Councilors veto or disagreement on a national law by a two-thirds majority. In the past the decorum of the House of Representatives was frequently such as to undermine popular respect for its judgment of that body. This is perhaps not without parallel in countries with longer experience in representative government. Although the early sessions in the Occupation indicated that the war interval had not entirely eradicated the unfortunate tendency to frenzied oratory and hysterical outbursts, there has been every evidence of a sincere attempt to rise to the new responsibilities. Statesmanship can only come from the actual practice of government and the exercise of authority.

The internal organization of special committees, maintenance of records, party organization, and parliamentary procedure is not unlike that of Occidental countries and need not be examined here in detail. The basic powers are, however, pertinent. Under the new *Constitution* the Diet (and under the circumstances noted above this means the House of Representatives alone) controls the passage of national laws, the establishment of a national budget, the conclusion of treaties, the conduct of investigations bearing on national affairs, the expenditure of money, the maintenance of reserve funds, the floating of loans and assumption of financial obligations, the auditing of expenditures, the amendment of the *Constitution*, and the supervision of the conduct and eligibility of their own members. Councilors are elected for terms of six years, and representatives for terms of four. Article XIV of the new *Constitution* provides for the absolute equality of citizens, and the new Election Law grants the right to vote to women and lowers the age of voting to 20 years from the former 25, and the age for candidacy to membership in the Diet from 30 to 25. As a result of the General Elections of 10 April 1946 the Japanese Diet for the first time in its history seated women members.

The third vertical administrative channel is that of the cabinets. There are two: the Imperial Cabinet (*Naikaku*) established by the *Imperial Rescript on Cabinet Organization* issued 23 December 1889 at the time of the adoption of the old *Constitution;* and the Privy Council (*Sūmitsu-in*) founded by the Imperial Ordinances of 30 April 1888 and 8 October 1890. Of these two, the Imperial Cabinet, composed of the several chiefs of the executive Ministries together with certain Ministers without Portfolio and the Prime Minister or Premier, is by far the more important.

The Imperial Cabinet (*Naikaku*), as created in 1889, had nine Ministries represented: Home Affairs, Foreign Affairs, War, Navy, Justice, Finance, Education, Agriculture and Commerce, and Communications. It was headed by a Minister President, counterpart of the modern Prime Minister or Premier. The Ministry of the Imperial Household was not included in the Cabinet at that time, nor has it been included in any government down to the present time. Prior to the war the Imperial Cabinet had been enlarged to include besides the Prime Minister, and certain Ministers without Portfolio, 13 executive Ministries represented by their chiefs, namely, War (*Rikugunshō*), Navy (*Kaigunshō*), Home Affairs (*Naimushō*), Foreign Affairs (*Gaimushō*), Finance

(*Ōkurashō*), Agriculture and Forestry (*Norinshō*), Commerce and Industry (*Shōkōshō*), Communications (*Teishinshō*), Railways (*Tetsudōshō*), Education (*Mombushō*), Justice (*Shihōshō*), Welfare (*Kōseishō*), and Overseas Affairs (*Takumushō*).

During the war there were a number of Cabinet changes, some of which created or dissolved executive Ministries. During September and October 1942 the Ministry of Greater East Asia (*Daitōashō*) was established and powers over that area of Foreign Affairs were transferred from the *Gaimushō*. In October and November 1943 the Ministry of Overseas Affairs was eliminated, and the Ministries of Commerce and Industry, Communications, Agriculture and Forestry, and Railways were replaced by the three new Ministries of Munitions (*Gunjushō*), Transportation and Communications (*Unyu Tsūshinshō*), and Agriculture and Commerce (*Nōshōshō*).

Capitulation and the necessity of demilitarizing Japan in accordance with the surrender terms brought the greatest of all changes. The Ministries of War and Navy were dissolved and two temporary administrative organs, known as Demobilization Ministry No. I (*Fukuinchō Dai-ichibu*) and Demobilization Ministry No. II (*Fukuinchō Dai-nibu*), replaced them to carry out the technical details of complete demobilization, disarmament, and destruction of all military potential. In keeping with this reorganization and the causes which produced it Article IX of the new *Constitution* states:

Aspiring sincerely to an international peace based on justice and order, the Japanese people forever renounce war as a sovereign right of the nation and the threat or use of force as a means of settling international disputes.

In order to accomplish the aim of the preceding paragraph, land, sea, and air forces, as well as other war potential, will never be maintained. The right of belligerency of the state will not be recognized. (United States Department of State trans.)

By March 1946 when the United States Education Mission was in Tokyo, if the YOSHIDA Shigeru Cabinet may be taken as an example of the organization of the Cabinet under the Occupation, the Ministries had been stabilized in a manner similar to the prewar form. There were represented the Ministries of Foreign Affairs, Home Affairs, Finance, Justice, Education, Welfare, Agriculture and Forestry, Commerce and Industry, Transportation, and the two temporary Demobilization Ministries. A need for a new Ministry of Labor was also recognized.

The functions of the Imperial Cabinet have changed with the various reorganizations and with the gradual evolution of the government. Article LV of the old *Constitution* provided that:

The respective Ministries of State shall give their advice to the Emperor, and be responsible for it.

All laws, Imperial Ordinances and Imperial Rescripts of whatever kind, that relate to the affairs of State, require the counter signature of a Minister of State.

The "Commentaries" of Prince Itō Hirobumi, head of the commission which originally drafted the *Constitution*, states what was intended by the writers and is generally considered to be the authoritative interpretation:

First, that the Ministers of State are charged with the duty of giving advice to the Emperor, which is their proper function, and that they are not held responsible on His behalf; secondly, that Ministers are directly responsible to the Emperor and indirectly so to the people; thirdly, that it is the Sovereign and not the people that can decide as to the responsibility of Ministers, because the Sovereign possesses the rights of sovereignty of the State; fourthly, that the responsibility for Ministers is a political one and has no relation to criminal or civil responsibility, nor can it conflict therewith neither can the one affect the other. (United States War Department trans.)

The *Imperial Rescript on the Functions of the Cabinet*, Articles II and V, issued on 23 December 1885, detail the functions of the Cabinet and establish the limits of responsibility by stating that it shall, in compliance with Imperial instructions, have general control over the various branches of the government, and that it shall have cognizance over the drafts of laws, administrative ordinances, the execution and enforcement of regulations and laws, financial estimates, budgets, settled accounts, expenditures, treaties, all national questions of importance, inter-Ministerial disputes, petitions from the people (via the Throne or the Diet), and the appointment, promotion, and removal of officials of the *chokunin* rank, two highest levels in the regular civil service.

The major changes made in the position of the Imperial Cabinet by the new *Constitution* were that it transferred executive power from the Emperor to the Cabinet (Article LXV); that the Cabinet was to be collectively responsible to the Diet (Article LXVI); that the Prime Minister was to be designated by a resolution of the Diet and not by Imperial appointment on recommendation of an extraconstitutional body such as the *Genrō* or *Jūshin* (Article LXVII); and that the Prime Minister might remove Ministers of State as he chose (Article LXVIII). This latter change, together with the renunciation of war and consequent dissolution of the Ministries of War and of the Navy, is of profound significance. Under the old system of government the Prime Minister nominated all Ministers of State except those representing the Army and Navy, who had to be a general and an admiral corresponding to American three-star rank or higher. These military officers could at any time force a fall of the Cabinet by the simple device of resigning, and the military services could prevent the formation of a new Cabinet by "finding it impossible" for any general or admiral to accept the post.

The old *Constitution*, Article VII, gave the military representatives direct access to the Emperor (*iaku jōsō*) on all matters relating to military secrecy and command (*gunki gunrei*). As a result the old form of the Cabinet consisted of a powerful military cabinet within the authorized political one, and the military services were in effect granted veto power over all governmental functions. When exercised, this military control demonstrated the paralyzing power of a strike of key public officials. Under the new *Constitution* such a paralysis is presumably difficult or impossible.

The second of the two cabinet-type agencies for executive control was the Privy Council (*Sūmitsu-in*). Article LVI of the old *Constitution* stated the responsibility of the members of this organ as being that of "deliberation upon important matters of State, when they have been consulted by the Emperor." The Privy Council immediately before the war was composed of a President and Vice-President and 25 Councilors, all appointed for life by the Emperor and all holding *shinnin* (Imperial Investiture Civil Service) rank. The Councilors were men of 40 years of age or more, and were frequently members of the House of Peers but were not permitted to hold concurrently a Cabinet post. In November 1945 the size of the Privy Council was reduced to ten members and the new *Constitution*, drafted between 6 March and 22 April 1946, contains no mention of the organ.

Although in the past it had no direct application to the educational system, mention should perhaps be made of the Japanese judicial system, which completes the Executive-Legislative-Judiciary organization of the government. The old judicial system was bifurcated in character: the Court of Administrative Litigation (*Gyōsei Saibansho*) which under authority of Article LXI of the old *Constitution* was autonomous and had jurisdiction over all cases involving the administrative authorities; and the Courts of Law (*Shihō Saibansho*), which under authority of Articles LVII through LX of the old *Constitution* had jurisdiction over all other legal matters. These latter were under the supervision of the Minister of Justice (*Shihō Daijin*) as established by Article 135 of the Law on the Constitution of the Courts of Justice (*Saibansho Kōsei Hō*), No. 6 of 10 February 1890. The Courts of Law were headed by a national Supreme Court (*Daishin-in*), located in Tokyo which was divided into a number of divisions sitting on both criminal and civil cases concurrently. Below this court, in descending order of jurisdiction, were courts of appeal (*Kōso-in*), located in Tokyo, Osaka, Nagoya, Hiroshima, Nagasaki, Miyagi, and Sapporo; district courts (*Chihō Saibansho*) located in 52 districts; and local courts (*Ku Saibansho*) located in 283 localities but in 1939 maintaining in addition 1,790 branches where routine matters of registration and arbitration were handled but no cases were tried. In addition to this system of law courts there were police courts (*Keisatsu Shobun*), juvenile courts (*Shōnen Shimpansho*), and special types of courts established by law under the authority of Article LX of the old *Constitution*, namely, courts martial (*Gumpō Kaigi*), prize courts (*Hokaku Shinkenjo*), consular courts (*Ryōji Saiban*), colonial courts, such as *Nanyōchō Hōin* for the South Sea Islands' jurisdiction, and courts for mariners (*Kaiin Shimpanjo*).

A detailed analysis of the internal organization and operating procedures of these various legal bodies is clearly unnecessary, but a brief note as to the limitations of the judiciary system may provide a side light on the governmental and political philosophy which is indeed pertinent to the thesis of this volume. Most prominent of the deficiencies in the legal system, from the Occidental point of view, was the complete absence of any power to establish the constitutionality or to investigate the content of a law (*hōritsu*). The procedure by which a law was passed, with ultimate sanction by the Emperor, made it final and unquestionable authority. This deficiency did not extend to ordinances (*chokurei*) which were issued from the various Ministries of State without Diet approval or Imperial sanction, but it did to all treaties (*jōyaku*) which are considered to be laws but of a higher authority than *hōritsu*. Of a less technical nature, a marked deficiency in the practical operation of the judiciary system has been the excessive literalness of decisions. This is both a result of the lack of interpretive power mentioned above and also of the formalistic education to which the judges have been subjected.

Article LXXVI of the new *Constitution* provides that the Supreme Court shall be vested with the "whole judicial power" and specifically prohibits the establishment of extraordinary tribunals and prohibits any branch of the Executive (vested in the Cabinet by the new *Constitution*) from exercising final judicial power. Article LXXXI states that the Supreme Court shall be the court of last resort with "power to determine the constitutionality of any law, order, regulation, or official act."

Within this organization of government the Emperor, the Diet, the Cabinet, the Ministries of Education, Finance, and Home Affairs, and the subordinate prefectural governments (under the Ministry of Home Affairs) with their subordinate local governments in municipality, city, town, and village, exercise controls over the educational system. The relevant details of each of these governmental entities will be examined in detail as their particular educational control is analyzed. For the purpose of considering the effect of Occupational control on education this brief summary of the national echelon will suffice.

The Formulation of Policy Under the Occupation. One of the quaint misconceptions of the American lay public is that the foreign policy of the United States is exclusively formulated somewhere in the mysterious fastnesses of the "Government in Washington." It is not the purpose of this study to examine foreign policy outside the field of the Occupation of Japan. Even within this delimited area only educational policy is a primary concern. But in so far as American foreign policy has to date affected the control and rehabilitation of the educational system of Japan, the popular conception of a precise and comprehensive foreign policy emanating from a central organ of the national government can be categorically denied.

There is an official policy but it is one which has been evolved. In its incipient stages it is the discernible trend of the personal actions and attitudes of the Occupation personnel. It is a pattern of local decisions made by individual officers in the field. It is the framework of interpretations and implementations of fragmentary evidences of American policy, sometimes cryptic War Department or Department of State orders, sometimes remarks made by public officials in news conferences or radio broadcasts, sometimes recommendations made in newspaper editorials, or the findings of commercial public opinion polls. It is the entire complex structure of SCAP directives, a very considerable portion of which were initiated in the Occupation Headquarters and could only be linked to superior governmental authority by some tortuous connection with the much abused omnibus provision of the *Potsdam Declaration* which stated: "The Japanese Government shall remove all obstacles to the revival and strengthening of democratic tendencies among the Japanese people." There have been formal statements of Occupational policy but with few exceptions these have followed and legitimized existing operational procedure and have not preceded and inspired those procedures. American policy in the Occupation has been formulated by at least six different methods: by directive, by interpretation, by example, by nudge, by review, and by mistake.

American policy by directive comes the closest to coinciding with the popular conception of a formal statement enunciated by one of the executive departments of the national government. The Far Eastern Subcommittee of the State-War-Navy Co-ordinating Committee (SWNCC) in Washington was charged with formulation of basic Occupational policy which when completed was submitted by the Secretary of State to the President for final approval and then forwarded by the Joint Chiefs of Staff (JCS) to the Theater Commander. The technical preparation of this policy, which in practice virtually predetermined the ultimate decision, was the responsibility of the Office of Far Eastern Affairs in the Department of State, of the Civil Affairs Division in the War Department, and of the Office of Military Government in the Bureau of Naval Operations in the Navy Department. Because the Occupation of Japan was originally considered primarily a military operation and during the first two years did in fact remain essentially a military responsibility, the two service components of this triumvirate early assumed the major responsibility for producing a plan or detailed statement of policy. A Joint Civil Affairs Committee under the wartime Joint Chiefs of Staff issued military government policy directives to Theater Commanders and advised swncc on the military elements of Occupational policy. The resultant swncc plan was almost identical, even in phraseology, with the jcs plan on most major points of policy, including those on education. This organization was continued after Surrender and formalized by a swncc Directive dated 8 April 1946 entitled, "Organization and Procedure for the Development and Promulgation of United States Policy with Respect to Occupied Areas." It provided that directives should be forwarded to the United States representative on the Far Eastern Commission (fec) or "where appropriate" directly to the Supreme Commander for the Allied Powers. The Far Eastern Commission, of course, was empowered to formulate its own policy, Allied rather than limited to the United States, which it sent directly to the Supreme Commander for the Allied Powers (scap).

In outward appearance at least such a machinery would appear to be eminently capable of producing a detailed statement of Occupational policy. This appearance proved deceptive. During the entire wartime existence of both Naval Schools of Military Government (at Columbia University and Princeton University) neither the officers under instruction nor the faculty were able to secure a single official statement of occupation policy from the Department of State. A similar condition must be assumed for the six Army Civil Affairs Training Schools (cats) at the Universities of Chicago, Harvard, Michigan, Northwestern, Stanford, and Yale although it is today impossible to verify this assumption.

Key wartime officials of each of the military government divisions in the War and Navy Departments openly indicated their dissatisfaction at transferal from combat duty to military government and privately confessed their lack of interest and fear that it would prove a disastrous handicap in their military career. Many of the trained military government officers who served in technical capacities in these two planning units frankly stated that they were not permitted to plan, "until they had a policy directive from higher authority." The conception that they were the persons responsible for initiating that policy was not only not accepted but openly ridiculed. A measure of the indifference or lack of foresight of the responsible military officials may be taken from the fact that the administration and faculty of the Naval School of Military Government at Princeton University, which graduated 986 Army and Navy civil affairs officers or approximately one third those trained for the entire Pacific, was ordered to refrain from holding any classes dealing with the area of Korea on the grounds that "we probably will never go in there anyway." This body of officers, who actually were to constitute a major proportion of the trained military government personnel in the occupation of Korea, received what training in that area they got because a junior naval officer turned his deaf ear to the order and scheduled such classes in their spare time. Out of more than 240 class hours, receiving 9 semester hours of graduate credit, only one lecture of an hour and a half was permitted in the field of education.

Three official statements of policy for the Occupation of Japan were issued before the Headquarters of the Supreme Commander for the Allied Powers was established in Tokyo. Two were Top Secret undated parallel directives of SWNCC and JCS which were issued during the early summer of 1945 as alternative plans for a contested and an uncontested invasion of the home islands of Japan. The sections concerning education in Japan consisted of a paragraph of about five short sentences. Essentially the same content was carried in a SWNCC Directive dated 13 October 1945 and a JCS Directive dated 3 November 1945, both of which also carried Top Secret classification. A direct quotation of the unclassified compilation of the education provisions of all these directives as contained in the Basic Educational Plan of the Civil Information and Education Section, GHQ, SCAP, follows:

1. To *eliminate* militaristic and ultra-nationalistic propaganda, official sanction of and support of Shinto, and unacceptable teachers.
2. *To introduce* democratic ideas and principles, democratic tendencies in social organizations, information on the Japanese defeat and its implications, and knowledge of the responsibility of the Japanese to maintain their own standard of living without assistance.
3. *To safeguard* religious freedom, and within the limits of security, freedom of opinion, speech, press, and assembly.
4. *To control* the curricula of educational institutions, the eligibility of persons to hold public office or important positions in private organizations, and the opening of schools.

The "Initial Post-Surrender Policy for Japan" prepared jointly by the State, War, and Navy Departments (SWNCC) on 29 August 1945 and approved by the President on 6 September 1945, besides certain statements of the ultimate objectives of the Occupation which will be considered in detail later, had only the following specific reference to education:

Militarism and ultra-nationalism, in doctrine and practice, including para-military training, shall be eliminated from the educational system. Former career military and naval officers, both commissioned and non-commissioned, and all other exponents of militarism and ultra-nationalism shall be excluded from supervisory and teaching positions.

On 27 March 1947 the Far Eastern Commission approved a basic educational policy, "Policy for the Revision of the Japanese Educational System," formulated by the Department of State. Until that time the formal educational policy of the Occupation was limited to that contained in SCAP Directive AG 350 (22 Oct 45) CIE, entitled "Administration of the Educational System of Japan" which was written in its entirety by a junior naval officer in the Civil Information and Education Section, GHQ, SCAP, and approved and issued by the Supreme Commander. The FEC policy statement essentially formalized the contents of this document and the operational policies which had been evolved in practice.

American policy by interpretation can be explained most clearly by tracing a specific instance from the initial policy directive to an implemented policy in the field. The highly explosive abolition of government sponsorship of Shinto will serve as an example. In both the alternative pre-Surrender plans for the Occupation of Japan there appeared somewhat cryptic and ambiguous statements to the effect that Shintoistic propaganda should be eliminated and that official sanction and support of Shinto should be abolished. These plans were classified Top Secret and in at least this provision had no effect on policy in Japan. The 29 August 1945 "Initial Post-Surrender Policy" prepared by SWNCC made no specific mention of Shinto and carried only a line bearing obliquely on the subject which said: "The Japanese people shall be encouraged to develop a desire for individual liberties and respect for fundamental human rights, particularly the freedoms of religion."

At the time of the drafting of the Basic Educational Policy, SCAP Directive AG 350 (22 Oct 45) CIE, all reference to Shinto was deleted on the grounds that no specific directive had yet required it and that the *Potsdam Declaration* had specifically guaranteed the establishment of freedom of religion. Tentative staff studies were begun merely as an insurance against possible embarrassment in the event of a sudden demand for technical information. On the morning of 8 October 1945 the *Pacific Stars and Stripes* carried headlines "Shintoism Will Be Eliminated as Jap State Religion," followed by a feature story from the Associated Press in Washington quoting John Carter VINCENT, Chief of the Office of Far Eastern Affairs in the Department of State in a radio broadcast. A frantic exchange of signals with the State Department brought the following clarification on 13 October 1945 from Secretary of State James BYRNES:

. . . Shintoism insofar as it is a religion of individual Japanese is not to be interfered with. Shintoism, however, insofar as it is directed by the Japanese Government and is a measure enforced from above by the Government, is to be done away with. People would not be taxed to support National Shinto and there will be no place for Shintoism in the schools. Shintoism as a State religion, National Shinto, that is, will go. Our policy on this goes beyond Shinto. The dissemination of Japanese Militaristic and ultra-Nationalistic ideology in any form will be completely suppressed and the Japanese Government will be required to cease financial and other support of Shinto establishments.

This was the policy. How was it to be interpreted and implemented? There were at least three kinds of Shinto, one being the heritage of a primitive animistic religion, another being a series of 13 officially recognized but autonomous religious sects, and the third being the official "national cult" which consisted of a mixture of ancient political rituals and nationalistic philosophy derived from the mythology of primitive Japan. This latter, known officially as *Kokka Shintō* or *Jinja Shintō*, was obviously the object of the Department of State's policy. But each of the three types were so intertwined that it was almost impossible to attack the national cult without violating the Occupation's often reiterated policy of encouraging freedom of religion. The *kamidana* or god-shelf, for example, which has traditionally been found in Japanese homes, schools, and offices, is *Shintō*, though whether religious or national is frequently not known by the owner himself. Some of the greatest national parks, such as the Tokugawa Shrine at Nikko (*Tōshōgu*), contained both Buddhist temples and

Shinto shrines. Removal of tax support would be somewhat comparable to a renunciation of Yellowstone National Park because Christian services had been held in a chapel located in its bounds. Many Japanese, devout Buddhists and Christians among them, looked upon the Yasukuni Shrine (*Yasukuni Jinja*), where the souls of the military dead are supposed to be enshrined, much in the same way that Americans look on Arlington Cemetery. The Ise Grand Shrine (*Ise Dai Jingū*) honoring the Sun-Goddess *Amaterasu Ōmikami*, mythological founder of Japan, has both a historical and religious heritage. It is a Jerusalem, Mount Vernon and Vatican in the eyes of the Japanese. Historically the 13 religious Shinto sects (*Shūha Shintō* or *Kyōha Shintō*) were derived from the same philosophers who had led a revival of ancient Shinto (*Fukko Shintō*) during the eighteenth century. Many of the devotees did not recognize the legal distinction which existed between their worship and their national patriotism.

The enunciated policy of the Department of State postulated a problem. The interpretation of this policy, largely by a most able junior naval officer in the Religions Division of CI&E, GHQ, SCAP, who worked for weeks with the Japanese leaders of all prominent religious bodies, examining details and compromising differences, provided the solution. The result of this brilliant staff work was SCAP Directive AG 000.3 (15 Dec 45) CI&E, "Abolition of Governmental Sponsorship, Support, Perpetuation, Control, and Dissemination of State Shinto," which actually established a working policy which has successfully separated national Shinto from the State without any observable Japanese resistance and has even occasioned highly commendatory co-operation of the various religious elements concerned.

This manner of policy formation through interpretation has not been uniformly successful. The "Initial Post-Surrender Policy" Directive of 29 August 1945 stated that "Japan is not to have . . . any civil aviation." An enthusiastic and impetuous staff officer in the Economic and Scientific Section dashed off a directive, AG 360 (18 Nov 45) ESS–E, which was approved and issued to the Japanese. It directed that by 31 December 1945 all organizations which had in any way been engaged in aeronautical training, research, or operation should be dissolved, and barred any group or individual Japanese from owning or operating any aeronautical equipment including models. Had this directive been strictly enforced it would have closed virtually every secondary and higher school in Japan and would have provided the Occupation personnel with the delightful pastime of chasing some nine million small boys reputed to own model airplanes. The author of the directive became ill. Two months after issuing it was almost impossible to find a copy of the directive. Six months after issuing the Imperial Aeronautical Research Laboratory was permitted to salvage much of its equipment and to make available to other laboratories and universities its incomparable staff for work in approved disciplines.

American policy by example is best illustrated by the conferences and report of the United States Education Mission to Japan in March and April 1946. As a result of a staff study prepared in the Education Division of CI&E, GHQ, SCAP, General MacArthur requested the State and War Departments to invite to Japan a body of distinguished American educators, to confer with members of his staff and to advise him on basic educational policy.

The Mission of 24 educators was accompanied by Col. John Andrews, as Military Liaison Officer, Dr. Harold Benjamin of the United States Office of Education, and Dr. Gordon Bowles of the Department of State. The chairman was Dr. George Stoddard, then Commissioner of Education for New York State and President-elect of the University of Illinois. In response to the request of General MacArthur the Mission was divided into five committees: Aims and Content, Administration, Teaching and Education of Teachers, Language Reform, and Higher Education. These committees were respectively directed by Dr. Isaac L. Kandel, Professor of Comparative Education at Columbia University, and Editor of School and Society; Dr. Alexander J. Stoddard, Superintendent of Schools in Philadelphia; Dr. Frank N. Freeman, Dean of the School of Education in the University of California, and President George W. Diemer of Central Missouri State Teachers College serving as co-chairmen; Dr. George S. Counts, Professor of Education at Teachers College, Columbia University; and President Wilson M. Compton of Washington State College.

The remaining members of the Mission were Dr. Leon Carnovsky, Associate Dean of the Graduate Library School in the University of Chicago; Dr. Roy DeFerrari, Secretary-General of Catholic University; Dr. Kermit Eby, Director of Research and Education, CIO; Dr. Virginia C. Gildersleeve, Dean of Barnard

College and United States Delegate to the United Nations Conference at San Francisco; Dr. Willard E. GIVENS, Executive Secretary of the National Education Association; Dr. Ernest R. HILGARD, Executive Head of the Department of Psychology at Stanford University; Monsignor Frederic HOCHWALT, Director of the Department of Education, National Catholic Welfare Conference; Mrs. Douglas HORTON, President of Wellesley College and former Director of the WAVES; Dr. Charles S. JOHNSON, Professor of Psychology and President-elect of Fisk University; Dr. Charles H. McCLOY, Professor of Physical Education at the University of Iowa; Dr. Ethelbert B. NORTON, Commissioner of Education for Alabama; Dr. T. V. SMITH, Professor of Philosophy at the University of Chicago and formerly Chief of Education in the Occupation of Italy; Dr. David H. STEVENS, Director of the Division of Humanities of the Rockefeller Foundation; Dr. William Clark TROW, Professor of Educational Psychology at the University of Michigan; Mrs. Pearl WANAMAKER, Superintendent of Public Instruction for the State of Washington; and Miss Emily WOODWARD of the University System of Georgia. Mr. Paul STEWART of the Department of State served as Mission Secretary General.

This Mission did not have the authority to enunciate official policy. It could only informally advise the Japanese representatives named by the Ministry of Education to work with it, and could recommend policy to the Supreme Commander. The details of its recommendations are considered elsewhere in this volume. It made policy, however, by example. Because of the unassailable technical ability of its members and because of the prestige of their professional positions, the Japanese accepted their educational findings as Occupation policy, despite repeated warnings to the contrary by the Headquarters. Where they have not followed the recommendations the Japanese have used the same tactics of evasion employed to avoid sincere compliance with an official SCAP directive. The Department of State Publication No. 2671, *Occupation of Japan: Policy and Progress,* presents on pp. 156–163, a digest of the report, and on p. 35 calls the report of the Mission "still another of SCAP's achievements in redirecting the education of the Japanese youth and people."

American policy by nudge, or more formally, by "direct liaison," is authorized by Paragraph 2 c of SCAP General Order

No. 4 of 2 October 1945 and Paragraph 3 c of SCAP General Order No. 27 of 3 June 1946. These direct the Civil Information and Education Section to maintain liaison with the Japanese Ministry of Education, educational institutions, and various organizations "to insure their understanding of and co-operation with the . . . education objectives of the Supreme Commander."

In practice the mere indication of interest in a particular educational problem by any responsible official in Headquarters has been sufficient to establish that educational matter as a priority problem for the Japanese officials. This method of formulating policy was first consciously tried out and met its most spectacular success in the elimination of the military arts.

One of the essential parts of the old *samurai* tradition was the practice of the so-called military arts (*budō*) which consisted of Japanese swordsmanship, archery, horsemanship, wrestling, and a form of self-defense known as *jujitsu*. In modern Japan a number of sports have carried on that tradition. *Kendō*, a form of fencing with bamboo swords, *naginata*, a girls' sport similar to *kendō* and usually translated "halbert," and *judō*, a modern refinement of *jujitsu* or trick wrestling, have been the most popular. Japanese wrestling, or *sumō*, is equally popular but is not a part of the formal *budō* discipline. As sports they are no better and no worse than their Occidental counterparts. But the manner in which they were perverted by the militaristic clique in Japan may be noted from the following quotation from *Nippon Today* (Sports), published sometime early in the war by the East Asia Travel Corporation, a sponsored agency of the Japanese Government:

Kendō, or the Nippon style of fencing, is based on the sword which is linked with the soul of the warrior. It lays emphasis on a rigorous spiritual training even more than on physical skill in the art. In other words, *Kendō* is the means by which attention is riveted on the spiritual training of the warrior and to the manhood that he represents. It fosters the type of fighting spirit which allows the enemy to get in a flesh-cut in order that a bone-splitting blow may be delivered in return, and cultivates the unique mental attitude of entertaining no fear of death where the cause of the Emperor is at stake. It is this pervading spirit of *Kendō*, applied to the use of up-to-date scientific warfare, that has enabled Nippon to score her impressive series of victories over the forces of America, Britain, and Chungking.

Fearful that such propaganda might mislead the Occupation Forces and cause them to prohibit all exercise of the sport, the instructors of *kendō* submitted an article, "Zen and Swordsmanship" translated from the volume, *Zen Buddhism and Its Influence on Japanese Culture,* by Suzuki Daisetzu Teitaro, to support their contention that *kendō* should be retained in the curriculum of the schools. This article said in part:

The sword is the soul of the samurai: therefore when the samurai is the subject of a talk of any kind, the sword inevitably comes with it. The samurai is asked when he wishes to be faithful to his vocation, to rise above the question of birth and death, and to be ready at any moment to lay down his life, which means either to expose himself before the striking sword of the enemy or to direct his own towards himself. The sword thus becomes most intimately connected with the life of the samurai, and has become the symbol of loyalty and self-sacrifice. The reverence paid universally to it in various ways proves it.

The sword has thus a double office to perform: the one is to destroy anything that opposes the will of its owner and the other is to sacrifice all the impulses that arise from the instinct of self-preservation.

At the same time the instructors in *judō* submitted a reprint of Professor Kano Jigorō's lecture, "The Contribution of Judo to Education," delivered at the University of Southern California during the Tenth Olympic Games, to support their contention that *judō* should be retained in the curriculum of the schools. It said in part:

The kinds of attack were chiefly throwing, hitting, choking, holding the opponent down, and bending or twisting the opponent's arms or legs in such a way as to cause pain or fracture.

. . . so that *Jujitsu* means an art or practice of gentleness or of first giving way in order ultimately to gain the victory; while *Judō* means the way or principle of the same.

. . . *Judō* is a study and a training in mind and body as well as in the regulation of one's life and affairs.

After studying the case presented by the supporters of the military arts, the Education Division, which until then had not placed the physical education program on a very high priority, decided that perhaps a housecleaning was in order. Many of the instructors were former military officers or noncommissioned officers likely to be eliminated by the proposed purge. A considerable volume of letters from Japanese students urged that the sports be removed from the curriculum. But a scap directive forbidding boys to wrestle or play at swords with sticks seemed somewhat lacking in dignity.

On 3 October 1945 in a report to the newly formed Education Division of CI&E, GHQ, SCAP, the Ministry of Education had stated that they were revising the physical training program to eliminate "militarism." On 16 October 1946 a meeting was held with the Chief of the Physical Education Section of the Secretariat of the Ministry of Education. He was not ordered to make any changes, since only the Supreme Commander could issue a directive, but in a friendly and informal way it was suggested that if the Ministry saw fit to eliminate the sports from the school programs it would probably not be necessary for the Headquarters to take official notice and issue a prohibitory directive. It was hinted that if such a directive were issued it would almost certainly outlaw all private clubs and public exhibitions as well. On 6 November 1945 the Ministry issued Order No. 80 eliminating *kendō*, *judō*, and *naginata* from school curricula and prohibiting their practice under school auspices or on school premises. By Order No. 100 of 26 December 1945 the Ministry of Education directed the complete disposal of all sports equipment formerly used in these military arts. Policy had been made—by nudge.

American policy by review is too well understood by citizens of a democracy to warrant description. Public opinion forced a reversal of the policy which destroyed the Japanese cyclotron. The pressure of scientific opinion secured the reversal of the policy which closed all research laboratories until they had been surveyed and determined completely innocuous. A brilliant international scientist pointed out that it was naïve to think that you could command a man to stop thinking or that any series of inspections could preclude the mathematical research which is the most potent of war potential. It was charged that while the laborious and ineffectual survey was dragging on, the intellectual and industrial life of the nation was being crippled. International public opinion reviewed and forced the reversal of the original policy denying the importation of food and prohibiting the continuation of the nitrate industry for fertilizers. The Far Eastern Advisory Commission (FEAC) and later the Far Eastern Commission (FEC) and the Allied Council for Japan (ACJ) provided a channel through which basic

Occupation policy came to be scrutinized by the people of the Allied Nations. It was no longer easy to establish a policy in a secrecy justified by "military security." The constant threat of adverse world opinion helped to form policy.

American policy by mistake is a method of formulation which is often forgotten or tacitly ignored. Sometimes policy is made by such a ludicrous accident as that of a typist forgetting to copy a line, as occurred in the SCAP Directive AG 350 (30 Oct 45) CI&E, "Investigation, Screening, and Certification of Teachers and Educational Officials." Fortunately most such errors, as in this particular case, do little more than cause temporary confusion. The Japanese officials were bewildered at the peculiar wording until they decided to translate the newspaper accounts rather than the official copy.

There occur other errors, however, which have far-reaching policy results. Early in the Occupation, while military units were still disorganized and before the General Headquarters of SCAP had officially been formed, a young naval officer from one of the ships in Yokosuka thumbed his way to Tokyo and visited the Tokyo Imperial University. Since he had been a university student in New York prior to his naval service and was interested in social problems he asked to meet the most liberal professors so that they might discuss Occupational policy and in particular, educational policy. Any American uniform looked impressive to the Japanese in September 1945 and the top-drawer talent of the university was soon assembled. One professor, who spoke English and had traveled extensively in Europe and South America acted as interpreter and so impressed the young officer with his "sincerity and liberal point of view" that he wrote a brief report on their conversation and handed it in to an army officer in Advance GHQ, USAFPAC, connected with the Education Section and known to the student by reputation. The young officer was casually encouraged to continue his interviews with this Japanese, which he did until a sizable dossier had been compiled and until he had missed his ship. The naval lieutenant was assisted in overtaking his ship and in explaining his absence on the basis of "a special project with the Army," and the army officer in Headquarters carried on the series of interviews. This sudden attention for an able professor but relatively unknown political figure could only mean one thing to the Japanese. Within a matter of days the Tokyo Imperial law professor, Dr. TANAKA KŌTARŌ, was named Chief of the Bureau of Schools in the Ministry of Education. Faced with the reality of public office he reverted to conservatism and shelved many of his liberal policies. Before the first year of the Occupation was over he was made the Minister of Education. Probably no single man in the Japanese education system had greater influence on the Japanese formation of policy in the first two years of the Occupation than this man, snatched from obscurity because the Japanese thought the Allied Powers were interested in him.

Explanation of the Japanese side of the complex system of policy channels is relatively simple. SCAP directives were handed to the Central Liaison Office (*Shūsen Renraku Chūō Jimu Kyoku*) of the Imperial Japanese Government. From that office they were directed to the appropriate Japanese Ministry where action was taken exactly as if the policy statements had been handed down from the Imperial Cabinet. All policy statements transmitted by liaison went directly to the appropriate echelon in the Japanese hierarchy. They were the "cross-talk" in the telephone network of the Occupation, having no official force but being too important to be wholly ignored.

The Battle for the Japanese Mind

The minds and personalities of the Japanese, with all their obvious contradictions, shortcomings, and defects, are the most precious asset which the nation has. As the salvage of war and defeat is appraised, one cannot but feel that all else is relatively unimportant.

Defeat is only in part a physical condition. It is also a condition of mind. The history of the world is studded with examples of men and of nations beaten to their knees, apparently helpless before the might of an enemy, yet who were not defeated, simply because they would not admit defeat. Some of these nations, like England in the Battle of Britain and Russia in the Siege of Stalingrad, were supported by a sublime faith in the right of their cause and the certainty of their victory. Some, like the Undergrounds of France and Norway, fought on in the knowledge that help would come. Some, like Paraguay, which twice in its history fought until it had practically eliminated the adult male population, were driven by a spirit of nationalism which made death seem honestly preferable to surrender. The military leaders of Japan were aware of these great urges and of the character of defeat. They twisted even so innocent a thing as a primitive animistic religion to their use and exploited the supernatural to urge the people to ever greater efforts. They counted upon winning the war through a superior spirit, rather than through superior arms.

These leaders were stupid as well as criminally responsible. The physical defeat of Japan was inevitable. No amount of spirit could have continued the physical war to anything but a conclusion of national obliteration. The Emperor and his advisers were, belatedly, wise in surrendering. But surrender marked only a partial defeat. This was a war of philosophies as much as one of armies and of people. Japan had been reduced to military impotence, but had the minds of the people been changed?

Japan in the Occupation inevitably became a battleground of ideas. Pressure groups, both Japanese and foreign, have continued to fight for the Japanese mind. Only when this struggle is completed will it be clear where lies victory and where defeat.

Paradoxically the Occupation Authorities, up to a certain point, appeared to have welcomed this battle. The terms of the historic *Potsdam Proclamation*, made public on 26 July 1945, are so familiar that there is hardly need for quotation. The tenth article, however, is so fundamental a keystone in all postwar policy affecting Japan, that it may be well to examine the exact wording:

10. We do not intend that the Japanese shall be enslaved as a race or destroyed as a nation, but stern justice shall be meted out to all war criminals, including those who have visited cruelties upon our prisoners. The Japanese Government shall remove all obstacles to the revival and strengthening of democratic tendencies among the Japanese people. Freedom of speech, of religion, and of thought, as well as respect for the fundamental human rights shall be established.

It should be noted that this *Proclamation* was in a large measure the product of the United States and the United Kingdom, the USSR still being at peace with Japan and China being informed through dispatches. This, then, is primarily an expression of the social and political philosophies of two nations which are themselves committed to a democratic form of life. Democracy cannot be forced on a people. It is something which must come from the desire of the governed. The signatories recognized that any attempt to compel acceptance of representative government, with all its social implications, would only substitute a foreign military oligarchy for the discredited Japanese military. The Japanese people would continue in ignorance and political serfdom. The *Proclamation* did not order the establishment of a democracy, it directed that obstacles to a free choice by the people should be removed. And it held out to them a promise of freedom when they had made their choice.

12. The occupying forces of the Allies shall be withdrawn from Japan as soon as these objectives have been accomplished and there has been established in accordance with the freely expressed will of the Japanese people a peacefully inclined and responsible government.

The United States, at least, is clearly committed to this policy. The "United States Initial Post-Surrender Policy for Japan" which was prepared jointly by the Department of State, War Department, and Navy Department and which was radioed to Gen. Douglas MacArthur on 29 August 1945 and later approved by President Harry Truman on 6 September 1945, states that the ultimate objectives are:

(a) To insure that Japan will not again become a menace to the United States or to the peace and security of the world.

(b) To bring about the eventual establishment of a peaceful and responsible government which will respect the rights of other states and will support the objectives of the United States as reflected in the ideals and principles of the Charter of the United Nations. The United States desires that the government should conform as closely as may be to principles of democratic self-government but it is not the responsibility of the Allied Powers to impose upon Japan any form of government not supported by the freely expressed will of the people.

What have been the forces which have contended for the Japanese mind? Among the Japanese two political minorities represented opposite extremes. One was a sort of intellectual Underground, conservative, secretly fighting every reform, hoping for a return to something similar to Japan before the China Incident. Time, custom, conservatism, and nostalgia were their allies, and delay, compromise, the fumbling of the Japanese Government, and the discord of the Allies were their weapons. They fought a silent, insidious war but they should not be underestimated as opponents. The other was a flamboyant and vocal radical element, openly committed to the philosophy of communism. Russia was their example and their tutor, and strikes, mass meetings, the misery of the people, and the discrediting of the past were their weapons.

Between these extremes were the great majority of Japanese people, stratified from the inert, politically uninformed masses to the middle-of-the-road intellectual who recognized that Japan could never return to her prewar feudalism but was yet unconvinced that it was ready for a real representative government. And over all these was the official structure of the Occupation Forces, acting as a referee which demanded fair play and interpreted the rules.

Outside Japan were the victorious nations which ostensibly were collectively represented by the Occupation Forces, but which individually differed as greatly in their political philosophies as did the forces within Japan. The United States dominated both policy making and implementation, and the Headquarters of the Supreme Commander for the Allied Powers was in fact an American military headquarters. The military security of the Occupation Forces and the presumed desirability of protecting postwar Japan from disturbing outside ideological influences during its period of infancy, lent plausible justification to the rigid censorship of all mass education media and the exclusion of all but a trickle of innocuous foreign importations. Even American thought, though overwhelmingly favored, was filtered through a highly selective Occupational censorship. Japan had in fact exchanged its Oriental military dictatorship for an Occidental one. This obviously could not long continue.

Not all of the Occupation was undesirable, even from the point of view of the Japanese themselves. It introduced foreign ideas and institutions which might otherwise never have been known or experienced. Because it was a military dictatorship it had the inherent strengths of such a dictatorship. When a decision had been made quick action was possible regardless of cost or opposition. It was presumably possible to enforce compliance with at least the externals of any directed reform until the people had a chance to decide whether it was worth while or not. It lessened, if it did not eliminate, many of the hampering influences which characterized the prewar educational structure—the vested interests, the antagonism to Western ideas, the conservatism, and blind adherence to the traditional.

But it appears highly probable that the undesirable elements of any occupation bring greater disadvantages than its acknowledged efficiency counterbalance. Any occupation tends to bring dependence. It brings fear of taking any action which is not sanctioned by the occupation authorities for fear of reprisals. It reduces or nullifies the powers of the nation's officials and thus discourages the development of real leadership. If the occupation is a military one it almost inevitably brings the disadvantages which seem to be a frequent if not an inherent characteristic of military organizations—mediocre personnel, delay, red tape, conservatism.

As the barriers to their individual participation in the Occupation were gradually lowered, each nation attempted through every permissible medium to influence the decision in this basic contest for the Japanese mind. Their motion pictures, books, magazines, news services, radio, commercial and cultural contacts became munitions of the battle. The struggle continues.

In one matter nearly all Japanese and foreign elements are in agreement. Education is the instrument through which the battle of philosophies will be won. It is, therefore, the most important factor in the final results of the Occupation and in Japan's survival. Re-education of virtually the entire population is the solution to Japan's basic problem of cultural survival. But what form shall this re-education take?

The Rules of Thought Warfare

Ashes or opportunity? This is the greatest decision which the Japanese people must make. Shall they choose to drift passively back into the old discredited pattern of their prewar culture, or shall they choose to seize upon the opportunity furnished by this greatest of all disasters to seek a cultural renaissance? Shall they be supine pawns in the world battle of ideologies or shall they be dignified connoisseurs, accepting only what is best from the cultures of other nations, creating in their own society indigenous cultural resources which may later serve as an inspiration to other nations?

Implicit in this great decision is the problem of how the judicial selective action shall take place. Is it possible to draw the outlines of a plan which will be acceptable both to the nations of the world and to the Japanese people? Is it possible to formulate a strategy which will survive the impact of antagonistic philosophies in the battle for the Japanese mind? Is it possible to plant today the seeds of an inner cultural growth which the Japanese people themselves will tomorrow recognize as being to their own advantage to continue?

In its broadest sense education embodies everything in the culture of man. It is the impact upon the individual of all the countless thousands of stimuli arising from his contact with his surroundings. There is no completely uneducated man. He is conditioned by his sight, his hearing, his smell, his taste, his touch, even by the perception of bodily position, heat, and pressure. The government, the social structure, the home, the economy, the situations arising from his family, business, religious, and other influences, teach him the lessons he must master if he is to survive. Man is educated by the great events of his lifetime, by the wars, famines, the social reforms, the technological advances, the memories and traditions of the past. In the struggle for cultural survival and in the battle for the Japanese mind, all of these instruments will be used. The emancipation of women, for example, will be approached not only through propaganda deliberately issued to influence this decision but by the social reforms and economic pressures which give the woman liberties and demand that she use them.

But there is a narrower sense in which education may be considered. It is the formal discipline of the mind and character, the training of thought habits, the imparting of information, the systematic conditioning of the individual, which is accomplished through the schools and institutions linked with them. It is an instrument convenient to large-scale, rapid, and efficient indoctrination of a people. It is to this latter and admittedly limited conception of education that this study must of necessity be confined.

The traditional educational system of Japan is not acceptable. It was the tool, if not an actual cause, of the thinking which led to Japan's career of militarism. Changes will have to be made in three elements of the formal system. Fundamental to all will be the changes in the goals of education. This is the problem of philosophy and implies a reversal of long-established traditions of the sublimation of the individual to the state, fundamental in both the doctrines of *Shintō* (The Way of the Gods) and *Kōdō* (The Imperial Way). There will have to be changes in the instruments of education, both designed to bring the structure into conformity with the new philosophy and designed to establish a structure which will exhibit internal resistance to possible future manipulation. And there will have to be changes in the educational processes. Education for democracy is a process of experiencing the rights and responsibilities of self-direction. It can only be accomplished through the stimulation of the thinking and through the inner growth of the people. It cannot be imposed from above as a political system which must be accepted through fear.

Democratic control in education, as in all other social and political areas, is founded on a basic faith in the potential worth of every individual. It would be comparatively easy for a ruthless occupying power or for a totalitarian Japanese government to establish in Japan the outward aspects of a democratic state. But the very compulsion which established "democracy" would be a denial of the essential concept of democracy. This is the obvious handicap under which the United States, first as the dominant occupying power and later as an adviser, must operate. But there is a strength as well. If democracy can be taught, its survival value is much higher than imposed totalitarian philosophy. It becomes a self-generating force.

Two methods of teaching the democratic principle, while accomplishing the necessary changes in education, are basic. The first is by avoiding compulsion. Persecution, whether in religion, politics, or education, usually strengthens rather than weakens the opposition. In Japan, where the Emperor, the military leadership, the foundations of the State, the school system, even the characters in the writing system are inextricably interwoven with mythical and often fanatical religious beliefs, this is particularly true. The second is the complementary method of stimulating desire. The Japanese people must come to recognize that there is necessity for change. They must then be assured of the possibility of accomplishing the change they desire. And finally there must be made available to them those elements which are necessary if the elected change is to be successful. This presupposes an adroit public relations campaign. It must go beyond the usual methods of propaganda. It must set up situations such that the only apparent solution teaches the lesson. It must lead and not force.

There are many forms which an acceptable plan for the rehabilitation of the Japanese educational system might take. Each is the product of a series of interlocking decisions, each new problem hinging on the solution of the previous. A measure of their quality may be found in the degree of consistency which is found in the separate solutions as the plan progresses from the establishment of a basic philosophy of education to the details of finance, administration, and teaching. Three criteria might be applied to each decision: Is it acceptable? Is it desirable? Is it practical?

Acceptability as a criterion should be based on the generally accepted minimum standards of the enlightened nations of the world. Japan, merely because it was a defeated and occupied nation, should not be compelled to adopt standards which are neither adopted nor complied with on the part of the nations which defeated her. Adoption of such changes in the traditional patterns of Japanese life should be elective and not compulsory. Japan should not be made the testing ground for social and political theory which the conquerors are unwilling to experience in their own countries.

Desirability as a criterion, on the other hand, should be based on the generally accepted maximum standards of the enlightened nations of the world. Japan should be encouraged to aspire to the best in each of the societies which have defeated her. In using this criterion there may arise a danger of blind acceptance of all that is foreign. This mental attitude was evident in the first years of the Meiji Restoration, and subsequent disillusionment made the nation swing back to a conservatism which need never have occurred if the westernization process had been more gradual and more judicial. Japan embarked on a somewhat similar wave of foreignism in the first year of the Occupation, but an increased sophistication made the inevitable rejection occur earlier in the process than in the Meiji Restoration. An adequate plan for reeducation should guide this force, and limit it.

Five rules might well assist in applying this criterion. Every effort should be made to salvage as much as possible, rather than to discard unthinkingly, traditional Japanese educational patterns. Where problems exist and there is a choice of solutions, the

Japanese-inspired solution should be elected in preference to one coming from foreign culture. Real efficiency should be the test of desirability rather than slavish uniformity, even though uniformity may enable a superficial economy in time and money. Where a problem exists and there is a choice of solutions, the one which has a record of successful application should be elected in preference to the one which exists only in theory. Finally, originality of solution is to be preferred to a patchwork of traditional patterns. This last may appear to be a contradiction of the others. It is not so intended. Where it is possible to preserve some desirable part of the Japanese tradition or to solve a problem by seeking out a little-known or isolated example in Japanese experience, this should be done. But in order to break with the fettering traditions of the past, no opportunity should be overlooked to inspire the Japanese people to seek new and original educational paths. Growth should be the deciding factor.

Practicality as a criterion is likely to be employed mainly in determining the economic possibility of desirable reforms. There are two questions which must be asked: can the desired education be economically justified in the light of Japan's probable future poverty; and is the educational reform in question one which is desirable in the light of Japan's probable future economy? If Japan is to be a democratic nation, and the very recognition of the necessity of re-education presupposes this goal, a certain level of popular education must be provided regardless of its cost. Beyond this indispensable minimum, however, the burden of proof lies with the advocate of the additional elements. Each element of the educational plan should be required to demonstrate its contribution to the evolving economy.

Ashes or opportunity? Does the will to survive, to seek improvement, to aspire to a cultural renaissance, to make great sacrifices for their re-education—does this will exist in the new Japan? This is the fundamental problem. All possibility of reform must be predicated on the assumption that it does.

II

"OF EMPERORS AND MEN"

The Problem of Philosophy

ON Wednesday, 24 October 1945, less than two months after the collapse of the Japanese war machine, the Tokyo English edition of *The Mainichi* carried a headline:

"People's Ultra-Nationalistic Thought
To Be Stamped Out by HQ of Allies:
Japanese Thought to be Completely Rectified"

It has often been said that if man can know everything about a single thing, no matter how small, he can know the universe. The physician from an analysis of a smear of blood can diagnose the disease which ravages the entire body. The mathematician from an infinitely small characteristic part of a function, the differential, can expand or integrate his knowledge to a complete description of the entire function. The physicist in analyzing the dark lines in the spectrum of the sun's rays can discover the existence and predict the physical properties of a chemical element not known upon the earth. In this simple headline there are the essential characteristics of Japan's second great educational problem, that of her philosophy.

The educational system, like the monetary, the judicial, the legislative, executive, and other essential public services, is a governmental organ. As such it is controlled by political policies which may or may not represent the will of the majority of the people in the state. It is almost inevitable that these policies and the far more fundamental philosophy which is basic to them should become so merged that their separate identities are lost. But policy, whether political or educational, is no more than a course of action determined by the government or its people. Philosophy, however, is the great body of principles which underlie a form of government or society. In the first three years of the Occupation the political policy of Japan fundamentally changed five times. It will inevitably change many more times in the future. But it is doubtful if the political philosophy of Japan has essentially changed even through the War, Defeat, and Occupation. Superficial evidences of a possible change have appeared: a revised *Constitution;* a reformed Diet; a temporal ruler; a compliant people. But only the future actions of Japan can give the final evidence on the sincerity and permanence of these changes.

An educational philosophy for Japan is more than a mere statement of contemplated reforms. It includes the basic political philosophy of the nation and defines its implications for the discipline of education. It has a body of content, a codification, a literature of interpretation, and a precedent of application. An educational philosophy must be appraised both in terms of the authority which established it and the procedures through which it is applied. Two identical statements, if determined respectively by an authoritarian oligarchy and by the elected representatives of a free people, become two utterly different philosophies. A philosophy must be the pattern of the rights and duties, the goals and the reasons, of a society.

Japan, if it is to survive, must have a new philosophy. Such a philosophy might come by evolution, through the gradual re-education of the people by years of contact with the demands and realities of postwar internationalism. Once before the Japanese were suddenly catapulted into involuntary and violent competition with Occidental nations centuries further advanced in an industrial and scientific evolution. They revised their philosophy. They chose railroads and airplanes and were not content to make better sandals for walking. Today Japan is faced with an equally compelling necessity to overtake the social evolution of the democratic Occidental powers. It might be done by slow evolution but the price appears impossibly high. The operation is in progress and the patient is dying. Japan must change its goals, it must realign its rights and duties, and if it is to be sane it must seek new reasons.

The Elements of Japanese Nationalism

Of all revolutions, the revolution which takes place in man's thought is the most significant. The Japanese have experienced such a revolution. During the last few disillusioning weeks of the second World War and the first two years of the Occupation the thinking of the Japanese people underwent profound modification. The most fundamental tenets of their political and social philosophy were subjected to frantic and searching reappraisal. It was much more than the forced realization that they had failed in an attainable program of expansion. It was much more than the realization that they had been misled by their leaders with regard to a series of verifiable facts and that as a result they had built a false and unsubstantial political structure and been led to the brink of national obliteration. It was the renunciation of the very goals in their philosophy of life and the very axioms of their system of thought.

> Precious are my parents that gave me birth,
> So that I might serve His Majesty.

Thus ran the lines of the oft-quoted Japanese poem by SAKURA Azumao.

"The Japanese Government shall remove all obstacles to the revival and strengthening of democratic tendencies among the Japanese people."

Thus ran the lines of the *Potsdam Proclamation*. But this was an ultimatum handed by a conqueror to the vanquished and was political rather than educational. What of the change in educational philosophy?

. . . the Emperors hand over the august injunctions of the Imperial Ancestors, and thereby make clear the great principle of the founding of the nation and the great Way which the people should follow. Here lies the basic principle of our education. Wherefore, education too is in its essence united with the religious rites and government. In short, religious rites, government, and education, each fulfilling its function, are entirely one.

These were the statements of basic prewar Japanese educational philosophy in the *Kokutai no Hongi* ("Cardinal Principles of the National Entity of Japan"), official Ministry of Education policy publication.

"Dissemination of Japanese militaristic, National Shintoistic, and ultra-nationalistic ideology will be prohibited." And these last were the initial lines of educational policy in the pre-Surrender plan for the military government of Japan. But again, this is a directive dictated by a victorious foreign power. Have the Japanese accepted this fundamental change in goals?

The *Guide to New Education in Japan*, published by the Ministry of Education in May 1946 as an expression of Japanese educational philosophy after Surrender, at least during the Occupation, says in the official English edition:

As the weaknesses and shortcomings of the Japanese nation were wrought over a lengthy period, it will take time to correct them. It is also a task relative to the basic principles of outlook on life or thought. The most effective way of establishing a new Japan is to cultivate and develop the new life and thought particularly of youths, boys and girls. This is no other than education. (P. 9.)

To construct a New Japan, it is necessary, first of all to remove obstacles in the way. Two of the most important ones are militarism and ultra-nationalism. (P. 11.)

What should be done to eliminate Militarism and Ultra-nationalism? (1) First of all, militarists and ultra-nationalists are to be eliminated from among those who have been in the leading position in the army, politics, economic circles, as well as in the world of thought, and in the press. . . . (2) It is moreover necessary to set free or put back into office those who have been confined or driven out of their offices on account of their being liberalists and oppos[ed] to militarism and ultra-nationalism. . . . (3) But, in order to destroy, fundamentally and for all time to come, militarism and ultra-nationalism, the education of the people must be depended upon. . . . There must be no instigation to be vexed at the defeat and to brood vengeance. . . . The custom of beginning to fight at the slightest provocation must also be stopped. . . . Whatever it may be about, it is not well to obey blindly orders from above. . . . And the truth must be thoroughly inculcated that each person must make himself a worthy man by developing his real abilities and by letting live his characteristics, that is, to complete his individual personality. (Pp. 21–23.)

. . . it is by reorienting the attitude and sentiment of the Japanese people, and by no other means, that militarism and ultra-nationalism can fundamentally and eternally be eliminated. (P. 23.)

This may have been a sincere statement or it may have been calculated propaganda. There is little question that the authors were sincere and were doing their honest best to understand the reasons for the collapse of their old structure of educational thought and to meet the demands for a new. But there are some grounds for doubt that the official agency, the Ministry of Education, which sponsored this *Guide to New Education in Japan* was equally sincere. At least for the duration of the Occupation, however, it stood as Japanese official philosophy. And as the months passed and the puzzled and dependent teachers in the schools received no conflicting blueprint of official *Mombushō* philosophy, the seeds of democratic ideology contained within it may have germinated.

These three epithets, "Militarism," "Ultranationalism," and "National Shintoism," are the tag titles of Allied propaganda. They are the convenient labels attached to all the Japanese nationalistic ideology which has become repugnant to the Occidental Powers. Today these terms are unquestioningly accepted as the baser element in a dichotomy, while "Peace-Loving," "Democratic," and "Free" are adjectives used to describe the opposite. Through repetition and the compulsion of SCAP directives both Japanese and the Allied Powers have come to use these terms freely. What do they mean?

What Is Militarism?

Perhaps as pertinent an interpretation of what is meant by "Militarism" as may be found is that which the Japanese themselves have concluded is the meaning of the term. Quoting again from the *Guide to New Education in Japan:*

What is militarism? It is a principle on which a State, anticipating war, exerts its utmost effort to the repletion of armaments, concentrates on it all its domestic organizations, and, toward other countries, tries to carry through its claims by means to war. But in order to comprehend concretely what militarism signifies, it is essential to consider what peculiarities a militaristic state possesses.

(1) A militaristic State makes the greatest possible endeavor to complete its armament, presupposing war. . . .

(2) In a militaristic State, soldiers occupy a high position in society and also grasp practical power in administration. . . .

(3) In a militaristic State, economy gets connected with military preparations, and the financial groups tend to be related with war. . . .

(4) In a militaristic State, culture is controlled for purposes of war and speech and thought are oppressed. Mythology and philosophy approving wars of invasion, sciences aiming at the invention of new war weapons, motion pictures, dramas, music with the purpose of heightening the fighting spirit and stimulating the hatred for the enemy, religious praying for victory and surrender of the enemy— these constitute the culture of a militaristic State. Hence those

branches of culture which do not serve directly as instruments of war are neglected and oppressed, or [are] distorted into such forms as will serve as such. And it is a matter of course that thoughts and speeches opposing to war or criticizing militarism are oppressed, and those who express them are driven out of office or put into prison. If, in this case, those in high positions, retaining in them remnants of feudalism, are inclined not to respect the human nature, the personality, the individuality of the people, and the people, on their part lacking critical spirit, blindly obey, the militarists take advantage of this defect and execute controls and oppressions all the more. . . .

(5) A militaristic State attempts to solve international problems by means of war. In other words, when a dispute occurs on account of clash of interests between countries, it resorts to war for the solution, instead of trying to solve it by peaceful negotiations according to the international law. Because a militaristic State, presupposing war from the outset, prepares armaments, and organizes and educates its people for purposes of war, it is quite natural, when a troublesome question arises, for the State to try to carry through its intentions by means of war. (Pp. 11–13.)

It is evident, and hardly surprising, that these five characteristics of "Militarism" closely parallel the requirements for "disarmament and demilitarization" which the Occupying Powers imposed upon the Japanese Government. Rearranged in an order similar to that of the Japanese *Guide*, the requirements of the *Potsdam Proclamation* are as follows:

(7) [Japan shall be occupied until] . . . there is convincing proof that Japan's war-making power is destroyed. . . .

(9) The Japanese military forces, after being completely disarmed, shall be permitted to return to their homes. . . .

(6) There must be eliminated for all time the authority and influence of those who have deceived and misled the people of Japan into embarking on world conquest. . . .

(11) Japan shall be permitted to maintain such industries as will sustain her economy and permit the exaction of just reparations in kind, but not those which would enable her to re-arm for war. To this end, access to, as distinguished from control of, raw materials shall be permitted. . . .

(10) . . . Freedom of speech, of religion, and of thought, as well as respect for the fundamental human rights shall be established.

(12) . . . there has been established in accordance with the freely expressed will of the Japanese people a peacefully inclined and responsible government.

The "United States Initial Post-Surrender Policy for Japan," prepared by SWNCC on 29 August 1945 and approved and issued by the President on 6 September 1945, stated the same five requirements in the form of objectives of the Occupation. They have been rearranged to make their order conform to that of the Japanese *Guide:*

(b) Japan will be completely disarmed and demilitarized. . . .
(b) The authority of the militarists and influence of militarism will be totally eliminated from her political, economic, and social life. Institutions expressive of the spirit of militarism and aggression will be vigorously suppressed.
(d) The Japanese people shall be afforded opportunity to develop for themselves an economy which will permit the peacetime requirements of the population to be met.
(c) The Japanese people shall be encouraged to develop a desire for individual liberties and respect for fundamental human rights, particularly the freedoms of religion, assembly, speech, and the press. They shall also be encouraged to form democratic and representative organizations.
Part I. The ultimate objectives of the United States [are] . . . to bring about the eventual establishment of a peaceful and responsible government which will respect the rights of other states and will support the objectives of the United States as reflected in the ideals and principles of the Charter of the United Nations. . . .

Article I of the "Draft Treaty on the Disarmament and Demilitarization of Japan," made public 21 June 1946 by the Department of State, provided that all Japanese armed forces and paramilitary organizations in whatever guise should be disarmed, demobilized, and disbanded; that the "establishment, utilization or operation for military purpose of all military structures, installations and establishments" should be prevented; and that a similar prohibition should apply to "all factories, plants, shops, research institutions, laboratories, testing stations, technical data, patents, plans, drawings, and inventions" which were designed or intended for military use.

The implementation of these principles will be considered in detail in later portions of this volume where the direct effect of that implementation upon the educational system of Japan is considered. At this point it will be sufficient to note that within the first 45 days after Surrender approximately 4 million soldiers and sailors located in the home islands of Japan, out of the total military strength of approximately 7,400,000, had been demobilized. A year and a half after Surrender General MACARTHUR in his first postwar press conference stated that demobilization and demilitarization were complete. In a series of directives known as the "Purge Orders," beginning with SCAP Directive AG 091-1 (4 Jan 1946) GS, "Removal and Exclusion of Undesirable Personnel from Public Office," the militaristic clique were removed from all positions of influence. In a series of SCAP directives the manufacture and sale of arms, ammunition, implements of war, the operation of war plants, and the production or use of aeronautical equipment were prohibited, culminating in SCAP Directive AG 004 (6 Nov 1945) ESS/ADM, "Dissolution of Holding Companies," which directed the Japanese Government to proceed with the dissolution of the *zaibatsu* or family economic combines, the great industrial interests which provided the war potential in pre-Surrender Japan. The series of directives begun with the so-called "Japanese Bill of Rights," SCAP Directive of 4 October 1945, guaranteed, on paper at least, the political, civil, and religious liberties.

One of the equivocal and at times ludicrous aspects of the Occupation has been the mental gymnastics necessary to enable military officers of the Allied Powers to preach a doctrine denouncing militarism and deriding the military machine of the defeated nation. The most powerful military machine the world has yet seen was commissioned to be the missionary of peace. At the time that the President and a considerable proportion of the military and political leaders of the United States were vigorously advocating the establishment of compulsory military service, increased budgets for the armed forces, and the unification of Land, Sea, and Air Forces in order to increase military efficiency, the officers of those three services were directed to convince the Japanese public that a military machine was intrinsically wrong.

Early in the Occupation one general became so dismayed at the "Militarism" displayed by the Japanese in marching their students into the classroom, in requiring the students to wear uniforms, and in continuing the custom of having students identified by a cloth badge sewed on the left breast and bearing strange cabalistic symbols, that it was necessary to conduct an extensive investigation and prepare a staff study to ease his mind. A teacher with from 35 to 50 students may be excused the custom of marching her charges into the school, a device copied from peace-loving and neutral Sweden. The custom of wearing uniforms is considered in Japan, and in most of Latin America and several of the European countries which fought on the side of the Allies, to be an evidence of "democracy" since it removes the painful disparities in costume which otherwise would obtain between the wealthy and the poor. The identification badge, with symbols in *kanji* or Chinese ideographs which one must ruefully admit are cabalistic to the majority, was a means of sorting out mangled bodies after an air raid and corresponded roughly to the fingerprinting of American school children.

There were mistakes made, as in that awful affair when the Japanese pointed out that the Occupation Headquarters had banned as "militaristic" a piece of beautiful, and singable, Japanese music which all through the war had been the theme song of the American propaganda radio broadcasting to Japan. But not all the mistakes were made by the officers of the Occupation Forces. There was the Japanese official who had to be tactfully corrected for his overenthusiasm in deleting a picture of a Roman helmet from a textbook of ancient history and for dismounting all public figures in official illustrations on the grounds that the horses of Japan were bred by the Army Remount Service.

Somehow the Occupation Forces managed to convince the Japanese that militarism was inherently wrong and that the presence of Allied military forces was no denial of this principle. Article IX of the new *Constitution* of Japan, in which war is renounced forever, is a tangible proof. General MacArthur in his 17 March 1947 press conference at the Tokyo Correspondents' Club stated:

Japan on her initiative and without coercion has completed a constitution which takes the great step of renouncing war. There was a great deal of criticism when this first appeared, but it remains. . . . She also has abolished military installations under the Potsdam Declaration.

Therefore they will be unprotected when we withdraw. Who is going to protect them?

One method would be to back track and permit small military establishments. . . . But the Japanese are relying upon the advanced spirituality of the world to protect them against undue aggression. (From AP as reported in the *New York Times*, 18 March 1947.)

Is there a demonstrable difference between "military" and "militaristic"? The Japanese have pointed out that there is the difference between the point of view of a victorious and a defeated nation. The victorious nation can claim that it fought in defense while the defeated is the proven aggressor. The victorious military machine can justify its actions on the grounds of "military necessity," whereas the same action taken by the defeated army becomes the grounds for revenge and prosecution as a war criminal. The Japanese point out that no nation in modern times has ever admitted openly that its military structure was for anything but defense or the protection of its national rights. All modern military machines, whatever their avowed or secret principles, must in time of war adopt many if not all of the characteristics which both the Japanese and the Allied Powers have branded "militaristic." They must exercise censorship over all information media and channels of communication. They must stockpile for war and build up an industrial machine to supply the military forces. They must place military officials in positions of high authority and conduct a conscious campaign to influence the public to respect and admire their military leaders. They must organize the financial and industrial structure of the nation to gear with the military structure and must closely link the military leadership with that of the industrial, even to the extent of temporary military seizure. Finally, they must fight to win on the assumption that a military decision is the *sine qua non.*

If there is a discernible difference between the legitimate "military" and the illegitimate "militaristic," it is one of attitude. It has been charged that the Japanese *gumbatsu* or military clique was characterized by four basic mental attitudes. One was the constant appeal to force and not to reason. A second was the prominence of the revenge motif in their thinking. A third was the glorification of the brutal. And the last was the deification of power. Certainly no impartial observer who reviewed the physical resources of the Japanese war machine after the war could fail to be impressed by the stupidity of the army commanders. It has frequently been stated and there is much evidence in support of the belief that the Japanese Navy was far better informed and far more judicious in their self-appraisal. But there can be little doubt that the Japanese Army was officered by essentially stupid, uneducated, brutal, and uncouth men who did not even recognize their own pathetic inadequacy. Some of the foreign condemnation of Japanese military brutality and respect for force is undoubtedly traceable to a difference in social customs. But even within the frame of reference of their own society the military was looked upon, and sometimes even admired, as a tough, uncompromising, and manly service. Chapter VII in an astonishing little study, "My Army Life" by FUKUYAMA Kunio, a 22-year-old student at Waseda University, which was written in the spring of 1946 as an exercise in English composition, is quoted in full:

Chapter VII

The last soldier who got slapped in the Imperial Army

Much has been said about the discipline of the Japanese Army, particularly the beating and slapping of the lower class of army personnel. Being often told before I entered the Army that the slapping was not meant to mean any ill-feeling toward the new recruits, but to make them capable of enduring all hardships in the army life, and any small mistakes would be dealt by severe punishment from superior officers, I had been very much afraid of it inwardly.

Well, my first experience of this treatment was about two weeks after I had entered the Army. Inspection was held in our barracks concerning the cleanliness of shirts we were wearing then. Unfortunately two-thirds of our section, including me, had soiled shirts because of the heavy work we had to do. The probationary officer lined us who had failed to undertake washings and brutally beated us with a bamboo sword. It was so severe that my head was spinning as though it were a top. But we could do nothing but take it unflinchingly. If anyone tried to avoid the slap by so much as a turn of his head, the results would be far disastrous for him. After the punishment to my surprise we were to say, "Thank you, sir," bowing our heads because we were told by our superior officer that to be slapped was merely to be taken as a warning but to me it seemed too rough just as a warning.

From that day onwards, on the average we were punished two or three times at least a day, though I did not know why. Moreover some fellow comrades were slapped more than ten times a day. At least two months went by until we thought nothing of the beatings we were getting. The superior officers explained to us that by slapping it was sole purpose of building up our "soldier's morals" but I could not help thinking we were just like the castrated pigs put to work.

When an epidemic broke out in our company about four months after I enlisted, we were ordered to take our blankets out and air them out in the sun to be disinfected, every morning before we assembled for roll call. That was the time, I was never before so humiliated. On that morning we, like a wild cat, carrying the blankets on our shoulders ran to attention in front of the weekly officer. Having no time to carry my blankets along the passageway because of the crowd, I tossed them out of the window.

Now, this was one of the most strictly prohibited and unfortunately I was caught in the act by the weekly officer. "What are you doing, Fukuyama," "Yes sir," I answered, saying "Damn it!" in my heart. "What are you doing, you heard me!" "Yes sir, I . . . I just tossed my blankets out of the window." "I trust that you already know that it is strictly prohibited." "Yes sir, but I thought that was the quickest way." All of a sudden, I felt a blow across my face from a bamboo sword and another one, hearing the snappish words of "You meant to disobey our order!" And again. This time I was struck on my forehead and could not explain how outrageous I then felt.

Thinking that the coming blow would surely make me unconscious, I avoided in spite of myself, but it was my fatal mistake for ten or eleven blows were dealt to me without stopping, making me quite unconscious after that.

But to suffer by watching our fellow comrades getting whipped was to me, far more worse than to get the beating myself. It used to make me furious to see my friends endure sufferings caused by senior officers when everybody was around, especially at roll-call at night, but nothing could be done about it by us. After coming back to our own room where there weren't any superior officers, to speak ill of the senior officer who had slapped us on that day was our only diversion.

Strange to say, in the Japanese Army the superior had taken a special privilege of doing anything they wanted against their subordinates and said they were teaching them "Soldier's spirit" or "Military education." But those who were beaten used to cause their hatred against the superior only, but never take that punishment as an admonition not to repeat the same mistake again. Moreover some of the soldiers who had endured this brutal treatment were apt to make their mind up that they would revenge themselves by treating their own subordinates worse when they were superior officers, making full use of their privilege.

During my life in the Army, it is impossible to say how many times I was beaten. I have told you about my first experience of being slapped, so I will confess here, by the way, as to my last experience of it in the Army life. I was slapped on the very day when the Imperial Rescript declared the capitulation of Japan. As we had been bombed intensively from the day before, our needed sleep was often interrupted in the trenches by mosquitoes and intensive heat as well as bombs. In the morning, we were ordered by a weekly officer to fall in assembly, but I was late from lack of sleep. As punishment I received a hard blow on my face as usual. The scar as the result of it is still visible on my face but I now think little of it because I'm rather proud to think that the last person to be slapped in the Imperial Army was myself.

Translated into larger terms, the attitude of militarism becomes a generalized pattern of thinking, a virus which seeps downward from the military commander to poison even the civilian masses. The military machine stands like a coiled spring in constant explosive potential. Its leaders know that if it is not periodically used, in real and not simulated war, its temper will be fatigued and its strength dissipated. The military ideal of "discipline and smartness" is realized only when each individual member of the machine reacts efficiently, automatically, and unthinkingly. There is no place for self-direction, the very essence of democratic government, in any except the highest officer ranks. The moral code, far from being strengthened by military discipline as is claimed by the military apologist, is altered in its very goals. It is not the protection of the weak and the attainment of justice which is taught, but the amoral accomplishment of a military objective, impersonal obliteration of any opposing force. The complete incompatibility of the militaristic and democratic philosophies at the individual level is the difference between killing your opponent and amicably compromising a disagreement with him. At the national level it is the difference between an invasion and a reciprocal treaty.

What Is Ultranationalism?

The Four Divine Elements. If it were profitable to examine the Japanese analysis of militarism perhaps it will be equally profitable to examine the post-Surrender Japanese ideas on ultranationalism. A rather extended passage from the Ministry of Education's 1946 publication, *Guide to New Education in Japan,* will illustrate the present official position:

What is ultra-nationalism? It is ultra-nationalism that, in alliance with militarism, drove Japan to war. Ultra-nationalism is an attitude of loving one's country too much, which causes the sacrifice of individual welfare under the pretext of serving the country and the neglect from the standpoint of other countries. This will be explained in more detail.

(1) Ultra-nationalism is a principle of putting the State above everything, which regarding the State next to nothing, sacrifices everything else to it. A State is the most perfect form of society, as a member of which a man can live a life of the most orderly cooperation. The love of one's fatherland is a man's natural feeling. It is one of high virtues to devote oneself to one's fatherland.

But man does not exist for the sake of the State, but the State exists for man. Ultra-nationalism forgets this and does not respect humanity, the personality, and the individuality of the people. It is in letting these grow without distortion, the nature inherent in man, his ability, the human nature as a requisite, that the object of life lies. And the personality which consists in uniting and activating such a human nature with a free will is nothing but the qualification, the value of man as man. It is a crime to ignore this human personality and to utilize man like a machine, or a slave. Moreover, each individual has peculiar characteristics of its own, distinguishing him from others. In developing the individuality of each person, helping each other, and going on establishing a rich, lofty culture, lies the happiness of life. But ultra-nationalism, under the pretext of serving the State, in reality from the prejudices of the leaders, makes grow the human nature of the people in a specific, crooked direction (for instance, in the direction of war) and suppresses its growth in any other direction. Moreover, ultra-nationalism, ignoring the personality of the people, suppresses their free will and their critical spirit and wants them to obey their leaders blindly. In addition, telling the people to serve the great cause at the expense of the small self, ultra-nationalism gives no regard to the individuality of the people, and wants to put them into a uniform mould. In brief, ultra-nationalism attaches more importance to the State as a whole than to the individual, and requires service to the whole at the sacrifice of the freedom and rights of the individual. These are also characteristics of a totalitarian State. (Pp. 13–14.)

* * *

(2) Ultra-nationalism imbues the people with the feeling of superiority and does harm to international comity. As a matter of fact, a State is a State in the world, different States holding diplomatic relations with one another, carrying on trades between one another, one State learning the superior culture of the other State thereby supplementing its own shortcomings, becoming more and more prosperous all together. How miserable a State is when it is isolated from inter-

national relations is driven home to us concerning Japan of the present day. But ultra-nationalists think their own country is the only fine country in the world, and boast of the philosophy and culture of their country as the most excellent. In this respect it is also called fascistic nationalism. It finally goes so far as to conclude that it is a good thing to spread to other countries the policies of its own country and to rule other countries. In Japan, the Divine Country idea, taught by Shintoism involved such a feeling of national superiority. And as ultra-nationalism has recently become more influential, this idea has become increasingly strong. In other words, the emperor of Japan, being a descendant of gods, is a living god and is superior to the sovereigns of other countries. This idea has recently been denied by the Emperor. The Japanese people, too, were born of gods and the Japanese troops are the Divine Troops, guiding and saving other nations. Japan's land, being the Divine Isles also born of gods, is everlasting. The doctrines developed in this way until, finally, it was being preached that, as is shown in the words "Making a House of the World" [*hakkō ichi-u*], for the world to become like one house under Japanese rule was the ideal of mankind. Such a feeling of superiority is what gave rise to war and incurred defeat. It is shown by this fact that ultra-nationalism does more harm than good to the State. (P. 15.)

Japan's ultranationalist political philosophy, known as *kōdō* or the Imperial Way, has been inextricably intertwined with the ideologies of the national cult, *Shintō* or the Way of the Gods, and the national polity or national entity known as *kokutai*. Is it possible to extract the philosophical essence from this mixture of mythology, religion, and political absolutism? There appear to have been four major concepts in *kōdō:* Divine Origin, Divine Characteristics, Divine Leadership, and Divine Mission. The Divine Origin is mythology from the misty prehistorical days of the *kami* or gods, traditionally set as the period before 660 B.C. The Divine Characteristics are the *Yamato damashii*, the peculiar endowment of the race of Japanese people derived from their genealogical succession from the gods. Both of these elements are Shinto in origin. Divine Leadership is the mixture of Confucian respect for ancestors, be they gods or humans, and Shinto religious belief in the divine origin of the line of Japanese Emperors. The Divine Mission is the almost inevitable resultant of the other beliefs. It is a sort of Japanese noblesse oblige; it is *hakkō ichi-u*, literally meaning "The Whole World under One Roof" but politically meaning the mission of extending the benefits of the Emperor's enlightened rule over all the inferior, and mortal, races surrounding Japan.

In order to understand the mystical but vigorously political philosophy of ultranationalism which is best known to Occidental students by its major policy manifestation, the Greater East Asia Co-Prosperity Sphere, it will be necessary to examine in some detail the Shinto, Buddhist, and Confucian contributions to that philosophy. This may conveniently wait a consideration of the nature of the National Shinto (*Kokka Shintō*) as an element in Japanese nationalism. It may be profitable at this point, however, to review briefly the salient beliefs in the mythological tradition of the creation of Japan, the land, the people and the Ruling Family.

The Contribution of Mythology. The earliest existent historical record of the Japanese people is the *Kojiki* ("Records of Ancient Matters") compiled by Ō NO YASUMARO. It was completed in the fifth year of the *Wadō* era of Emperor GEMMYŌ (A.D. 712) and is based entirely on oral sources. The preface of the work states that Emperor TENMU had ordered a person named HIEDA NO ARE who was gifted with a remarkable memory to collect and memorize the folk tales and traditions dealing with the foundation of Japan. Ō NO YASUMARO then reduced the memorized words of HIEDA to writing. Paralleling this record is one written in Chinese completed in the fourth year of the *Yōrō* era of the Emperor GENSHŌ (A.D. 720), entitled the *Nihon-shoki* (or *Nihongi,* "Chronicles of Japan"). The *Nihongi* was compiled by Prince TONERI, third son of Emperor TENMU, assisted by Ō NO YASUMARO, the compiler of the *Kojiki*. It is known that other written sources, as well as the oral traditions which are the basis of the *Kojiki*, were used in its compilation but these sources have not survived. With the exception of certain abbreviated cross references to Japan in the literatures of China and Korea, and certain archeological evidences, Japanese history until that age is entirely based on these two records. It is almost axiomatic that the traditional history earlier than one or two generations prior to these first recorded histories should be most untrustworthy, a blend of historical fact, mythology, and the storytellers' license. Commenting on the authenticity of early Japanese history in an article, "Early Japanese History," in *Transactions of the Asiatic Society of Japan* (Yokohama, 1899), Vol. XVI, First Series, p.

73, W. G. Aston finds that the earliest date of the accepted Japanese chronology which is confirmed by external evidence is A.D. 461 and concludes that Korean and Chinese chronology are more trustworthy than Japanese for the period prior to that date. The traditional date of B.C. 660 marking the coronation of Emperor Jimmu, founder of the Imperial House, is admitted to be highly problematical even by Japanese scholars and the date B.C. 25 has been suggested.

Both of these basic records have been translated into English by various Japanese and European scholars but two translations have been so widely read that they have become almost as well known as the original. These are:

Chamberlain, Basil Hall, trans., "Kojiki, or Records of Ancient Matters," *Transactions of the Asiatic Society of Japan*, Vol. X, Supplement 1882. Reprinted 1906; republished 1920 by the Japan Times Publishing Co., Tokyo.

Aston, William George, trans., "Nihongi" (2 vols.). *Transactions and Proceedings of the Japan Society of London*, Supplement I, London. The Society, 1896.

A convenient condensation of the story of the prehistorical period, an amalgamation of the folk tales contained in both of these records, is presented by the great Japanese religious scholar, Dr. Anesaki Masaharu, in *Mythology of China and Japan*, Vol. VIII in the series, "Mythology of All Races" (Boston, Archeological Institute of America, 1928).

The legend of the creation of Japan, upon which the whole structure of Japanese ultranationalism is based, begins with the universe in a misty, chaotic mass containing certain germs of life. The purer part separated into heaven and the grosser element settled down and became the earth, which at first floated in the nebulous mass of the heavens like a fish sporting in the water. The first life was produced in a reedlike growth which was transformed into a god. This was followed by a number of other spontaneously created male gods, having neither father nor mother, existing arrested in time and suspended in space, imbued with human characteristics of personality. The first creation of a physical world begins with the episode of two gods, *Izanagi no Mikoto* (His Augustness the Male-Who-Invites) and *Izanami no Mikoto* (Her Augustness the Female-Who-Invites), standing on a bridge floating in the heavens. They dipped a jeweled spear down into mists and found the ocean. When they withdrew the spear the brine from the waters dripped from the point and coagulated to form an island, the first of the land. This scene has been depicted frequently on wall scrolls (*kakemono*) and other objects of art, and is as well known to the Japanese child as the Manger Scene or the Crucifixion are to children in the Christian tradition. *Izanagi* and *Izanami* descended to this island and lived there as husband and wife, creating by birth a series of islands, the sea, the rivers, the mountains, and finally the ancestors of trees and herbs. In the primitive animism of *Kami Nagara no Michi*, the ancient precursor of modern *Shintō*, each of these were considered *kami*, loosely rendered "gods."

The creation of life and death in these ancient legends centers about a myth in which *Izanami*, while giving birth to the Fire-God, was severely burned and died. She descended into a terrifying place of darkness, a nether-land, where she underwent putrefaction. Her mate, *Izanagi*, followed and despite her plea that he should not look the male god disobeyed and looked upon her, felt loathing, and as a punishment was driven away pursued by a horrible female deity from the denizens of this nether-land. In purifying himself after this encounter *Izanagi* washed himself. In the *Shintō* tradition this corresponds to the ritual of *misogi* (cleansing) in which contamination with the unclean, death, and blood are washed away in free-running water or by the sprinkling of salt. In this process of washing *Izanagi* the male god created *Amaterasu Ōmikami* (the Sun-Goddess, or literally, Heavenly-Shining-Great-August-Deity) from the drippings from his left eye. Similarly he created the Moon-God, *Tsuki-yomi*, from his right eye; a dwarfed leech-child that was abandoned; and finally from the drippings of his nose, a male god, *Susano-o no Mikoto* (Swift-Impetuous-Male-August-Deity), frequently rendered the "Storm-God," but in the Japanese mythology a god occupying the position of obstreperous masculinity and unpredictability. The Sun-Goddess, *Amaterasu Ōmikami*, had a luster which "shone throughout all the six quarters" and because of her manifest superiority to all the other gods was sent to heaven to rule. Her younger brother *Tsuki-yomi*, the Moon-God, was sent to heaven to become her consort and to share in the government of the heavens.

The symbols of Imperial succession are the Three Sacred Treasures, the Sacred Mirror of *Yata*, the Sacred Jeweled Necklace of

Yasakani, and the Sacred Sword of *Murakumo*, which in the *Shintō* philosophy stand respectively for Truth, Mercy, and Justice. These three famous Imperial regalia are supposed to have been given by the Sun-Goddess to her grandson, *Ninigi no Mikoto* (His Augustness the Prosperity-Man, or Ruddy-Plenty), on the occasion of his descent to earth, and have been handed down from Emperor to Emperor to the present time. The origin of these three Sacred Treasures is the subject of two myths, one dealing with the withdrawal into seclusion of the Sun-Goddess and the other dealing with the banishment of the Storm-God to *Izumo*, an earthly nether-land geographically located on the Sea of Japan side of the southwestern portion of the main Japanese island of Honshu.

Susano-o, the Storm-God, who had withered the trees and shaken the mountains and caused great trouble, was on the verge of being expelled by order of *Izanagi* from the earth to the nether-land where the shade of his mother, *Izanami*, had gone. He went instead into the heavens and by his uncouth actions disgusted the Sun-Goddess, *Amaterasu Ōmikami*, his sister. She was so frightened that she retired into a rock cave in the heavens and closed the door and made it fast, and night descended on the "whole Plain of High Heaven and all the Central Land of Reed-Plains." In this eternal night there was only the sound of the voices of the gods raised in woe. To meet the crisis the "eight hundred myriads of Deities" assembled and made plans to entice her to come out. They made an eight-handed iron mirror and a curved string of 500 jewels. Assembling all the "long-singing birds of eternal night" they bade them sing and draped the jewels on the branches of a tree and hung the mirror from the middle of the tree. Then one of the older goddesses put on a girdle of moss and a hat made out of an uprooted tree and holding bamboo grass as if it were flowers began to do an absurd and obscene dance. The assembled gods were convulsed with mirth and began to laugh. The Sun-Goddess, curious and a little piqued at the gaiety, when the darkness should have caused only gloom, opened the door a crack to see why they were making merry. One of the goddesses replied that they were rejoicing because they had found a deity whose radiance was more splendid than that of the Sun-Goddess, and held the mirror so that *Amaterasu Ōmikami* looked out and saw her own reflection. She edged forward to see it better and one of the gods took her hand

and drew her out; then they put a rope across the doorway and said she must not go further back than that. And so the Sun-Goddess was prevailed upon to return to the open heavens.

Susano-o, the Storm-God, on being banished to the nether-land of *Izumo* for having frightened his sister the Sun-Goddess, traveled first to Korea and on return to Japan stopped at the headwaters of a river and found an old man and woman, earthly deities, weeping for the eighth and last of their daughters, destined to be devoured in the eighth annual foray of a ferocious eight-headed serpent. The Storm-God made a compact with the parents that he should receive the girl as a wife if he were able to kill the serpent. He did so by arranging eight tubs of *sake* or Japanese rice wine so that each of the eight heads of the serpent might drink and become intoxicated and finally fall asleep. While the serpent was in its drunken stupor the Storm-God killed it and chopped it into small pieces, until on one of the eight tails his sword was nicked. Splitting open the tail he found there imbedded the Sword of *Murakumo*, named for the clouds which always formed where the serpent was, and later known as the grass-cutting sword, *Kusanagi*, because the Storm-God used it to mow the grass of a field. *Susano-o* married the daughter of the earth gods and had 81 sons, thus founding the earthly race which stood in apposition to that descending from JIMMU, first Japanese Emperor and great-grandson of *Ninigi no Mikoto*, himself the grandson of the Sun-Goddess.

The link between the gods of heaven, or more exactly, of *Takama-ga-Hara* (Plain of High Heaven), was established by the legend of the descent to earth of this *Ninigi no Mikoto*, son of *Amano-Oshihomimi* and grandson of *Amaterasu Ōmikami*, the Sun-Goddess. According to the accepted Japanese mythology the Sun-Goddess issued a Divine Oracle (*Shintaku*) which said: "The Luxuriant Land of Reed Plains is the country which our descendants are to govern as monarchs. Go forth, therefore, Ye Imperial Grandson, and rule over it! May Ye fare well. Our Imperial lineage shall continue unbroken and prosperous, co-eternal with heaven and earth."

Ninigi no Mikoto, however, was both wise and prudent and before descending to earth himself sent two lesser gods to deliver the Divine Oracle to *Ōkuninushi no Kami* (Deity-Master-of-Great-Land), the most powerful of the 81 sons of *Susano-o*, the

Storm-God, and the leader of the rival earthly tribes. *Ōkuninushi* and his son, *Kotoshironushi no Kami*, rulers of *Izumo* or the nether-land, agreed to the sovereignty of the chosen grandson of the Sun-Goddess and in return received a beautiful palace, today marked by the *Izumo Taisha* Shrine. Reassured by the reports of his envoys, *Ninigi no Mikoto* then descended to earth on Mount Takachiho in what is the modern Prefecture of Miyazaki in eastern Kyushu, and proceeded with his duties of ruling the land. The instrument of this extension of the Sun-Goddess' rule was JIMMU, son of *Ugayafukiaezu*, grandson of *Hikohohodemi*, and great-grandson of *Ninigi no Mikoto*. Being thus the fifth generation descendant of the Sun-Goddess, JIMMU is both a god and the first Emperor. There seems little doubt that some historical figure known as JIMMU actually existed, although it is considered by Occidental and some Japanese scholars that he probably lived about five centuries after his traditionally assigned era. As to his divinity there is rather more than skepticism.

Whatever the physical and spiritual ancestry of this early Japanese tribal leader, the story of his ascension to the throne is basically that of a powerful clan chieftain who subjugated one of the three large populated areas of the Japanese home islands. JIMMU came from *Hyūga* (in modern Miyazaki Prefecture), in eastern Kyushu, and sailed across the Inland Sea to *Naniwa* (modern Osaka), where he prepared to mount an expedition against the tribes in *Yamato* (modern Nara Prefecture). He found stubborn resistance and detoured via *Kii* (modern Wakayama Prefecture), conquering all tribes, and finally was enthroned at *Kashiwara* Palace at the foot of Mount Unebi, near the city of Nara, on 11 February B.C. 660, commemorated as *Kigensetsu* (Empire Founding Day). The tribes that he conquered are traditionally considered to be descendants of the Storm-God *Susano-o* who was banished to and ruled *Izumo* (modern Shimane and Tottori Prefectures). It will be noted that by this device of dual descent from the original gods who consolidated the land, *Izanagi* and *Izanami*, through their children the Sun-Goddess, *Amaterasu Ōmikami*, and the Storm-God, *Susano-o no Mikoto*, the Japanese explain the obvious ethnological differences in the Japanese people and yet retain the twin ultranationalist fictions of racial purity and divine origin.

Japan the political entity is called *Nihon* or *Nippon*. Japan the spiritual entity is called *Shinkoku*, the Land of the Gods or the land of the *kami*. Another ancient expression for the country is *kami nagara mo waga ko no shiroshimesu kuni* (the country which our children govern as *kami*). What does *kami*, rendered loosely as "gods," really signify? It does stand for the deities of prehistoric Japanese mythology. It also stands for the deities of foreign religions, being Jehovah of the Hebrews and God of the Christians, though the term *hotoke* is used for the Buddhas in the pantheon of Buddhism. This peculiar elasticity in meaning for the term *kami* has enabled Japan to practice the syncretism with Confucianism, Taoism, Buddhism, and recently Christianity, which is so marked a characteristic of her philosophy. Any definition of *kami* written in the immediately prewar years could not fail to have political overtones. But a brief note on the term written half a century ago by Professor KUME Kunitake in his article, "Japanese Religious Beliefs: Shintō—the Kami," in Count ŌKUMA Shigenobu's work, *Fifty Years of New Japan* (London, Smith, Elder & Co., 1909), II, 23–24, may be pertinent:

"Kami" is a comprehensive term applicable to anything high or above oneself, such, for example, as "a deity," "an emperor," "a feudal chief," "an elevated place," or "a hair on the head." As the very focus of *Shintō* is thus a vague and indefinite term applied alike to gods and heroes, or to natural phenomena, *Shintō* offers no direct opposition to the other religions. The Emperor is conceived as a living *kami*, under whom lies a gradation of *kami* and *shimo*, namely the higher and the lower, the elder and the younger, the father and the son, the protector and the protected, down to the lowest peasantry in their weather-beaten huts. What, then, is the greatest *kami* revered by Shintōists? It is then the very *Ruler of the Universe*.

But despite this nebulous quality of the term *kami*, invariably advanced by Japanese apologists to the Occidental observer in explanation of a situation which otherwise would appear impossibly mystical and somewhat akin to psychopathic self-adulation, the people of Japan look upon *kami* unless qualified by context as the gods of the prehistoric era. Count ŌKUMA Shigenobu on p. 2 of Vol. I of the work just quoted states:

Early in the ninth century the Japanese Government compiled a "New Record of Family Names" (*Shinsen Shōji Roku*). This consisted of extracts from the genealogies of the 1882 noble families then existing in the Imperial capital, Kyōto. It was divided into three parts, namely, (*a*) the Imperial Families (*Kwo-betsu*), or descendents of the first Emperor Jimmu, (*b*) the descendents of the *kami* prior to Jimmu (*Shin-betsu*), and (*c*) families who had immigrated from other lands (*Ban-betsu*). As regards the first two classes, the first was originally composed of the main branch of the second. Japan was at that time under the control of these three classes of nobles, and as the first two were practically one and the same, it follows that Japan was under the rule of the *kami* and to this day the masses of the people firmly believe that the right of sovereignty remains in the hands of the descendents of the *kami*.

It was almost inevitable that the theory of Divine Origin should lead to the conclusion that the people were of holy extraction, and hence enjoyed Divine Characteristics and that they enjoyed Divine Leadership through the line of Imperial succession tracing its genealogy back to the Sun-Goddess, *Amaterasu Ōmikami*. The textual evidence of these beliefs is overwhelming. It will suffice to quote from three or four recognized Japanese authorities to illustrate the concept.

Katō Genchi in his book, *A Study of Shintō, the Religion of the Japanese Nation* (Tokyo, Meiji Japan Society, 1926), p. 208, states:

The vital essence of Shintō manifests itself in an expression of that unique spirit of the national service of the Japanese people, which is not only mere morality but is their religion, culminating in Mikadoism or their peculiar form of loyalty or patriotism towards the Emperor, who is at once political head and religious leader in a government constitutional yet theocratico-patriarchal.

Baron Kikuchi Dairoku in his lectures given at the University of London entitled *Japanese Education* (London, John Murray, 1909), p. 4, says:

. . . this fundamental character may be briefly said to consist in the unique relation between the Imperial House and the people, which is not simply a relation between the present Emperor and the people, but one which has existed between the two for generations, through more than twenty centuries; this is the reason why there is such repeated reference to the Imperial Ancestors and forefathers of the people.

and again on pp. 7–8 states:

From the first Emperor, Jimmu, there has been *an unbroken line of descent* to the present Emperor. This unique character of our Imperial dynasty, together with the fact that all Japanese (with the insignificant exception of the subjugated aborigines and naturalised Coreans and Chinese) are regarded as either descended from the Imperial family or from those who came over with it from Takama-ga-Hara, may be said to constitute the fundamental character of our nationality, as distinguished from other nations. Our nation is, as it were, one family, of which the Emperor is the head or patriarch, and this relation has subsisted from the first foundation of our Empire down to the present time. Never, during the whole long period of our history, has there been a single instance of a subject presuming to attempt to place himself on the throne, and never have we been conquered by a foreign invader. This relation between the Imperial House and the people, I repeat, is the most important factor in the development of our national character, and, as stated in the Rescript, is the basis of our education.

KUME Kunitake in his article, "Japanese Religious Beliefs: Shintō—the Kami" (*op. cit.*), states on p. 30:

To this day devotees of *Shintō* pray only for the Emperor's welfare, not for their own, and the Emperor offers his daily prayer for the welfare of his subjects. He is regarded as a living *kami*, loved and revered by the nation above all things on earth, and himself loving and protecting the nation, who are deemed sons of *Kami Nagara* and are entrusted to his care by the *kami*. This mutual understanding obtains between every individual Japanese and the Emperor. The Sovereign studies our needs and feels our sorrows. What more have we, then, to ask from the *kami* directly? Thus *Shintō* (doctrine of the *kami*) is *kundō* (doctrine of the Emperor), for *Shintōism* is *Mikadoism*. "The *kami's* will is the Emperor's will" is a maxim inscribed on the heart of every Japanese. Herein one may see the fountain-head of our patriotic spirit, whose marvelous activity has served to raise Japan in these fifty years to the level of the first-rate Powers of the world.

Count ŌKUMA Shigenobu (*op. cit.*), I, 6, states:

From the idea that Japan is the country of the *kami*, her people have been led to believe that she is under the special protection of these heavenly beings. There is, of course, no theoretical certainty for this belief. Yet events which have occurred during her long career as the *kami's* country have, not unnaturally, been attributed to favours of the unseen.

HOZUMI Nobushige in his famous legal study, *Ancestor Worship and Japanese Law* (Tokyo, Maruzen Kabushiki Kaisha, 1912), pp. 87–88, states:

The Emperor holds the sovereign power, not as his own inherent right, but as an inheritance from the Divine Ancestor. The government is, therefore, *theocratical*. The Emperor rules over the country as the supreme head of the vast family of the Japanese nation. The government is therefore, *patriarchal*. The Emperor exercises the sovereign power according to the Constitution, which is based on the most advanced principles of modern constitutionalism. In other words, the fundamental principle of the Japanese government is *theocratical-patriarchal constitutionalism*. This tripartite character of the government presents the curious meeting of the Past and Present.

The *Kokutai no Hongi,* fundamental policy statement of the Ministry of Education published in 1937 and banned by the Occupational Authorities in 1945, is devoted almost in its entirety to an analysis of how the three fundamental ultranationalist concepts of Divine Origin, Divine Characteristics, and Divine Leadership shall be applied to the routine governmental and educational duties. Two brief quotations from the English translation by John Owen GAUNTLETT and Robert King HALL, *Kokutai no Hongi* ("Cardinal Principles of the National Entity of Japan") (Cambridge, Harvard University Press, in press), will serve to illustrate this portion of the argument. On Ms. p. 20 it says:

The Imperial Throne is the Throne of a line of Emperors unbroken for ages eternal, and is the Emperors' Throne of a truly single line. The Imperial Throne is the Throne of the Sovereign Lords who are the deific offspring of the Imperial Ancestor, who inherit the Land founded by the Imperial Ancestors, and make it their great august task to govern it peacefully as a peaceful Land, and is the station of the Emperors who, one with the Imperial Ancestor, manifest their great august Will even until now, and who cause the Land to prosper and care for the people. The subjects, in looking up to the Emperor, who is deity incarnate, reverence at the same time the Imperial Ancestors, and under his bounty become the subjects of our country. Thus, the Imperial Throne is a Throne of the utmost dignity and is the foundation of a Land eternally firm.

And on Ms. pp. 184–186 it says:

All the laws in the Imperial Constitution on forms of government are but extensions and transmissions of this principle of direct Imperial rule. For instance, stipulations on the rights and duties of Sovereign and subject are different from those which exist among Western nations where a system of free rights serves to protect inherent rights

of the people from the ruler, for the stipulations are the fruit of the
Emperor's fond care for his people and his great august spirit to provide them with equal opportunities for assisting the Throne without feelings of barrier. The triune subsistence, for example, of the
Government, courts of justice, and the Diet, is different from the
mutual independence of the legislature as it exists among Western
nations, which aims at depriving the one holding sovereign power of
judicial and legislative powers, giving recognition only to, yet at the
same time curbing, his administrative power, with a view to restrain-
ing the powers of the ruler; for in our country segregation is not in
respect of the rights of a ruler, but applies merely to the organs for
the assistance of the direct Imperial rule, whose object is to make ever
more secure the assistance extended to the direct rule by the Emperor.
The deliberative assembly, too, is, in a so-called democratic country,
a representative organ of a people who are nominal rulers; while in a
so-called monarchy, where the sovereign and the people govern the
nation together, the assembly is a representative organ of the people
whose object is to hold the caprices of the sovereign under restraint
and to provide a means by which the ruler and the people may govern
the nation together. Our Imperial Diet, on the other hand, is completely different; since it was instituted with the one object of providing the people with a means of assisting the Emperor's direct rule
in special ways in regard to special matters.

The Sacred World Mission. If the ultranationalist philosophy of
Japan had stopped short of foreign application, if it had confined
itself to this foregoing conception of a divine absolutism, it might
have remained the unpalatable and disappointing excursion into
modern representative government of an essentially feudalistic
nation but need not have become an unacceptable ideology for a
member of the community of nations. But one of the dangers of
the Messianic complex, whether the delusion be that of a Christ or
of a *kami*, is that he who considers himself divine soon considers
his ambitions sacred. Japan had a Divine Mission and this mission
was the epitome of the entire philosophy of ultranationalism. Irrefutable evidence of this mission has been compiled in the interminable sessions of the war crimes trials in Tokyo. It is recorded
in literally hundreds of thousands of volumes and millions of
copies of newspapers which carried the official propaganda line.
From the plethora of material only three statements will be
quoted. The first is the statement of the expansionist policy in
Greater East Asia, as reflected in *Ji Kyoku Eigo Mondai Shū*

("Collection of English Questions Asked in College Level Entrance Examinations"), compiled by INOE Masahira and ŌHARA Miyao (Tokyo, Tai Bun Do, 1940). This interesting document is organized in the form of a series of questions and answers, in both Japanese and English, based on actual examination questions which had been asked in leading colleges in 1938–39. In the preface it stated that in 1937 only 7% of the questions "reflected the times" but that in 1938–39 nearly half of the questions dealt with the times (i.e., the war in China). A few questions from pp. 1–6 will serve as examples:

If there is anyone who thinks that with the fall of Canton, and Hankow, peace will come soon, he does not realize the meaning of the incident. Japan wishes to undertake the construction of a new East Asia and has now entered the period of establishing a new life among the people. In this sense the true war was just begun. (Tokushima Higher Technical School.)

What Japan seeks is the establishment of a new order which will insure the permanent stability of East Asia. In this lies the ultimate purpose of our present military campaign.

This new order has for its foundation a tripartite relationship of mutual aid and co-ordination between Japan, Manchoukuo and China in political, economic, cultural and other fields. Its object is to secure international justice, to perfect the joint defence against Communism, and to create a new culture and realize a close economic cohesion through East Asia. This indeed is the way to contribute toward the stabilization of East Asia and the progress of the world. (Nagasaki Medical School, College of Pharmacy.)

It goes without saying that Japan at all times is endeavouring to maintain and promote her friendly relations with foreign nations, but at the same time we consider it only natural that to keep peace and order in East Asia we must even act alone on our own responsibility, and it is our duty to perform it. At the same time there is no country but China which is in a position to share with Japan the responsibility for maintenance of peace in East Asia. (Meiji College, in Harbin.)

Japan's ambition is to contribute to the great social heritage of mankind and through her unique gift to enrich the accumulated civilization of humanity. This can only be attained by the realization of the one hope in the Japanese mind that is the amalgamation of the civilizations of the East and the West. (Kōtoku Gakuin, in Manchuria.)

The *Kokutai no Hongi* ("Cardinal Principles of the National Entity of Japan"), published in 1937, concludes with two paragraphs entitled "Our Mission."

Our present mission as a people is to build up a new Japanese culture by adopting and sublimating Western cultures with our national entity as the basis, and to contribute spontaneously to the advancement of world culture. Our nation early saw the introduction of Chinese and Indian cultures, and even succeeded in evolving original creations and developments. This was made possible, indeed, by the profound and boundless nature of our national entity; so that the mission of the people to whom it is bequeathed is truly great in its historical significance. The call for a clarification of our national entity is at this time very much in the fore; but this must unfailingly be done by making the sublimation of Occidental ideologies and cultures its occasion, since, without this, the clarification of our national entity is apt to fall into abstractions isolated from actualities. That is to say, the adoption and sublimation of Occidental ideologies and the clarification of our national entity are so related as to be inseparable.

The attitude of the Japanese in the past toward the cultures of the world has been independent and yet at the same time comprehensive. Our contributions to the world lie only in giving full play more than ever to our Way which is of the Japanese people. The people must more than ever create and develop a new Japan by virtue of their immutable national entity which is the basis of the State and by virtue of the Way of the Empire which stands firm throughout the ages at Home and abroad, and thereby more than ever guard and maintain the prosperity of the Imperial Throne which is coeval with heaven and earth. This, indeed, is our mission. (Trans. from GAUNTLETT and HALL, *op. cit.*, Ms. pp. 210–211.)

The *Shinmin no Michi* ("The Way of the Subject"), the other of the two basic Japanese policy documents banned by SCAP directive in 1945, contains two paragraphs in which the Mission of Japan is specifically stated. The text as presented in translation in the appendix to Otto D. TOLISCHUS' *Tokyo Record* (New York, Reynal & Hitchcock, 1945), p. 415, is quoted in part:

Japan's mission of world historical significance is revealed by the Imperial spirit embodied in this Rescript. [The September 1940 *Rescript Announcing the Japan-German-Italian Tripartite Treaty*.] The fundamental spirit, as is seen from the opening passages of the Rescript, is to let all nations seek their proper places, which is made a prerequisite condition to lasting peace. Japan's guiding position in

East Asia has thus been firmly implanted beyond dispute, and the spirit of the founding of the Japanese Empire, which is symbolized by the embracing of the six cardinal points and covering of the eight cords so as to form one roof [hakkō ichi-u], is made clear as the basic conception of the construction of a new world order.

Viewed from the standpoint of world history, the China Affair is a step toward the construction of a world of moral principles by Japan. The building up of a new order for securing lasting peace of the world will be attained by the disposal of the China Affair as a steppingstone.

It may perhaps be a novel point of view to the Occidental observer, but it is one which has been advanced by thoughtful and apparently sincere Japanese, that the four sacred tenets of Japanese nationalist philosophy—the Divine Origin, Divine Leadership, Divine Characteristics contributed by mythology, and the Divine Mission contributed by modern interpretation of that mythology—are not necessarily objectionable. Certainly the Allied case against them cannot be accepted a priori nor has it been established solely by defeat.

These Japanese point out that the belief in the Divine Origin can be paralleled by similar myths and folk legends in virtually all the European nations. The Christian tradition of Genesis is based on an ancient Hebrew legend which is no more susceptible to scientific verification than that of the "Consolidation of the Land" by *Izanagi* and *Izanami*. The theory of Divine Characteristics can be matched with the "chosen people" of the Jewish tradition, the "pure Aryan race" of the Germans, the "white supremacy" of the Southern states of America, and the "white man's burden" of the British. Concededly many of these are outmoded or even objectionable beliefs among the enlightened nations of the world, yet a pride in race and culture would hardly constitute valid grounds for foreign intervention if that sense of superiority were not accompanied by some overt act. The very political theory of "sovereignty," which is basic to all government, is essentially ethnocentric in character. The Japanese conception of Divine Leadership is almost an exact counterpart of the old European theory of "divine right of Kings." The concept of the Emperor as a human descendant of the gods does not materially differ in educated Japanese eyes from the sacred position claimed for the Pope in the Roman Catholic Church. The ritual of the Emperor reporting to his Divine Ancestors the progress of his temporal policies is paralleled by the Occidental appeal through prayer for divine intervention in political matters. It is pointed out that President Harry S. TRUMAN in his radio address on 1 September 1945 at the time of the Surrender ceremonies in Tokyo Bay, said:

To all of us there comes first a sense of gratitude to Almighty God Who sustained us and our Allies in the dark days of grave danger, Who made us to grow from weakness into the strongest fighting force in history, and Who now has seen us overcome the forces of tyranny that sought to destroy His civilization.

God grant that in our pride of the hour we may not forget the hard tasks that are still before us; that we may approach these with the same courage, zeal, and patience with which we faced the trials and problems of the past four years. . . .

God's help has brought us to this day of victory. With His help we will attain that peace and prosperity for ourselves and all the world in the years ahead.

Can it be, ask these sophisticated Japanese, that defeat has proven the Christian and Hebrew God to be more powerful than their pantheon? Or does the Allied antipathy to the Japanese conception of Divine Leadership establish the criteria between the true (Allied) and the false (Japanese) gods? Or perhaps, if Allied avowals of religious tolerance may be accepted at face value, it is not an attack on either the strength or authenticity of the Japanese gods but merely a denunciation of the subject matter of the prayers. And if this be so, they argue, does it follow that political appeals to Japanese Divine Leadership in matters unobjectionable to the Allied Powers shall be considered acceptable and tolerated? Shall the Occupation Authorities, then, establish a censorship board to screen the prayers?

It is evident that if the policy of the Allied Powers is to be consistent it must attack the philosophy of ultranationalism not on the basis of the historic truth or rationalism of the Japanese concepts of Divine Origin, Characteristics, and Leadership, but rather on the basis of the political unacceptability of the Japanese Divine Mission. The former constitute essentially an internal problem and one which is properly the province of Japanese scholars and scientists. These concepts will be reduced to their appropriate level as myths when the freedoms of research and publication make possible to the Japanese themselves a critical scrutiny. But the latter, since it is the goal or objective for practical political action in the international field, is a matter of concern for all responsible World Powers.

In what way was the Japanese Mission unacceptable? In what manner did it differ from Occidental internationalism which is respected or condoned among the Allies? Many Japanese and some impartial foreign observers would say that it differed very little. They would point out that Western internationalism varies from traditional imperialism to world government in the United Nations model. Even in imperialism there are many forms. At one extreme is British colonialism which avowedly works to educate the native populations to the point of responsible self-government, and at the other pole is traditional Dutch colonialism which has attempted to protect native populations from the impact of European civilization, even going to the extent of retaining native legal and financial structures in addition to the imported Dutch systems. They would characterize French colonial policy as systematic official exploitation through monopolies. To many Americans who have never considered that their nation was an empire they would present the illuminating concept that almost all of Latin America has been a part of colonial America, bound by the exclusion of European political influences under the Monroe Doctrine, by economic dependence upon the United States for loans and imports, and by the covert threat of military intervention. Would the United States tolerate for a single moment, they would ask, a government in one of the Caribbean nations which actively threatened the security of the Panama Canal? And between the extremes of colonial imperialism and the United Nations there exists the great interlocking structure of favored-nation treaties, reciprocal trade agreements, and hemispheric solidarity policies. What, ask the Japanese, is the essential difference between the Good Neighbor Policy and the Greater East Asia Co-Prosperity Sphere Policy?

There is a difference but it is not one apparent in the explicit statement of the two policies. The difference lies in the sincerity of the statement and in the means employed for implementing the policies. Japan as a nation has given concrete evidence of insincerity in its formulation of the Greater East Asia Co-Prosperity Sphere Policy and it must be assumed that this insincerity extends equally to all ramifications of the Japanese conception of a Divine

Mission. Thus, Japanese aims, as stated in INOE and ŌHARA's compilation of examination questions (*op. cit.*, pp. 3–5), were:

China now is completely in Japanese hands. But Japan's genuine wish cannot be the downfall of China. Rather must it be its restoration and rebirth. It cannot be the conquest of China, but co-operation with it. Japan can have no other wish than to go hand in hand with a China that has awakened as an Oriental people to build a really stable world of East Asia. (South Manchurian Higher Technical School.)

Japan does not aim at making China solely dependent on Japan; she does not want her territory, but her cooperation, in order to bring about a new era of fruitful development and constructive prosperity, which will benefit not only China and Japan but all nations of the world. (Hamamatsu Higher Technical School.)

But it would be the naïve person indeed who could accept such statements as anything but propaganda in the light of the history of Japan during the period from 1932 to the Surrender in 1945. The Greater East Asia Co-Prosperity Sphere Policy and the Divine Mission of World Leadership alike must be measured in terms of the actions of the Japanese in attempting to implement those policies. On this basis they are unacceptable to Japanese and foreigner alike.

A common justification for ethically unacceptable actions which is advanced by apologists in all nations is that "the end justifies the means." In Japan this might be reworded, "the Divine End justifies any means." But the end and the means are not independent entities. The particular means selected to achieve an end almost inevitably determine to a considerable degree what that end shall be. Thus Japanese "control" of their sources of raw materials in Manchukuo could have been any of several kinds of control. It could have been an economic control derived from incentive prices, or reciprocal trade agreements, or yen loans, or favored geographical position, or private investments. Any of these would have conformed to the practices of the Allied nations and would presumably have been acceptable. It actually was a political control derived from military occupation and domination of a puppet government. This was unacceptable. The means by which the control had been established determined to a major degree the kind of control.

Japanese leadership in the world will be determined by the means by which it achieves that leadership. If Japan had aspired to its Divine Mission of world leadership through pre-eminence in science and industry, in scholarship and ethics, in the arts and cultural pursuits, it almost certainly would have attained the way station of leadership of Greater East Asia. It might eventually have achieved its ultimate goal. Reasoning from its failure, is it possible to detect the weaknesses in the means it employed? There appear to be two: internally it subordinated the individual to the State, and externally it attempted to reach world leadership through military conquest. Both of these might be acceptable in a totalitarian police state but they are quite incompatible with the standards set by the democratic nations of the world and they are unacceptable in a philosophy of education for the new Japan.

What Is National Shinto?

A Religion, Philosophy, Cult, or Conspiracy? National Shinto (*Kokka Shintō*), also known as Shrine Shinto (*Jinja Shintō*), is the former official cult of Japan which has been banned since 15 December 1945. For a philosophy which has been the subject of such searching and critical analysis on the part of its opponents and such voluminous exposition and emotional adulation on the part of its adherents, National Shinto is singularly lacking in a clear-cut definition. Is it a religion? Officially, no. But in the eyes of the simple Japanese peasants, and even in the minds of many of the educated Japanese, there is no essential difference between this and their religion. Is it a system of ethics? No, although it closely parallels much of the Confucian ethics and is the basis of a considerable portion of the training in *Shūshin*, the formal course in Japanese ethics formerly required of all students. Is it a system of rituals? Historically this appears to have been its major political function, and recently its liturgy has been a prominent part of most public functions, but that is only an important though not indispensable portion of National Shinto. Is it a political philosophy? Is it a conspiracy?

Foreign visitors to prewar Japan and readers of Dr. Daniel Clarence HOLTOM's definitive volume, *The National Faith of Japan: A Study in Modern Shintō* (London, Kegan Paul, Trench, Trubner & Co., 1938), are familiar with the usual threefold division of *Shintō* into (1) primitive animism, (2) the 13 recognized religious sects, and (3) State or National Shinto. Dr. HOLTOM in an earlier volume, *The Political Philosophy of Modern Shintō* (Chicago, University of Chicago Libraries [private edition of an earlier TASJ monograph], 1922), had clearly considered it "the State Religion of Japan." But National Shinto, as it was known during the war and the Occupation, was rather more than merely one of the three modern branches of an ancient religion. The term "National Shinto" as one of the three unacceptable elements in the nationalist philosophy of Japan has come to be a counterpropaganda title for all those quasi-religious manifestations of Japanese nationalism which in the Occidental mind are linked with political and military fanaticism. It is much more than *Shintō*. It is in part the ethics of *Bushidō*. In part it is the discipline of *Zen* Buddhism. In part it is the filial piety and ancestor worship of Confucianism. In this sense "National Shinto" might profitably be considered not from the viewpoint of Dr. HOLTOM's trisection but from that of three other divisions: what the people of Japan consider it to be; what the former Japanese Government claimed that it was; and what foreign observers have come to believe it to be. One thing is certain, its roots are in the religions of Japan and its modern form cannot be understood without some knowledge of the organization and history of the religions which have fed it.

There are four religions which have a wide following in Japan and which have profoundly influenced Japanese thought: Shinto, Buddhism, Confucianism, and Christianity. The final one of these, Christianity, has had little effect on National Shinto other than in the negative way of inciting powerful official resistance to westernism, and has made its major contribution to Japanese philosophy through the introduction of Occidental science and learning. It is considered in a later portion of this volume in this connection. Confucianism by many Japanese is considered not a religion but rather a moral philosophy. It is frequently pointed out that some of the ablest Confucian philosophers have been Buddhist or Shinto priests and that many devout followers of Shinto and Buddhism acknowledge their adherence to the ethics expounded in the Confucian classics. This is hardly a denial of its religious qualities but is merely another evidence of the religious syncretism which has enabled Japanese to accept without intellectual conflict or emotional disturbance the beliefs of several religions.

The Contribution of Confucianism. Japanese tradition has it that Confucianism was introduced into Japan from China, via Korea, in the 16th year of the reign of Emperor Ōjin (A.D. 285) by a Korean scholar, WANI. The King of *Kudara* (Pekche), one of the three ancient Korean principalities, had sent an envoy, ACHIKI, to the Court of Emperor ŌJIN who interested the Emperor in both the Chinese classics and in the Chinese system of writing. At his suggestion the Emperor sent for WANI to serve as tutor to his son and Crown Prince, WAKIIRATSUKO. Among the teaching materials which WANI brought with him were the *Rongo* (Lun Yü, or "Analects") and the *Senjimon* (Ch'ien Tzu Wen, or "Thousand Ideographs"). Modern scholars tend to discount this tradition, recorded in the *Kojiki*, with regard to details —holding that WANI probably arrived about A.D. 405, that Chinese writing was known in Japan before his arrival, and that the *Senjimon* was not compiled until a century after the arrival of the Korean scholars. Whatever the historical truth of the tradition, it is certain that by A.D. 500 both the *Rongo* and the *Senjimon* were known in Japan. From that day to the present students of the Chinese writing system and its Japanized form (*kambun*) have studied not only the calligraphy of the Chinese but also the content of the Confucian classics. The masses, who never were able to read these difficult writings, were indoctrinated with the content of the classics through popular stories that included their teachings.

The history of Confucianism in Japan is generally divided into four periods: the first producing mainly philological commentaries and lasting from the highly problematical date of A.D. 285, marking the traditional introduction until about 1298; the second extending for the following 303 years and marked by the introduction of the teachings of the Sung School by a Chinese priest, *Nei-issan* (Ning i Shan), in 1299; the third constituting the 265 years of the Golden Age of Confucianism under the Tokugawa Shogunate ending in 1867; and the last period dating from the Meiji Restoration until the present.

Confucianism influenced the philosophy of National Shinto in at least three ways. In the earliest period there was either a strengthening of indigenous beliefs in filial piety and ancestor worship or else the actual introduction of those beliefs. The precise influence is lost in the half millennium of unrecorded history following the introduction and preceding the writing of the *Kojiki* and *Nihongi*. The second of the ways in which Confucianism has influenced the philosophy of National Shinto has been by the almost imperceptible indoctrination of the educated classes through centuries of reading Chinese texts and studying Chinese writings. This has been in the main an unconscious, almost osmotic, infiltration of Chinese allusions, logic, and ethics. But during the Tokugawa period there came the third and most powerful influence, that of the schools of Confucian philosophy. There were at least six of these schools, the most influential one being the *Shushi Gakuha* or Chutsze School deriving its philosophy from CHUTSZE, the Chinese scholar of the Sung dynasty. Among the founders of this system of thought were FUJIWARA Seika (1561–1619), HAYASHI Razan (1583–1657), and the famous educator, KINO-SHITA Junan (1621–98). ARAI Hakuseki (1657–1725), who had acquired some European learning and was the author of 160 volumes of philosophical and political studies, NAKAMURA Tekisai (1629–1702), author of the famous *Hime Kagami* ("Lives of Virtuous Women"), a treatise on the education of women, and KAIBARA Ekken (1630–1714), author of *Taigiroku* ("Great Doubts") and *Shinshiroku* ("Meditations"), had a profound influence on the thought of their day. This school existed as a powerful force almost to the end of the Tokugawa Shogunate, with SATŌ Issai (1772–1859) and RAI Sanyō (1780–1832) being the last great leaders.

A second of these schools was *Yōmei Gakuha*, or the Wang-Yangming School, deriving its philosophy from the teachings of WANG-YANGMING, Chinese scholar of the Ming dynasty. The Japanese founders of this system of thought were NAKAE Tōju (1608–78) and KUMAZANA Banzan (1619–91). The *Ko Gakuha* or Classical School was founded independently by YAMAGA Sokō (1622–85), the advocate of *Bushidō* and author of *Seikyō Yoroku* ("Compendium of Confucius"), and by ITŌ Jinsai (1627–1705), the author of *Seigakuhen* ("Exposition of Confucius"). A weak but typically Japanese attempt to compromise the dogma of all schools was the basis of *Setchū Gakuha* or the Eclectic School, founded by KI Heishū (1728–1801), and an equally typical Japanese attempt to return to the classic writings and draw modern conclusions from them was the basis of *Kōshō Gakuha* or the Philological School, which was in reality not a formal school but merely a group of scholars who emphasized careful source studies. The last of the six main schools was the *Dokuritsu Gakuha* or Independent School founded by MIURA Baien (1723–89) and continued by NINOMIYA Sontoku (1787–1856).

It has already been mentioned that Japanese ordinarily do not consider Confucianism a religion. Professor INOUE Tetsujirō in his monograph "Japanese Religious Beliefs: Confucianism," in ŌKUMA (*op. cit.*), II, 42, says:

Regarded from its outward form, it appears to be a religion, but, while religion deals mostly with spiritual conceptions, Confucianism concerns itself principally with secular morality, and, unlike religion, is free from ritual observances and superstitious notions. In this respect Confucianism is rightly regarded as a moral system, clearly distinguished from religion.

Certainly it is as a system of ethics and not as a religion that Confucianism has affected National Shinto. Two principles derived from the five Confucian relationships between sovereign and subject, father (or mother) and child, husband and wife, elder and younger brother (or sister), and friends are prominent in all National Shinto literature. These are the principles of loyalty and of filial piety. In Japanese Confucianism two additional relationships have been added, that of the elder for the younger (without necessarily implying blood relationship) and that of master for pupil. Baron SUYEMATSU Kencho in his monograph, "The Ethics of Japan," *Journal of the Royal Society of Arts* (London), Vol. LIII, No. 2729, March 10, 1905, reprinted in *Smithsonian Institution Annual Report* for the year ending June 30, 1905 (Washington, Government Printing Office, 1906), p. 295, says:

The idea of the best virtue that a sovereign can have is "jen" [*jin*], meaning to be as humane as possible to his subjects, detesting oppression, giving the best administration to his country. . . .
    The idea of the best subject is loyalty. The idea of that of father and son is filial piety on the part of the child and strictness on the part of the father, which is modified in the case of the mother toward tenderness. . . . The idea which governs the relationship between man and wife is harmony. . . . The idea of that of brothers and sisters is brotherly friendship. . . . The idea of that of friends is trustworthiness. . . . The elder and the younger in general are expected to respect each other as the case demands, and the relationship between them is to be regulated by a term which is equivalent to the English word "order"; that is to say, the younger should not seek to supersede the elder, but to pay respect to him, while the elder is ex-

pected not to take advantage of the younger, but to treat him with kindness. The relationship between master and pupil is also regarded as very important. The pupils are expected to respect their masters almost as much as their parents, while the master is expected to treat his pupils with parental kindness; no businesslike thought is to enter their minds.

It would be both presumptuous and of doubtful value to attempt to summarize here the complex structure of the Confucian ethical system. Suffice it that among the human virtues such attributes as wisdom (*chi*), humanity (*jin*), courage (*yū*), filial piety (*kōkō*), loyalty (*chūgi*) and self-restraint (*shūshin*) are frequently advocated. Superficially these ethical principles would appear to be quite acceptable in any philosophy developed for the postwar Japanese educational system. But it would seem there exists a danger. In Christian ethics "love" is considered to be an absolute and to be universal. But in Japanese ethics, tracing its Confucian interpretation to the great Chinese philosopher MENCIUS (Meng-tse, B.C. 372–289?), the motivating factor "love" is considered a variable in time and space and hence one which properly may be modified according to the circumstances. Thus it has been held that where a conflict of interests occurs one should love a nearer object more than a distant one, a neighbor more than a foreigner, a fatherland more than a foreign country. The implications in a state emerging from feudalism into internationalism are obvious.

The Contribution of Buddhism. The greatest of the religious contributions to Japanese culture, as measured in followers, artistic production, wealth, and political influence, has been Buddhism. Tradition credits the formal introduction of Buddhism to Japan to a mission from the King of *Kudara* (Pekche) in Korea to the Court of Emperor KIMMEI in 552, which brought as gifts certain of the sacred books and an image of Buddha. Prince SHŌTOKU, the actual ruler during the reign of Empress SUIKO (593–628), acted as the patron of Buddhist learning and by the time of his death Buddhism was firmly established in the Japanese islands. A brief resume of the history of Japanese Buddhism may be of value.

Buddhism as a religious philosophy began during the 45 years of the wandering ministry of SIDDHĀRTHA, known as Sakyamuni or the Gautama Buddha (B.C. 557–477?), in India. SIDDHĀRTHA was apparently the son of a lesser noble in the Gautama branch of the Sakya clan who was raised by his mother's sister whom his father

married. When he was 29 this young man who was to become the
Gautama Buddha abandoned his wife and son, Rāhula, and began wandering in search of religious peace. He practiced trances,
self-mortification, and asceticism, finally abandoning these disciplines, and after about seven years found enlightenment and began
his active ministry. His philosophy, which denied the elaborate
rites and mysticism then common in the Brahman religion, is most
succinctly stated in the Sermon of Benares and is known as "The
Four Noble Truths" (Jap. *Shitai*, San. Catuāri Āryāsatyāni); and
"The Noble Eightfold Path" (Jap. *Hachi Shōdō*, San. Āryāstānga
Mārga). "The Three Law Seals" (Jap. *Sambōin*, San. Trividyā),
not a part of the Sermon of Benares, are conceptions or fundamental philosophical premises underlying his entire system. He believed in the impermanence of all existence (Jap. *shōgyō mujō*,
San. anitya), in the universality of human suffering (Jap. *nehan
jakujo*, San. dukha), and the nonexistence or nonreality of the ego
(Jap. *shōhō muga*, San. anātmā). The Four Noble Truths establish
the universal existence of pain or suffering (Jap. *ku*, San. Dukha),
the origin of suffering in the cravings for gratification of the senses,
future life, and prosperity, which is known as Accumulation (Jap.
shū, San. samudaya), the passing away of pain through the complete denial and renunciation of this craving, known as Extinction
(Jap. *metsu*, San nirōdha), and finally the method of achieving
this complete cessation of pain, known as the Way (Jap. *dō*, San.
mārga). The Way is by The Noble Eightfold Path which consists of eight ethical virtues: Right Views, Right Aspirations,
Right Speech, Right Conduct, Right Mode of Living, Right Effort, Right Mindfulness, and Right Rapture or Contemplation.

The Gautama Buddha's teachings were modified markedly by
his followers, who quickly reassumed much of the ceremony
which he had despised and adopted the mysticism which was a
characteristic of Hinduism. So completely did Buddhism revert to
the practices of Brahmanism and Hinduism that it ultimately was
unable to compete with this latter religion, disappeared from India,
the locale of its founding, and has survived until today only in
the surrounding Asiatic countries in two forms: Hīnayāna (Lesser
Vehicle, Jap. *Shōjō*) and Mahāyāna (Greater Vehicle, Jap.
Daijō). These two streams of Buddhism are separated on both historical and canonical grounds. Hīnayāna Buddhism under the
patronage of King Asoka (Priyadarsin) about B.C. 240 spread over

all of Southern Asia and survives today in Southeast Asia as "Southern Buddhism." Mahāyāna Buddhism is traditionally considered to have been founded by ASVAGHOSHA, a Brahmin who wandered widely throughout India and finally settled in Benares sometime between B.C. 100 and A.D. 300. The writings of ASVAGHOSHA, many of which probably were written by other priests and attributed to him, together with those of NĀGĀRJUNA, became the basis of the division of Mahāyāna into sects. ASANGA, one of the great Mahāyāna writers of the fifth century A.D., laid the foundation for syncretism and the absorption of competing religions by the process of identifying their gods with the deities in the expansive Buddhist pantheon. Japanese Buddhism, as represented by the sects which have survived, is Mahāyāna, Greater Vehicle, the "Northern Buddhism." The theory of syncretism has made it ideally suited to an amalgamation with Confucianism and Shinto.

The voluminous writings of early Buddhist leaders were canonized in the four great Councils or Synods of Rajagriha, Vaisālī, Pātaliputra, and Jalandhara. The first two are recognized by both branches of Buddhism. The third, the Synod of Pātaliputra (*circa* B.C. 295), was convened by King ASOKA of Magadha in India, and is considered by Hīnayāna Buddhists to be of equal authority. King ASOKA became the patron of this school and spread it by official missionaries over Ceylon and the area now known as Afghanistan. The last of these councils, the Synod of Jalandhara (*circa* A.D. 250), was called by King KANISHKA of Scythia, and is recognized by the Mahāyāna Buddhists to have authority second only to the first two. King KANISHKA played much the same part as protector and patron of Northern Buddhism that King ASOKA had held in Southern Buddhism. Based on the findings of these four synods the Buddhist Canon is separated into the two great divisions which have given their name to the Southern and Northern Buddhists: Lesser Vehicle (Hīnayāna), and Greater Vehicle (Mahāyāna). Each of these canons is divided into three subsections: the collected sayings of Buddha and his immediate disciples (Jap. *Kyōzō*, San. Sūtra-pitaka), the rules given for the priesthood (Jap. *Ritsuzō*, San. Vinaya-pitaka), and collected commentaries and monographs on the sayings of Buddha (Jap. *Ronzō*, San. Abhidharma-pitaka). The language of the Gautama Buddha was Magadhi but the oldest written records are in the so-called

Pali Canon written in Pali and the basis of the transliteration into
the Burmese and Siamese alphabets and the less frequent translations of the Lesser Vehicle into Burmese, Siamese, and other
Southeast Asiatic languages. The *Dai Nippon Kōtei Daizōkyō*
("The Canon of Japan"), which is recognized as the most scholarly Buddhist work produced in that nation, is a compilation of
Japanese Tripitaka based on four older canons: the *Kōraibon*, published in Korea in the eleventh century, the *Sōzō* and the *Genzō*,
published in China in the thirteenth century, and the *Minzō*, published in China in the sixteenth century. Many of these are derived from the Sanskrit texts which in major part formed the
Greater Vehicle, though much of the Chinese Canon consists of
original Chinese works. August Karl REISCHAUER, in his book,
Studies in Japanese Buddhism (New York, The Macmillan Company, 1917), pp. 158–170, states that of the 6,771 books which are
reputed to be in the Japanese Canon, some are missing and the vast
number have never been translated into a form that any but the
scholars can read. As a result the practice has arisen of merely
twirling them on a revolving stand or leafing rapidly through them
to gain merit. In practice most sects use only a few of the canonical
scriptures.

Mahāyāna Buddhism went from India into Central Asia, especially the Tarim Basin, and from there reached China about 65
A.D. Chinese Buddhism was augmented by direct importations of
Indian Buddhism from time to time, as for example by the immigration of BODHIDHARMA [who is traditionally considered to
be an Indian, though some scholars feel he may have been a Per-
sian], the founder of contemplative Buddhism and its chief modern
example the *Zen* Sect, who arrived about 520. Chinese Buddhism
was influenced by Confucianism and Taoism, both indigenous
Chinese philosophies, and during the thirteenth century was mixed
with a stream of debased Buddhism, the Lamaism of Tibet and
Mongolia, which originally had been exported to those countries
from China itself. Buddhism was carried into Korea both from
China directly and via Mongolia. From there it was taken to Japan,
arriving according to tradition in 552 and being firmly established
as a State-sponsored religion by 622, when Prince SHŌTOKU died.
In these travels Buddhism had changed and developed, or deteriorated, from the teachings of the Gautama Buddha. Following the
death of Prince SHŌTOKU, though in no way caused by that event,

there began to appear in Japan divergent sects, similar to those existing in China, whose philosophies were frequently antagonistic. The influence of Buddhism on the philosophy of State Shintoism was the influence not of the original stream of Mahāyāna Buddhism but of the interpretations made by each of these sects.

The first sects to be formed in Japan, known as the "Six Sects of the Southern Capital" (*Nara*), were Chinese in character. The *Sanron* Sect was introduced from China via *Koma* (Koryo, one of the three main kingdoms in ancient Korea) in 625 by EKAN (Ekwan). It was not properly Mahāyāna Buddhism but was of the so-called Mādhyamika School and held the belief that all phenomenal existence was unreal, as well as the belief of the Gautama Buddha that the ego was unreal. The *Jōjitsu* Sect, known also by its Sanskrit name of Satya-siddhi-sastra Sect, was introduced from China also in 625 and believed in subjective idealism. This was a sect of Hīnayāna or Lesser Vehicle Buddhism and it never secured much of a following in Japan. The *Hossō* Sect, or Dharma-lakshana Sect, was introduced from China in the fourth year of the reign of Emperor KŌTOKU, 653, when the Japanese priest DŌSHŌ returned from studying the doctrine of idealism (Jap. *Yuishiki*, San. Vijñāna-matra) under HIUEN-TSANG. This was of the Yoga School and is important in the history of Japanese religion because it introduced the belief in syncretism, which led to harmonization with the Shintoists, and the development of *Ryōbu Shintō* (Double Aspect Shinto), largely through the work of the three priests, GYŌGI, KŪKAI, and SAICHŌ in the eighth and ninth centuries. The *Kusha* Sect, or Abhidharma-kosa-sastra Sect, a form of Hīnayāna Buddhism, was brought from China in 658 by two Japanese priests, CHITSU and CHITATSU. This sect believed in the nonreality of the ego but attempted to explain all phenomena on a psychological basis. The *Kegon* Sect, or Avatamsaka-sūtra Sect, the only true form of Mahāyāna Buddhism found in the six Nara sects, was introduced from China in 736 by the Chinese priest DŌSEN (Tao Hsüan) and the Indian priest BODHISENA, who brought over the *Kegonkyō* (Avatamsaka-sūtra). A Korean priest, SHINSHŌ (or JINJŌ), arrived in Japan from *Shiragi* (Silla, one of the three main kingdoms of ancient Korea) about 740 to lecture on these sacred writings and is commonly credited with founding the sect. The *Ritsu* Sect, or Vinaya Sect, was introduced from

China in 753 when the Chinese priest GANJIN (Chien Chen) visited Japan and preached the doctrine of Discipline (Jap. *Ritsu*, San. Vinaya). It was of the Hīnayāna School of Buddhism and in time virtually disappeared, although a few thousand adherents still are found in Japan. The *Sanron, Jōjitsu*, and *Kusha* sects have completely disappeared.

The first two characteristically Japanese sects to be formed were the *Tendai* and *Shingon*, founded in 805 and 806, respectively. The *Tendai* Sect, named for the Chinese T'ien-t'ai Sect, was founded by SAICHŌ (or DENGYŌ Daishi) and the *Shingon* Sect, known also as the Vairochana Sect because it believed that man could only attain Buddhahood through identification with the Eternal Buddha Vairochana, was founded by KŪKAI (or KŌBŌ Daishi). These two sects, known as the Heian (or Kyoto) sects, were the natural result of two evident needs. Buddhism, after experiencing a period of great popularity and official sanction during the reign of Emperor SHŌMU (724–749), had become corrupted and had degenerated into Court intrigue and political spoils. A religious reformation was obviously needed to parallel the political reforms introduced by Emperor KAMMU. The other need was to secure some kind of philosophical compromise with *Shintō*. Both SAICHŌ (767–822) and KŪKAI (774–835) were truly remarkable men. The latter is credited by tradition with the invention of *hiragana*, the cursive form of the Japanese syllabary, and with founding the *Sōgei Shuchiin*, first public school for the masses. These two priests and their followers completed the task of identifying the main gods in the Shinto pantheon with those in the Buddhist, thus enabling loyal Japanese to continue their classic reverence for the mythological creators of the nation while at the same time accepting Buddhism. When completed this compromise was later known as *Ryōbu Shintō* or Double Aspect Shinto and resulted in so complete an amalgamation that Buddhist priests were actually attached to Shinto shrines and took part in official rites.

This syncretism was begun, however, at least a century before by priests of the *Hossō* Sect. Tradition has it that in 735 there was a smallpox epidemic which made the Japanese people wonder if they were being punished for having adopted Buddhism. Emperor SHŌMU, who was then contemplating erecting the *Nara Daibutsu* or Great Buddha of Nara, was afraid to do so unless the native gods were placated. He sent GYŌGI Bosatsu to the Grand Shrine in Ise to ask the Shinto Sun-Goddess, *Amaterasu Ōmikami*, if it were propitious to begin this work. GYŌGI, who appears to have been shrewd as well as devout, spent a week and then came back declaring that the Sun-Goddess had revealed that she herself was identical with Vairochana, the Eternal Buddha.

It was inevitable that a religious movement with such power as that exercised by the *Tendai* and *Shingon* sects during the first four centuries of their existence, or to about 1200, should become corrupted. The Court officials maneuvered to use the Buddhist sects to their own ends and the Buddhist priests interfered in politics. Morality degenerated, priests became arrogant and even criminal to the point of flouting the authority of the Emperor, and culture was debased. And again there came about a religious renaissance to meet this threat of secularism. This renaissance gave rise to the Six Sects of the Great Awakening, *Yūdzū Nembutsu*, *Jōdo*, *Shin*, *Zen*, *Nichiren*, and *Ji*. All have survived to the present, and the *Zen* Sect is represented by three large divisions, the *Rinzai*, with fourteen subsects, the *Sōtō*, and the *Ōbaku*.

Four of these Six Sects of the Great Awakening are commonly known as the Amida sects, named from a common element in their dogma that salvation can only come through faith in the name of *Amida Butsu*, and repetition of the prayer "*Namu Amida Butsu*" (I adore Thee Thou Buddha of the Eternal Life and Light). The first of these Amida sects to be founded was the *Yūdzū Nembutsu* Sect founded by RYŌNIN (1072–1132), a priest who had studied in the *Tendai* monasteries. The date of its founding is variously given as 1117, 1124, 1126, and 1132. The relatively unimportant *Ji* Sect was founded by IPPEN Shōnin (1239–89) in 1276. The remaining two of the Amida sects are also known as the Pure Land sects because their doctrine includes a concept of a Paradise or a Pure Land. One is the *Jōdo* Sect founded by GENKU (HŌNEN Shōnin) in 1175. HŌNEN (1133–1212) was a student of *Tendai*. The other of these Pure Land sects is the extremely powerful *Shin* Sect, or *Jōdo Shinshū* Sect, founded by HŌNEN's greatest disciple SHINRAN Shōnin (1173–1262) in 1224.

The *Shin* Sect is today the most powerful of all Japanese Buddhist Sects and enrolls approximately one third of all believers in Japan, about one fifth of the total population. It is somewhat analogous to the Protestant division of the Christian Church, permitting its priesthood to marry and imposing no restrictions on food and drink. Unlike most other Japanese sects the *Shin* Sect regards life as illusory. In concord with other Japanese Buddhist sects it views life as transitory and miserable, and believes in the Three Treasures (Jap. *Sanbō*, San. Ratnatraya), of the Oneness with the Perfect Person (Jap. *Butsu*, San. Buddha), the Truth or the Ultimate Law of the Universe (Jap. *Hō*, San. Dharma), and the Priesthood or Community (Jap. *Sō*, San. Sangha). Being in addition an Amida Sect it conceives of the doctrine of salvation through the transfer of merit by the compassion of *Amida Butsu*. Being a Pure Land sect it also believes in a life after death or a Paradise (Jap. *Jōdo*, a limited form of the San. Nirvāna). It has a well-defined theory of reincarnation progressing through ten stages: (1) Hell, (2) Hungry Spirit, (3) Beasts, (4) Asura, (5) Man, (6) Heavenly Beings, (7) Śravaka, (8) Pratyeka-buddha, (9) Bodhisattva, and (10) Buddha. The position of Chief Abbot (*Hosshu*) of the order is invariably held by the blood descendants of SHINRAN, the founder, and to these Abbots is attributed something of the infallibility as that attributed to the Pope in the Roman Catholic Church. It was the powerful political and religious influence of the Chief Abbots of the two major subsects of *Shin*, MYONYO of the *Hompa Honganji* and GENNYO of the *Ōtani-ha-Honganji*, which succeeded in modifying the 1869 decree establishing Shinto as the State religion, which in its original form would have stripped Buddhism of all of its power and might have forced its suppression in Japan, and secured the recognition of freedom of religious worship in 1876. UTSUKI Nishu in his volume, *The Shin Sect: A School of Mahāyāna Buddhism* (Kyoto, Hompa Honganji, 1938), p. 2, states as one of the special features of the *Shin* Sect: "The nature of the teaching is not nationalistic but universal, and therefore applicable to any nation and people, regardless of sex, caste, time and place."

The two remaining sects of the Great Awakening were the *Nichiren* Sect founded in 1253 by NICHIREN Shōnin (1222–82) and the *Zen* Sect introduced from China in 1191 in the form of a subsect, *Rinzai*, by the priest EISAI (1141–1215) and in 1228 in the form of a subsect, *Sōtō*, by DŌGEN (SHŌYŌ Daishi) (1200–1253). A third subsect of *Zen*, *Ōbaku*, was founded in 1653 by a Chinese monk INGEN (Yin Yüan).

NICHIREN, founder of the sect bearing his name, had studied

under the *Shingon* and *Tendai* sects and profoundly hated the Amida sects and their doctrine. He felt that they were creating unnecessary divisions in Buddhism and were undermining the glory of the Gautama Buddha and transferring this glory to the Amida Buddha. He urged a return to the original teachings of SAKYAMUNI, though it is doubtful if his scholarship was perfect enough for him to have an accurate historical knowledge of those teachings. His bitterness against other Buddhist sects may be summed up by his oft quoted statement, *"Nembutsu muken; Shingon bōkoku; Zen temma; Ritsu kokuzoku"* (The *Nembutsu* Sect is hell; *Shingon* is national ruin; the *Zen* are devils; and the *Ritsu* are traitors to the country).

In 1260 NICHIREN completed his first great politico-religious work, an essay in the form of a dialogue, entitled, *Rissho Ankoku Ron* ("The Establishment of Righteousness and the Security of the Country"), which included a prediction of a foreign invasion as the ultimate of the current political disasters, dramatically fulfilled in his own lifetime by the attempted conquest of Japan by KHUBLAI KHAN in the autumn of 1274 and the destruction of the Mongol armada at Hakata in 1281. This same essay renounced religion as an individual faith and identified it with nationalism. NICHIREN's bitter denunciation of other Buddhist leaders included the plea that the government suppress all sects but his own and went so far as to advocate the suppression of heresy, especially the worship of Amida Buddha, by the death penalty, holding that the killing of a heretic was not murder. He was repeatedly mobbed, twice exiled—to the Izu Peninsula in 1261 and to the island of Sado in the Sea of Japan in 1271—and once was miraculously saved from the death sentence at Tatsu-no-kuchi in 1271. During his exile to Izu in 1262 NICHIREN formulated his famous five theses, which adopted the Lotus Sutra (San. Saddharma-puṇḍarîka) as the sole and final religious authority and Japan as the land where true Buddhism should prevail and from whence it should be spread to all the world. In his essay, *Kyō-ki-ji-koku shō* ("Treatise on the Doctrine, the Capacity, the Time, and the Country"), written in that year, he says, "One who would propagate the Buddhist truth, by having convinced himself of the five principles, is entitled to become the leader of the Japanese nation." Despite the vigorous opposition which his militant preaching and writing stirred up, he attracted to his views many of the

political and military figures of his age and must be credited in a
large measure with awakening Japan to the danger of a foreign invasion and with uniting it for defense.

The *Zen* Sect, though neither the wealthiest nor the largest, enrolling only about one fifth of the Buddhists in Japan, has exercised a profound influence on Japanese nationalist philosophy and
has frequently contributed the ideas which in Occidental minds
have been associated with National Shintoism and mistakenly attributed to *Shintō*. *Zen* is probably the most thoroughly Japanese
in character of all Buddhist sects. It has contributed very
markedly to the system of ethics known as *Bushidō*, The Way
of the Warrior. It has been an outstanding example of Japanese
syncretism, absorbing Confucian philosophy and adapting it from
the Chinese milieu of reverence for scholars and contempt for soldiers to the Japanese environment which has honored the military
class as the rulers of the nation. It has given great prominence to
the virtues of individual discipline, courage, perseverance, and
clear insight, all highly desirable attributes in a military state, and
has contributed a considerable portion of the teachings found in
the school subject known as Japanese ethics (*Shūshin*). Despite
claims by such *Zen* scholars as Nakariya Kaiten, author of *The
Religion of the Samurai: A Study of Zen Philosophy and Discipline in China and Japan* (London, Luzac & Co., 1913), that its
origins are possibly traceable to pre-Buddhistic sources such as
the Brahmanic practices of meditation (Jap. *Zazen*, San. Dhyāna)
recorded in the Upanishads, and certainly to the founder of Buddhism, Sakyamuni, who found enlightenment while absorbed in
meditation under the Bodhi Tree, no less an authority than Sir
Charles Eliot, author of *Japanese Buddhism* (London, Edward
Arnold & Co., 1935), states categorically that no clear Indian
origin for *Zen* can be discovered.

The Chinese origins of *Zen*, however, are historically obvious.
According to *Zen* tradition Sakyamuni, the Gautama Buddha,
passed on to his disciple, Mahākāsyapa, the secret of enlightenment through meditation, thus making him the First Patriarch. It
was then handed down from one noble mind to another through
a succession of patriarchs until it was revealed to Bodhidharma,
the 28th Patriarch, who according to tradition journeyed from
India into China about A.D. 520. Bodhidharma is supposed to have
insulted Emperor Wu of the Liang dynasty, gone into seclusion

for nine years in the Shao Lin Monastery, where he so incurred the hatred of the other Buddhists that his life was attempted on three occasions, and finally left China after converting a Confucianist, SHIN-KŌ (Shang Kwang), who had taken the Buddhist name E-KA (Hui K'e), and giving to him both the secret of enlightenment and his own dark green cloak as a sacred symbol of the transmission of the law. This second of the *Zen* Patriarchs in China in turn passed it on to SŌ-SAN (Sang Tsung), who first reduced *Zen* teachings to writing in *Sin Jin-mei* (Sin Sin Ming, or "On Faith and Mind"). The green cloak was handed on until the Fifth Patriarch in China, KŌ-NIN (Hung Jen), the Abbot of the Hwang Mei Monastery, held a poetry contest to determine who was to be his successor. JIN-SHŪ (Shen Tsung), the leading disciple of the 700 contestants felt he had won, but a lowly rice-pounder in the monastery E-NŌ (Hui Neng) secretly wrote one that the Fifth Patriarch thought was by far the best. As a result he passed on the Kachāya, or symbol of the transmission of the law in the form of the old green cloak, to the rice-pounder, but being a realist, suggested he had better flee before it was discovered. The disciples pursued and caught this Sixth Patriarch, but when they were going to fight to take the cloak he told them it was a symbol of patriarchal authority, not something to fight over. They tried to take it but could not lift it, so that many were converted and followed him to form the Southern School of *Zen*. The disgruntled JIN-SHŪ would not admit defeat and founded the Northern School of *Zen*. This was the start of many divisions into subsects which gradually undermined the strength of *Zen* in China.

From China it was introduced into Japan on at least three occasions before it finally took root in the work of EISAI in 1191 and DŌGEN in 1228. DŌSHŌ (629–700), a Japanese priest who had studied under GENJŌ (Hsüan Tsang) and E-MAN (Hui Man) in China in 653 returned to practice *Zen* contemplation in the *Gan-gō* Monastery in Nara, but it occasioned no particular interest. The Chinese *Zen* teacher GI-KU (I Kung) came to Japan in 810 and the Japanese priest KAKU-A returned to Japan in 1174, after three years study of *Zen* under BUK-KAI (Fo Hai). Their work also left no lasting effects in Japan. It is perhaps significant that EISAI himself was neither markedly successful nor free from the persecution of the *Tendai* and *Shingon* priests until he wrote his famous book, *Kozengo Kokuron* ("The Protection of the State by the Propagation of *Zen*"). Following this "his merit was appreciated" and the Emperor TSUCHI-MIKADO (1199-1210) bestowed on him a royal purple robe and the highest rank in the Buddhist priesthood (*Sō Jō*).

Of all the Oriental religions *Zen* is perhaps the most difficult for an Occidental to describe and for an unbeliever to understand. The sect has produced a most voluminous literature, and *Zen* priests kept mass education alive for centuries in the *terakoya* or temple schools, yet the true believer in *Zen* looks on learning with mild contempt. It has attracted the military class in Japan and has been called the "religion of the *samurai* (warriors)," yet it is avowedly one of quiet meditation. It is possible to quote the adjectives applied to it by the greatest modern students of comparative Oriental religions, Japanese and foreign, and they merely add to the mystery—esoteric, contemplative, mystical, austere, disciplined. The sincerely sympathetic Occidental who reads the sacred writ of *Zen* either in Japanese or in translation, or who talks with the chief abbots of the *Zen* monasteries today, is left with the feeling that he has understood the words but not the sentences, that he has listened to a plausible lunatic. Finding this firsthand evidence meaningless it is necessary here to quote or paraphrase the second-hand evidence of Japanese students of the sect.

There are supposed to be three major elements to *Zen*: the method of practicing meditation known as the *Zen* contemplation (*zazen*); the body of *Zen* doctrine not systematized but best presented by the "Sayings" (*goroku*) which are found in the *Zen* literature (*Hekiganshu, Rinzairoku, Mumonkan, Kidōroku, Kaian-Kokugo*, etc.); and the expression of *Zen* in action, known as *Zen* activity, a kind of device for stimulation (*kufū*, i.e., "device," including the *Kōan* or "catechism"). The ultimate objective of these three elements is the attainment of a peculiarly *Zen* or intuitive form of enlightenment known as *satori*, which is wholly divorced from logic and intellect.

The first of these, *zazen*, is familiar to students of Indian Yoga. As practiced in *Zen* two postures are permitted, the full cross-legged sitting or Lotus Seat, and the half cross-legged sitting, both with the tip of the nose and the navel in a perpendicular line, hands resting in the lap with palms up and thumbs touching. The person in meditation consciously goes through three steps in his mental training: he masters his sensual desires and withdraws himself from worldly desires; he masters his physical body by rigorous self-discipline, by *zazen*, and by austerity; and he masters his mind by erasing any of the conflicting thoughts, illusions, passions, and desires. He puts aside anger, fear, sorrow, worry, jealousy, hate, and love, and attempts to achieve a quietude and a complete loss of inhibition. This is the goal which *Zen* swordsmen achieved when they countered an opponent's stroke and made their own killing riposte without consciously knowing that they had even been attacked. To achieve this goal of complete enlightenment may require a few days or many years of meditation. The mind is supposed to go through five stages known as the "Five Ranks of Merit" (*Kō-kun-go-i*) in reaching this goal, known as Merit over Merit (*Kō-kō*), in which the believer no longer merely sits in contemplation (Jap. *Zen*, San. Dhyāna) but naturally lives in contemplation at all times.

The second of the elements, *Zen* doctrine, is almost impossible to bring to a sharp focus, since the method of teaching precludes precise statements of dogma or detailed analysis of accepted beliefs. ANESAKI Masaharu, possibly the greatest living authority on the Japanese religions, in his book, *History of Japanese Religion* (London, Kegan Paul, Trench, Trubner & Co., 1930), pp. 208–210, has described *Zen* doctrine:

Zen is an intuitive method of spiritual training, the aim of which consists in attaining a lofty transcendence over worldly care. The Zennist is proud to see in his method an unwritten tradition directly transmitted from Buddha to his great disciple, Mahā-Kāsyapa, and then successively to the masters of Zen. Not only does the Zennist defy reasoning and logic, he takes pride in transcending the usual channels of thinking. He denounces any idea to formulate tenets, for any formulation deadens the soul and life. Zen aims at giving an intuitive assurance of having discovered in the innermost recess of one's soul an ultimate reality which transcends all individual differences and temporary mutations. This reality is called the mind or soul, or the fundamental nature, or the primeval feature (of the world and the soul) [Jap. *shin*, San. chitta, Eng. mind, or soul]. It means the fundamental unity of existence underlying and pervading all particular beings and changes, which is, however, not to be sought in the external world but directly and most clearly in one's own inner heart. Like the Ātman of the Upanishad, it is the ego, not individual but cosmic, which at the same time is to be realized in every soul. When one realizes this through training in Zen, he has absorbed the universe into himself, which amounts to identifying himself with the cosmos.

Formulated in this way the philosophy of Zen is idealism, though the best Zennist is pragmatic enough not to lose himself in barren abstractions, but to test his spiritual attainment in life activity and to express it in art and poetry. The moral attainment lies in moral life, especially in straightforward action and daring conduct not bewildered by circumstances, whether in weal or in woe. The soul which has attained this eminence of spiritual illumination identifies itself with the whole cosmos, and is therefore no more troubled by particular incidents or vicissitudes; not disturbed, therefore neither caring for gains and pleasures, nor afraid of encountering calamities and adversities. The life of an ideal Zennist may be compared, as the Zennist is proud to say, to a solid rock standing in the midst of a raging sea and defying the surging billows. He can jump into the whirlpool of life and not be overwhelmed. His calm resolution has something like resignation, but all is the result of tranquil self-possession and so there is always firm fearlessness in his action. Morality or life activity is for the Zennist not an end in itself, but a test of his spiritual attainment, a natural expression of the noble loftiness of his mind, Reflections of moonlight in the waters may be agitated but the moon itself always remains serene and pure; so the moon of the Zen spirit is undisturbed in spite of its reflections in the waters of human life.

Parenthetically it should be noted that it is this body of *Zen* doctrine which made the sect so attractive to the *samurai* and the military class. Training in strict discipline, in the enduring of physical privation and pain without a murmur, in respect for "honest poverty" and denial of riches achieved by any expedient or ignoble means, in masculine severity and dignity often approaching rudeness or brutality, in unflinching courage, in hatred of dishonor—all these were contributions of *Zen* to the ethics of the military class, or were perhaps that class's contribution to *Zen* doctrine. It should be remembered that the famous 47 *Rōnin*, vassals of Akō who were led to their impoverishment, misery, and death by Ōishi Yoshio (1659–1703) in a monstrous vendetta to avenge their master's dishonor according to the code of *Bushidō*, were driven by the religious spur of *Zen*, not of *Shintō*.

The last of the three elements, *Zen* activity, is the peculiar pattern of words and actions used by *Zen* priests to teach their doctrine. It was Chinese in origin and, to the uninitiated at least, rude or inexplicable in the extreme. The most common form is a sudden loud cry of *"Katsu"* ("Hoh") made popular by the Chinese *Zen* priest RINZAI (Lin Tsi). It has been manifest in many ways: by killing a cat with a single stroke of the knife, by pointing to any convenient near-by object, by turning one's back on a questioner, by slapping the face of an Emperor (HWANG PAH striking Emperor SUEN TSUNG), and above all by the use of brusque insulting or unintelligible remarks (BODHIDHARMA insulting the Emperor WU). It appears to be a method of stimulating the novitiate to think for himself and to reason, or more properly to meditate, his way to enlightenment. D. T. SUZUKI, priest and professor of *Zen* and author of the well-known *Introduction to Zen Buddhism* (Kyoto, The Eastern Buddhist Society, 1934), has translated into English an exhortation of RINZAI to his disciples. It is reproduced in E. STEINILBER-OBERLIN and MATSUO Kuni's volume, *The Buddhist Sects of Japan* (London, George Allen & Unwin, 1938), pp. 143–144. These words from the Chinese founder of one of the major *Zen* subsects convey more than many pages of explanation:

O you disciples who aspire after the truth, if you wish to obtain an orthodox knowledge of Zen, take care not to deceive yourselves. Tolerate no obstacle, neither interior nor exterior, to the soaring of your spirit. If on your way you meet Buddha, kill him! If you meet the Patriarchs, kill them! If you meet the Saints, kill them all without hesitation! That is the only way of reaching salvation.

Do not allow yourselves to be entangled in any arguments whatsoever. Place yourselves above them and remain free. So many men come to me pretending to be disciples of Truth, who are not even freed from the vanity of a goal, of a prejudice which dominates them. Therefore when I see these men I strike them down. Such a one has confidence in his arms? I cut them off. Another counts on his eloquence? I make him hush. Yet another believes in his foresight? I blind him.

I have never seen one who was completely free—who was *unique*. Most of them have filled their minds very uselessly with the farces of the old masters. What have I to give them? Nothing! I try to remedy their evil by delivering them from their slavery.

O you, disciple of truth, strive to make yourself independent of all objects. Here is my thought. Since five or ten years I have vainly awaited a free soul. None has come to me. I can say that I have only seen the phantoms of beings, contemptible gnomes haunting the woods or the bamboo groves, pernicious spirits of the desert who nibble at stacks of filth. O you with the eyes of moles why do you waste all the pious donations of the devout? Do you believe yourself worthy of being called a monk of the Zen doctrine if you possess such an erroneous idea of it? I tell you: No Buddha! No teaching! No discipline! No demonstrations! What are you ceaselessly seeking in the house of your neighbor, O you with the eyes of moles? Do you not understand that you are placing another head over your own? What do you therefore lack in yourself? That which you are using at this very moment differs not from that of which Buddha is made. But you do not believe me and you seek elsewhere. Renounce this error! There is no exterior truth. And now you attach yourself to the literal sense of my words so that it is much preferable that we should end this discourse, and that you should be nothing at all.

Buddhist ethics are not as precise or as detailed as Confucian. They are more philosophic doctrines and less the practical regulations of the individual's daily life. If the ethics of all the Japanese Buddhist sects may be generalized they may be said to set as the primary vice ignorance that admits the reality of the self and sets self-interest as the primary motive of conscious action or as the valid end of all action. The negation of this ignorance, through enlightenment rather than through the commonly accepted educational processes, is the primary virtue. SAKYAMUNI'S Way (Jap. *michi* or *dō*, San. mārga) is the foundation stone of positive ethics for acquiring this enlightenment. It is found by the Noble Eightfold Path of Right Views, Right Aspirations, Right Speech, Right Conduct, Right Mode of Living, Right Effort, Right Mindfulness, and Right Rapture or Contemplation. Erected upon this cornerstone is a complicated structure of positive virtues of which two have direct relation to the Japanese psychology of nationalism. These are the Five Organs (Jap. *Go-kon*, San. Indriya), Faith, Exertion, Mindfulness, Contemplation, and Wisdom; the Four Benevolences (Jap. *Shi–on*, San.—), Parents, Ruler, People; and the Three Treasures (Jap. *Sampō*, San. Ratnatraya) of The Buddha, The Laws, and The Priesthood. For the general follower the virtues of Sympathy, Gentleness, Piety, Mercy, Kindness, Clear Conscience, Sense of Shame, Conscientiousness, and Thoughtfulness are established as virtues but for those who seek to become Bodhisattvas and ultimately Buddhas it is necessary to aspire to Charity, Morality, Patience, Forbearance, Exertion or Diligence, Meditation, and Wisdom. But it is generally conceded even by

Buddhists that the ethics of the sects are primarily negative. They are injunctions to avoid the vices. Most fundamental of these vices are the Three Poisons (Jap. *San-doku*, San Saṁyojana) of Lust, Anger, and Folly. These basic vices are the cornerstone for another elaborate structure of vices to be avoided: the Five Greeds, the Five Lusts (physiological), the Seven Fetters, the Five Crimes, the Seven Prides, the Five Hindrances (psychological), and the Five Impurities.

As a practical code of ethics, Buddhism offers the Ten Warnings (Jap. *Jukkai*, San. Sīla) paralleling the Christian Ten Commandments: Thou shalt not Kill, Steal, Commit Adultery, Lie, Exaggerate, Slander, Use a Double Tongue, Be Greedy, Be Angry, Be Heretical. To these vices and virtues which were recognized by all Buddhist sects in general there should be added the vices of Dishonor, Cowardice, and Disloyalty; and the virtues of Bravery, Loyalty, Imperturbability, Stoicism, Fortitude, Cleanliness (bodily and psychological), and Simplicity of *Zen*. It is this list of virtues, combined with the ethics of loyalty and filial piety contributed by Confucianism and with the rituals and certain myths of divine characteristics of Shinto, that became first *Bushidō* (The Way of the Warrior), which was a standard of behavior, and later *Shūshin*, Japanese ethics which was a required course in a curriculum and not a code of ethics.

The Contribution of Shintō. The ancient indigenous religion of Japan was a primitive animism which, according to the *Nihongi* ("Chronicles of Japan") compiled in 720, came to be known as *Shintō* to distinguish it from the imported religions of Confucianism and Buddhism. This archaic form of Shinto was probably not a systematic religion but a body of faith and superstition. In its earliest known form natural objects such as mountains, groves of trees, rocks, waterfalls, rivers, and especially trees were used as sanctuaries but man-made shrines (*miya*) were constructed long before historic time. The oldest known *kami* (rendered "gods or superior beings" by CHAMBERLAIN, ASTON, and numerous Japanese scholars, but recently considered by HOLTOM to have the primary meaning, "occult force,") were the deities of the ancient mythology of Japan, the Sun-Goddess, the Storm-God, the Moon-God, the Gods of Fire and Thunder and Lightning, and all the "eight hundred myriads of Deities." But they were also foxes, badgers, albinos, trees, rocks, springs, and other natural objects.

Worship consisted of festivals largely connected with the agricultural seasons and with the act of procreation. There was probably no professional priesthood but only the leaders of families
or clans. Offerings of rice (considered a quasi-sacred food somewhat akin to bread in the Christian faith), vegetables, fish, fowl,
and animals killed in the hunt were offered as gifts to the gods.
Religious dances and songs became a part of the rites of worship
and phallic symbols, outlawed in modern times, were erected as
shrines.

It is difficult if not impossible to separate this early animism from
its corrupted, or at least modified, form after the introduction of
Confucianism and Buddhism. Both of these religions were well
established in Japan long before the compilation of the *Kojiki*
(712) and *Nihongi* (720) the earliest written sources. It is almost
certain that the Confucian concept of ancestor worship and filial
piety profoundly influenced Shinto belief, and produced the dual
elements of nature worship (*tennen sūhai*) and ancestor worship
(*sosen sūhai*) which today characterize Shinto. There is evidence
that competition with the religious beliefs and ceremonial rites of
these two imported religions led to the development or at least
sophistication of a professional Shinto priesthood. By the end of
the prehistoric period there was a priesthood composed of *Nakatomi* (ritualists), *Imibe* (abstainers), *Urabe* (diviners), and
Sarume (musicians and dancers, probably also Temple prosti-
tutes). The ritualists chanted the *norito* or prayers, involving
poetic imagery but not conforming to standard Japanese forms of
poetry, and on occasion pronounced a curse (*noroi*) or a blessing
(*ukehi*), the latter also being a formal poetic oath. The abstainers
practiced personal abstention from certain acts or contacts considered unclean or leading to religious defilement, and conducted
ritualistic ceremonies to ward off pollution or to restore a suppli-
cant to his former purity. Sickness, sexual contact, excrement, perversion in any form (such as incest), and contact with anything
involving blood (such as menstruation, wounds, childbirth, the
butchering of animals, the dead) were considered unclean. Purification was accomplished by three procedures which in time developed into ceremonial rites: by burning in fire (*hiwatari*), by
casting away into running water or washing in salt water (*misogi*),
and the blowing away by winds (*harai*). The transferal of contamination from a living person to some material object, usually

an image cut out of paper roughly corresponding to a paper doll, which could then be destroyed by fire or water was practiced. In the modern form these rites of ablution are highly formalized: abstention (*imi*) being practiced by the priesthood and involving the avoidance of contact with unclean things, cleansing (*misogi*) being practiced by the sprinkling of salt or water and the ceremonial washing of the hands, and exorcism (*harai*) being performed by the waving of a wand with paper strips attached (*gohei* or *ō-nusa*) over the person to be purified by a member of the priesthood. Offerings are customarily food and drink (*shinsen*), and occasionally paper representing cloth, attached to a twig of the *sakaki* tree (cleyera ochnacea) and placed before the altar or god-shelf (*kamidana*). The diviners practiced divinations (*saniwa*), ordeals, especially by boiling water, (*kugatachi*), and incantations (*norito*) copied from the Chinese Shamanism known as *On'yō dō*, which had come from Korea at about the time of the introduction of Chinese writing. The musicians and dancers perform to this day highly formalistic dances in exquisite and elaborate costumes.

The history of Shinto in Japan is both vague and complex. Dr. D. C. HOLTOM, the eminent American student of *Shintō*, in his volume, *The Political Philosophy of Modern Shintō. A Study of the State Religion of Japan* (Chicago, Private ed. of the University of Chicago Libraries, 1922), p. 6, has divided it into four periods: from mythology to the end of the sixth century in which he characterizes it as being a primitive, animistic, agricultural religion concerned with food supply, government tranquility, and pure ceremonies; from 552 when Buddhism was introduced until 1737 when KAMO Mabuchi began to publish his researches in ancient Japanese literature characterized by syncretism with Buddhism and the development of *Ryōbu Shintō* (Double-Aspect Shinto); from 1737 to 1868 characterized by the awakening of national consciousness, the rise of the TOKUGAWAS, and the literary revival which produced *Fukko Shintō* (Revival-of-Ancient-Learning Shinto); and the period from the Meiji Restoration in 1868 to the writing of the book (1922) characterized by a division of Shinto into *Shūha Shintō* (Sect Shinto) and *Jinja Shintō* (Shrine Shinto), the avowedly "nonreligious" official cult of Japan. To these four there may now be added a fifth, the period of suppression of National Shinto and the separation of the Japanese Church and State which began on 15 December 1945 and continues through the present. Without attempting to follow the tortuous turnings of Shinto history through these five periods it will suffice to examine briefly the major changes which occurred in the philosophy of Shinto.

The fusion of Shinto with Confucianism occurred before recorded history and can only be surmised from fragmentary archeological and legendary evidences. The nature of this amalgamation has already been noted. The second of the five great events, the fusion of Buddhism and Shinto, is amply documented. This syncretism has also already been mentioned, in connection with the work of the Buddhist priests GYŌGI of the *Hossō* Sect, SAICHŌ of the *Tendai* Sect, KŪKAI of the *Shingon Sect*, and their followers. The *Tendai* priests developed a philosophy known as *Sannō Ichijitsu Shintō* (Mountain-King-One-Reality Shinto) in which it was held that there was an eternal and absolute Buddha and under this a multitude of manifest buddhas who appeared from time to time in the form of the gods and goddesses of other religions. Thus *Amaterasu Ōmikami* of traditional *Shintō* was identified with Vairochana, the eternal Buddha, and a similar correspondence was established for the lesser deities. The *Shingon* priests led in the development of the philosophy of *Ryōbu Shintō* (Double-Aspect Shinto) in which the same ultimate objective of identifying the two pantheons of gods was accomplished through the principle of *honji suijaku* (source-manifest-traces) by which it was held that the original source or reality which is inherent in Buddhism can be detected by traces which are manifested in other religions.

The importance of these two compromises with foreign religions cannot be overemphasized. After a struggle lasting centuries a workable solution was found in dividing the functions of a State religion into three areas: Shinto retained its historic position of dominion over public ceremonies, Buddhism became the living religion of Japan, and Confucianism dominated Japanese ethics. Shinto was to remain relatively quiescent for nearly half a millennium as the major motivating factor in Japanese Government but its all-important link with political activity was assured. If further proof of this ancient characteristic of Shinto were needed the philology of the Japanese word for "government," *matsurigoto*, which literally means "affairs of worship," should suffice.

The third of the great events in the history of Shinto was the

development of *Fukko Shintō* (Revival-of-Ancient-Learning
Shinto) which attempted to expurgate all Confucian and Buddhist
doctrine and to revert to the pure and ancient forms of the Japanese religion.

At least three schools preceded *Fukko Shintō* in the Shinto
Renaissance which occurred during the latter part of the Tokugawa Shogunate. The first of these was *Yui-itsu Shintō* (Only-One Shinto) which was developed in direct opposition to the
Ryōbu Shintō or Double-Aspect Shinto. It was developed by the
Urabe and Yoshida families, hereditary Shinto priests of the
Kamakura period and was crystallized by Urabe Kanetomo
(1435–1511), who in all probability must also be credited with
the coining of the name *Ryōbu*. As the name implies *Yui-itsu
Shintō* denied the Buddhist premise and proclaimed the individuality and absolute eternity of the Shinto deities. Two other
Shinto schools of philosophy, with marked traces of Confucianism
evident despite their professed return to original Shinto, were
Watarai Shintō usually identified with Watarai Nobuyoshi
(1615–90) and *Suiga Shintō*, founded by Yamazaki Ansai (1618–82).

Fukko Shintō itself was pioneered by Kada Azumamaro (1669–1736) and Kamo Mabuchi (1697–1769) but it is usually associated
with the names of its two greatest writers, Motoori Norinaga
(1730–1801) and his pupil Hirata Atsutane (1776–1843).
Motoori Norinaga was a student of the great ancient writings of
Japan, the *Kojiki*, *Nihongi*, and *Manyōshū*, and a profound hater
of the Chinese revival in Japan in the seventeenth century. He
wrote a commentary on the *Kojiki*, the *Kojiki-den*, in which he
exalted Japanese language, customs, and religion. His pupil Hirata
Atsutane was a prolific writer who continued Motoori's adulation
of things Japanese and his contempt for those foreign. W. G.
Aston in his volume, *Shinto: The Way of the Gods* (London,
Longmans, Green & Co., 1905), p. 373, points out, however, that
Hirata's antiforeignism did not prevent him from believing in
the immortality of the soul (a Buddhist contribution), filial piety
(a Confucian contribution), the ethical code of China (although
he claimed it was really unnecessary since Japanese are created by
nature intuitive), and an identification of Buddhist deities in the
Shinto pantheon (though in an inferior position).

Dr. D. C. Holtom in his study, *The National Faith of Japan:*

A Study of Modern Shintō (London: Kegan Paul, Trench, Trubner & Co., 1938), p. 51, summarizes the characteristics of this vital religious-political movement as follows:

. . . Fukko Shintō in its most noteworthy specific characteristics is a revival of loyalty to the Emperor as over against the shōgun and the local daimyō. It declares that in the great national family of Japan filial piety is merged in loyalty, and in this respect departs from traditional Confucianism, which, from the standpoint of Japanese conceptions, exaggerates filial piety within the family at the expense of a higher and wider devotion to the state. It finds assurance of security and continuity for its institutions by an idealization of the past similar to that of the Taika Reform of the seventh century and persuades itself that the peculiar organization of the emperor-centered state life of Japan has kept the land immune from the revolutions and changes of dynasty that have disorganized foreign countries and, in particular, China. It substitutes the *Kojiki* and *Nihongi* for the sutras as sources of authority and interprets the early mythology in such a way as to make the Sun Goddess, Amaterasu-Ōmikami, the founder of the state and the head of the royal line. Fukko Shintō derives from the old literatures the materials out of which to build a resistance against an over-rapid foreign acculturation and, in particular, forges from its ancient sources the instruments of an attack on the Tokugawa usurpation. It relies on a rationalization of history in order to develop the two-fold thesis of a *jure divino* sovereignty in an Imperial Line unbroken from divine ages and destined to rule Japan eternally and a divine Japanese race which, by virtue of the directness of its genealogical connections with the *kami*, is braver, more virtuous and more intelligent than all other races of mankind. The god-descended Japanese Emperor is divinely destined to extend his sway over the entire earth; the Japanese race is divinely endowed to do the right thing at all times without the need of the formal and external precepts which less favored peoples are obliged to depend upon. Fukko Shintō thus follows well known patterns in finding the basis of its national pride in the conceptions of a great tradition, a superior culture, a superior racial stock, an unbroken continuity and a beneficent destiny guaranteed under the aspect of eternity.

If this summary applied only to a minor school of religious philosophy of more than a century ago it would have little meaning. But it is notable for two reasons: it almost exactly describes what the Japanese militarist clique actually attempted to foster as an official national policy in the *Kokutai no Hongi* in 1937, and it represents the judicial opinion of the Occidental scholar whose work probably more than any other single thing influenced the Allies' policy on National Shinto after Surrender.

The fourth great event was the adoption of the philosophy of *Fukko Shintō* as a national cult and the consequent legalistic squirmings to maintain the fiction of freedom of religion while compelling the Japanese people of all faiths to participate in its ceremonies and to accept its beliefs. On 10 February 1868 the Meiji government established the *Jingi Kan* (Office for Shinto Religion) and gave it a rank above all other departments of the government. On 20 February 1868 the privileged position which the Buddhist Church had enjoyed under the Tokugawa Shogunate was abolished by order of the *Daijōkan* (Council of State) and much of its property was confiscated. What impelled the new government to take such a radical and potentially dangerous step at a time when it was barely established and still occupying a tenuous position?

Many foreign observers, Dr. HOLTOM among them, have openly charged the Japanese Government with a carefully planned policy of using the framework of ancient Shinto, as revived in *Fukko Shintō*, as the device for securing political stability for the newly restored Imperial Government. This stability was achieved by the religious reverence for the Emperor as the lineal descendant of the Sun-Goddess, endowed with infallibility, holding temporal and spiritual power through the inalienable power of sovereignty handed on through ages eternal. The ancient folklore, the beliefs in racial uniqueness and divine destiny, the intense nationalism, the great body of religious ritual could be, and it is claimed they were, diverted to a cynical and pragmatic end. They could whip up the religious fervor and inspire the fanatical patriotism of the great masses of the people to the point where they would submit without complaint to the hardships which were inevitable if Japan were to become a modern industrial nation within a generation.

There can today be little doubt that such a manipulation of the religious heritage of Shinto actually took place. The question remains, however, whether or not it was a conscious, deliberate plot on the part of the advisers of the youthful Emperor MEIJI, or whether it was a relatively unintentional growth of the ideas basic in *Fukko Shintō*, a philosophy which had personally inspired these men to attack the Shogunate and to seek the Imperial restoration. Dr. KATŌ Genchi, formerly Professor of Shinto at the Tokyo Imperial University, in a monograph entitled, "A Trait of the Religious Character of the Japanese People in Close Connection with Their Institutional Life, as Illustrated by Shinto: A Study of the National Faith of the Japanese," trans. by K. F. NAKAJIMA and published in the *Young East* (publication of the International Buddhist Society), Vol. VII, No. 4, 1938, pp. 15–16, states:

In the upheaval of the *Meiji* Restoration in 1868, Japan experienced various extraordinary events; despite the historical fact that the word "Shinto" designates the nationalistic Shinto in all ages, the *Meiji* government being anxious to suppress the conflict between Shinto and Christianity, then a new foreign power, declared at home and abroad that the nationalistic Shinto was not a religion. Reducing that Shinto into the role of the simple moral code of the Japanese nation and of official rites without any religious meaning, the government endeavoured to reconcile Christianity and Shinto, otherwise which might come into a head-on collision, protecting thus the existence of the latter.

A third and plausible explanation may be advanced. It is possible that this philosophy of nationalism grew imperceptibly until it was suddenly recognized as a useful tool by the political leaders of the Meiji Restoration and that only then was there conscious use made of the people's acceptance of these mystical and mythical beliefs. Some credence may be accorded this view on the grounds of the relatively innocuous and unimportant position the national cult apparently played in the early years of the Restoration. No less an authority than W. G. ASTON writing in 1905 in his volume, *Shinto: The Way of the Gods*, p. 376, concluded that the official cult of that day, which he recognized was substantially the Pure Shinto of MOTOORI and HIRATA, *Fukko Shintō*, had "little vitality" and was "almost extinct." It was probably the worst guess in Shinto history! Not even the disaster of total military defeat in the second World War has breached the four tenets which Shinto nationalists have advanced: the Emperor still exercises sovereignty; the people still are at liberty to, and a vast majority probably still do in actuality, look on the Sun-Goddess as their divine ancestress; the Emperor is still infallible; and only the method of accomplishing Japan's sacred mission, not the mission itself, has been discredited.

Whatever the truth of the charges of a deliberate plot to use this religion for nationalistic ends may be makes very little difference in the realities of postwar Japan. The people will never be argued away from a religious belief on the basis of historical logic. The belief itself, and not the motives of the people who propagated it, must be attacked. And the attack must be dignified, just, subtle, and indirect. Fortunately one of the implements which the Meiji nationalists forged lies ready at hand. It is the separation of Shinto into *Jinja Shintō* (Shrine Shinto) and *Shūha Shintō* (Sect Shinto).

The separation of Shinto into a religion and a "nonreligious national cult" took place gradually and for a time imperceptibly over a period of 70 years. It culminated in what is known as *Jinja Mondai*, the "Shrine controversy." It began in 1868 with the abolition of the *Jisha Bugyō* (Board of Commissioners for Temples and Shrines), which from the middle of the seventeenth century had exercised supervision over all religious bodies. This was replaced by the *Jingi Kan* (Office of Shinto Religion) on 10 February 1868, which in turn was made the *Jingishō* and given the status of one of the eight Ministries on 22 September 1871. Meanwhile a division of the *Mimbushō* (Ministry of the People), called the *Shajigakari* (Office of Shrines and Temples), had been established on 6 August 1870, which handled the nonreligious affairs not delegated to the *Jingishō*. The cleavage had begun to be apparent. It became more marked very rapidly. On 21 April 1872 the *Jingishō* was replaced by the *Kyōbushō* (Ministry of Religion), which had charge of all legally recognized religious bodies. This was attached to the *Mombushō* (Ministry of Education) later that year, on 25 November 1872, and in January 1877 the *Kyōbushō* was formally abolished by Order No. 4 of the *Daijōkan*, or Department of Home Affairs, and its functions were transferred to a new office *Shaji Kyoku* (Bureau of Shrines and Temples) in the Department of Home Affairs. Meanwhile the religious status of Shinto was receiving official recognition. On 10 September 1872 Shinto priests were granted the right to be *Kyōdō Shoku* (teachers of religion and ethics) and to conduct ceremonies at the shrines. On 3 May 1875 the two religions, Buddhism and Shinto, were formally separated, forbidden to unite, required to worship in separate places—and *Ryōbu Shintō* was officially dead.

But paralleling this recognition of Shinto as a religion were acts which established Shinto as a national cult. On 1 July 1871 the government established a system of grades of public shrines, which with minor changes existed in force until 15 December 1945. On

13 April 1875 the government established by law the form of rituals and ceremonies which should be held in Shinto shrines. Two acts completed the legal separation of Shinto: on 15 May 1882 Shinto institutions were separated into *Jinja* (shrines) and *Kyōkai* (churches), the former containing the graded shrines established in the 1 July 1871 order, and the latter containing all local sects which were not granted that recognition; and by Imperial Ordinance No. 163 of 26 April 1900 the *Shaji Kyoku* (Bureau of Shrines and Temples) in the Ministry of Home Affairs was abolished and two organs, the *Jinja Kyoku* (Bureau of Shrines) and the *Shūkyō Kyoku* (Bureau of Religions) were established to take its place. The Bureau of Shrines had cognizance over the official shrines and national cult; the Bureau of Religions had jurisdiction over all religions and the private Shinto sects. On 13 June 1913 this latter was transferred to the Ministry of Education and the separation was complete.

Although legally consummated the separation was still the source of unending and acrimonious disputes among leaders of the religious orders. Probably no more concise statement of the official position could be found than that of the noted Japanese jurist, Ariga Nagao, in his article, *Shintō Kokkyō Ron* (Shinto as a State Religion) in the *Tetsugaku Zasshi* ("Philosophical Magazine"), Vol. XXV, No. 280, June, 1910, p. 702:

In the case of a civilized country there must exist freedom of faith. If Shintō is a religion, however, the acceptance or refusal thereof must be left to personal choice. Yet for a Japanese subject to refuse to honor the ancestors of the Emperor is disloyal. Indeed a Japanese out of his duty as a subject must honor the ancestors of the Emperor. This is not a matter of choice. It is a duty. Therefore this cannot be regarded as a religion. It is ritual. It is the ceremonial of gratitude to ancestors. In this sense the government protects the shrines and does not expound doctrine. On the other hand since it is possible to establish doctrines with regard to the (Shintō) deities, it is necessary to permit freedom of belief in Shintō considered as a religion. Hence there has arisen the necessity of distinguishing between Shintō regarded as the functioning of national ritual and that Shintō which proclaims doctrines as a religion. (Trans. and quoted by D. C. Holtom in *The Political Philosophy of Modern Shintō*, pp. 24–25.)

When it is remembered that the greatest of all shrines, the *Ise no Daijingū* which is dedicated to *Amaterasu Ōmikami*, the Sun-

Goddess of *Shintō* and the Imperial ancestor of Japanese nationalism, was considered officially to "stand quite peerless in sanctity
and be worshiped with profound reverence," the incompatibility
of this position with the religious beliefs of Christians, and some
Buddhists, is apparent. The almost equally famous *Yasukuni Jinja*
in Tokyo, dedicated to the deified souls of those who had rendered great service to their country and especially those who had
died in battle, came close to idolatry in the eyes of many non-
Shintoists. But the practical problem which faced any minority
religion in Japan could not be evaded. If Christianity, for most
Buddhists could take philosophical refuge in some variation of
Ryōbu Shintō, were to be anything but a clandestine and persecuted sect it would have to find some compromise between the demands of its own monotheism and Japan's nationalism. The Roman Catholic Church on 25 May 1936 found it possible and
expedient to admit such a compromise in its *Instructions* by the
Sacred Congregation of Propaganda Fide. It said in part:

The Ordinaries in the territories of the Japanese Empire shall instruct the faithful that, to the ceremonies which are held at the Jinja
(National Shrines) administered civilly by the Government, there is
attributed by the civil authorities (as is evident from the various
declarations) and by the common estimation of cultured persons a
mere signification of patriotism, namely, a meaning of filial reverence
toward the Imperial Family and to the heroes of the country; therefore, since ceremonies of this kind are endowed with a purely civil
value, it is lawful for Catholics to join in them and act in accord with
the other citizens after having made known their intentions, if this be
necessary for the removal of any false interpretations of their acts.
(English trans. of the Latin text. Quoted in full in D. C. HOLTOM,
The National Faith of Japan, pp. 298–299.)

This effectually settled the "Shrine controversy" and the separation of *Kokka Shintō* or *Jinja Shintō*, representing the official national cult, from *Shūha Shintō* or *Kyōha Shintō*, the 13 recognized
religious sects, was complete. Buddhists and Christians complied
with compulsory visits to shrines and participation in official
Shinto ceremonies with outward composure though perhaps with
inward tremors of conscience. The uneasy peace was held until
the Occupation brought true liberty of conscience and freedom
of religion.

What were the 13 officially recognized Shinto sects which composed *Kyōha Shintō?* They were 13 local sects of Shinto which were granted official recognition, a sort of incorporation or charter, under the provisions of the *Shūkyō Dantai Hō* (Religious Bodies Law), Law No. 77 of 8 April 1939. They were admittedly religions, but did their teaching materially differ from that of the national cult? Basically it did not.

Three of them, *Shintō Honkyoku* (or *Shintō Kyō*), *Taisha Kyō*, and *Shinri Kyō*, claim no founders and maintain that they derive their teachings from the ancient religion of Japan. Their philosophy is Pure Shinto, however, a direct extraction from the teachings of MOTOORI and HIRATA, and hence almost identical with the nationalist teachings of the official cult. Actually *Shintō Honkyoku* was organized as a sect by Viscount INABA Masakuni (1834–98) and was officially recognized in 1885; *Taisha Kyō* was organized as a modern sect by Baron SENGE Takatomi (1848–1918) and was chartered in 1876; and *Shinri Kyō* was organized by SANO Tsunehiko (1834–1906) and was made a separate sect in 1894.

Three more of the sects, *Jikkō Kyō*, *Fusō Kyō*, and *Mitake Kyō* derive their central philosophy from the ancient worship of mountains, *Fuji* and *Ontake*. Both *Jikkō Kyō and Fusō Kyō* trace their origin to HASEGAWA Kakugyō (1541–1647) but the modern organization of *Jikkō Kyō* is attributed to SHIBATA Hanamori (1809–90) and its recognition as a separate sect dates from its charter in 1885, while the modern organization of *Fusō Kyō* was accomplished by the *Shintō* priest SHISHINO Nakaba (1844–84) and its legal recognition dates from 1882. The *Mitake Kyō* was organized as a sect by SHIMOYAMA Ōsuke (?–1882), a business man in Tokyo, and was recognized as a separate sect in 1882.

Two sects, *Shinshū Kyō* and *Misogi Kyō*, are frequently referred to as the Purification sects because they magnify the purification rituals of ancient Shinto, especially that of *misogi* or washing away pollution. *Shinshū Kyō* was legally recognized as a separate sect in 1884 and was largely the work of YOSHIMURA Masamochi (1839–1915); while *Misogi Kyō*, named for the *Shintō* purification rite of that name, was made a separate sect in 1894 and recognizes INOUYE Masakane (1790–1849) as its spiritual founder, although his teachings, embodying *Zen* Buddhist teachings and Confucian ethics, were relatively unsystematized at his death and no distinct religious group had up to then been organized among his followers.

Direct descendants of the ancient shamanistic cults of Shinto mixed with Chinese *On'yō dō* are *Kurozumi Kyō*, *Konkō Kyō* and *Tenri Kyō*. Their doctrine centers in faith healing and may be characterized by emotionalism and revelations. One of these, *Tenri*, is frequently called the "Christian Science of Japan" from certain similarities of creed. *Kurozumi Kyō*, legally recognized in 1876, takes its name from its founder, KUROZUMI Munetada (1780–1850); *Konkō Kyō* was legally recognized in 1885 and was founded by KAWATE Bunjiro (1814–83); and *Tenri Kyō*, founded by MAEKAWA Miki, later known by her married name as Mrs. NAKAYAMA Zembei (1798–1887), was given legal recognition in 1888 but did not achieve complete independence until 1908.

Probably furthest away from the Pure Shinto which is the basis of the national cult are the two sects, *Taisei Kyō* and *Shūsei Ha*, which openly recognize strong Confucian contributions and make no claim to the purity which MOTOORI sought in his philological studies of Ancient Shinto. *Shūsei Ha*, recognized in 1876, was founded by NITTA Kuniteru (1829–1902), who was also known as TAKEZAWA Kansaburō and as TŌYŌ; and *Taisei Kyō*, recognized as an independent sect in 1882, was founded by HIRAYAMA Shōsai (1815–90).

Yet every one of the 13 sects believes in the essential tenets of the official Shinto which is basic to ultranationalism: Divine Origin, Divine Characteristics, Divine Leadership, and Divine Mission. The Occupation Authorities and the majority of Occidental scholars were scrupulous in advocating that full religious protection be accorded these sects, but there can be little doubt that at least a part of this tolerance was traceable to the fact that they did not realize to what extent the sects propagated the objectionable philosophy of the national cult.

The policies and procedures which led to the abrogation of the Religious Bodies Law, the abolition of governmental sponsorship of *Kokka* or *Jinja Shintō*, and the separation of Church and State on 15 December 1945, have already been considered in connection with the operation of the Occupation machinery of control. As the fifth of the great historical events in the development

of Shinto it may be profitable here to note some of the provisions
of the mandatory change. SCAP Directive AG 000.3 (15 Dec 45)
CIE, "Abolition of Governmental Sponsorship, Support, Perpetuation, Control, and Dissemination of State Shinto," stripped of
certain causal and penalty paragraphs, provided that:

1 a. The sponsorship, support, perpetuation, control and dissemination of Shinto by the Japanese national, prefectural, and local governments, or by public officials, subordinates, and employees acting in
their official capacity are prohibited and will cease immediately.

b. All financial support from public funds and all official affiliation
with Shinto and Shinto shrines are prohibited and will cease immediately.

(1) While no financial support from public funds will be extended
to shrines located on public reservations or parks, this prohibition will
not be construed to preclude the Japanese government from continuing to support the areas on which such shrines are located.

(2) Private financial support of all Shinto shrines which have been
previously supported in whole or in part by public funds will be permitted, provided such private support is entirely voluntary and is in
no way derived from forced or involuntary contributions.

c. All propagation and dissemination of militaristic and ultra-
nationalistic ideology in Shinto doctrines, practices, rites, ceremonies,
or observances, as well as in the doctrines, practices, rites, ceremonies,
and observances of any other religion, faith, sect, creed, or philosophy,
are prohibited and will cease immediately.

d. The Religious Functions Order relating to the Grand Shrine of
Ise and the Religious Functions Order relating to State and other
Shrines will be annulled.

e. The Shrine Board (*Jingi-in*) of the Ministry of Home Affairs
will be abolished, and its present functions, duties, and administrative
obligations will not be assumed by any other governmental or tax-
supported agency.

f. All public educational institutions whose primary function is
either the investigation and dissemination of Shinto or the training of
a Shinto priesthood will be abolished and their physical properties
diverted to other uses. Their present functions, duties, and administrative obligations will not be assumed by any other governmental or
tax-supported agency.

g. Private educational institutions for the investigation and dissemination of Shinto and for the training of priesthood for Shinto
will be permitted and will operate with the same privileges and be subject to the same controls and restrictions as any other private educa-

tional institution having no affiliation with the government; in no case, however, will they receive support from public funds, and in no case will they propagate and disseminate militaristic and ultra-nationalistic ideology.

h. The dissemination of Shinto doctrines in any form and by any means in any educational institution supported wholly or in part by public funds is prohibited and will cease immediately.

(1) All teachers' manuals and textbooks now in use in any educational institution supported wholly or in part by public funds will be censored, and all Shinto doctrine will be deleted. No teachers' manual or textbook which is published in the future for use in such institutions will contain any Shinto doctrine.

(2) No visits to Shinto shrines and no rites, practices, or ceremonies associated with Shinto will be conducted or sponsored by any educational institution supported wholly or in part by public funds.

i. Circulation by the government of "The Fundamental Principles of the National Structure" (*Kokutai no Hongi*), "The Way of the Subject" (*Shimmin no Michi*), and all similar official volumes, commentaries, interpretations, or instructions on Shinto is prohibited.

j. The use in official writings of the terms "Greater East Asia War" (*Dai Toa Sensō*), "The Whole World under One Roof" (*Hakkō Ichi-u*), and all other terms whose connotation in Japanese is inextricably connected with State Shinto, militarism, and ultra-nationalism is prohibited and will cease immediately.

k. God-shelves (*kamidana*) and all other physical symbols of State Shinto in any office, school, institution, organization, or structure supported wholly or in part by public funds are prohibited and will be removed immediately.

l. No official, subordinate employee, student, citizen or resident of Japan will be discriminated against because of his failure to profess and believe in or participate in any practice, rite, ceremony, or observance of State Shinto or of any other religion.

m. No official of the national, prefectural, or local government, acting in his public capacity, will visit any shrine to report his assumption of office, to report on conditions of government or to participate as a representative of government in any ceremony or observance.

*   *   *

So that there might be no possible misunderstanding about the purpose of this powerful prohibitory directive from the Allied Occupation Forces there is included a specific statement of purpose:

The purpose of this directive is to separate religion from the state, to prevent misuse of religion for political ends, and to put all religions, faiths, and creeds, upon exactly the same legal basis, entitled to precisely the same opportunities and protection. It forbids affiliation with the government and the propagation and dissemination of militaristic and ultra-nationalistic ideology not only to Shinto but to the followers of all religions, faiths, sects, creeds, or philosophies.

It is evident that it was not solely the official national cult *Kokka* or *Jinja Shintō* which was the object of the attack but the much larger, and Occidental, concept of National Shinto. *Dai Toa Sensō* is an expression of ultranationalistic and militaristic philosophy. *Hakkō Ichi-u* is an expression which has been known since the earliest extant writings in Japanese, but one which was so infrequently used that until the rise of the militarist clique in modern Japan even fairly large-sized dictionaries did not include the term. It has been used both in Shinto and in Buddhist writings but became a propaganda term of the ultranationalists in the two decades prior to Surrender. The *Kokutai no Hongi* is an exposition of Confucian, Buddhist, and Shinto philosophies blended into a statement of ultranationalistic policy. Although the Allied Powers had gone so far as to prohibit certain elements of philosophy should they appear in the creeds and dogma of any religious order, thus in effect trespassing on the liberty of faith which had been assured in the SCAP Directive of 4 October 1945, on "Removal of Restrictions on Political, Civil, and Religious Liberties," they had not directly attacked Shinto but only the "militaristic and ultranationalistic elements" of Shinto. Paragraph 2 e (2) of the 15 December 1945 Directive specifically assures freedom and protection to *Jinja Shintō* when it is practiced as a private religion and not as a compulsory national cult. It is clear then that "National Shinto" as conceived of by the Occupation Powers came closer to what the Japanese call *Kokutai* (National Entity or Polity) or *Kokumin Dōtoku* (National Morality) than it did to the narrow limits of *Fukko Shintō*. Fortunately the exact extent of this unacceptable portion of Shinto has been delineated by the 15 December 1945 Directive:

Militaristic and ultra-nationalistic ideology, . . . embraces those teachings, beliefs, and theories which advocate or justify a mission on the part of Japan to extend its rule over other nations and peoples by reason of:

(1) The doctrine that the Emperor of Japan is superior to the heads of other states because of ancestry, descent, or special origin.
(2) The doctrine that the people of Japan are superior to the people of other lands because of ancestry, descent, or special origin.
(3) The doctrine that the islands of Japan are superior to other lands because of divine or special origin.
(4) Any other doctrine which tends to delude the Japanese people into embarking upon wars of aggression or to glorify the use of force as an instrument for the settlement of disputes with other peoples.

Stripped of these objectionable elements and separated from the foreign contributions of Confucian ethics and Buddhist philosophy, Shinto proves remarkably sterile. Dr. Karl FLORENZ in his monograph, "Ancient Japanese Rituals," in *Transactions of the Asiatic Society of Japan*, Vol. XXVII, First Series, deals at some length with the ancient Shinto concept of *tsumi* (crime, or sin). In the text of the *norito* or ritual prayer of the *Ōharai* (*Oho-harahe*) or Great Purification Ceremony of Ancient Shinto two types of these ethical offenses were listed: heavenly sins (*ama tsu tsumi*), and earthly sins (*kuni tsu tsumi*). The heavenly sins were apparently a partial list of those offenses which *Susano-o no Mikoto*, the unruly Storm-God of ancient mythology, had committed and which were applicable to behavior of men on earth, namely:

breaking down the divisions of the rice-fields, filling up the irrigation channels, opening the flood-gates of the sluices, sowing seed over again, setting up pointed rods (in the rice-fields), flaying alive and flaying backwards, evacuating excrements (at improper places).

The earthly sins included:

cutting the living skin, cutting the dead skin, albinos [*shira-hito*, or "white men," variously interpreted by Japanese scholars as referring to "white leprosy"; "white ring-worm"; *shira-hage*, a skin disease which makes the head bald; and even as people from *Shiragi*, the ancient kingdom of Silla in Korea—surely an evidence of racial discrimination!], being affected with excrescences, the offense of (a son's) cohabitation with his own mother, the offense of (a father's) cohabitation with his own child, the offense of (the father's) cohabitation with his step-daughter, the offense of (a man's) cohabitation with his mother-in-law, the offense of cohabitation with animals, calamity through crawling worms, calamity through the gods on high, calamity through birds on high, killing the animals [Florenz considered this to be restricted to other people's animals, but it seems likely in view of the history of the *eta* class that it was the act itself that was a sin], the offense of using incantations.

In its ancient form Shinto's major ethical teaching was the principle of *makoto* (truth). Yet even this simple doctrine was twisted to the nationalistic ends, which are now forbidden. Professor KUME Kunitake in his article "Japanese Religious Beliefs: Shintō —the Kami," p. 38, states:

That one word, *makoto*, is the foundation of all Japanese morals, a foundation on which is to be raised a grand edifice of the True Religion. . . . Theology is for the learned, contemplation for the gifted, and the sacred formulae for the pious. But a man must first of all be true—true to himself, true to the Emperor, true to the faith he professes. That one word *makoto* is the foundation of Japanese morals, religion, and government, truthfulness towards the *kami* and the Emperor having developed ultimately that matchless moral standard *Bushidō*.

The Educational Legacy of Nationalism

The formulation of an educational philosophy within the matrix of Japanese nationalism was evidenced by an almost limitless mass of actions, statements, episodes. Yet so tenuous is the formation of an idea that it is often difficult to focus upon a single concrete datum which can be presented as irrefutable proof. Japanese educational philosophy was evidenced by the turn of a phrase in the convocation of school assemblies, by the use of extreme honorifics of speech in teaching anything which impinged on any of certain political areas, by the taut emotionalism exhibited by the school officials and transferred to the students during certain official ceremonies. It was evidenced by hundreds of little side references in the content of the textbooks: in a beautiful poem to a flower, but the flower was the chrysanthemum, symbol of the Imperial Family; in the kindergarten coloring of a fish, but the fish was the crimson carp, symbol of the Boys' Festival or Iris Fete of 5 May (*Shōbu-no-sekku*); in a tale of a boy's staunch courage in the face of the cold and exposure of winter, but the boy was to grow to be Japan's most famous modern general. But it is in the literature of Japan that the most lasting evidences of this amalgamation of nationalism and educational philosophy are found. They are the scores in the rocks left after the glacier has melted. Of these evidences in literature only three will be considered: the *Imperial Rescript on Education*, the *Kokutai no Hongi*, and the textbooks of Japanese ethics or *Shūshin*.

The Imperial Rescript on Education. It appears likely that the most frequently quoted document in all Japanese history is the *Imperial Rescript on Education* issued by Emperor Meiji on the 30th day of the 10th month of the 23d year of Meiji, otherwise 30 October 1890. It has been reprinted hundreds of millions, possibly billions of times. It was committed to memory by millions of school children and is known in detail by virtually every mentally competent Japanese living today. It was considered so sacred that copies of it in every school were kept in a place of honor and security, frequently a special safe, and were brought forth periodically with great ceremony for public readings that had quasi-religious pomp and emotionalism. It has been repeatedly charged, and investigations by the Occupation Forces verified at least some of the charges, that school officials who stumbled over the reading of a single word were subjected to humiliation, discipline, and frequently dismissal. There are recorded instances of such officials committing suicide in expiation, and of school children driven to suicide or self-mutilation in a frenzy of patriotic emotionalism following one of these readings. It contains the distillate of every nationalistic philosophy objectionable to the Allied Powers, yet the Occupation Authorities scrupulously avoided any official notice of its content, authority, or public presentation. It says:

Know ye, Our Subjects:
Our Imperial Ancestors have founded Our Empire on a basis broad and everlasting and have deeply and firmly implanted virtue; Our subjects ever united in loyalty and filial piety have from generation to generation illustrated the beauty thereof. This is the glory of the fundamental character of Our Empire, and herein also lies the source of Our education. Ye, Our subjects, be filial to your parents, affectionate to your brothers and sisters; as husbands and wives be harmonious, as friends true; bear yourselves in modesty and moderation; extend your benevolence to all; pursue learning and cultivate arts, and thereby develop intellectual faculties and perfect moral powers;

furthermore, advance public good and promote common interests; always respect the Constitution and observe the laws; should emergency arise, offer yourselves courageously to the State; and thus guard and maintain the prosperity of Our Imperial Throne coeval with heaven and earth. So shall ye not only be Our good and faithful subjects, but render illustrious the best traditions of your forefathers.

The Way here set forth is indeed the teaching bequeathed by Our Imperial Ancestors, to be observed alike by Their Descendants and the subjects, infallible for all ages and true in all places. It is Our wish to lay it to heart in all reverence, in common with you, Our subjects, that We may all thus attain to the same virtue. (Complete official English trans.)

What has given this apparently innocent, even innocuous, statement its incalculable power in Japan? Two situations are immediately apparent: the original meaning of the document has long since been lost in the maze of militaristic and ultranationalistic interpretations and commentaries, and the instrument itself has become cloaked with a sacrosanctity based on the adulation of fanatical patriots. It is in effect no longer merely a political document but has become the basic sacred writ of modern National Shinto.

The *Rescript on Education* was not always accorded such a position of infallibility. We have the detailed account of Yoshi-kawa Akimasa, Minister of Education in 1890 and actual author of the *Rescript,* to the contrary. Yoshikawa published a statement on the background and writing of the *Rescript* in the 5 August 1912 issue of the *Kokumin Shimbun* and on the following day an English translation of his statement appeared in the *Japan Advertiser*. He states that the process of westernization had proceeded to such a point in Japan prior to 1890 that persons who "advocated the virtues of righteousness, loyalty and filial duty" brought down upon themselves cynical laughter and derision. This naturally evoked a violent rebuttal from the more conservative writers and editors and in the annual meeting of prefectural governors at the Ministry of Home Affairs in 1890, witnessed by Prince Yamagata as Minister and himself as Vice-Minister of Home Affairs, the situation was considered and it was decided that since it dealt with "people's thoughts" it should be made the responsibility of the Ministry of Education. Emperor Meiji immediately directed Viscount Enomoto Takeaki, then a Cabinet

Minister, to frame some principles on education which might be used to guide the people. He made some notes but resigned before completion and YOSHIKAWA Akimasa himself, as the new Minister of Education, completed the work. He consulted Viscount INOUE Ki frequently on the legal aspects of the draft and conferred directly with Emperor MEIJI on the ethical principles to be incorporated "in the new moral standard of the nation." YOSHIKAWA's revealing statement on the content of this moral standard follows:

As people know, the Imperial Rescript on Education was based on the four virtues: benevolence, righteousness, loyalty, and filial piety. The making of these four virtues the foundation of the national education was, however, strongly criticized at that time, and some scholars even declared that these virtues were imported from China and ought never to be established as the standards of the nation's morality. Others again said that, should such old-fashioned virtues be encouraged among the people, it would mean the revival of the old form of virtue typified by private revenge, etc. But I strongly upheld the teaching of these four principal virtues, saying that the essence of man's morality is one and the same irrespective of place or time, although it might take different forms according to different circumstances, and that therefore the aforesaid four virtues could well be made the moral standard of the Japanese people.

The Imperial Rescript was issued in its original form, and in spite of the criticism and opposition before its promulgation, which caused much fear about its future, the Rescript, once issued, soon came to be the light of the people in their moral teaching and is now firmly established as the standard of the nation's morality. (Trans. as given in the *Japan Advertiser*.)

Perhaps the easiest way to summarize the militaristic, ultranationalistic, and National Shintoistic interpretations which have become an inseparable part of the psychological context of this historic document is that of noting from which broad streams of Japanese philosophy each of the ideas contained within the *Rescript* were drawn.

The opening line, "Our Imperial Ancestors have founded Our Empire on a basis broad and everlasting . . . ," is taken directly from *Fukko Shintō*. It has been interpreted by ultranationalists to establish official sanction of the belief that the Japanese nation was physically created by the deities of ancient mythology, and that it has been endowed with a characteristic of unchangeable government, inescapable and eternal Imperial succession. The next line, "Our subjects ever united in loyalty and filial piety . . . ," is lifted directly from Confucian ethics. It has been intrepreted to mean that Japan enjoys Divine Leadership which the people should revere and that the citizen should be inferior to the State in a paternalistic (or patriarchal) form of government. "This is the glory of the fundamental character of Our Empire . . . ," is taken from *Fukko Shintō*. Its ultranationalistic interpretation is that Japan enjoys a "unique character" as a state. The term "fundamental character" (*kokutai no seika*) has become a propaganda tag title used to inflame patriotic emotionalism.

The major portion of the next sentence is composed of a series of homely virtues taken from Confucian and Buddhist sources. Needless to say there is a striking parallelism with the virtues of *Bushidō,* The Way of the Warrior, but this is explainable on the grounds of a common source rather than a conscious quotation. The line, ". . . be filial to your parents, affectionate to your brothers and sisters; as husbands and wives be harmonious, as friends true; . . . ," consists of the last four of the Five Relationships of Confucian ethics: Sovereign and Subject, Parent and Child, Husband and Wife, Elder and Younger Brother (or Sister), and Friends. The line, ". . . bear yourselves in modesty and moderation . . ." is based on Confucian self-restraint, modesty, and decorum in relationship to the organized community, and on *Zen* Buddhism's ideals of simplicity and dignity. The line, ". . . extend your benevolence to all . . ." is based on Buddhist charity, mercy, and kindness, and on Confucian humanity, sympathy, and goodness. This innocent appearing statement has been interpreted by Japanese ultranationalists as authority to extend to all nations the benefits of Japan's unique heritage and rule, and by Japanese militarists the right to impose this benefit through military force. The line, ". . . pursue learning and cultivate arts, and thereby develop intellectual faculties and perfect moral powers . . ." is taken from Wisdom, the first of the three basic attributes of men in Confucian philosophy, and from the Buddhist concept of wisdom as the last of the Five Organs and, in many sects, the method of enlightenment.

The latter part of the sentence just noted is probably inspired by shrewd practical politics, ". . . advance public good and promote common interests; always respect the Constitution and observe the laws. . . ." But the final statements are unquestionably inspired by National Shinto, the political philosophy, not the religion, ". . . should emergency arise, offer yourselves courageously to the State; and thus guard and maintain the prosperity of Our Imperial Throne coeval with heaven and earth." The _Kokutai no Hongi_, basic blueprint of Japanese ultranationalism, states in commentary on this line:

In the great august Will and great august undertakings of the Emperor, who is deity incarnate, is seen the great august Will of the Imperial Ancestors, and in this Will lives the endless future of our nation. That our Imperial Throne is coeval with heaven and earth means indeed that the past and the future are united in one in the "now," that our nation possesses everlasting life, and that it flourishes endlessly.

. . . And this is brought to fruition where the subjects render services to the Emperor—who takes over and clarifies the teachings bequeathed by the Imperial Ancestors—accept the august Will, and walk worthily in the Way. Thus, sovereign and subject, united in one, take shape and develop eternally, and the Imperial Throne goes on prospering. Truly, the Imperial Throne, which is coeval with heaven and earth, forms the basis of our national entity; and that which in the beginning of the founding of the nation firmly established this, is the Oracle coeval with heaven and earth. (Trans. in GAUNTLETT and HALL, _op. cit._, Ms. pp. 19–20.)

The line, ". . . So shall ye not only be Our good and faithful subjects, but render illustrious the best traditions of your forefathers . . ." is a direct appeal to the filial piety taught alike in _Fukko Shintō_ and Confucianism. It establishes patriotism to the Imperial Throne on a religious and ethical basis. Equally an attempt to secure the religious incentive of linking the _Rescript_ with Shinto doctrine is the major portion of the final paragraph, "The Way here set forth is indeed the teaching bequeathed by Our Imperial Ancestors, to be observed alike by Their Descendants and the subjects, infallible for all ages and true in all places." Japanese ultranationalists have interpreted this as indicating that the Way of the Imperial Ancestors, in practice the policy of the ruling clique, is something which is sacred, infallible, eternal, and something which it is the obvious duty of all Japanese to extend to "all places."

One of the peculiar policies which marked the first two years

of the Occupation was that which has preserved inviolable this
document. In October 1946 the Ministry of Education discontinued authorization for the ceremonial reading of the *Rescript* but
permitted its retention by schools. Why wasn't it banned by the
Shinto Directive? Why hasn't it been censored from all textbooks?
There can be no positive answer, even from those directly and
intimately connected with formation of policy. In part it was because of the active opposition to such a prohibition on the part of
staff officers in the Occupation. Their objections were threefold:
there is nothing intrinsically wrong with the *Rescript;* any attack
on it would be an attack on the Confucian ethics, Buddhist philosophy, and Shinto mythology which would be interpreted as an
attack on religion; and it is convenient for those who are in authority in a military occupation, essentially a dictatorship, to have
some centrally dictated statement of goal or aim.

Early in 1946, however, after official sanction of Shinto had
been prohibited and the Emperor had voluntarily denied his divinity, the possibility of having the present Emperor issue a new
Imperial Rescript on Education was seriously considered. Such
a solution would have had the advantage of sweeping away the
context of all the multitudes of militaristic and ultranationalistic
commentaries which have colored the old. It would also have retained the good elements which undeniably exist in the original,
and would have given the Occupation Authorities the opportunity of dictating some solid educational policy through the Emperor's lips, thus securing the efficient, and blind, obedience to
those policies which the masses of Japanese have traditionally accorded the Emperor's rescripts. This policy had progressed to the
point where a number of tentative drafts of such a Rescript had
been written, and through the good offices of an influential member of the Jesuit Order an informal channel had been established
to a Catholic convert in the Imperial Household through which
suggestions might be passed. The Ministry of Education had independently considered the content of a possible new Rescript. Certain members of the United States Education Mission to Japan,
however, were violently opposed to any proposal that the Emperor should be given the prestige of issuing any "Educational
Code" even if virtually dictated by the Occupation Authorities.
Among the Japanese the *Kyōsantō* (Communist party) in a statement to the press on 28 March 1946 objected to the proposal,

which had become public knowledge through some of the information leaks in the Ministry of Education, on the grounds that "it would be flagrantly undemocratic to impose on the people principles of education by such methods as the granting of an Imperial Rescript." For once the Communist party propaganda line coincided with the opinion of a considerable proportion of the Occupation Authorities and was supported by non-Communist educational leaders in the Allied Powers. Plans to bring out a new Rescript were abandoned.

But the logical corollary of abolishing the old *Imperial Rescript on Education*, also advocated by the Communist party, independently by several members of the United States Education Mission to Japan, and by numerous scholars in the Allied Powers, has not been acted upon. Meanwhile the *Rescript* stands as the highest expression of educational philosophy in Japan and the Japanese, as indicated in the 29 March 1946 issue of *Jiji*, printed in the 31 March 1946 edition of the *Nippon Times*, ponder:

The Rescript . . . sets up an absolute standard to which all other virtues are relative. This standard is the "prosperity of the Imperial Family," which is "coeval with heaven and earth" in the terms of the rescript. Under this scheme, human virtues have no independent basis, but are means to an end. Why should the moral life of men and women be governed by the absolute standard mentioned above? This is the weakness of the whole system.

The *Kokutai no Hongi*. Reference has frequently been made to a truly remarkable Japanese policy document, the *Kokutai no Hongi* ("Cardinal Principles of the National Entity"), which was published by the Ministry of Education on 30 March 1937. The purpose of this document is given in its opening paragraph, "Consciousness of Our National Entity." It is quoted in full:

Paradoxical and extreme conceptions, such as Socialism, Anarchism, and Communism, are all based in the final analysis on individualism which is the root of modern Occidental ideologies, and are no more than varied forms of their expressions. In the Occident, too, where individualism forms the basis of their ideas, they have, when it comes to Communism, been unable to adopt it; so that now they are about to do away with their traditional individualism, which has led to the rise of totalitarianism and nationalism and incidentally to the springing up of Fascism and Nazism. That is, it can be said that both in the Occident and in our country the deadlock of individualism has led alike to a season of ideological and social confusion and crisis. We shall leave aside for a while the question of finding a way out of the present deadlock, for, as far as it concerns our country, we must return to the standpoint peculiar to our country, clarify our immortal national entity, sweep aside everything in the way of adulation, bring into being our original condition, and must at the same time rid ourselves of bigotry, and strive all the more to take in and sublimate Occidental culture; for we should give to things basical their proper place, giving due weight to minor things, and should build up a sagacious and worthy Japan. This means that the present conflict seen in our people's ideas, the unrest in their modes of life, the confused state of their civilization, can be put right only by a thorough investigation by use of the intrinsic nature of Occidental ideologies and by grasping the true meaning of our national entity. Then, too, this should be done not only for the sake of our nation but for the sake of the entire human race which is struggling to find a way out of the deadlock with which individualism is faced. Herein lies our grave cosmopolitan mission. It is for this reason that we have compiled the *Kokutai no Hongi* ("Principles of the National Entity of Japan"), to trace clearly the genesis of the nation's foundation, to define its great spirit, to set forth clearly at the same time the features the national entity has manifested in history, and to provide the present generation with an elucidation of the matter, and thus to awaken the people's consciousness and their efforts. (Trans. in GAUNTLETT and HALL, *op. cit.*, Ms. pp. 6–7.)

The original draft of the *Kokutai no Hongi* was prepared by HISAMATSU Sen-ichi, Professor at Tokyo Imperial University and outstanding scholar in the Japanese classics. This original manuscript is unavailable, hence its contents can only be surmised. It was submitted to an official Compilation Committee and in the course of three conferences on the wording and content was very substantially changed, to the outspoken displeasure of Dr. HISAMATSU.

The composition of this Compilation Committee is significant. Besides Dr. HISAMATSU there were YOSHIDA Kumaji, KIHIRA Masami, and INOUE Takamaro, members of the *Kokumin Seishin Bunka Kenkyūjo* (National Spirit Cultural Research Institute or NSCRI); WATSUJI Tetsurō, FUJIKAKE Shizuya, and UI Hakuju, Professors of Tokyo Imperial University; KUROITA Katsumi, Professor Emeritus of Tokyo Imperial University; SAKUDA Sōichi, Professor of Kyoto Imperial University; YAMADA Yoshio, Professor of Tohoku Imperial University; KŌNO SHŌZŌ, President of

Kokugakuin University; ŌTSUKA Takematsu, official compiler of materials for the History of the Reformation; IIJIMA Tadao, Professor of the Peers' School; and MIYAJI Naokazu, official in charge of Historical Researches. This official committee was assisted by a board of ten specialists who were charged with doing research: OGAWA Gishō, Chief of the Investigation Section, Thought Control Bureau; YAMAMOTO Katsuichi, ŌGUSHI Toyo-o, and SHIDA Nobuyoshi, members of the NSCRI; KONDŌ Toshiharu, YOKOYAMA Shumpei, and SHIMIZU Gishō, school inspectors; and FUJIOKA Tsuguhei, SANO Yasutaro, and FUJIMOTO Manji, supervisors of libraries. Three of these men had died (YOSHIDA, KIHARA and KUROITA) and seven (INOUE, YAMADA, ŌGUSHI, SHIDA, OGAWA, KONDŌ, and SHIMIZU) had been purged, or forbidden to hold political or educational positions, though not for participation in the authorship of this volume, by the end of the second year of the Occupation.

A possible explanation of the apparent official indifference evidenced by the Occupational Authorities to these men who were presumably responsible for the writing of one of the two documents specifically banned by name in the SCAP Shinto Directive may be found in the procedure of editing. It is possible, though unlikely, that their basic ideology was changed. It is certain that a major part of their manuscript was rewritten. The chief Editor, ITŌ Enkichi, Chief of the Bureau of Thought Control and later Vice-Minister of Education, made such drastic changes in the manuscript, even to rewriting large portions while the document was in galley proof, that it is generally conceded to represent his personal labors. Mr. ITŌ, had he lived, would unquestionably have been purged on any of several counts including leadership of the bureau officially credited with instigating more than 60,000 arrests for "improper thoughts." Death, however, spared him this indignity.

The first printing of the *Kokutai no Hongi* in March 1937, numbering 300,000 copies, was distributed to the teaching staffs of public and private schools from the university level to the lower cycle of the elementary school. A notification was sent by the Vice-Minister of Education to all prefectural governors, university presidents, and principals of the *kōtō gakkō* (higher schools preparatory to the university) and *semmon gakkō* (college level technical schools) directing them to exert every effort to place the book before the public. The Cabinet Printing Bureau published successive editions and up to March 1943, the last date for which publication statistics are available, had sold approximately 1,900,000. In the same period 28,300 reprints by private presses had been sold and approximately 51,200 reproductions of the *Kokutai no Hongi* had appeared in other books. Portions of the text had been reproduced in the textbooks of the middle schools and *seinen gakkō* (youth or continuation schools). It was required reading in *kōtō gakkō* (higher schools) and *semmon gakko* (colleges or technical schools) and was studied critically by student teachers in the normal schools. Teaching staffs were required to form self-study groups and to read and discuss the material in it. It was quoted in official ceremonies and portions were read to school assemblies. It was itself a commentary on the *Imperial Rescript on Education* yet its content was so abstruse, and the language in which it was written was so vague and difficult, that the *Kokutai no Hongi* itself became the object of a considerable number of commentaries. One of the best known, that of MIURA Tōsaku, published in Tokyo by the *Tōyō Tosho Kabushiki Gōshi Kaisha* on 25 July 1937, went through 93 printings in the first two years, each containing an annotated copy of the *Kokutai no Hongi*.

Yet so obviously objectionable was the content of the *Kokutai no Hongi*, even in the eyes of the Japanese after defeat, that it was virtually impossible to secure a copy following Surrender.

The *Kokutai no Hongi* preaches from a simple text. It is "to guard and maintain the prosperity of Our Imperial Throne." Building on the premise that "religious rites, government, and education are entirely one," it argues along the well-worn path of ultranationalism. It retells the story of the Divine Origin with all the implications of Divine Characteristics of the Japanese people and nation. It traces the Divine Leadership, popularly known as the *Tenno* System, from the sacred Oracle by which the Sun-Goddess, *Amaterasu Ōmikami*, delegated the power to rule the earth to her grandson; through the sacred Imperial Succession which has handed on this Divine Authority through an "unbroken line" to the present Emperor, HIROHITO, the 124th in the succession founded by Emperor JIMMU; to a culmination in the theory of the *kokutai* or National Entity as an immutable law, which shall characterize Japan for eternity and shall perpetuate the Imperial line for ages eternal. It argues that all activity, and in particular scholarship and intellectual activity, is both a gracious gift of the Emperors and a part of the patriotic and sacred duty of the subject who is to support the Emperors. It links all duties with the traditional ethical concepts of the people, loyalty and filial piety, and with the great religious motivation, Shinto. It performs an adroit metamorphosis on the other element of the philosophical dichotomy and reduces the rights of the subject to the privilege of performing these duties. Finally it establishes the whole structure of its political ultranationalism as the *raison d'être* of education.

For the sake of brevity it may be permissible to extract from the rambling, repetitive text a few concise quotations, admittedly taken out of context but presented in a sequence which it is felt faithfully illustrates this argument. With this as a frame of reference the complete quotation of the chapter devoted to education will have added meaning. The following are from the translation in GAUNTLETT and HALL, *op. cit.*:

1. That the Emperor who accedes to the Throne is descended from an unbroken line of sovereigns is the basis of the founding of the Land, and is that which the Oracle clearly sets forth. Namely, that the offspring of *Amaterasu Ōmikami* accede to the Throne from generation to generation is a great law which is for ever unalterable. (Ms. pp. 20–21.)

2. . . . the Imperial Throne is acceded to by one descended from a line of Emperors unbroken for ages eternal, and is absolutely firm. Consequently, the Emperor, who sits upon such an Imperial Throne, is naturally endowed with gracious virtues, so that the Throne is so much the firmer and is also sacred. That the subjects should serve the Emperor is not because of duty as such, nor is it submission to authority; but is the welling, natural manifestation of the heart and is the spontaneous obedience of deep faith toward His Majesty. (Ms. pp. 21–22.)

3. Filial piety in our country has its true characteristics in its perfect conformity with our national entity by heightening still further the relationship between morality and nature. Our country is a great family nation, and the Imperial Household is the head family of the subjects and the nucleus of national life. The subjects revere the Imperial Household, which is the head family, with the tender esteem they have for their ancestors; and the Emperor loves his subjects as his very own. (Ms. pp. 59–60.)

4. Since our ancestors rendered assistance to the spreading of Imperial

enterprises by the successive Emperors, for us to show loyalty to the Emperor is in effect a manifestation of the manners and customs of our ancestors; and this is why we show filial piety to our forefathers. In our country there is no filial piety apart from loyalty, and filial piety has loyalty for its basis. (Ms. p. 60.)

5. Verily, loyalty and filial piety as one is the flower of our national entity, and is the cardinal point of our people's morals. Hence, national entity forms not only the foundation of morality but of all branches of such things as politics, economics, and industry. Accordingly, the great Way of loyalty and filial piety as one must be made manifest in all practical fields of these national activities and the people's lives. We subjects must strive all the more in loyalty and filial piety for the real manifestation of the immense and endless national entity. (Ms. p. 63.)

6. Scholastic pursuits in our country have from the beginning progressed through the august patronage of the successive Emperors, and it is to their patronage that we owe the advancement which we see today. That is to say, the Emperors adopted, from of old, Confucianism and Buddhism as well as the allied cultures of the Continent, giving them due attention and patronage. (Ms. p. 159.)

7. Our scholastic pursuits one and all find their culmination in our national entity and see their mission in guarding and maintaining the prosperity of the Imperial Throne. The carrying out of researches in the face of tremendous difficulties when the *Edo* Period saw the introduction into our country of such sciences as medicine and ballistics, and the assiduous application and efforts made in the adoption of many Occidental sciences following the *Meiji* Restoration, were things made possible by keeping up the Way of the subjects whose principle is to guard and maintain the prosperity of the Imperial Throne. Nevertheless, in the scholastic pursuits of our day in which foreign cultures are being imported at a tremendous pace and great advancements made in every field, we cannot say for certain that there is no danger of unconsciously losing sight of this focal point. (Ms. p. 162.)

This, then, is the frame of reference. A mere description of the application of this political philosophy to education would seem to the Occidental educator too fantastic for credence. But it was applied. And the application was an intensely practical one that colored the most commonplace details of instruction. Only by sampling the actual instructions officially directed to the teachers is it possible to understand fully the mystical and religious quality which saturated the educational philosophy of Japan. The chapter on education in the *Kokutai no Hongi* is quoted in full, as translated in Gauntlett and Hall, *op. cit.*, Ms. pp. 163–169:

That education in our country is also wholly based on our national entity, that it makes the manifestation of this national entity its focal point, and that it has its distant source in the Way handed down to us since the founding of the Empire, is a fact we have seen to be equally true in the case of scholastic pursuits. In the old days, when clan chiefs rendered services at the Imperial Court, taking their parishioners with them, education consisted in the handing down of the history of services rendered by their ancestors. For example, we see in the genealogy of the *Takahashi* family how they gave injunctions to their posterity and thereby instilled fervour into their sense of duty by relating step by step how their ancestor, *Iwakamutsukari no Mikoto*, excelled in loyal service to the Emperor *Keikō* (A.D. 71–130), and how subsequently generation after generation carried on the family vocation and served as Imperial Household officials in the Imperial Court. Genealogies that have followed are all of this type. In the education of the knights in later generations, too, importance was laid on family education according to this tradition and instructions were always given to preserve the family name. What appears in the written pledge of *Kikuchi Takemochi*, which forms the family precepts of *Kikuchi*, a loyal subject of the *Yoshino* Court, is a good example:

"Since I, *Takemochi*, born of a family of knights, do render service at the Imperial Court, do pray that the Three Treasures may see my way to establishing myself in the world through the benevolence of the Imperial Court, I myself doing honour to my family name by following the laws of honesty in compliance with the Way of Heaven. I hope, besides, never to be a knight that forgets righteousness or makes light of shame through his own ambitions or greed with a heart taken up with the affairs of the world."

Education in recent times has owed much to the activities of the Shintoists, scholars of Japanese classics, Confucianists, Buddhist scholars, moral philosophers. Among these activities reverence for the Purification Ceremony of *Nakatomi* among the Shintoists or the studies and dissemination of our classics among scholars of Japanese classics are the most noteworthy. Hand in hand with contributions by these people go the reading aloud of poems before the deities at the shrines and the offering of tablets, even including votive tablets that have to do with computations. The rise of the various pursuits is traced to the deities; for instance, in the setting up of guardian deities as founders of various artistic pursuits, the revering of the *Hachiman* shrine as enshrining a military deity, the looking up to *Temman Tenjin* as a man of letters, and in the tracing of the origin of the *waka* to the sacred poem of *Yakumo* by His Augustness *Susano-o no Mikoto*.

Just as the word *oshi* signifies to love, *oshie* (to teach) means *to rear tenderly;* and it means the rearing of mankind in compliance with the Way on the basis of man's natural affection. *To guide* means the guiding of your children so that they may reach the Way. Just as the Emperor *Meiji* enjoined in the Imperial Rescript on Education, our education, for one thing, comprises the spirit of guarding and maintaining the prosperity of the Imperial Throne by following the august spirit manifested in the founding of the Empire in keeping with our national entity. Hence, this is entirely different in its essence from the mere development and perfection of oneself such as is seen in the idea of self-realization and perfection of one's character as set forth in individualistic pedagogics. In short it is not a mere development of individual minds and faculties set apart from the nation, but a rearing of a people manifesting the Way of our nation. Education whose object is the cultivation of the creative faculties of individuals or the development of individual characteristics is liable to be biased toward individuals and to be led by individual inclinations, and in the long run to fall into a *laissez-faire* education, and so to run counter to the principles of the education of our country.

Education must be such that it treats knowledge and practice as one. Education that lays one-sided emphasis on knowledge and lacks in practical application by the people is in contradiction to the true aim of our nation's education. That is, it is to be noted that the true object of our national education is seen in walking the Way of the founding of our Empire with knowledge and practice united in one. All systems of knowledge take shape only through practice and in this manner fulfil their object: and at the base of inductive knowledge there should always be a deep conviction that is linked with our national entity and practice related thereto. Hence, national conviction or application gains in accuracy and develops more and more through inductive knowledge; so that in our education, too, inductive or scientific knowledge must be given attention and encouragement. And this knowledge must, at the same time, contribute to the true advancement of our national civilization by keeping it under the influence of national conviction and practice. In other words, we should devote our efforts on the one hand toward the development of the various fields of the numerous sciences and on the other take heed to their synthesis, elevate them into practice and thereby fulfil the aims of those spheres of knowledge, giving expression to their special features.

The Emperor *Meiji* graciously says in 1897 in the Outline of Education and Studies:

"It is the teaching of Our Ancestors, the spirit of our national laws, and what is looked upon by the entire nation as a model of teaching, to count as most vital in education and studies the following of the

Way of mankind by clarifying the Way of humanity and justice and of loyalty and filial piety, by exhausting the resources of knowledge and of talent and accomplishments."

Howbeit, there have of late been not a few who have given weight solely to knowledge, talent, and accomplishments, not fathoming the real purport of civilization and enlightenment, breaking the laws of ethics and corrupting public morals. This is to be accounted for by the fact that toward the early part of the *Meiji* Restoration the good points of Western countries were at one time assimilated and daily progress made with the excellent idea of breaking away in the main from old abuses and of adopting knowledge from all over the world. Nevertheless, it is feared that if, as an unfortunate result, foreign ways are copied without due thought—with ideas of humanity, righteousness, loyalty, and filial piety set aside—the great principle binding the Sovereign and his subjects, and the fathers and their children, will in course of time be forgotten. This would not be in keeping with the primary purpose of our education and studies.

This behooves us indeed to reflect matters deeply, with the present times viewed in the light of these factors.

From Bushidō to Shūshin. The course of study in the Japanese curriculum which by Occidentals has popularly been considered the ultimate in the extremes of Japanese nationalism is *Shūshin* or Japanese ethics. So powerful was the Allied popular sentiment against the continuation of this subject that it was made the initial object of educational reform by the Occupation Forces after Surrender. A rapid survey of the contents of the *Shūshin* textbooks published during the progress of the war was actually begun in Tokyo before the establishment of SCAP on 2 October 1945 and was completed before the enunciation of basic educational policy in the 22 October 1945 SCAP Directive. Yet so apparently innocuous were the major portions of the text of these books that the Occupation Authorities were in an admitted quandary as to their proper course of action. There was a constant and vigorous pressure to ban the *Shūshin* courses in their entirety, yet the staff officers charged with the preparation of the official studies felt that their analysis of the actual contents of the books failed to reveal sufficient objectionable material to justify this drastic action before an impartial reviewing authority. To ban an innocent text might have had, and in fact later did have, serious repercussions on the grounds of "book burning" and "textbook censorship," which were inconsistent with the avowed aims of the Occupation.

It was only after a most exhaustive scrutiny and line-by-line textual analysis that the Occupation Headquarters finally on 31 December 1945 suspended the courses in *Shūshin* by SCAP Directive AG 000.8 (31 Dec 45) CIE, and then only until new and suitable instructional materials could be prepared.

Actually how objectionable were the textbooks on *Shūshin?* The immediate reason for banning *Shūshin*, other than that of acceding to popular pressure, was the practical though unpublicized reason that physical censorship of the existing textbooks would both leave tattered and unserviceable volumes and would direct the attention of the Japanese to the deleted portions. The Japanese authorities themselves recognized these difficulties and requested but were refused authorization to suspend temporarily the use of the textbooks. The reason advanced for this peculiar policy decision on the part of Occupation Headquarters was that Japanese teachers did not have the intellectual power or teaching experience to teach adequately without a textbook. A more fundamental reason openly recognized within Headquarters was that such a voluntary step would have robbed the Occupation Authorities of the credit for a popular and spectacular punitive action. The basic charge that Japanese ethics as a discipline was intrinsically unacceptable to a democratizing Occupation Force was never satisfactorily sustained.

In January 1945 two officers under instruction in the Civil Affairs Training School (CATS) at the University of Chicago, Capt. E. N. LOCKARD, AC, and Lt. Paul D. EHRET, USNR, completed a detailed study of the ethical teachings or "morals" contained in the *Shūshin* textbooks used in the six years of compulsory education immediately prior to the war. These two officers were later the Chief and Assistant Chief, respectively, of the Education Division of Military Government in Korea. They analyzed the current editions of the six official volumes, including 152 stories and 150 illustrations, and found that 39 basic moral teachings were included. Of these 39 moral teachings, 20 were on the theme of serving the community and nation; 18 were on honoring and respecting the family; 12 each were on helping those in need and on the Emperor or the Imperial Family; 8 were on perseverance in the face of difficulties, and 5 each were on obeying the law, being loyal, and keeping healthy and clean. The remaining 67 stories dealt with such virtues as being trustworthy, avoiding waste, accepting blame, being honest, being brave, being self-reliant, respecting others, admitting wrong, meeting obligations, being kind, forgiving mistakes, being polite, and being modest. The two analysts concluded that the content of the entire course might be divided into three overlapping areas: the acceptable behavior pattern of the child with relation to other children, parents, the school, and his immediate surroundings; the Emperor institution and the benefits accruing from that form of government; and the child's relationship with the community and nation. Their recommendations, made months before Capitulation, are interesting and pertinent:

The stories of the first type, relating to the child's personal conduct are for the most part simple, direct, and appropriate for the age level of the child. In this group there is no moral concept with which military government will be required, because of military necessity, to take issue. The teachings of these principles will have no adverse effect on the occupying forces and is consistent with the encouragement of a friendly, post-war Japanese people.

Stories relating to the Emperor are of interest. . . . If the institution of the Emperor is abolished during the period of occupation, these stories will be most inappropriate. If, however, the institution is retained, and used by the occupying forces, this group of stories, as written, would not endanger the security or success of military government.

The group of stories relating to service to the community and nation are concentrated for the most part in the last two books. Many of these stories are not unlike stories in our elementary school textbooks; they relate tales of heroism and begin a study of elementary civics, with discussions of taxes, the obedience of laws, elections, serving when drafted, etc.

* * *

This set of textbooks has a moderate amount of nationalistic doctrine in it. The loyalty, devotion, and sacrifice of heroes of the past, including military heroes, are naturally used as examples for youth— just as the lives of national heroes are used in other countries for the same purpose. There are also in these books references to the great of other nations: Socrates, Ben Franklin, Florence Nightingale, etc. Some stories touch upon the need for international cooperation and peace, and discuss other nations favorably.

In the spring and summer of 1945 a thorough study of the content of all *Shūshin* and national language texts and most of the other Japanese textbooks, used in the *shō gakkō* and *kōtō shō gakkō* (later the two levels of the *kokumin gakkō* or national elementary school) at the outbreak of the war, was conducted by the Education Division of the Planning Staff at CASA, Monterey, Calif. Complete translations were made of the major successive editions of *Shūshin* textbooks used in Japan beginning with the 1906 editions and ending with the 1941, published after the report of the Ministry of Education committees on the nationalization of education. After study it was concluded that if any charge should be leveled against the *Shūshin* textbooks it would have to be the charge of triteness, unsophistication, and maudlin sentimentality. Good was very good, the pure was pure, and the virtues were rewarded. There was, however, a discernible trend toward nationalism in the successive editions appearing between 1932 and 1941. Thus, in the February 1940 edition of the Sixth Book (*Jinjō Shōgaku Shūshin-Sho*) for example, there appeared such chapters as "The Great Imperial Shrine," "The Imperial Household," "The People's Duties," "National Development," and "Foreign Relations." It was prefaced with the *Imperial Rescript on Education* of 30 October 1890 and the *Imperial Rescript Given Young Students* of 22 May 1939, and the tone of the text is established by the latter:

The duty of Our subjects to foster national entity (*kokutai*), to cultivate national power, and thus eternally maintain the trend of our national growth is heavy and its road far. The realization of these aims is upon the shoulders of you students, young in age. We command you to respect valour and virtues, put honor above all things, consider the history of the present and the past; and by observing the trend of Our country and of the world clarify your own thinking, deepen and widen your outlook, and never lose sight of balance and the sense of justice in the realization of your aim; and by fully understanding your own talent and duty, cultivate your literary power, learn military discipline, and cultivate and muster the spirit of fortitude and manliness; thus accomplishing the Great Duty that has been placed upon your shoulders.

In the editions of *Shūshin* textbooks which appeared during the progress of the war there were the obvious propaganda inserts dealing with the attack on Pearl Harbor, the necessity of working harder and keeping up one's spirits, and apologia for the Chinese fiasco and the Greater East Asia Co-Prosperity Sphere Policy. There appeared in some of the final editions prior to Surrender premonitions of military disaster and almost pathetic attempts to explain the strategic and technological causes of continuing and apparently inevitable defeat. These evidences of a Japanese educational philosophy may be readily dismissed. They marked only a transient phase of the military operation, not basic philosophy. But the nationalistic evidences in the 1940 editions cannot so easily be disregarded. Two major themes are evident: a code of ethics based on *Bushidō* and emphasizing loyalty, filial piety, bravery, and a somewhat chauvinistic honor; and the ever recurring pattern of militarism, ultranationalism, and National Shintoism.

Bushidō, The Way of the Warrior, was originally the uncanonized code of honor or rule of conduct of the *samurai* or military class of medieval Japan. It grew from instructions given by military leaders such as MINAMOTO Yoritomo (better known by the first name, Yoritomo) (1148–99), the first of the Kamakura Shogunate, who directed his men to:

1. Practice and mature the military arts.
2. Be not guilty of any base or rude conduct.
3. Be not cowardly or effeminate in behavior.
4. Be simple and frugal.
5. The master and servants should mutually respect their indebtedness.
6. Keep a promise.
7. Share a common fate by mutual bondage in defiance of death or life. (As summarized by Baron SUYEMATSU Kencho in his volume, *The Ethics of Japan*, p. 301.)

This code of ethics has been eulogized by Japanese. It might perhaps be argued that it is somewhat primitive and incomplete yet it would not generally be considered unacceptable to Occidental students. It has been from the fanatical and bizarre applications rather than from the inherent character of its teachings that the objectionable character has evolved.

In the *Shūshin* texts *Bushidō* as the ethical standard of Japan was both directly advocated and was indirectly taught by historical example. Thus in the February 1940 edition of the Sixth Book, the last edition of the final compulsory year published prior to the outbreak of war and analyzed here as a typical example, the chapters on loyalty and filial piety are based around an incident in the life of KUSUNOKI Masashige (1294–1336) one of the Emperor GODAIGO's vassals from Kawachi. Masashige was ordered to subjugate a rebel chieftain named Hōjō Takatomi and vowed to the Emperor that come victory or defeat he would never rest till he had carried out the order. He suffered severe losses but ultimately by his example attracted other generals to his assistance and won. He later lost his life in a suicidal cavalry charge, ordered against his judgment by the Imperial Court, against the overwhelmingly superior forces of ASHIKAGA Takauji. Before going to his death he had a premonition, called his son, Masatsura, charged him with continuing to serve the Emperor loyally, and sent him home to Kawachi with a short sword which had been given him by the Emperor. After Masashige's death the son, overwhelmed with grief, attempted suicide (*seppuku*) with the Imperial sword and was stopped by his mother, who said:

Though you may be young, you are your father's son. Listen well to me. The reason that your father had sent you back home from Sakuroi no Eki was because he wanted you to follow in his footsteps to destroy the enemies of the Emperor and set his August mind at ease. That was your father's last will and you yourself have told me about it. Have you already forgotten it? How can you ever accomplish your father's ambition and serve the Emperor loyally!

The son suffered remorse, grew up, served faithfully, attained great eminence and the favor of the Emperor, and finally committed suicide in battle when much of his force was lost against a superior enemy. Lest the moral be missed the two lessons close with a proverb, "Loyal subjects come from families where filial piety is observed faithfully" (*Chūshin wa kōkō no mon ni izu*).

The emerging pattern of modern nationalism, present in all the editions of *Shūshin* but occupying a more prominent place than the traditional *Bushidō* in the immediate prewar years, was taught directly and by implication. The fundamental credo of the Divine Origin of Japan occupies the opening paragraph of the Sixth Book as a geographical description: "The Great Imperial Shrine, where the Imperial Ancestor Great Sun-Goddess *Amaterasu Ōmikami* is enshrined, is located in the city of Ujiyamada in Ise. Its compound is located at the foot of Mt. Kamiji along River Isuzu. The compound is filled with 'holy atmosphere,' and once a person enters this area he cannot help but feel purified within himself."

Again to ensure that no one can miss the moral, a poem of Emperor MEIJI is appended to the lesson, "On this day when I worship at the shrine beside River Isuzu, I feel that I have again entered the heavenly circles" (*Hisakatano ameni noboreru kokochishite Isuzuno miyani mairu kyōkana*).

The major issue of "The People's Duties" occupies three lessons in the Sixth Book selected for analysis. It begins: "We, the Japanese people, are by nature peace-loving people. However in case of a national crisis we, as the people, have made it our duty to serve the country courageously unmindful of our personal sacrifice."

It pleads the threefold obligation of a citizen: to be trained and ready to fight, to pay taxes to support the Army and Navy, and, oddly, to exercise the franchise so that the members of the Diet will truly represent the people. The equally vital issue of linking education with the national entity or *kokutai* is considered in the final four chapters. The first of these deals with education and consists of an adroit sales talk designed to encourage the graduating youth to continue in his education either through one of the secondary schools or through the part-time continuation or youth school (*seinen gakkō*). The last three of these chapters deal with the *Imperial Rescript on Education.* To the extent that the *Rescript* itself is nationalistic and objectionable the interpretation is also nationalistic and objectionable. It is, in effect, merely a slightly amplified paraphrase written in simpler language for the school children. If the *Rescript* can be preserved it is a little absurd to ban so innocent and parallel an interpretation.

One chapter in the Sixth Book selected for analysis is devoted to "Foreign Relations." Written after the invasion of China, published after the adoption of the plan for the nationalization of the schools, here if anywhere one should find subversive ultranationalist ideology if it truly formed an intrinsic part of the basic Japanese educational philosophy. So that no possible omission will change the context, the entire lesson is translated and quoted:

It is needless to emphasize the necessity of people living in the same neighborhood cooperating with each other to increase their common happiness. Similarly, it is necessary for the countries of the world to have friendly intercourse among them and by helping each other to increase the happiness of the peoples of the world and to maintain peace throughout the world. It is for this reason that the countries of the world today exchange ambassadors and ministers with each other and formulate various treaties among themselves.

Emperor MEIJI, too, had deep concern for the friendly intercourse among the nations of the world. In an Imperial Rescript given the people in the 41st year of MEIJI (1908), Emperor MEIJI commanded the people to cultivate international relations and receive the benefits of civilization along with other countries.

When a peace conference was held in Paris at the termination of the European War [first World War], Japan participated in this conference. At this conference a peace treaty was formulated, and as a part of this treaty the covenant of the League of Nations was agreed upon. When the League of Nations was established in the 9th year of TAISHŌ [1920], Emperor TAISHŌ gave an Imperial Rescript to the people commanding the people to realize the peaceful aim of the League of Nations and to make efforts to cultivate our national power and to make progress along with the world.

The present Emperor, too, is deeply concerned with the peace of the world. When he was the Crown Prince, the Emperor made a tour of the European countries and cultivated our amicable relations with the various countries of the world.

In this manner our nation has made it our national policy to maintain world peace and to develop civilization. Therefore we have cooperated earnestly with other countries since the inception of the League of Nations, but at the time of the establishment of Manchukuo, our government had a difference of opinion with other powers concerning the policy of maintaining peace in East Asia, so in the 8th year of SHŌWA [1933] we withdrew from the League of Nations. At that time, the present Emperor gave the people an Imperial Rescript commanding the people to establish an international peace in accordance with national belief and conviction.

To establish an international peace it is necessary for us to maintain the stability of East Asia. Consequently, we have formed a treaty with Manchukuo pledging each other to maintain our friendly relations and to defend our respective countries by cooperating with each other. Now we are making efforts to increase friendly and peaceful relations with China and to maintain the stability of East Asia by cooperating with each other, thus realizing our common prosperity. Only by so doing can we bring about the peace of the world.

We must not forget the importance of foreign relations. We must make every effort to understand the trend of the world and to have the world understand the conditions in East Asia. In our relations with foreigners let us make it our business to understand each other and thus bring about an increased happiness for the people in general.

There are two possible explanations of the apparently innocuous character of the vast majority of the *Shūshin* textbooks. One is that although the material is innocent the language in which it is presented is inflammatory and insidiously nationalistic. To a limited extent this charge may be substantiated. In those portions of the text where political or distantly historical matters are concerned the words that are used are necessarily ones which have certain propaganda value: the National Entity (*Kokutai*), Land of the Great Eight Islands (*Ōyashima no Kuni*), Peaceful Land (*Yasukuni*), Greater East Asia War (*Dai Toa Sensō*), World under One Roof (*Hakkō Ichi-u*), Land of the Rising Sun (*Hinomoto no Kuni*), etc. Although originally these terms were not emotion-loaded words, by the outbreak of the war with the United States in 1941 they had taken on color from their use in propaganda. It is also true that where reference is made in any manner to the Emperor Institution the honorifics of the Japanese language make of each word a propaganda title: Deity Incarnate, i.e., the Emperor (*Akitsumikami*), August-Child-of-the-Deities-in-Heaven (*Amatsukami no Miko*), the Sacred One (*Hijiri*), Heaven and Earth, i.e., Japan (*Ametsuchi*), Land of the Gods (*Shinkoku*), etc.

The second explanation is that although the text itself is reasonably free from ultranationalism, the teacher is officially charged with inflammatory interpretations in his teaching. This is an accusation readily investigated. Two basic instructions were given the teachers of Japan: the propaganda volume, *Kokutai no Hongi*, which has already been considered, and a set of teachers' manuals to accompany the official textbooks in *Shūshin*. There can be no doubt of the ultranationalism of the *Kokutai no Hongi* though there can be very grave doubts as to its effectiveness in influencing the teachers. If for no other reason it was ineffective because it was written in language too difficult for the majority to understand. But if any instrument should give evidence of the basic educational philosophy of Japan the instructions to teachers on how they were to explain the lessons in Japanese ethics certainly should be that one. A number of editions of these teachers' manuals beginning with 1906 were analyzed and the ones in use at the time of the outbreak of the war were translated. It will perhaps be most revealing to consider the manual which accompanied the February 1940 edition of the Sixth Book which has already been noted.

From a technical point of view the teachers' manual is more than adequate, even superior. It is divided into a number of chapters coinciding with the lessons to be taught. Each chapter contains: (1) a statement of purpose, (2) a copy of the students' lesson with detailed notes on factual content, such as dates, first names, geography of places mentioned, etc., (3) a series of important teaching points or things to emphasize, and (4) supplementary material to assist the teacher who does not have access to libraries or other sources, such as full copies of the *Constitution*, laws, famous speeches, historical sketches pertinent to the lesson, even explanations of difficult grammatical or orthographical passages with notes on the semantics and philology of the section.

The opening lesson, "The Great Imperial Shrine," is presented for the following "purpose": "The purpose of this chapter is to teach the children the Imperial Household's deep reverence and the nation's high respect for the Great Imperial Shrine, and to deepen the children's veneration for the founder of the Empire."

Two notes are pertinent to this analysis, the first revealing a National Shintoistic bias and the second reiterating the theme of loyalty to the Emperor Institution:

7. The people must also place a hemp idol in their homes and dutifully respect the founder of our country; and even those who live in inconvenient parts of the country should make a pilgrimage to the Ise Shrine at least once in their lifetime.

8. We, born as subjects of Imperial Japan, must always respect the founder of our country, endeavor to make our country an eternity, know the reason for our nation's solemnity, and guard and maintain the prosperity of our eternal Imperial Throne.

Rapidly reviewing the stated "purpose" at the beginning of each lesson it becomes apparent that the basic philosophy is that of loyalty to the Emperor Institution; all other ethical standards are subordinate:

Chapter 2—The Imperial Household
The purpose of this Chapter is to understand the solemnity of the throne and the greatness of the Imperial Household, and to inspire the true loyalty of the students to the Emperor.

Chapter 3—Loyalty
The purpose of this Chapter is to strengthen one's determination to exert full devotion and faith in one's sovereign and to fulfill the great cause for the sake of our Emperor, and have the children practice this effort in their everyday life.

Chapter 4—Filial Piety
The purpose of this Chapter is to teach the students that loyalty and filial duties are one and the same thing in our country and to encourage them to [venerate] the idea of loyalty and filial piety.

Chapter 13—Duties of the People
The purpose of this Chapter is to teach the students about compulsory military service and to fulfill the duties of protecting the country and enhancing Imperial prestige.

Chapter 16—Foreign Relations
The purpose of this Chapter is to instruct the students in the importance of diplomatic relations in extending Imperial influences throughout the world and in promoting the great cause.

There is no need to continue a systematic review of the propaganda theme which is woven throughout all the teachers' manuals. It is indicative of the fundamental educational philosophy of Japan, but it is not novel. It is the theme of Divine Origin, Divine Characteristics, Divine Leadership, and Divine Mission. It is the theme of ultranationalism, the theme of the Imperial Institution supported by the quasi-religious mythology of National Shinto. It is a detailed application of the philosophy of the *Imperial Rescript on Education,* and all its militaristic and ultranationalistic interpretations, applied to the everyday classroom teaching of the most remote instructor in the school system. It is the incontrovertible proof of Japan's educational philosophy of extreme nationalism.

The Impact of Defeat

The psychological and physical impacts of defeat which made such remarkable changes in the outward characteristics of the educational system have not been equally effective in modifying the basic philosophy of education.

There have been at least five influences which have tended to reform the prior educational philosophy. The first and most obvious one of these has been the official SCAP directives on education, principally the AG 350 (22 Oct 45) CIE Directive, "Administration of the Educational System of Japan." The second most important of these influences has been the *Report of the United States Education Mission to Japan*. The third has been the enunciated statement of policy made by the United States Department of State and the Far Eastern Commission on behalf of the Occupying Powers. The fourth has been the series of statements made by official or semiofficial educational conferences and bodies in the Allied Powers which have been convened for the purpose of planning the renaissance of education in the postwar world. These presumably represent the extracted essence of the great body of tradition, educational and sociological, which has existed in the responsible and progressive nations of the world. And the final one is the expression of awakened Japanese thought.

The Educational Policy Directive. The SCAP Directive AG 350 (22 Oct 45) CIE, "Administration of the Educational System of Japan," is a policy document. Officially it was issued to inform the newly formed Cabinet of Baron SHIDEHARA Kijuro of the "objectives and policies of the occupation with regard to Education." Actually the officers in the Civil Information and Education Section of Headquarters who initiated this directive were motivated at least as much by the desire to crystallize Occupation policy along more constructive and less punitive lines than that which was feared would be the form of an educational policy written by the career military officers who were expected to replace the reserve officers being demobilized after Surrender. This directive was, therefore, something of a liberal and constructive hedge against an opposing philosophy of retribution and rigid control. Because it is the most fundamental document bearing on education to appear in the Occupation, the body of the text is quoted in full:

1. In order that the newly formed Cabinet of the Imperial Japanese Government shall be fully informed of the objectives and policies of the occupation with regard to Education, it is hereby directed that:
   a. The content of all intruction will be critically examined, revised, and controlled in accordance with the following policies:
      (1) Dissemination of militaristic and ultra-nationalistic ideology will be prohibited and all military education and drill will be discontinued.
      (2) Inculcation of concepts and establishment of practices in harmony with representative government, international peace, the dignity of the individual, and such fundamental

human rights as the freedom of assembly, speech, and religion, will be encouraged.

b. The personnel of all educational institutions will be investigated, approved or removed, reinstated, appointed, reorientated, and supervised in accordance with the following policies:

(1) Teachers and educational officials will be examined as rapidly as possible and all career military personnel, persons who have been active exponents of militarism and ultra-nationalism, and those actively antagonistic to the policies of the occupation will be removed.

(2) Teachers and educational officials who have been dismissed, suspended, or forced to resign for liberal or anti-militaristic opinions or activities, will be declared immediately eligible for and if properly qualified will be given preference in reappointment.

(3) Discrimination against any student, teacher, or educational official on grounds of race, nationality, creed, political opinion, or social position, will be prohibited, and immediate steps will be taken to correct inequities which have resulted from such discrimination.

(4) Students, teachers, and educational officials will be encouraged to evaluate critically and intelligently the content of instruction and will be permitted to engage in free and unrestricted discussion of issues involving political, civil, and religious liberties.

(5) Students, teachers, educational officials, and public will be informed of the objectives and policies of the occupation, of the theory and practices of representative government, and of the part played by militaristic leaders, their active collaborators, and those who by passive acquiescence committed the nation to war with the inevitable result of defeat, distress, and the present deplorable state of the Japanese people.

c. The instrumentalities of educational processes will be critically examined, revised, and controlled in accordance with the following policies:

(1) Existing curricula, textbooks, teaching manuals, and instructional materials, the use of which is temporarily permitted on an emergency basis, will be examined as rapidly as possible and those portions designed to promote a militaristic or ultra-nationalistic ideology will be eliminated.

(2) New curricula, textbooks, teaching manuals, and instructional materials designed to produce an educated, peace-

ful, and responsible citizenry will be prepared and will be substituted for existing materials as rapidly as possible.

(3) A normally operating educational system will be re-established as rapidly as possible, but where limited facilities exist preference will be given to elementary education and teacher training.

2. The Japanese Ministry of Education will establish and maintain adequate liaison with the appropriate staff section of the Office of the Supreme Commander for the Allied Powers, and upon request will submit reports describing in detail all action taken to comply with the provisions of this directive.

3. All officials and subordinates of the Japanese Government affected by the terms of this directive, and all teachers and school officials, both public and private, will be held personally accountable for compliance with the spirit as well as the letter of the policies enunciated in this directive.

The reactions to this statement of policy, and of equally fundamental educational philosophy, were varied. The Supreme Commander looked on it and found it good and issued the directive without a change. The "tough peace" school of the Occupation Headquarters looked on it and found it bad and set about stiffening its punitive measures by counterintelligence raids and similar administrative devices. Some of the teachers in New York City were reported to have cynically remarked that it gave the Japanese a degree of academic freedom they themselves did not enjoy. Some of the teachers in Tokyo admitted frank bewilderment —they neither knew the words nor the concepts. One immediate result was evident. To the propaganda terms of opprobrium, "militarism" (*gunkokushugi*) and "ultranationalism" (*kokusuishugi*), two new ones of laudation were added, "democracy" (*minshushugi*), and "freedom" (*jiyū*). It is interesting that the English word "liberty" is usually rendered as *minshushugi,* thus making it synonymous with "democracy." No one seemed to have a very clear idea of what "freedom" meant, but it was felt that if anything were linked with that nebulous term it would receive the sanction of the Occupation Headquarters. School children striking against an unpopular teacher, an emotional college student interrupting a class to deliver a stump speech in a political campaign, a struggling private school pre-empting former military barracks by squatter's right, a professor using his class to excoriate the existing government and deliver a diatribe against the present

Emperor—all of these were evidences that Japan would have to build a psychological context in which the terms of this directive would have meaning. And in the process the terms of "democracy," "liberty," and "freedom" might diverge markedly from their meanings in Occidental nations.

The Report of the United States Education Mission to Japan. The composition, organization, and prestige of the USEMJ has already been considered. One of its five committees was that on the Aims and Content of Japanese Education working under the inspired chairmanship of Dr. Isaac L. KANDEL, Professor of Comparative Education at Teachers College, Columbia University, and Editor of *School and Society*. While the Mission's report has never been accepted as the official policy of the Occupying Powers, it has exerted an influence over Japanese educational thought in some ways more powerful than that of official directives. It was prepared with the assistance of the best available Japanese educators and has been consciously followed in the preparation of most of the subsequent Japanese educational reforms. The statement on "The Aims of Education" is quoted in full:

Before the reconstruction of education in Japan can be undertaken, it is imperative that the bases of a philosophy of education in a democracy be clarified. To repeat constantly the word "democracy" is meaningless unless it is clothed with content.

A system of education for life in a democracy will rest upon the recognition of the worth and dignity of the individual. It will be so organized as to provide educational opportunity in accordance with the abilities and aptitudes of each person. Through content and methods of instruction it will foster freedom of inquiry, and training in the ability to analyze critically. It will encourage a wide discussion of factual information within the competence of students at different stages of their development. These ends cannot be promoted if the work of the school is limited to prescribed courses of study and to a single approved textbook in each subject. The success of education in a democracy cannot be measured in terms of uniformity and standardization.

Education should prepare the individual to become a responsible and cooperating member of society. It must be understood, too, that the term "individual" applies equally to boys and girls and to men and women. In building for a new Japan, individuals will need the knowledge which will develop them as workers, citizens, and human beings. They will need to apply that knowledge in a spirit of free inquiry as society members participating in the manifold aspects of its organization. All this is in harmony with the fundamental principles laid down in the Charter of the United Nations Organization and in the draft Constitution of the United Nations Educational, Scientific, and Cultural Organization.

It follows that the central authority should not prescribe content, methods of instruction, or textbooks, but should limit its activities in this area to the publication of outlines, suggestions and teaching guides. As soon as they have been suitably prepared for their professional work, teachers should be left free to adapt content and methods of instruction to the needs and abilities of their pupils in various environments and to the society in which they are to play a part.

The reorientation of Japanese education involves not only the negative aspect of a complete elimination of militaristic, ultra-nationalistic, and other objectionable features of instruction, but a careful appraisal of those aspects of the culture that will enrich the new program. For example, in such subjects as history, ethics, geography, literature, art and music, consideration must be given to what can be retained that will increase cooperation between Japan and other nations.

Education cannot proceed in a vacuum, nor is a complete break with a people's cultural past conceivable. There must be some continuity even in a crisis such as the present. It should be the task of all engaged in the educational activities of Japan to analyze their cultural traditions in order to discover what is worth preserving as humane ideas and ideals that will give a strength to the new plans. Here the Japanese will find a legitimate and inspiring basis for loyalty and patriotism. The injunction of the Meiji period to "pursue knowledge everywhere" is well taken, but a frame of reference must be found in the consciousness of a worthy national culture, so as to avoid the dualism that comes from the constant addition of new elements.

The essence of this discussion of the aims of education is that freedom of teaching and of inquiry must be encouraged not only for the preservation but for the enrichment of the national culture of Japan. The ability to distinguish between fact and mythology, between the real and the fanciful, flourishes in a scientific spirit of critical analysis.

This means a shift from the aim, foremost in the minds of parents, students, and teachers, of passing examinations. A system of education that is dominated by preparation for examinations becomes formal and stereotyped, it makes for conformity on the part of teachers and students. It stifles freedom of inquiry and critical judgment, lending itself readily to manipulation by the authorities in the interests of a narrow bureaucracy rather than of society as a whole. Finally, the system engenders an abnormal competitive spirit that may lead at times to cheating and corruption, or to an unhealthy frustration.

Nevertheless, there is a place for new types of examinations that do not make the future of youth dependent upon the hazard of chance. This problem was the subject of an international inquiry in which some ten countries participated from 1931 to 1938. The study of the examination issue requires agencies of criticism and the creation of centers for educational research. Every possible device must be employed, if an accurate knowledge of a student's abilities is to be obtained. It is not an accident, but the direct result of the ideal of providing equal educational opportunity for all, that guidance and counseling are given such a prominent place in many post-war plans for educational reconstruction.

Education, of course, is not confined to the school alone; the family, the neighborhood and other social structures have their part to play in it. Education in the new Japan should seek to open as many sources and methods as possible for acquiring meaningful knowledge. Unless the learner is an active participant in the process of education, that is, unless he learns with understanding, education becomes an accumulation of items to be forgotten as soon as examinations are over. (Pp. 7–9, official copy.)

Department of State Policy. The opening paragraph of the Department of State "Policy for the Revision of the Japanese Educational System," approved by the Far Eastern Commission (FEC) on 27 March 1947, contains a statement of "Guiding Principles and Objectives." It is quoted in full:

1. Education should be looked upon as the pursuit of truth, as a preparation for life in a democratic nation, and as a training for the social and political responsibilities which freedom entails. Emphasis should be placed on the dignity and worth of the individual, on independent thought and initiative, and on developing a spirit of inquiry. The inter-dependent character of international life should be stressed. The spirit of justice, fair play, and respect for the rights of others, particularly minorities, and the necessity for friendship based upon mutual respect for people of all races and religions, should be emphasized. Special emphasis should also be placed on the teaching of the sanctity of the pledged word in all human relations, whether between individuals or nations. Measures should be taken as rapidly as possible to achieve equality of educational opportunity for all regardless of sex or social position. The revision of the Japanese educational system should in a large measure be undertaken by the Japanese themselves and steps

should be taken to carry out such revision in accordance with the principles and objectives set forth in this paper.

The remainder of the statement of official policy deals with the application of the fundamental philosophy just quoted to the mechanics and procedures of the educational system. The prior authorship and influence of the *Report* of the USEMJ and the SCAP Educational Policy Directive are discernible in the text. The policy statements contained in this document are of three types. One canonizes and lends official sanction to operational policy which had been in effect for months. Thus Paragraph 2 directs that the teachers be screened and those objectionable on ultranationalistic, militaristic, or totalitarian grounds be forbidden to teach—after the screening of the more than half a million teachers had been completed; and Paragraph 8 directs that textbooks be censored and new ones substituted for the objectionable ones—after more than 190 million new texts had been distributed. The second type of policy statement generalizes upon a specific policy which until the publication of this document had been enforced only within restricted limits. Thus this document directs that the "classical sports such as *kendō*, which encourage the martial spirit, should be totally abandoned"—after *budō*, which includes *kendō* and the other military arts, had been voluntarily banned from tax-supported schools by the Japanese. Perhaps the most interesting element, however, is the third, that of defining educational philosophy by implication. Three paragraphs, 7, 11, 17, are especially pertinent.

7. Teaching of ultra-nationalism, state Shintoism, veneration of the Emperor, exaltation of the state over the individual, and race superiority, should be eliminated from the educational system.

The Emperor is retained, and his position as "symbol of the State" and *de facto* Executive Chief of the nation is written into the new *Constitution* with the approval and guidance of the Occupation Forces, yet by this policy statement the schools are forbidden to teach the students that they shall "venerate," shall regard with admiration and deference, their leader. The Japanese have been assured that the Allied Powers will not "impose upon Japan any form of government not supported by the freely expressed will of the people," yet by this document the schools are forbidden to teach the political concept that the State is superior to the individual, one which in the past the Japanese have accepted and which at the present many of the World Powers do themselves accept. The philosophy of democracy has brought about a shift in political policy. The Japanese may elect any form of government they wish, so long as it is a democracy. And this ambivalence produces a perplexing ideological anomaly. What is the Emperor? He is not a god, for he disclaims this himself. And he is not the sovereign, for the new *Constitution* locates sovereignty in the people. What force, then, can his Imperial rescripts have?

This policy states:

11. Imperial rescripts should not be used as a basis of instruction, study, or ceremonies in schools.

Yet the *Imperial Rescript on Education* is still the basic codified Japanese educational philosophy and Imperial rescripts are the basic core of the legal structure. Shall the school be forbidden to teach respect of the law?

17. The Japanese Government should exercise such control over the educational system as will ensure the achievement of the objectives of the occupation, particularly the reforms called for by this policy decision. Subject to the foregoing, and to maintenance of standards prescribed by the Government, the responsibility for the local administrations of educational establishments should in due time be decentralized. Japanese parents and citizens should be encouraged to feel a sense of individual responsibility for the achievement of the objectives set out in paragraph 1. Where practicable they should be associated with the control, development, and work of the schools and other educational institutions.

Here again, in the policy of decentralization to secure democratic direction and to preclude totalitarian usurpation, is the theme of education for representative government. Whether or not the Japanese sincerely accept or merely temporarily accede to these ideological demands, it is certain that the pattern of American democracy will constitute a major part of the philosophical impact of Defeat and Occupation.

The Foreign Educational Tradition. Japan has not been totally isolated from the great educational traditions of the Occident. The library of one private school near Tokyo, the *Tamagawa Gakuen*, which survived the war contains nearly 100,000 volumes on education collected from the literatures of America and Europe. For

70 years there has been a constant stream of Japanese students returning from study abroad and introducing into Japan Occidental educational theories. One of the first constructive moves undertaken by the Occupation Headquarters in the rehabilitation of education was the establishment of a free library in the center of Tokyo in which virtually all the major titles in English which had appeared during Japan's wartime cultural blackout were made available to any Japanese who could read the language. Japan after defeat was like a dry sponge eager to soak up the ideas of the victor.

It might appear both presumptuous and superfluous to attempt in this brief account a summary of what these foreign traditions of educational philosophy are. Presumably the official statements already considered faithfully translate these traditions into concise canons of educational thought. But at the risk of repetition one or two statements made by national or international bodies of educators will be noted since they conveniently exemplify the thinking of their respective nations.

The Educational Policies Commission of the National Education Association of the United States (NEA) in May 1943 published a short report, *Education and the People's Peace*, in which they recalled the words used in the so-called "peace convention" held by the NEA in Milwaukee in July 1919. They quoted: "If our ideals of humanity and democracy are to continue, *even for ourselves as an American people*, it is essential that we . . . *demand from all nations the education of their people in the fundamental ideals and principles of good government*." Written in the second year of America's participation in the second World War, *Education and the People's Peace* attempts to define the basic issue of the war and of education. On pp. 17–18 it states:

We intend not only that our free way of life shall survive, but also that it shall spread and flourish.

We are not yet clear and unanimous as to what the free way of life means. But we see some of the principles upon which it rests. We see that recognition of these principles is essential in order that our broader war aims may be attained.

One of these is the principle of earned security, the principle that all men and women should have an opportunity, thru their own exertions, to achieve mental and economic security for themselves and their children. This security is not given as charity from one person to another. It is something to be achieved. It is the *opportunity* to achieve it that must be universal, equitable, unalienable, and genuine.

Another is the principle of peaceful change. Warfare has hitherto been one of the great means of bringing about changes, sometimes highly desirable changes, in human relations. Since we propose to try to end war, we must provide some other means of bringing about constant and necessary changes thru cooperative, orderly, peaceful procedures. The only method of peaceful change that has been reasonably successful has been the method of open, cooperative discussion and action. Hence, it will be necessary to accompany any proposed peace plan with plans for the extension of freedom of discussion and teaching and for the provision of universal education.

A third principle requires the full use of science and technology in the production of wholesome goods and services. If we limit the term "essential" merely to the minimal provisions of food and shelter, there is no longer any need for scarcity of the essentials of life. But if we include in the term "essential" the various refinements of living—of food, of clothing, of shelter, of cultural life—then scarcity will never be removed, because the capacities of people to want and use goods and services are all but unlimited. Every new invention satisfies some needs and creates others.

A fourth principle relates to intellectual and religious freedom. People have a right to think and believe as they please, subject to the one, but crucial, condition that their opinions and beliefs shall not lead them to actions which destroy the liberties of other people. In practice, this principle means free access to knowledge, untrammeled teaching, and the universal availability of educational opportunity.

This is perhaps as direct a statement of basic goals as is available. Most thinking evidenced by the educators of the United Nations has been of the negative type leading to eradication of recognized abuses in totalitarian systems. Typical of this viewpoint is the opening paragraph of the section entitled "Proposals for the Reconstruction of the Educational Programs of the Axis Countries" in the study, *Education for International Security*, prepared by the International Education Assembly at the Harpers Ferry meeting in September 1943:

The political philosophy of the nazis, fascists and Japanese militarists permeates and dominates the cultural life of the axis peoples. Their systems of education glorify war, perpetuate the myth of racial superiority, and subordinate the individual to the interests of the state and party. More important still is the fact that education is made the means of giving permanence to the regimentation which has been established by force. Those elements of the axis populations and of conquered peoples who are regarded only as workers are denied access to all schooling above the elementary level except vocational training. On the other hand, those elements of the axis populations who are regarded as the ruling group are given special training in every field of learning. In effect, therefore, the essential characteristic of nazi, fascist and present Japanese educational systems is the denial of the fundamental principle of the democratic social order, namely, individual development through free access to the entire body of knowledge.

Yet even this attack on the totalitarian educational philosophy reveals a structure of irreducible minimum in the democratic system which must be met by the Japanese if their postwar education is to be acceptable to the democratic nations. Similarly an analysis of the recommendations made for an international educational organization by such groups as the Universities Committee on Postwar International Problems in its pamphlet, *Education and World Peace* (Boston, the Committee, 1943), and later incorporated in the *Charter* and *Constitution* of the United Nations Educational, Scientific, and Cultural Organization (UNESCO), reveals a background pattern of educational philosophy which has never adequately been codified but which exists as a powerful and recognizable tradition. This is the belief which is stated in the Preamble of the UNESCO *Constitution*: ". . . the States Parties to This Constitution, believing in full and equal opportunities for education for all, in the unrestricted pursuit of objective truth, and in the free exchange of ideas and knowledge."

How to implement this basic philosophy is a problem not only perplexing to the Japanese but also to the signatory powers in UNESCO. The Department of State publication, *UNESCO: A Provisional Program* (Washington, Office of United States Public Affairs, October 1946 [Mimeo.]), pp. 12–13, states:

How best to direct the process of education beyond national and away from selfish ends is far from clear. It will be necessary to find ways of turning feelings of aggressiveness, combativeness, jealousy, anxiety into constructive channels; of fostering cooperativeness, tolerance, kindness, goodwill; of softening or eliminating national, dogmatic or racial tensions and conflicts, often rooted in age-long traditions.

Awakened Japanese Thought. There can be little doubt that one of the potentially most powerful, and promising, impacts of Defeat upon the traditional educational philosophy of Japan has been the impact of awakened Japanese thought. Its presence is obvious, its sincerity imponderable, its effects undetermined. An attempt to evaluate it faces the problem recurrent in the chemical and biological sciences of having positive qualitative proof of existence without the availability of an accurate quantitative analysis. For each public expression of this changed educational philosophy may be nothing more than a calculated tactic of evasion or an unconscious repetition of Occupational-sponsored Occidental beliefs. Were the Japanese not quite conscious of this possibility, and hence prone to discount the sincerity of such statements, it would make little practical difference, since the impacts of Japanese liberal statements over an extended period of time cannot fail to have a profound influence on the thinking of Japanese educators.

The pattern presented is a reasonably accurate reproduction of the pattern of Occidental thought which has been considered in terms of Occupational policy and statements of responsible organs in the Allied Powers. Thus the *Guide to New Education in Japan,* an official publication of the Ministry of Education in May 1946, after advocating the elimination of militarism and ultranationalism presents a positive program for the inculcation of "respect for Human Nature, Personality, and Individuality" and for the "development of Scientific Standard and Philosophical and Religious Culture." The objective of education in the new Japan is stated in the chapter on "The Construction of a Peaceful, Cultural State, and the Mission of Educators." Two passages are directly in point:

For the establishment of a peaceful, cultural state, it is necessary to carry out democratization in politics, economy, society, and many other fields, and thereby to make the national life just and equitable, bright and cheerful, and secure and stabilized. . . . (P. 59.)

When the buds of the mind of the youth fostered by present day educators have made a splendid development after five, ten, or twenty years time, militarism and ultra-nationalism will have been cleanly wiped out; the real power intrinsic to human nature, personality and individuality, will have been given full play to, with scientific sureness, philosophical breadth, and religious depth; the principles of democracy will have universally been carried out; a peaceful cultural state will have been established; and the mankind of the world will be enjoying eternal peace and happiness. Not to let these high and distant ideals pass away as a mere dream, to realize them surely step by step through the daily activities of education—thereon rests the hope and joy of educators. (P. 65.)

While this philosophy obtains, profound changes are being accomplished. It is possible that these changes will erect barriers against retrogression into the traditional pattern of Japanese thought which will be sufficiently strong to weather the resurgence of conservatism which must be expected after prolonged Occupation and the resumption of self-direction. It is also possible that the ideas which official Japan is now selling under duress may be so attractive to a people emerging from feudalism and thought control that the ideas may survive through their own intrinsic merit. That there exists a powerful and not always clandestine opposition to these new ideas is certain. The concept of *kokutai* is not dead. In November 1946, after review by the Bureau of Legislation (*Hōsei Kyoku*), the Japanese Imperial Cabinet published a booklet entitled *Shin Kempō Kaisetsu* ("Exposition on the New Constitution") in which the government took the position that the *kokutai*, the national entity, had not undergone any change. While the *kokutai* remains, the fundamental philosophy is unchanged and reform is an illusion.

Kōdō—The Destiny of a Lonely Man

After a searching scrutiny of the philosophical tenets which have in the past been officially held, and those which today appear to have currency in Japan, the pattern of a developing philosophy which would be acceptable to the other nations of the world becomes fairly clear. At least in the present circumstances it appears equally acceptable to the Japanese. Militarism, in the sense of blind and arrogant use of military might to accomplish a disputed end, shall be rejected. Ultranationalism, in the sense of a Divine Mission to become the political and economic ruler of the world, justified on the grounds of a Divine Origin, Divine Leadership, and the Divine Characteristics of nation and people, shall also be rejected. The concept of National Shintoism, as a quasi-religious ethical standard imposed upon the people through political force, shall be prohibited. The inherent dignity of the individual shall be recognized and certain political and social rights shall be respected. These rights shall include freedom of religion, freedom of speech and assembly, freedom of access to knowledge and the truth, protection from police and political oppression, the right to organized self-government, recognition of the equality of sexes, races, economic and social groups in the law, and a stabilized economy which provides the individual with a reasonable expectation of freedom from want. As applied to education this philosophy postulates the existence of full and equal educational opportunities for all people, freedom of research and the pursuit of objective truth, and freedom of communication and the exchange of ideas.

But fundamental in this mass of principles and applications drawn from the Anglo-Saxon form of democracy which has evolved in the past millennium, is one concept which has not yet been honestly faced. Democracy in the Occident could only succeed when the political theory of Divine Right of Kings was discarded. Democracy in Japan can only succeed when the traditional form of the Emperor Institution is equally discarded. A mere renunciation of divinity by the Emperor is not enough. The concept of a *kokutai*, of a sort of unique national characteristic which is inherent and immutable, which is not only capable but divinely destined to eternal survival, makes any such statement of expediency of no consequence. Can a god, however sincerely he may speak, become less than a god by a mere denial?

The Emperor was retained because the Allied Powers considered that his value as a puppet for the control of the civil population outweighed his demerits as the symbol of a discredited ideology, as the responsible leader of a defeated nation, and as an active participant in the war crimes for which other leaders have been tried and executed. The Occupying Powers openly stated that he was being retained to be manipulated. The Occupation Forces took a gamble in which they risked a possible future political impasse in order to ensure that they would not suffer the losses of a contested invasion nor the harassment and attrition of a fanatical Underground. The gamble was won but perhaps at too great a price. Even a puppet has a continuing influence and when that puppet is truly revered by the civil population his position as buffer between the foreign invaders and the people is not without dignity and prestige. The Emperor of Japan could not today be attacked as a war criminal, even if his guilt were established, without discrediting the victors who have in effect been his allies in the government of Japan. Only the Japanese themselves could consistently remove this constant threat of an Emperor who has only superficially been stripped of his power and who continues to enjoy the complete loyalty of the vast majority of his people.

The solution which the Occupying Powers obviously desired was public acceptance of the Emperor as a respected but not as a religiously revered benevolent monarch. They hoped that he would be divested of virtually all power but would retain that indefinable aura of traditional leadership which in the British Commonwealth has so effectively unified its diverse peoples under the English king. They gambled that this devaluation of the Emperor could be compressed into a single generation and not require the slow evolution which characterized European adoptions of constitutional monarchies. Perhaps they were right but the evidence to date does not appear to support their hopes.

This vital and unsolved problem underlies almost every philosophical dilemma which today confronts the educators of the nation. What to do with the *Imperial Rescript on Education* is still as unsolved as on the day of Capitulation. How to treat loyalty to the Emperor is still a question mark. Lip service to democracy is demanded, but the question of what shadow or substance Japanese democracy shall be is still unanswered.

III

"A BULWARK NEVER FAILING"

The Problem of Organization

THE Japanese educational system has continued as potentially dangerous as it was before Pearl Harbor. Unacceptable teachers and officials have been purged but can tomorrow be recalled. Hundreds of millions of textbooks have been censored but can tomorrow be republished. The rights of students have been proclaimed but can tomorrow be revoked. Curricula have been revised but can be revised anew. A philosophy of democracy and freedom has been stated but a philosophy of totalitarianism and repression can as easily be enunciated. The most basic reform of all, the achievement of accessibility to knowledge through a fundamentally revised writing system, promises eventual capacity for self-government, but has met with indifference or antagonism from the Occupational Authorities and obstruction from the vested Japanese interests. The Japanese people have failed to achieve that absolutely essential factor in educational reform, direct control of their school system. They exchanged a Japanese military dictatorship for an Occupational military dictatorship. The old was brutally jingoistic while the new was benevolently paternalistic. Both manipulated the school system to their own ends. Reforms have been made, but as long as the existing educational organization remains intact, the school system will remain an inviting tool to whatever group is temporarily in power.

Reorganization of the educational system is the third serious and immediate problem facing Japanese educators. This has been recognized alike by Japanese and foreign observers. More effort has been concentrated on solving this problem than on any other educational reform since the Occupation began. Reorganization of the administrative system held top priority in the Education Division of Occupation Headquarters from early in the spring of 1946. The United States Education Mission to Japan in April 1946 recognized its fundamental importance. The Japanese Ministry of Education and the Japanese Education Reform Council, established to work with the Ministry and the United States Education Mission, publicly stated that this problem was the most pressing and the most important. On 19 January 1947 the Headquarters of the Supreme Commander for the Allied Powers and the Japanese Ministry of Education simultaneously announced a sweeping organizational reform which presumably was considered a solution of the problem, at least in principle. Evidence exists, however, that would indicate that this plan of reform, admittedly unrealizable for several years, has failed to solve the essential problem of overconcentration of control, even in principle.

Administrative reform of the educational system is indissolubly linked with a vast number of other educational decisions. Primarily it involves efficiency, expense, and controls.

Efficiency is a complex condition. In its simplest form it can be measured by an administrative index, such as the per capita cost of providing a standard instructional program, or the time elapsed between enunciation of a policy and its realization in the field. It can be increased by better accounting methods, more efficient use of personnel, and development of effective mass instructional methods. Beyond this simple administrative efficiency, however, there is a more refined form of educational efficiency. Traditionally this has been measured by the reduction in the illiteracy rate, lessening of the attrition between grades in school, elimination of loss in transfer from one type of program to another. Measured in such terms Japan in the past has enjoyed an efficient school system. Even with the chaotic conditions that are an aftermath of the war, the Japanese system ranks high in comparison with most foreign and all Asiatic nations. In a democratic system, however, education is something more than the mass production of a predetermined and uniform citizen unit destined to serve the State. Education searches for and develops creative talent. It recognizes individual differences. It attempts to create knowledge and not merely to pass on knowledge. Here efficiency is measured in the tenuous terms of leadership. Japan must determine how it can increase the over-all efficiency of its educational system. Maintenance of its standard of administrative efficiency is desirable. But development of efficiency in detecting and promoting the growth of nascent leadership, creative ability, and intelligent self-direction is absolutely essential to survival.

Expense in educational reform is connected with but not necessarily a simple function of efficiency. Increased business efficiency may be expected to lower the cost of education, but increased instructional efficiency almost inevitably increases it. Prewar Japan traditionally spent more for education than for all its military services combined. In the light of the nation's material destruction and the probability of long-enduring burdens of reparations, an increased educational allocation for any extended period appears both improbable and undesirable. Reform costs money, yet failure is the most expensive program of all. Japan must determine whether it can afford its projected program of educational reform. It must equally decide whether it can afford not to have reform.

These are the elements which both the Japanese and the Allied Powers have considered. But the problem of control, though recognized, has not been met so squarely. The extreme centralization of the existing educational system has made possible an amazing record of efficient demilitarization of the schools since the Surrender. It was perhaps unrealistic to expect the Occupational Authorities to destroy so convenient, and so typically military, an instrument for policy dissemination and control. It is naïve to expect the Ministry of Education and its subordinate prefectural educational bureaus to officiate voluntarily at their own abdication. The unorganized, uninformed, and unrepresented people of Japan are incapable of accomplishing such a decentralization of educational control. The present leaders of Japan, both the sincerely democratic Japanese and the thoughtful foreign advisers, must ask themselves one question: "Does the added efficiency of a highly centralized educational system outweigh the danger of leaving intact a tool by which a small power clique can control the schools?"

Out of Ages Past

The formal educational system of Japan is almost entirely a product of the past 80 years. It dates from the beginning of the Meiji Restoration and specifically from three events of overwhelming importance: the *Charter Oath of Five Articles* (6 April 1868), in which the Emperor enunciated the principle of seeking foreign knowledge; the *Educational Code of 1872*, which established in principle a national, tax-supported, and compulsory educational system having extreme centralization of control; and the *Imperial Rescript on Education* (30 October 1890), which established the policy of nationalism and loyalty to the Imperial Institution.

So completely had the educational structure discarded the forms of pre-Meiji education that an impartial observer in 1935 would have been hard put to it to find even vestigial traces. But the cultural heritage of a nation seldom is completely supplanted and almost never dies. By 1937 there was clearly apparent a reawakening of the intellectual isolationism and extreme nationalism which had characterized Japan under the Tokugawa Shogunate (1603–1867). It was paced by a revival of Pure Shinto, or Revival of Ancient-Learning Shinto (*Fukkō Shintō*) made famous by MOTOORI Norinaga (1730–1801) and his contemporaries. From the publication of the notorious *Kokutai no Hongi* ("Cardinal Principles of the National Entity of Japan") by the Bureau of Thought Control in the Ministry of Education in 1937 until the initiation of the National School Reform in April 1941, there was clearly evident a resurgence of ancient or at least a modern nationalistic interpretation of the ancient, cultural patterns of Japan. The war and later the Occupation prevented the continued development of this into an educational system, but the threat of changes made or contemplated is sufficiently alarming to warrant a brief review of the pre-Meiji educational tradition.

Despite Japanese claims to the contrary, formal education did not occupy an important position in Japan before the close of the Tokugawa Shogunate. From time to time culture and individual scholarship did. Historical references to schools are relatively few and fragmentary, and until 712–720 when the *Kojiki* and *Nihongi* were compiled, are nonexistent. Sweeping and at times quite unjustifiable deductions as to what must have been the educational structure of the country have been based on isolated events and inconclusive documentary references. The historical exactness of these traditions, however, need not concern us here. Since they are generally accepted by the Japanese it makes little practical difference, in so far as their effect as traditions is concerned, whether they are historically true or not.

Pre-Meiji Education. Five basically different educational periods are discernible: the preliterary age of tribal and clan government (B.C. 660–A.D. 285); the age of the introduction of Chinese

learning and Court and temple tutors (A.D. 285–701); the age of
the *Taihō-ryō* (Law Code of the Great Treasure, compiled in
A.D. 701 in the reign of Emperor MOMMU) (A.D. 701–1185); the
age of military ascendancy (*buke jidai*), and educational stagnation notable only for Buddhist temples acting as repositories for
the intellectual heritage (A.D. 1185–1603); and the age of Tokugawa isolationism and cultural renaissance, marked by the *terakoya*
(temple schools) and clan schools (A.D. 1603–1867).

Education in the earliest period, before the introduction of
Chinese ideographs, is known only by inference and tradition.
The legends and myths of a primitive people were handed down
to succeeding generations, so it must be presumed that there was
some means of teaching these myths. Japanese society had progressed to the point of a rudimentary specialization of trades, so
the simple tasks of their daily lives must have been taught, possibly by an apprenticeship system. K. YOSHIDA and T. KAIGO in
their volume, *Japanese Education*, Tourist Library No. 19
(Tokyo, Maruzen, copyright 1937), p. 9, present the official
Japanese guess:

The recognized social organization of Japan was that of the paternal
or family basis. Those of the same blood formed a single family;
families in union formed a national group, with the Imperial Household as its head, thus creating one great, national family. There grew
up, very naturally, the custom of perpetuating the family occupation.
In order to make this possible there developed a certain form of education for the children of the various clans. As yet, however, there was
no such educational organization as might be termed a school.

The second period in Japanese education (A.D. 285–701) is remarkable for three great events: the introduction of Chinese
ideographs, the introduction of Confucian philosophy, and the
introduction of Buddhism. The Japanese Ministry of Education
in 1876 in an *Outline History of Japanese Education* prepared for
the Philadelphia Exposition, advanced the claim that Chinese characters were introduced from Imna (Jap. *Mimana*), a part of
modern Korea, during the reigns of Emperor KAIKA (B.C. 158–
98) and Emperor SUIJIN (B.C. 97–30). Most historians, however,
date the introduction of the ideograph from the arrival of a scholar,
WANI, from Pekche (Jap. *Kudara*) in what is modern Korea,
who was to serve as tutor for Prince WAKIIRATSUKO, son of Emperor ŌJIN. The traditional date is A.D. 270 or 285, although

Western scholars on the basis of textual analysis and cross references in the literatures of other Asiatic countries frequently place this at A.D. 405. Whatever the date of his arrival WANI was also apparently responsible for first introducing Confucian philosophy, since among his teaching materials were the *Rongo* ("Analects of Confucius") and, according to less reliable tradition, *Senjimon* ("Thousand Ideographs"). Buddhism in Japan dates from 552 when King SEIMEI of *Kudara* (Pekche) sent among other gifts to the Emperor of Japan, KIMMEI, a gold and copper image of Buddha together with a number of the Buddhist sutras and a letter praising the religion.

Tradition has it that the Emperor was at first undecided on his course of action and asked advice from his *Ō-omi* (chief of chiefs) SOGA NO INAME. This ambitious leader of the SOGA family recognized the opportunity to undermine the prestige of the NAKATOMI clan, hereditary Court ritualists in the religion now known as *Shintō*, and the MONONOBE clan, who because of their military prowess were charged with the protection of the Imperial Palace. He accordingly advised the adoption of Buddhism and when other Court factions demurred converted his home into a temple and began to preach. An epidemic occurred at about that time and the people, incited by the rival NAKATOMI and MONONOBE families, interpreted this pestilence as evidence of the wrath of the native *kami* (gods). They burned his temple and threw the Buddha into a canal in *Naniwa* (modern Osaka). The Great Hall of the Imperial Palace is supposed to have burned sometime after this sacrilege and this event was interpreted as evidence that Buddha was equally displeased. The image was fished out of the canal and worship was resumed. SOGA NO INAME appears to have reverted to his worship of native gods, but his son, SOGA NO UMAKO, *Ō-omi* under the succeeding Emperor, BITATSU, continued steadfast in his teaching of the imported religion and hence is generally conceded to have been the real founder of Buddhism in Japan. The following Emperor, YŌMEI, was a nominal Buddhist, and Prince SHŌTOKU (572–621), Regent during the reign of Empress SUIKŌ, became the patron of the imported religion.

It was Prince SHŌTOKU's intense interest in Buddhism which led to the great educational awakening of this period. Transplanting so developed and sophisticated a religion in primitive Japanese society required creative effort of the first order. Japanese nuns and priests had to be trained to conduct the rituals. Japanese work-men had to be trained to construct the temples and create the vestments and ecclesiastic paraphernalia. Scribes had to be taught to copy the sutras. Three events of educational significance marked this period: large numbers of Korean and Chinese teachers and artisans were brought to Japan, and larger numbers of Japanese students were sent to China to study; the first Japanese code of laws, really a statement of Chinese ethics which are recognizable in modern Japanese educational policy, were issued by Prince SHŌTOKU in 604; and the first formal schools were founded in Japan. The *Hōryū Gakumonji* or Learning Temple, constructed in 608, is considered by the Japanese to be the first formal school designed to train the priesthood, but the first known lay schools were founded at *Ōtsu*, near modern Kyoto, between 668–672, by Emperor TENCHI. Since one of these schools was of university level, and since two students, TAKAMUKU Kuromasa and a priest named BIN, were appointed to the position of professors in 645 after returning from study in China, there is presumptive evidence that schools actually existed much earlier. In 672 the first-known astronomical observatory was established. In 664 a Korean, KISHITSU Shushi, was named *Fumiyano-kami* (Superintendent of Education).

The year 701 marks the establishment of a formal educational system in Japan, and the beginning of the third of the great pre-Meiji educational eras (A.D. 701–1185). There had been a legal code promulgated by Emperor TENCHI in 662 as an outgrowth of the Taika Reform of 645–650. It has not survived and little is known of its contents other than that the two professors, TAKAMUKU and BIN, contributed from their knowledge of Chinese codes and that the Sui and T'ang codes were used as models. In 701 the famous *Taihō-ritsuryō* (Code of *Taihō* era, or of the Age of the Great Treasure) was completed by FUJIWARA NO FUBITO and his colleagues in the Court of Emperor MOMMU. This code was revised in 718 and afterward was known as the Code of *Yōrō*. It consists of two sections: the *Taihō-ritsu*, a twelve-volume compilation of criminal laws or prohibitions, and the *Taihō-ryō*, a thirty-volume compilation of civil laws or injunctions on various cultural and social matters. Two volumes were devoted to education and public officials and these constitute the first detailed educational plan known to have existed in Japan.

The *Taihō-ryō* provided for a governmental structure remarkably similar to that of twentieth-century Japan. Under the Emperor was a Great Council of State (*Dajō-kan*), headed by a Chancellor and two Ministers of State, and a Council of Religion (*Jingi-kan*) having equal rank. The Council of State handled political and lay matters while the Council of Religion was in charge of festivals, rituals, and all ecclesiastic matters concerned with the native gods. Eight subordinate Ministries—of the Imperial Household (*Kunaishō*), of Ceremonies (*Shikibushō*), of Civil Affairs (*Jibushō*), of the Central Office (*Nakatsukasa*), of Popular Affairs (*Mimbushō*), of War (*Hyōbushō*), of Justice (*Gyōbushō*), and of the Treasury (*Ōkurashō*)—served as technical advisers to the Chancellor. Administration outside the capital was delegated to provincial governors appointed by the Emperor and Chancellor. Each province was divided into districts, which in turn were subdivided into townships.

The educational provisions of the *Taihō-ryō* probably were not put into effect for several years and may never have been fully carried out. As a code they were impressive and remarkably parallel to the organization established 12 hundred years later under Emperor MEIJI. The center of the educational system was to be a national university (*daigaku*) at the capital, to which children of families holding the Fifth Court Rank or higher were admitted automatically and children of families as low as the Eighth Rank might be admitted on application. In addition certain hereditary retainers, such as the descendants of the first scholars to introduce Chinese ideographs, WANI and ACHINO-OMI, known as *Yamato-Kawachi no Fubitobe* (Learned Men of the Nara-Osaka Region), were admitted. Each prefecture was to have a school (*kokugaku*) for the children of local officials, though this was apparently not to be of university level, and quotas of from 20 to 50 students, depending on the size of the prefecture, were established. The instruction in these schools was designed to prepare governmental officials. The priesthood, both Buddhist and Shinto, were to be trained in temples and at shrines. Control of the educational system was through the national university by a board appointed by the Court. Teaching in the prefectural schools was to be restricted to residents of that area, headed by the governor himself if he was considered capable. The university had a qualified professional faculty. Financing of this system was accomplished by private endowment, by the income from government loans, and by grants of public domain.

In addition to the private ecclesiastic schools in temples and the governmental system of *daigaku* and *kokugaku*, this period produced the first of the great clan schools, created by the noble families such as SUGAWARA, TACHIBANA, FUJIWARA, and ARIHARA to provide education supplementing that of the *daigaku*. They were ordinarily restricted to the children of the family, and bore such names as *kōbunin, kangakuin, shōgakuin*, and *monjōin*. The first-known school for the common people, the *Sōgei Shuchiin*, was modeled after the Chinese village school and established in Kyoto in 827 by the *Shingon* Buddhist priest KŪKAI (also known as KŌBŌ Daishi), who is credited by tradition with the invention of *kana*, the phonetic syllabary. The first-known Japanese library was founded in 775 by ISHIGAMI Iyetsugu. The flow of Japanese students to China continued unabated until the early 900's and then lessened until by 1185, taken as the close of this period, it had practically ceased.

The fourth educational period was that of military ascendancy (A.D. 1185–1603). It was a period marked by civil wars, a decay of culture, economic misery, and the growth of feudalism. Two cultural developments emerged from this period of the "dark ages" and have contributed indirectly to the educational heritage of Japan: one was a remarkable advance in the arts, the other was the development of an ethical code of the military caste, known by the modern term *Bushidō* (literally, military-knight-way). This unwritten code, like the codes of European chivalry, idealized honor, truth, justice, benevolence, politeness, courage, and loyalty. These virtues, however, as practiced by the Japanese warriors of that period, would have been scarcely recognizable to the Occidental student of ethics. Honor meant the right of a noble or one of his swordsmen to kill any commoner who crossed his path. Loyalty meant the obligation to kill one's own child or sell one's wife into harlotry or undergo an excruciating form of suicide in order to demonstrate unswerving fealty to a feudal chief. Based on Chinese Confucian ethics and the esoteric and mystical philosophy of the *Zen* Sect of Buddhism, *Bushidō* at its best was a primitive moral code and at its worst, from the Occidental viewpoint, a cruel and often psychotic feudal ethic.

Virtually no direct contribution was made to education. The Imperial University at Kyoto burned in 1177. The *Sōgei Shuchiin*, only school for the common people, was discontinued. Of the great clan schools, only that of the ASHIKAGA, founded in 1160, appears to have survived, and this was largely devoted to training the children of the *Shōgun's* family for military and Court duties. Frank Alanson LOMBARD, in his volume, *Pre-Meiji Education in Japan* (Tokyo, Kyo Bun Kwan, 1913), p. 67, sums up the educational contribution of these 500 years with the statement:

. . . education had not ceased to exist; but it flourished only in the retirement of temples and under the fostering care of those who escaped the enervating luxury of the Court on the one hand, and the rude might of unorganized soldiery on the other. The slender thread of literary culture was held unbroken by Buddhist priests who made their abiding place a school and gathered into careful keeping books that would otherwise have been lost.

The fifth period of Japanese education, that of the 265 years of isolationism under the Tokugawa Shogunate (A.D. 1603–1867), contributed relative peace, a revived interest in scholarship, governmental encouragement of the Buddhist temples and centers of learning, and a fairly high economic level. Three direct contributions to education can hardly be overestimated: the development of government schools, the spread of *terakoya* or temple schools for the common people; and the introduction of fragmentary elements of Occidental learning, primarily Dutch medicine.

The Tokugawa Shogunate arose as a result of the successive military and political efforts of ODA Nobunaga (1533–83), TOYOTOMI Hideyoshi (1536–98), and TOKUGAWA Ieyasu (1542–1616), and is named for the family of this last general. It is common to speak of the genius of these three military rulers of feudal Japan. They undoubtedly were remarkable military commanders. But their genius bears a singular resemblance to that of modern dictators. Overwhelmingly ambitious, absolutely ruthless, clever to the point of slyness, brilliant organizers, and intelligent administrators, they brought the benefits of a *Pax Romana* and the efficiency of a Fascist police state. Nobunaga was a feudal chieftain in *Owari* (modern Aichi Prefecture containing Nagoya), who succeeded in defeating the surrounding clans and demonstrated his military ability to such a degree that in 1567 the Emperor ŌGIMACHI secretly invited him to come to Kyoto and supplant the failing *Shōgun* of the ASHIKAGA family. Nobunaga did so, although he established ASHIKAGA Yoshiaki as puppet *Shōgun* or Chancellor, a position he held titularly until 1597. In 1582 when Nobunaga was murdered by one of his own generals, he had subjugated approximately half of Japan.

One of Nobunaga's most able generals was Hideyoshi, son of a foot soldier employed by the family of ODA to which Nobunaga belonged. Hideyoshi had risen from the ranks to the position of most-trusted general and after Nobunaga's death continued the military campaigns. In 1584 he was named Regent (*Kampaku*), a position inferior to *Shōgun*, but in fact he assumed complete political power. He conducted a brilliant and bloody series of campaigns, subjugated the island of Kyushu, and even in 1592 conducted a year-long campaign in Korea, which finally drew the condescending and contemptuous attention of the Chinese. Although Hideyoshi withdrew to the southern tip of Korea and fought a bloody but ineffectual war of attrition, this venture was a conceded failure but still unterminated when Hideyoshi died in 1598. It was immediately abandoned.

Although Hideyoshi had succeeded in reducing Japan to a nominal peace it was in fact an armed peace with the great rival clans forced to admit his sovereignty only through fear of his arms. On his death there took place a bloody war of succession from which TOKUGAWA Ieyasu emerged victorious after the great battle of *Sekigahara* (in the modern Gifu Prefecture, north of Nagoya) in 1600. Ieyasu was a relatively unimportant vassal of one of the feudal lords, IMAGAWA, early subjugated by Nobunaga. He had become an active ally of Nobunaga, linked his family with the ODA clan by the marriage of his son to the daughter of Nobunaga, and had fought ably with Nobunaga and later Hideyoshi in their campaigns for the consolidation of Japan. In 1603 Ieyasu was named *Shōgun*, went to *Edo* (modern Tokyo), and established his *Bakufu* or seat of the Shogun government. Ieyasu fought a number of other battles, culminating in the annihilation of the TOYOTOMI clan in the siege of Osaka in 1615, in order to compel subordination of rival clans, but from the establishment of the Court in *Edo* until the Meiji Restoration in 1867 the

TOKUGAWA family exercised absolute and virtually undisputed rule over the nation.

One of the early educational moves of this family was the expropriation of the private clan school of the HAYASHI family and conversion of it in 1690 to a governmental school, the *Shōheikō* named for the birthplace of Confucius. The HAYASHI family was named *Daigaku no Kami* (Lord of the University) and given administrative power over it in perpetuity. This school was impregnated with Confucian philosophy and colored all educational thought for two centuries. In addition the shogunate established a series of other official schools, such as the *Wagaku-sho* (School for Japanese Studies), *Igaku-kan* (School for Japanese and Chinese Medicine), *Igaku-sho* (School for Dutch Medicine), *Rikugun-sho* (School for Military Science), *Kaigun-sho* (School for Naval Science), and *Bansho-shirabe-sho* (School for Foreign Studies).

Four other types of schools supplemented the governmental schools which the Tokugawa Shoguns established for the education of their family and the training of Court officials. These were the *hangaku, kyōgaku, shijuku,* and *terakoya*.

The *hangaku* were clan schools established by the feudal lords (*daimyō*) in their own prefectures and supported by their local governmental funds for the purpose of training the children of the noble class (*kuge*) and the military class (*buke*). The *kyōgaku* was a similar institution located in the territories of the next subordinate feudal official (*taifu*) and in prosperous towns devoted to the instruction of the children of the military classes and in some instances the farmer class (*hyakushō*) and townspeople (*chōnin*). The fifth and lowest class, the outcasts (*eta* or *hinin*), of course received no formal education whatever. Some of these schools were supported by the feudal family and some by public taxation. The courses were usually from six to seven years in length and Confucian ethics (similar to modern *Shūshin*), reading, calligraphy, and simple arithmetic were taught. Physical education and military training, including the military arts (*budō*), were basic parts of the training of the upper classes and the standards of all work were higher for them than for the children admitted from the lower classes. Critical evaluation was discouraged and the schools were characterized by a rigid scholasticism typical of the traditional Chinese instruction.

Education for the common masses, the lowest military classes, the farmers, and the townspeople, was provided by two levels of private schools. The best known were the *terakoya* (temple schools) which were elementary level schools usually established in the Buddhist monasteries and temples and taught by priests, doctors, or impoverished swordsmen known as *rōnin* or warriors without a feudal lord. They taught reading, calligraphy, arithmetic, and simple Buddhist philosophy. These schools were financially supported by gifts from the students, who occupied a peculiarly intimate personal relationship to their teachers, something akin to that of a disciple to a sage. The Japanese Ministry of Education estimates that there were approximately 15,000 *terakoya*, often co-educational and ranging in size from a half dozen to as many as 500 or 600 pupils, in existence at the close of the Tokugawa era. It was on this tradition of common education and with the physical assistance of their personnel and material resources that the dramatic creation of a national governmental elementary system was possible after 1872. The second of the two private schools was the *shijuku*, secondary level schools offering the Chinese classics, advanced reading, literary composition, and similar studies, but otherwise similar to the *terakoya*.

The most fascinating educational development of the Tokugawa era was the osmotic introduction of Occidental learning. This introduction was not a continuous process but one marked by three distinct waves, or more descriptively, by three distinct seepages. A fourth period was indeed a wave, that of the feverish introduction of Western culture in the first 30 years of the Meiji Restoration. First of the three Tokugawa periods was that of the Christian influence from the discovery of Japan about 1542 by the Portuguese until the suppression of Christianity with the *Shimabara* Rebellion in 1638. The second period (1637–1854) was marked by the surreptitious infiltration of science through the Dutch officials attached to the Dutch East India Company factory permitted to exist on the artificial island of *Deshima* in the harbor at Nagasaki. The last of the three periods (1854–67) was characterized by the arrival of European and American missionaries, linguists, and scientists and by the crumbling antagonism toward foreign culture evidenced in the expiring years of the shogunate.

Mendez PINTO claimed to have discovered the Japanese islands in 1542 but this honor is usually attributed to three adventurers who were blown north from the island of Macao (near modern Hong Kong in Southern China) to make landfall on the small Japanese island, *Tanegashima* (southeast of Kagoshima, off the southern coast of Kyushu), approximately 1542. By 1548 Portuguese ships were calling with some frequency and on 15 August 1549 Francis Xavier landed at Kagoshima after calls at Malacca and Canton en route from the College of St. Paul at the Portuguese settlement at Goa, India.

Xavier spent 27 months in Japan and thoroughly laid the groundwork for Jesuit missions. At first they were received with tolerance and even eagerness but a series of episodes antagonized the Buddhist priests (*bōsan*) and finally Toyotomi Hideyoshi, the military Regent, himself. The Roman Catholic version is that Xavier was militaristically evangelical and if reproved for preaching an unpopular doctrine, such as that sodomy is a vice, he would make a violent issue and preach in the streets, incite the crowds, and openly condemn the Japanese officials and nobles. His example was followed by succeeding Jesuit missionaries and came to a crisis in 1587. It is claimed that Hideyoshi became infuriated when Japanese Christian girls refused his procurer. A series of questions were sent the same night to the Vice-Provincial, Father Coelho, demanding to know why the Jesuits forced Japanese to become Christians, why they destroyed temples, why they persecuted Buddhist priests, why they violated the Japanese custom by eating meat, and why they enslaved Japanese and carried them to India. Despite a courteous, and to the Jesuits a satisfactory, reply by Father Coelho, Hideyoshi published his famous order of 25 July 1587. The English translation found in Otis Cary's *A History of Christianity in Japan* (New York, Fleming H. Revell Company, copyright 1909), p. 9, follows:

Having learned from our faithful counsellors that foreign religious teachers have come into our estates, where they preach a law contrary to that of Japan, and that they have even had the audacity to destroy temples dedicated to our *Kami* and *Hotoke;* although this outrage merits the most extreme punishment, wishing nevertheless to show them mercy, we order that under pain of death they quit Japan within 20 days. During that space of time no harm nor hurt will be done them, but at the expiration of that term, we order that if any of them be found in our states, they shall be seized and punished as the greatest criminals. As for the Portuguese merchants, we permit them to enter our ports there to continue their accustomed trade, and to remain in our estates provided our affairs need this; but we forbid them to bring any foreign religious teachers into the country, under penalty of the confiscation of their ships and goods.

Roman Catholic records themselves would appear to substantiate some of the claims made by Japanese historians in justification of the continued persecution of the Christians and of the Portuguese and Spanish. Father COELHO got a six months' stay on the grounds that there was no shipping space, but when finally forced to comply sent only three persons, prevailed upon the ship's captain to lie as to the overloading of the ships, and concealed his followers with the Christian feudal lords in Kyushu. The Jesuits and the Franciscans carried on an open and violent conflict, despite a brief from Pope GREGORY XIII which in 1585 forbade under pain of major excommunication any but Jesuits to perform religious functions in Japan. So flagrant were the violations of this order that Pope CLEMENT VIII in 1600 published a bull officializing the clandestine traffic already going on, by permitting other orders, primarily Dominicans and Franciscans, to preach in Japan if the missionaries went via Goa, India, and under the Portuguese flag. An English pilot, WILL ADAMS, arrived on the first Dutch ship in 1600 and was violently attacked by the Portuguese and Spanish missionaries but was protected and raised to a position of great influence as an adviser to the Court by the *Shōgun* TOKUGAWA Ieyasu. On 27 January 1614 Ieyasu issued his famous decree against Christianity, a portion of which is reproduced here from the translation in CARY's volume (*op. cit.*), pp. 176–178.

Christians have come to Japan, not only sending their merchant vessels to exchange commodities but also longing to disseminate an evil law and to overthrow right doctrine so that they may change the government of the country and obtain possession of the land. This is the germ of great disaster and must be crushed . . . the Missionaries disbelieve in the way of the gods, blaspheme the true law, violate rightdoing, and injure the good. . . . These must be instantly swept out, so that not an inch of soil remains to them in Japan on which to plant their feet, and if they refuse to obey this command, they shall pay the penalty.

Persecution continued until 1637, with any discovered Christian put to death by burning or by the hideous French torture of

fosse in which the victim was suspended head down in a pit of
dung while his circulation was gradually stopped by twisted cords.
Buddhist priests were organized to assist in the search for believers.
In 1630 all foreign books were banned. In 1635 all Japanese were
forbidden to leave the country or to have any intercourse with
foreigners, other than the Dutch in *Deshima* and the Chinese, on
pain of death. In the latter part of 1637 there took place the so-
called *Shimabara* Revolt in which 37,000 Christianized Japanese
were besieged in *Hara* Castle (on the Shimabara Peninsula south
of Nagasaki on the west coast of Kyushu). On 11 April 1638 they
were defeated with 17,000 dead and their heads were displayed
in Nagasaki as a symbol of the complete eradication of the foreign
faith. It also marked the eradication of practically all Occidental
knowledge thus far introduced.

The period from 1637 to 1854 was marked by the laborious and
perilous seepage of Dutch learning past the vigilant isolationist
defenses of the Tokugawa Shogunate. Learning was introduced
by two means: personal contact with the Dutch scientists who
accompanied the chief factor from the Dutch settlement in Nagasaki on his annual courtesy visit to the *Shōgun* in *Edo* (modern
Tokyo), and by translation of foreign books.

Dr. Engebert KAEMFER, who arrived in 1690, and Philipp Franz
von SIEBOLD, who arrived in 1823, are the most notable examples
of the Dutch scientists who influenced the Japanese. The latter
served nominally as physician to the Dutch factor but devoted
much of his energies to the study of Japanese natural history. In
1829 he was expelled from Japan for accepting secretly a map of
Japan from the Japanese astronomer TAKAHASHI at the Observatory in *Edo*.

It is ironical that the first systematic Western learning to influence the Japanese came from a member of the hated class of
expelled missionaries, a Franciscan priest who arrived in Kyushu
in 1709 and was interviewed at the command of the *Shōgun*
TOKUGAWA Ienobu by the Japanese scholar, ARAI Hakuseki
(1657–1725). ARAI published these interviews in the two works,
Sairan Igen (1713) and *Seiyō Kibun* (1715), so that although the
priest was kept in confinement in *Edo* his influence was widely
felt. In 1720 the *Shōgun* TOKUGAWA Yoshimune removed the prohibition on importation of foreign books, except those on religion,
and became so fascinated by the foreign works on astronomy, es-

pecially a book presented to him by the Dutch factor in 1738, that he ordered AOKI Bunzō (1698–1769) to begin the study of the Dutch written language. This was quite a departure from earlier Tokugawa policy, which had maintained a school for Dutch interpreters in Nagasaki but had forbidden them to learn to read. AOKI only learned about 500 words. However, MAENO Ryōtaku (1723–1803), a Japanese physician, became a pupil of his and, together with SUGITA Gempaku (1733–1817), by almost unbelievable deception and effort learned about 700 words. They secured a Dutch dictionary and a book on anatomy, *Tafel Anatomia*, which they checked with the secretly dissected body of a criminal. Aided by six other physicians they translated this book in three years and published it in 1774 under the Japanese title of *Kaitai Shinsho* ("New Anatomy"), ushering in the so-called Dutch medicine.

In 1808 the Nagasaki School for interpreters added the study of English and the next year Russian. In 1838 a medical school was established in Osaka and both Dutch medicine and the Dutch language were taught. When Japan was opened to international commerce by the treaty with the United States in 1854, Western learning, at least in the Dutch language, and in the field of science, was well established.

The years 1853–67 were years of frantic efforts on the part of the TOKUGAWA family to stave off a rising antagonism to their rule. In 1857 a school for the study of foreign books, first in Dutch, and later in English, Russian, French, and German, was established in *Edo* and became the nucleus of what is today Tokyo Imperial University (*Tōkyō Teikoku Daigaku*). The following year, 1858, FUKUZAWA Yukichi, greatest Japanese educator of the nineteenth century, founded Keiō University (*Keiō Gijuku*), in Tokyo, in which English learning and language supplanted Dutch. In 1863 selected students were sent to Holland, Russia, and England. When the fall of the shogunate came, although the Tokugawa government was castigated for having had contact with Western countries, hardly one of the shogunate's critics who became a prominent leader of the Meiji Restoration had not been influenced by foreign learning, primarily, of course, Dutch.

The Meiji Restoration. The remarkable group of men who served as advisers to the Emperor MEIJI could not help being influenced by the educational tradition which they inherited. Japanese education included in this tradition recognition of mass education of the common people, both by governmental schools and by the *terakoya;* acceptance of the prominent place of religious philosophy in education, both Confucian ethics and Buddhist mysticism; marked interest in the esthetic, both in the arts (including calligraphy and the *Nō* drama), and in the social customs (such as the tea ceremony); acceptance of the dominating position of the ideographic writing system; sense of inferiority to foreign culture, historically Chinese but immediately Occidental; and acknowledgment that the educational process was primarily an instrument for influencing political and social affairs and not a procedure for the development of the individual. In addition to these basic conceptions Japanese educational tradition cluttered the opening years of the Meiji Restoration with a wealth of rather inconsequential trappings such as the segregation of sexes, scholastic formalism, elevation of the master to a quasi-reverential position of authority by his students, and fee payment as a device of finance.

The tremendous influence which this period of Japanese history has had on educational thought and the role it plays in any plan for the rehabilitation of postwar Japan has been considered in detail in the section on philosophy. It will be sufficient here to consider briefly the creation of the administrative organization. Two problems faced the government: to determine what part the educational system should play in the restoration of Imperial prestige and the establishment of a modern Japan, and to determine what physical structure most effectively would implement this policy. *Four great Decisions* The decision to use the educational system as the primary instrument for transforming a feudal society to a modern industrial state may be said to be the greatest decision of the early Meiji government. Hugh KEENLEYSIDE and A. F. THOMAS in their *History of Japanese Education and the Present Educational System* (Tokyo, Hokuseidō Press, 1937), p. 73, state:

. . . these statesmen were forced to call into action every resource of character, sentiment, training and religion which was likely to unify and strengthen the power of the nation. The policies adopted were carefully evolved and courageously applied. Nothing was left to chance, and nothing was overlooked. The fundamental objectives were clearly visualized and vigorously pursued. They may be summarized in the terms of *national unification, unquestioning loyalty, the acquirement of modern scientific and economic technique* and *the perfection of national defense.*

To achieve these objectives it was necessary to import Occidental knowledge, and the decision was made to send students abroad and to bring contract teachers to Japan. It was clearly desirable to have an educational system which cleanly broke with the old conservative Chinese traditions and which could be economically and efficiently manipulated by the national government, so the decision was made to establish a national, tax-supported, centrally controlled system modeled on the French structure. Finally it appeared desirable if not absolutely necessary to link the education with some powerful motivating force such as a popular religion, so the ancient cult now known as *Shintō*, The Way of the Gods, was resurrected and made the dominant influence in school ceremonies, curricula, and educational philosophy.

The opening gambit in achieving this policy trilogy was made by Emperor MEIJI on 6 April 1868 in the Throne Room of the Imperial Palace in Kyoto, when he took the *Charter Oath of Five Articles*, enunciating the basic principles upon which he intended to base his rule. The fifth of these articles reversed the traditional Japanese policy of isolation, practiced under the Tokugawa Shogunate:

(V) Knowledge shall be sought among the nations of the world and the Empire shall be led up to the zenith of prosperity.
  (Original official trans. Later official translations: "Wisdom and ability should be sought throughout the world for the purpose of promoting the welfare of the Empire"; "Wisdom and ability should be sought after in all quarters of the world for the purpose of firmly establishing the foundations of the Empire.")

The next five years witnessed a feverish attempt to realize the fullest implications of this statement. Because of the civil disturbances many of the school buildings had been occupied by the military forces as headquarters and hospitals. In November 1868 the School of Foreign Languages which the Tokugawa government had founded in *Edo* (modern Tokyo) was reopened under the Meiji government in the same city. The old *Shōheiko*, or Confucian College, was reopened and in June 1869 was renamed

Daigaku (university) and placed at the head of the educational system in a position analogous to the Napoleonic University of France. An Educational Board created in 1868 directed all governmental education until June (also given as July and January by various sources) 1871, when it was replaced by a Department of Education (*Mombushō*). In February 1869 the Educational Board took charge of all newspaper publication and in May 1870 it was given supervision over all book publication. In October 1869 a Bureau of Translation was established in the School of Foreign Languages for the purpose of translating foreign textbooks and of writing foreign language texts. An Educational System Investigation Bureau was also established in 1869, headed by Mori Arinori and Kato Hiroyuki, to investigate the construction of a national system. In July 1870 the most promising younger scholars from each prefecture were sent to the School of Foreign Languages for study at government expense as *Koshusei* (tribute youths), and in the next three months the most advanced students from that school began to leave for America, England, and France to study literature and science. At the same time gifted medical students from the School of Medicine began to leave for foreign study, principally in Germany. In November 1871 Tanaka Fujimaro, Chief Secretary of the Department of Education, was sent to the United States as an Embassy official to study American education.

The second fundamental move in achieving the Meiji educational policy was made in August 1872 when the *Educational Code of 1872* was officially announced. Preparation, of course, had been going on for more than a year. In August 1871 the old feudal political divisions (then totaling 263) were abolished and 75 prefectures were established. In June 1872 the *Daijōkan* or State Council had issued an order that all children, male and female alike, should be given an education; foreign books should be translated; commercial and vocational schools should be created; and children of intellectual promise should be given preferential education. A sum of two million yen had been appropriated to finance the *Mombushō* (National Department of Education) and the schools which were to be under its control. Existing schools, previously under the local governments of the old feudal districts, were notified that they were to be converted to or replaced by schools regulated by the National Department of Education and were to follow prescribed courses of education.

In November 1872 an educational convention was held in the *Mombushō* to which the officials of local governments were invited. Two far-reaching decisions were reached, which have influenced Japanese education since that date almost as much as the *Educational Code* itself. A Bureau of Superintendence was created within the *Mombushō* and charged with responsibility for inspecting and supervising the schools which were thereafter to be under the National Department of Education. It was further decided to establish an annual appropriation of national tax monies to the local governments, in proportion to the population, for aid in the support of elementary schools. The quota established at that time was nine tenths of a yen per capita.

The *Educational Code of 1872* was almost a direct copy of the French educational system. YAMASHITA Tokuji in his volume, *Education in Japan* (Tokyo, Kenkyusha, 1938), p. 11, writes:

The new system was established after the example of the French system. The nation was divided into eight university districts by the Educational Ordinance [changed to seven university districts in April of the 6th year of Meiji, 1873], each of them consisting of 32 secondary school districts. Each secondary school district was again divided into 210 elementary school districts or one for each 600 of population on the basis of . . . a population of 33,000,000. In other words the new system called for establishment of 8 universities, 256 secondary schools and 53,760 elementary schools.

The French system was followed because its strong policy of centralization attracted the attention of the Meiji Government, which desired to unify the education of the nation.

The importance of the *Educational Code of 1872* did not rest solely on the somewhat grandiose scheme of more than 54,000 schools. It was in fact a code, a systematic body of laws regulating all details of educational structure, finance, and control. The elementary schools were to be eight years in length, divided symmetrically into two cycles of four years each, and ordinarily attended by children from the ages of six to thirteen. Middle schools, including vocational continuation and foreign language schools, were to be six years in length, divided into two equal cycles of three years each. Curricula for both levels were to be established by national regulation both as to time and content, and national uniformity, by concurrent interpretation of the *Code*, was to be maintained by federal inspectors. Schools were to be financed by student fees, local taxation, and federal subsidies. Private schools meeting certain standards were to be controlled through a federal licensing system.

Exceeding even the importance of these specific regulations, however, was the importance which the *Educational Code of 1872* allocated by implication to the *Mombushō*, or National Department of Education, later the Ministry of Education. The *Constitution* of the *Mombushō*, established in June 1871 and revised in November 1876, states in part:

The business of the department is divided into two classes. The business of the first class is transacted by the minister after the approval of the General Government. The business of the second class is conducted at the discretion of the minister, who is, however, responsible for all the business of the first and second classes.
Business of the first class:— To devise and establish systems of education; to make and revise educational regulations; to establish school taxation; to regulate the grants of money to local school-districts; to establish government schools; to send officials of the department to foreign countries; etc.
Business of the second class:— To present educational measures to the General Government; to issue notifications concerning the business of the department; to supervise the local authorities in regard to educational matters; to confer academic degrees; to regulate the disbursement of government grants to the school-districts; to collect books and apparatus conducive to the progress of science and the arts; to collect and diffuse information in regard to education; to summon conventions of inspectors of school-directors, or of school-teachers and school-experts, for the purposes of discussion of educational questions; to send students to foreign countries and to superintend the same; to engage native and foreign teachers, and to regulate their salaries; etc. (*Mombushō* trans. See also *An Outline History of Japanese Education*, pp. 177 f., prepared by the Japanese Department of Education for the Philadelphia International Exposition [New York, D. Appleton & Co., 1876].)

The 24 July 1891 Imperial Ordinance No. 93, "Official Regulations for the Department of Education," stated in part:

Art. I. The duties of the Minister of State for Education are to control all affairs connected with education and learning. *over*

Art. II. The following business shall be under the control of the Minister's Cabinet, besides those points enumerated in the General Regulations.

Business concerning:

1. The appointment, promotion, dismissal, and social position of public school officials.
2. The licensing of teachers.
3. The examination of books and charts for school use.
4. The compilation of books and charts useful for education.
5. Pensions for teachers, and for the families of deceased teachers.
6. Foreigners employed by the Department of Education.
7. Students in foreign countries.
8. Petitions. (*Mombushō* trans.)

The *Mombushō* has changed its internal organization on numerous occasions since its organization into three bureaus (Special Education, Common Education, and Technical Education) in the first year of the *Educational Code of 1872*. It was reorganized not less than five times in the first year of the present Occupation. Departments or bureaus were added or lopped off to meet immediate professional and political demands. In September 1874 there were five bureaus (Schools, Finance, Publications, Copyright and Press Laws, and Public Health), and in 1946 there were five and a Secretariat (Schools, Social Education, Scientific Education, Physical Education, and Textbooks). But the actual powers and duties of the Ministry of Education today are startlingly similar to those which are listed above.

It quickly became evident that the *Educational Code of 1872* was impossible of immediate realization. The nation simply did not have the physical, personnel, or financial resources to create such an educational empire over night. In addition to this inadequacy, however, implementation of the *Code* may be criticized on two theoretical bases. Japan had no widespread tradition of universal education, and mere establishment of a national policy did not create a popular demand for education. It is doubtful if the schools could have been effectively used even had it been possible to construct them. The second basic theoretical objection to the *Code* was the inflexible geographical distribution of schools. Barring a highly developed system of transportation, not then available in Japan, which would permit movement of students to educational centers at some distance from their homes, it is necessary to locate schools with relation to concentrations of population. The geometrical subdivision of university districts made an imposing plan but one which had little contact with reality. Despite these shortcomings the *Educational Code of 1872* has been basic to practically all educational control, organization, and finance down to the present time. Once a privilege has been openly offered to the people subsequent denial is almost a political impossibility, and abrogation must come through progressive modification.

It was inevitable that the *Code* should proceed through a series of reforms. The first came in 1873 when the eight university districts were reduced to seven (Aichi, Hiroshima, Miyagi, Nagasaki, Niigata, Osaka, and Tokyo). By 1879 the impracticality of the *Code* had become so evident that a major reform was considered necessary. In September the *Educational Decree of 1879* replacing the *Code of 1872* was promulgated and was in turn modified the following year. This *Educational Decree* abolished the arbitrary school districts established in the 1872 *Code* and delegated authority to establish elementary schools to the local (*chō* or *son*) officials. Local, elected school committees were authorized. Federal subsidy of local education was abolished (temporarily) and the local authorities were required to finance the elementary schools, a practice which led to accentuation of the student fee system. Elementary education was nominally continued as an eight-year system, though only the first three years were compulsory and sufficient loopholes were left in the *Decree* to permit evasion of all but 16 months of that. In 1886 control of the elementary schools was given to prefectural (*ken*) officials, while federal control of the middle and higher school system was established by the *University Decree of March 1886*, the *Normal School Decree of April 1886*, the *Middle School Decree of April 1886*, and the *Elementary School Decree of April 1886*. A minimum of four years compulsory education was established by the last of these.

It would be of doubtful value to examine in detail the subsequent reforms and revisions which have continued into the periods of *Taishō* and *Shōwa*. They are available (in English) in the annual reports of the *Mombudaijin* (Minister of Education) published by the Japanese Ministry of Education, a complete file of which is deposited in the United States Library of Congress, and partial files of which are available in major American university libraries, notably Harvard, California, and Columbia. Among the most important were the *Elementary School Revision of 1890*, based on the new *Constitution;* the *Middle School Regulation of 1899,* compelling each prefecture to maintain at least one boys' and one girls' middle school; the *Amendment to the Elementary School Decree in 1907*, which raised the period of compulsory education from four to six years; the *Higher School Decree of 1911;* the *University and Higher School Acts of 1918*, including the recommendations of the series of Educational Investigation Committees first formed in 1913; and the *Elementary School Regulations of 1921*. Five recent reforms, however, must be considered briefly if the present problem of organization is to be understood. These are the proposed HIRAO Plan of 1936; the Official System of 1937, which may be taken as the last normal year in Japanese education; the *National School Reform of 1941;* the Educational System of the Occupation of 1946; and the *Educational Reform of 1947*. These will be examined as elements in the modern system of education.

The third of the great strategic moves in creating the educational system of the Meiji Restoration was the issuance of the *Imperial Rescript on Education* on 30 October 1890. A detailed analysis of this document and the part it played in linking the emotional drive of the national cult of *Shintō* to the political and educational reconstruction of Japan has already been presented in the section on philosophy. With regard to its influence on the organization of the school system it will suffice to note that it categorically establishes the centralization of all control of education in the Imperial Tradition. "Our Imperial Ancestors have founded Our Empire on a basis broad and everlasting, and have deeply and firmly implanted virtue; Our subjects ever united in loyalty and filial piety have from generation to generation illustrated the beauty thereof. This is the glory of the fundamental character of Our Empire, and herein also lies the source of Our education." (Official trans.)

The Meiji *Constitution of the Empire of Japan*, which was put in force in the same year, though granted on 11 February 1889, and which has continued in effect until the adoption of the *New Constitution of the Empire of Japan*, promulgated on 3 November 1946 and made effective on 3 May 1947, established the legal principle enunciated above. Articles I, III, IV, V, X, and LV are pertinent:

Art. I   The Empire of Japan shall be reigned over by a line of Emperors unbroken for ages eternal.

Art. III   The Emperor is sacred and inviolable.

Art. IV   The Emperor is the head of the Empire, combining in himself the rights of sovereignty, and exercises them, according to the provisions of the present Constitution.

Art. V   The Emperor exercises the legislative power with the consent of the Imperial Diet.

Art. X   The Emperor determines the organization of the different branches of the administration, and salaries of all civil and military officers, and appoints and dismisses the same. . . .

Art. LV   The respective Ministers of State shall give their advice to the Emperor, and be responsible for it. (Official trans.)

The chain was forged. By these three great moves the advisers to Emperor Meiji had created what was to prove one of the most effective propaganda machines of modern times. The authority came from the gods of the mythological ages; was handed down from Emperor to Emperor through the line unbroken for ages eternal; assumed the infallibility of sacred and inviolable utterance; was implemented by legislative power, sovereignty, and executive determination of governmental organization, including complete control of the appointment and dismissal of officials; was guided by ministerial advice while evading responsibility for errors in that advice; was handed on to the Minister of State for Education as delegated authority through Imperial ordinances; and reached the school in the form of blanket administrative authority which covered finances, licensing, appointments, publication of textbooks and materials, construction of buildings, inspection, supervision, establishment of curricula and standards, granting of degrees, direction of research, even control of thoughts. . . . There is an element of pathos in the inclusion of Article XXIII in the new *Constitution*, written in the first year of the Occupation, when this house of cards had come tumbling down:

"Art. XXIII Academic freedom is guaranteed."

The Tyranny of the Machine

When Emperor HIROHITO assumed the throne on the death of his insane father, Emperor TAISHŌ, on 25 December 1926, he came to a nation which despite the disastrous earthquake of 1923 was enjoying greater financial security and political prestige than at almost any other period in modern times. The parliamentary system was functioning with a greater degree of real authority than at any time before or since. The educational system was internationally recognized to be one of the most efficient mass instructional programs in the world. In the first ten years of his reign Japan very nearly approached a working Occidental version of a constitutional monarchy. Increasing social unrest caused by the world depression constituted the gravest problem. Unemployment in the highly industrialized home islands of the Empire focused the attention of educators on both the ultimate goal and the organization of the educational system. The result was a series of proposed educational reforms culminating in the famous HIRAO Plan of 1936, a reform which was never put into effect but which influenced educational thought then and may again in the face of technological unemployment in postwar Japan.

HIRAO *Plan of 1936.* The Minister of Education, Mr. HIRAO Hachisaburo, was a prominent business leader and not an educator or politician. He approached the problem of widespread unemployment of secondary and higher school graduates with the unemotional and uncomplicated attitude of the traditional industrialist facing a problem of overproduction. If there is a surplus of students, reduce the number by limiting future production. The American solution of increasing consumption of the educational product was considered visionary. There was apparently improper distribution rather than overproduction of graduates. A Japanese trained for a profession or the so-called "salary man" positions felt a social obligation to refuse manual employment in one of the trades or crafts. In 1936 only 17,000 of the 30,000 university graduates were able to get employment, while the technical schools were able to supply only 16.4% of the 17,630 technicians then needed in industry.

Elementary education in the HIRAO Plan was to be increased. Compulsory education was to be extended from six to eight years and the entire elementary system was to be extended to ten years, divided into an initial cycle of six years (*shō-gakkō*) offering "education essential to the general public," and the upper cycle of four years (*kōtō shō gakkō*) offering a curriculum modified to meet local needs and designed to achieve "cultivation of character." The traditional secondary schools of Japan (*chū gakkō*), which in the past had served primarily as institutions preparatory to higher education, were to be reduced in number to a maximum of one per prefecture, were to be reduced in length of course from five years to three, and were to be supplemented by parallel secondary institutions offering terminal courses in commercial, industrial, and agricultural subjects. The higher school (*kōtō gakkō*), traditionally a three-year post-secondary course sometimes attached to a four-year secondary course to make a total of seven years' training leading to the university, was to be reduced to a total of five years with six months of the traditional final three-year post-secondary course devoted to vocational training. The number of universities (*daigaku*) was to be reduced, with private universities the particular target for attack. In an effort to reduce the intense competition for admission to the more desirable universities and to avoid concentration of students in large cities, the plan contemplated a geographical redistribution of universities permitted to continue, together with regulations designed to discourage attending a university outside the student's residential district.

Certain philosophic and curricular policies inherent in the Hirao Plan need not concern us here. Three organizational features are pertinent.

The first concerned the feasibility of geographical redistribution of postelementary education. If national secondary schools offering preparatory courses for admission to the universities were to be artificially restricted to one per prefecture, and if an adequate system of dormitories for nonresident students were to be provided (this latter was not contemplated), such redistribution by prefecture appears practical. But arbitrary decentralization of the university facilities of the nation, in view of the fact that 22 of the country's 45 universities were then located in Tokyo, appears highly impractical. Physical plants representing hundreds of millions of yen could not be abandoned. The universities had originally sought locations advantageous to the concentrations of population and to the locale of correlative cultural institutions.

The second organizational problem arose from the inadequacy of the existing supply of teachers. The HIRAO Plan recognized that the decrease in secondary schools would not make available a fraction of the number of teachers required to staff the expanded elementary system. To provide these needed teachers the Plan required each prefecture to maintain one normal school and proposed a change in the requirements for licensing to permit secondary school graduates with three years' practice teaching the right to teach in elementary schools.

The final and disastrous problem which the Plan faced was that of financing. It was estimated that an extraordinary expenditure of approximately 42 million yen would be necessary to initiate the plan, and that an annual increase in appropriation of about 22 million yen would be necessary to carry it out. These figures, representing respectively only 7% and 3.7% addition to the actual educational expenditure of 596,529,255 yen in that year, exclusive of private grants, were considered absurdly impractical and the Plan was shelved.

The "Normal" System of 1937. It is fortunate that the year 1937, taken as the "normal year" for international educational statistics by the United Nations, and generally conceded to be the most typical prewar year in Japanese education, should also be the year when a series of international educational and professional conferences were held in Tokyo. A record of these significant conferences on educational problems is available in English in the seven-volume report of the world Federation of Education Associations. Because of the influx of foreign visitors the Ministry of Education prepared perhaps the most comprehensive study of the current educational structure which has ever been compiled in Japan. Three materials in English provide the American student with an accurate though condensed picture of the 1937 system. They are: *A General Survey of Education in Japan* (Tokyo: Department of Education, 1937); *Education in Japan under the Department of Education: Administration and Work* (charts and statistical tables) (Tokyo, Department of Education, 1937); and *Japanese School Life through the Camera* (photographs) (Tokyo: Kokusai Bunka Shinkokai, 1937). A brief summary of this "normal" system may be of value.

At the head of the educational system of Japan was the powerful national Ministry of Education (*Mombushō*), first organized in 1871, holding Ministerial rank since 1885, and basically reorganized in the reforms of 18 June 1915 and 2 June 1934. It was divided into eight bureaus, a Secretariat, two permanent and several special committees. It functioned according to the traditional plan of line and staff organization. The functions of the *Mombushō* in 1937 were only slightly changed from what they had been during the Meiji Restoration. The old powers were retained and to them had been added preservation of national treasures (including parks, works of art, and historical objects); control of religious bodies (including their physical properties, temples, shrines, churches, and schools); supervision of thought through investigation, propaganda, and punitive action; and expanded administrative duties arising from the extension of Japanese education to areas such as hygiene, adult education, mass information media, and research, which had not been a part of the system in the Meiji period.

The head of the Ministry of Education was the Minister of Education (*Mombudaijin*), appointed by the Emperor on the advice of the Prime Minister, and holding by reason of this Imperial investiture the highest civil service rank, that of *Shinnin*. Because the Minister was a member of the Imperial Cabinet, his tenure was subject to the political exigencies of the dominating party, with the result that the extensive powers nominally bestowed on this appointee were in fact relatively unimportant. Hugh KEENLEYSIDE and A. F. THOMAS in their *History of Japanese Education and Present Educational System*, p. 20, describe this difficulty:

In order for a Minister of Education to effect any serious reforms he would have to be in office for a long time, and increasingly empowered. But the life of Japanese cabinets during the past few years has been short. Moreover, with the powerful opposition in certain educational and other factions in Japan to any far-reaching reforms, a Minister of Education would not survive long any determination to insist upon any radical changes, even if the cabinet of which he was a member were to remain in office. The vested interests would force his resignation by one way or another. Thus the vicious circle makes a double turn, and in the meantime the educational system becomes stagnant. These frequent changes of the cabinet are of course the strength of those who oppose reforms. It is therefore safe to conclude that under the present regime in Japan's politics, few changes of any importance can be made in her system of education.

To provide professional continuity in the executive direction of the Ministry, the Vice-Minister of Education (*Mombujikan*) was appointed by the Minister in the name of and with the consent of the Emperor presumably to serve indefinitely. The Vice-Minister held the rank of *Chokunin* of First Rank, corresponding to the first or highest of the nine regular civil service ranks (*kōtōkan*). Civil service rank should not be confused with Court rank (*ikai*) which was an honor granted by the Imperial Household to peers and their heirs, officials, military officers, and distinguished public citizens. Actually, Vice-Ministers of Education in practice changed almost as frequently as did the Ministers, usually because the Vice-Minister found that it was impossible to work conscientiously with a succeeding incumbent and consequently resigned. The duties of the Vice-Minister of Education were more closely analogous to those of the chief of staff of a military commander than to those commonly associated with a vice-president or vice-governor in Occidental politics. He was charged with the detailed direction of the Ministry of Education and actually assumed most of the responsibilities of the Minister, even to issuing all but basic policy orders, since the Minister was generally uninformed of the technical details of education and was largely occupied with political responsibilities, such as answering questions in the Imperial Diet (*Teikoku Gikai*), attending sessions of the Cabinet (*Naikaku*), and presenting budgets and proposed legislation for approval.

Two other executive posts in the Ministry of Education were designed ostensibly to give continuity despite falls of the Cabinet, but perhaps more realistically had been created to give offices to unattached statesmen who had a claim against the 1924 coalition Cabinet of Viscount Kato Kōmei. These two posts were the Parliamentary Vice-Minister (*Seimujikan*), who served as a policy level liaison officer between the Diet and the Ministry, and the Parliamentary Councilor (*Sanyo*), who served as a liaison officer between the Diet and the Ministry, with particular authority over budgetary matters. Both held the rank of *Chokunin* of the First Rank and both were appointed by the Prime Minister on the recommendation of the Minister of Education.

In common with the 12 other Executive Ministries the Ministry of Education in 1937 had a Minister's Secretariat (*Daijin Kambō*), which controlled all functions not specifically delegated to one of the eight permanent bureaus (*kyoku*), with the exception of federal school inspection and certain research in the field of laws and ordinances. At the head of the Secretariat was a Chief Secretary (*Kambōchō*), not to be confused with the Minister's private secretary whose political influence though indirect was profound. The Chief Secretary who held *Sōnin* rank was the administrative director of five sections (*ka*): Personnel (*Kambō ka*), handling promotions, pensions, retirement, ranks, employment of foreigners, custody of seals, supervision of ceremonies, festivals, Imperial portraits and rescripts, and internal control of the Ministry; Archives (*Bunsho ka*), handling official correspondence, filing, compilation of reports and statistics, translation, and isolated administrative matters such as traveling rebates; Accounts (*Kaikei ka*), handling preparation of the budget, accounting, inspection of books, custody of government properties, and all lawsuits; Architecture (*Kenchiku ka*), handling construction, repair, and planning for all schools, the Ministry, libraries, and museums; and Physical Education (*Taiiku ka*), handling school hygiene, hygiene education, physical training, preventive medicine, health statistics, physical training tests, research and competitions, and control of schools for the handicapped.

Two other divisions of the Ministry existed outside the eight permanent bureaus. One was the Division of Superintendents (*Tokugakuhan*), which included 17 roving federal school inspectors holding civil service rank of *Chokunin*, Second Rank, who were charged with spot inspections of educational administration in prefectural schools, and general inspection of school facilities, hygiene, accounts, and teaching in federal schools. Supervision as a separate function of education did not exist in the form familiar to American teachers. The rigid federal control of curriculum, methods, textbook preparation, teachers' manuals, and teacher preparation, together with the inflexible line and staff organization tended to make supervision an administrative rather than a professional function. Thus, with the exception of seven full-time inspectors in the field of social education, supervision depended upon the regular staffs of the Secretariat and the eight bureaus. In 1937 there was a permanent Inquiry Committee on Laws and Ordinances, which was expected to draft educational ordinances, laws, and regulations and to recommend legal revision in accordance with educational policy of the Ministry. It has been traditional for similar Ministers' committees (*iinkai*) to be established from time to time to investigate and recommend policy on a special educational or cultural problem. Among such special committees functioning between 1937 and the outbreak of the second World War were the Committee on Romanization of the Japanese Language, the National Language Committee, the Textbook Committee, the National Treasure Preservation Committee, and the Earthquake Disaster Prevention Committee.

The eight permanent bureaus (*kyoku*) in the 1937 Ministry of Education were headed by Bureau Chiefs (*Kyokuchō*) usually holding the civil service position of *Chokunin* of either the First or Second Rank. Although not always trained specialists in the discipline of education, they were usually educators in the broad sense that they had extensive experience either on university faculties, in public school administration, or in lesser educational bureaus. The general functions of the complex educational system were allocated to the various bureaus on two bases: one, structural, with higher, secondary, and elementary education considered separately; and the other, functional, with religion, textbooks, thought control, social and technical education established as divisions. Below the Bureau Chiefs were a broadening base of bureaucratic technicians, researchists, and clerks holding civil service tenure and ranks from *Sōnin* of the Third Rank down to *Hannin* of the Fourth Rank. Translated into terms more familiar to Americans this means that in higher brackets of the bureaucratic hierarchy were relatively competent technicians, usually graduates of an Imperial University and predominantly of Tokyo Imperial University, and in the lower brackets were the pathetic teen-age girls who brought tea, and the threadbare, defeated, myopic government workers who listlessly copied figures and filed papers and waited for retirement.

Most powerful of the eight bureaus was the Bureau of General Educational Affairs (*Futsū Gakumu Kyoku*), which was divided into two sections: The Section of School Affairs (*Gakumu Ka*), which had charge of all matters concerning kindergarten, primary schools, normal schools, boys' and girls' middle schools, schools for the blind, deaf, and dumb, sanctioned schools in foreign countries, special educational institutes, compulsory education, military education in public schools, and tests and certification of teachers above the elementary level; and the Section of

General Affairs (*Shomu Ka*), which was charged with responsibility for federal grants and subsidies to local units in connection with compulsory education, for elementary education, normal school education, education for the blind, deaf, and dumb, entrance examinations to special schools, civil service examinations, and for certain legal matters concerned with schools and employees in this level of education.

The Bureau of Higher Educational Affairs (*Semmon Gakumu Kyoku*) was also divided into two sections: The Section of School Affairs (*Gakumu Ka*), which had charge of universities (*daigaku* and *semmon gakkō*), higher schools (*kōtō gakkō*), various special schools of university level, a number of semi-autonomous cultural institutions (such as the Astronomical Observatory, Institute for the Study of Infectious Diseases, Research Institute for Metals, the Earthquake Research Institute, and the Institute for Chemical Research), Japanese students abroad, Chinese students in Japan, tests and certification of higher schoolteachers, and various federal grants; and the Section of Arts and Science (*Gakugei Ka*), which was concerned with the Imperial Academy, the Imperial Academy of Fine Arts, scientific committees, research, and conferences, the granting of degrees, titles and honors, and with meteorological and geodetic services.

The Bureau of Technical Education (*Jitsugyō Gakumu Kyoku*) was divided into two sections: the Section of Commercial and Industrial Education (*Shōkō Kyōiku Bu*), and the Section of Agricultural Education (*Nōgyō Kyōiku Bu*), charged with responsibility for technical, vocational, commercial, nautical, fishery, and agricultural schools, the training of suitable teachers in these fields, the handling of federal grants and subsidies, and the testing and certification of instructors.

The Bureau of Social Education (*Shakai Kyōiku Kyoku*) was divided into three sections: Adult Education (*Seijin Kyōiku Bu*), concerned with libraries, museums, and an adult education program outside the schools; Youth Education (*Seinen Kyōiku Bu*), in charge of continuation schools, youth societies, the Boy Scouts, and the youth schools (*seinen gakkō*) begun on 1 April 1935 ostensibly to give physical and moral training to young men so as to "foster their citizenship" but actually used as a propaganda tool of the militarists and ultranationalists; and General Affairs (*Shomu Bu*), frequently called the Motion Picture Section (*Eiga*

Ka) to differentiate it from the section of the same name in the Bureau of General Education, with responsibility for a regulation and approval of books, popular amusements, and the motion pictures in the public interest.

The Bureau of Textbooks (*Tosho Kyoku*) was divided into two sections: Editorial (*Henshū Ka*), in charge of investigation of the national language and compilation of standard textbooks; and Publications (*Hakko Ka*), which investigated, approved, and certified nonofficial textbooks prepared for use in the schools (usually middle schools and technical schools), and which supervised the publication by private monopolies of the official textbooks compiled in the bureau. In addition there were various compilation or editorial officials (*tosho kanshūkan*) and a permanent Textbook Committee composed of advisers from the Army, Navy, professional, and commercial groups (*Kyōkayō Tosho Iinkai*).

A relatively unimportant subdivision of the Ministry, having bureau status in 1937, was the Bureau of Educational Research (*Kyōiku Chōsa Bu*), which was charged with studying foreign educational methods, systems, and publications with a view to adoption in the Japanese system.

The two final bureaus in the 1937 Ministry of Education have been dissolved and their functions suspended as a result of the Defeat and Occupation.

The Bureau of Thought Control (*Shisō Kyoku*), sometimes called the Bureau of Education and Training (*Kyōgaku Kyoku*), was in charge of molding the people's thoughts to the pattern approved by the military regime in power. This bureau was a propaganda agency and was militantly punitive in nature. It worked in close co-operation with the infamous *Kempei Tai* and other secret police organs. The bureau was divided into two sections: the Section of Thought Problems (*Shisō Ka*), which was charged with "guidance and control of thought problems in schools and social educational institutes, and control of thought problems in other directions," served as the propaganda section and worked with the National Spiritual Culture Research Institute (*Kokumin Seishin Bunka Kenkyūjo*); and the Section of Investigations (*Chōsa Ka*), which operated under a mandate to "investigate thought problems in schools and social educational institutes . . . in other directions . . . at home and abroad . . . and in books." This bureau was the one which produced the basic ultra-nationalistic policy books, *Kokutai no Hongi* ("Cardinal Principles of the National Entity of Japan") and *Shimmin no Michi* ("The Way of the Subject"), both banned by SCAP Directive AG 000.3 (15 Dec 45) CIE, "Abolition of Governmental Sponsorship, Support, Perpetuation, Control, and Dissemination of State Shinto." It was also the bureau which the Japanese had eliminated voluntarily in anticipation of Allied punitive action prior to the formal beginning of the Occupation.

The Bureau of Religions (*Shūkyō Kyoku*) was divided into two sections: the Section of Religious Affairs (*Shūmu Ka*), which supervised all religious sects, denominations, churches, temples, cathedrals, priests, missionaries, and other matters pertaining to religion; and the Section of Preservation (*Hozon Ka*), charged with responsibility for the preservation of national treasures, historic spots, scenic beauties, and art treasures. This bureau was given the added responsibility of jurisdiction over all matters contained in the Religious Bodies Law (*Shūkyō Dantai Hō*), Law No. 77 of 1939 promulgated on 8 April 1939, which forced all recognized religious bodies, including the 13 sects of Sect Shinto (*Shūha Shintō* or *Kyōha Shintō*), to become juridical persons, a sort of legal incorporation but granted certain tax immunities which previously had been enjoyed only by the Buddhist sects. The official national cult of Japan, State Shinto (*Kokka Shintō* or *Jinja Shintō*), was not considered a religion and was regulated by the Shrine Board (*Jingi-in* or *Jinja Kyoku*) of the Ministry of Home Affairs (*Naimushō*). The Bureau of Religions was unobtrusively dissolved in the autumn of 1945 under pressure from the Occupation Headquarters and as a result of the abrogation of the Religious Bodies Law by the SCAP Directive of 4 October 1945, commonly known as the "Japanese Bill of Rights." It was permitted to continue functioning on an unofficial and interim basis, however, during the preparation and implementation of the SCAP Directive on Shinto, and during the preparation of a new Religious Bodies Law which was found necessary in order to straighten out the financial tangle occasioned by the precipitate abrogation of the earlier one.

A peculiar triple form of control was exercised by the National Ministry of Education (*Mombushō*) over subordinate educational institutions. Certain schools, such as the schools for the blind, deaf, and dumb, the higher normal schools, the higher schools (*kōtō gakkō*), certain special and technical schools, and the universities were directly under the control of the Ministry. Even the Imperial universities, which enjoyed the highest degree of autonomy of all Japanese tax-supported educational institutions, were nominally under the control of the Ministry of Education and in certain extremely important matters, such as granting of degrees, were actually under its control. A second group of schools, including the middle schools, normal schools, and certain special and technical schools directly under the prefectural (*ken*) authorities, were controlled indirectly by the Ministry of Education through the Education Section (*Kyōiku Ka*) of the Prefectural Department of Education (*Gakumu Bu*). A third group of schools, including kindergartens, elementary schools of both levels, youth schools (*seinen gakkō*), and a small number of middle schools and technical schools, were controlled through the local village (*mura*), town (*machi*), city (*shi*), and municipality (*to* or *fu*) educational departments.

The channels of authority from the Ministry of Education down to the individual schools resemble the parallel system in use in most military organizations: basic policy and administrative orders were analogous to the military command channel and went from Minister to prefectural governor to local mayor to head of the school; minor policy and internal administrative regulations were analogous to the technical channels of a military engineering or medical department and went from the appropriate bureau chief in the national ministry either directly to the schools or via the pertinent sub-section of the educational department of prefecture, city, town, or village. Basic policy was established by national laws (*Hōritsu*), which according to Article XXXVII of the Meiji *Constitution* required the consent of the Imperial Diet (*Teikoku Gikai*), and by Imperial ordinances (*Teikoku Chokurei*), which were issued by the Emperor but were prepared by the Minister of Education and bore his countersignature. Basic policy of a more transient nature or administrative decisions not requiring the prestige accorded a law or Imperial ordinance were ordinarily put in the form of Ministry of Education orders (*Mombushōrei* and *Mombushō Kunrei*) which approximated executive orders in American governmental procedure. The compilation of all these laws, ordinances, and orders, together with their periodic amendments and technical interpretations, constituted the *Mombuhōrei* or Ministry of Education regulations which were the final standard in Japanese education. Below these basic legal instruments were a vast number of technical and administrative regulations or instructions, corresponding to the technical instructions of a military organization, issued by bureau chiefs in the Ministry and by the educational officials in subordinate political units.

Because the type of control exerted depended both upon the academic level of the school to which it was intended and also upon the particular educational element (curricula, textbooks, administration, personnel, and finance) under consideration, a detailed examination of these channels must be delayed until the school structure has been reviewed.

The school structure of Japan in 1937 was almost entirely under the Ministry of Education. It is true that a few isolated schools were independent of that Ministry and were both supervised and financed through other governmental agencies. Thus, the Peers' School and the Peeresses' School were under the Ministry of the Imperial Household (*Kunaishō*); the various military and naval academies were under the Ministries of War (*Rikugunshō*) and Navy (*Kaigunshō*), respectively; various technical schools in forestry, sericulture, and fishing were under the Ministry of Agriculture and Forestry (*Norinshō*); and the police academies were under the Ministry of Home Affairs (*Naimushō*). It is also true that even among the schools under the control of the Ministry of Education, a majority were indirectly affected by other ministries. Thus the Ministry of Home Affairs appointed the prefectural governors (*Kenchiji*), who in addition to their other political responsibilities, were the legal educational deputies of the national Minister of Education, and as such controlled the elementary system with approximately three quarters of the 15,201,485 students enrolled in 1937. The Ministry of War controlled the military officers who served as instructors in virtually all public secondary schools under the provisions of Ministry of War Order No. 19 of 1935. The Ministry of Finance (*Ōkurashō*) had final control over all public budgets and immediate control over two of the most important sources of educational funds, the general distribution tax (*bun-yo-zei*) and the educational subsidy (*haifu-kin*). But authority over the Japanese educational system was so completely conceded to lie with the Ministry of Education that for the sake of brevity only those schools under its control will be noted.

The 1937 "normal" school system was somewhat arbitrarily divided into three levels (elementary, secondary, and higher education) on the basis of advancement up the educational ladder, and into a fourth area (special education), based not on the level but on the type of subject matter. This latter was composed of schools concerned primarily with continuation, vocational, and nonacademic instruction.

Elementary education was offered in three types of schools: kindergartens (*yōchien*), which after 1930 included nursery schools (*takujijo*); ordinary elementary schools (*jinjō shō gakkō*); and higher elementary schools (*kōtō shō gakkō*).

The kindergarten was only vaguely controlled by the Ministry of Education, since it was not a part of any official system, and, with the exception of a few isolated examples attached to teacher training or research institutes, was neither the object of official inspection and supervision nor the recipient of tax support. Kindergartens were established by private individuals, philanthropic groups, religious orders, and the local governments of cities, towns, and villages. Their internal organization and curriculum was copied from the German original.

The ordinary elementary school constituted the core of the Japanese educational system in 1937 and despite reforms still does. At that time the regulations requiring six years of compulsory education, which had been established by the reform of March 1907 and put into effect on 1 April 1908, were still in effect. Official statistics indicate that for the years 1935-39 no less than 99.59% of all children of compulsory school age actually attended school, a figure which if true would place Japan above all other nations in this regard. The school course was six years and the school year was rather longer than is customary in Occidental countries, only 90 holidays, including vacations, national holidays, and Sundays, being permitted. The curriculum was entirely prescribed and approximately 40% of instructional time was devoted to learning the mechanics of the written language. On the basis of time allotment arithmetic, with 20% of the instructional time, was second in importance and Japanese ethics (*Shūshin*), and a number of other classes, ranked third with only about 8%. On the basis of the importance accorded a subject regardless of its time allotment, *Shūshin* almost certainly would have ranked first in all curricula from the beginning of the twentieth century to Surrender. The objective of this basic elementary education was defined by the Ministry of Education as being: ". . . to instil into the youthful minds the elements of moral and general education, and the knowledge and ability essential for the conduct of life, care being taken at the same time to develop the physique of the children." (Trans. by KEENLEYSIDE and THOMAS, *op. cit.*, p. 175.)

Despite the fact that the compulsory school laws did not require attendance beyond the ordinary elementary school, that school was not considered terminal in character. An extension of the elementary school, corresponding to the upper cycle in most systems based on the French model, was provided in the form of the higher elementary school. This was a two- to three-year, noncompulsory, terminal course offering advanced work in the same subjects taught in the ordinary elementary school and in addition an introduction to vocational education which occupied about 20% of the instructional time. Graduates of this higher elementary school either left the educational system or had the option of continuing in vocational schools, normal schools, the girls' middle schools, or (by examination) the boys' middle schools. Of the 25,906 elementary schools in 1937 approximately 26.9% were ordinary, .7% were higher, and the remainder, or about 72.4%, included both levels. It is significant that 99.3% of these schools were maintained by cities, towns, and villages, under supervision by the prefectural authorities, while the insignificant remainder were private schools and tax-supported institutions attached to higher governmental schools. It is also significant that the two levels of the elementary school enrolled 11,792,738 or about 77.4% of the 15,201,485 students in all Japanese formal education that year. There was a total of 268,686 teachers, with almost exactly twice as many men as women.

Secondary education was offered in three basic secondary schools (*chūto gakkō*), enrolling students of roughly parallel age groups but offering widely different curricula: the boys' middle school (*chū gakkō*); the girls' middle school (*kōtō jo gakkō*), sometimes known in English as the girls' higher school; and special or technical schools (*jitsugyō gakkō*), which included secondary level trade, technical, vocational, commercial, and normal schools, and institutions for the handicapped. This latter group of special schools should not be confused with the special schools maintained by Ministries other than that of education and designed to train specialized personnel employed in the subordinate echelons of those Ministries.

Traditionally the most important of the secondary schools was the boys' middle school (*chū gakkō*). It was not expressly designed to be a university preparatory school and in fact approximately 74.1% of its graduates did not go on to further schooling. But in effect, at least in the large cities, it did become a preparatory school, since both the curriculum and the tradition of the school emphasized preparation for entrance into the higher school (*kōtō gakkō*), which was solely concerned with university preparatory study, or with entrance directly into a military or technical school of post-secondary level. In 1937 the five-year boys' middle school was divided into two integrated levels: the lower being a two-year generalized course offering many of the same subjects as those taught in elementary schools but given with greater detail, and in addition elementary military training and language study; and the upper being a three-year specialized course including civics, military education, foreign language, and laboratory science in addition to those courses continued from elementary school. English, French, and German were offered as language electives but English predominated about ten to one, with German second, largely elected by premedical and scientific students. This upper level was in turn divided into two sections: the *Dai Ichibu*, or First Section, which was strictly preparatory to entrance into a higher school; and the *Dai Nibu*, or Second Section, which was a terminal course. Because the prestige of the school depended to a major degree on the percentage of the students who were sent to the higher school, the preparatory section, *Dai Ichibu*, normally set the pace.

Admission was difficult, with only about 55.8% of the applicants accepted. This becomes more significant when it is realized that by official statistics approximately 99.6% of the students who had enrolled in the first grade of the elementary school in 1932 actually graduated from the six-year course in 1937, and that of those graduating (both boys and girls) only 9.7% applied for the boys' middle school. Once admitted, the student found competition most intense. It was common knowledge that only about 87.4% would survive the five-year course; that of those graduates only 7.7% would be admitted to a higher school and thus virtually assured of later admission to a university; and that of this tiny residue only about half would be admitted to a higher school which had the reputation of securing a high percentage of admissions to one of the much desired Imperial universities. There were other roads to the university but that of the boys' middle school was the usual even though difficult way. In 1937 there were 563 of these schools with 14,312 teachers and 364,461 students.

The feminine counterpart of the boys' middle school was the girls' middle school, sometimes literally translated girls' higher school though it was not on the same academic level as the *kōtō gakkō.* This was also a five-year course nominally offering much the same curriculum as the boys' middle school. In actual practice, however, many schools offered only a four-year course and the work accomplished was generally considered to be of inferior quality to that expected in the boys' middle school. Some three-year girls' middle schools existed, but these required graduation from the higher elementary school (eight years) rather than from the ordinary elementary school (six years) for admission. The girls' middle schools were also highly selective at entrance, though less competitive than the boys' during their course and at graduation because there were far fewer opportunities to go on to higher education with the result that a preponderance of the students considered them terminal in character. The girls' middle school compared favorably with the boys' statistically, though equally indicating a very marked falling off of students beyond the elementary level. Thus approximately 12.5% of the graduates of the lower schools applied for admission, as compared to 9.7% for the boys, and 62% of these applicants were accepted, as compared with 55.8% for the boys. In 1937 there were 996 schools, 16,887 teachers, and 444,535 students. Slightly more than half of the teachers were men, while almost 100% of the teachers of the boys' middle school were male.

The third major type of secondary level school was the technical school, sometimes translated into English as special school. This was a generic term for any of the considerable variety of vocational, commercial, and trade schools which existed as separate institutions offering two- to four-year courses in one or more specialties. Five types of these schools occurred in sufficient numbers to be considered classes in themselves: agricultural school (*nōgyō gakkō*), commercial school (*shōgyō gakkō*), fisheries school (*suisan gakkō*), industrial school (*kōgyō gakkō*), and trade or vocational school (*shokugyō gakkō*). In addition to these there were relatively autonomous individual schools for the blind (*mō gakkō*), for the deaf and dumb (*mōa gakkō*), and, although they were not on the secondary level, for art (*bijutsu gakkō*) and music (*ongaku gakkō*). In 1937 there were 1,355 of the vocational schools with 20,879 teachers and 447,449 students, while there were 140 schools for the handicapped, with 1,383 teachers and 3,586 students. There were 848 of all the other special schools lumped together, with 10,896 teachers and 159,190 students.

The youth school (*seinen gakkō*), created by Imperial ordinance on 1 April 1935, had by 1937 become an important part of the educational structure and a powerful political instrument. It was designed to be a continuation course, either full or part time, for graduates of the elementary schools who could not continue in the regular secondary schools. Because it was not an entirely new school but rather an adaption and consolidation of previously existing technical continuation schools for young men, the youth school had been predominantly concerned with various forms of vocational education. By 1937 it was enrolling a small percentage of young women students and had shifted its emphasis to moral education and physical training. The moral education was nationalistic in character and included Japanese ethics.

The youth school was two to seven years in length and rather informally divided into three levels. The lowest level consisted of two years of elementary level extension work designed to parallel the higher elementary school, and to enroll graduates of the six-year ordinary elementary school. The middle of the three levels was five years in length, quasi-secondary in difficulty of subject matter, and enrolled graduates of either the lower level of the youth school or of the higher elementary school. A one-year postgraduate course was occasionally offered in the larger cities and constituted the highest of the three levels. The youth school was not a part of the compulsory educational system in 1937 (it became so in 1939), but the pressure of public opinion plus a certain attractiveness of program led to the somewhat impressive enrollment of 1,764,472 students (68.3% of them young men), and the employment of 75,849 teachers. The official claim of 17,337 schools was somewhat misleading, since these did not necessarily indicate separate buildings, many being located in conventional day schools, used in the evenings, or in spare rooms in large industries.

Higher education in 1937 was offered in four fundamentally different types of schools: normal schools (*shihan gakkō*), higher schools (*kōtō gakkō*), colleges or technical institutes (*semmon gakkō*), and universities (*daigaku*).

The normal school was really four institutions rather than one. The ordinary normal school (*shihan gakkō*) was a five-year training course for prospective elementary schoolteachers. It enrolled students graduated from the higher elementary school, or transferred from the middle schools at an equivalent level, so that in its lower grades it was really a secondary level school. The five years were divided into two cycles, the upper one being three years in length and distinctly post-secondary in curriculum. A second and highly specialized normal school was the normal school for youth schoolteachers (*seinen shihan gakkō*), which was three years in length and enrolled graduates of the middle schools. Two parallel schools, the higher normal school for men (*kōtō shihan gakkō*) and the higher normal school for women (*joshi kōtō shihan gakkō*), offered four-year post-secondary training courses for prospective secondary schoolteachers. These two types of schools admitted graduates of the respective middle schools. Only four of these schools, with 349 teachers and 2,692 students, existed in 1937, a clear statistical indication that the majority of secondary schoolteachers were recruited from other sources, primarily universities and *semmon gakkō*, some of which offered no pedagogical or professional training. In addition to the four formal types of normal schools there were a number of teacher-training institutes (*kyōin yōseijo*), which gave three-year courses to teachers of various technical subjects. Exclusive of the six higher normal schools, there were 154 schools, 2,402 teachers, and 32,-669 students in the 1937 teacher-training system of Japan. It should be noted that a considerable but indeterminate proportion of the women students (about one third of the total) attended these schools with no intention of going into the teaching profession but merely for cultural reasons.

The other of the two types of schools classified as higher but actually serving many of the functions of a secondary school was the higher school. It was the three-year penultimate segment in the rapidly tapering educational pyramid, enrolling only male graduates of their own four-year preparatory department, or graduates of the *Dai Ichibu* Section of the boys' middle schools by examination after four or five years' training. Mention has already been made of the selective entrance examinations and high rate of disqualification for admission which was used effectively to limit the number of candidates for university admission. The higher school was considered purely a university preparatory institution. By some it is claimed that tradition made it somewhat relaxed in the academic standards demanded of students who had been admitted—a sort of semiholiday filled with final adolescent pranks sandwiched in between the brutal academic cramming of the boys' middle school and the serious study of the university. It is quite possible that the obvious disregard of some of the social conventions and the affectation of sloppy clothes and manners were relatively superficial characteristics and not truly indicative of the academic standards maintained. In 1937 there were 32 higher schools, 1,438 teachers, and 17,017 students.

The Japanese college or technical institute (*semmon gakkō*) was a three- to five-year school offering work definitely higher than secondary institutions, frequently of better academic quality than the higher schools yet not accorded quite the recognition given university work. Students were admitted upon graduation from the boys' middle school or by very severe competitive examination if they did not hold that diploma. As the name indicates, they were "specialty" schools offering intensive work in one or more technical specialties and in the arts and sciences. In 1937 there were 213 of these schools (140 of them private), with 9,763 teachers and 121,280 students. They constituted the source of a very large percentage of skilled technicians upon which the Japanese industrial and commercial structure was based.

The highest level of Japanese formal education was given in the university (*daigaku*). There were 45 universities in the four main islands of Japan in 1937, with 5,041 teachers above the level of student assistants, and 51,396 students. It is significant that there were no universities for women, no recognized women faculty members, and only 210 women students. Private universities sometimes had a preparatory department (*yobi ka*) corresponding to a *kōtō gakkō*, or dependent colleges (*semmon gakkō*), attached. The Japanese university proper was organized in semi-autonomous faculties (*gakubu*), each of which was represented on a university council if the university had more than one faculty. After three years of *gakubu* the student could go on to a higher division or graduate level of the faculty, known as the *kenkyū ka*, which in the larger universities were united in a kind of school of higher studies or *daigakuin*. The internal organization was more similar to the French, Italian, or Latin-American universities than to British or American. Courses of study were quite formalized and ranged from four to seven years in length. Curricula were almost entirely prescribed with electives being limited to such minor choices as the selection of a major foreign language from a very restricted list, English and German predominating. Japanese universities were divided into four classes, based on the criterion of financial support. These were the six Imperial universities (*Tōkyō, Kyōto, Tōhoku, Kyūshū, Hokkaidō,* and *Ōsaka* in descending order of prestige and importance), which were essentially autonomous and had several faculties; the 12 government universities, which were accorded nearly the same support and autonomy as the Imperial universities but which consisted of single faculties in commerce, medicine, engineering, and literature and science; two public universities, offering work in commerce and medicine and supported and supervised by governmental bodies other than the Imperial Government, in this case the municipal governments of Osaka and Kyoto; and 25 private universities, some of which were fairly truthful copies of American and European prototypes.

National School Reform of 1941. In December 1938 the Educational Council (*Kyoiku Shingi Kai*), one of the special technical committees organized to advise the Minister of Education, submitted a proposal for the nationalization of the compulsory school system. Bureaus of the Ministry of Education made a careful study during the following year and in March 1940 the Ministry announced that the plan was to be initiated in all parts of the Japanese educational system beginning with the next school year, in April 1941. Had it not been interrupted by the outbreak of World War II this reform would have been the most far-reaching of any of the reforms proposed officially since the writing of the *Educational Code of 1872.* It was interrupted, however, and at the time of Surrender its provisions were almost indiscernible except in the substitution of the name national school (*kokumin gakkō*) for the traditional elementary school (*shō gakkō*); an official claim to eight years of compulsory education in a school system with nearly all schools closed; and a few tattered wartime textbooks reflecting belligerent ultranationalism and militarism. Basically the *National School Reform of 1941* was a curriculum and ideological reform, rebelling against Western culture, "foreignism" and "individualism" in any form, and advocating militant nationalism. Perhaps no more concise statement of the objectives of this reform may be given than that which was stated in the Ministry of Education announcement, Bulletin No. 9, March 1940, "A Reform of Primary Education":

The aim of the National School System is to effect expansion and improvement of primary education and to lay the foundation of a new educational system in Japan. In order to give the rising generation a more thorough basic training as Japanese subjects and make them the vital force behind future national development, the term of compulsory education will be prolonged from six to eight years. The inculcation of the principles on which the Japanese Empire has been founded will be made the principal object of primary education, and for this purpose, uplifting of national spirit, development of intellectual faculties, and elevation of the physical standard will be promoted by carrying out improvements in the quality of education and securing correlation of teaching matter. In a word, the proposed system aims at making the future generation robust enough in mind and body to augment the national strength and display the spirit and ideals of the Japanese nation which have as an end the bringing of the world together into one happy family.

From an organizational viewpoint the plan did not impose any particularly difficult burden. Of the approximately 1,593,000 school children who completed the basic six-year elementary school (*shō gakkō*) in March 1938 about 83% continued on into the higher elementary school (*kōtō shō gakkō*) or went into the middle schools. Thus, at the time of the promulgation of the plan in 1940, when these 1938 graduates and all succeeding classes were affected by the new compulsory education laws, something less than 16% were actually not enrolled in a standard full-time school. In 1939 the youth schools (*seinen gakkō*) were made compulsory for those who had left the regular system, so that even

these 16% presumably were being supplied some part-time education. Absorption of the 16% into existing elementary schools
would have meant only an average increase of ten students per
school. Thus there was not contemplated any immense increase in
enrollment with extraordinary demands on school construction.
The division of the new nationalized schools into two cycles of
six years for the national school (*kokumin gakkō*) and two years
for the higher national school (*kōtō kokumin gakkō*), exactly
paralleling the old ordinary and higher elementary schools, effectively eliminated the reorganizational problems which would
have been probable had a more contrasting plan been adopted.
Finally, the curriculum itself differed more in orientation and
emphasis than in actual subject changes. Thus there was little if
any fundamental reorganization in facilities, such as laboratories,
which would have been expected had a fundamentally different
methodology been contemplated.

Five years later many of the common people still called the
schools *shō gakkō* and the reform was a dead issue.

The Educational System under the Occupation, 1946. Between
8 December 1941 and 2 September 1945 Japanese Education
underwent inevitable wartime changes, many of which were
equally observed in American schools. The secondary school
courses were lowered from five years to four and all vacation periods were eliminated. University students exempted from compulsory military service were required to give increasing proportions of their time to war industries, principally shipbuilding, until
the universities and colleges had practically closed except for certain forms of research. Elementary school children were required
to work in war gardens and were formed into air-defense corps.
Military officers who held relatively unimportant positions on
the faculties as physical training instructors and leaders in the
youth groups assumed authority over the students greater than
even the heads of the schools. Evacuation of children from the
major cities, both on a systematic official basis and by individual
initiative, produced housing problems in rural areas. Bombed out
schools were moved to shrines, temples, public offices, and private
homes.

One wartime change, however, had potential significance. It
was a move to decentralize the powerful controls held by the
Ministry of Education. On 11 July 1945 Radio Tokyo announced

in a broadcast beamed to Greater East Asia that the Ministry of Education was to be reorganized with a 30% cut in staff; with the creation of a new bureau, the Bureau of Student Mobilization (*Gakuto Dōin Kyoku*), established by Imperial Ordinance No. 407 of 11 July 1945, to have special cognizance over the youth corps (*Seinen Dan*) and student war participation; and with the decentralization of many of the Ministry's functions and transferal of some of its important personnel to the newly created regional superintendence generals (*Chihō Sōkan*). These regions had been created as a result of the administrative reorganization of 1943 accomplished under the emergency wartime authority delegated to the Prime Minister in January 1943 by the Diet. According to the "Regulations Relative to Regional Superintendence Generals" (*Chihō Sōkan Kansei*) of 10 June 1945, the four main islands of Japan were divided into nine regions, each containing from two to eight prefectures, which roughly coincided with but were not at all identical with the university districts created in 1872. Karafuto was attached to the Region of *Hokkaidō* and Okinawa was attached to *Kyūshū*, as overseas possessions still under the control of Japan and approximating prefectures in organization. The other seven regions were: *Tōhoku*, centered around Miyagi; *Kantō*, the great plain surrounding Tokyo; *Hokuriku*, with its center at Niigata; *Tōkaidō*, named for the ancient road between the Palace at Kyoto and the Shogun's *Bakufu* in *Edo*; *Kinki*, with center at Osaka; *Chūgoku*, with center at Hiroshima; and *Shikoku*, the island bounding the south of the Inland Sea.

The avowed purpose of transferring many of the powers from the central government to these regions was alleged to be increased efficiency, a claim which perhaps had some merit as transportation and communication lines became disrupted in 1945. But it appears clear that the real purpose was to prepare for an expected invasion of the homeland, when one section of the nation might be cut off completely from the rest, and to disperse vital governmental records and personnel in the face of increased air raids. Actually, however, the dispersal of Ministry of Education functions consisted more in evacuating personnel and matériel to near-by rural areas than it did in decentralizing basic controls. The Compilation Section of the Bureau of Textbooks, for example, was located in a women's higher normal school on the outskirts of Tokyo at the time of its occupation by Allied troops, but the vital control over the nation's textbooks continued to be located in the Ministry of Education. As for the regions, within two months after Surrender their importance, if it had ever existed, had so faded that it became a minor research problem to discover from educational officials exactly where the boundaries had been set and what the delegated powers had been. The Occupation wiped out an embryonic tendency to decentralization and re-established a concentration of administrative control which probably exceeded anything that had existed prior to the war.

It would be very easy to fall into the error of discerning too many reforms and changes in the educational system during the first two years of the Occupation. In the first year there were five reorganizations of the Ministry. In January 1947 there was inaugurated, in theory, the basic reform which conservative Japanese delight in terming the *Shōwa* Restoration. Actually these changes have been very slight and have tended to be more the mere reshuffling of boxes in an organization chart than real reforms of the physical school system. For the sake of brevity the organization which existed at the time of the United States Education Mission to Japan, in March and April 1946, will be taken as standard.

Of all elements in the school system the Ministry of Education differed most from the 1937 organization. There was still a Minister (*Mombudaijin*) at the head of the Ministry, appointed by the Emperor on the recommendation of the Prime Minister and still holding the highest civil service rank of *Shinnin*. He was still preoccupied with the political maneuvering of vital issues rather than the routine administrative direction of the Ministry or the school system. There was also a Vice-Minister (*Mombujikan*), who was presumed to be a nonpolitical appointee of the Minister, though there were actually more Vice-Ministers in the first two years of the Occupation than there were Ministers. He still held *Chokunin* rank and was charged with the major executive responsibility. But the two liaison positions, the Parliamentary Vice-Minister (*Seimujikan*) and the Parliamentary Councilor (*Sanyo*) of the 1937 system, no longer existed.

The greatest change in the organization of the Ministry, of course, was the elimination of the Bureau of Religions (*Shūkyō Kyoku*) and the Bureau of Thought Control (*Shisō Kyoku*), which had been prominent in the 1937 organization. But of some importance to the school system proper was the revised organization of the bureaus which had direct control over the schools themselves.

The old bureaus of General Educational Affairs (*Futsū Gakumu Kyoku*), Higher Education (*Semmon Gakumu Kyoku*), and Technical Education (*Jitsugyō Gakumu Kyoku*) were combined into a single organ, the Bureau of School Education (*Gakkō Kyōiku Kyoku*), which became something of a little Ministry of Education within the Ministry. It was divided into five sections: university (*Daigaku Kyōiku Ka*), college (*Semmon Kyōiku Ka*), normal school (*Shihan Kyōiku Ka*), secondary school (*Chūtō Kyōiku Ka*), and elementary and continuation school (*Seishonen Kyōiku Ka*). In practice this combined bureau was found to be quite unwieldy and inefficient.

Another bureau change in the Ministry was the expansion of the old Section of Physical Education (*Taiiku Ka*) of the Minister's Secretariat into a full Bureau of Physical Education (*Taiiku Kyoku*), probably inspired by the emphasis on physical education occasioned by the suppression of the military arts (*budō*) through pressure from SCAP Headquarters in the early months of the Occupation. In addition to the promotion of athletics, physical education, and school hygiene which had concerned the original section in the Secretariat, the new bureau added a fourth, the Labor Service Section (*Kinro Ka*), which had charge of school gardens and similar programs aimed at alleviating the disastrous food shortage which was the nation's principal problem during the first year of Occupation.

The old Bureau of Social Education (*Shakai Kyōiku Kyoku*) was continued and three new sections were added. These were the Investigation Section (*Chōsa Ka*), which continued the functions of the extinct 1937 Bureau of Educational Research (*Kyōiku Chōsa Bu*), and the two sections of Religious Affairs (*Shūmu Ka*) and Art (*Geijutsu Ka*), which were taken over from the suppressed Bureau of Religions (*Shūkyō Kyoku*) and charged with liquidating its long-term responsibilities. The other three sections, holding the same responsibility as in the 1937 Bureau of Social Education, were those of Social Education (*Shakai Kyōiku Ka*), Civic Education (*Kōmin Kyōiku Ka*), and Cultural Education (*Bunka Kyōiku Ka*).

A new Bureau of Scientific Education (*Kagaku Kyōiku Kyoku*) was created in the 1946 Ministry of Education. It was charged with a few of the functions of the old Bureau of Vocational Education (*Jitsugyō Gakumu Kyoku*) but was essentially concerned with scientific rather than vocational or trade education. The Japanese were disillusioned by their poor showing in vital scientific research during the progress of the war and perhaps uncritically placed much of the blame for the defeat on this deficiency. The Vice-Minister of Education under Minister ABE Yoshishige of the SHIDEHARA Cabinet and later under Minister TANAKA Kōtarō of the YOSHIDA Cabinet was YAMAZAKI Kyōsuke, distinguished engineer and professor at Tokyo Imperial University. Professor YAMAZAKI was convinced that Japan could only survive restrictions of heavy industry if it developed an entirely new economy based on highly skilled trades and light industry such as watchmaking, optical instruments, textiles, and eventually radio and electronic equipment. Under his direction first as Bureau Chief and later as Vice-Minister, this bureau assumed considerable importance. It was divided internally into four sections: Scientific Education (*Kagaku Kyōiku Ka*), Cultural Science Research (*Jinbun Kagaku Kenkyu Ka*), Natural Science Research (*Shizen Kagaku Kenkyu Ka*), and Research and Reports (*Chōsa Ka*).

The last of the five bureaus in the 1946 organization of the Ministry of Education was the Bureau of Textbooks (*Kyōkasho Kyoku*). It was charged with identical duties and organized in much the same manner as in 1937 except that the Compilation Section had for administrative reasons been divided into two sections: one in charge of actual preparation of official textbooks (*Dai-ichi Henshuka*), the other in charge of "investigation and sanction" of commercially produced textbooks for use in secondary and higher level schools (*Dai-ni Henshuka*). A General Affairs Section (*Shomu Ka*) and a Research and Reports Section (*Chōsa Ka*) had also been added. In 1937 the thought control investigators had performed the function of sanctioning commercially produced texts, to satisfy the demands of the Japanese military clique who feared "individualism." In 1946 the textbook compilation functionaries continued this work in compliance with the requirements of the Allied Military Occupation Forces who feared "ultranationalism." Perhaps the motives of the latter were more defensible. But the textbooks of the nation were still being filtered through the facilely manipulated orifice of a bureaucratic editorial board.

There is a certain deceptive ease about paper reforms. In the monthly reports which the Ministry of Education submitted to the Civil Information and Education Section (CI&E) of the Headquarters of the Supreme Commander for the Allied Powers, these changes in the Ministry seemed both impressive and laudatory. But in the realities of the Ministry itself much of this reform appeared nebulous and transitory. A page from the informal personal notes of the naval officer in charge of Educational Reorganization, made just prior to the arrival of the United States Education Mission in Tokyo on 5 March 1946, may prove revealing:

Visited the *Mombushō* from 0800 to 1530 today. Expected the place to be a hive of activity just before the Mission arrives. Wrong again. No different from what it was before I left for Korea. All the evidences of the war are still here. The building is cold, grimy, cluttered. In the courtyard there is still the same old air-raid shelter, three beatdown [Pacific Theater slang, i.e., badly strafed or deteriorated] charcoal burning sedans, piles of rubbish. The front door was locked and nobody but the Vice Minister and about twenty janitors and tea girls were on the job before 0930 and the rest straggled in up till about 1100, coming from the suburbs on the rickety trams and underground. Everyone is shabby, unshaven, dirty and dejected. But the war alone can't account for a lot of the inefficiency. In part it is due to an economy of cheap labor, in part due to their inefficient writing system, and in part it's just plain bureaucracy! It is a little difficult to reconcile their war effort and industrial efficiency before the war with this example of a people fighting for existence. It is more like the waiting room in an old-time RR station with a few characters dozing on the benches than the nerve center of an educational system of nearly 18 million students.

They have no system of screening visitors, and Bureau Chiefs and even the Vice Minister spend half their time seeing any school teacher or principal who drifts into the capital with his own little problem. I checked on the files in two sections again today to see if my indicators have been disturbed in the past month. They not only haven't been discovered and hence the files haven't even been opened, but there is a mouse nest in one! So help me! With every English teacher in the country dependent on the *Mombushō* if they ever want to teach again, they still haven't a translator pool and are limping along with about six fairly proficient translators. The ex-Minister's daughter is by far the best but they've almost killed her off with overwork. They have over 900 employees now, more than before the War, but the bales of documents and files that have been brought back here are still unsorted. In the latest reorganization they just pasted up new paper signs on the doors; didn't even have the old personnel change desks. They are terribly overcrowded in the bureaus but there are about a dozen large "conference rooms" that are empty and idle. There were only six persons using the Japanese typewriter, and two women using western or *romaji* typewriters. How an organization of this size can expect to get its work done with every document having to be copied by hand is beyond me.

On the morning of 9 March 1946 the United States Education Mission to Japan and the Japanese Education Committee assembled in the auditorium of the Peers' Club in Tokyo to be briefed on the problem of reorganization. All officials of the Ministry of Education from the Vice-Minister to sub-section chiefs were assembled on the platform. The Minister was absent, answering questions in the Diet. The following is a quotation of the stenographic record of the last part of the briefing by the American naval officer:

What is wrong? You will hear the Vice Minister in just a moment speak of what the Ministry of Education itself considers is wrong with the system.

I cannot present the public's case. I am an officer of another nation. No one who is outside the teaching profession in Japan is really competent to make such a statement. No one who is in the teaching profession of Japan, and wishes to stay in it, dares speak frankly.

Perhaps, however, I can analyse for you the letters to this Headquarters—letters of criticism. These letters charge that the *Mombushō* is staffed with civil service bureaucrats, and the lowest level of them at that; that the *Gakubatsu*, the Old *Teidai* Tie [refers to the Japanese educational clique, drawn from *Teidai*, Japanese colloquial for *Tōkyō Teikoku Daigaku* or Tokyo Imperial University], controls education; that all the reforms are paper plans but that there is no realization of these plans in the schools; that the *Mombushō* stifles freedom of the individual; that this staff sitting on the stage before you harbours militarists in temporary hiding. . . . And then many of the letters end with a request for appointment to the very staff they condemn!

Occasionally criticisms of the Ministry of Education would appear in the public press. One of the most detailed was a long feature article by NISHIZAWA Eiichi, entitled "Education in the

Past Marked by Government Interference: System of Teaching Was Completely Deprived of Vitality and Initiative by Bureaucrats," which ran from 6 to 8 November 1945 in the *Nippon Times*. A quotation of a part of the concluding section highlights the danger of military domination:

. . . the Minister of Education came to have a highly unenviable epithet conferred upon him by the sarcastic portion of the public, that is, the "Parasite Minister," feeding upon the sweat and blood of other cabinet ministers and having the ministerial portfolio given to him only by the exigencies of the constitutional politics of the country. This state of things inevitably brought about in time the highly undesirable method of giving the post of Education Minister to a person who belonged to either of the two armed services, and who possessed, of course, neither understanding nor sympathy for education or matters connected with education. The following instances substantiate this statement: there were in the earlier years of the Meiji era, Marquis TsUGUMICHI [SAIGŌ Tsugumichi], who was Admiral of the Imperial Navy, followed by Count Sekunori KABAYAMA, who was also an Admiral, Vice-Admiral Viscount Takeaki YENOMOTO, Marshal Prince Iwao OHYAMA, General Prince Taro KATSU, General Count Gentaro KODAMA, and finally General Baron Sadao ARAKI. In most recent days, another instance was furnished by Lieutenant General Harushige NINOMIYA. [Occidental students would include in this list other outstanding militarists, among whom Gen. TŌJŌ Hideki, Japan's wartime Premier who assumed the portfolio of Minister of Education following the Cabinet reorganization in April 1943, would occupy a prominent, if infamous, position.]

* * *

It is really a great disadvantage and loss to the State that the important porfolio of Minister of Education has for many years been occupied by men lacking in foresight and enthusiasm, constantly living under the influence of Bureaucracy.

A few of these criticisms toyed with the idea that the authority of the Ministry should be drastically reduced. Such was HOASHI Riichiro's article, "Scheme to Place Education on Democratic Basis Bared: Government Control Should Be Ended in New Setup, Writer Proposes," which appeared in the 26 March 1946 issue of the *Nippon Times*. Professor ŌNISHI Masao's article, "Education Ministry Criticized as Being Inept and Feudalistic," appearing in the 28 January 1946 *Nippon Times*, concluded that "the complete disbandment" of the Ministry of Education is the indicated solution. Most of such suggestions, however, were more rebellion against some abuse by the Ministry than a dispassionate conclusion that that central organ was inherently dangerous and undesirable. Typical of this viewpoint was the conclusion reached by 18 fairly prominent schoolmen in Tokyo, reported in the article, "Educationalists Hit Education Ministry," appearing in the *Nippon Times* for 27 November 1945. According to this article, they felt:

. . . that the educationalists in Japan had never been allowed to carry on education in accordance with ideas or creed of their independent thinking. They had been forced to teach what officials of the Education Ministry, who included young university graduates, would like them to teach. Under these circumstances, officials of the Education Ministry, who during the war had whipped the teaching staff of the schools all over the country to militarism, had no right to request resignation of the educationalists unless the officials themselves first retire from public life.

ABE Yoshishige, then Minister of Education and formerly head of the First Higher School in Tokyo, represents the highest type of traditional Japanese educator. He was considered something of a liberal before the war, was universally respected as a man of integrity and intellect, and was considered highly acceptable by the responsible officials in the Occupation Headquarters. His attitude toward the position of the Ministry of Education may have been somewhat colored by his official position, but was representative of a very large percentage of the professional educators of Japan. Writing in the *Shukyo-to-Bunka* he held:

The Education Ministry has carried the least weight among the governmental ministries, and the portfolio of Education has been held in less regard than any other portfolio. This anomaly must be remedied by making the position of the Education Minister weightier and stronger. It may further be suggested that the permanence of position like that assured for judicial officials should be guaranteed to educators, with due care taken to prevent stagnancy settling in the educational world on that account. (Trans. by *Nippon Times*, reprinted 27 March 1946.)

Perhaps there has been no more illuminating commentary appear in public print in Japan during the Occupation than that which was stated by ABE Shinnosuke, Adviser to the *Mainichi*, in his article, "Shidehara Cabinet Analyzed," which appeared on 31 October 1945:

I am given to understand that the Education Office is soon to gather the principals of normal schools in Tōkyō to give them a short course in democratization of educators. I do not know how long the course would be, but one must not take it for granted that a course lasting two or three days could repaint the face of the education.

What I actually think is that even such [a] short course is not necessary. In fact, I believe just a brief official instruction ordering them to "democratize the education from now on," would be sufficient. Why? Because the educators in this country do not value such [a] thing as "ism" in their education. They would carry out whatever they are told to by the Education Office, regardless of totalitarianism or democracy.

So long as they were directed from the Education Office, they would follow the order to a T. Therefore, the attempt to reform them into democratic educators on the surface would not be worth the stamp that has to be put on the official letter addressed to them.

Next in importance to the vital problem of what organization and authority the Ministry of Education was to hold was the question of what should be its personnel. This was a problem which concerned not only the teaching profession and the Japanese people but the Occupation Authorities as well. The formal screening of public officials and purge of politically unacceptable incumbents will be considered in a later portion of this volume. It is enough to note at this point that the screening process was negative in nature, designed to eliminate those who were dangerous and not to detect and encourage those who could make a positive contribution to the democratic re-education of Japan. The first three years of the Occupation proved singularly disappointing in this larger mission, at least in so far as the Ministry of Education is concerned.

The first Minister of Education with whom the Occupation Forces had to deal was MAEDA Tamon, brilliant and suave former Director of the Japanese Institute in New York who was repatriated on the S.S. *Gripsholm* and became Governor of the Prefecture of Niigata and President of the Hokuriku Regional Council until his removal on 25 February 1944. Although MAEDA Tamon resigned his postwar position as Minister of Education in anticipation of being purged under the provisions of the first SCAP Removal and Exclusion Directive, AG 091-1 (4 January 1946) GS, it was generally considered that his unacceptability was based on a technicality (formal membership in certain banned Imperial assistance societies which had automatically accompanied his wartime post as governor), and that his tenure of office as Minister of Education had been marked by full co-operation with the Occupation Forces and by a policy of considerable liberalism. He had replaced most of the bureau and section chiefs in the Ministry with professors, educators, and public figures who had records of democratic tendencies and in some cases active opposition to the expansionist policies of the prewar militarists. These educators worked diligently, and one, Dr. TANAKA Kōtarō, Professor of Law at Tokyo Imperial University, rose to be Minister of Education in the YOSHIDA Cabinet. But it was apparent to foreign observer and Japanese alike that they were defeated in their efforts by the delaying tactics and active obstruction of the entrenched bureaucrats who made up their staffs.

On one occasion during the tenure of Minister ABE Yoshishige in the spring of 1946 it was necessary to censure Dr. TANAKA Kōtarō, then serving as Chief of the Bureau of School Education, because he appeared for a scheduled official conference at Occupation Headquarters completely unprepared with the information which was required, and had to be briefed by his subordinates in the presence of the waiting Allied officers. It was positively known by those Allied officers that Dr. TANAKA had been placed deliberately in this compromising and humiliating position by his own assistants, who had untruthfully professed ignorance of the agenda and had made temporarily unavailable the necessary data.

How well the established bureaucrats were able to defeat the evanescent evidences of educational liberalism may be inferred from a personal letter to an American naval officer from one of the most able Japanese officials, a man who continuously from the first of the Occupation held a position which enabled him to know the highest level of policy making. His name, for obvious reasons, is withheld. This letter was dated 10 March 1947 at the time when Dr. TANAKA Kōtarō had just left the YOSHIDA Cabinet:

. . . Dr. Tanaka has resigned from his post. . . . It is my great disappointment that he left from his post before he accomplished his plan about Japanese Education. Do you know who succeeded Mr. Yamazaki's position? It must be a great surprise to hear that Mr. Arimitsu was the man. I have too many things to tell you about the procedure. But now I want to tell you just that all the personnel whom Mr. Maeda invited to *Mombushō* have left it now and all the positions in *Mombushō*, except that of Head of the School Education Bureau, are in the hands of *Mombushō* people again.

Mr. YAMAZAKI was the able, sincere, and liberal Vice-Minister who has already been mentioned and Mr. ARIMITSU, his successor as Vice-Minister, was a petty bureaucrat who was caught red-handed by the American naval officer to whom this letter was sent in a flagrant violation of the Occupation controls on textbook publication and was publicly reprimanded, fined, and temporarily suspended. His appointment as Vice-Minister was both a commentary on the short memory or indifference of the Occupation Forces and on the power and arrogance of the traditional Japanese bureaucrats. The claim advanced in a 20 January 1947 press release from the Public Relations Office of General Headquarters, Far Eastern Command, that one third of the wartime personnel of the Ministry of Education had been removed or persuaded to resign voluntarily, appears to have been somewhat oversimplified.

Below the level of the national Ministry of Education, the educational system of 1946 was little different from that of the "normal" year of 1937. The prefectural educational departments differed in minor details but were essentially still subordinate reflections of the national Ministry. In the major cities and municipalities there were still educational departments which were organized on a bureau basis, operating in their restricted areas as did the prefectural departments and national Ministry. In the smaller cities, towns, and villages there were still the relatively impotent nonprofessional Councils of Education which rubber-stamped the actions of the headman (*chō*). The Ministry of Home Affairs still controlled the selection of prefectural governors, who still acted as chief educational deputies of the national Minister of Education. The Ministry of Finance still controlled the vital National Distribution Tax (*bun-yo-zei*) and Educational Subsidies (*haifu-kin*). The Purge, only slightly effective in the early part of 1946, had reached down increasingly into the personnel of the various administrative levels during 1947, but was ineffective against the educational danger which was far greater than an occasional rabid militarist—the great entrenched mass of conservative bureaucrats.

Under constant prodding from a foreign invader, itself a grave educational hazard, the Japanese Government had apparently cleared from the school system most known militarists and ultranationalists by the end of the first two years of Occupation. But the superficiality of such a forced procedure may be suggested by the first major Japanese housecleaning conducted by the Ministry of Home Affairs on 27 October 1945, only 55 days after unconditional Surrender, when prudence as well as repentance dictated faithful compliance with the spirit of Occupational policy. No less than 32 of the 47 prefectural governors and a total of 130 prefectural department chiefs were removed in a single sweeping order. What happened to them? Thirteen governors were dismissed. Four new governors were appointed from "civilian circles," though the impartial observer would note that one had been a consul general and another had been the Tokyo Metropolitan Defense Chief. The rest were reappointed in different localities.

The Shōwa Restoration, 1947. President NAMBARA Shigeru of Tokyo Imperial University is credited with coining the effective paraphrase, *Shōwa* Restoration, in his *Kigensetsu* or Empire Founding Day address, 11 February 1946, when he held that: "The Shōwa Restoration, in a real sense, must be realized through the rejuvenation of the Japanese spirit. Intellectual and religious reformation is more vital than a reformation of the political and social structures."

If this term may be applied to any educational reform of this period it most appropriately applies to the administrative reform plan which the Japanese Ministry of Education announced simultaneously with the Civil Information and Education Section, GHQ, SCAP, on 20 January 1947. The legal basis of this reform was established by the Fundamental Law of Education passed by the Diet on 31 March 1947 and the School Education Law passed on 29 March 1947. The reform, initiated at the start of the new academic year, 1 April 1947, but probably destined to very imperfect realization for an indeterminate period in the future, was the outgrowth of nearly a year's study and planning following the recommendations made by the United States Education Mission to Japan. One of the five committees of the Education Mission was that concerned with "Administration of Education at the Primary and Secondary Levels." Its chairman was the distinguished Superintendent of Schools in Philadelphia, Dr. Alexander J. STODDARD. The official summary of the somewhat extended recommendations made by this committee and adopted unanimously by the entire Mission appears in the *Report of the United States Education Mission to Japan*, submitted to the Supreme Commander for the Allied Powers, in Tokyo on 30 March 1946, pp. 65 f. Because of its importance it is quoted here in full:

The principle is accepted that, for the purposes of democratic education, control of the schools should be widely dispersed rather than highly centralized as at present. The observance of ceremonies in the reading of the Imperial Rescript and obeisances to the Imperial Portrait in the schools are regarded as undesirable. The Ministry of Education, under the proposals of the Mission, would have important duties to perform in providing technical aid and professional counsel to the schools, but its direct control over local schools would be greatly curtailed.

In order to provide for greater participation by the people at local and prefectural levels, and to remove the schools from the administrative control by representatives of the Minister of Home Affairs at the local level, it is proposed to create educational agencies elected by popular vote, at both local and prefectural levels. Such agencies would be granted considerable power in the approval of schools, the licensing of teachers, the selection of textbooks—power now centralized in the Ministry of Education.

There is proposed an upward revision of compulsory education in schools to be tax-supported, co-educational and tuition-free, such education to cover nine years of schooling, or until the boy or girl reaches the age of sixteen. It is further proposed that the first six years be spent in primary school as at present, and the next three years in a "lower secondary school" to be developed through merging and modifying the many kinds of schools which those completing primary school may now enter. These schools should provide general education for all, including vocational and educational guidance, and should be flexible enough to meet individual differences in the abilities of the pupils. It is proposed further that a three-year "upper secondary school" be established, free of tuition costs, in time to be coeducational, and providing varied opportunities for all who wish to continue their education.

Together, the lower and upper secondary schools would continue the varied functions of other tax-supported schools now at this level:

higher elementary schools, girls' high schools, preparatory courses, vocational schools, and youth schools. Graduation from the upper secondary schools would be made a condition of entrance to institutions of higher learning.

Private schools under the proposal would retain full freedom, except that they would be expected to conform to the minimum standards necessary to assure ready transfer by the pupil from one school to another, whether public or private.

The Occupation Forces' evaluation of the plan actually produced by the Ministry of Education and its advisory body, the Japanese Education Reform Council (*Kyōiku Sasshin Iinkai*), established to implement the recommendations of the United States Education Mission, and headed by ABE Yoshishige, ex-Minister of Education, has been stated in a press release dated 20 January 1947 by the Public Relations Office, GHQ, FEC, USA. Quoting the present Chief of the Education Division, CI&E, GHQ, SCAP, it says in part:

Of great importance are the basic reforms of administration and structure of the school system which the Ministry plans to introduce at the start of the new school year. A Fundamental School Law has been drafted by the Ministry and spells out the implications of the new constitution for the field of Education. In addition to stating the aims of education, it provides for equal educational opportunity, the approval of coeducation, compulsory education through nine years of schooling, academic freedom and the freedom of the schools from political influence.

A second law of significance is one on School Administration. Japan's educational system has hitherto been under the rigid control of the national government through the extreme degree of power given the Ministry of Education to determine educational practice everywhere in the country. This machinery constituted a ready-made device for the militarists when they decided to place the thinking of the Japanese people under their control.

The new proposal of the Ministry of Education establishes boards of education with members elected by the people and responsible directly to the people. This fundamental principle of any really democratic system of education will constitute a major advance in the democratization of Japan's educational system. It will result in a decentralization of the power and control previously exercised by the central government and will permit the adaptation of school programs to local and prefectural needs.

A new School Education Law has been proposed by the Ministry which will define the nature of the new school system. Gone is the old pattern of one set of schools for the select few from the privileged class while the masses of students received a different and inferior education. Common, general education will continue through nine years, rather than the six now in practice, and this common schooling will be compulsory. Entrance to the upper reaches of the school system will no longer be restricted to the privileged class, but will be open on an equal basis to all students.

While it is true that limited facilities will require selection of those who go beyond the ninth year, the methods of selection have been democratized by increasing the number of students who can be accommodated, and developing methods which will result in the selection of a better type of student in higher institutions of learning.

No definite evaluation of the plan, or of the sympathetic Occupation Forces' summary, can be made for some time. The Japanese themselves have hastened to point out publicly that many of the objectives of the reform cannot be realized for years. It was evident from the opinions voiced in committee sessions during the Japanese deliberations leading to the recommendation of these laws that most of the Japanese educators considered that the new 6-3-3 organization of education and the formal elevation of compulsory education to nine years were the fundamental elements of the reform. It would perhaps be pessimistic to suggest that neither of these objectives is particularly novel to the Japanese scene nor likely alone to work a major rehabilitation of the Japanese people. Equally, it would perhaps be unkind to point out that the Occupational presentation of this projected reform was either naïve or deliberately optimistic.

Equal educational opportunity had been an avowed policy in Japan since 1872, and had been an actual realization in the past 50 years to a degree beyond any of the nations which had defeated her with the possible exception of the United States. Compulsory education, if part time be included, was set at nine years in 1939, and full-time compulsory education was raised to eight years in 1941. Actual attendance beyond the eighth year has dropped off not because of the alleged pattern of education for the privileged class being distinct from that of the common people but because of the very system of competitive examinations which is now advanced as the remedy. On the statute books at least discrimination on the basis of religion, race, or social position has been outlawed for more than half a century. Even people of the *eta* class, once considered untouchables, have been given full protection of the law and equality in education for more than 15 years, as evidenced by the Bureau of Social Education Order No. 22 of 30 October 1932 and Baron Araki Sadao's Minister of Education Order No. 24 of 29 August 1935. Japanese academic freedom has been traditionally less than in the more progressive local systems of the United States but has not compared unfavorably with that permitted in Middle Eastern, European, and South American nations which have similar adaptations of the centralized French educational system. As for establishing the freedom of the schools from political influence, the very claim is callow. Tax-supported public schools are themselves political institutions. Their stated purpose is to produce acceptable citizens in the political organization that supports them. The problem facing the Japanese people, the Occupation Forces, and the world, was not that of severing the schools' link with their political source, but rather of linking them to a new and more acceptable political organization while at the same time establishing safeguards to protect them from slipping back under the domination of the discarded one.

The proposal to establish boards of education with members elected by the people is certainly the most significant portion of the reform. Yet the assumption that this is an innovation is erroneous. At the local level have been municipal (*to* or *fu*), city (*shi*), town (*machi*), and village (*mura*) governments. With the exception of Tokyo, the only *To*, and Osaka and Kyoto, the only *Fu*, which have organizations almost exactly like prefectures, the local units are governed by a mayor or headman (*Shichō, Chōcho,* and *Sonchō*, respectively), who is elected by the assembly, though in cities the nomination is made by the prefectural governor. Each of these mayors is advised by technical bureaus, which include one charged with educational matters (*Kyōiku Kyoku,* in cities). Pertinent to this proposed reform is the fact that the assemblies (*Shikai, Chōkai,* and *Sonkai,* respectively), which elect the mayor and which constitute with him the joint executive and legislative bodies at the local level, have been popularly elected. At the city level the *Shikai* is supplemented by an additional popular body, the city council (*Shi Sanjikai*), elected from within the assembly and charged with control of finances. At the level of the wards (*ku*) in municipalities and cities, and in all towns and villages there were revived shortly before the war the long dormant five-

and ten-family groups which are now known as neighborhood groups (*tonari gumi*). Although misused by the Japanese militarists as a device for establishing mass responsibility and allotting group punishment, the *tonari gumi* were once representative government organs and today potentially offer the vital local control recommended. It would appear that it is not the existence of local government bodies representative of the people but their actual control over education which will be a true measure of the success of the proposed 1947 reform of the *Shōwa* Restoration.

Educational Finance—Control by Anemia

Legal Basis of Educational Finance. The ultimate legal basis for all control of finances rested in Chapter VI, Articles LXII through LXXII, of the old or Meiji *Constitution of the Empire of Japan*, and now rests in Chapter VII, Articles LXXXIII through XCI of the new *Constitution*. Although the new *Constitution* is considerably changed from the provisions of the earlier one, it does not materially affect the financial structure and controls which have already been established for the educational system. There is a strengthening of the power of the national Diet over all phases of national finances, but the Cabinet is still charged with preparation of the budget which the Diet must approve. Unless specifically changed by law no change may take place in the tax structure, and no money may be expended or public obligation be undertaken except as authorized by the Diet. The two greatest changes, that of expropriating all property of the Imperial Household other than hereditary estates and of specifically prohibiting appropriation of public monies for religious or private purposes, have only slight effect on the educational system.

Below the *Constitution* the basic financial regulations in the educational system are a series of Imperial ordinances for the various levels of schools.

The National Elementary School Ordinance (Imperial Ordinance No. 148 of 1 March 1941 as amended by No. 199 of 1943 and No. 635 of 1943) contains three articles (XXXIII through XXXVI) which direct that national elementary schools (*kokumin gakkō,* now again called *shō gakkō*) shall be financed by the municipality or municipal school union except that where the prefectural governor deems it necessary a prefectural subsidy may be paid. It also specifically prohibits the collection of tuition fees except in the special course (*tokushuka*), in which case the fees are considered receipts of the municipality and are administered according to regulations of the Ministry of Education. These regulations are contained in Ministry of Education Order No. 4 of 14 March 1941 as amended by No. 39 of 1941, No. 33 of 1943, No. 66 of 1943, No. 72 of 1943, and No. 6 of 1944. They provided that in the event such exceptional tuition fees have to be collected (exclusive of those for the *tokushuka*) they shall be limited in cities and city-town-village school unions to 20 sen per month and in towns, villages, and town-village school unions to 10 sen per month. This corresponded to about one and one-third cents and two-thirds cents, respectively, in the early part of the Occupation, to less than one third of that by the end of the first two years of Occupation, and to less than a fifteenth of that by the end of the third year.

The Youth School Ordinance (Imperial Ordinance No. 254 of 26 April 1939 as amended by No. 155 of 1941, No. 110 of 1943, No. 199 of 1943, No. 636 of 1943, and No. 81 of 1944) provides that youth schools (*seinen gakkō*) shall be financed by the local municipality or municipal school union except those youth schools founded by the prefecture in areas which otherwise could not support them, in which case the prefecture assumes the cost. Tuition fees are banned except in prefectural youth schools which are permitted in rare cases to collect such fees if approved by the Ministry of Education. In all other details the youth school funds are treated similarly to those of the elementary schools.

The Secondary School Ordinance (Imperial Ordinance No. 36 of 21 January 1943 as amended by No. 199 of 1943) provides simply that tuition fees and other money for expense in secondary schools (*chūtō gakkō*) may be collected in accordance with rules prescribed by the Ministry of Education. These regulations are contained in the Ministry of Education Orders Nos. 2 and 3 of 2 March 1943 as amended by No. 33 of 1943, which provides that tuition and entrance fees may be collected in public schools by permission of the prefectural governor and in private schools by permission of the Minister of Education. Vocational schools (*jitsugyō gakkō*) are subject to a regulation containing the same provisions, Ministry of Education Order No. 4 of 2 March 1943 as amended by No. 33 of 1943. Since secondary schools may be founded by municipal governments and other tax-supported educational institutions as well as by prefectures, the usual controlling agency; main financial support comes from tax monies available through the regular financial channels of the appropriate government echelon.

Higher normal schools (*kōtō shihan gakkō* and *jōshi kōtō shihan gakkō*) as well as the normal schools for youth school teachers (*seinen shihan gakkō*) and ordinary normal schools (*shihan gakkō*) are prohibited from levying tuition fees by the Normal Education Ordinance (Imperial Ordinance No. 109 of 8 March 1943 as amended by No. 199 of 1943 and No. 81 of 1944). Private higher schools (*kōtō gakkō*) are required to be legal corporations and to have equipment and endowment (set at 500,000 yen) sufficient to enable them to give a standard of work equivalent to that given by national higher schools, which are tax supported. All colleges (*semmon gakkō*) are directed to levy tuition fees except in special cases where they are permitted to remove the fee or fail to levy it, by the College Ordinance (Imperial Ordinance No. 61 of 27 March 1903 as amended by No. 8 of 1928 and No. 39 of 1943). Private universities (*daigaku*), by the University Ordinance (Imperial Ordinance No. 388 of 6 December 1918 as amended by No. 7 of 1928 and No. 40 of 1943), are required to be legal corporations and to deposit with the Ministry of Education an amount of legal tender or negotiable securities sufficient to guarantee their financial responsibility and a standard of work comparable to Government and Imperial universities, which are tax supported.

All private schools, which are regulated in the most minute details of their internal administration by a mass of Imperial ordinances and Ministry of Education orders, are required to be legally incorporated, to demonstrate financial responsibility, to submit proposed budgets, and to render annual financial reports to the Ministry of Education, in accordance with the basic Private School Ordinance (Imperial Ordinance No. 359 of 3 August 1899 as amended by No. 218 of 1911, No. 19 of 1919, No. 381 of 1923, and No. 156 of 1941). By Law No. 38 of 5 April 1919 as amended by No. 12 of 1941, private schools are exempted from land taxes on property actually owned and used for educational purposes.

National responsibility for financing education is established by a series of laws and Imperial ordinances, which are implemented at each educational and governmental echelon by ministerial, bureau, departmental, and school ordinances. Law No. 13 of 28 March 1914 as amended by No. 70 of 1921 and No. 40 of 1939 states that: ". . . those people in a school district who are obligated to pay city, town or village taxes shall bear the expense of district schools and kindergarten used primarily by district inhabitants."

The basic legal authority for this financial aid is established by the Law Placing Responsibility on the National Treasury for Meeting the Expenses of Compulsory Education (Law No. 22 of 29 March 1940 as amended by No. 11 of 1941 and No. 30 of 1943). This law provided that one half the expenses for salaries, longevity allowances, special allowances, bonuses, governmental death grants, and travel expenses for the faculties of national elementary schools (*kokumin gakkō*), now again called *shō gakkō*, supported by prefectures, municipalities, and the Government of the Territory of Hokkaido, shall be met by the National Treasury. Imperial Ordinance No. 240 of 1 April 1940 as amended by No. 344 of 1941 and No. 217 of 1943 directed the payment of this subsidy in four installments during April, July, October, and January of each year. A similar provision for youth schools (*seinen gakkō*) was made by Law No. 22 of 24 March 1939 as amended by No. 31 of 1944. An Imperial Ordinance No. 108 of 8 March 1943 as amended by No. 82 of 1944 apparently stopped this subsidy and there is no record of its being reinstated, but the budgets of post-Surrender academic years indicate that the subsidies are still being paid and the basic legislation is still in force.

There are other national subsidies paid local educational bodies to encourage various forms of training. Among the most important is the subsidy for vocational education established by Law No. 9 of 23 March 1914 as amended by No. 31 of 1920 and No. 22 of 1939. This provides that the National Treasury shall pay on the advice of the competent Minister a subsidy not to exceed an amount equal to that borne by the founder of the local vocational school, such grants normally running for three years. A similar subsidy is paid by the National Treasury to encourage school attendance by impoverished school-age children, as provided in the Ministry of Education Instruction No. 18 of 4 October 1928 and amended by No. 16 of 1930 and No. 19 of 1933. This money is used to provide textbooks, supplies, clothing, and food for children who would otherwise not be able to attend compulsory schools. The latter subsidy originated with a grant of money from the Emperor on the occasion of his marriage on 26 January 1924.

The Sources of Educational Funds. The tax structure of Japan is perhaps no more complicated than that of other great powers. It is sufficiently complex, however, so that a brief description of the national system may be necessary if the portion which is applicable to education is to be understood.

Taxes are collected and administered on three governmental levels in Japan: national, prefectural, and municipal (municipality, city, town, and village). Governmental revenues are of two types: taxes, ordinarily constituting the greater source of income; and extraordinary revenues from various nonrecurring receipts, earnings on government property, and government borrowings, especially in the form of bond issues. The tax portions of these governmental revenues are of three types: tax monies which go into the general pool of governmental receipts and there lose their identity; earmarked taxes which retain their identity and must be used for a specific purpose in a specific locality or institution; and equalization taxes which are allocated to lower echelons of the governmental structure on the basis of local need. General pooled tax monies are allocated on the basis of budgets, whose preparation, approval, and execution are set by law; and earmarked taxes are redistributed in accordance with the law authorizing their collection. Equalization taxes are distributed on the basis of a rather complicated formula of population, local financial need, and geographical distribution. This latter type is one of the most important sources of educational revenues and constitutes one of the most powerful controls over local education exerted by the national Ministries.

The Local Tax Allocation Law (Law No. 61 of 29 March 1940) provides in detail for the payment by the National Government to the governments of prefectures and lesser governmental echelons of two types of equalization taxes: grants-in-aid (*bun-yo-zei*), also known as national distribution taxes, and subsidies (*haifu-kin*).

There are two types of grants-in-aid: the transfer grant (*kampu-zei*) which consists of land, house, and business taxes; and the allocation grant (*haifu-zei*), which consists of income taxes, "juridical persons" tax (a kind of corporation tax), admission taxes, and amusement taxes (on eating and drinking establishments). The transfer grant is returned in its entirety to the particular prefecture which originally collected it, and hence constitutes little more than a bookkeeping transaction which permits the national government to supervise the expenditure of the money. The allocation grant, however, is distributed without regard to the original source of the money both to prefectures and to municipal governments, on the basis of a formula established in the October 1944, "Regulations Relative to the Local Tax Distribution Law" of the Local Government Bureau (*Chihō Kyoku*) of the Ministry of Home Affairs (*Naimushō*). This formula includes, besides the relatively mechanical factors of economic capacity of the subordinate echelon based on the tax rate per capita and the financial demands on that echelon based on such considerations as the number of students, the highly subjective factor of the "broad judgment of the Home Minister." It should be noted that the allocation grant also differs in that not all of the tax monies originally collected are redistributed but only a portion of each, varying annually according to local need. It should be further noted that both types of these grants-in-aid are paid to the lower governmental echelon to aid their finances generally and as such are absorbed into their general revenues, a portion of which is again redistributed to educational institutions.

The other form of equalization tax, the subsidy, is a specific grant from the national government to a prefecture, lesser government, echelon, or individual school, to aid that organization in accomplishing some specific objective, usually one of primary interest to the national government. The funds for these subsidies are drawn from the general pool of national revenues and hence have lost all identity. The allocation of all equalization grants made from the National Treasury is done by the Local Tax Allocation Committee (*Chihō Bun-yo-zei Iinkai*) of the Ministry of Home Affairs. The Minister of Home Affairs is the chairman of the committee, which includes in its membership the Vice-Minister of Finance, the Chief of the Local Government Bureau of the Ministry of Home Affairs, and 11 members of the Diet. Seven secretaries from the Ministry of Finance and four from the Ministry of Home Affairs are in charge of the technical details of the committee. Policy rests largely with the Ministry of Home Affairs while the routine administrative work involved in handling these funds rests with the Financial Section of the Local Bureau (*Chihō Koku Zeisei Ka*) of the Ministry of Finance. Since the grants-in-aid are payments to the general funds of the subordinate governmental echelon (usually prefectures) there are only the relatively minor controls exercised by the national Ministry over all expenditures. The use of subsidies, however, is minutely detailed and supervised.

The original sources of revenue at each of the three pertinent governmental echelons are not dissimilar to those of other industrialized nations. Of the ordinary revenues at the national level approximately two thirds come from taxes with personal income taxes accounting for about half. In addition there are "juridical persons" taxes of two types, inheritance taxes, taxes on mining property, custom duties, transportation taxes, demurrage charges, a series of luxury taxes (amusement, horse racing, admission, liquor, and soft drinks), sugar excise tax, textile consumption tax, and taxes on financial transactions (Bourse, security transfer, and commodity). Mention has already been made of the three taxes on land, houses, and business received from and returned to the prefectures as transfer grants. Other ordinary revenues are receipts from the sale of stamps, income from government forests, prison receipts, income from other national property, fines, payments under the pension laws, profits from the Bank of Japan, and miscellaneous income. Excess profits tax revenues, receipts from commodity price adjustments, payments for public works, and receipts from special accounts controlled by the national government are considered extraordinary revenues, frequently more than double the amount of the ordinary.

It is difficult to present a recent national budget which has much meaning in view of the spiraling inflation of the war and post-Surrender years. The National Budget for 1946 was later amended in the light of extraordinary demand occasioned by the Occupation Forces and the rising cost of living, but in its original approved form reflects the added expenses which accompanied the war yet avoids the distortion of the relative positions of various expenditures resulting from uncontrolled inflation. As a result this budget probably best illustrates what may be considered a relatively "normal" post-Surrender income.

Anticipated ordinary revenues totaled 19,817,467,462 yen with extraordinary revenues amounting to 35,245,827,749 yen, thus making a total anticipated income available to the national government of 55,063,295,211 yen. Of the ordinary revenues, taxes accounted for 12,230,158,000 yen or 61.8% (of which the income tax alone amounted to more than half or 6,783,338,000 yen); grants-in-aid or national distribution taxes came to 228,801,000 yen or only 1.15%; stamps brought in 337,711,000 yen; receipts from government properties and public undertakings totaled 6,447,569,078 yen, and miscellaneous items added 573,227,484 yen. Of the extraordinary revenues, the excess profits tax was expected to bring in 501,700,000 yen and "miscellaneous revenues" (largely bond issues and sale of government properties) totaled 34,344,127,749 yen. It is interesting that there was an anticipated national income of 66,200,494 yen from educational institutions and services, such as experimental farms, hospitals, vaccines, royalties on State-approved textbooks privately published, and State-owned scientific research rights.

The educational expenditures of the Ministry of Education constituted the immensely greater portion of the total educational expenditures made on the national level. The cost of operation of a small number of highly specialized schools for police, fishermen, foresters, merchant marine officers and, formerly, for the military services, was imbedded in the budgets of the other Ministries and cannot be accurately assessed. In relation to the educational expenses of the nation these amounts were trivial. Two Ministries other than Education, the Ministry of Home Affairs, and the Ministry of Finance, exercise some indirect control over the schools through finances. There are certain expenses, such as a portion of the salaries of prefectural governors and other officials appointed by the Ministry of Home Affairs yet charged with certain educational administrative duties, and a portion of the operating expenses of prefectural and municipal offices proportionate to their use in educational administration, which might properly be designated as an educational expenditure. Both of these indirect expenses, however, are not ordinarily considered a part of the cost of education in Japan but rather a part of the over-all governmental administrative cost. As such they are unidentifiable in the budgets of the respective Ministries. By far the most important of the educational expenditures for these two Ministries, however, are those made as grants-in-aid or subsidies to lesser governmental units. Since the funds are administered locally they will be considered in the frame of reference provided by the budgets of the local units, where their relative position in proportion to other governmental expenditures will have meaning. Exclusive of this major federal equalization expenditure, the only educational expense on a national basis which is worthy of note is that of the Ministry of Education.

The Ministry of Education in 1946 had a budget of 672,737,742 yen total expenditure, composed of 354,111,163 yen ordinary expenditures and 318,626,579 yen extraordinary expenditures. This represented approximately 1.22% of the national budget. It is highly significant that the budget for 1948, approved by the Diet after a bitter partisan struggle on 25 March 1947, was for 4,369,-875,000 yen which represented 3.77% of the 1948 national budget. The increased net appropriation reflected inflation but the increased proportional appropriation reflected a profound faith in and commitment to education. The ordinary expenditures were divided into three categories: general expenses of 35,746,734 yen covering the cost of running the Ministry itself, maintaining certain subordinate offices, conducting scientific research, and granting miscellaneous subsidies to various local organizations for education; transfers to special accounts of 134,630,281 yen for the support of Imperial universities, government universities and colleges, and schools directly under the control of the national Ministry; and supplementary expenditures of 183,730,148 yen for subsidies in support of compulsory education, subsidies for teachers of youth schools (*seinen gakkō*), and certain minor disbursements. The extraordinary expenditures were also divided into the same three standard categories: general expenses of 197,-106,712 yen covering certain administrative expenses, miscellaneous building and repairs (in the Ministry itself), and nonrecurring or exceptional subsidies; transfers to special accounts of 23,994,321 yen for the same classes of schools mentioned above; and supplementary expenditures of 97,525,546 yen primarily to cover special family allowances to teachers.

Certain individual items in the 1946 Ministry of Education Budget deserve mention. Of the ordinary expenditures those for scientific research (18,700,000 yen), administration of the Ministry itself (5,463,503 yen), and miscellaneous subsidies (9,174,-

326 yen) are the largest but are still relatively small compared with the immense expenditure for semi-autonomous schools (37.8% of the total ordinary expenditures), subsidies in support of compulsory education (42.7%), and subsidies for youth school teachers (9.1%). Of the extraordinary expenditures an item of 23,360,000 yen or 7.3% of the total extraordinary expenditure was for research. Two very large items, 140,886,335 yen (44.3%) for group evacuation of school children and 95,873,787 yen (32.5%) for special allowances to teachers, were obviously war measures which have not been necessary in succeeding budgets. But a considerable part of the unprecedented 1947 Ministry of Education Budget of 1,041,448,604 yen (compared with 672,-737,742 yen for 1946 and 142,678,000 yen for 1936) was in the form of subsidies amounting to 362,555,000 yen or 36.4% for extra salaries, allowances, and bonuses to elementary school-teachers necessitated by the rising cost of living. The 1946 Budget was based on an official rate of exchange of 15 yen to 1 dollar United States currency, and the 1947 Budget was based on the revised official rate of 50 yen to 1 dollar.

On the prefectural level revenues are from five sources. National subsidies and grants-in-aid have already been mentioned. In addition the prefecture collects a surtax on the national tax on land, houses, business and mine properties; a series of earmarked "work" taxes, usually including one for town planning and one for irrigation assessed as special surtaxes on acreage, land, homes, and businesses; a number of independent prefectural taxes which are not in any way controlled by the national government and which usually include an acreage tax, taxes on ships, motor cars, and electric poles, and taxes on hunting and fishing licenses, licensed *geisha* (not a tax on prostitution but an indirect entertainment tax), and taxes on the acquisition of real property (a modified sales tax). Outside the tax structure the prefecture has a number of revenues from rents, fees (including student tuition fees), business licenses, and income from the sale of prefectural bonds and prefectural properties. Since the national equalization grants vary widely from prefecture to prefecture depending upon local needs it is impossible to generalize with very much meaning as to the relative importance of subsidies and grants-in-aid in the total receipts. Kanagawa Prefecture, which includes the city of Yokohama and is one of the wealthiest and educationally the most progressive of the prefectures, receives from the National Treasury approximately one half of its total revenue.

The budget for Kanagawa Prefecture covering the same period as that mentioned for the national government, 1946, will perhaps serve as an illustration of prefectural finances. Of the total anticipated income of 58,172,599 yen, 38,340,902 yen was considered ordinary revenue and 19,831,697 yen was considered extraordinary. Of the ordinary revenues the prefectural taxes constituted much the largest item with 21,369,354 yen of which 16,818,080 yen were from the distribution taxes. Other items were 165,875 yen income from prefectural properties; 1,918,763 yen from various service charges (1,519,825 yen of which was expected from school tuition fees); receipts from the National Treasury amounting to 13,252,574 yen representing various types of subsidies; and miscellaneous revenues to the extent of 1,634,336 yen. The extraordinary revenues of Kanagawa Prefecture in 1946 were expected to include 11,215,743 yen for subsidies of various kinds; 4,932,100 yen from sale of prefectural bonds; and a number of minor items to total the 19,831,697 yen.

The 1946 Kanagawa Prefectural Budget anticipated a total expenditure for education of 16,818,579 yen or 28.8% of the total income. Of this amount 16,790,823 yen were ordinary expenses and represented 43.8% of the ordinary revenue of the prefecture. Of the total educational expenses, 98.5% was spent on three types of schools: prefectural schools (boys' middle schools, girls' middle schools, technical schools, agricultural and fisheries schools, and schools for the blind, deaf, and dumb), 2,296,497 yen; youth schools, 2,177,589 yen; and aid for elementary schools (salaries, allowances, travel, and death benefits), 11,816,842 yen. It should be noted that the prefectural schools were themselves a source of income to the general treasury of the prefecture to the extent of 1,484,725 yen from secondary school tuition fees (averaging about six yen per month or 40 cents United States currency at the then prevailing rate of exchange), 28,000 yen from entrance fees, and 42,000 yen from examination fees. This total of 1,554,725 yen constituted about 9.25% of the total educational expenditure or about 4.05% of the total ordinary revenue and 2.67% of the total revenue of the prefectural government from all sources.

On the municipal level the tax structure varies much more

because of the extremes in size and wealth of the various units. The largest is the municipality with *Tōkyō To* having a prewar population of 6,274,000, *Ōsaka Fu* with 3,092,000, and *Kyōto Fu* with 1,177,000. Cities (*shi*) range in size from the minimum 30,000 population required to satisfy the legal definition to Yokohama, with 2,652,000. Towns (*machi*) vary in size from 4,000 to 55,000 and villages (*mura*) have populations from a few farm families to over 4,000 persons. In addition to the grants-in-aid and subsidies from national and prefectural governments, the revenue of these municipal corporations is received from four tax sources: surtaxes on national land, house, business and mining property taxes; surtaxes on prefectural acreage, ship, motor car, electric pole, acquisition of real property, fishing, and *geisha* taxes; independent municipal taxes on householders, boats, bicycles, carts, safes, electric fans, dogs, butchershops, and miscellaneous services; and special surtaxes for town planning, irrigation, and land utilization. Outside the tax structure the municipal corporations receive revenue from such properties as electric railways, bus lines, waterworks, rental of municipal property, fees, and municipal bond issues.

Tōkyō To is selected as an example of municipal financing, despite its obvious uniqueness, because it is by far the most important educational center in Japan and because it alone has represented every element of educational financing found in the nation. The same budget, 1946, chosen to illustrate the national and prefectural levels has been chosen for the municipal. Of the total anticipated income of 436,146,205 yen, 202,236,000 yen represented ordinary revenue and 233,910,205 yen was considered extraordinary revenue. Of the ordinary revenue the metropolitan tax with 118,910,557 yen was by far the greatest single item (44,842,504 yen being surtaxes on national taxes). The second largest item, 47,920,835 yen, represented payments from the national government (41,606,712 yen being distribution taxes and the rest subsidies). Of the extraordinary revenue, national subsidies amounted to 41,713,365 yen; municipal bond issues totaled 133,588,000 yen; and certain transferred reserve funds represented 50,414,000 yen. Miscellaneous minor accounts brought the total to the 233,910,205 yen cited.

The 1946 Tokyo Municipal Budget anticipated a total expenditure for education of 74,463,662 yen, of which 72,855,594 yen were ordinary and 1,608,068 yen were special or extraordinary expenditures not presumed to be recurring. Thus the ordinary educational expenditure constituted 36% of the ordinary revenue and the total educational expenditure represented 17.1% of all expenditures in the municipality even during the period of great financial distress. Of the ordinary expenditure of 72,855,594 yen by far the largest single item was the 32,368,252 yen allotted to national elementary schools amounting to 44.4% of the ordinary educational expenditure. Industrial schools received 5,579,-125 yen or 7.66%; youth schools received 3,068,811 yen or 4.21%; boys' middle schools were given 2,374,284 yen or 3.26%; girls' middle schools got 1,785,011 yen or 2.45%. A general fund of 25,904,683 yen, representing 35.6% of the total ordinary educational expenditure, was used for expenses relating to schools but not restricted to any specific type. Minor amounts were allocated for higher schools (*kōtō gakkō*), special schools, schools for the blind, deaf, and dumb, teacher training institutes, libraries, art exhibition halls; social education, school hygiene (including medical and dental services), physical culture, and nursery schools.

Administration of Educational Funds. Since financial control constitutes one of the most powerful controls exerted over the educational system by the various governmental agencies, it may be profitable to examine somewhat in detail the machinery of its administration. Perhaps the least complicated method of presenting these controls is to trace the money from its original source to the school which ultimately benefits under the administration of each of the various governmental agencies.

At the national level, three Ministries are concerned: the Ministry of Finance, of Home Affairs, and of Education. They will be considered in turn.

The Ministry of Finance (*Ōkurashō*) functions as the general fiscal agent, operates a mechanical control over all governmental spending, and serves as the ultimate authority in deciding the appropriate portion of national funds which should go to educational institutions, subject of course to Diet approval. Its procedure differs somewhat from one part of the educational structure to another, depending upon the type of school concerned and the source of funds.

At the level of higher education the Ministry of Finance collects funds from the income on land, student fees, hospital receipts, income from bonds, and similar educational sources. Each university (*daigaku*) keeps its own funds and does not surrender them to the Ministry, but merely submits a financial statement. Each college (*semmon gakkō*) surrenders its funds to a general pool (accounted for by the Ministry of Education) from which they are redistributed in accordance with the need and contribution of the individual school. Since all normal schools (*shihan gakkō*) are government schools they are treated as government colleges. Private universities get certain subsidies paid through the Ministry of Education by the national government, final veto power being held but seldom exercised by the Ministry of Finance. Private and prefectural colleges do not get such subsidies in general. Allocation of these funds is done by budget, with the exception of earmarked university funds whose identity has never been lost. The budget is prepared by the school, approved by the Ministry of Education, and finally approved by the Ministry of Finance. Either the Ministry of Education or the Ministry of Finance could veto the school's budget but in practice few are questioned. The Bank of Japan is the financial agent and keeps all detailed books. If the income from the land, fees, hospital receipts, income on bonds, and other special holdings of the universities and higher institutions is not sufficient to meet the budget, the Ministry of Finance pays the difference from the general pool of tax monies held in the National Treasury. If a balance exists at the end of any fiscal year the surplus funds are put into the general school fund held by the Ministry of Finance. The Ministry of Finance does not inspect the educational institution but accepts the recommendation of the Ministry of Education. It does not exercise any educational control but does supervise the keeping of financial records and exerts final veto control over the budget.

At the level of secondary education the fiscal procedures differ markedly according to the type of school. The government middle schools (*kanritsu chu gakkō* and *kanritsu kōtō jo gakkō*) are attached to higher normal schools (*kōtō shihan gakkō*) and accordingly are treated as the government colleges described above. Prefectural middle schools (*kenritsu, furitsu,* or *toritsu chutō gakkō*) are financed by the prefecture with funds drawn primarily from local taxation which is never surrendered to any higher governmental echelon and with funds from the national distribution tax or grant-in-aid paid by the Ministry of Finance through the Ministry of Home Affairs. It will be recalled that this type of tax is really an equalization fund composed of partial or total repayments of prefectural taxes. In the event of a deficit the national government through the Ministry of Finance pays the difference from the general funds of the National Treasury. The Ministry of Finance has final control over these national funds, restricted by the mechanical provisions of the distribution formula, and supervises the keeping of records but does not exert any educational control or conduct any inspection of educational institutions receiving the funds. In addition to the above the Ministry of Finance pays the educational subsidies, previously discussed, on recommendation by the Ministry of Education and regulated by law. Approximately half of these are earmarked for buildings and equipment, half for teachers' salaries. The money is paid through the Ministry of Education to the prefectures. Private middle schools (*shiritsu chutō gakkō*) receive national funds from the Ministry of Finance in the form of equipment subsidies and pension-matching subsidies. Approximately one fourth of the pensions paid by the Pension Association (*Ōnkyū Kumiai*) are paid from national funds.

At the level of elementary education the Ministry of Finance exercises virtually no control, acting only as fiscal agent for the national government in making certain payments to the prefectural and municipal governments. Prefectural and local government youth schools (*kōritsu seinen gakkō*) are under the prefectural Department of Education and are financed almost entirely by the prefecture. Until 1945 the national government paid a subsidy of approximately one half the salary of the teachers but beginning with 1946 this was supposed to be stopped except in exceptional cases. Private youth schools (*shiritsu seinen gakkō*) receive no federal subsidy. What the future financing of these schools or their successors will be is not yet clear, and will depend in a considerable measure on the extent to which the Japanese authorities are able to convince their foreign advisers that the youth schools have in fact been purged of their objectionable prewar characteristics. Those elementary schools (formerly called *kokumin gakkō* and now renamed *shō gakkō*) which are attached to normal schools and higher normal schools as experimental and practice schools are financially treated as ordinary colleges, with the exception that their funds come from federal funds. The vast majority of elementary schools, however, are public, tax-supported institutions nominally under the local governmental unit (municipality, city, town, village, or union school district). The salary and allowances of teachers is paid by the respective prefectural governments. Of this money approximately half is paid through the prefecture from the Ministry of Education, using the Ministry of Finance as agent. This is a subsidy and is controlled as are the other subsidies mentioned above. Other special subsidies for food, physical examinations, repairs, and extraordinary expenses (usually at the rate of one fourth the cost) are paid in the same manner and in amounts determined each year in the budget.

The Ministry of Home Affairs (*Naimushō*) has relatively little educational control but occupies an important position in the chain of financial control of the schools of Japan. It functions as a general fiscal agent over schools administratively under the prefecture or municipal echelons of government. It has final authority over the redistribution of tax monies collected by the prefectures and paid into the National Treasury, through its domination of the committee which allocates national distribution taxes. And it exercises a very powerful influence over the budget of the prefecture by advice given the Financial Section of the Local Bureau (*Chihō Koku Zeisei Ka*) before the budget is submitted to the prefectural assembly (*Kenkai*), which has the ultimate authority. One of the strongest controls is that of exercising judgment as to the appropriateness of the self-taxation of the prefecture, one of the basic elements in the formula for redistribution of *bun-yo-zei* funds. The Ministry of Home Affairs also maintains an independent set of books, checking the prefectural books and the books of the Bank of Japan, on these educational accounts.

The Ministry of Education (*Mombushō*) has by far the greatest educational control but acts only as an advisory and dispensing agent in the financial control of the schools of Japan. Broadly speaking it makes direct grants of monies to meet all expenses to the individual schools at the higher educational level (*daigaku, semmon gakkō,* and *shihan gakkō*) while exercising very little actual educational control over them. Conversely it makes indirect grants and subsidies through the prefectural government (and in the case of elementary schools through the municipal government in addition) to assist in a particular service or to meet an individual item in the budget of secondary and elementary level institutions (*chutō gakkō, seinen gakkō*, and *kokumin* or *shō gakkō*). This general pattern applies, of course, only to government schools, and the variations which obtain with private and certain affiliated public institutions have already been noted in connection with the Ministry of Finance controls. Since the mechanics of collection, allocation, and distribution of funds has been considered in connection with the Ministry of Finance, only the controls exercised by the Ministry of Education need be examined here.

At the level of higher education, the Ministry of Education has theoretical veto power over budgets of the universities but in practice seldom exercises it. Its veto power over the budgets of colleges and normal schools is both theoretical and actual, and is exercised when necessary. The Ministry administers the earmarked university funds and pays various subsidies and grants-in-aid authorized by the Ministry of Finance from the National Treasury. The Ministry of Education keeps separate financial records for schools under its direction and submits these to the Ministry of Finance for auditing. Control through inspection is not exercised over universities but is exercised in the case of colleges and normal schools. Educational administrative control, although theoretically authorized, is applied only through general policy directives and suggestion in the case of universities, but direct control is imposed on colleges and normal schools through approval of curricula, textbooks, and faculty appointments.

At the level of secondary education, the Ministry of Education allocates funds from the general resources of the National Treasury in the form of subsidies for certain specific services. The Ministry submits to the prefectural government a list of subsidies it is willing to pay and the prefectural government then makes application for those it is entitled to and wishes. The Ministry of Education approves the amount and type and on its recommendation (regulated by law) the Ministry of Finance pays the money to the prefectural government which in turn allocates to the individual schools. The final control over these items in the national budget rests with the Ministry of Education, and the funds when sent to the prefecture are completely earmarked so that no latitude is permitted in their distribution. The Ministry of Education maintains independent books on the funds and reports to the Ministry of Home Affairs, whose personnel at the prefectural level are charged with direct administration of the money. The prefectural bank (*Kenkinko*) acts in the same capacity for these funds as did the Bank of Japan for the grants-in-aid and national funds. The Ministry of Education maintains a fairly rigid inspection of the schools using the funds and exercises a powerful control through teachers' licenses, validation of textbooks, approval of curricula, and supervision of certain studies.

At the level of elementary education, the Ministry exercises much the same type of financial control as it does over secondary schools, except that the final recipients of the funds are one stage further removed. Thus it recommends to the Ministry of Finance the payment of subsidies amounting to approximately half the teachers' salaries which are paid through the prefectural government, and certain other subsidies for such things as dental care, physical training programs, food and clothing for poor children, care for orphans, school lunches, repairs, building, evacuation of children from disaster areas, etc.

Below the national and above the prefectural echelons of government there has from time to time in Japanese history been a regional (*chiku*) government. The only one recent enough to have any bearing on present and future educational organization is that of the nine regional blocs created as a result of the January 1943 delegation of authority to the Prime Minister by the Diet as a war measure. It is rather doubtful that these regional offices ever really attained much control over education, despite the announcement by the Ministry of Education of 11 July 1945 to that effect. On 6 November 1945 all the regional offices were closed in compliance with an order from the Headquarters of the Supreme Commander for the Allied Powers dated the day before.

The prefectural echelon of government, however, has exerted in the past a very powerful financial control, and if the provisions of the 1947 Reform Plan are carried out this control will be accentuated. The prefectural government administers all funds going to secondary and elementary schools located within the bounds of the prefecture (with the exception of a small number of such schools affiliated with national or autonomous institutions). Since the financial procedures do not materially differ between schools it will be convenient to consider the prefectural control from the point of view of types of revenue rather than types of schools as was done at the national level.

National funds are paid from the National Treasury on order from the Ministry of Finance. No funds come directly, however, but are paid through the Ministry of Education or Ministry of Home Affairs and are subject to their recommendations and veto.

Basically the funds from the Ministry of Education are subsidies drawn from the general tax pool of the national government and delivered to the prefecture as earmarked subsidies allowing little leeway for administration. The procedure for allocating and distributing these funds has already been described. When the prefectural government in turn distributes the money it is done either in the form of a direct payment to the individual teacher or to the representative of the school at the prefectural office or through the local office of the prefecture (*Chihō Jimusho*), depending on convenience. The prefecture has virtually no control other than that of requesting the items needed on the approved list of available subsidies. The financial control is exercised by the Ministry of Education. But the prefectural government supervises the records, maintains a fairly thorough inspection of the recipient schools, reports to the Ministry of Education, and exercises a powerful educational direction, bounded, of course, by the limitations imposed by national laws and the directions issued by the Ministry of Education.

The funds from the Ministry of Home Affairs are fundamentally grants-in-aid or national distribution taxes, which are delivered to the prefecture in the form of a lump sum to aid several governmental services, education being among them. The procedure for allocating and distributing these funds has already been described. A considerable control is exercised by the prefectural government in administering the funds. The various sections of the prefectural government, including the Education Section (*Kyōiku Ka*), submit their individual budget requests to the General Affairs Section (*Shomu Ka*), which combines and revises them and presents the unified budget to the governor (*Kenchiji*), who submits it with his recommendation to the Ministry of Home Affairs for approval. Although this Ministry has the authority to veto such a budget it does not in practice exercise this right but only offers advice. The approved budget is then submitted by the governor to the prefectural assembly (*Kenkai*) for approval and the bank of the prefecture is directed to disburse the monies on the governor's authority and in accordance with the budget. The prefecture keeps detailed financial books on the funds and reports to the Ministry of Home Affairs. The inspection, reports, and educational direction over services rendered are similar to those in connection with the subsidies of the Ministry of Education.

Prefectural funds are handled in exactly the same way as the grants-in-aid from the Ministry of Home Affairs, other than that their source is different. The governor asks the prefectural assembly to authorize taxes adequate to meet the proposed budget. The upper limit on rates and the type of taxes permitted is set by a national law passed by the National Diet and known as the Local Tax Law (*Chihōzeihō*). Once the money has been collected and pooled it loses its identity and is indistinguishable from the national funds.

The prefecture exercises some control over local or municipal funds. The individual school requests a certain sum of money to finance a proposed educational service. The mayor (*Shichō, Chōchō*, or *Sonchō*) sets the amount and rate of the tax, limited by law (*Chihōzeihō*) by the National Diet, though occasionally exceeding that rate by a limited amount on authorization of the prefectural governor, and submits the proposed budget to the local assembly (*Shikai, Chōkai, Sonkai*). If passed by this body, it must be reviewed by the chief of the prefectural local office (*Chihō Jimusho Chō*) for reasonableness and legality. Advice, but no veto, is authorized for a breach of the former and a veto is mandatory in the event of a flaw in the legality. The funds are retained locally, only accounts being rendered to the prefectural government and the full amount of the collected funds is used in the locality where collected, no redistribution on the basis of equalization being permitted.

The next smallest political subdivision, the county (*gun*), exists as a geographical unit but not as an administrative unit. It neither levies nor administers taxes.

Below the county in size is the municipal echelon which is divided into two types, based on size and complexity of government: the municipality (*to* or *fu*), and the city, town, and village (*shi, machi*, and *mura*). Tokyo, the only *to*, and Osaka and Kyoto, both *fu*, are organized and exert financial control in exactly the same manner as prefectures. Money, from sources identical to those described for prefectures, is sent to wards (*ku*) in the built-up metropolitan parts of the municipality for the youth schools and elementary schools, and to the schools individually for secondary schools and colleges. These funds are sent to the city, town, or village government of subordinate municipal governments within the limit of the municipality but not in the central metropolitan area. The internal organization of the municipality has a Bureau of Education (*Kyōiku Kyoku*), which is divided into four sections: Elementary Schools, Social Education, Welfare, and General Affairs. The financial control rests in the Finance Section (*Zaimu Ka*), a subdivision of the Secretariat (*Kambō*), and is identical with that of the prefecture.

Except for size the city, town, and village financial control is the same. On the secondary level there are a very few boys' and girls' middle schools (*chutō gakkō*) which are entirely financed with local tax money and with minor fees collected, pooled, and redistributed without reference to the original source. No prefectural funds, other than loans in emergencies, are paid to these schools. By far the greater number of schools under local control, however, are the elementary schools, which are supported by three types of funds: local, prefectural, and national. The collection, allocation, and distribution of local tax monies has been described with reference to the controls which the prefectural governments exercise. The local government and the school have no control whatsoever over prefectural funds and in fact seldom handle them. Thus the teacher is paid either at the prefectural office or the local prefectural office.

The local governmental echelon actually receives national funds in two forms: hidden subsidies and distribution tax monies paid through the prefectural office, and direct loans from the Ministry of Finance paid through the Bank of Japan. The first of these two types of funds has so completely lost its identity in passing through the prefectural controls that frequently the city officials are quite unaware that they originated in national Ministries. The second, direct loans, are borrowed from the prefectural governor who is authorized to act for the Minister of Home Affairs, and are approved by the Minister of Finance.

The financial structure of the educational system would perhaps be oversimplified if some mention were not made of the autonomous schools under federal governmental support. The Tokyo Imperial University and its affiliated institutes will serve as an example, both because it is by far the most important institution of higher learning and also because it involves every factor of autonomous financing found in any of the government schools.

The university is financed with two types of funds: national taxes, amounting to a little more than one half the total income, and local university funds. The funds from national taxation are drawn from the general pool of national revenue and paid by the Ministry of Finance through the Bank of Japan on authorization by the Ministry of Education, as a part of the national budget, the procedure for which has already been examined. In theory the Ministry of Education, Ministry of Finance, and Diet in turn could exercise veto power over the proposed budget of the university, but in fact usually only the Ministry of Finance exercises this power. The National Auditor (*Kaikei Kensain*) inspects the books for accuracy. There is no educational inspection and in practice the university enjoys almost complete autonomy. The National Diet does exercise certain policy controls through laws (*hōritsu*) and the Ministry of Education directs certain technical matters through various types of laws and regulations (*shōrei, kunrei*, and *tsūchō*). Local university funds come from student fees of all sorts; interest on investments and endowment; income from services such as the university hospital; income from the sale of certain products such as lumber, farm produce, and vaccines; fees from the manufacture and research done for private concerns; and small royalties and patents' fees from items produced by the university, such as scientific equipment. The identity of these funds is maintained, deposited to the credit of the president of the university in the Bank of Japan, and when redistributed some effort is made to return them in proportion to their sources, though a major part is pooled for general university expense. The controls are essentially the same as that for national funds allocated to the university.

Decentralization—Defense in Depth

What are the educational controls of Japan? Where are they located? How do they operate? What are their characteristics—

their strengths and weaknesses? And who shall exercise them?

The Japanese Ministry of Education has controlled the educational system through five direct techniques: it has written the basic laws and orders; it has directed the administration and supervision, including school inspection; it has exercised basic administrative control over the finances; it has maintained a monopoly in the educational services such as radio, film, textbooks, recordings, special teaching institutes, and research; and it has directed the punitive and restrictive measures of Thought Control. It may be protested that this last is an outmoded and illegal procedure but it is evident that the power to license and to "screen" the teachers, the uncontested right to determine curricula and to censor teaching materials, and the sole authority to admit, exclude, promote, and discipline students would give essentially the same control if abused.

But are there not other and indirect techniques of control which are equally powerful and equally susceptible to the manipulation of a powerful and unscrupulous minority? Three are readily discernible: tradition, ignorance, and prestige.

Tradition is an integral part of the educational thought of Japan. The link between Shinto ritual and political action has known a history of more than a millennium and has been one of the most dominant characteristics of modern Japan. Confucian philosophy has placed a reverence for the past and a respect for the thoughts and actions of ancestors on the highest moral plane. Even in post-Surrender Japan, when the past might be presumed to be discredited, the first premise of the governmental propagandists is that the policy is in no wise antagonistic to the "unique national entity of Japan," to the *kokutai*.

Ignorance is the powerful weapon of any police state or authoritarian government. The masses of people must be kept docile through ignorance of the true facts if they are to remain submissive to the manipulation of the ruling clique. This was true in prewar Japan when the *zaibatsu* (economic clique) and the *gumbatsu* (military clique) were in power. It was true in the Occupation when a foreign military force was in power. And it is likely to continue to be true, no matter what type of national administration ultimately comes to Japan, if the entrenched bureaucracy, the *gakubatsu* in the Ministry of Education, retains its hold on the governmental services.

Prestige is an intangible but effective control. The Ministry of Education has suffered the most intensive and sustained attack of its history. But evident through almost all the caustic criticism and violent denunciation of the Ministry has been an acceptance of the commanding position of that organ. The Ministry still has the power to influence the thinking of the vast majority of Japanese educators. It is the rare person in public life who would not be honored to be consulted by it on policy. Positions in the Ministry, though not perhaps as esteemed as those in certain other Ministries, are still eagerly sought by Japanese educators. There may be vocal disagreement with enunciated policy of the Ministry, but whatever that policy may be it is respected.

There are two basic arguments against continuation of the overwhelming centralization of power in this body. The first is an attack upon the internal characteristics of the Ministry, an argument for free enterprise as opposed to government-controlled monopoly. The second is an attack against the external controls manipulated by the Ministry, an argument against an easily manipulated and highly centralized administrative machinery.

The Ministry has become a body of entrenched bureaucrats. All educational reform is subjected to the stultifying influences of their cautious and proprietary scrutiny. Their power depends upon maintaining their own indispensability even at the cost of destroying competitive talent outside the *Mombushō*. There is a loss of competition in almost everything connected with the school system. The methods are standardized and originality is penalized. The buildings are stereotyped replicas of one adequate but undistinguished official model. The textbooks are monuments to mediocrity. There is a sort of spurious efficiency of the whole, but archaic methods and lack of competition combine to bring inefficiency of the parts. Administrative procedures in many parts of the system are identical with those of nearly a thousand years ago. Education is almost universally respected, but the school has about the same personal appeal to the parent as does the post office or fire station. It is a governmental service, recognized to be worthy and necessary, but removed from the dominating interest that comes only with active participation.

It may be advanced that the 1947 *Reform* postulates a decentralization of power. Evidence to date would indicate that the Japanese have paid lip service to a popular policy of the foreign advisers, while retaining almost intact the basic powers and controls of the Ministry. Perhaps they are guilty of "looking at the ceiling through a reed" (*Yoshi no zui kara tenjō nozoku*). Perhaps it is a deliberate circumvention. Whatever their motives it seems clear that a far more drastic revision is essential.

It would be incorrect to dismiss the present system of educational controls in Japan as being an unqualified failure. There are at least three distinct advantages which must be credited to the high degree of centralization: uniformity and economy, equalization of funds and educational opportunity, and susceptibility to rapid change.

The efficiency of centralized control is binodal in character. It is true that the Ministry of Education, with approximately 900 total employees, controls approximately 18 million students at an administrative cost much below that which can be approached by a democratic and decentralized system. But the real efficiency of an educational system, as pointed out at the beginning of this section, must be measured in terms of the quality and suitability of the end product. As long as it was Japanese policy to produce a very small minority of gifted and productive intellectual leaders and to restrict the remaining mass of the population to a stenciled reproduction of an approved governmental model, the existing centralized system proved more than adequate. It mass-produced citizen puppets. But if it is to train thinking, self-governing, productive citizens, the present system would appear to be inadequate and inefficient.

The financial structure of the present centralized system has provided in the past a level of educational facilities that has been outstanding in the world. The equalization provisions have avoided many of the defects which traditionally have characterized decentralized systems, such as that of the United States and of the elementary system in Brazil. It has been tacitly assumed by Japanese educators, and by many foreign observers, that a decentralization of the educational controls would entail a parallel decentralization of the financial controls, with attendant and obvious loss in efficiency and equalization of educational opportunity. A study of the financial structure would appear to indicate that this assumption is not necessarily correct. There seems to be no obligation to decentralize, or even to change markedly, the existing financial structure. The most autonomous educational

institutions in Japan, the Imperial universities, have the highest
degree of centralized, national financing. It is clear, of course, that
no political subdivision can be permitted to rebel against the established policy of the whole, and if a majority of the Japanese people
wished to change an educational policy it would be possible to do
so through the enactment of law. But in the absence of basic
legal changes there appears to be no reason why educational control equal to that now enjoyed by the universities might not be
centered in local or prefectural governmental echelons, while
retaining the existing national and prefectural financial controls
without prejudice.

The world has recently learned the desirability and even necessity of governmental machinery which permits rapid revision
of policy and adaptability to external change. War mobilization, perhaps the most spectacular of crises, no longer is a leisurely
process of months or even years, it is a matter of days and may
become one of hours. Participation in such critical national efforts
is no longer limited to a small professional minority, but is rapidly
becoming, if it has not already reached, complete population
mobilization. Education which enlists the largest numbers, and
frequently entails the largest expenditure, of any industry in a
modern nation, increases rather than diminishes in importance
in such emergencies. The educational system which can rapidly
be transformed to meet the demands of a national emergency is
obviously desirable. In this regard the existing system in Japan
is without peer. It could be, and was in 1941, converted into a
machine almost entirely devoted to furthering the war potential
of the Empire in a matter of hours.

Perhaps the most dramatic educational somersault in modern
times occurred during the three weeks following Surrender. By
the time the Civil Information and Education Section of General
Headquarters, AFPAC (later transferred to General Headquarters,
SCAP), had been established on 22 September 1945 the Japanese
Ministry of Education had carried out in principle at least prac-
tically every school reform which the Occupation Authorities
had planned to demand. The first educational officers to reach
Japan were met with a *fait accompli* and spent the first weeks of
the Occupation trying to check on the actual enforcement of
Japanese instituted reforms. So completely had the Ministry of
Education foreseen probable Allied directives and forestalled

them by voluntary reforms that as late as the first quarter of 1946 there were conducted staff meetings in General Headquarters to analyze systematically the possible omissions of the Japanese and to plan new demands.

There are distinct advantages to an organization which can be manipulated with such speed. In the hands of a benevolent dictator such a system permits rapid reforms which might be indefinitely delayed in a democracy. But the very efficiency in reversing its established policies which drew from General MacArthur an expression of congratulation on the occasion of his issuing the Basic Educational Policy Directive on 22 September 1945 constitutes the greatest danger of the present system. The Allied Powers, and the Japanese people, dare not preserve so dangerous a tool for the manipulation of the schools and the thought of the nation.

IV

CHINESE CHARACTERS OR ROMAN
LETTERS?

The Problem of the Written Language

AN educated and literate citizenry is the fundamental prerequisite of any form of modern representative government or
democratic society. This principle is so much a part of the Anglo-
Saxon tradition that it is rarely questioned in countries where this
tradition has dominated the social organization. It is the justification advanced for universal, tax-supported, compulsory education. Unless a citizen can read he cannot be informed. Unless he
is informed he cannot intelligently make the decisions which
his self-government demands. Truth, as conceived in the democratic tradition, is a verifiable fact and not the expression of
superior authority. Accessibility to truth, in the same tradition,
is obtainable only through freedom of communication and the
critical evaluation which is the mark of the educated man.

Freedom of communication was not always measured in terms
of literacy. In colonial New England, for example, people solved
their problems in the open debate of the town meeting, in which
all men whether literate or not might test their views with those
of their neighbors. But geographical expansion, immense increases
in population, and technological advances have created a new
society where men must delegate their powers of governmental
decision and must trust to the integrity of technical experts in
securing information. The citizen in a modern democracy at best
exercises selective judgment and collectively holds veto power. It
is perhaps possible that society may some day reach a level of
technological advance such that sound recording and transmission
will completely replace the printed word as a record of the past
and as the channel of current information. But that day is not
here and is not in the discernible future. For the present the written language is the basic channel of communication and literacy is
the measure of the effectiveness of this channel.

Japan is in a process of social revolution. It is avowedly committed to a democratization of society and to a system of representative government. In the process of reform the literacy of the common people will be a crucial factor. For 50 years the astonishingly efficient Japanese educational system and the official claims of an extremely high rate of literacy have stood as the unexplained paradox in an obviously undemocratic nation. The Anglo-Saxon recognizes that while education is a necessary component of the democratic state it does not assure the existence of that state. But Japan has had the outward forms of self-government. Have these literate and educated people denied to themselves the rights which their knowledge should have secured?

There exists evidence that the majority of the Japanese people are unable to read writing necessary to the development of their democratic tendencies. It has been charged that this is caused by the excessive difficulty of the written form of the Japanese language rather than by the absence of an adequate system of compulsory education. It is claimed that the development and adoption of a markedly simplified writing system alone can provide a solution. Japan, if it is to attain its goals of democratization, must sort these charges and seek some solution to the problem of the written language. A rational solution can come only through an orderly and systematic investigation of three distinct phases of the basic problem.

Japan must first determine in what ways the present system of the written language is an obstacle to the development of democratic tendencies among the people. If the existing writing system is in fact found to be unsatisfactory, Japan must then determine a practical and effective simplification. Having determined the necessary linguistic reforms which must be accomplished Japan must finally adopt a practical and effective method of accomplishing the change-over from the present to the new system of the written language.

The Burden of the Ideograph

China's Sorrow and Japan's Misfortune. There is no record of the ancient Japanese language having any written form, and it is generally believed that the ancient tongue was first reduced to writing with the introduction of Chinese culture about the fourth century A.D. Japan in its two millenniums of history has copied many things from the cultures of many nations. It copied the Chinese ideographic system of writing. It is quite possible that this was the most disastrous of all its importations.

To the Occidental student of Western language, all written in some variant of a phonetic system, it may be difficult to appreciate fully the monstrous handicap which the Japanese writing system has imposed on that people. It is possible to understand only if the dual natures of the Chinese and Japanese languages are appreciated. For in loosely descriptive lay language there are two Chinese and two Japanese languages—the written and the spoken forms.

To the modern linguistic scientist the "language" of a people is the spoken tongue. What is popularly known as the "written language" is nothing more than a notation system to stand for the sounds of the spoken language. Disregarding for the moment the minor stylistic differences which have occasionally developed in the written forms of Occidental languages, the spoken tongue and the written matter when read aloud should be identical. If through some improbable set of circumstances the "written language" should incorporate words and grammatical constructions which did not exist in the "spoken language," and if the percentage of these dissimilar elements should be increased to the point where the written matter when read aloud was quite unintelligible to a person well grounded in the spoken tongue, the modern linguist might argue that they were in fact two "languages"—one, the normal spoken language, and the other, an artificial spoken language which had adequately been reduced to a notation in the written form but which was not adequately understood in the spoken form. This conception of language is based on the premise that all thought is ultimately reducible either to uttered or to subvocal meaningful sounds. The possibility of a system of written communication entirely dissociated from the spoken language is categorically denied.

Starting from this basic premise that the spoken tongue is the foundation of all communication, the sound structure is analyzed into three units: morphemes, phonemes, and allophones. Morphemes are held to be the speech-sound units that are left after all possible grammatical analysis has been accomplished, and hence are the smallest units of meaningful speech sound. They are the stems, prefixes, infixes, and suffixes of words. In Occidental writing systems these units are normally indicated by the notation for syllables or groups of syllables which have basic meaning. Phonemes are held to be speech sounds which in any given language function in the same way and hence are the smallest unit of distinctive speech sound. In Occidental writing systems these units normally are indicated by letters and diacritical marks. In those languages which are popularly spoken of as "phonetic," such as Spanish, Portuguese, Finnish, Hungarian, Czech, and Polish, the letters and diacritical marks approach the ideal phonemic system of writing in which there is one and only one symbol for each phoneme and only one phoneme for each symbol. In lay terms the language is written as it is pronounced. Allophones, the third class of speech-sound units, are of less importance to this problem, since they are the sounds which compose the phoneme, and hence are the ultimate phonetic material of the language. They are of two types: fixed allophones which in any given language always occur in certain sound situations, and free allophones which are the chance variations in the pronunciation of the phoneme. In lay language these are the sounds which give speech an "accent" or "overtones." They are ordinarily written in phonetic symbols such as those of the International Phonetic Alphabet.

This theory of language is widely accepted among Occidental scholars. It is presented in Leonard BLOOMFIELD's *Language* (New York, Henry Holt & Co., copyright 1933); in Bernard BLOCH and George L. TRAGER's *Outline of Linguistic Analysis* (Baltimore, Linguistic Society of America, Waverly Press, 1942); and in Edgar H. STURTEVANT's *An Introduction to Linguistic Science* (New Haven, Yale University Press, 1947). If it were universally accepted there would be no linguistic problem of the Japanese written language, for by the basic premise there would be no difference between the "spoken language" and the "written language," and the adoption of an adequate phonemic notation would present no particular difficulties. But this theory of language is not universally accepted among students of Chinese and Japanese, and whether linguistic, political, or economic in origin the difficulties of a reform of the writing systems are manifest and inescapable.

In the opinion of many able Occidental students of these languages, and of the majority of educated Chinese and Japanese, the two "written languages" have progressed, or deteriorated, according to the viewpoint, far beyond even the hypothetical stage described above. These people hold, in contradiction to the theory of most modern linguists, that in the extreme forms the two-writing systems permit intelligible written communication which when read aloud is unintelligible even to persons versed in the notation system. They contend that the languages may in fact sound like nothing but plausible gibberish. Perhaps these people are wrong. Perhaps, as the linguistic scientists suggest, despite their admitted practical command of the language they are quite ignorant of its phonemic structure. But since these are the people who must make the change if it is to be made, their opinions cannot be shrugged off. Their arguments, even though initially rejected on a theoretical basis, must be systematically sifted, investigated, and answered.

The initial difficulty in understanding the problem of the Japanese written language is in understanding the notation system. A notation system may be constructed with its signs standing either for sounds without meaning or for meaning unrelated to sounds. The former is an alphabet or syllabary, with the symbols known as letters. The latter is some variant of primitive picture writing with the symbols known, if they have become sufficiently stylized, as characters or ideographs. The writing systems of both Chinese and Japanese are based primarily on this latter, or ideographic, form of notation and incorporate only a secondary, though complicated, overlay of the former, or alphabetic notation. Both systems are highly inefficient. Of the two the Japanese copy is undeniably inferior.

The Chinese spoken language which was originally reduced to a written form with ideographs was a nearly monosyllabic language, that is, its morphemes or smallest meaningful units were individual syllables. It was also an analytical or isolating language, with few or no inflections or "word endings," and therefore depended primarily upon the meaning and position of the words in the sentence to indicate the grammar. Most modern linguists contend that any language can, and for reasons of efficiency should, be reduced to an alphabetic, or approximately phonemic, notation. But if the ideographic notation is to be used, there can be little question but what ancient Chinese was ideally suited to that system of writing. Thus, in its theoretically simplest form, there was one specific symbol or ideograph for each separate word in the language. Since none of the words were altered by inflection the ideograph stood invariably for that meaning, and incidentally for the conventional sound of the word also having that meaning.

But Japanese in its ancient form was a highly inflected language, depending primarily on the modification of the sounds attached to the root of a word to indicate the grammar. A fixed symbol or ideograph could, it is true, be assigned to the root meaning of a word, but some purely phonetic notation would have to be added to represent the indispensable grammatical inflection. It was, therefore, a type of language totally unsuited to a writing system in which characters stood for meaning. Japanese was also polysyllabic, that is, made up of morphemes which were not necessarily monosyllables; it was agglutinative, with words made up by joining a series of other words; and it was essentially an open syllable language, that is, composed solely of vowels and syllables ending with vowels. Although in theory these latter characteristics would not preclude an ideographic notation specifically designed for the language, they did present great difficulties when the ideographs of another language were used.

This became evident as soon as the Japanese scholars attempted to adopt the Chinese system of writing as a system for writing spoken Japanese.

A Chinese character could be used to stand for the meaning of a Japanese word, if an equivalent Chinese word existed. When the character had an ideographic value and stood for a meaningful sound, or morpheme, it was called a *mana* or by the modern term, a *kanji*. When it was phonetic in value and stood for a vowel or open syllable, regardless of whether that was by chance a morpheme, it was called a *kana*. Thus, the same character, 山, used as a *kanji* or ideograph, would express the word "mountain" in both languages. When read aloud in the Japanese language this character could be pronounced either in the native Japanese (*yama*) or in the Japanese imitation of the Chinese word *san*. But some additional system had to be derived to represent Japanese words, names, and place names for which no counterpart existed in Chinese. This could have been done by the invention of new characters which were different from anything in Chinese. Many Japanese *kanji* (known as *kokuji*) were in fact invented in this manner and are quite unintelligible to the Chinese reader. More important, however, was the invention of some system of notation to represent the sounds of the inflections which carried no root meaning, and hence could not be represented by a Chinese character, but which were indispensable to the grammar. This was accomplished with the invention of the phonetic syllabaries (*kana*). Certain characters in Chinese were adopted as symbols, not of meaning, but of the sound which the Japanese would make in attempting to reproduce the Chinese reading. As long as the ideograph was retained in its original form they were called *manyōgana*, named for a famous Japanese poetical collection *Manyōshū*, written in such characters. But the shapes of these characters were gradually modified and stylized until they reached approximately the form of the two *kana* in common use today. KIBI NO MABI is traditionally credited with the invention of *katakana*, a block or printed form, in the eighth century, and KŌBŌ Daishi is credited with the invention of *hiragana*, a cursive form, in the ninth century.

What eventually evolved was not one system of writing but many. As an aid to understanding the confusing variations and complicated cultural ramifications of written Japanese it may be well to note briefly the salient features of that form of notation which has most nearly become the standard. It is presented as a conscious and deliberate oversimplification. The system is known as *kanamajiri*, that is, a mixture of ideographs (*kanji*) and phonetic syllabary (*kana*). The Chinese characters or *kanji* stand for the root meanings of basic words, while the phonetic script or *kana* stand for the sounds of certain grammatical particles such as postpositions, of inflected endings, and of words for which no ideograph is readily available. Many words, almost exclusively nouns, are composed of combinations of two or more ideographs, known as Chinese compounds (*gōseigo*), while most verbs and adjectives are composed of combinations of ideographs and *kana*. Difficult words are frequently explained in a parallel phonetic script known as "sidewriting in *kana*" (*furigana*), which enables the person with a limited knowledge of ideographs to read the passage phonetically. The closest approximation to the Japanese *kanamajiri* to be found in Occidental writing is one of the standard shorthand systems where certain frequently recurring words are assigned fixed symbols while the remaining words are recorded with a quasi-phonetic script. It is also somewhat analogous to an

English sentence liberally interspersed with mathematical symbols standing for nouns and verbs, or to a child's reading book with pictures of trains, ships, animals, and other objects replacing the written words for those things in the sentences. The closest approximation to the Japanese *furigana* to be found in Occidental writing is the text of one of the old-fashioned Latin "ponies," with an interlinear English translation of the Latin sentences.

The charge has often been made that written Japanese is the most difficult language in common use today. This difficulty is directly traceable to the unfortunate importation of the Chinese writing system, but it is equally traceable to difficulties introduced periodically through the continuation of that system. As spoken Japanese became enriched with the intellectual growth of the country, the writing system became increasingly unsatisfactory. When the Meiji Restoration opened Japan to Occidental knowledge the inadequacy of the traditional system became obvious. Japan was then faced with a choice between attempting to patch up the old system so that it might limpingly serve, or of discarding it for a modern phonetic system. It is one of the conceded tragedies of that era that the choice was made to preserve the old. The traditional forms of Japanese were distorted with compromise and unwieldy linguistic repairs without succeeding in devising a truly adequate system. What was a well-grounded suspicion before the recent war has become a widely recognized fact. The written form of Japanese is simply too inefficient to be continued if Japan is to compete on a basis approximating equality with Occidental nations. It may well be that her cultural survival is at stake.

The structural difficulties. Structurally, modern written Japanese suffers from five basic difficulties: the writing symbols, the format, the stylistic forms, the multiple readings, and the abbreviated forms. By far the most critical of these is the first, that of the incredibly complex writing symbols. Analyzed solely from this point of view Japanese is commonly written in five different basic systems: *kanji, kana, kanamajiri,* sidewriting, and romanized Japanese.

Japanese can be written in characters (*kanji*) alone. In the past 50 years this form has seldom been used in other than on memorial tablets, in textbooks on *kambun,* or the Chinese classics, and in certain scholarly writings, but prior to the Meiji Restoration many texts were written in this manner. The characters are used, however, in the standard writing system today. There are five forms of these *kanji* in relatively common use: the "block form" (*kaisho*), a modified printed script form used in handwriting (*gyōsho*), a cursive or "grass writing" form (*sōsho*), "seal writing" (*reisho*) used on *han* or seals, and the old form of "seal writing" (*shōten*). In addition scholars in certain historical disciplines must have a knowledge of the "archaic form" (*kobun*) and an archaic form sometimes called "middle Japanese" because it comes between *shōten* and *kobun* (*taiten*). Two distinct types of *reisho* are still in use in seals, the *korei* and the *hachiburei*. The *sōsho*, *reisho* (*korei* and *hachiburei*), *shōten*, *taiten*, and *kobun* are sufficiently different from the first two forms (*kaisho* and *gyōsho*) so that a reading knowledge of one does not imply a reading knowledge of the other. The Japanese scholar who hopes to master the language will discover (for example, in 壽, *kotobuki*) at least 106 distinct variations in the writing of a single character. It should be emphasized that these are not mere variations in type but actual symbol changes, such as reversal or inversion of two parts of the character to make it appear artistic or symmetrical.

Japanese can be written in the phonetic syllabary (*kana*) alone. There are two main forms in common usage: a printed or block form (*katakana*), which is the first system taught small children and which is used rather restrictedly in some books, for foreign names, for legal and scientific writings, and in the handwriting of some adults; and a cursive form (*hiragana*), which has come to be used in nearly all communication where *kana* is used. They are sufficiently different so that knowledge of one does not imply knowledge of the other. In addition there is a minor form (*hentaigana*), which is often mixed with *hiragana* and used in literary writings, especially in women's writing and in pre-Meiji books, to produce a feeling of style. A form of primitive *kana* (*manyōgana*), using Chinese characters to stand as phonetic symbols, is almost never used in modern writing except in quoted passages of ancient writing and in names.

Japanese can be written in a mixture of characters and phonetic syllabaries (*kanamajiri*). This is the standard form of modern written Japanese. It may be *kanji* and *hiragana*, as in most newspapers and popular literary works; *kanji* and *katakana*, as in legal writing, public documents, and some technical studies; or *kanji* and a mixture of both *hiragana* and *katakana*, as in certain textbooks and literary works. The most difficult form is the grasswriting (*sōsho*) form of *kanji* mixed with *hiragana* and *hentaigana*, as commonly used in artistic works, such as wall hangings (*kakemono*), and in letters written by educated women.

Japanese can be written in a mixture of standard Japanese (*kanamajiri*) with the more difficult characters explained by notes in *kana* written along the side. This form is known as *furigana* and is in common use in newspapers, popular magazines, and some textbooks. Any of the several forms of *kana* can be used but *hiragana* is most commonly employed. A very rare form (*furikanji*) in which *kanji* are written alongside the *kana* is sometimes used in children's textbooks as a means of teaching characters. It has been advocated as a transitional step in the process of changeover to a phonetic system as a device for clarifying ambiguities arising from homonyms. Another rare form is *okurigana*, a type of sidewriting which supplies postpositions and other grammatical aids to help the reader read Chinese in Japanese (*kambun*), a required subject at the secondary school level.

Japanese can be written in any of a number of systems of transcription in Roman letters (*romaji*). The earliest of these were based on Spanish, Portuguese, and Dutch pronunciation and were used from the middle of the sixteenth century until the re-opening of Japan in 1853. In 1867 Dr. J. C. HEPBURN published his *English-Japanese Dictionary* using a romanization of Japanese based on English spelling. This system (*Hebonshiki Romaji*) was revised in 1886 by a committee of the Roman Alphabet Society (*Romaji Kai*) and was called the *Romaji Kai* System, and later the *Hyojunshiki* or Standard System. This system, with a few changes and known as the *Hiromekai Romaji*, is the system best known in America and the one used on foreign maps. It was the standard system used by the Allied Powers in the Occupation. Dr. A. TANAKADATE, famous physicist of Tokyo Imperial University, has developed and publicized a form of romanization known as the *Nihonsiki Romazi*, which was adopted as the standard Japanese form by the Imperial Japanese Cabinet in its *Naikaku Kunrei 3* dated 21 September 1937. This system has been widely accepted in Japan and in a very slightly modified form, known as the Yale System, in the United States.

The second of the basic structural difficulties of the written form of standard Japanese (*kanamajiri*) is the direction of writing or the format. It can be written vertically from top to bottom, it can be written horizontally from right to left, and it can be written horizontally from left to right. Most literary forms are written vertically in the traditional manner. Both *kana* and *kanji* were designed for this direction of writing. Scientific and mathematical writings are ordinarily horizontal from left to right so that mathematical and chemical formulae, Arabic numerals, and diagrams can be accommodated. Foreign language textbooks are printed according to the custom of the language being studied.

The third of the structural difficulties of written Japanese is the multiplicity of stylistic forms. Four are in common use: *kōgotai*, *bungotai*, *sōrōbun*, and *kambun*.

Vernacular style (*kōgotai*) is by far the most common style used in writings directed to the masses and to students. It is a close approximation to the form of the spoken language and accordingly is most readily understood. In its simplest form it can be understood easily when read aloud since it is identical with the common spoken language, although in its more literary form there may be ambiguities. It has commonly been stated by educated Japanese that these misunderstandings arise from the existence of homonyms whose meaning is not clear in the spoken form but would be clear in the written form because of the different appearance of the *kanji*. It seems highly probable, however, that this is an erroneous explanation. When such misunderstandings occur in *kōgotai* it is almost certain they are caused by the fact that the listener simply is unfamiliar with the word, although in the written form he might guess at the meaning from the appearance of the *kanji*. One thing is certain, however. These ambiguities, if they occur, are quite unnecessary and creep into the writing because the author, accustomed by habit to depending upon the appearance of the *kanji* to carry meaning, has not bothered to write in the way he would speak the same thought.

Literary style (*bungotai*) was until after Surrender the common form used in legal writings, erudite literary writings, certain types of historical and political writings, and, less commonly, for learned papers. Following the writing of the new *Constitution* in the vernacular, however, it has been used much less frequently even in official or learned writing. It is sufficiently different from the spoken language so that it is often somewhat difficult to understand when read aloud. It is not basically different from *kōgotai*, however, and the claim that it is quite unintelligible when read aloud is a gross exaggeration. Classes in literature frequently read extended passages aloud without misunderstanding. Only when rare words appear, when the reading readiness of the listener is quite insufficient, or when a deliberate attempt is made to introduce an ambiguity through distortion or elimination of the context, will there be unintelligibility.

Epistolary style (*sōrōbun*) was the common form used in letters of educated people, in formal business correspondence, and in similar writing. In recent years it has gradually been discarded in the pronounced popular trend toward the vernacular but it is still not uncommon among older people. It varies greatly from the spoken form of the language, but the charge that it is not perfectly intelligible when read aloud appears to be without substantiation. Part of the text of *Nō* drama is frequently in *sōrōbun* and is readily understood when read on the stage. Letters read aloud to the assembled family are not unintelligible.

Chinese classics style (*kambun*) is a relatively rare form of written Japanese, ordinarily encountered only in certain courses in the middle, higher, and university levels of the educational system. It is really a system of reading Chinese by means of diacritical marks, called *kaeriten*, which tell in what order to read the Chinese characters. By reading the Chinese characters in this order and by giving them Japanese sounds it is possible to guess what would have been the Japanese inflection of the word if it had been written in Japanese instead of Chinese. This system, of course, is completely unintelligible when read aloud; unless the order is changed, the missing postpositions are supplied, and the inflected endings are added to the roots. All of these transformations are required of a reader in *kambun*, so that the process demands a separate reading skill. It is in reality a means of decoding a foreign language without translating it.

A fourth structural difficulty of written Japanese, and one which applies to every literary style, is the multiplicity of readings, or pronunciations, which can be given a *kanji*. The character 生 (*ikiru*) with the basic meaning, "to live," is possibly the most difficult *kanji* to read. In compounds, names, inflected forms, and sound shifts, this character can be pronounced with 80 different sounds. The name of the former Minister of Education in the Shidehara Cabinet, Mr. Abe Yoshi-shige, is written 安部能成. Most people, including the Ministry of Education before Mr. Abe was named Minister, read it as *Nōsei*. Some read it as *Yoshi-nari*. The correct reading, *Yoshi-shige*, could be determined only by inquiring of the Minister himself. The reading of names written in *kanji* is so difficult that Article 17 of the Ministry of Education Order No. 32, 26 November 1908 (revised 1944) states that all applicants for teachers' examinations must write their names phonetically in *kana* beside the Chinese character.

There are three major ways of reading *kanji* in common usage: *kunyomi*, *onyomi*, and *atejiyomi*.

Japanese reading (*kunyomi*) is the reading of the ideograph, either a Japanese character (*kokuji*) or a Japanese copy of a Chinese character (*kanji*), with the sound of a Japanese word. The ideograph 山 ("mountain"), for example, is read *yama*.

Chinese reading (*onyomi*) is the reading of a Japanese copy of a Chinese character (*kanji*), with the Japanese rendition of the Chinese sound for that character. The ideograph 山 ("mountain"), for example, is read *san*. There are three main types of Chinese readings: *go-on*, *kan-on*, and *to-on* or *to-in*. *Go-on* are readings that are based on the pronunciation of the Chinese word in the *Go* (Wu) Province during the Eastern Shin dynasty in the fourth century A.D. This form is used on occasion in all standard Japanese, but is almost exclusively used in Buddhist writings. *Kan-on* are readings that are based on the pronunciation of the Chinese word during the *Han* dynasty, in the period from the second century B.C. to the second century A.D. *To-in* are readings based on the pronunciation of the Chinese word during the *Tang* dynasty, from the seventh to the tenth century A.D. The ideograph 行 will serve as an example. In the inflected form 行く (*yuku*, "to go"), it has the *kun* reading *yu(ku)*. In the compound 修行 (*shugyō*, "asceticism"), it has the *go-on* reading *gyō*. In 行為 (*kōi*, "act, deed"), it has the *kan-on* reading *kō*. And in 行燈 (*andon*, "paper lantern"), it has the *to-on* reading *an*.

Weird reading (*atejiyomi*) is the reading of a *kanji*, either Japanese or Chinese in origin, by some sound that has no connection with the meaning of the character. This truly weird method of reading is accomplished in two ways. One method is that of reading a difficult or sophisticated word written in *kanji* with the sound of a common Japanese spoken word which is an approximate synonym. The compound 判然 meaning "clearly" would be read *han zen* in its sophisticated form but is sometimes read *hakkiri* in the vernacular. This type of reading is common in scientific writings where coined words are extensively used. Also it is possible to read a difficult or unfamiliar word written in *kanji* with the sound of a foreign word, usually in English, which has the same meaning. The characters 麥酒 stand for the word for "beer" and mean literally "wheat brew." If read in Japanese they would be *bakushu*, a very uncommon word for the drink. They are ordinarily read, therefore, with the Japanized pronunciation of the English word, rendered "*biiru*."

The final structural difficulty of written Japanese arises from the elimination of some of the strokes normally found in the *kanji*. The most obvious type of this elimination is "grass writing" or *sōsho*, in which the character is formed by a continuous cursive stroke (although the line may be broken by lifting the brush slightly), which suggests rather than actually marks the various strokes which would go into the printed character. Some of the block (*kaisho*) and cursive (*gyōsho*) characters have abbreviated forms (*ryakuji*) in which certain of the strokes are omitted. These *kanji* have the same meaning as the full form (*honji*) and are clearly derivatives of the full form, but quite often are so markedly changed that they really constitute an entirely new *kanji* which must be memorized as if it were a different word. The character 國 meaning "country" and read *koku* or *kuni*, is an example. In the *ryakuji* form it is 囯 . In the *sōsho* form it is 𣏟 . The effect of these abbreviated forms inserted in the text of standard written Japanese is somewhat analogous to English written with a sprinkling of shorthand and mathematical symbols substituted for words. As the abbreviated forms become common they tend to replace the complete form of the *kanji*, which in time becomes obsolescent.

It should not be presumed from this brief summary of the structural difficulties of written Japanese that these five exhaust the list of undesirable characteristics of the system. The most formidable of practical difficulties, for example, is the barrier of memorizing thousands, and for scholars in the fields of literature, Chinese classics, and certain areas of philosophy, tens of thousands, of the ideographs (*kanji*). A little recognized but serious deficiency is the relative absence of semantic causal nexus. The Japanese sentence consists of a series of word pictures, each with a relatively precise central idea surrounded by gradually dimming psychological context, strung together by the integrating power of the reader's mind. Although learned Japanese contend that in this respect the Japanese writing system is no different from others, it appears that there is some ground for the charge on the basis of degree. Japanese, at least in some forms, is analogous to English written solely in elliptical sentences. Such a writing system, while it may lend itself to somewhat mystical poetic forms, is hardly an adequate vehicle for precise technical thought. While there are a number of possible explanations, it is perhaps significant that some of the propaganda prepared in Japan and directed to learned circles in China during the war was in English, not in the Chinese characters, and technical papers produced in wartime research laboratories in Japan were on occasion written in English or had English abstracts.

Nor should it be presumed that these structural difficulties are of equal gravity. Modern written Japanese may be taken as that array of styles, format, writing symbols, readings, and even literatures which the normal Japanese citizen may be expected to encounter in his daily life. There is, of course, the constant change observable in any living language, and within certain limits these changes are reflected in the written forms. Some of the structural difficulties which have been enumerated are unquestionably in the process of evolutionary reform. Thus the various seal forms of the *kanji* are almost unused except in signatures, monuments, and similar formal and limited application. Since the Meiji Restoration, with the exception of a few minor and ineffective conservative revolts against the popular trend toward abandonment of all the complex style forms in favor of the vernacular, first *kambun*, then *sōrōbun*, and after the rewriting of the new *Constitution* in the vernacular, even *bungotai* have gradually given way to *kōgotai*. But even if full allowance of these natural trends toward simplification is made, two unanswerable facts remain: the Japanese who wishes education beyond the secondary school still must be familiar with the full array of the forms enumerated; and if the natural evolutionary simplification were to be carried to its logical conclusion and only one style, one format, one form of ideograph, and one form of phonetic syllabary were to survive, the complexity of the writing system would still be overwhelmingly greater than that of any other nation with the possible exception of China. Truly China's sorrow has become Japan's greatest cultural handicap.

In Recognition of Defect. Written Japanese is extremely difficult to read. Sir George SANSOM, one of the greatest living Occidental authorities on Japanese culture, in his volume, *Historical Grammar of Japanese* (Oxford, Clarendon Press, 1928), p. 4, states: "One hesitates for an epithet to describe a system of writing which is so complex that it needs the aid of another system to explain it. There is no doubt that it provides for some a fascinating field of study, but as a practical instrument it is surely without inferiors."

Hugh KEENLEYSIDE and A. F. THOMAS, in their *History of Japanese Education and Present Educational System,* p. 92, in speaking of the educational problems of the Meiji Restoration, state:

It is difficult to exaggerate the difficulties experienced by the Japanese students who, in addition to the terrific impact of a whole new form of civilization, were faced with the necessity of maintaining the fundamental traditions of their own culture, and in particular of using their own incredibly complicated written language. . . . The reaction against the use of the Chinese characters found its strongest champion in Viscount Mori, the versatile and energetic Minister of Education between the years of 1885 and 1889.

Professor Basil Hall CHAMBERLAIN, translator of the *Kojiki* and world-famous Japanese scholar, says in his *Things Japanese* (London, Kegan Paul, Trench, Trubner & Co., 1927), pp. 469–470: ". . . and the result is the most complicated and uncertain system of writing under which poor humanity has ever groaned. An old Jesuit missionary declares it to be evidently the invention of a conciliabule of the demons to harass the faithful."

Professor W. H. SHARP, writing in his official report to the Director General of Education of India, *The Educational System of Japan,* Occasional Report No. 3 (Bombay, Government Central Press, 1906), p. 401, says:

. . . the Japanese child has a formidable task before it in merely learning to read and write something of its own tongue—a task so considerable indeed that it swallows up a disproportionate part of the primary stage of instruction, whilst the hundreds of Chinese characters so laboriously acquired soon fade from the mind if not constantly reviewed. The nature of the language thus places a considerable stumbling-block in the way of education, both by the time required to master its inherent difficulties, and by the effect upon the intellect of the mere memorizing of characters.

Dr. Frank Alanson LOMBARD, in his volume, *Pre-Meiji Education in Japan*, p. 241, says:

. . . Japan is a unity in government, language and people; yet by the character which she has borrowed she has burdened herself and her children with a greater task of mere memory in acquiring the ability to read and write than is undertaken by any other modern people, and besides has completely isolated herself from the understanding of the Western world. The Japanese student never ceases to study his letters and he never has them all learned.

Professor J. Ingram BRYAN, holder of the Order of the Sacred Treasure, 16 years a teacher in Japan, and lecturer at Cambridge University in Japanese Studies, says in his book, *Japan from Within* (New York, Frederick A. Stokes Co., 1924), p. 201:

A unique handicap under which the Japanese education labours is the necessity of the child devoting the earlier years of school life to the drudgery of memorizing the thousands of ideographs, a command of which is essential to reading, and to acquirement of knowledge. The difficulty might be obviated by substituting the Roman alphabet for the native characters, but as yet prejudice against such a change is too strong. The enslavement of the young mind to this memorizing of word pictures develops memory at the expense of reasoning power, and stunts rational growth.

The Hon. John Harrington GUBBINS, former First Secretary and later Japanese Secretary of the British Embassy in Tokyo, in his book, *The Making of Modern Japan* (Philadelphia, J. B. Lippincott Company, 1922), p. 299, writes:

How greatly education is hampered by the difficulty of the language will be understood when it is mentioned that a Japanese youth who goes through the whole educational course provided by the State is still studying it when on the threshold of the University; and that if he desires to attain any real literary scholarship he must continue this study for some time after his education is completed.

Dr. C. Burnell OLDS, long a resident of Japan and a student of the Japanese educational system, writing in the October 1942 issue of *Foreign Affairs*, says in his article, "Education for Conquest: The Japanese Way":

Then he is put through the daily and long-continued wrestling bout with the writing brush, so that he may teach his fingers to coordinate with his brain. His thinking power, the while, is being subjected to, and is exhausting itself in, the mechanical memorization of innumerable ideograms. . . . Is the mere mastering of 4,000 complicated Chinese characters that originated as many years ago, and coming to understand their multifarious usages, education? Every day is filled full and vacations are few and far between. . . . Even blind men who cannot see at all may be better educated than those who can, if for no other reason than that they do not have to spend the best part of their days learning an interminable number of complicated ideographs.

It is self-evident that any problem which has evoked such widespread and continuing comment from foreign observers would have been recognized and thoroughly explored by Japanese leaders. Out of a considerable literature on the subject four quotations have been chosen to illustrate the importance given to the problem of the written language by Japanese who have been recognized by their own people as leaders in modern Japan. The first is taken from the official history prepared for the Philadelphia International Exposition by the Japanese Ministry of Education, *An Outline History of Japanese Education* (New York, D. Appleton, 1876). It says on p. 13:

At the lowest estimate a schoolboy was required to learn one thousand different characters. In the Government elementary schools at the present time about three thousand characters are taught. A man laying any claim to scholarship knows eight or ten thousand characters; and those who pass for men of great learning are expected to be acquainted with many tens of thousands. [It should be noted that while this was possibly true three quarters of a century ago, the number required today is probably less.]

These characters have each their distinct meaning, so that the learner has not merely to learn the mechanical act of making it, but also its meaning and its proper place and use in a sentence. Many years of the boy's life are mainly spent in this task of learning to write and to use the numerous letters of his alphabet.

Marquis SAIONJI Kimmochi in 1907 in "National Education in the Meiji Era" (quoted in ŌKUMA, "Fifty Years of New Japan," *op cit.*, II, 173, and in KEENLEYSIDE and THOMAS, *op. cit.*, p. 104), wrote:

The greatest difficulty of all connected with education in Japan is the extreme complexity of the Japanese language. Japanese students to-day are attempting what is only possible to the strongest and cleverest of them, that is to say, two or three in every hundred. They are trying to learn their own language, which is in reality two languages, blended or confused the one with the other, according to the point of view, while attempting to learn English and German and in addition studying technical subjects.

Baron KIKUCHI Dairoku, one-time Privy Councilor and President of the Imperial Academy, in his book, *Japanese Education* (London, John Murray, 1909), p. 167, says:

You will probably now have got some idea of how enormously the labour and difficulty of learning our language is increased by the admixture of Chinese ideographs; you will perhaps wonder why we have not done away with them altogether: all I can say is that it is very hard to sweep away usages of many centuries all at once. It might possibly have been done at the beginning of the Meiji era, if the statesmen of those days had seen fit, for those were the days of radical reforms; but they had been educated in the old days when the only study considered worth while cultivating was the study of Chinese classics and history, and education meant knowledge of Chinese; they could not dream of such a thing as the expulsion of the Chinese ideographs.

Dr. NITOBE Inazo in the posthumously published collection of his American and Canadian lectures, *Lectures on Japan* (Tokyo, Kenkyusha, 1936), p. 297, in commenting on the inefficiency of education, says:

The use of Chinese ideographs is the root of all evil in this respect. A large part of the school-life is spent in mastering some 4,000 ideograms, most of which are pronounced in three or four ways and written in at least three ways. The waste of energy thereby incurred is worthy of the most serious consideration, and can be prevented only by the adoption of transliteration, i.e., the use of the Roman alphabet instead of Chinese ideograms.

Mere complexity is insufficient ground for condemnation. The present theories of nuclear physics can scarcely be characterized by simplicity, yet no thinking man of this age would condemn them solely on that ground. The modern physical philosopher recognizes the error of the early twentieth century oversimplification. Merely because the standard writing system of Japanese is complex is not of itself justification for radical and costly change. Postwar Japan cannot afford the luxury of reform for reform's sake. If the Japanese writing system is inadequate it must be judged so because of social and educational limitations and not because of mere linguistic deficiencies.

Is the System Inadequate? Japanese have charged that the written form of the language constitutes a major barrier to the reconstruction of the educational system and to the democratization of the country. A synthesis of these charges made in letters, interviews, and the Japanese language press may perhaps serve as a point of focus for a detailed investigation of the several inadequacies of the writing system.

It is contended that the democratization of Japan is jeopardized because the excessive difficulty of the writing system makes most information inaccessible to the masses of the people. It is held that the present system requires such a disproportionate amount of the available school time that students do not have the opportunity to study subject matter essential to their development as citizens in a representative government. It is charged that the necessity of long study in order to acquire any degree of facility in the present writing system tends to perpetuate a highly stratified social structure at times approaching a caste system, based upon the financial ability to acquire the necessary training.

It is charged that the efficient rehabilitation of the country is jeopardized because the excessive complexity of the present writing system makes modern business efficiency impossible. It is pointed out that it has barred the use of efficient typewriters, teletype, linotype, filing systems, dictionaries, and duplication processes. It is stated that the use of ideographs makes excessively difficult the development of a scientific literature and the adoption of scientific and technical terms in international use.

Finally, it is argued that the present writing system is a barrier to international understanding and amity because it makes the acquisition of a foreign language imperative for any person who is to be educated, yet imposes an unnecessary difficulty in acquiring the foreign language, with the exception of Chinese and Japanized

Korean. It is pointed out that the excessive difficulty of the writing system has made Japanese culture relatively inaccessible to Occidentals.

How valid are these charges?

The charge that the traditional system of written Japanese is unsatisfactory as a system of communication designed to be used by the masses appears to be substantiated by the evidence. The writing system has failed on both linguistic and educational grounds. All significant democratization reforms have been delayed and many may be defeated unless a more efficient system is adopted. The traditional system appears to have been unsatisfactory both from the point of view of the Occupational Authorities and from the point of view of the Japanese themselves, though the spokesmen of both groups have never publicly admitted its inadequacy.

The masses of the people were not adequately reached by the information services of the Occupation Authorities. SCAP directives were legal documents and the official text was in English. In theory the Imperial Japanese Government was bound by the English text alone. A considerable number of the most important of these directives, however, contained a clause which stated in effect: ". . . all citizens and residents of Japan will be held personally accountable."

This provision necessitated a Japanese text which could be understood by the people who were to be held accountable. In practice the translation of such a Japanese text was found to be difficult if not impossible. An analysis of the Chinese characters appearing in four major SCAP Directives—[AG 350 (22 Oct 45) CIE, "Administration of the Educational System of Japan"; AG 091 (4 Oct 45), "Removal of Restrictions on Political, Civil, and Religious Liberties"; AG 000.3 (15 Dec 45) CIE, "Abolition of Governmental Sponsorship, Support, Perpetuation, Control, Dissemination of State Shinto (*Kokka Shintō*) (*Jinja Shintō*)"; and AG 091.1 (4 Jan 46) GS, "Removal and Exclusion of Undesirable Personnel from Public Office"]—indicated that 31.1% of these *kanji* were outside the radius of *kanji* presumed to be understood by half the graduates of the compulsory educational system on the basis of prior statistical studies of the attainment of such graduates.

A study conducted by the Director of the *Kanamoji Kai* (Kana

Alphabet Society) was made of 1,453 workers in 14 factories located in Tokyo, Kanagawa, Chiba, and Saitama Prefectures. This study indicated that only 29% of the workers could read simple sentences and only 17% could read difficult sentences taken from the text of the officially sponsored history, *From the Mukden Incident to the Signing of the Surrender Documents on the Missouri*, which had been published in installments by all Japanese newspapers between 7 December 1945 and 20 December 1945. The same workers were tested on their ability to read 40 *kanji* selected at random from the history. The subject was asked to "read," i.e., give the approximate pronunciation of the character in the simple phonetic notation, *kana*. It was, therefore, merely a test of the ability of the workers to transform the written notation (*kanji*) into an approximate phonetic utterance, here recorded in the simple *kana* for convenience. It was assumed that if the subject were unable to render even an approximate phonetic equivalent for the word he could not be considered to know its meaning. This assumption is subject to certain modifications which will be considered in detail in a later analysis of Japanese literacy, but for the purposes of this test the scores may be taken as the maximum percentage of the total of different, not running, ideographs whose meaning might be understandable to the worker.

Workers' Education	Average for Males	For Females
11 years plus schooling	86%	80%
9–10 years' schooling	72%	57%
8 years' schooling	56%	52%
6–7 years' schooling	36%	19%

This test would indicate that the reading deficiency of workers was not merely the familiar situation found in the United States with readers unfamiliar with the meanings of some of the words. The situation was rather analogous to that of an American child confronted with a page to read in which blank spaces, or more properly cabalistic symbols, were liberally interspersed so that from a quarter to two thirds of the words were missing. Such passages appear as "completion tests" in some mental examinations.

An analysis was made of the *kanji* used in the official news release of the Supreme Commander, Gen. Douglas MacArthur, on the Yamashita war criminal trial. It was found that 29% of the *kanji* used were outside the presumed reading level of half the graduates of the six-year school system. A rough interrogation check in downtown Tokyo indicated that approximately one adult in ten could read the names of war criminals who had been arrested and tried by the Allied Powers. No claim is made that these were more than indicative of a serious reading disability in the public. Combined with the substantiating evidence of much more exhaustive Japanese studies of reading ability, they appear to indicate quite clearly that Occupational propaganda—it was officially known as "information"—was not reaching the people.

The most vital reason why the present writing system is unsatisfactory from the point of view of the Japanese people themselves is essentially the same as that for an Occupation Force. The people do not have adequate access to those documents necessary to informed citizenship. Professor Doi Kōchi, holder of the Chair of English Literature at Tohoku Imperial University and inventor of Basic Japanese, in an article in the *Asahi Hyōron*, translated and quoted in Media Analysis Division, *Publication Analysis* No. 43, 22 May 1946, CI&E, GHQ, SCAP, says:

In order that democracy may be realized, each citizen must be able to choose for himself proper representatives. This means that a majority of the people must be able to understand home and foreign affairs, the conditions of society, and broad economic principles. In order to give the general public such a knowledge, a national language which is plain and simple is necessary.

*   *   *

Our citizens, both male and female, have been given the right when they reach a certain age to select political representatives. In order to make the greatest and best use of this right, it is necessary to educate the people. This education requires a sensible language which the people can understand perfectly.

The process of learning to read requires a disproportionately high percentage of the student's time. This allocation of time to the mechanics of reading leaves a correspondingly lower percentage of time for acquiring the learning itself. An interesting evidence of the waste in learning time in acquiring the traditional system of writing with *kanji* is given by the schools for the blind. The Tokyo Governmental School for the Blind, for example, teaches the same material to blind students as the regular national elementary schools teach normal seeing students. Blind secondary school students take the standard secondary school course, including ethics, civics, Japanese language, English or German, mathematics, history, geography, natural history, physics, chemistry, domestic science (for the girls), singing, and gymnastics—in four years instead of the five normally required for students who can see, and who must memorize *kanji*. The textbooks used are direct translations into Japanese Braille, a phonetic alphabet, of the official Ministry of Education textbooks.

In the regular Japanese schools supervised by the Ministry of Education in 1944 a total of 69 hours (the unit is one class hour per week for one academic year, i.e., annual hours) out of the total of 172 spent in the six-year compulsory school system was devoted to learning to read and write Japanese. In 1937, a total of 76 hours, or 42% of the total of 156 were spent in learning to read and write. This might be a defensible percentage if the process of learning to read were terminated at that point. However, tests indicate that the average student just graduated has acquired only 600 of the 3,500 *kanji* actually used by newspapers making a conscious effort to limit the number of characters. The process of acquiring *kanji* is a continuing one. The General Affairs Committee of the Japanese Diet found that 4,052 *kanji* were used in the records of the first 25 sessions. Between 8,000 and 9,000 must be recognized if university reference books are to be read. *Giles's Chinese-English Dictionary*, intended to contain only characters in common use, lists 13,848. The *K'ang-hsi Dictionary* lists 39,753 with an appendix of 7,463 rare *kanji*. Two of the commonest standard Japanese dictionaries, *Daijiten* and *Jigen*, contain 14,924 and 10,373 characters, not words, respectively. Between 20 and 30,000 *kanji* must be mastered if the reader is to acquire a scholar's knowledge in the opinion of members of the Faculty of Literature of the Tokyo Imperial University. The pupil studying mathematics is sometimes unable to solve a "problem" because he cannot read it. All content courses devote a certain proportion of the time to mastering *kanji* which are common only to that material. Teachers' manuals contain detailed directions of how certain key *kanji*, often having a political connotation, are to be explained. Advanced law students in their final year at the university must systematically memorize new *kanji* encountered in their studies. This does not correspond to the acquisition of new words in a particular subject field in an Occidental language, since the acquisition of *kanji* is necessary even when the word is known. Japanese frequently compare this constant process of memorizing new *kanji* with the necessity of learning to spell in a writing system which is imperfectly phonetic, as in English. The argument is spurious, however, for the two are not at all comparable in degree.

The ability to read Japanese rapidly disappears unless constantly practiced. In a study of 762 males in 14 factories, with only 8 years of schooling, the tests of recognition of *kanji* indicated an average improvement of 9.1% from the end of schooling to the peak (between 30 and 39 years of age) and then a drop of 15% bringing the reading level of persons over 40 years of age considerably below the level of those recently graduated from school. S. TAKADA, in a study, "Survey of Students' Retention and Misuse of *Kanji* on the Basis of School Years" in *Kyōiku Shinri Kenkyū* ("Study of Educational Psychology"), Vol. XII, No. 7, found that in the elementary school grades "*kanji* learned once does not mean that it is accurately retained indefinitely, but with constant application such *kanji* can be retained."

Although only fragmentary quantitative evidence is available, ample qualitative evidence exists that a rapid loss takes place. A Caucasian school inspector with 27 years' experience in the school system of Japan, for example, was unable to read during two years' imprisonment in World War II and found that he had lost so many *kanji* that he was able to read a Sixth Grade Reader only by constant reference to a dictionary. His ability to read English and to speak Japanese had suffered no appreciable loss during the same period. Japanese prisoners taken early in the war found great difficulty in reading difficult parts of newspapers or propaganda leaflets when repatriated. The former Executive Editor of the *Asahi*, Japan's foremost newspaper, Mr. SUZUKI Bunshiro, with 25 years' newspaper experience, confesses that he cannot write a feature story without reference to a dictionary. Japanese women, with their writing confined largely to personal letters after graduation from school, are traditionally unable to write these letters without reference to a *kanji* dictionary. Prince TAKAMATSU, younger brother of the Emperor, in January 1946 told a naval officer from the Education Division, CI&E, GHQ, SCAP, that he must use a dictionary frequently in order to write his personal diary.

The Imperial Government of Japan found that when it needed communication with its people this communication was missing. There exists some evidence that during the war the Japanese supply system on occasion broke down because of the inability of personnel in the lower echelons to read the official directions. On 15 August 1945 when the recording of the Emperor declaring the close of the war and directing that his people lay down their arms was sent over the air, it was ambiguous and had to be followed by an interpretation and commentary. In Nagano Prefecture many of the people understood the Imperial Rescript to say that Japan had won the war, and demonstrated in the streets for more than an hour in celebration. This communication breakdown was caused by the fact that the manuscript, an Imperial Rescript, was written in *bungotai*, a style that only the educated could read, and in this particular instance few if any could understand when read aloud.

Business efficiency is very low. A Japanese *kanji* typewriter—the *Nihon* will be taken as an example—has 2,005 characters plus a reserve of 858 in the rare-type drawer, bringing the total to 2,863. Operation of this machine is relatively simple, but speed is virtually impossible. An average graduate of the eight-year elementary school system in the United States learns to type 35 words per minute without errors in 54 hours of instruction. A rated typist or secretary in the United States types from 60 to 70 words per minute. Prizewinners type as much as 100 words per minute. A skilled foreign typist, unfamiliar with Japanese, typing stroke by stroke, typed the romanized Japanese text of the SCAP Directive, AG 091 (4 Oct 45) GS, "Removal of Restrictions on Political, Civil, and Religious Liberties," at the rate of 63 *romaji* words per minute, or the equivalent of 199 *kanji* per minute. The ablest *kanji* typist in the Ministry of Education, tested on the same material, typed 33 *kanji* per minute on the *Nihon kanji* typewriter. These tests were conducted in the usual manner over a period of 15 minutes' typing time.

All type must be set by hand in printing establishments. It is true that linotype machines capable of handling 800 symbols have been designed, but allowing for *katakana*, *hiragana*, *romaji*, numerals, and necessary signs and symbols, they are capable of handling only 500 *kanji*. Such machines, however, would be excessively expensive and would lose much of the speed which constitutes the major advantage of the linotype machine. The 500 *kanji* linotype would be able to set only 77.3% of the *kanji* appearing in the running text of the average Tokyo newspaper. It is obvious that such a machine would have little practical use, so little, in fact, that it has never been adopted. A standard linotype machine can, of course, handle *romaji* perfectly; a standard linotype machine with one extra keyboard can handle both *romaji* and *kana*.

Indexing is very complicated and inefficient. It has been an acute problem in China where library catalogues, dictionaries, and general filing have been hopelessly handicapped, and typewriters and business machines have been so complicated as to be virtually worthless. Modern systems have been devised by the librarian WAN Kuo-ting; the former Minister of Education, Dr. CH'ÊEN Li-fu; the President of the *Commercial Press*, Mr. Y. W. WONG; the Dean of Yenching University, Dr. William HUNG; and by the great Chinese philosopher and writer, LIN Yutang. This latter student of the problem has experimented with four systems: classification by sequence of strokes, which demands a precise knowledge of the mechanical construction of the character; by a phonetic syllabary classification, unsuitable at least in China because of dialect fluctuations; by a numerical classification depending upon recognition of four "corners" or discernible patterns in the character; and a top and bottom form classification, the basis of the mechanical classification system used in arranging the relatively limited number of characters in his Chinese typewriter.

The basic Chinese indexing system, however, is still the etymological one of the *K'ang-hsi Dictionary* which compressed the 540 radicals, or discernible patterns, of the *Shuowen* (a Second-Century Study of Chinese Philology) into 214, and supplied a subclassification by counting additional strokes. This is the basis of the traditional radical and stroke-count method. Three systems are used in modern Japan: indexing by radical and stroke count, indexing by sound, and indexing by spelling.

Indexing by radical and stroke count is the system used in most *kanji* dictionaries, *Ueda's Daijiten*, for example, some encyclopedias, card files of materials, or names expressed in rare *kanji*. The system depends upon recognizing in the *kanji* some subordinate pattern of strokes, known as the "radical," which is a commonly repeated portion of a large group of different *kanji*. The majority of these radicals are in themselves *kanji* capable of being used alone to stand for a single meaning. Each of the 214 groups of *kanji* which include these radicals are again subdivided into lesser groups which are written with one, two, three, etc., extra brush strokes. Each of these subgroups may have scores—or in a large filing system or dictionary, hundreds—of entries which must be scanned to find the particular entry desired. All such systems must have an additional category in which are recorded all *kanji* in which a radical cannot easily be recognized. This group is usually arranged by counting total strokes. Small indexing systems, such as small dictionaries or small files using this system, may disregard the radicals and index directly under the total number of strokes in each character.

Indexing by sound is the system commonly used in office filing systems, dictionaries of relatively common terms, encyclopedias, lists of names, and other indices whose reading is known. It has the advantage that every entry can be immediately and directly located, as in an alphabetical index in European languages. It has the very serious disadvantage that entries can only be located if their pronunciation is known. The most common order is that of the 49 basic syllables of *kana*, with appropriate subdivisions also based on the *kana*. Even this order is given in two different ways. The *iroha* order, invented by the Buddhist priest KŪKAI and based on a 47-sound poem which uses each of the syllables only once, is widely used in Japan in older indices. The more modern system is the *a-i-u-e-o* order taken from the order of the *gojū-on* or "50-sound" table.

Indexing by spelling is possible only in cataloguing romanized material which, of course, can be indexed alphabetically in the same manner as in Occidental languages.

Handwriting is excessively difficult to read. Standard block form (*kaisho*) *kanji* are written with from one to at least 48 brush strokes (No. 14,886 of *Ueda's Daijiten*, read *tatsu yuku* "dragon goes"; *kan-on* is given as *tō*, *go-on* is given as *dō*). Characters with as many as 20 strokes are relatively common. In handwriting the cursive or "grass-writing" (*sōsho*) form is frequently used and these strokes are compressed into a flowing stroke which only remotely approximates the multiple strokes of the printed *kanji*. It is inevitable that writing in this cursive form should be difficult. Most large Japanese dictionaries include a section in which examples of standard variations on the more common characters are listed. Recognition of *kanji* is akin to recognition of non-literal communications signs such as the black and white diagonal bars that stand for a railroad crossing in the Occident. Differentiation between a limited number, perhaps one or two hundred, is relatively easy. It is the inevitable and increasing multiplicity of these symbols which makes their recognition a major memory feat.

The system of writing Japanese with *kanji* and *kana* (*kanamajiri*) makes the learning of foreign languages unnecessarily difficult. The vertical eye movement learned in standard Japanese makes horizontal reading appear fatiguing. Dr. INOUE Tatsuji, famed Japanese ophthalmologist, however, in an article in the 29 April 1946 *Yomiuri* wrote that his experiments had indicated that traditional Japanese was both slower and more fatiguing, because of the multiplicity of strokes and the vertical eye movement. CHANG Chung-Yuan, in his monograph, *A Study of the Relative Merits of the Vertical and Horizontal Lines in Reading Chinese Print*, Archives of Psychology No. 276 (New York, 1942), p. 56, concludes "that for reading purposes the horizontal arrangement of characters offers definite advantages over the vertical."

The system of writing Japanese in *kanamajiri* almost certainly erects a cultural barrier between Japan and the Occidental world. Spoken Japanese is relatively easy for any foreign student to acquire. The acquisition of even a superficial knowledge of the written language, however, is so difficult that few but people who are to be professional linguists or who intend to spend a lifetime in Japan can afford the time and effort to learn it. The Naval Language School at Boulder, Colo., at first accepted only students who already possessed a good working knowledge of spoken Japanese or else were single men under 30, who were in the upper 10% of their university graduating classes and had demonstrated ability in language. Later the pressure of the war necessitated some relaxation of these standards. With even this highly selected talent it presumably required 10–12 hours per day, 6 days per week, for 9 to 14 months, to acquire an elementary reading knowledge. Although it was officially claimed that graduates could read all parts of a Japanese newspaper with facility, this claim was found to be somewhat excessive among newly graduated officers. After six months or a year of experience in the field, however, most graduates had far surpassed the claim. It has been estimated by one of the ablest Japanese linguists connected with the naval program that a serious and mature student, with demonstrated language ability, one year prior residence in Japan, and a knowledge of spoken Japanese to the level of approximately 2,500 words, could acquire a reading knowledge sufficient to understand a daily newspaper such as the *Asahi* in 300 hours of personal tutoring if the most modern techniques, such as the use of mechanical flash cards, were employed. This was advanced in support of the claim that the writing system was easy, not that it was difficult. Even if this estimate be accepted the difficulty as compared with a phonemic system is obvious. Estimates made by Occidental scholars of the time required to acquire anything like a command of cultural Japanese vary from three to seven years. Sir George Sansom, in his *Historical Grammar of Japanese*, p. 43, states: ". . . it is not an exaggeration to say that absolute certainty in reading Japanese texts, whether ancient or modern, is almost unattainable."

Can a Japanese Be Literate?

What is literacy? The ratio of literacy is the standard yardstick by which all nations measure their cultural and political level. Their people can be effective citizens only if the government has continued in direct contact with them through the media of writing. In a representative government, in which the people in effect make policy, literacy becomes of overwhelming importance. Japan has officially claimed 99.6% adult literacy. This, if true, would be the country's most remarkable achievement and would put Japan far ahead of any other nation in this respect. Actually, however, the myth of Japanese universal literacy is based on a translation error and a fallacious method of determining literacy. The official statistics on children under 14 years of age attending school for the years 1935–39 averaged 99.59%. In Japanese statistics these figures are given as the "ratio of those attending school" (*shūgaku ritsu*). There does not appear to be any specific term for "literacy" in Japanese and in reports which the *Mombushō* has translated into English this term is apparently rendered as "literacy," since the percentages given are identical or are rounded off to the nearest decimal place. That this translation error was not unconscious must be assumed from the fact that these figures were supplied for the compilation of international literacy statistics. It appears, therefore, that it was assumed that all those students who attended school would become literate. In order to understand the dubious value of such an assumption, it may be well to glance briefly at the extensive and somewhat disappointing array of methods which have been used for determining literacy in other nations.

Other nations measure their literacy by:

(1) Determining the percentage of the adult population who have completed a level of schooling which may be presumed to ensure that the graduate is able to read with comprehension. This has been used in nearly all countries and has been the common method used in Argentina, Brazil, Chile, and certain states of the United States.

(2) Determining the percentage of the adult population who are able to read: (a) the *Constitution;* (b) common laws such as traffic ordinances; (c) editorials in newspapers; (d) political feature stories in newspapers. This has frequently been erroneously considered one of the requirements for naturalization in the United States, and at one time even led to the practice of the courts and the official examiners testing applicants for their ability to read material of this level, until the Regulations of 1 January 1936 (File 25/127) of the Immigration and Naturalization Service, re-established the policy of strict observance of the Act of 29 June 1906, which made the sole educational requirements for naturalization the ability to speak English and to sign one's name in one's own handwriting.

(3) Determining the percentage of the adult male population who as conscripts, army recruits, persons liable to military service, veterans, or voters are capable of passing an official test of literacy based on materials officially considered essential to citizenship. This system has been used in Argentina, Japan, Sweden, the Soviet Union, and the United States.

(4) Determining the percentage of those people who are able to make a signature by writing and not by a "mark" on applications for marriage license. This has been the traditional method of England, Wales, Scotland, the Netherlands, Switzerland, and Uruguay.

(5) Determining by test the percentage of the adult population who can write a letter to a friend and read the answer to it. This was the basis of census statistics in British India.

(6) Determining the percentage of the adult population who can write in some language, not necessarily the official language of the nation. This was the traditional method used in the United States, but it has been replaced by mere census interrogation.

(7) Determining by census interrogation what percentage of the adult population make an unsupported claim to ability to "read" or to "read and write." This is the present method used in the United States.

Not one of these seven methods seems to meet adequately the demands of the Japanese situation. The first two taken in conjunction most nearly approach a solution. Yet even this combination only approximately measures the gross results. Literacy in Japanese is too complicated a skill to be measured by such crude procedures. It is probable, although there is no supporting evidence available, that 99.6% of the Japanese adults can read simple material written in the phonetic syllabary, *kana*. Since virtually no materials are written solely in *kana* such an accomplishment can hardly be considered a demonstration of functional literacy. It is true that there have been some light readings, mainly novels and newspapers, which have had practically all *kanji* paralleled by *kana* "sidewriting," which amounts to a phonetic transliteration, but the trend for more than two decades has been away from "sidewriting." Similarly, ability to read *romaji* is an inadequate proof of literacy, since a much smaller percentage of Japanese have in the past mastered this simple system. All other common forms of writing Japanese involve the use of Chinese ideographs, *kanji*. Yet mere knowledge of a specific number of *kanji* appears to be an inadequate measure.

If recognition of *kanji* is taken as the guide it must be assumed that even adults with no formal education are partially literate, since tests of Army conscripts reveal such persons can recognize an occasional *kanji*, learned like the American road signs for a curve or a railway crossing. Similarly, Y. Kubo in his article, "Measurement of Education by Reading Ability," in *Jidō Kenkyūsho Kiyō* ("Child Study Bulletin"), No. 6, reports that in testing pre-elementary school children on the list of symbols (*kana* and *kanji*) used in the first six grades, it was found that

31% of middle-class children and 10% of lower-class children recognized all of the 51 *katakana* symbols; 5% and 0%, respectively, read all of the *hiragana* symbols; and the average number of ideographs (*kanji*) recognized was 4.3 and 2.0 respectively, with the maximum 73.

The problem arises as to what constitutes recognition of an ideograph. An impression of the meaning can sometimes be deduced even though the "reading" or pronunciation of the Japanese word is unknown. Conversely, people can sometimes "read" the word by giving it its proper pronunciation without having any knowledge of the meaning. Since *kanji* have both multiple readings and multiple meanings, the question arises as to whether a person "knows" a *kanji* when he is able to give one of the readings and one of the meanings.

The number of *kanji* which must be "known" in order to be literate also poses a problem. In phonetic systems of writing, once the phonetic values of the symbols are learned, new words can instantly be recognized if the reader knows the word in his spoken vocabulary. Parenthetically it may be added that even in writing solely with *kana*, the system of notation is not perfectly phonetic, or more accurately phonemic, since there are 109 basic syllables in Japanese and only 49 *kana* symbols and two diacritical marks, requiring approximately 35 conventional and nonphonemic combinations to represent other syllables. This is not true with ideographs. The *kanji*, or compound, for each new word, even though the word in its spoken form is quite familiar to the reader, must be separately memorized. As a result, the learning process of the mere mechanics of reading and writing is never completed. Expert Japanese opinion as to what level of *kanji* recognition constitutes literacy has varied from 500 to 3,500 with 1,356 and 2,669 most frequently advanced. The actual *kanji* included in these lists have varied from year to year. The permissible readings and meanings of each of these *kanji* have also varied.

Finally, the style in which a person is competent to read with understanding or to write unambiguously constitutes a problem. Readers who have an excellent command of *kōgotai*, or simple vernacular, may be quite unable to read understandingly *bungotai*, *sōrōbun*, or *kambun*. Mere knowledge of the *kanji* appearing in *kambun*, for example, is insufficient for understanding reading. A definite reading skill, enabling the person to determine the order and to supply the postpositions and inflected endings, must be acquired.

Much has been written of the "functional illiteracy" of the American public, of the inability of the average reader to understand what he reads, of the startling inability of the masses to read intelligently. The basic difference between literacy in an Occidental language and literacy in Japanese, however, can best be appreciated when it is noted that the average Japanese has no chance to understand what he reads. The simple acquisition of 25 to 30 phonetic symbols opens up to the Occidental reader access to any concept which he is linguistically and psychologically prepared to understand. If he knows what the word means when he hears it, he knows what it means when he sees it. But no Japanese, however erudite, ever completely masters the system of notation itself. At some level of difficulty in written communication he will find gaps in the manuscript with key words missing, not by reason of his unfamiliarity with their meaning but solely by reason of his unfamiliarity with the particular notational sign or *kanji* which stands for that concept. The percentage of these blank spots decreases gradually as the education, and hence reading skill, increases. But such a situation poses the pregnant question, "Can any Japanese be truly literate in such a system?"

Are Japanese literate? If Japanese literacy is measured on the basis of the last four standards which have been applied in other countries it would rate very high, possibly as high as official claims. Thus no Japanese would be judged illiterate on the signature test, since traditionally signatures are made with a *han*, or personal seal. Similarly the census question, "Can you read?," would be answered affirmatively by the vast majority, since no normal person living in Japan can fail to memorize a few *kanji* as signs. The test of ability to write a personal letter and the test of ability to write in some language, not necessarily his own, would also reflect a very high rate of "literacy" since virtually all native Japanese know *kana* and since prewar Japan (1938) had only 28,857 foreign residents (presumably exclusive of Chinese and Koreans), or an insignificant .047% of the total population. Obviously these tests do not apply to the Japanese problem and their results are meaningless.

But if Japanese literacy is measured on the basis of any of the other standards, the official ratio of literacy must be considered in error.

As was noted above Japanese literacy as measured by attainment presumed to be synonymous with school attendance (*shūgaku ritsu*) is superficially high (99.6%) but upon inspection is found to be startlingly low.

The compulsory educational system of Japan, as well as of every country, has as its primary objective the teaching of reading and writing. Economic and social pressures prevent this compulsory education from being indefinitely extended. In Japan it has ranged from 4 to 8 years, with 6 years being the practical level for the past 30 years. In 1935 with 6 years of compulsory education the school system taught 1,356 *kanji*. The *Kanamoji Kai* (Kana Alphabet Society) and the *Hattori Koko Kai* (Hattori Public Duty Society) during March 1935 tested 1,479 urban graduating sixth-grade pupils in a seven-hour examination which indicated that one half of them could not write in a recognizable form (i.e., with certain permissible errors) more than 600 *kanji;* that only 15% could write more than 1,000 *kanji;* and that only one tenth of 1% could write as many as 1,300 *kanji*. This dictation type test is one of the standard methods used to determine whether the student has acquired a reasonable recognition and reproduction skill. It is a notation test, not a vocabulary test, since the meanings of the *kanji* and their compounds are not required. Silent reading comprehension is ordinarily measured by testing the student's grasp of essential points (*yatenhasoku*) and grasp of the outline (*taiihasoku*), as, for example, in T. YAMAMOTO's "Study of Silent Reading Comprehension," in *Kyōiku Shinri Kenkyū* ("Study of Educational Psychology"), Vol. V, No. 7, in which he tested 2,200 students in the fourth, fifth, and sixth grades. S. OTOMO, in an investigation of 5,081 rural and urban elementary school children distributed among the first eight grades, found that rural schools were approximately two years behind urban schools in the upper grades, as reported in "Educational Measurements of Book Reading Ability," in *Nomura Kyōiku Kenkyūsho Hōkoku* ("Nomura Educational Research Institute Bulletin"), No. 1.

The list of 1,356 *kanji* was continued essentially intact until 4 July 1942, when the number of *kanji* officially required to be taught in the compulsory education system was raised to 2,669

by the Japanese Cabinet. This enormous increase of nearly 97%
in the teaching load was accompanied by a reduction of 13 hours
in the number of hours devoted to learning to read the Japanese
language, a matter of 20% reduction in time. No appreciable
change in teaching techniques compensated for this increased
load. Although no class trained under the new system was graduated, since Defeat and the Occupation caused abandonment of
the plan, it must be presumed that actual mastery of the *kanji*
would have been no higher and probably would have been far
less than that of those tested in 1935. Measured on this basis,
Japanese who have been graduated from the compulsory education system cannot be considered functionally literate.

Literacy measured by ability to read politically necessary documents is also disappointing. Japanese newspapers, as in other countries, vary widely in the difficulty of their writings, and vary
widely within a single publication in the difficulties of various
types of news.

Standard Japanese (*kanamajiri*) is almost exclusively used. In
1923 newspaper offices by common consent embarked on a program of limitation of the number of *kanji*. They were not agreed
upon what that number should be nor which specific *kanji* should
be used, but they agreed to hold the number to between 2,000
and 3,000. Among the numerous studies which have been made
to determine the actual compliance with these restrictions mention might be made of OKAZAKI Tsunetaro's study, *Kanji Seigen
no Kihonteki Kenkyū* ("Basic Studies on the Limitation of Chinese Characters") (Tokyo, Matsumura Sanshōdō, 1938); and
OKAZAKI Tsunetaro and MATSUSAKA Tadanori's study, *Shimbun
no Kanji Shiyō Dosū Shirabe* ("An Investigation into the Frequency of Kanji Used by Newspapers") (Tokyo, Shōwa Tō-
shadō, 1941). The *Asahi Shimbun*, Japan's leading newspaper, attempted to limit its main stories to 3,307 *kanji* in 1943, and the
Nichi Nichi, now the *Mainichi*, restricted its news stories to 2,528
kanji in the same year. These limitations were gradually relaxed,
and after Surrender the editors of papers admitted they used from
5,000 to 6,000 different *kanji*. A study made in 1935, which may be
considered a normal peacetime year, indicated that 3,542 different
kanji were used but that 500 of these represented 77.3% of the
total and that 1,000 *kanji* represented 91.7% of the total.

Sidewriting (*furigana*) has also commonly been supplied as

a means of explaining difficult *kanji* in simple *kana* for the benefit of "partial illiterates." In 1926 the political and social news stories of the *Asahi Shimbun* supplied 52% of the *kanji* with a phonetic transcription in *kana*. This also has decreased until during the first year of the Occupation the *Asahi Shimbun* supplied only 9% of the *kanji* with *kana* sidewriting. Because the number of difficult and rare *kanji* has increased with the introduction of many foreign and technical terms and the wide use of foreign names as a result of the War, Defeat, and Occupation, this reduction in the percentage of *furigana* is even more serious than the reduction from 52% to 9% would indicate. The *Minshu Shimbun* ("People's Gazette"), a paper directed to the masses and enjoying the backing of the Social-Democratic party, carried no *furigana* whatsoever. In 1936 (which may be considered a normal peacetime year) the *Asahi Shimbun* supplied 31% of the *kanji* with *kana* sidewriting.

All major newspapers use the vernacular (*kōgotai*) in everything but isolated feature articles. However, certain types of news, such as editorials, letters to the editor, and political feature stories are commonly written in a more difficult literary type of the vernacular. Such articles are frequently beyond the reading skill of any but people with middle school education or above. On this basis, approximately 85% of the adult population cannot be presumed to be functionally literate.

The Japanese have themselves recognized that the official language used in public documents presents a formidable barrier to democratization. On 30 March 1946, the *Nippon Times* carried an editorial on this subject. It said in part:

An elementary school teacher reports that out of an entire class of sixth grade pupils, only two were able to read and reasonably understand the new draft Constitution for Japan. It is a question, of course, as to how well even pupils in the sixth grade of American Schools can read and understand the Constitution of the United States, so the poor performance of the Japanese youngsters need not occasion too much surprise. But it does pose some uncomfortable questions concerning the prospects for democracy in Japan.

It must be realized that about 80 percent of the entire Japanese population receive no more than six years of formal schooling so that the average Japanese citizen possesses little more education than these sixth grade pupils who found the new draft Constitution so puzzling.

* * *

. . . the Japanese written language and its whole system of orthography, including the use of the Chinese ideographs, may need to be simplified and rationalized in a sweeping campaign of language reform.

As early as 21 November 1945 the *Mainichi*, in an editorial, "Change the Constitution into Colloquial Style," had publicly called for not only a simplification of legal language but a rewriting of the *Constitution*, all laws, bulletins, regulations, and official notices in the vernacular. It said in part: ". . . The cardinal point of the political education of the people is to let them familiarize themselves with state politics and legal institutions. For this purpose the authorities concerned should first set the example by changing the Constitution into the spoken language."

At 1 P.M. 17 April 1946 the Imperial Japanese Government made public the text of the revised draft of the new *Constitution*. It was written in *kōgotai*, or simple vernacular style, and had a high percentage of *hiragana*, or cursive phonetic syllabary, used with the *kanji*. It was still a long way from *romaji*, or a substantially phonemic text, but it was a giant stride in the direction of simplification. Public reception of the new draft was almost entirely favorable. The 20 April 1946 editorial of the *Nippon Times* was characteristic:

. . . the changes in the actual contents are quite minor and without particular significance. But the fact that the style has been transformed from the difficult formal literary style traditional with official documents to an easier popular style more closely approaching the colloquial speech is a fact of tremendous significance to those who are familiar with the particular characteristics of the intricate Japanese language. It signifies that the great mass of the common people, heretofore unable to comprehend a good part of most official documents, will be able to understand this constitution to a singular degree. It is an important contribution to the assurance that the government under the new constitution will rest on the democratic basis of the understanding and support of the people.

It may be argued that since literacy is a political as well as educational phenomenon, it could validly be defined as anything the interested political unit wished it to be. A similar argument could be advanced in psychology by saying that "intelligence" is that which is measured by an "intelligence test." Just as in a temperature scale, there are no theoretical minimum or maximum points, so that the units are merely arbitrary subdivisions (usually on a linear scale) of the pure quantity measured between two convenient verifiable points on that scale. Japan has attempted such a measurement of "literacy."

An official test of "Comprehension of the National Language" was given 567,915 young men of 20 years of age inducted into the Japanese Army at the beginning of the war (1941). This group might be expected to show a higher literacy than the general population because it was made up of physically selected males who had attended school during the period when the Japanese schools were at their highest efficiency. The test required for a perfect score (100%) a language ability less than that required to read perfectly the basic Japanese papers (Imperial rescripts, Japanese *Constitution*, common laws, and simple news items from the daily newspapers) and established its zero point as complete failure to answer any part of the examination correctly. The average score on the test for graduates of the six-year compulsory course was 39.1%; for graduates of the additional two years of the higher course of the elementary school, 56.7%; and for persons graduating from the main course of the continuation school (*seinen gakkō*) 60.8%. Figures for the corresponding age groups in the 1937 conscription list, considered the last normal prewar year, were 37.7%, 56.6%, and 58.4%, respectively.

Perhaps the result of these annual tests which was considered most significant by the Japanese officials was the apparent discovery that graduates of the six-year compulsory course did only 65% as well on languages as they did on national history and 79% as well as on mathematics based on a comparison of the relative positions of comparable age groups on the two arbitrary scales. The average scores for all conscripts revealed a marked though lessened disparity between language and subject-matter attainment. Thus the average for conscripts of all educational levels showed only 72% the attainment in language as compared with attainment measured in ethics and national history and only 90% that attained in mathematics. These tests are subject, of course, to the obvious criticism that the officially required standards may not have been, and almost certainly were not, comparable. The tests do show, however, a serious failure to meet official minimum standards, and a markedly more serious failure to attain these standards in the field of language.

What Are the Explanations? The Japanese rate of literacy has not lacked for official and unofficial apologists. Three basic arguments are advanced to explain the poor showing of Japanese students, conscripts, and workers in view of the long-maintained official claim of 99.6% literacy: there has been too little instruction, the quality of instruction has been too low, and the materials that the masses are expected to read are too difficult.

Has there in fact been too little instruction? It might be argued that education like the good things of this life can never be had in too abundant quantities. But from a practical point of view there are economic and social limits to what even the most favored nation can provide. Judged on this basis Japan does not appear in an unfavorable light.

The percentage of time in the curriculum which is devoted to language instruction is very high. Japanese schools in 1937 devoted 76 hours out of a total of 156 (annual hours, as defined previously), or 42% of the time, in elementary schools to formal instruction in reading (*yomikata*) and writing (*kakikata*). In 1944, despite the pressure of war, these schools devoted 69 hours out of a total of 172 or 40% to acquiring the tools of reading. Comparison with the United States is rendered difficult because in recent years a large percentage of the schools have not used standardized curricula and many have used core curricula in which formal instruction in reading has been merged with instruction in subject-matter fields. In a study of the time allotments in elementary school subjects, published by C. H. MANN of Teachers College, Columbia University, in 1928, and quoted by J. H. DOUGHERTY, F. H. GORMAN, and C. A. PHILLIPS on p. 49 of their volume, *Elementary School Organization* (New York, Macmillan, 1945), 1,763 units were devoted to reading out of a total of 9,153 units in the first six grades or 19%.

The length of the compulsory school year is more than adequate. Japanese schools have a school year extending from 1 April to 31 March, with authorization for holidays not to exceed 130 days, thus making a minimum school year of 235 days, approximately 30% longer than in the United States. The United States has, in most states, a standard school year of 36 weeks or 180 days established by law. In 1937 the average number of days actually attended in the compulsory school system was 173 days.

The length of compulsory education is comparable with enlightened Occidental nations. Japanese schools established the period of compulsory education as four years by the *Educational Code of 1872.* This was extended to six years by the *Elementary School Reform of 1907.* The period of compulsory education was extended to eight years by the *National School Reform of 1941* which remained in effect until April 1947 when the Occupation-inspired administration reorganization went into effect, with frank public announcement that the nine-year compulsory education provision was a dream for the future and not an enforceable immediate reality. Under the 1941 revision the last two years of the compulsory eight might be taken in a part-time extension school of indifferent quality (*seinen gakkō*), so that the Japanese compulsory educational system continued to be commonly referred to as one of six years. Of the 664,680 conscripts tested in 1941, approximately 88% had completed eight years of some form of formal education. The United States varies from state to state with regard to the period of compulsory education. The age of 14 is the minimum release date, thus making eight years of schooling the minimum compulsory education. In 1940 the average attendance at school at the age of 14 was 92.5%; at 15 was 87.6%; at 16–17 was 68.7%; and at 18–19 was 28.9%. The 1940 Census indicated 82.4% of the population 20–24 years of age, and therefore roughly comparable to the Japanese conscripts, had eight years of schooling or less; and that 60.4% of the population 25 years and older had eight years or less.

The percentage of children of school age that actually enroll in compliance with the compulsory school laws is remarkably high. Japanese schools in 1944 enrolled 10,619,558 out of the total of 10,641,153 children of school age, or 99.77%. It is very doubtful if any other nation in that war year could claim an equal figure. The United States in 1940 enrolled 15,034,659 out of the total of 15,828,035 children of a corresponding age (7–13 inclusive), or 94.9%. The United States Census of 1920 reported 90.6%, and the Census of 1930 reported 95.3% of this age group. Argentina, most literate of the South American nations, for example, in 1937 had a potential school population of 2,552,212 yet despite compulsory school laws only 1,852,327 or 72.7% were matriculated.

The percentage of children of school age that are in average daily attendance is also remarkably high. Japanese schools in the war year of 1944 reported an average daily attendance of 97.9%. For over 20 years the average daily attendance was better than 96% of the potential school population. The United States enrolled proportionately fewer than attended in the Japanese system. The record of average daily attendance of those enrolled in compliance with compulsory school laws in the United States ranged from 80.6% in 1925 to 84.2% in 1943. Argentina in 1937 had an average daily attendance of 1,543,317 or 83.2% of those enrolled and 72.7% of those eligible.

Has the instruction in fact been of too poor quality? It can be argued with considerable truthfulness that the level of teaching in Japan is quite low when judged by Occidental standards. But this argument is based on foreign criteria of evaluating teaching quality, not on proficiency within the accepted standard of the nation concerned. For what he was intended to do the traditional Japanese teacher has been very efficient. In the fields of drill activity, one of the few methodological areas where valid comparisons can be made, the Japanese teacher does not suffer by comparison. In the indirect measures of teacher quality, the percentage of the national income devoted to education, the ratio of students to teacher, and the amount of training required for certification, Japan has been outstanding rather than laggard.

Japan has spent a very high percentage of its national income on education. In 1938 the Japanese national income was 23,424,-000,000 yen and the 1938 total taxes were 2,779,233,000 yen or 11.8% of the national income. In the same year, the total tax-supported educational expenditure was 557,925,843 yen or 2.3% of the national income. In 1938 the United States had a national income of approximately 64 billion dollars and spent approximately 2,344,049,000 dollars on tax-supported education, or 3.6% of the national income. It should be noted that since the United States proportionately spends more tax money on middle and higher education than does Japan, the disparity between the level of elementary school instruction, pertinent to the written language problem, is correspondingly less.

The percentage of national income spent on the education of each student is also a measure of presumed quality. Japan in 1938 (based on the 1937 budget) spent 28.55 yen or 1.2 units (10 to the minus 10%) of the national income on each student in the compulsory educational system. The United States in the same year spent 92.16 dollars or 1.43 units of the national income per student enrolled in the compulsory educational system. Again the higher compulsory levels in some states (5–17 taken as average) and the higher cost per student of secondary and higher education, make the American average appear disproportionately higher.

The ratio of students to teachers in the entire compulsory educational system of Japan in 1938 was approximately 39.2 and in the United States (1937–38) was 29.5. Because the American system employs a much higher percentage of special subject teachers, the actual average size of classes is nearly comparable in the two countries. In 1944 despite war conditions the Japanese ratio was down to 38.5.

The amount of training required for certification of Japanese teachers is somewhat less than that in the best Occidental countries, but is presumably sufficiently high to ensure the minimum linguistic techniques necessary for teaching elementary reading and writing. Japanese teachers are certificated under provisions of Article 97, Book I, Chap. IX, Topic 2, of the Elementary School Ordinance of the *Mombuhōrei* (Ministry of Education Laws and Ordinances). With the exception of emergency certification, the minimum standard has been the equivalent of graduation from the secondary schools with at least 11 years' schooling beyond the kindergarten. The United States in 1921 had only 4 states which required anything beyond secondary school and these required less than one year of advanced work. By 1937 two thirds of the 48 states required work beyond the secondary school graduation, according to an article, "Trends in Certification of Teachers," by B. W. FRAZIER in the January 1939 issue of *School Life,* and to W. A. SAUCIER in the volume, *Theory and Practice in the Elementary School* (New York, Macmillan, 1941), p. 449.

Finally, are the materials really too difficult? The difficulty of the materials which the masses are expected to read may arise from either of two causes: the content may be too difficult, or the language may be too difficult.

The compulsory educational system is presumed to prepare

for citizenship. This presupposes that the contents of the news-papers, official papers, and other information sources necessary to representative government will be accessible to graduates of the system. If this condition does not obtain, the solution lies in a change of the educational system, not in a change of the subject-matter content of public informational materials. It has been seen that the Japanese educational system has more than met standards which have been found adequate for teaching the lin-guistic elements of citizenship in other countries. If it has failed, the only solution is to simplify the language.

Attempts and Failures, Forays and Alarms

The Attempts to Simplify the System. The Japanese them-selves made many attempts to simplify the written form of Japa-nese. At one time or another virtually every theoretical possibility for the simplification of the written form has been explored and in a limited degree tried out. The only simplification which has come into nearly universal usage is that of writing in the vernacu-lar (*kōgotai*). Aside from this reform in style, already well ad-vanced, there are three possible methods of simplification: the limitation of *kanji*, the increase of *furigana*, or the adoption of a phonetic system.

The method of simplification through limitation of *kanji* is based on the assumption that it is advisable to retain the general structure of the written form of Japanese but to simplify it by limiting the number of *kanji* which must be memorized in order to read and write the language. It has been attempted repeatedly and has invariably failed. Such a simplification, if conscientiously carried out, produces an impoverished form of *kanamajiri* some-what analogous to Basic English as an extracted portion of normal English.

The Ministry of Education has at various times selected lists of *kanji* considered to be the essential ones for the use of the general public. This has usually been done as a control in selecting the material which goes into graded official textbooks. The texts in use at the time of Surrender used the list of 1,356 *kanji* adopted in 1938, and all *Mombushō* lists prepared since that date have used the 1938 list as a basis. In June 1942 the Society for the Investiga-tion of the National Language (*Kokugo Shingi Kai*) published its *Hyōjun Kanji Hyō* ("Table of Standard Kanji"), in which were listed:

1134 common *kanji* selected on the basis of frequency and use in the daily lives of the people.

1320 supplementary *kanji* selected on the basis of relatively high frequency and use in the daily lives of the people.

74 special *kanji* appearing in the Imperial House Law, the Imperial Constitution, posthumous names of Emperors, the Imperial Message, the Imperial Message to Servicemen.

The Imperial Japanese Cabinet on 4 July 1942 passed a formal agreement that all governmental documents would, wherever possible, use the *kanji* from the Ministry of Education list, so that "the government's policy toward the people as a whole will be easily comprehensible." This had not been observed and until the revision of the *Constitution*, after Surrender, official writings had been notoriously difficult to read.

In September 1943 the Ministry of Education published an official list, *Hyōjun Kanji Benran* ("A Manual of Standard Kanji"), based on the recommendations of the Society for the Investigation of the National Language and 80 optional *kanji*, totaling 2,749. This list was primarily designed to canonize the indispensable minimum of *kanji* and thus provide a standard for the preparation of graded materials for the schools. Indirectly it was expected to serve as an official limitation imposed on the *kanji* used in other governmental writing, with the purpose of ensuring their simplicity and availability to persons of limited education. The limitation was not observed, however, and no restriction on *kanji* was apparent in the 1945 textbooks. Under pressure from liaison officers of the Education Division, CI&E, GHQ, SCAP, to produce an understandable teachers' manual for the reorientation of the teachers, the Ministry of Education on 20 February 1946 agreed to restrict the language in the proposed manual to the 1,134 common *kanji* of the 1942 list of the Society for the Investigation of the National Language. In the *Jiji Shimpo* of 19 January 1946, the head of the Textbook Bureau of the Ministry of Education, Mr. J. ARIMITSU, stated:

However, with the termination of the war, it has become absolutely necessary to have a limited number of *kanji* for efficiency in national life and science. . . . If a goal is set, the limit will be set at 1,300 *kanji* or so, but proper names will be excepted, it is presumed. So, it is thought that by the end of March, with the compilation of *Kokumingakkō* textbooks awaiting, this plan will be followed.

An inspection of the Ministry of Education, conducted on 30 April 1946, revealed that a total of 166 official textbooks had been approved for publication and 96 had actually been printed, with no attempt at any control of *kanji*. It was stated by the Chief of the Language Investigation Section of the Textbook Bureau, during the inspection, that there were no controls contemplated and no plan had been worked out by which such a control might be exercised. The opportunity to simplify the next year's textbooks had been lost or avoided.

The pressure of mounting public interest in language reform was forcing the Ministry of Education to take some action, however, and a Special Investigation Committee on the National Language had been set up with official sponsorship. On 28 April 1946 the plenary meeting of the Society for the Investigation of the National Language (*Kokugo Shingi Kai*) refused to approve a tentative list of 1,295 *kanji* which this committee had prepared and submitted as the list to be used in textbooks of schools within the compulsory education level and in all public writings. The *Nippon Times*, on 14 May 1946 in reporting this (KYODO) story, stated:

It was the opinion finally reached by the Council that the original plan of using 1,295 characters would be difficult to enforce in all walks of life. It was said that even after the adoption of the system, characters not included in the list would gradually come into use again in various quarters. It was particularly demanded that the restriction on the use of Chinese characters should be studied separately for scientific, newspaper, and official terms, and others.

The Ministry of Education, however, did not relax its efforts and other lists of characters continued to be prepared in its research bureaus. There is some ground for suspecting that concentration upon this phase of the problem of simplifying the notational system was a deliberate attempt to evade an open recognition of the desirability of a phonemic system and a calculated policy of delay until popular interest died. The obvious impossibility of selecting any radically limited number of *kanji* and canonizing them as the "only essential" ideographs of a living language was never faced nor admitted.

The method of compiling the lists made their value even more dubious. They suffered from at least three limitations. First, they were essentially frequency counts based on too narrow a sampling of textual material. In general they were rough tabulations of the frequency of appearance of characters in the running text of a newspaper. For reasons of economy the tabulation was usually made by weighing the type fonts returned to the bins after breaking up a form. In comparison with the vast quantity and diversity of materials studied in the compilation of such a word count as Professors Edward Lee THORNDIKE and Irving LORGE's study, *The Teacher's Word Book of 30,000 Words* (New York, Teachers College, Columbia University, 1944), the 1946 *Mombushō* list was based solely on one month's text in one newspaper, overlaid on the existing 1938 and 1942 word lists. Second, the units that were being counted were not words but symbols which stood either for meaning or for sounds. The frequency tabulation represented, therefore, an indistinguishable mixture of semantic, morphemic, and phonetic (not phonemic) frequencies, perhaps somewhat comparable to Helen Slocomb EATON's *Semantic Frequency List for English, French, German, and Spanish: A Correlation of the First Six Thousand Words in Four Single-Language Frequency Lists* (Chicago, University of Chicago Press, 1940). Finally, since the presumed use of the ultimate list was to limit the appearance of *kanji* in all public writings, it was essential that certain structural words be included even though not justified on the basis of frequency tabulation. This necessitated a radical and subjective modification of the original list by a board of presumed experts in language. The result was somewhat analogous to *The Interim Report on Vocabulary Selection for the Teaching of English as a Foreign Language*—FAUCETT, PALMER, THORNDIKE, and WEST, compilers (London, P. S. King & Son, 1936). The Japanese proverb *Mae e futa-ashi ushiro e mi-ashi* ("Two steps forward and three steps backward") would seem to describe the *Mombushō* procedure.

There have been a number of unofficial attempts to limit the number of *kanji* in common use in the interest of simplifying the writing system. Thus Tokyo newspapers in 1923 agreed among themselves to limit their text to between 2,000 and 3,000 *kanji*. Tests made in 1935 on the five leading newspapers indicated that in 447,575 running *kanji* 3,542 different characters appeared. In 1943 the *Asahi Shimbun* published *Yoji Yōgo Rei* ("List of Characters and Words in Use by the Asahi") establishing 3,307, including the 2,669 of the Ministry of Education list, for use in nontechnical, nonquoted, nonofficial news items. Imperial rescripts, orders, laws, regulations, legal terms, quoted material, technical terms, place names, personal names, and special matter supplied by the government or from overseas, were exempted from any restrictions. The *Nichi Nichi*, now the *Mainichi*, published at the same time *Hyōjun Kanji Ichiran Hyō* ("Catalogue of Standard *Kanji*") listing 2,528 *kanji* which it proposed to use in a similar manner. All such attempts have failed or been disregarded, possibly because the other *kanji* type pieces were not physically removed from the composing room. Editors of two Tokyo newspapers, the *Asahi* and the *Yomiuri*, explained that it was the path of least resistance to use rare *kanji* rather than re-word the sentence. The *Nippon Times* on 19 February 1946 carried an announcement that the *Yomiuri* would voluntarily cut the *kanji* use from its current 4,600 to 2,300, difficult *kanji* in personal names excepted. The Managing Editor of the *Yomiuri*, Mr. SUZUKI Tomon, in an interview with the officers of the Education Division, CI&E, GHQ, SCAP, stated that this plan of limitation of *kanji* was the first in a series of steps contemplated by the newspaper in reaching its announced goal of romanization.

The invention of Japanese typewriters has imposed a mechanical limitation on general business writing. Mention has already been made of the *Nihon* typewriter which has 2,005 *kanji* plus a reserve of 858 in the rare-type drawer. This limits anything written on the machine to a maximum of 2,863 *kanji*. Because the majority of books, magazines, and newspapers are set in type from handwritten manuscript, however, this limitation fails to affect the mass of printed material directly. Few, if any, authors compose on the Japanese typewriter, using it if at all as a mere mechanical device for copying their handwritten manuscript. The typewriter accordingly has little effect even as a psychological limitation.

Certain Japanese writers have consciously attempted to limit themselves to a minimum use of *kanji*. Mr. YAMAMOTO Yūzō, one of Japan's best-known modern authors, member of the Imperial

Academy and of the House of Councilors, has experimented with writing in the media of a very restricted number of *kanji*. His famous book, *Fujaku Shimmyō* (from the Buddhist expression roughly translated as "Not Slighting One's Life," explained by the author's son as expressing a denial of the common Japanese practice of committing suicide over trivial matters), is both a remarkable *tour de force* written in 817 *kanji* (in the 3d edition) and at the same time one of the most perfect examples of modern Japanese prose—clear, simple, and stylistically beautiful. Mr. YAMAMOTO recognizes, however, that such limitation could never solve the basic problem because each new subject field would demand a new 800 *kanji* list.

It has been suggested that the writing system might be simplified by increasing the percentage of *furigana*. If Japanese written in the vernacular (i.e., as people speak) had 100% *kana* sidewriting (*furigana*) it would presumably be understandable to a Japanese who knew no *kanji* at all. The higher the percentage of *furigana*, therefore, the more accessible would be the text to people with limited knowledge of *kanji*. That *furigana* exists at all is evidence that the Japanese publishers have recognized the need. The trend, however, has been toward decreasing rather than increasing the percentage of *furigana*. In 1938 the Police Bureau (*Keihokyoku*) of the Home Ministry ordered all publishers of magazines for the young to discontinue the use of *furigana*. The motive behind this order is not today clear, but at the time it provoked a considerable controversy among Japanese writers amply documented in *Furigana Haishi Ron to Sono Hihan* ("On the Abolition of *Furigana* with a Critique"), published by *Hakusui Sha, circa* 1939. The public appears to have been apathetic. In a study of the *Asahi Shimbun*, it was found that in 1926 52% of all *kanji* had sidewriting in *kana;* in 1936 this percentage had dropped to 31%; and in 1945 only 9% had *furigana*. During the first year of the Occupation social news carried a markedly greater percentage (from 10% to 100%) of sidewriting than did political news, thus limiting the accessibility of the material most pertinent to the Allied Powers. Mr. ONO Shunichi, President of the *Minshu Shimbun*, a paper ostensibly directed to the masses, explained the fact that his paper had no *furigana* whatsoever on the grounds that the *rubitsuki*, or special type which carries both the *kanji* and the *kana* sidewriting, is too small to be read except with great difficulty. The argument is also advanced that the really hard *kanji* seldom have this sidewriting because maintaining a double stock of type (one *kanji* and the other *rubitsuki*) is uneconomical for seldom-used characters.

The adoption of a phonetic system of writing is the final of the three structural methods proposed for simplification of the writing system. Japanese and foreign students of Japanese have experimented with phonetic, or more accurately semiphonemic, systems of writing the Japanese language from the time of MURA-SAKI Shikibu, authoress of Japan's most celebrated classical work, *Genji Monogatari* ("The Tales of *Genji*"), which was written in *hiragana* in the tenth century. All phonetic systems of writing Japanese are based on the principle of adopting a very limited number of symbols which alone or in combination are able to indicate the sounds in the Japanese spoken language. The only fundamental difference between these systems is the choice of the symbols which are to stand for the sounds. There are six major systems, each of which has several variations: a phonetic syllabary, an international phonetic alphabet, a Japanese phonetic alphabet, a Japanese Braille, a Japanese shorthand, and a romanized transcription or alphabet.

By far the most common, of course, is the syllabary (*kana*) which is the traditional phonetic transcription, derived from *manyōgana*, or Chinese characters used phonetically. Because it is so commonly used in conjunction with *kanji*, it is frequently forgotten that the *kana* may be used quite alone as a notation system complete in itself. It is in fact used alone in telegrams, in certain types of military dispatches, and in simple stories for children. Most educated Japanese adults, however, look upon material written only in *kana* as rather tiring to read, and as rather childish in style. It is advocated by the *Kanamoji Kai* (Kana Alphabet Society).

The International Phonetic Alphabet, while occasionally used as a scholar's notation in the study of the language, is not advocated as a standard writing system by any leading Japanese because the sounds in spoken Japanese are few enough and similar enough to common Occidental languages to make diacritical marks and extra symbols of an international phonetic alphabet unnecessary. If used as a phonetic description it is adequate, since there are discernible differences between the sounds of Japanese and those of other languages. But if used as a phonemic transcription (i.e., as an alphabet), then it would become little more than an ordinary Latin alphabet as most of the differentiating symbols would be unnecessary and would disappear.

There have, however, been occasional phonetic alphabets expressly designed for the Japanese language proposed by individuals. None of these alphabets has been adopted. Thus, in 1919 Mr. Inatome Masakichi published his study, "As Substitutes for *Kanji* New Japanese Characters and Their Spelling," which presented a semicursive alphabet designed to be written horizontally. A system of cursive *kana* designed to be written horizontally is proposed by Mr. Ōno Kazuyoshi. No literature has yet been published in either style. An extremely complicated phonetic alphabet using new symbols for both vowel and consonant sounds is advocated by Mr. Kamiya Tatsugorō. An interesting feature of the system is that, like the ancient phonetic Korean notation revived following the liberation from Japan, the syllables are constructed by merging the vowel and consonantal symbols in a nonprogressive order, thus leading to a distortion presenting little difficulty when written by hand with a brush but making the use of type difficult and typewriters virtually impossible. The effect is unlike that of an alphabet in which one letter follows another and is more like that of the component portions (*hen, tsukuri,* and *kammuri*) of a Chinese character, which are compressed into an approximate square regardless of the effect on relative sizes and shapes. The magazine, *Meishō Moji* ("Meiji-Shōwa Script"), a monthly publication edited and published by Mr. Kamiya, is written in this system. Its files extend from 1 January 1930 through 15 September 1938.

Japanese Braille is perhaps the most remarkable phonetic system for transcription of Japanese. It was invented in 1890 by Mr. Ishikawa Kuraji, instructor in the Tokyo Government School for the Blind and Deaf, and is described in his study, *Nihon Kummō Tenji* ("The Point System for the Japanese Syllabary adopted from Braille's System"), publisher and date not given. It is based on the standard system invented in 1829 by Louis Braille by which 63 combinations of the six dots ($\vdots \vdots$) can be used to stand for sounds. In the Japanese system these combinations stand for the Arabic numerals, mathematical and grammatical symbols, roman letters, and Japanese *kana*.

Japanese shorthand is an entirely practical, widely used phonetic system. There are five shorthand systems in use, all based on Japanese *kana:* Nakane System; Tagusari System; Kumazaki System; Mori System; and cursive Kana System. The best known is the Nakane System devised by NAKANE Masayo, former principal of the Kyoto Ryoyo Middle School. It is similar in appearance to Pitman's System in English, and requires a six months' course to attain an average speed of 220 symbols, not words, per minute. Outstanding students have attained 250 symbols per minute, or the amount required of secretaries in the Imperial Japanese Diet, in five months' study. It is significant that the most important writing in Japanese, the Diet *Proceedings*, are taken down phonetically, and later transcribed for the permanent record.

Romanized transcription (*romaji*) has been advocated by various foreign and Japanese students of the language since the middle of the sixteenth century. Systems have been constructed based on English, French, German, Spanish, Portuguese, and Dutch pronunciations. At present only two systems have any major currency: the *Hyōjunshiki Romaji* (Standard System), based on the so-called Hepburn System invented by Dr. J. C. HEPBURN in 1867 and advocated by the *Romaji Hirome Kai* (Roman Alphabet Propagating Society of Japan); and the *Nihonsiki Romazi* (The Japan System), given wide publicity by Dr. A. TANAKADATE, adopted as the official system in Japan by the Imperial Japanese Cabinet in 1937, and advocated by the *Nippon Romazi Sya* (also known as *Nippon Romaji Kai*—Japan Romanization Society).

Why Have These Attempts Failed? Why has the traditional writing system, *kanamajiri*, been continued? There is an overwhelming body of evidence to prove that it is difficult. An almost equally great body of evidence indicates that democratization of Japan depends upon a simpler method of communication. The necessity of a simplification has come to be recognized by practically all educated Japanese, conservative and radical alike. There has been a continuing and well-supported effort to secure the adoption of some simpler system dating from the early years of the Meiji Restoration. With the exception of a gradual trend toward simplification of style and the adoption of the vernacular in writing, which have incidentally lessened the number of *kanji* ordinarily used, all attempts have thus far failed. Why?

There appear to be eight reasons. These are: inertia, pedantry, ignorance, vested interests, ultranationalism, indifference, emotion, and honest intellectual doubt. Since each of these alleged reasons merely represents the opinion of an individual or group of individuals, an evaluation of them must rest upon the credibility of expert testimony. These eight reasons constitute a synthesis of the opinions expressed in 49 unsolicited letters at the time of the United States Education Mission to Japan; 41 interviews with acknowledged leaders in Japan chosen from authors, educators, linguists, officials, business and professional leaders; 104 newspaper articles and editorials appearing in the Japanese press between the Surrender and the announcement of the *Report* of the Education Mission; the minutes of the Japanese and American committees on Language Revision which met during the study of the Education Mission; statements of the seven most influential linguistic societies, namely the *Kanamoji Kai* (Kana Alphabet Society), *Nippon Romazi Sya* (Japan Romanization Society), *Romaji Hirome Kai* (Roman Alphabet Propagating Society of Japan), *Kokugo Shingi Kai* (Society for the Investigation of the National Language), *Kokugo Kyō Kai* (National Language Association), *Nippon Kokugo Kai* (Japan Language Society), and the *Gengo-gaku Kai* (Philological Society of Tokyo Imperial University); and opinions voiced at meetings of the *Nippon Shuppan Kyō Kai* (Japan Publishers' Society).

It is charged that inertia is the primary cause for failure. It is easier to do nothing than to make the effort to take positive action involving continuing self-discipline. This charge is supported only by the expressed opinion of numerous leading Japanese but it is so common a characteristic of social reform that it appears likely to be well founded.

It is charged that pedantry accounts for much of the opposition to reform. Educated Japanese accept involved style, difficult words, and rare characters as an indication of the profundity and brilliance of the writer. Japanese not infrequently have published material which they recognize cannot be understandingly read by the people to whom it is addressed.

An episode in the early months of the Occupation will illustrate this peculiar custom. Dr. TANAKA Kōtarō, formerly Chief of the Bureau of School Education and later Minister of Education in the YOSHIDA Cabinet, is a widely traveled professor of law at

Tokyo Imperial University. He is an excellent practical linguist and has published materials in Italian, Spanish, French, and English as well as in his native Japanese. He has a national reputation of being a "liberal." Yet in a meeting with the Education Division Staff, CI&E, GHQ, SCAP, on 26 January 1946, he officially opposed writing the Headquarters-inspired teachers' manual in simple understandable Japanese on the grounds that if the Japanese teachers could read it without difficulty they would be "insulted." He advocated bringing out the manual in the traditionally difficult form, and then bringing out a second manual or commentary to explain the first. Despite objection by liaison officers of the Headquarters, the Ministry of Education proceeded on this basis and on 7 February 1946 the Program Director of Radio Tokyo, controlling all radio programs in the Empire, revealed that he had been requested by the Ministry of Education to rewrite the projected manual in a manner that would be understandable by the teachers, and to broadcast an explanation of the official manual before it was released. It was planned to send all teachers the simplified unofficial edition of the manual as an aid to understanding the official version. During the conference with the Ministry of Education editorial staff which was called the following day as a result of this revelation, the Japanese editor presented the novel defense that even though the teachers could not understand the official manual, they would be "inspired" by it, knowing that it was the product of intellectuals.

Ignorance has, of course, been a prominent barrier to reform. Among the common people of Japan, who have suffered most from the intellectual barrier erected by the traditional system, there are few who have sufficient linguistic training to recognize the handicaps imposed by the system and to perceive the advantages of alternative writing systems.

Approximately 81.6% of the 664,680 conscripts called up in 1941, for example, had had eight years of schooling or less. They had been exposed to 1,356 *kanji* in the textbooks and classes of the compulsory educational system, then six years in length, and had studied approximately 450 additional *kanji* in the seventh and eighth years of their schooling. The numbers and specific *kanji* varied slightly according to the type of school. The number of *kanji* with which such a group might be presumed to have some familiarity was increased to 2,669 with the publication of the 1942 textbooks, still too superficial a command of the writing system to permit any valid judgment of the inherent characteristics of that system. This is not an unrepresentative group. Only approximately 12.6% of the total school population continues beyond the six-year elementary school into some type of school which includes instruction in foreign language where a contact with other notation systems would be available. The remainder, or approximately 87.4%, either leaves school or goes on to a school without foreign language requirements. Having no formal instruction in linguistics or in foreign languages they simply do not have the education necessary to recognize the problem.

It has frequently been charged that vested interests have stood in the way of reform. Among people who have acquired a relatively thorough knowledge of the traditional form of writing, this knowledge constitutes a very considerable investment, which consciously or unconsciously they are loath to jeopardize. It is charged that these people, including Buddhist and Shinto priests, critics, editors, writers, language scholars, lawyers, professors of the humanities, and public officials, have tended to protect their investment by opposing any fundamental change in the system. There is no doubt that the main objections to language simplification have come from these people, and that the pressure for reform has come from scientific, industrial, and professional groups, but it should also be noted that among the leaders in the various movements for language simplification are some of the leading figures in the former fields.

The explanation that ultranationalist influences were responsible for opposition to reform has also frequently been advanced. It is claimed that militarists and ultranationalists sponsored a definite program of intensifying the narrow nationalism of the masses of the Japanese by manipulating the language in such a way as to prevent access to pertinent political writings. In some instances, it is charged, this was the deliberate goal. In others it was the natural result of a conservatism in linguisitic reform which was occasioned by a desire to maintain an isolation of the national culture. The accusation has most frequently been made by students of Japanese who are of the viewpoint that some fundamental language simplification is a vital necessity. Thus, for example, Mr. SAEKI Kōsuke, Managing Director of the *Nippon Romazi Sya*, also known as *Nippon Romaji Kai* (Japan Romanization

Society), in an undated letter received in the Headquarters of the Occupation Forces on 7 November 1945, says:

Driving out Chinese ideographs from daily use will benefit every class of our people. The military, however, were blind to this fact. They kept low the cultural standard of our people in order to drive them in whatever direction they might choose. Indeed the learning of Chinese ideographs was quite sufficient to keep and develop the feudalistic tendency of the people, that is, the tendency of obeying unconditionally the established authorities.

This serious charge can be supported by a considerable body of evidence. School textbooks under the influence of the militarists reverted to more difficult literary forms, adopted classical allusions, introduced less frequently used *kanji* which had previously been eliminated, and increased the number of *kanji* from 1,356 in 1938 to 2,669 in 1942. Members of the *Nippon Romaji Kai* and *Kana-moji Kai* (Kana Alphabet Society), testify that they were warned by military and police representatives that printing of Imperial rescripts in either *romaji* or *kana* would be considered an act of lese majesty. Militaristic and ultranationalistic inspired articles were published designed to stop simplification of the language. A quotation from *Kokugo no Songen* ("Dignity of the Japanese Language"), published in May 1943 by YAMADA Yoshio, member of the House of Peers and ex-President of the *Jingu Kōgaku-Kan*, a government *Shintō* college, will illustrate their position:

Both the National Entity and the national language make progress through the Divine Will, and are indeed the Way of the Gods. The Way of the Gods is the peculiar property of the Divine Will, so that needless to say, to make changes through the will of the people, or even to make speculations are things that can by no means be allowed.

One of the most puzzling evidences of the militaristic and ultra-nationalistic position on language is that of the language used in *Kokutai no Hongi* ("The Fundamental Principles of the National Entity of Japan") and *Shimmin no Michi* ("The Way of the Subject"), notorious propaganda books prepared for the official indoctrination of the teachers which have frequently been referred to in this volume. Paradoxically, the language used in these two volumes is so difficult that few elementary schoolteachers were able to read them with understanding, apparently defeating the purpose of the propaganda. The only explanation which appears in the least to make sense is that suggested by Mr. OKIMOTO Isoji, an educational official of the Central Liaison Office, to the effect that the propaganda was never intended for the common teachers but rather for the relatively well-educated school heads, inspectors, and officials who were to interpret the "Divine Will" to the others.

The persecution of persons advocating language reform under the provisions of the *Chian Ijihō* (Peace Maintenance Law) and the punitive action of the Thought Control Police has already been mentioned. In its 26 January 1946 editorial on "Language Problems" the *Yomiuri-Hochi*, leading Tokyo newspaper, charged: "A Japanese language reform movement with MINAMI Hiroshi as the leader has had some success but it was banned by the militarists for the reason that Communists such as TAKAKURA Teru were taking an active part in it."

At official request Mr. MINAMI came to Tokyo to present his evidence of this persecution by the Thought Control Police at a time when he was a high official in the Ministry of Education. Unfortunately Mr. MINAMI died suddenly less than a half hour before he was to meet the representatives of the Occupation Forces for this interview.

There is still evident an organized opposition to language reform. In its 22 April 1946 news article, "Language Reform in Nippon Opposed," the *Nippon Times* reported:

Among the forces which are opposed to Romanization is the Society for the Study of the National Language (*Kokugo Shingi Kai*).

The position of this society on the language issue was expressed by Keita KODAMA and Professor KOBATA of the Literature and Science University in addresses delivered at a meeting of the society at the Nippon University on April 13.

Both held that it would not be the right thing to adopt the Roman alphabet in Japan from various points of view, especially that of maintaining the independence of a racial culture.

How successful the conservative forces in Japan have been in continuing this opposition may be illustrated by an episode which occurred during the visit of the United States Education Mission to Japan. It had been evident to the Ministry of Education from the wording of the published charter to the Education Mission that the problem of language revision would receive some attention. A Special Language Section (*Kokugo Ka*) had been set up in the Ministry ostensibly to do research in this field, although repeated inspections indicated that less than 10% of its personnel even bothered to come to the office and the "research" was little more than a thinly camouflaged attempt to divert and delay all action in this field until popular interest had died. The Japanese linguist who was selected by the Ministry of Education and surprisingly was approved by Occupation Headquarters as the one to represent the Japanese nation in this matter during the meetings with the American members of the Mission, was Dr. ANDO Masatsugu, philologist, former President of Taihoku Imperial University in Formosa, former professor in the *Jingu Kōgaku-Kan*, a government *Shintō* college, and member of the Imperial Academy. He was at that time banned from holding public office or educational position by the 4 January 1946 SCAP Purge Directive (Appendix A, Category G) and was under investigation by the Civil Intelligence Section, GHQ, SCAP, for alleged complicity in a plot to misinform and nullify the recommendations of the United States Education Mission.

Dr. ANDO's presentation apparently was not too convincing to the 27 distinguished American educators, for their *Report* recommended romanization. But the conservatives were not defeated. Delay was their tactic. On 9 May 1946, during an official inspection of the *Kokugo Ka* at the Ministry, Mr. KUGIMOTO Hisaharu, Chief of the Section and apparently personally an able and sincere researchist, admitted to officers from the Education Division of Headquarters that his section had not even secured nor bothered to read a copy of the Education Mission's recommendations on language revision, despite the fact that this extremely important document had been released to the Ministry of Education 35 days previously and had been released to and appeared in the Japanese newspapers 33 days previously.

Indifference also contributed to frustrate attempts at reform. The great masses of people have been so engrossed in the routine of their daily lives that they have not bothered to inform themselves. Many do not recognize that any problem exists and many of those who do have not bothered to consider possible solutions for it.

The impartial observer cannot but be impressed by the degree of emotion exhibited in the controversy over reform of the writing system. People who have recognized on an intellectual level the desirability of a fundamental change in the writing system have been unwilling to accept such a change because of powerful personal feelings. There can be no question that many Japanese feel a strong emotional attachment to the ideograph. It is considered an expression of art, and calligraphy is practiced by some almost as a religious ceremony. There is present also the attachment of antiquity, a feeling that the ideograph is a heritage of the classic ages. The traditional writing system is defended by the same argument which American classicists once used in defense of the formal discipline of Latin. A letter to the Supreme Commander for the Allied Powers from MAMORI Minoru, an instructor in Kumamoto City, received and translated by ATIS on 11 April 1946, states in part:

In regard to the simplification of the written language, we have a strong objection to that. The difficulty in the study of the language does not lie solely in the written words. The language itself is difficult. Supposing a full concession were made on the point that the learning of Chinese characters is difficult. To evade learning on such a ground is cowardly and retrogressive. Instead we should muster our courage to go forth and tackle that which is difficult. In this manner the cultivation of the mind should be planned and a misfortune should be turned to a blessing. . . . He who grieves over the difficulty of *kanji* has the spirit of a green tradesman who begrudges the investment of capital.

Finally, honest intellectual doubt of the efficacy of linguistic reform must not be discounted. Some people sincerely believe that the advantages of the traditional system of writing Japanese outweigh the advantages of any of the proposed alternatives.

"And how stand ye, brother?" Japanese language revision was one of the most controversial of proposed reforms in the Occupation. One of the peculiar aspects of the controversy was the conservatism, and on occasion emotional prejudice, evidenced by some officers in the American Occupation Forces and by some of the officials in the Department of State. This minority of American representatives attacked any proposal of language revision with a vehemence that no Japanese publicly revealed. Perhaps their antagonism was traceable to a nostalgia for the charming prewar Japan in which some had lived. Perhaps linguistically they were characterized by the old Japanese proverb, *Shōchi wa bodai no samatage* ("A little knowledge is a hindrance to the full knowl-

edge of the truth"). Perhaps they felt a natural resistance to any change which would increase their already considerable labors. Perhaps they feared criticism as "academic tinkerers" and preferred the easier acclaim of punitive action against Japanese war criminals and big business. Perhaps they were honestly convinced that it was an unsound movement.

The official case against language reform is in part unobtainable and in a large measure unrevealable. The Hon. Eugene DOOMAN, then Special Assistant to Assistant Secretary James Clement DUNN of the Department of State, on 6 July 1945, wrote to Maj. Gen. J. H. HILLDRING, then Director of the Civil Affairs Division of the War Department, on the subject. His "informal comment," characteristically classified "Confidential," effectively ended all official study of the subject at the time the military occupation of Japan was being planned. The remaining evolution of official policy in the Department of State, the War Department, and the Headquarters of the Supreme Commander for the Allied Powers, is effectively concealed behind the curtain of classification, military orders, and unrecorded staff decisions.

The unofficial case against any revision in the writing system may be quickly summarized. It was argued that any language revision was "a matter for the Japanese to decide"; that the Occupation Forces "had no right under the Potsdam Declaration" to impose such a reform; that any change would cause social unrest; that Japan was too complex an industrial nation to sustain such a reform without being reduced to a state of "chaos"; that the "high percentage of homonyms would make any phonetic system of writing impractical and the written language unintelligible"; that advocacy of such a reform was "cultural imperialism"; and that the only people, Japanese or foreign, who were advocating such a change were "crack-pots, visionaries, and fanatics."

There was, of course, no official case in favor of language reform but the unofficial case is obtainable and impressive. Between the entrance of the Occupation Forces into Japan and the publication of the *Report* of the United States Education Mission, a number of articles on the subject of language reform in Japan appeared in the American press.

The *New York Times'* correspondent Burton CRANE, who speaks and to some degree reads Japanese and who before the war was a correspondent for the *Japan Advertiser*, filed two stories, "Japan's Literacy Just Propaganda" on 23 November 1945 and "Making Japanese Easy" on 24 March 1946. A quotation from the latter of these articles is typical of the reaction of the press:

Romaji is not just a dream. That is the considered opinion of a growing proportion of Japan's academic world these days, and what it means is that the half-century-old movement to substitute the Roman alphabet for Chinese characters in writing Japanese is currently enjoying more favor than at any time in Japan's history. If finally successful, the effect of the change will be to make what is now the world's most difficult language not much harder for a foreigner to learn than German.

The reasons advanced for Romanization are the same as they have always been: Written Japanese is so difficult that Japan's school children have little time to learn much else and even few adults know more than a thousand of the fifty-six thousand Chinese characters in which formal Japanese is written.

In the past all attempts to simplify Japanese have failed because of the force of tradition and the fact that the Government did not consider a fundamentally ignorant populace any detriment. Now it is generally admitted that democratization needs informed people.

The articles, "Romanization of Japanese," 9 January 1946 by Mack JOHNSON of the *New York Herald Tribune;* "Japanese Language Romanization," 15 January 1946 by Robert B. COCHRANE of the *Baltimore Sun;* "Shift to Letter Language May Teach Japs to Think," 4 February 1946 by Maj. Compton PAKENHAM of *Newsweek;* and "Revising Japanese Language," 19 February 1946 by Audrey MENEFEE of the *Christian Science Monitor*, were equally friendly to the reform.

On 16 January 1946 the *Philadelphia Record* ran an editorial entitled "Basic Japanese." It is quoted in part:

It's taken defeat in a major war to do it. But the Jap people may some day be able to read their own newspapers. For the average Jap, reading a newspaper has been as difficult as working out a cross-word puzzle.

* * *

The shift [to a Roman alphabet] may bring about a more fundamental change in the Japanese than breaking up the feudal land system or democratizing the big business setup. The average Jap, now illiterate in all language, will be able to find out what is going on in his own country and the world.

There would be no point in our enforcing freedom of the press if only a few could read it. Defeat may eventually make Japan a modern state.

Articles and editorials on the subject of the revision of the Japanese written language have been numerous since the publication of the *Report* by the United States Education Mission to Japan. Perhaps the most thorough is "A Modern Language for Japan" by John ASHMEAD, Jr., in the January 1947 issue of the *Atlantic*, Vol. 179, No. 1, pp. 68–72. Mr. ASHMEAD was one of the ablest Japanese language officers in the naval service and was intimately connected with a study of the writing system conducted by the Civil Information and Education Section, GHQ, SCAP, during the Occupation. He wrote in part:

> We have not hesitated to direct the Japanese to disarm, to break up the big trusts, to begin land reforms, and to rewrite their textbooks. Surely, unless the Japanese masses are reasonably literate and educated, these reforms will vanish from Japan with our Armies. If we continue to allow writing in characters, only the 15 percent or so of the Japanese who can afford a higher education will ever become literate. Why should we hesitate to direct the Japanese to write in a phonetic alphabet—a method of writing which their own liberals have advocated for over sixty years, which has been successfully employed since the beginnings of writing in Japan, and which will make widespread literacy possible?

One of the political elements which concerned American officials in the Occupation was the probable attitude of China to any attempted language reform. China's own history of widespread illiteracy might be presumed to preclude her from any position of prominence as a linguistic adviser. But China has clung to the tradition of being the great exporter of culture to Japan and has recognized the economic advantages of maintaining the present parallelism of ideographic writing systems. An episode which occurred in the first year of the Occupation is illuminating.

On 12 November 1945 an investigation and staff study on the entire problem of simplifying the written language was begun in the Education Division, CI&E, GHQ, SCAP. This work was of course confidential but the mere process of collecting materials for the study inevitably revealed the official interest in it. The personnel of the Central News Agency, a semi-official Chinese organ actually representing the Kuomintang, learned of the official study and without consulting any representative of Headquarters conducted a private investigation through Japanese sources. On 18 January 1946 this agency filed a story, "Plans to Replace Present Way of Writing Nippon Language by Alphabet," which was published widely throughout China. Quotation of a portion of the English text filed for cabling follows:

Actual experiments conducted by those studying this problem show that writing based on Chinese characters takes more time to learn and is more difficult to use than romaji. Experts have discovered that Japanese claims of high percentage of literacy among their people have been completely false. It is discovered that the average Japanese cannot read an entire newspaper which employs only eighteen hundred characters on an average according to an agreement made in 1927 among newspapers which were then attempting to broaden the reading public.

The study shows that primary school graduates should know 1,356 characters but on an average the number which are familiar to "educated" persons selected at random from the streets of Tokyo is only six hundred.

Those making the study have come to the conclusion that the low rate of literacy is due mainly to difficulty in mastering the Chinese type of language.

The figures were only approximately correct but the trends were accurate. Reaction in Occupation Headquarters, when the press clipping from China arrived, bordered on dismay.

On 30 April 1946 Brig. Gen. Ken R. DYKE, then Chief of the Civil Information and Education Section of GHQ, SCAP, was called to testify before the Allied Council for Japan (ACJ), Tokyo representatives of the Far Eastern Commission (FEC). During the meeting he was questioned as to official policy regarding the elimination of Chinese characters (*kanji*) from the Japanese writing system, by China's representative, Lt. Gen. CHU Shih-ming. General DYKE had been in the United States on leave at the time of the United States Education Mission to Japan and had been represented by his deputy and later successor, Lt. Col. Donald R. NUGENT, USMC, an outspoken critic of language revision. Although the *Report* of the Education Mission had unequivocally recommended revision and the adoption of *romaji*, General

DYKE's reply to the question of the Chinese representative, as reported in the 1 May 1946 *Pacific Stars and Stripes*, was that language reform was a matter which the Japanese themselves would have to decide.

Just what is American policy on this matter?

The official Department of State Publication No. 2671, *Occupation of Japan: Policy and Progress*, Far Eastern Series No. 17, in the section on education, p. 36, states:

The report [of the United States Education Mission to Japan] places great emphasis on the need for substituting some type of the Roman alphabet for the involved ideographs used by the Japanese. In contrast to the 26-letter alphabet in use in the United States and western European countries, the Japanese writing system contains thousands of ideographs. A knowledge of at least 2,000 Japanese ideographs is necessary to read even a newspaper, and the average Japanese knows far less than that number. The educators concluded that, if the Japanese people were to be able to read their papers and books intelligently and acquire the information needed to understand political, economic, and social issues, they must have a writing system which will not require the excessive time now necessary to master the ideographs.

The 30 March 1946 *Report* to the Supreme Commander for the Allied Powers of the United States Education Mission, so frequently alluded to, is worthy of careful study. In releasing it to the Japanese public, Headquarters emphasized the fact that the *Report* was a technical recommendation to Gen. Douglas MAC-ARTHUR as the Supreme Commander for the Allied Powers and not a statement of official policy. General MACARTHUR in his official press release stated that: "The report may well be studied by all educators regardless of individual aspects. Some of the recommendations regarding education principles and language reform are so far reaching that they can only serve as a guide for long range study and future planning."

The chapter on "Language Reform" was prepared by a subcommittee of the Mission under the chairmanship of Professor George S. COUNTS, Head of the Division of the Foundations of Education, Teachers College, Columbia University, and noted authority on Russian Education. The subcommittee included a psychologist, a professor of English who has been connected with numerous international programs of language simplification, a scholar with a thorough knowledge of both spoken and written Chinese and extended residence as a professor in the Orient, and a Caucasian who was raised in Japan and speaks the language bilingually. The pertinent portions of the chapter are quoted:

. . . we recommend a drastic reform of the Japanese written language.

Clearly the question of language reform is basic and urgent. It casts its shadow over practically every branch of the educational program, from the primary school to the university. If no satisfactory answer can be found to this problem, the achievement of many agreed upon educational goals will be rendered most difficult.

*   *   *

The Japanese language in its written form constitutes a formidable obstacle to learning. Practically all informed persons agree that the memorizing of Kanji, in which the Japanese language is largely written, places an excessive burden on the pupils. During the elementary years they are required to give a very great part of their study time to the sheer task of learning to recognize and write the language characters. During these initial years, time that might be devoted to the acquisition of a vast range of useful linguistic and numerical skills, of essential knowledge about the world of physical nature and human society, is consumed in a struggle to master these characters.

The results achieved by the inordinate amount of time allotted to recognizing and writing Kanji are disappointing. On leaving the elementary school the pupils may lack the linguistic abilities essential to democratic citizenship. They have trouble in reading common materials such as daily newspapers and popular magazines. As a general rule, they cannot grasp books dealing with contemporary problems and ideas. Above all, they usually fail to acquire a degree of mastery sufficient to make reading an easy tool of development after leaving school. Yet no one who has visited Japanese schools can deny that the pupils are mentally alert and remarkably diligent.

*   *   *

. . . the Mission believes that in time Kanji should be wholly abandoned in the popular written language and that a phonetic system should be adopted.

*   *   *

In the judgement of the Mission, there are more advantages to Romaji than to Kana.

*   *   *

. . . we propose:

1. That some form of Romaji be brought into common use by all means possible.

2. That the particular form of Romaji chosen be decided upon by a commission of Japanese scholars, educational leaders, and statesmen.

3. That the commission assume the responsibility for coordinating the program of language reform, during the transitional stages.

4. That the commission formulate a plan and a program for introducing Romaji into the schools and into the life of the community and nation through newspapers, periodicals, books, and other writings.

5. That the commission study, also, the means of bringing about a more democratic form of the spoken language.

6. That in view of the study drain on the learn-time of children, the commission be formed promptly. It is hoped that a thorough report and a comprehensive program may be announced within a reasonable period. (Pp. 20–23.)

Eighteen months after the beginning of the Occupation, nearly a year after the Education Mission, the Department of State had completed a revision of policy based on this Mission's recommendations. It submitted it to the Far Eastern Commission and on 27 March 1947 it was approved and published as, "Policy for the Revision of the Japanese Educational System." It included every important recommendation made by the Education Mission, with one significant exception. On language reform there was not a single word.

To all appearances the forces of conservatism had won. The great mass of Japanese—uninformed, conservative to the point of being reactionary, strongly tied by emotion to the traditional ideographic writing system—and a small number of vested Japanese interests had succeeded in maintaining the *status quo* in the face of an inspired but politically weak drive for reform by a handful of Japanese liberals. And the conservative or indifferent mass of high-ranking officials in the Occupation military government had demonstrated once again that a technical recommendation by a low-ranking officer gets very short shrift if it runs contrary to the traditional channels of the military mind. The naval officer who had "stirred up all the trouble" was conveniently banished. The Japanese were told that it was a decision for them to make. What responsible Japanese Government would dare to initiate such a fundamental social change in the face of obvious Allied disapproval? The adoption of *romaji* was dead.

But a strange thing has happened. The seeds of phonetic writing planted over a millennium ago and then crushed by the weight of Chinese literary eminence; resurrected a century ago with the impact of European culture on the Tokugawa Shogunate and the Meiji Restoration but crushed under the traditionalism of Japanese nationalism; and now revived by a foreign officer in the Occupation Headquarters supported by a small coterie of dedicated Japanese scholars, only to be crushed again by the conservatism and active antagonism of the Allied military forces of the Occupation—these seeds have refused to die.

The volume *Education in Japan* published on 15 February 1946 by the Education Division, CI&E, GHQ, SCAP, for briefing the United States Education Mission to Japan, was not permitted to carry a line on the subject of simplification of the language and writing system. The two-volume work *Education in the New Japan* published in May 1948 by the same part of the Supreme Commander's Headquarters, carries an entire chapter (XXI) on "Language Simplification," in which it says:

With the present interest shown by the Ministry of Education, by the press both metropolitan and prefectural, and by local elementary school teachers, it is possible to look forward to a transformation as a result of which the Romaji movement will no longer be of a more or less sectarian character but a general social development participated in by individuals who may never have had any previous connection with the movement. The introduction into the school curriculum of an officially sponsored course in Romaji will also give the movement a public character which it has lacked in the past.

In the United States Department of State *Documents and State Papers* (Vol. I, No. 1) of April 1948 the following statement of policy appears: "SCAP's attitude is that the reform of the Japanese writing system and the methods by which such a reform is to be achieved are problems to be decided by the Japanese Government, and it favors the adoption of any suitable language form that will contribute to the intellectual development of the Japanese people and the healthy growth of democratic tendencies."

What brought about this remarkable though perhaps grudging shift in Occupation viewpoint? It was the continued interest of a growing number of responsible Japanese. The *Romaji Kyōiku Kyōgo Kai* (Romaji Education Advisory Council) recommended to the Ministry of Education on 22 October 1946 that a 40-hour minimum course in *romaji* should be given in all school years above the third or fourth beginning with the 1947 academic year. The opening sentence of this recommendation is significant: "It is a matter of necessity in order to effectively conduct education in the national language, to improve the efficiency of social life, and to promote the cultural level of the nation, that the nation in general should acquire the practical habit of reading and writing its national language expressed by means of the Roman letters." (Trans. by *Mombushō*.)

On 28 February 1947 the Vice-Minister of Education issued Instruction No. 7 from the Bureau of Textbooks entitled "Concerning Teaching Romaji in Elementary Schools" in which it was stated that beginning with the 1947 academic year elementary schools were to carry out what was essentially the program recommended by the Romaji Education Advisory Council, but on a voluntary rather than compulsory basis. Occupation Headquarters reports that 90 per cent of the elementary schools voluntarily adopted the program and that 13 per cent expressed the desire to begin the course in the third instead of the fourth school year.

Can this Japanese-sponsored movement survive in the face of continuing Occupation indifference and covert antagonism? Can it survive the incessant attacks of Japanese conservatives? Has the seed of phonetic writing at last been nurtured to the point where the plant may survive? Only time, the inexorable critic of all social change, will conclusively tell. There is, however, already one tiny straw in the wind.

The 2 September 1948 issue of *Yomiuri Shimbun* in an article entitled "Romaji Education Is Started," stated:

On September first, the first day of the new school term, the historical beginning of *romaji* education was started. This is not to be mistaken for teaching children *romaji;* it is teaching them in *romaji*. It is an experiment looking towards the elimination of *kanji* and *katakana* or any other form of Japanese writing. Throughout the country 86 schools will participate and will carry on curricula in *romaji*, under the supervision of the Committee on Romaji Experiment of the *Mombushō*. In Tokyo, the fourth grade pupils of the Otaku Kuhara Primary School, the fifth graders of the Minato-ku Hirowo Primary School, all the children in the third, fourth, and fifth grades of the Tanishi School in the Nishi-Tama District will be in the experimental group.

A visit by the *Yomiuri* reporter at the Hirowo School revealed that the pupils involved were studying arithmetic, science, and social studies in *romaji*. Both the teacher and the children were writing *romaji* on the blackboard and in their notebooks.

This bold venture is based upon the recommendation of the United States Education Mission that visited Japan in the spring of 1946.

The contents of the various textbooks are identical with those in Japanese, but they are written in *romaji*. Where this is not possible, the teacher has "translated" the texts from the original into *romaji*.

In the past, problems of arithmetic were not understood by some children because of *kanji*, but this handicap under *romaji* has disappeared, and the parents are with the children in rejoicing about it. The relief of the boys and girls is quite visible.

After forty hours of study [of *romaji*] some bright pupils can read 125 words per minute, the speed of the average adult reading the usual Japanese language material.

For the benefit of the *romaji*-children throughout the country a newspaper entirely in *romaji* will be published in Tokyo beginning October 1. It will be a bi-monthly publication. (Trans. by Toru MATSUMOTO.)

Can the Chinese Loan Be Funded?

The Precedent of China. Japan imported the basic elements of its traditional writing system from China. Can it now import a solution to the problem which the system has created?

The parallelism between the problems of the written language in the two countries is striking. Chinese is written with ideographs which with but few exceptions are almost identical with Japanese *kanji*. China has many styles of characters, each roughly paralleled by Japanese forms. Thus the Chinese *kai-shu* or *chen-shu* (formal script) which was developed in the early Han period and reached its peak in the Tsin dynasty is probably the common origin of both modern Chinese printed ideographs and Japanese *kaisho*, while *ta-tsao* (greater cursive script), developed at about the same time, and *hsing-tsao-shu* (walking-running style), which reached its peak about 375 A.D., are the probable precursors of Japanese "grass writing" (*sōsho*). China has its classical literary style of the written language (*wen-li*) corresponding to Japan's *bungotai*, and its simpler vernacular (*pai-hua*) corresponding to Japanese *kōgotai*. Both Chinese and Japanese traditional written languages are relatively difficult to understand when read aloud and depend, at least in part, upon the appearance of the characters to remove the ambiguities arising from the many homonyms. Both nations have experienced profound literary revolutions leading to the adoption of the vernacular (*pai-hua* in China and *kōgotai* in Japan) in common writing for the press and popular fiction.

China's problem of illiteracy, officially estimated at between 75% and 90% during the 30 years prior to the Surrender of Japan, is immensely more troublesome, both because China has no commonly used phonetic script comparable to *kana* and also because China has suffered a lack of financial support for the school system which is unknown in modern Japan. But both nations are equally handicapped by a linguistically imposed business inefficiency with lack of typewriters, linotypes, and efficient filing systems, dictionaries, and indices. Chinese children are condemned to the same exhaustive, inefficient, and unproductive memorization of characters. Chinese scientists are faced with the same problem of developing a modern scientific vocabulary and literature in a writing system which is inadequate to the demands of a modern world. China has erected the same barrier between its culture and that of the Occidental world. And China has attempted the same solutions that have been tried or advocated in Japan: simplification of style, limitation of characters, use of a phonetic syllabary, and romanization.

The simplification of style through adoption of the vernacular in writing was begun centuries ago but in its modern form dates from 1 January 1917 when Dr. Hu Shih, a philosopher educated in the United States and later Chinese Ambassador to the United States, published his famous eight principles of literary reform in an article, *Wen-hsüeh Kai-Liang Ch'u-Yi* ("Some Suggestions for the Revolution of Chinese Literature"). He held that the only Chinese writings which had been written in recent centuries and which had any claim at all to being considered classics, were those which had been written in the spoken language of the common people, *pai-hua*.

He predicted that *pai-hua* would become the vehicle for literary writing in the future and urged established writers to drop the classical allusions, pedantic style, obsolete characters, and tortuous literary expression which had marked the *wen-li*. Dr. Hu's principles, though hardly new, were a novel idea to the mass of Chinese literati and students. The conception that a great scholar should write as he spoke was caught up and made an integral part of the revolutionary student movement, which became the New Culture Movement (*Hsin Wen-hua Yün-tung* or *Hsin Su Chao*). By the end of 1919 approximately 500 newspapers and magazines were being published in this written style. Student magazines and popular fiction shifted to the vernacular style. Distinguished literary figures, such as CHOU Shun-jen, who wrote under the pseudonym of LU Shun and was the author of the famous *Ah Q Cheng Ch'uan* ("Real Story of Ah Q"), wrote in *pai-hua* and lent prestige to the movement. In 1920 the Ministry of Education made *pai-hua* the official style to be used in all elementary school textbooks, and many secondary schools voluntarily adopted the vernacular. The movement is amply documented in HU Shih's book, *Pai-hua Wen-hsüeh Shih* ("History of Vernacular Literature"), published in Shanghai in 1934. Thirty years after his original article it was evident that Dr. HU Shih's revolution in style had unqualifiedly succeeded. *Pai-hua* is the common written language of the masses.

The simplification of the written language through limitation in the number of characters is identified with the Chinese Mass Education Movement (*P'ing-Min Chiao-Yü Yün-Tung*) of Yang Ch'u James YEN. Mr. YEN, also a representative of the scholarly class of Chinese and one who had received an American education, left Yale University in 1918 to go to France as a YMCA worker in charge of 5,000 Chinese coolies in Boulogne. These were a part of the 200,000 Chinese laborers recruited in the Provinces of Chili and Shantung to work for the Allies during the first World War. Mr. YEN was profoundly moved by the inherent dignity and intelligence of these workers despite their obvious lack of education. He determined to establish literacy classes so that they might write to their people in China and as an experiment published a camp newspaper, *Hua Kung Chou Pao* ("The Chinese Laborer's Weekly") in *pai-hua*. He found that the average adult could learn to recognize 1,000 characters in about four months if taught by intensive methods. Mr. YEN returned to China in 1920 and spent four years experimenting with literacy classes in cities and conducting a statistical analysis similar to a frequency count of words, of 1,600,000 running ideographs recorded in more than 200 types of literature and popular publication in *pai-hua*. On the basis of this study he was able to establish a list of 1,300 basic characters considered a foundation vocabulary in *pai-hua*.

He then published four readers, known as the *Ping Min Chien Tzŭ K'o* ("People's Thousand Character Readers"), which were designed to teach these 1,300 ideographs and a minimum skill in reading to the average intelligent illiterate in 96 hours of classroom work. In March 1922 the first extensive educational campaign was begun in Changsha, in the Province of Hunan, Central China. The results of the experiment became a national sensation. Madam Hsiung Hsi-Ling, wife of the former Premier and elder statesman of China, devoted her full time to this work from August 1923 until her death. Her prestige helped to lift what was a typical missionary-type mass education project to the stature of a cultural revolution.

Mr. Yen and his assistants recognized that approximately 80% of China's population lived in the 1,900 rural districts or *hsien*. It was decided to attempt a very large-scale experiment in one of these *hsien*, and Tinghsien, about a hundred miles south of Peiping, was chosen as the site. The purely anti-illiteracy objectives of the movement were expanded to include civic, health, and vocational education. The health program was built around simple first aid, and medical instruction was given to prominent local residents, who then became part-time lay practitioners. The vocational education program included local agricultural research and demonstrations in home trades, animal husbandry, and improved agricultural methods. Census taking, always a difficult technical problem in China, was made the instrument for introducing civic consciousness in a rural society traditionally patriarchal.

Although the Mass Education Movement has been brilliantly publicized and although it has unquestionably done an immense amount of good as an adult education program, it presents very little that is novel as a method for solving the problem of the written language. The sergeant-teachers trained in Rancho Boyeros in Cuba and the famous Educational Missions in Mexico used a similar and equally effective adult education program. The *Instituto de Información Campesina* founded by Srta. Graciela Mandujano in Chile provided the same and additional services with what appear to be more efficient and original educational techniques. The "Each One Teach One" program of literacy education which Dr. Frank C. Laubach worked out while a missionary at Dansalan, Lake Lanao, in northern Mindanao, P.I., is equally effective as a teaching method and immensely more efficient linguistically since it uses a phonetic rather than an ideographic system of writing. Even the Laubach program is hardly original, being a modern adaptation of the monitor principle worked out in the slums of England and the schools of India by Lancaster and Bell more than a century earlier. The Rowan County "Moonlight Schools" made famous by the work of Cora Wilson Steward, later head of the Anti-Illiteracy Crusade in the United States, used a teaching technique similar to the language education in the Mass Education Movement in China. The Russian "liquidation of illiteracy" was based on a system of decentralized self-education directed by university students and practice teachers who spent their vacations in the villages.

These were primarily programs for providing low-cost education where formal schools had not been available in sufficient quantities. Japan, even with the loss of facilities from war damage, is not faced with a serious lack of schools. Its illiteracy is caused by a linguistic difficulty rather than an economic or social one. Only the principle of limitation of characters would appear to be applicable directly to the Japanese problem. As used in China, this limitation was restricted to a teaching device and was not generally considered a fundamental simplification of the nation's written language.

There has been no lack of attempts to reduce written Chinese to a phonetic system. Various forms of romanization introduced in the past by foreign scholars and missionaries have failed, linguistically, because of the excessively complex system of diacritical marks to handle the tonal system and because of the monosyllabic form of traditional written Chinese. The new Yale System, essentially a phonemic system, has very few diacritical marks and appears to be very efficient.

Written in ideographs, the 44,449 characters, which in Chinese are morphemes since they may be used singly as words as well as in compounds, listed in the *Imperial Dictionary* of *K'ang-hsi* are recognizable without ambiguity. This basic list, more than two centuries old, has been augmented by many thousands of modern and technical words, each represented by a distinctive ideograph or more commonly by a compound of two or more existing characters. In the Peiping dialect, however, there are only about 420 monosyllabic sounds. Thus each sound is represented on an average by about 105 meanings. In the Wade System of romanization the sound *chi* has at least 165 characters and *i* has 178, though within these numbers they are further differentiated by tones. It is evident that if *wen-li*, the classical style, is retained it is possible that there might arise ambiguities caused by homonyms, even though tone marks are added. It is a widely accepted theory of linguistic science, however, that any language which is understandable when spoken is understandable when written in an adequate phonemic system. In Chinese it is admittedly possible to write the vernacular *pai-hua* in a nonideographic notation. Ambiguities are clarified, as in spoken Chinese, by linked compounds, stress, tone, and context. About 40 phonetic, actually semiphonemic, systems have been attempted in the past century, and in limited usage, such as the romanization of the Holy Bible in southern Formosa, have proven somewhat unwieldy but effective writing systems. Two such systems, which have received official recognition, will serve as examples. These are the syllabary *Chu Yin Tzu-Mu* and the Peiping Ministry of Communication's System of Romanization, devised in a large measure by WANG Chingchun, former Managing Director of the Peiping-Hankow Railway.

Chu Yin Tzu-Mu is a set of 39 symbols consisting of 24 initials, 12 finals and 3 medials. Like *kana* in Japanese these Chinese phonetic symbols are simplifications of, or more exactly stylized fragments of, common Chinese ideographs whose basic pronunciation is well established. Also like *kana* these symbols have been used side by side with the traditional characters to teach pronunciation in dictionaries and elementary school textbooks. Although *Chu Yin Tzu-Mu* was officially recognized by Order No. 75, of 23 November 1918, after approval by a congress of representatives from all provinces called by the National Ministry of Education, this system has failed to do more than assist in the establishment of a uniform national pronunciation based on the Peiping dialect.

The Peiping Ministry of Communication's System was officially adopted in February 1918 for telegraphic communication. It was designed primarily to be used as a means of sending the Chinese language over internal telegraph and foreign cable systems without the excessive cost and loss of time involved in using the four-cypher code which had traditionally been used. It was estimated by the Ministry of Communication that an average 25-word coded Chinese cable required about one half hour to write or decode as compared to the two minutes for an open message in an Occidental language. The cost was approximately double. The Ministry of Communication's System was really a simple phonetic code. In order to standardize pronunciation, the Peiping dialect with a four-tone scale was adopted. The tremendous difficulty of homonyms was solved by a combination of phonetic and semantic systems composed of three elements. First, the sound of the word was written phonetically in a slight modification of the Wade System but without the diacritical marks. To this was added a single letter (q, v, x, or z) to represent the appropriate tone. Next was added the phonetic rendition of the sound of the radical, spelled backward to indicate that it stood for meaning and not sound. The standard 214 radicals or etymologically differentiating elements which appear as recognizable patterns in the ideograph were reduced to 102 and it was hoped that ultimately this number might be reduced to about 40 without introducing ambiguity into standard Chinese. The word *yivok* in the system, for example, would mean one of the many Chinese words pronounced as *yi*; limited to the smaller group of those pronounced with the second tone, here rendered by the letter *v*; and still further limited by the basic idea of the radical pronounced *ko* (*k'ou* in the Wade-Giles System) (which gives the idea of "mouth" and which would appear as a recognizable pattern of strokes in the ideograph if the word were written in the traditional form), here rendered by the letters *ok*—thus giving a final meaning of "giddy laughter"!

Where there was no probability of homonymic ambiguity, as in the case of definite and crystallized compound words which had meanings rendered as single words in Occidental languages, the phonetic rendition together with the tone sign was written but the reversed phonetic rendering of the radical was omitted. The result was a system which could be written in roman letters, but which variously assigned these letters to the properties of a sound, of a diacritical mark, and of the meaning of a limiting portion of the ideograph. Obviously even the most difficult *wen-li* could be accurately transliterated, but equally obviously the Peiping Ministry of Communication's System served merely as an additional code linked to the cumbersome traditional ideographic method of writing. If the writer did not know the character he could not use this quasi-phonetic writing.

Why has China not produced some system of simplified writing system which can help Japan meet its problem of the written language? Two quotations from authoritative Chinese, since they apply almost equally well to Japan, may be illuminating.

Mr. Yang Ch'u James YEN, speaking before the 66th Annual Meeting of the National Education Association in 1928, said:

. . . China has been a monarchy for many centuries and under a monarchy education for the entire people was not considered either necessary or desirable. In fact the idea of giving an entire people education is a comparatively recent one in any country! Furthermore, the Chinese emperors of the dynasties had deliberately discouraged people's education. They wanted to practice what we call in Chinese the "Ignorance Policy" and they succeeded very well.

Dr. CHEN Chih-mai, Counselor of the Chinese Embassy in Washington, D.C., in a letter to the author dated 5 December 1946, wrote:

The chief difficulty, I feel, in launching any reform at present is that the person who happens to have learned the simplified language will find himself unable to read the books written during the last four thousand years and therefore he will have to learn the traditional language also, with the result that instead of making the process of learning simpler it really means a certain duplication of effort. I really do not think that any Chinese is prepared either to part company with his rich historical heritage or to take the trouble of having the old books re-written in the simplified language. Such things as Tang poetry, for instance, would lose its place in our culture, which I for one [would] consider a major calamity.

The Precedent of Turkey. There exists for the serious student of the written-language problem in Japan one large-scale experiment in language simplification which is strikingly parallel and very significant. That is the shift which was made in Turkey from the Ottoman Turkish (*Osmanlı*) to the romanized "language of strength" (*Türkçe*).

Ancient Turkish, like Japanese, was a language rich in folklore but impoverished or devoid of an indigenous written literature. Turkey imported its written language as well as its religion from the Arabs and Persians, as Japan imported its from the Chinese and Koreans. The spoken Turkish language was unsuited grammatically and phonetically to the alien written form, as ancient spoken Japanese was unsuited to the ideographic writing system of China. Spoken Turkish has eight vowels while Arabic has three and in the written form omits the symbols for these sounds. In adapting the Arabic system to Turkish the eight Turkish vowel sounds (hard *a, i, o, u* and soft *e, i, ö, ü*) were sometimes rendered by a system of Arabic diacritical marks (*harèkès*) placed above or below the consonantal symbols, and sometimes were simply omitted. The religious and classical literatures of Arabia and Persia dominated Turkish culture for centuries; as *Mahāyāna* Buddhism and Confucianism from China dominated Japanese culture. Educated Turks read Arabic and Persian classics and overlaid their native Turkish with an expanding vocabulary of Arabic and Persian words; as Japan has traditionally drawn upon Chinese literature and language. The Turkish student was faced with the imposing task of learning the 612 symbol *Osmanlica*, somewhat less of a hurdle than the memorization of thousands of *kanji* in Japanese, but still sufficiently formidable so that nearly 90% of the citizens were illiterate.

Every argument against simplification of the language which has been advanced in Japan was equally advanced by learned Turks. Change from Arabic would be an affront to Islamic culture and religion. The adoption of roman letters would be sacrilegious, since the *Kuran* ("Koran"), fundamental religious document of Islam, was originally written in Arabic. Romanized Turkish would make it impossible for people to read the great Turkish classics. Children would be cut off from the culture of their father; elders would refuse to read the transliterations of familiar books. The traditional Arabic script was artistic and beautiful while Roman letters were monotonous. The reader was able to get the idea quickly from the old script, but would have to puzzle over the romanized version. Many of the most important words in intellectual communication were of Persian or Arabic origin and were not adaptable to romanization. Change to the new system would make Turkey revert to an impoverished ancient language unsuited to modern needs. All changes should be made slowly. Great care should be taken to select the best alphabet if any change were made. A romanization of the language would be undignified, an aping of European nations, a loss of national stature. Increased illiteracy, rather than improvement, would result from such a change. There would be great economic loss to those with business investments involving the traditional script.

In one element Turkey after the Revolution and Japan after the second World War are not parallels. Turkey had as its leader one of the most brilliant—and possibly ruthless—personalities of modern times. He was domineering and authoritarian, but he was also paternalistic. It is probable that some of the advisers of the Emperor Meiji during the Restoration may have enjoyed similar gifts, but no one in Japan under the Occupation was remotely comparable in stature to the first President of the Turkish Republic, the Gazi, Mustafa Kemal Atatürk.

Mustafa Kemal was the creator of the nationalization movement, Kemalism (not to be confused with the racially more nationalistic Pan-Turkism, *Türkçülük*, of Ziya Gök Alp) which sought to replace the feeling of inferiority and dejection which characterized the closing years of the Ottoman Empire with a dynamic pride. His policy was one of nationalization, secularism, and industrialism. His objective in nationalization was to achieve homogeneity and national consciousness, and not to expand his territorial possessions. His objective in industrialization was to build up those industries needed for security, and to remove control from foreign owners, not to eliminate the characteristically agrarian economy of the nation. He conceived of a national industry which was partly State owned and partly private enterprise.

He clearly recognized the impossibility of building a modern nation, representative or otherwise, on a foundation of 90% illiteracy. He appreciated that the very core of nationalism is the language, and he set about creating a pure Turkish (*öz Türkçe*) which would serve as a vehicle for his political, economic, and social reforms. Romanization would accomplish three objectives in his program of nationalism: it would make it impossible for the newly educated to read the literature in the old script, thus setting up a barrier against return to old ideas; it would make learning to read relatively simple, thus cutting down the percentage of illiteracy and making the minds of the masses available to governmental propaganda; and it would make possible a new business efficiency with typewriters, linotype machines, better filing systems, etc., thus clearing the way for the economic rehabilitation of the nation. But he recognized that in addition to romanization his language reform would have to cut many of the ties with Arabic and Persian. In an introduction which Mustafa KEMAL contributed to the important Turkish linguistic work, *Türk Dili Içün* ("For the Turkish Language"), by Sadri MAKSUDI, published in 1930, which has been translated and quoted by Sir Telford WAUGH in "A Far Reaching Turkish Plan," in *Journal of the Royal Central Asian Society*, Vol. XX, Pt. IV, October 1933, p. 580, and by Henry Elisha ALLEN, *The Turkish Transformation* (University of Chicago Press, 1935), p. 114, he says:

The tie between national sentiment and language is very strong. A rich national language has great influence on the development of national feeling. The Turkish tongue is one of the richest of all; it only needs to be wisely used. The Turkish nation, which has known how to establish its government and its high independence, must free its tongue from the yoke of foreign words.

Three elements of the Turkish language reform are of particular interest as a possible guide to solution of the Japanese problem: the linguistic changes involved, the method of introducing those changes, and the social results of those changes.

The linguistic changes involved in the language reform were two: the writing system was changed from Arabic script to a 28-letter Latin script or romanization; and the vocabulary and grammar of the language, both spoken and written, were to a large degree purged of Arabic and Persian influences and replaced with newly created Turkish words or revived forms taken from ancient folk literature.

The new Turkish alphabet is almost perfectly phonemic. Each phoneme has a symbol and each symbol has only one phoneme. It omits the letters *q, w,* and *x* of the English alphabet but adds *ç, ş, ı* (without the dot), *ö* and *ü*. The forms *ğ, â, î,* and *û* are not considered separate letters of the alphabet but standard forms modified with a diacritical mark. The Commission on Latin Characters had commenced its task on 26 June 1928 with the official injunction that it was to discover the most logical means of romanizing the writing system and was not to waste time discussing the desirability of romanization. Despite this clear-cut mandate, the commission by the end of July was still unable to agree upon an alphabet and was talking of a gradual change-over that would require 20 to 25 years. Tradition has it that Mustafa Kemal became impatient with the prolonged and academic discussions as to the technical intricacies of the proposed alphabet. He is said to have sat up all one night and the next day emerged with the highly satisfactory alphabet which is today in use. Whatever the accuracy of this story, never officially denied, it is a historical fact commemorated on Turkish postage stamps that on 9 August 1928, Mustafa Kemal set up a blackboard in Sarayburnu Park in Istanbul and introduced the new writing system to his people.

The substitution of Turkish words for the traditional Arabic and Persian loan words was largely the work of the Society for Turkish Linguistic Studies and Research (*Kurultay*) established 12 July 1932. This organization searched ancient Anatolian folklore; made comparative studies of Sumerian and Hittite; sought ancient word lists of pure Turkish origin, such as the eleventh-century dictionary of Mahmud Kâşgarli; consulted dictionaries of pure Turkish words, such as the partially completed *Osmanlı-Turkish Dictionary* of Huseyin Kadri Bey, the *Osmanlı Dictionary* of Velid Çelebi Bey, the *Turkish-Osmanlı Dictionary* of Süleyman Hurşhit Bey, and Comdr. A. Vahid Bey's *English-Turkish Dictionary*. It compiled lists of international technical terms. The First Great Turkey Linguistic Congress was convened in Ankara on 26 September 1932 to map out a program of research. Two years later, the Second Congress met at the *Dolma Bahçe*, one of the surviving palaces of the former Sultan in Istanbul. In that period it had collected over 100,000 words of pure Turkish origin. In March 1935 the Society published a pocket glossary, the *Osmanlıca-Türkçe*, and shortly afterward its counterpart, the *Türkçe-Osmanlıca*, containing about 8,000 equivalents in the old language and the new.

The method of accomplishing the change-over to the new system may be characterized by a period of careful preparation; by a dramatic presentation to the people as a completed system backed by the prestige and authority of the President; by a powerful and effective propaganda; by a realistic time schedule which allowed a minimum of time for the defenses of conservatism to become intrenched; and by the active participation of the masses.

The people of Turkey were prepared for the violent psychological upheaval marked by the abandonment of the Arabic script through a series of social reforms. Shortly after the turn of the century the public offices in European Turkey had abandoned the ancient reckoning of hours, in which the 12 hours of the day ended at sunset and the 12 hours of night were divided into watches. On 1 January 1926 the two ancient Turkish methods of dates were abandoned: the religious year based on MOHAMMED's flight from Mecca to Medina in 622 A.D. and the civil year introduced by MAHMOUD the Reformer which corresponded to the lunar year beginning on the first of March. Old Turkish 1342 became 1926 A.D. On 1 June 1928 the international number system was made the official system. Even the romanization of Turkish was not entirely a novelty before Mustafa KEMAL's dramatic presentation. As early as 1924 chemical formulae had been officially written in roman letters. In 1926 the names of foreigners in official correspondence were listed in Roman letters. The Congress of Turkology held in Baku in February and March 1926 had with a single dissenting vote (Kazan) pronounced itself in favor of Latin characters. The Turkish press had given great prominence to the deliberations of the Commission on Latin Characters which had been called on 26 June 1928.

Propaganda for the change really began with the often quoted 9 August 1928 speech of Mustafa KEMAL. He left very little doubt in anyone's mind what was his wish:

Fellow countrymen! In order to express our beautiful language we are adopting new Turkish characters. We are under this obligation to emancipate ourselves from the incomprehensible characters which have placed our heads in an iron frame. We want to understand our language by all means, and we shall understand it surely with these new characters. Now the time has come for work. My own conviction is that hereafter there is no need either for me or you to talk much. No more words, but action, activity and marching forward. We have accomplished much. But today there is an important task, though not the last, to be accomplished. Learn quickly the new Turkish characters. Teach them to the whole nation. Take this as a patriotic task and realize it. If only ten per cent of the nation can read and write and the great majority remain illiterate, it is a thing of which to be ashamed. . . .

I want the activity of the whole nation applied to this task. In a year or two, the whole Turkish nation shall learn these new characters. Our nation with its alphabet and mentality shall prove that she constitutes a part of the civilized world.

When the Gazi spoke, few in Turkey dared to differ. The Prime Minister, Ismet Inönü (then known as Ismet Paşa), gave a historic speech in Malatya on 13 September 1928 in which he told the people that Mustafa Kemal was going through the country, teaching the new alphabet in the streets, in the squares, in the schools. The Ankara Teachers' Union (*Muallimler Birliği*) on 25 August 1928 pledged its members to teach only in the new characters. Mustafa Kemal knew how to catch the people's imagination. A deputy in the National Assembly, the proprietor of the newspaper *Cumhuriyet*, Yanus Nadi Bey, on presenting himself to the President to secure leave to go abroad on an official mission, was required to submit to an examination in the new alphabet before the assembly. His examination, with the President's nine corrections in thirteen lines, was published in his own newspaper. The President's Cabinet was invited to his summer home for their vacation and to study the new alphabet. On 1 November 1928 Mustafa Kemal made the need for alphabet reform his major topic in the opening address to the Grand National Assembly. It caused little surprise when two days later on 3 November 1928 the Grand National Assembly officially adopted Mustafa Kemal's new Turkish alphabet. On 11 November 1928 the same Assembly ordered the opening of national schools (*Millet Mektepleri*) to teach the new system of writing to both literate and illiterate adults under 40.

The time schedule was a vital part of the change-over program. Newspapers, magazines, motion pictures, advertising, statistics, and schools were expected to shift immediately to the new alphabet with 1 December 1928 set as the dead line. The official adoption of the new system in all departments of the government was set for 1 January 1929, exactly two months after the passing of the law. Certain legal papers such as marriage licenses, arrests, processes, and court proceedings could be written in the old system up to 1 June 1929. All other documents, official or private, might be written in the old form until 1 June 1930.

What were the results of this fundamental language simplification?

The great masses of Turkish people welcomed the change. The *Millet Mektepleri* were highly successful folk schools. By setting the upper age limit for those required to attend at 40, Mustafa Kemal had shrewdly played on his people's vanity. It is said that few men and almost no women stayed away from the classes for fear of being considered beyond that age.

Over 20,000 of these folk schools were actually set up by 1 January 1929 and enrolled 625,000 men and 420,000 women, 60% of whom are reported to have learned to read and write during the first term. Illiterates enjoyed the undreamed-of social distinction of being able to read. By 1936 Turkey officially claimed 3 million literate adults (30% of those above primary school age) and Donald E. Webster, author of *The Turkey of Atatürk* (Philadelphia, American Academy of Political and Social Science, 1939), and later Cultural Attaché in the United States Embassy in Ankara, feels that it is a reasonable claim. The most remote village school was not safe from a surprise visit from the President and the highest or lowliest official might expect to be publicly examined at any time. Local committees in the People's Houses (*Halkevi*) collected old Turkish words and decentralized the effort to discard Arabic and Persian roots while seeking pure Turkish. With the powerful personality of Mustafa Kemal urging the movement on, romanization of the writing system and Turkification of the vocabulary was both popular and feverish.

The linguistic and social gains have been less spectacular but equally encouraging. Students learn the new system as if it were the only writing system Turkey had ever known. They look on *Osmanlı* Turkish as American students do on Middle English. The phonetic system has lived up to most of the linguistic claims made for it, in efficiency both in business and education. Illiteracy, though exact statistics are unobtainable, is officially considered to be rapidly declining. Although the desirability of extreme nationalization of the language by eliminating loan words may perhaps be questioned by the foreign observer, there can be no doubt of the success of that element of the program. It is claimed that Halid Zıya Bey, born in 1866 and considered the father of Turkish fiction, lived to see the language change to the point where his writings were almost unintelligible to the reading public even when transliterated into the phonetic alphabet. Modern Turkey reads almost exclusively modern authors. Turkish expatriates who have had no contact with the language since the reform find even the spoken tongue almost incomprehensible. University graduates whose entire education has been conducted in the new romanized writing system have demonstrated by their postgraduate studies abroad that they have suffered no appreciable cultural handicap by the total discard of the old Arabic script.

One adverse element in the reform might have been predicted. There was a sudden drop in circulation of newspapers, periodicals, and books immediately after the reform was put into effect. Educated persons, once the novelty wore off, preferred to read in French, the common second language, rather than to struggle with the unfamiliar *Türkçe*. It took several months before the decrease in illiteracy made itself felt in equal and finally increased markets. The amount which these papers dropped in circulation is difficult to determine exactly, partly because circulation is one of the bases of taxation. Yakup KADRI Bey, Turkish deputy and prominent author, writing in *Milliyet*, 5 April 1929, estimated that several popular weeklies with circulations of 30,000 had dropped off to 2,000, 1,000 and even 500, finally forcing their publishers to close. Professor Georges COURTIN of the Turkish Lycée of Smyrna, in an article, "Un essai d'orthographe phonétique: la réforme turque" in *Mercure de France*, Vol. CCIX, No. 764, 15 April 1930, writes that some of the newspapers fell 25% to a maximum of 50% in circulation. Professor OKUBO Koji, Japanese President of the Society for Scientific Research in Islamic Civilization (*Isuramu Bunka Kyōkai*) in Tokyo, and lecturer on the Turkish Language in the Zenrin Foreign Language School, states that this "cultural depression" lasted only a year; within two years many journals and papers had increased their circulation by as much as tenfold; and that by 1936, seven years after the reform was initiated, no significant dislocation was apparent.

Is a Phonetic System Practical?

Seven basic reasons have been advanced against the adoption of a phonetic system in written Japanese: the possibility of ambiguity due to homonyms, the cultural loss, the cultural imperialism, the chaos in change-over, the inefficiency, the delay or postponement, and the difficulty in reading. What are the merits of these arguments?

Ambiguity and Homonyms. It is generally agreed among Japanese that the language contains such a high percentage of Chinese monosyllables that it cannot be understood when written in a phonetic writing system. The facts do not appear to support this objection.

Many books at every level of scholarship have been published in *romaji*. These books range from doctoral dissertations like NAGAO-Seturō's *Niyaku no Kikai*, in the field of mechanics, published in 1929, and technical books like *Netu Oyobi Netu-Kikwan* by KOGA-Kunio on internal combustion engines, to the simplest children's books. Religious books, including the Episcopal Prayer Book, and the Holy Bible, have been published in *romaji*. A number of journals, such as *Romaji*, the official organ of the *Romaji Hirome Kai*, have been published in *romaji*. Ten of the Reports of the Aeronautical Research Laboratory of Tokyo Imperial University were published in *romaji* (6 in German, 48 in standard Japanese, 265 in English). The greatest of Japanese classics, the *Nihongi*, the *Kojiki*, and the *Manyōshu* have been published with some editorial deletions in *romaji*. Modern foreign books, such as H. G. WELLS's *A Short World History*, several novels by Robert Louis STEVENSON, and GRIMM's *Fairy Tales* have been published in *romaji*. NATSUME Sōseki's famous Japanese novels, *Nihyaku-Tōka* ("The Two Hundred Tenth Day") and *Botchan* ("Young Master"), are published in *romaji*. Chinese classics (for example, *Rongo*, containing the discourses of CONFUCIUS to his disciples) have been transliterated into *romaji*. An equally imposing group of publications exists in *kana*.

It is generally conceded that any language which can be understood when spoken aloud can be understood when written phonemically. Japanese obviously can be understood when spoken aloud, and the daily conversations, radio, lectures, and speeches are not a phantasy. The mannerism of writing *kanji* in the air is a symptom of mental laziness of a person who does not trouble to rephrase an ambiguous sentence. It is a sort of physical parenthetical expression. A man who has lost his right hand does not become mute. The blind, who have never seen *kanji*, can speak and are educated. The Japanese controversy arises not from a denial that a spoken language can be represented adequately by an alphabet, but rather from the belief that the written form of Japanese is actually a different language, not in fact understandable when read aloud.

The Chinese morphemes, monosyllables, which have been introduced into Japanese with the use of *kanji* do not make the language unintelligible when uttered because of their high percentage of homonyms. Many of these Chinese monosyllables were not pure homonyms in the original Chinese because they were pronounced with the Chinese tonal scale. Since this tonal scale is not present in spoken Japanese, the Japanese rendition retains only the basic sound, modified to suit the Japanese phonetic structure, without the differentiation in tone. It is true that this contributes to the production of a large number of homonyms represented in the written system by individual *kanji*. If used as isolated monosyllabic words in Japanese, they would in many cases be ambiguous. Fortunately the great majority of them are normally used not as isolated monosyllables but as part of Japanese words known as Chinese compounds (*gōseigo*) when written in *kanji*. These polysyllabic words are seldom homonymic. When written phonemically the portion of the word represented by a Chinese monosyllable which is homonymic when standing alone causes no more trouble than does the syllable "poly—," taken from the Greek word, *polys*, which is found in scores of English words, such as "polyangular," "polyandrous," "Polynesian," "polygamy," etc., or the initial syllable "con—" in the word "condor" (bird) from the Quechua Indian language and in the word "conger" (eel) from the Latin and originally from the Greek word *gongros*.

Every language contains a certain number of homonyms. All languages, spoken Japanese included, clarify the possible ambiguities which might arise from the use of the homonyms by the adept use of context in the sentence. The famous Spanish sentence, "¿Como Como? Como Como Como," (written without diacritical marks) is a humorous recognition of the existence of homonyms. It is estimated that there are 250 common meanings for the English word "put" when used in combination with directional prepositions: Thus, "put in" is the equivalent of "insert," "interject," "pack," "dock," "beach," "write," "load," etc. The 13 verbs of Basic English in proper context express more than 3,000 meanings. The Japanese words for "bridge," "chopsticks," and "edge" are usually considered to be identically pronounced *hashi*. Actually they are not homonyms since they are accented differently, but the existing Japanese *kana* system, and even most *romaji* systems, do not indicate the differentiating morpheme, the accent, so that in the phonetic writing they appear to be equal. This example is commonly advanced by Japanese, however, to prove that a phonetic transcription would be quite ambiguous and hence impractical. If the *romaji* word *hashi* were used standing alone, completely divorced from all context, it would of course be ambiguous. But a reader would hardly interpret a sentence in context as "building a *chopstick* across a river," or "eating his rice with a suspension *bridge*." A more exact phonemic system which indicated the missing accent, would in this case, of course, make the words quite unambiguous even if standing alone.

Even context will not clarify ambiguities arising from homonyms if there is too high a percentage of these homonyms. It has been the uncritical contention of the opponents of a phonetic system that the percentage of homonyms is "impossibly large." Statistical studies, though perhaps not definitive, do not appear to confirm this.

A study of the homonyms existing in the complete literary language (based on the *Dai-Nippon Kokugo Jiten* of 200,000 words; *Dai-Genkai* of 70,000; *Gensen* of 250,000; *Ji-En* of 110,000; *Gen-En* of 79,000; and *Shin-Jikai* of 49,000) reported in the study *Dō Ongo Rui Ongo* ("Homonyms and Related Words"), published on 30 July 1931 by *Nippon Hōsō Kyōkai*, indicated that there are approximately 8,700 homonyms (not pairs), or about 3.6% in more than 250,000 words. A study of the homonyms existing in military and technical language, based on *Japanese Military and Technical Terms*, CINCPAC-CINCPOA Bulletin No. 18–45, 30 July 1945, indicated that there are approximately 1,430 homonyms (not pairs; this being a total of 569 homonymic sounds), or less than 4.9% in the 29,256 words. A study of the homonyms existing in the normal everyday language of educated Japanese, based on the broadcasts from Radio Tokyo during the month of May 1934 prepared by SATŌ Takashi, indicated that a total of 1,880 different homonyms were used, although 923 of these occurred only once during the month, and 1,500 or 80% occurred five times or less. A study of the number of homonyms which exist in the language which presumably can be written and read by graduates of the six-year compulsory educational system indicates that there are only 896 homonyms which are expressed solely by combinations of the 500 most common *kanji* (those determined in the 1935 study of the *Kanamoji Kai* and the

Hattori Hōkō Kai). Homonyms whose meaning would be clarified by writing in *kanji* outside the limit of this restricted number would presumably be unintelligible to the average graduate of the compulsory educational system.

It should be noted, of course, that comparisons of the relative density of homonyms in the structures of two different languages are quite misleading. Morphemes can be accurately determined and counted, but combinations of these morphemes in words vary so much that the determination of what are comparable "word" units in two languages is difficult or impossible. A count of "dictionary entries" in bilingual dictionaries gives a rough approximation but is subject, of course, to the criticism that the entries are determined by noncomparable factors, such as the subjective evaluation of the editor, the indexing system, and the convention adopted for separating root from derived meanings.

The substitution of a phonetic writing system for the traditional *kanji* would eliminate a major source of ambiguity arising from the multiple readings of the characters. The problem is the reverse of the homonym problem. In the case of homonyms, the meanings are different, sounds and phonetic writing are the same, and the *kanji* are different. In the case of multiple readings, however, the meanings are different, the sounds and phonetic writing are different, and the *kanji* are the same. Thus in the case of characters having multiple readings, far from clarifying ambiguities by the use of *kanji*, ambiguities are introduced. A typical example is 金 which stands for the Japanese *kane* (metal) and *kin* (gold). The two meanings, written in *romaji* as *kane* and *kin*, could not be confused.

Cultural Loss. It is argued that much of Japanese culture, its art, poetry, and style in literature, is linked with *kanji*. It is held that if a phonetic system of writing were substituted for the *kanji* this culture would be lost. In any modernization of a civilization it is inevitable that there will be certain losses. A compromise must be made between cultural loss and the practical gains in democratization, business efficiency, and education. The vast majority of Japanese under the present system do not have an education which permits them to enjoy the niceties of Japanese literary style. The actual cultural loss need not be great.

The traditional 17-syllable poem (*haiku* or *hokku*) and the 31-syllable poem (*waka* or *tanka*) have on occasion been written phonetically in *hiragana*. It is the opinion of many leading Japanese literary figures that Japanese poetry actually gains by being written phonetically.

Some of the greatest historical classics of Japanese literature are written phonetically. The most famous is probably *Genji Monogatari* ("The Tales of *Genji*") by MURASAKI Shikibu in 54 volumes done between 999 and 1011 A.D. Others are written phonetically in *hiragana*, *katakana*, or *manyōgana* with varying percentages of Chinese characters standing for meaning interspersed. A study of the language of the Japanese classics by Dr. HISAMATSU Sen-ichi, leading authority on literature at Tokyo Imperial University, completed 20 March 1946, indicated that 20 of the 35 best-known works had more than 85% of the symbols in their running text in phonetic writing. These predominantly phonetic writings included *Eiga Monogatari*, *Genji Monogatari*, *Ise Monogatari*, *Ochikubo Monogatari*, *Taketori Monogatari*, *Utsubo Monogatari*, *Yamato Monogatari*, *Makura no Sōshi*, *Sarashina Nikki*, *Tosa Nikki*, *Kokin Wakashū*, *Ōkagami*, *Manyōshu*, *Senzai Wakashū*, *Shin-Kokin Wakashū*, and *Shūi Wakashū*. Dr. HISAMATSU studied the oldest extant texts of each of the works. Modern editions frequently have ideographs used in place of the original phonetic symbols.

It is perhaps unnecessary to point out that in the event that a phonetic writing system should be adopted scholars and those who elected literary courses in the university would be able to continue their studies of the Japanese literature in the *kanji* notation. Modern English scholars read the Greek and Latin classics in the original but do not insist that the newspapers, magazines, popular books, scientific works, and textbooks be written in those languages. *Beowulf* in Old English, and Geoffrey CHAUCER's *Canterbury Tales* in Middle English are not denied to English and American school children, although only specialized scholars could read them in the original. All classic literature worthy of continued study could and would be translated into the vernacular and into the phonetic form, where it would in fact become far more accessible to the masses.

It seems probable that the adoption of a phonetic system would stimulate a new national literature. Use of the words of true Japanese origin would be stimulated since they would offer few problems of ambiguity because of homonyms. Literature springing from the folk tales of the Japanese people would tend to replace imitations of Chinese literary forms and the perpetuation of traditional Chinese stories. It is true, of course, that collections of folk literature have already been made by Japanese scholars, but a markedly wider interest in reading would inevitably broaden the base of authorship. For the first time in Japanese history the middle and lower classes would become articulate. Some Japanese unabashedly deny the desirability of encouraging these classes to express themselves.

The literature of a people is far more than the poetry, essays, novels, and other literary forms of writing. In a modern nation it includes the mass of scientific literature upon which the physical development of the nation is based. It is at least as necessary to have a writing system which adequately meets the need of this literature as it is to preserve the form of ancient writings.

Finally, the Chinese character as a medium of art would be continued. Artists could practice their *kanji* as Occidental artists practice laying a wash in water colors or study human anatomy in a life class. The lay appreciation of fine calligraphy need not be lost with the adoption of an efficient medium of communication.

Cultural Imperialism. It is argued that Japan has in the past received nearly all its culture from China; that any change in the system of writing Japanese with *kanji* would deprive Japan of its greatest cultural link with China; and that adoption of *romaji* would in effect force Occidental culture upon Japan.

The most direct answer to these charges is that the leading phonetic writing systems are in fact Japanese. One phonetic system of writing, *kana*, is a Japanese invention, is 1,000 years old, and is the medium in which some of the greatest Japanese literature has been written. Another phonetic system, *romaji*, has been used for 75 years, was studied officially as a result of Imperial Ordinance 222 of 26 November 1930 establishing the *Rinji Romaji Chōsa Kai* (Tentative Romaji Research Society), and was officially recognized and its spelling regulated in Imperial Cabinet Order 3 of 21 September 1937.

There is no major language change involved in the adoption of a phonetic system of writing. The basic language of Japan is obviously the spoken language. As was earlier indicated, a leading school of linguists would say that it was the only Japanese language. There would be no change to be expected in this spoken form with the possible exception of some slight modification of erudite speech resulting from the increased thinking in the vernacular on the part of highly educated people. The change in the writing system is primarily a change in notation.

The argument in favor of continuing Japan's cultural dependency upon China is less than realistic. Japanese cannot speak or read Chinese without studying it as a foreign language. It is true that they are able to understand the meaning represented by individual characters, but the structures of the two languages are so dissimilar that the Japanese who has not studied Chinese or *kambun* is quite unable to read even newspaper articles written in Chinese.

The choice of what foreign languages should be studied in the educational system is a matter which the Japanese feel should be left to them and should not be influenced by foreign groups. In the past the percentage of students studying each of the languages offered has fluctuated in a manner indicating direct correlation with Japanese foreign trade, diplomatic alliances, and cultural importations. The languages offered have been English, Chinese, German, French, Spanish, Portuguese, and Russian. According to *Mombushō* statistics, though the figures seem somewhat low, in the 30 years between 1915 and 1945 a total of 29,275 teachers of English, 416 teachers of German, 297 teachers of French, and 571 teachers of Chinese were licensed to teach in the middle schools and girls' high schools. During the same period 2,603 teachers of English, 564 teachers of German, and 172 teachers of French were employed in the higher schools (*kōtō gakkō*). Russian, Chinese, Spanish, and Portuguese were not included in the official subjects of institutions of higher learning (*daigaku, semmon gakkō*, and *kōtō gakkō*).

It is true that historically Japan employed a strong cultural importation from China. In the past 30 years, however, Japan has exported to China. Not fewer than 38,724 Chinese students studied in Japanese institutions of higher learning from 1927 to 1945, according to the registry in the Sino-Japanese Students' Association. During the same period only 66 Japanese students were issued passports for study in Chinese institutions. Five of these were governmental investigators. A small number of Japanese residents in China presumably attended Chinese educational institutions without formally registering with their own government. A study of the imports of books by MARUZEN, a major Japanese book importing house credited officially with handling approximately 85% of all books imported, indicates that in the ten years prior to Surrender, even with the European markets shut off during the war, the four countries of Great Britain, United States, Germany, and France represented 94% of all book imports (money value), while China and all other countries combined supplied only 6%. The Tokyo Imperial University Library acquired virtually no modern Chinese books during the 30 years between 1915 and 1945 with the exception of a very few acquired by official exchange agreements. The withdrawal records of that library indicate almost no use of modern Chinese books.

Chaos in Change-Over. It is argued that the Japanese people would rebel against any change, that the present high rate of literacy in Japan would be wiped out, and that there would be 50 years of chaos, with records disrupted and reference books made unavailable.

It is improbable that the Japanese people would rebel against such a change. The movement for language reform and for romanization in particular has had Japanese leadership for more than half a century, representing the highest political, social, economic, and intellectual levels. The entire population has been exposed to *romaji* in road signs, railway stations, billboards, and to a lesser degree in foreign language phrase books. The Occupation greatly increased the public use of *romaji* and the explicit recommendation of the United States Education Mission to Japan, even though in effect denied in official policy statements, greatly stimulated the popular interest in this system. The phonetic syllabary, *kana*, of course, is used daily by every Japanese who can read and write at all.

In the Tokyo newspapers having public distribution there were 44 articles and editorials on language reform between 1 January 1946 and the announcement of the *Report* of the United States Education Mission with its recommendation on romanization on 30 March 1946. In the same papers there were 75 articles and editorials on language reform during the month of April 1946 immediately following the release of the *Report*. The *Nippon Shimbun Hō* ("Japanese Newspaper News"), a biweekly trade paper for journalists, carried 13 articles between November 1945 and the announcement of the Mission's recommendations, and 8 articles during the month of April following the release of the *Report*.

An article in *Mimpo*, 11 May 1946 translated and quoted in ATIS *Press Translations*, Social Series 565, Item 3, stated:

A movement to reform Japanese script is progressing rapidly. Leaders of this movement think that the rise of more *Romaji* and less *Kanji* would make Japanese easier and would elevate the cultural level of Japan. Among many magazine publishers, including the *Chū-Ō-Kōron*, there has arisen the attitude that some 20 percent of the pages of each issue should be romanized. In this connection, HATANAKA Shigeo, chief editor of *Chū-Ō-Kōron*, said, "I believe that the adoption of Roman letters at this juncture will give a strong impetus to the establishment of a new form of expression. In the romanization of Japanese, there are some questions of techniques as to how the 'nuances' or 'delicacies' in essays on philosophy and thought can be expressed. However, we agree to the adoption of romanized letters. We will do our utmost to express naturally, in Roman letters, articles on topics which appeal to the masses rather than doing a special column in Roman letters. I want all magazine publishers to discuss this matter with one another in order to achieve romanization as soon as possible."

The *Nippon Shimbun Hō* on 22 April 1946, carried an article by KATAYAMA Satoshi, one of the editors of the *Yomiuri Shimbun*. It said in part:

. . . I believe that the cost of producing papers would be about one-third. I think it would be good in the case of Japan to set a limit [for romanization] of from 3 to 5 years.

. . . it is a mistake to say that romanization cannot be carried out unless changes [in style] are made. Unless reform is carried out hand in hand with the adoption of *romaji* it seems to me that the thing will never be accomplished. . . .

If *kanji* is completely lost, feudalism, whose medium is *kanji*, would be eliminated from society—and it was for this reason that reactionary politicians refused stubbornly to accept it.

* * *

. . . the adoption of *romaji* is not a preparation to changing over to a foreign language, though its adoption certainly means the simplification and purification of Japanese.

There is some danger of opposition from the literary men, but there is no reason whatever for opposition, since the social responsibilities of literary men will become more and more important if the people's ways of expression are enriched and literacy heightened among the people. Again, classics can be retained as classics.

*   *   *

In conclusion, it should be said that there may be a certain amount of confusion when romanization is carried out; but what is necessary is to see it put into practice. And since the newspapers cannot very well adopt *romaji* wholesale, I think the thing to do is to have a part set aside as a *romaji* column, and to keep the material written at a high standard and to work toward nothing but *romaji* in the end, in step with the people's acquisition of *romaji*.

The *Ōsaka Mainichi,* 22 April 1946, carried an article, "Kyōto Scholars Favor Romanization of Japanese to Foster Education," which stated in part:

The following comments represent the general opinion of the leading scholars of Kyōto:
(1) Seiichi Mizuno, research scholar of Tōhōbunka Kenkyūsho and a noted savant of Chinese ideography:
"My object in advocating romaji does not mean the abolition of the Japanese language in place of a foreign tongue. I merely favor the romanization of Japanese, as conceived and employed by the people, with the purpose of promoting a more rational system of written Japanese."
(2) Dr. Tatsuo Yatabe, eminent psychologist of Kyōto Imperial University:
"Language must keep in tune with the march of time. Consequently, the medium of Japanese expression must change from an ideographic stage to a phonetic stage in order to follow the latest scientific advancement. The invention of telephone, radio and other scientific devices has evolutionized the world from an eye age to an ear age."
(3) Dr. Hideki Yukawa, internationally known physicist of Kyodai [Kyōto Imperial University]:
"Science demands absolute exactness. Expressions via Chinese characters are too vague with too many phonetic similarities. The progress of ideographic expression has stopped. It is now on a downward trend with countless confusing abbreviated characters coming into existence.
(4) Dr. Hiroshi Suekawa, president of Ritsumeikan University:
"The foolish attempt of Japanese law students to inject artificial

prestige into judicial terminology through the overuse of difficult Chinese characters has resulted in the unpopularity of law expressions. Legal terms should be a part of everyman's pocket vocabulary like in the United States—here is where the romanization of Japanese comes in."

(5) Testsutaro YOSHIKAWA, professor of education of Doshisha University:

"The feudalistic education system of Japan needs to be revolutionized to meet the current situation. I believe that the romanization of Japan will do the trick for the 'brain racking' Chinese characters tending to enslave the students with undue formality are the basis of feudalism."

(6) Hisanosuke IZUI, assistant professor of orthography of Kyōto Imperial University:

"Five years is all that is needed to romanize the Japanese language, once the movement gets under way. The main issue is action— 'don't beat about the bush.' When the movement is in full swing it will be unnecessary to worry about artificial limitation of the language. The people themselves will decide that, in a natural way."

The adoption of a phonetic system would not make Japan illiterate, even temporarily. If *kana* were selected the changes could be made immediately without anyone who can now read being seriously handicapped. If *romaji* were selected the change would have to be made gradually in order to give time for the people who do not now read *romaji* to learn the letters and their sounds. The total population is made up of four groups presenting different problems. These four are: those under 14 years of age and under the control of the compulsory educational system, those who have had some middle school education and have been exposed to foreign language instruction, those who are university or higher school graduates, and those who are adults and have completed the compulsory educational program but have not gone on to higher education.

Approximately 37% of the total population is 14 years of age or below and hence still under the control of the compulsory educational system. The Japan Romanization Society (*Nippon Romaji Kai*) found in teaching 10,000 elementary school students *romaji*, that it required an average of 20 hours to teach sixth-graders to read and write as accurately as, but slightly less rapidly than, they were able to read and write in their traditional *kana-majiri*. Nearly all people who have completed one or more years in the middle school have learned to read *romaji* in conjunction with their study of foreign languages. University graduates and professional people can read *romaji*. The only major group which cannot be presumed to read *romaji* is the adult Japanese population which has left the compulsory educational system but has not continued its education. This is officially estimated by the Ministry of Education to be 47.4% of the total population, or about 85% of the "effective" adults.

The speed and ease of reading would be temporarily lessened, since even those Japanese who now read *romaji* in general cannot read it with the same facility as they do standard Japanese. Members of the *Kanamoji Kai, Nippon Romaji Kai,* and the *Romaji Hirome Kai,* however, maintain that they are able to read their respective forms of phonetic writing as readily as the standard Japanese.

Records need not be disrupted by such a change. Most filing systems make provision for gradually transferring items from the active file to the dead file. Files of correspondence become inactive in a matter of weeks or at most months. The card index in a library would not be seriously disrupted since the only people consulting works in traditional Japanese would be able to read the existing indices. As new works are added to the catalogs, the entries in *romaji* would be indicated by cards written in *romaji*. There are people of all age levels today who read the *kanji*. Such people by normal distribution would be found in all business, professional, commercial, academic, and cultural organizations and would be able to read the documents in traditional Japanese for the next 35 years. Books and papers more than 35 years in print have more historical than current importance.

Reference books need not become unavailable to the Japanese scholar. If the book is written in true vernacular, in the way people speak, it presents no problem at all, since it can be transliterated into either *romaji* or *kana* as easily as an Occidental secretary transcribes shorthand notes into full language. Since most Japanese books have been written in a modified form of the vernacular, with meaning carried in part by the individual *kanji* and not by the context and words alone, it might be necessary to rephrase certain sentences to clarify ambiguities caused by homonyms. Such a process would still be mere transliteration, however, and not translation. None of the problems which appear when one language is translated into another are present. Books which are only infrequently used need not be transliterated but when needed might be consulted in the original by persons competent in the traditional system.

Inefficiency. It is argued that despite statistics to the contrary the people can read unfamiliar *kanji* because they can "figure out the meaning" of unknown characters by their appearance, that the *kanji* really are more efficient because a word can be written by a single character and not by a series of phonetic symbols, and that books written in *kanji* take much less paper than those written in *kana* or *romaji*.

It is true that a person with a thorough knowledge of *kanji* can often guess at the meaning and the pronunciation of an unfamiliar *kanji* by analyzing its appearance. He cannot, of course, write such a *kanji* without looking it up in a dictionary. Guessing the meaning of a strange *kanji* depends upon the ability of the reader to recognize two basic elements: the radical or discernible pattern of strokes which is usually found to the left (*hen*) or at the top (*kammuri*) and which establishes the fundamental category of the meaning, and the modifying factor or *tsukuri* of the character, usually located on the right or lower side, which restricts, classifies, or otherwise narrows the meaning of the *hen* or *kammuri*. The pronunciation is guessed from the *tsukuri* alone, disregarding the *kammuri* or *hen*. However, it is frequently impossible to determine what is the *tsukuri*. Once determined it may itself be mistakenly read. At best such a system is guessing. Not even an educated Japanese can be sure of either the meaning or the reading without looking up the unfamiliar *kanji* in a dictionary. Such a guessing method is comparable to guessing the meaning of an unfamiliar English word, either by context or by recognizing some Latin or Greek root.

The claim for efficiency of *kanji* on the grounds that a word can sometimes be written by a single character is an oversimplification and misleading. It is true that a limited number of Japanese words are represented by a single character, which may be extremely complicated in its own internal construction. However in inflected forms, such as verbs and adjectives, where *kana* are used to indicate the inflection one symbol does not represent the word. Similarly, the majority of nouns are polysyllabic, and more important are polymorphemic, and are hence represented by Chinese compounds (*gōseigo*) with more than one *kanji*.

The claim that the *kanji* are more economical of space and hence saving of paper is equally unsubstantiated. It is true that individual words and individual literary works can be written in a more compressed form in *kanji* than in *romaji*. It is also true that some Japanese has been written in extremely small type, with a consequent saving of paper and increase in difficulty of reading. But in the normal Japanese publication the *romaji* form is no longer and on occasion is actually more saving in space than the traditional Japanese. In W. G. Aston's famous *Grammar of the Japanese Written Language* there are appended facsimiles of various styles of Japanese taken from historical documents and letters, together with a version in Latin letters. The *romaji* versions require half to six sevenths the space required for the original. *Romaji* transliterations of the 12 volumes of the Ministry of Education Reader (*Shōgaku Kokugo Tokuhon*) in use in 1941, and the six volumes of the Ethics (*Jinjo Shōgaku Shūshin-Sho*) required from one third as much to an amount of space just equal to that required by the *kanji* original, when using type sizes in the two writing forms considered appropriate for the various age levels. The typewritten (pica) *romaji* texts of three major SCAP directives required 20 pages while the typewritten *kanamajiri* texts of the same three, with the same margins, required slightly more than 33 pages.

Delay or Postponement. It is argued that even though a shift to a phonetic system is theoretically desirable, it should be delayed; that there should be more study of the problem; and that the style of the language should first be changed.

It is true that continued study might produce a more scientific romanization or *kana* writing. However the practical advantages of adopting a phonetic system immediately quite outweigh the presumed advantages of minor improvements in the system which might ultimately be adopted. The existing systems, while admittedly not perfect, are quite adequate. Slight changes in spelling romanized words would take place in the normal growth of the language regardless of what system is now adopted. The style of written Japanese will change to adapt itself to the phonetic system of writing only when it is widely used in phonetic writing.

Studies on what style should be are of academic interest but will have little effect on the writing of the nation. The practical problems of publication make the immediate the most desirable time to make the change-over. Each year that passes increases the economic and organizational difficulties which must be met if the change is to be made.

Immense numbers of books were destroyed by the air raids and fires in the war. The lack of paper and the destruction of machinery caused a severe shortage of books and delayed the replacement of those destroyed. The old and interim textbooks used in schools in Japan during the Occupation, numbering more than 200 million volumes, will gradually be censored, rewritten, and republished. The books which still are available on the market are badly dated. The importation of foreign books has been resumed in a limited degree after nearly a decade of prohibition. The majority of these, if they are to have any wide circulation, will have to be translated into Japanese. The system of writing into which they are translated will be a vital issue. A great deal of the printing equipment will have to be replaced. Some was destroyed in the air raids and fires; some was worn out. When this equipment is replaced it would be highly desirable to replace it with modern machinery.

The Japanese reading public is starved for new materials. Despite the disastrous economic condition obtaining in the country, the people are buying and reading everything in print. It is inevitable that during the change-over to a phonetic system the people who have acquired reading skill in *kanamajiri* would find the new system more tiring to read. It is advantageous to make the change when the new system would not have too much competition with the old system.

Difficulty of Reading. It is argued that *kana* and *romaji* are very difficult for Japanese people to read, that the reader must pause and think of *kanji* represented by the word before getting the thought, and that it is not precise enough for legal or important documents.

It is true that adults who have read the standard *kanamajiri* for years find that the reading of *romaji* which they have practiced only for a few hours is somewhat slower and more tiring. This is to be expected. Practice will to a considerable degree eliminate this difficulty. Young people and children, however, have been taught *romaji* and read it with great speed and ease. American language officers who censored radio intercepts (taken down in *romaji*) during the second World War read it with great speed and ease. Members of the *Nippon Romaji Kai*, almost the only adult Japanese who have had extended practice in *romaji*, state that they read romanized Japanese as rapidly as traditional Japanese. There is essentially no difference in the speeds with which a Japanese can read *kana* and the traditional *kanamajiri*, though with persons who have not practiced the simpler *kana* form the speed with which the ideas are recognized may be somewhat less.

It is true that people who have read standard *kanamajiri* for years find that they have to read difficult sentences in *romaji* twice or mentally visualize the appropriate *kanji* when first reading *romaji*. This also is to be expected. This disappears rapidly as they gain practice in the new system. People who have never learned *kanji*, or for whom *kanji* are difficult, read *romaji* of course without any mental image of the *kanji*.

It is not true, however, that *romaji* is inexact and that it cannot be used in legal and official papers. It has been used for three quarters of a century on the most important official documents. Treaties, instructions sent to an ambassador abroad, the reports sent back to Japan at critical moments, when they have not been sent in code, have been sent via the international cable and telegraph systems in *romaji*. The records of the Diet, Japan's highest governmental assembly, are recorded in phonetic shorthand based on *kana* or *romaji* and later transcribed to the traditional *kanamajiri*. The most exact writing in any language is that done in scientific reports. *Romaji* has been used for scientific books and papers, has been advocated by some of the leading scientists in Japan, and is currently being used in classroom lectures on scientific subjects by a number of professors. TERADA Torahiko's volume, *Umi no Butsurigaku* ("The Physical Phenomena of Oceans") (Tokyo, Nippon Romazi Sya, 1923); YAMAZAKI Kijūro's book, *Kōtō Sūgaku no Tehodoki* ("An Introduction to Higher Mathematics") (Tokyo, Reizo Kitō, 1934); and IKENO Seiichiro's *Jikken Idengaku* ("Genetics") (Tokyo, Kenkichi Noguchi and the Nippon Romazi Sya, 1927) are concrete evidences that an essentially phonemic notation—in this case *Nihonsiki Romazi*—is adequate in Japanese.

Which Phonetic System Is Best?

All of the proposed phonetic systems are adequate. None is perfect. The choice must be made on the basis of securing the most advantages with the fewest disadvantages. For practical considerations all but three may be ruled out: *kana*, *Nihonsiki Romazi*, and the Hepburn System of *romaji*. It has been one of the unfortunate characteristics of the language simplification movement in Japan that the major objectives have frequently been forgotten in rather undignified quarrels over the minutiae of rival systems. Each of the three named have several minor variations. These three, however, represent basically different approaches to the problem.

Kana. Those who advocate adoption of *kana* point out that *kana* is a Japanese invention. It represents the national spirit. It tends to preserve the national individuality of the Japanese. The *kana* is very easy to read. Everyone who can read Japanese at all can read *kana* since this is the first system taught children in schools. There would be no time lost in making the change-over to a phonetic system since there would be no necessity for re-education. They claim that *kana* would be an easy goal to reach in process of gradual limitation of the *kanji*. There would be no violent change to upset the people.

The advocates of *kana* further claim that *kana* is more efficient. Since the Japanese is an open syllable language, the *kana* syllabary is ideally suited to express it. Writing in *kana* would require fewer letters, fewer strokes on the typewriter. Actually *kana* is not more efficient. It is designed for vertical writing, and horizontal writing, necessary with arabic numerals and mathematical formulae, makes it very cumbersome. Typewriters in order to write the 109 common syllables in Japanese (represented by 49 basic *kana* symbols, 25 with diacritical marks added, and 35 formed by conventional combinations of pairs of the 49 basic signs) must have approximately twice the keys found on international typewriters using Latin letters, and hence become unwieldy and difficult to use by the touch system. In addition they must have a dead-key diacritical mark to give the ° or *seidakuon-ten* (or *han-nigori-ten*), and the ʺ or *dakuon-ten* (or *nigori-ten*), and thus strike twice for 25 of the *kana*. On the Royal typewriter, some experimental models of which were made in the United States for export to Japan, there are 47 *kana* available on a standard size keyboard, with *wi* (ヰ,ゐ) and *we* (ヱ,ゑ) omitted. Since there are no capitals, it has been possible to use the shift key to give 8 *kana* in the upper position, and 9 small-sized *kana* to use in the arbitrary combinations used to represent syllables for which no single symbol among the 49 is assigned. All 4 rows of type must be used.

The opponents of *kana* point out that *kana* is difficult for foreigners to read. It is obviously simpler than *kanji* but it is still something of a barrier between Japan and foreign countries. They state that *kana* would require the use of two typewriters, extra keyboards on linotype, and similar duplication in all schools, business houses, banks, transportation facilities, and other organizations which have contact with foreigners or with foreign languages. The *kana* is looked upon by many Japanese as a childish form of writing, somewhat as adults in Occidental countries look upon handwriting with crude printed letters.

Mention has already been made of the fact that there are insufficient symbols in the *kana* syllabary to represent the 109 syllables of the language. It is probable that when the *kana* were invented they were adequate for the sounds of the language as then spoken. In the more than a millennium that has elapsed, however, new sounds have been added and a device for representing them had to be adopted. Tradition has dictated certain formal combinations of the basic symbols that are quite unphonetic and very troublesome for both Japanese and foreign readers. The example of *shō* (ショウ) is often given. It can be written in *kana* as *se-fu* (セフ), as *shi-ya-u* (シヤウ), as *shi-ya-fu* (シヤフ), as *shi-yo-fu* (ショフ), and in several other ways.

Nihonsiki Romazi. Those who advocate the *Nihonsiki Romazi* claim that it preserves the regularity in the paradigms or tables of verb conjugations. Although it is a highly controversial point, the opponents of *Nihonsiki Romazi* hold that actually the verbs are not absolutely regularly conjugated. A system of national orthography can adopt nonphonetic symbols at will. The *Nihonsiki Romazi* uses nonphonetic, but it is claimed phonemic, symbols to secure regularity in the spelling of its paradigms. In lay language the *Nihonsiki Romazi* adopts the convention that the letters *h, t, s, z* before certain vowels shall take on changed phonetic values which in the Hepburn System are indicated by conventional English letter combinations.

The *Nihonsiki Romazi* also preserves the traditional organization of the "fifty sound" (*gojū-on*) table of *kana*. The *gojū-on* table has played an important part in Japanese study of their own grammar. It is, however, nothing more than a convenient mnemonic device in which the 47 fundamental vowel and unvoiced consonant plus vowel syllables of Japanese taken from the 109 total syllables, are arranged in a geometric pattern in the order of the vowels (*a-i-u-e-o*). The claim that it is derived from the open-syllable character of ancient Japanese is open to question.

It is further claimed that *Nihonsiki Romazi* is in fact a broad phonetic notation of Japanese. This is based on two studies. The first is an investigation by TAGUTI Riyūsaburō of the Tokyo Institute of Physical and Chemical Research reported by Professor A. TANAKADATE in the *Proceedings* of the Second International Congress of Phonetic Sciences in London, 1935, and presented in detail in *Rikagaku Kenkyūjo Ihō* ("Bulletin of the Institute of Physical and Chemical Research"), Vol. XII, No. 8, August 1933 and Vol. XIV, No. 4, April 1935. His full investigation of the phonemes of Japanese is presented in the *Nippon Gakuzyutu-Kyōkai Hōkoku* ("Reports of the Japan Science Society") for October 1935, December 1936, December 1937, and September 1938. In this investigation, Japanese words spelled in *Nihonsiki Romazi* were read backward, recorded on sound film, and played in reverse. Because they came out as normal Japanese words it was concluded that the notation system was scientific in that it had one symbol standing for one phoneme. The claim that the system is a broad phonetic notation is also based on a study that indicates that in certain localities in Japan each of the sounds represented by the syllables which are points of controversy with advocates of the Hepburn System are in fact used in the colloquial speech.

Nihonsiki Romazi has, of course, all the mechanical advantages of any system written in roman letters.

Opponents of *Nihonsiki Romazi* charge that it is really a syllabary, a sort of *kana* written with Roman letters, and hence has all the linguistic disadvantages of a syllabary. This objection is based on two facts: the advocates of the system have taught it with the letter combinations linked as a syllabary and not separated as an alphabet, and the spelling has deviated from accepted English phonetic notation in order to retain an apparent regularity in the *gojū-on* table of *kana*. They add that *Nihonsiki Romazi* is not as phonetic as the Hepburn System. It is difficult for foreigners, at least English-speaking people, to read without serious mispronunciation. It is confusing to Japanese students of foreign languages, especially of English, which is the almost universal choice. This objection is largely based on confusion arising from six syllables *fu, chi, shi, tsu, sha*, and *ji* which are rendered respectively as *hu, ti, si, tu, sya*, and *zi*.

Nihonsiki	*Hepburn*
Sintō	Shintō
Huzi-san	Fuji-san
Zinrikisya	Jinrikisha
Titibu	Chichibu
Tyōsen	Chōsen

The full list of differences in the two basic systems are:

Nihonsiki:
    hu,| ti,   tu, | si, | zi,| sya, syu, syo,| tya, tyu, tyo, | zya, zyu,| zyo.|
Hepburn:
    fu, | chi, tsu,| shi,| ji, | sha, shu, sho,| cha, chu, cho,| ja,   ju, | jo. |

The Hepburn System of Romaji. Advocates of the Hepburn System of *romaji* (*Hebonshiki Romaji;* or in a revised form *Hyōjunshiki Romaji*) claim that it is the oldest (based on English spelling) and most widely used romanization of Japanese. It has been used since its invention in 1867 by Dr. J. C. HEPBURN. The Hepburn System is relatively phonetic. It is easily read by foreigners, especially those with knowledge of English. Its use aids Japanese students in acquiring English to the extent of eliminating the confusing dual use of certain letters. It reduces to a minimum the cultural barrier between Japan and Occidental nations imposed by the Japanese language. There exists in the Hepburn System a considerable body of literature, though probably no greater than in the *Nihonsiki*, including the maps of the Occupation Forces, standard bilingual dictionaries, *romaji* references in foreign books, and practically all official writings prior to the official adoption of the *Nihonsiki Romazi* on 21 September 1937.

The advocates of the Hepburn System say that it is not inseparably linked with the *gojū-on* table. This claim is based on two facts: the advocates of the system have taught it as an alphabet and not as a *kana* written in inseparably linked pairs of Latin letters, and it does not deviate from English phonetic spelling in order to produce the appearance of regularity in the *gojū-on* table and paradigms.

The Hepburn System has, of course, all the mechanical advantages of any system written in Roman letters.

The major criticisms of the Hepburn System are that it is not "national" but is based on English orthography, and that it does not have regular paradigms. Advocates of the system reply that English is the nearest to an international language, and that the Japanese language itself does not have regular paradigms. They claim that the Hepburn System accurately represents the points of phonetic irregularity and that *Nihonsiki Romazi* produces the appearance of regularity in the written form by diverging from a phonetic transcription of the spoken language.

It is evident that the differences which exist between the two major types of *romaji* are slight compared with those between any alphabet system and the syllabary *kana*. Dr. Harold E. PALMER, internationally famous English phonetician and formerly linguistic adviser to the Japanese Ministry of Education, said in his volume, *The Principles of Romanization—with Special Reference to the Romanization of Japanese* (Tokyo, Maruzen Co., Ltd., 1930):

1. The Hepburnian system of Japanese Romanization is all that is required by foreigners and those who cater for their needs. It is long established, is embodied in numerous dictionaries almost without exception. It is in conformity with all the desiderata of a practical transliteration and, apart from details (such as the obligatory mark of vowel-length), can hardly be bettered.

2. The *Nihonshiki*, or *Japanese System*, of Romanization is in conformity with all the desiderata of a national orthography, and apart from details (such as *o* for *wo*) can hardly be bettered.

3. The alphabet of the International Phonetic Association with the addition of a few symbols . . . will provide the broadest or the narrowest notation that can be required by the most exacting of phoneticians.

The view of most students of the question, other than those whose advocacy of some particular form of linguistic revision is dictated by emotion or vested interests, is ably stated although not subscribed to by Dr. A. TANAKADATE, of Tokyo Imperial University, in his pamphlet, "Japanese Writing and the Romazi Movement" (London, Eastern Press, Ltd., 1920):

It is thought by many that the question of orthography is but of small importance compared with the outstanding national burden of the present system of writing, and that the Romanizers should rather sacrifice their personal views and reconcile themselves to any one of the systems now in use in adopting the universal method of writing, leaving small differences in the future to be improved and settled.

Which Change-Over Procedure Is the Best?

There have been three basically different methods of change-over from the traditional *kanamajiri* to *romaji* advocated: immediate adoption, gradual change in the entire literature as a unit, and gradual change with the new system applied to various portions of the literature at progressive intervals depending upon the age of the readers and the difficulty of the subject matter.

Those who advocate immediate change with the new system applied to all parts of the language simultaneously argue that the change-over period would hold disruption to a minimum; that only by making a complete break with past tradition quickly is it possible to ensure that there will not be backsliding, defection, and failure to comply; and that there is no linguistic reason for delay.

Opponents argue that immediate adoption would require that the change be made by fiat; that such a change would be distasteful to the people; that no Japanese agency is strong enough to make and enforce such a decree; that time is required in which to change the style of written Japanese to enable it to avoid homonymic ambiguities by context; and that the degree of disruption would be unnecessarily high.

Those who advocate gradual change with adoption of the new system delayed until the entire existing language had been progressively simplified by gradual reduction in the number of *kanji* used in *kanamajiri* and simplification of style, argue that the disruption during the change-over would be lessened although the period of change would be longer; that time is required to develop writers in the new writing system; that time is required to change the style of written Japanese to enable it to avoid homonymic ambiguities by context; that time is required to build up a volume of literature in the new system; that such a gradual change would be more acceptable to the people; and that it would not require change by fiat but by the action of "the people."

It is argued by opponents to this plan that for large areas of the language (mathematics, science, simple children's stories, light fiction, etc.) there is no reason for delay; that delay encourages backsliding, defection, and failure to comply; and that some central authority would have to bring to a focus the will of "the people" by setting a goal and enforcing compliance.

Those who advocate gradual change with the new system progressively adopted at various levels of difficulty and content in the literature argue that the disruption in the change-over would be held to a minimum; that there would be examples of the new system in the constant daily use, tending to discourage backsliding and encourage compliance; that a minimum amount of forced compliance by superior authority would be needed because the people would experience the benefits of the new system during the change-over; that time would be allowed for the development of new literary styles in difficult Japanese without delaying the adoption of the new system in those subject-matter areas in which no linguistic problems exist; that time would be provided for the development of writers in the new system and of a body of literature in the new system; that experience in writing in the fields of children's stories, popular literature, mathematics, science, and commercial writing, would give experience necessary for the development of serious literature, legal writing, social studies, etc.; and that a reading public in the new system would be developed. These advocates point out that every six years the compulsory educational system graduates approximately 14 million students or approximately one quarter of the adult population. One half the total population of Japan at any time is 20 years of age or less, hence is in school or has been graduated from the compulsory system within six years.

Opponents argue that with all its attractive features such a program would still require as a minimum that some central authority bring to a focus the will of the people by setting a goal, by setting up a time schedule, and by enforcing compliance until a sufficiently large reading public in the new system had been developed to support the movement without further aid.

Phonemic Phalanxes

It is customary for military staffs preparing a battle plan to digest the complicated and extensive technical intelligence upon which that plan is based, so that the commanding officer can see at a glance the essential findings. Perhaps in preparing a strategy for the battle for the Japanese mind a similar procedure may prove profitable.

What were the problems of the written language? They were three. Is the present Japanese writing system an obstacle to the development of democratic tendencies among the people? Is there available a practical and effective simplification? How shall the change-over to the proposed system be accomplished?

The present writing system (*kanamajiri*) is unsatisfactory and does constitute a barrier to the democratization of Japan. It is excessively difficult. It makes most information only partially accessible to the masses of the people. It requires a disproportionate amount of school time. It tends to perpetuate the highly stratified social structure. It makes difficult the extension of literacy. It constitutes a barrier to the efficient rehabilitation of Japan. It makes modern business efficiency difficult if not impossible. It makes the development of a scientific literature unnecessarily difficult. It constitutes a barrier to international understanding and amity. It makes the Japanese acquisition of foreign languages difficult. It makes Japanese relatively inaccessible to Occidentals.

Of the various available methods of simplification of the writing system, the evidence is overwhelmingly in favor of some form of a phonetic system. Such a system appears to offer the only solution to the problem which is practical, effective, and acceptable. Of the available phonetic systems, some form of romanized Japanese appears to offer distinct advantages over all others. While evidence in favor of *romaji* over *kana* is not as overwhelming as was the evidence of a phonetic system over an ideographic one, still it is sufficient to warrant a clear-cut decision in favor of romanization. Of the available systems of romanization, there appears to be little choice between those based on the Hepburn System and those based on the Japan System. The Hepburn appears to have some advantages of a practical nature and the Japan System appears to have some advantages of a linguistic nature. Either is acceptable. Both are practical. The evidence in favor of the Hepburn System appears sufficient to warrant an expression of preference, though not a clear-cut decision in favor of its adoption.

Of the various possible methods of accomplishing the adoption of *romaji* as the official writing system of Japan, a gradual change-over from the traditional system through a well-co-ordinated program of writing, transliterating, publicity, public relations, publishing, education, incentives, professional agreements, and official sanction appears to offer the greatest efficiency and to entail the least disruption. A period of five years in which to reach the goal of complete romanization appears to be a reasonable compromise between the disruption of too rapid and the stagnation of too leisurely an adoption. Enforced compliance with the provisions of the plan and governmental financial subsidy of the publishing industry during the period of change-over appear to be necessary provisions.

Of the various time schedules possible, a program of change-over in which the goal of complete romanization is attained at varying intervals depending upon the difficulties of style and content in each of the various kinds and levels of literature appears to have distinct advantages. Successive stages of *kanji* limitation appear to be desirable in the more erudite levels of literature to assist in style changes and the development of writers and a reading public. A rapid and complete change to *romaji* in elementary schools and secondary schools appears highly desirable to ensure the rapid production of a population mass which is literate but which is unable to read in the traditional *kanamajiri*, as an insurance against defection and backsliding in the program.

In any battle plan there must be a final choice of alternatives. This is the "sound military decision" of strategy. In the problem of the written language the Japanese themselves must make this final election. But if they be thoughtful, they can only arrive at one solution. Japan has available against the attrition of ignorance and the encroachment of nationalistic conservatism one of the most subtle and yet powerful allies of democracy—a phonemic writing system.

V

"GIVE US THE TOOLS . . ."

The Problem of Implementation

FULL and equal educational opportunities for all, freedom of research and the pursuit of objective truth, freedom of communication and the exchange of ideas—these, in the setting of a democratic social structure and a representative government, are the irreducible minimum of an acceptable educational philosophy for the new Japan. But these goals of the educational process will be vitiated unless constant vigilance is exercised to protect human rights and unless a conscious and continuing effort is exerted to apply these principles to the practical elements of the educational system. An ideal must be protected and it must be practiced if it is to survive.

Two basic reforms have been suggested as offering a bulwark against the erosion of conservatism, traditionalism, and nationalism. These are the establishment of a decentralized administrative structure less susceptible to the manipulation of a minority group, and the adoption of a writing system which would make possible facile communication and the development of an intelligent and informed electorate. The greatest defense of democracy against the inroads of totalitarianism is the broad dissemination of knowledge and the decentralization of governmental responsibilities.

But in the extension of these defenses against the resurgence of an unacceptable ideology there must also be a positive contribution of the democratic process to the educational system. The democratic ideal must be actively practiced in the daily operation of the school system, in the relationships between officials, teachers, and students, in the construction of curricula, and in the presentation of material. Democracy for the individual instructor must be removed from the high level of political theory and be exercised in the personal level of the individual class period. What democracy in education is to be in the new Japan will be determined by the hundreds of millions of practical applications at the lowest administrative and scholastic levels. Shall a student be permitted to attack the existing government during a class in a tax-supported school? Shall a teacher be removed from his teaching position without the opportunity to present a defense before an impartial board? Shall a teacher be forced to use only an official textbook or shall he be permitted to choose for himself his teaching aids?

The problem of implementation, by its inherent nature, reaches down into the trivia of the educational process. Democracy is an attitude of mind which does not force upon others in society a course of action which they are not freely willing to accept. This attitude of mind becomes the unconscious catalyst in the most insignificant actions of the teacher—unimportant separately but decisive in the aggregate. It is the unthinking conformity to a code of conduct and of intellectual integrity that, for example, denies a preferential position to a kindergarten child standing in line to have his coat put on, that permits the elementary pupils to choose for themselves the one to empty the wastebaskets, or that presents a minority opinion with the majority in a controversial report.

It would be very easy to be misled into an exhaustive, and exhausting, recital of these minutiae. Such a recital would not only be of dubious value but would in principle be incompatible with the educational philosophy advanced in this volume. Democracy is in its essence self-direction. Neither this present study nor any other should attempt to formulate for the teacher an "approved" reaction to every minor situation with which he will be confronted. This is not a traditional Japanese teachers' manual which details even the inflection to be used in reading key words. Conditions change and new situations arise, and it is a flexibility of mind and an inner resourcefulness that should be encouraged in the teacher to meet these changes. And so only five of the elements of the educational system will be considered: students, teachers, curriculum, method, and textbooks. And in each of these only a single fundamental problem will be analyzed.

Students. To determine to what extent and in what manner students in the past have been denied the civil liberties and equality of educational opportunity, and to decide how the abuses may be eliminated and a reasonable realization of these rights be assured.

Teachers. To determine what was wrong in the selection, training, supervision, and orientation of teachers in the past; and to decide how an adequate number of well-trained teachers, politically and professionally acceptable both to the Japanese and to the Occupying Powers, may be procured.

Method. To determine to what extent and in what manner the methods of teaching contributed to the manipulation of the educational process in the past, and to decide what reforms would make such control less likely to occur.

Curriculum. To determine how Japan's traditional curriculum was made a propaganda tool, and to decide what reforms must be instituted to make these abuses in the future difficult or impossible.

Textbooks. To determine to what extent and in what manner the textbooks were used as propaganda instruments in the past, and in what ways the preparation and publication contributed to this misuse; and to decide what reforms would make such manipulation by a minority group in the future difficult or impossible.

The new *Constitution* promulgated on 3 November 1946 and effective on and following 3 May 1947 devotes an entire section, Chapter III, to the rights and duties of the people. In the 31 articles of this chapter a pattern of democratic rights equal to and in some ways superior to those accorded the peoples of Great Britain and the United States are guaranteed the people. In addition to property rights, rights to redress under the law, rights to access to the courts, rights to protection from unlawful detention or police acts, and similar legal guarantees, there are a number which bear directly upon the educational process. Rearranged in an order which more clearly presents the new philosophy of freedom of education, these pertinent articles are quoted:

Art XXIII Academic freedom is guaranteed.

Art XXVI All people shall have the right to receive an equal education correspondent to their ability, as provided by law. All people shall be obligated to have all boys and girls under their protection receive ordinary education as provided for by law. Such compulsory education shall be free.

Art XIX Freedom of thought and conscience shall not be violated.

Art XXI Freedom of assembly and association as well as speech, press, and all other forms of expression are guaranteed. No censorship shall be maintained, nor shall the secrecy of any means of communication be violated.

Art XX   Freedom of religion is guaranteed to all. No religious organization shall receive any privileges from the State, nor exercise any political authority. No person shall be compelled to take part in any religious act, celebration, rite or practice. The State and its organs shall refrain from religious education or any other religious activity.

Art XIII   All of the people shall be respected as individuals. Their right to life, liberty, and the pursuit of happiness shall, to the extent that it does not interfere with the public welfare, be the supreme consideration in legislation and in other governmental affairs.

Art XIV   All of the people are equal under the law and there shall be no discrimination in political, economic or social relations because of race, creed, sex, social status or family origin. Peers and peerage shall not be recognized. No privilege shall accompany any award of honor, decoration or any distinction, nor shall any such award be valid beyond the lifetime of the individual who now holds or hereafter may receive it.

Art XVIII   No person shall be held in bondage of any kind. Involuntary servitude, except as punishment for crime, is prohibited.

Art XXIV   Marriage shall be based only on the mutual consent of both sexes and it shall be maintained through mutual cooperation with the equal rights of husband and wife as a basis. With regard to choice of spouse, property rights, inheritance, choice of domicile, divorce and other matters pertaining to marriage and the family, laws shall be enacted from the standpoint of individual dignity and the essential equality of the sexes.

Art XXVII   . . . Children shall not be exploited.

Art XV   . . . Universal adult suffrage is guaranteed with regard to the election of public officials. . . .

Art XXVIII   The right of workers to organize and to bargain and act collectively is guaranteed.

Within the frame of reference of these constitutional guarantees, what shall be the solution to the problems of implementation?

The Students—Equality of Educational Opportunity

The guarantee of equality of educational opportunity which is established in the new Japan by Article XXVI of the *Constitution* is hardly a new concept. It was basic to the compulsory educational laws passed in 1872. Yet it would be naïve indeed to advance the thesis that equality of opportunity had actually existed. The guarantee had been voided by a pattern of discrimination.

At a staff meeting held in the Education Sub-Section (later Division) of the Civil Information and Education Section (CI&E) of SCAP on 15 November 1945 study of the effect of discrimination on the school system was initiated. The purpose of this study was in part to check upon the degree to which the Japanese educational authorities had complied with the provisions of the SCAP Directive of 4 October 1945 on "Removal of Restrictions on Political, Civil, and Religious Liberties" and the SCAP Educational Directive of 22 October 1945 on "Administration of the Educational System of Japan." It was also in part to lay the groundwork for a systematic attack on discrimination in all elements of the educational system. Eight types of discrimination were examined: those against race, nationality, creed, sex, social position, wealth, political belief, and the handicapped. Of these eight areas in which discrimination was observed or could be established by historical evidence, only two appeared to be currently important either in extent or degree. These were discrimination against sex and political belief. The remainder, although some of them were given considerable publicity by the Headquarters of the Occupation Forces, possibly for political reasons, did not appear serious to the impartial foreign observer.

Race. The only racial discrimination, other than the transient wartime antipathies toward Occidentals, which could be established was that leveled against the *Ainu*, the apparently Caucasian aborigines of Hokkaido, whose traditional life is familiar to the English reader through Dr. John BATCHELOR's definitive volume, *Ainu Life and Lore: Echoes of a Departing Race* (Tokyo, Kyobunkwan, 1927). Yet even this area of discrimination was only established in the vaguest of terms, a sort of general recognition on the part of the Japanese that the *Ainu* were in some way "different." A personal investigation of the few remaining villages of these people led officers from the Education Division to the conclusion that the *Ainu* were almost completely absorbed into Japanese life, both by cultural assimilation and by miscegenation. Few of the *Ainu* even knew of the phonetic transcription of their language devised by Dr. BATCHELOR, and when questioned on relatively simple matters pertinent to the race, the village fathers, unable to supply the information, referred the investigators to the

Chief, Miyamoto Inosuke of Shiraoi Mura, near Noboribetsu, Hokkaido, and the Chief referred them to Dr. Batchelor's book for a final answer. Japanese is spoken by all, and even in family conversations Japanese with a considerable preponderance of *Ainu* loan words is commonly used. The children are educated in Japanese village schools, use official Japanese textbooks, are taught by Japanese teachers, and study unsegregated from Japanese children of the same neighborhood. Three full-blooded *Ainu* stood for election from their home districts in the 1946 elections, and Samo Kikuzō, a 53-year-old *Ainu* from Toyoura Mura, Hokkaido, relinquished his claim to a seat in the Lower House of the Diet in 1947 to run for election as Governor of Hokkaido and obtained a startling 11,286 votes although he was not elected.

Creed and Nationality. Much has been written in the foreign press about discriminations on the basis of creed and nationality. When traced to their sources these accusations are generally found to have originated either in commercial circles which resented the economic controls exercised by the Japanese Government over foreign business interests, or among missionaries who resented Japanese control of or active opposition to their educational and ecclesiastical labors. Only the latter source is pertinent.

The opposition to the spread of Christianity, even though freedom of religion was presumably guaranteed by Article XXVIII of the old *Constitution* and is specifically guaranteed by Article XX of the new *Constitution*, has an understandable historical origin in the expulsion of the Catholic orders following Toyotomi Hideyoshi's famous edict of 25 July 1587. This opposition became open and official following the rise of the militarist clique to power in the middle 1930's. Westernism, individualism, Occidental education, and Christianity have been considered an inseparable unity and identified in the minds of the Japanese nationalist with a direct attack on the *kokutai* or "national entity." It is true that during the war there were undeniable, but probably infrequent, acts of persecution against some Christians. A few leading Christian educators were removed but some of the most outstanding Christian educators served unmolested during the entire duration of the war. Christian services were not prohibited even during the war, though some Christian ministers, usually foreign, were confined. On the other hand some sects were quite sincere in their claim that Japanese educational laws made a violation of their freedom of conscience inevitable. The Seventh Day Adventists, for example, are a prominent and militant sect in Japan whose members brought considerable pressure on Headquarters of the Occupation Forces to compel the Japanese to prohibit the holding of school on Saturday, their day of rest. They held that this conflict of law and dogma was religious oppression and that the Japanese officials were guilty of religious intolerance. It is not improbable that an equal intolerance exists in certain parts of the United States against some of the beliefs which have been unacceptable to and have become the object of attack by the Japanese authorities. Whatever the merits of foreign accusations of Japanese religious persecution, and almost certainly they have been grossly exaggerated, this element of discrimination has been officially outlawed. Few, if any, Japanese students were barred from securing an adequate education in public institutions because of their personal religious beliefs.

Educational discrimination, however, cannot be so summarily dismissed. Complaints against such discrimination are mainly directed against two controls exercised by the Japanese Government: all private schools, including mission and church-supported institutions, were required to offer the official curriculum; and the educational and administrative direction of foreign-supported educational institutions immediately before the war had to be exercised by Japanese nationals rather than by foreign residents. Both of these requirements, although admittedly arising from a spirit of nationalism, are familiar controls in the majority of the Allied Powers where a centralized educational system and an official curriculum obtain—in virtually every Latin-American nation, for example. Additional subjects, in the form of a sort of enriched curriculum, have always been permitted in non-tax-supported schools, but the complaint of the private school heads has been that the official curriculum was so extensive that no time was left for extra studies when that had been complied with.

A most exhaustive investigation of discrimination against private schools, including the translation of every official order directed to such schools in the 50 years prior to the Occupation, failed to reveal any serious breach of civil and religious freedom with the exception of the well-known Ministry of Education Order No. 12 issued in 1899, which by interpretation in subsequent legal commentaries was held to prohibit the teaching of religion in both public and private schools. A little bit difficult to reconcile with this official position was the fact, amply documented, that some private schools did hold daily religious services up until the outbreak of the war with the United States. On 15 October 1945 the Ministry of Education issued Order No. 210, appending Order No. 8 in which private institutions were granted liberty to conduct religious services aside from the official curriculum specified by law.

The greatest discrimination, however, was the indirect one of discrediting the graduates of private schools and for all practical purposes of barring them from the desirable official appointments. In part it must be conceded that this attitude was justified by the very low quality of some of the private schools, operated admittedly for profit. But it was not justified in the case of many very excellent schools which were providing a highly necessary supplement to the official schools. It must also be conceded that this unfortunate discrimination, based not on official censure but on widespread public attitude, operated with equal inequity against the less popular Imperial universities and boys' higher schools, both official institutions. The impartial investigator noted, however, that where private, mission, and foreign schools had demonstrated by the excellence of their offerings and the proficiency of their graduates that they were really worthy of respect, these schools were accorded the same respect as the best of official institutions. Among universities, *Keio Daigaku, Waseda Daigaku,* and *Doshisha Daigaku;* among private Japanese progressive schools, *Seijō Gakuen, Seikei Gakuen, Jiyū Gakuen,* and the *Tamagawa Gakuen;* among mission schools the *Kansai Gakuin* and *Aoyama Gakuin;* and among women's colleges, *Tsuda College* and *Christian Women's College* are universally recognized in Japan to be of first quality and in some respects superior to official schools.

Social Position. Two extremes of the social scale have intrigued foreigners and attracted the scrutiny of the Occupation Forces. These are the *eta,* the traditional outcasts of Japan, and the *kazoku,* or peers.

The *eta* have been the subject of a considerable literature and are best known to Occidental students by the monograph, "An Inquiry Concerning the Origin, Development, and Present Situation of the Eta in Relation to the History of Social Classes in

Japan," by NINOMIYA Shigeaki, published in the *Transactions of the Asiatic Society of Japan*, Vol. X, Second Series, December 1933. Three theories of the origin of this social group have some currency: the theory that they are descendants of some foreign immigrants, probably from the Philippines or from Korea; the theory that they are descendants of some aboriginal tribe in Japan, either the *Orokko* who antedated the *Yamato* tribes from which the "Japanese" stem or else from a lost tribe of Hebrews who were supposed to have been the *Hafuri* tribe once located in the village of *Hōra* in Nara Prefecture; and the theory that they are descendants of the *etori*, an ancient class of people who killed animals to feed the hawks and dogs of the Court. This latter theory, most vigorously advanced by Dr. KITA Teikichi, is the most generally accepted. It holds that in addition to the *etori* or *tosha* (slayers of animals), four other groups were despised: *kawara-mono* (people of the river bank), *kawazaiku-nin* (leather workers), *ukarebito* (vagabonds), and persons without identity, including disgraced *samurai* or warriors who had not committed ritualistic suicide in expiation. The fact that this class of people have for over a thousand years been predominantly employed in menial and despised tasks such as scavengers, butchers, tanners, and undertakers lends credence to this theory. There is historical proof that the modern *eta* descends from the *tomobe-zakko* (artisan slaves), who came to be despised after the introduction of Buddhism and the prohibition on the killing of cattle and horses in 676. During the wars of anarchy before the Tokugawa Shogunate was established in 1603 the *eta* spread to all parts of Japan, chiefly as workers in leather. During the Tokugawa era (1603–1868) they were linked with the *hinin* (nonhumans) as the lowest social class, known as the *semmin* (despised people), lived as vagrants or were segregated into special villages, were permitted to engage only in certain menial tasks, were forbidden to marry outside their class, and were made the object of fantastic superstitions designed to prove them nonhumans.

The spirit of reform which accompanied and in part caused the passing of the Tokugawa Shogunate brought powerful agitation to abolish the discrimination against the *eta-hinin* and to grant them equal treatment with the *heimin* (ordinary people). The matter was brought to a head in 1869 when the problem of resurveying the land and standardizing the *ri*, a Japanese linear measurement today equal to 3.927 kilometers, was under consideration. Should the *eta* villages, known as *Tokushu Buraku* (Special Communities), be included in the computation of the distances? By a vote of 175 to 26 the *Kōgisho*, or assembly of representatives of the feudatories, voted to investigate and settle the whole question of the *eta* before considering the *ri*. On 28 August 1871 by its 61st decree the *Dajōkan* (Council of State) of the Meiji government proclaimed the emancipation of the *eta-hinin*.

But laws do not change public opinion and folk ways, at least not rapidly. By the turn of the century discrimination was still so little removed that a series of organizations were formed to sponsor equality of the *eta*, the most important of which was the *Dai Nippon Dōbō Yuwa Kai* (Japan Reconciliation Society). The Russo-Japanese War effectively stopped social agitation and the period until the close of the first World War was marked by little more than an increasing expression in favor of equalization appearing in the nation's journals. On 3 March 1922 in Kyoto there was held the First National Convention of *Suihei-sha* (Equality Association) marking the beginning of the *Suihei Undō* (water level, i.e., equality, movement). This organization adopted as its policy a militant program of direct action, freedom to choose their own occupations, and a linking of the movement with certain of the then radical political groups, unions, and communist organizations. Among the elements of their direct action was the policy of *tettei-teki kyūdan* (thoroughgoing censure), which led them to violent attacks, both propaganda and physical, against any person who allegedly had discriminated against the *eta*. By 1925 a radical faction in the movement, the *Zenkoku Suihei-sha Seinen Dōmei* (National Equality Association Youths' Union), was in power and had closely identified the *Suihei Undō* with the communist class struggle. It inevitably suffered the same police suppression, including the dispersal of the Seventh National Convention to have been held in May 1928, as did the *Nippon Kyōsan Tō* (Japan Communist party).

A careful scrutiny of the Japanese regulations and laws conducted by Headquarters of SCAP during the first year of the Occupation failed to reveal any official discrimination. There are instances of *eta* holding the most influential professional and political positions, though it must be admitted that few if any care

to make public their *eta* origin. That there has been some discrimination is revealed by such documents as Order No. 22 of
the Bureau of Social Education, 30 October 1932, directing the
heads of all schools to make a definite effort to teach "a feeling of
mutual respect," and Ministry of Education Order No. 24 of 29
August 1935 which condemns "an evil practice of inequality
among the Japanese which does grave injury to the harmonious
co-operation of the whole nation." Bureau of Social Education
Orders No. 37 and 38 of 4 December 1945 called a national meeting of prefectural officials and of the directors of key elementary,
youth, secondary, and normal schools to participate in a short
course of lectures on "harmonious co-operation" and "concilia-
tion education," and to arrange discussion groups in the separate
schools on the following topic: "Importance of arousing the people of outcast communities to raise their social status themselves
and of making them start their life afresh on an equal footing with
the rest of the nation."

But what discrimination exists is a social discrimination rather
than an official one. The facts are difficult to obtain, since even the
name *eta* is taboo and is today replaced by an imposing array of
euphemisms. Because *eta* are in fact unrecognizable except by
their poverty, residence, and professions, even their numbers are a
mystery. The 1,300,000 officially estimated by a number of
bureaus between 1920 and 1930 is less than half the number
claimed by the *Suihei-sha*, yet even this 2% of the total population then in Japan is meaningless. In the large cities where anonymity is possible the *eta* are absorbed and undetectable. In small
villages and rural areas there is still an undeniable public antipathy.
The people of Japan as a whole appear to look upon the *eta* with
sympathy but are unwilling to accept them when their origin is
known. Educationally there is no apparent discrimination but socially there is no open miscegenation.

The peers (*kazoku*) of Japan were an almost inevitable target
for an American Army bent on democratic missionary work. The
average officer with a background of service at Fort Dix, Fort
Sheridan, Fort Riley, and Fort Ord, looked with a deep suspicion
upon "all these Barons and Marquises and Court Rank and Orders
and things." His own position, standing two paces to the rear and
asking permission to speak or to leave a room when in the presence
of a superior, did not seem incongruous. The Japanese, however,

appear to have been equally suspicious, or compliant, for Article
XIV of the new *Constitution* prohibits peerage and denies the inheritance of honors, decorations, and distinctions. Frequent mention of two Japanese schools appeared in every pre-Occupation
study of Japanese education and became the focus of this zeal to
destroy all vestiges of a hereditary peerage. These were the Peers'
School and the Peeresses' School. The Occupation authorities concerned with education arrived prepared to stamp out some slimy
perversion of the people's rights, some arrogant militaristic tool
of the Imperial Institution, and were inclined to feel foolish when
a thorough investigation proved that these two schools not only
were innocuous but were among the most democratic and progressive schools in Japan.

The Peers' School (*gakushū-in*) was founded in Kyoto in 1847
for the purpose of educating Court officials but when the Court
was moved to Tokyo at the time of the Meiji Restoration the
school was temporarily closed and then reopened at Kanda,
Tokyo, in 1877 by the peers who contributed to its expense. It
was later transferred to the Ministry of the Imperial Household
(*Kunaishō*) and at the time of investigation, November 1945, was
receiving as income from the funds of the Imperial Household only
the amount of its annual deficit, 11% of its total running expenses
in 1945. The remainder of the expense of the school was met by
tuition fees and income from endowment, a fund originally subscribed to by the peers.

Almost equally surprising to the investigators was the fact that
only 32% of the students were peers, the remaining 68% being
commoners. With the exception of the provision that all princes
of the Imperial Blood should enter the school (actually only 9
students, including Korean princes, out of a total enrollment of
892, or approximately 1%) all students were admitted on the
basis of open competition. If the children of peers received some
advantage over commoners because of better prior education or
more ample economic resources with which to pay the tuition
fees, the Peers' School appeared to be no more antipathetic to
educational equality of opportunity than any other private school.
The curriculum meets all requirements of the Ministry of Education for public schools and in addition presents certain cultural courses, such as excellent work in English. Former Occidental teachers employed in the school and later serving as officers

in the Occupational Forces testified that until the outbreak of the second World War there was a definite antimilitaristic attitude evident among the students and no evidence of political interest other than a conservatism and desire to maintain the status quo. Even the translation of the name, *Gakushū-in*, as "Peers' School," upon investigation proved to have been misleading. The name, meaning literally "Hall of Learning," was derived from the Chinese ideographs in a passage in Chapter 1, Book 1 of the *Analects* of Confucius, in which the Master is reported to have said, "Is it not pleasant to learn with a constant perseverance and application?" The English public school is not for the public, Duke University is not a university for dukes, and the Peers' School is not exclusively for the children of peers. *Shiranu ga hotoke* (Ah! the sweet bliss of ignorance)!

The Peeresses' School (*Joshi-Gakushū-in*) was likewise found to be innocuous. It was founded in 1885 under the name of *Kazoku Jogakkō* and in 1906 was made a part of the Peers' School. In 1918 it was separated from the *Gakushū-in* and renamed the *Joshi-Gakushū-in*. Originally situated in Akasakaku, Tokyo, its buildings were burned in the air raid of 25 May 1945 and it was temporarily removed to emergency buildings in Toshimaku, and Koishigawaku, Tokyo, and to two schools for evacuated children in Kanomura, Tochigi Prefecture, and Shiobara, Tochigi Prefecture. It was open to commoners as well as the daughters of peers from the time of its establishment, and in November 1945 at the time of investigation approximately 50% of its students were commoners (7 Imperial princesses, 375 peeresses, and 389 commoners totaling 771 although only 466 were actually present at the school because of the evacuation). The Peeresses' School, because of lower income from fees and virtually no income from endowment funds, was primarily supported by the Imperial Household, which in 1945 made up the deficit of 94% of the total expenses. Its curriculum appeared equally innocent, however, although it suffered as did the Japanese public schools in an overcrowded curriculum and in a preponderance of the traditional ethical and esthetic training considered proper for a Japanese girl.

Wealth. Two other areas of possible discrimination, that of wealth and that of the physically and mentally handicapped can be quickly dismissed. The Occupation Forces made much of the fee system in the tax-supported institutions of Japan. Actually the fee system has probably been little or no deterrent to the poor student in his effort to secure education. The compulsory elementary schools have been tuition free for generations. Parents who elect to send their children to private schools or to public experimental schools attached to normal schools expect to pay a nominal tuition fee. In 1945 these ranged from 11 yen per year in attached institutions to 50 yen per year in the Peers' School, traditionally the most select private elementary school of the nation. At the then official rate of exchange these fees were $.74 and $3.35 United States currency, respectively. Secondary schools, not then compulsory, and tax-supported universities charged tuition fees varying according to the course and the institution, and reaching a maximum of 150 yen per year, or $10 United States currency, in the Imperial University. Kanagawa Prefecture, considered one of the most outstanding in its educational services, charged from 50 yen to 62 yen per year in its technical and secondary schools in 1945. To these tuition charges were added nominal fees for entrance, examination, and laboratory facilities. It is perhaps significant that *Tōkyō To* doubled the tuition fees for secondary schools in September 1947, as reported in the 13 September 1947 issue of *Dai Ichi Shimbun.* Elementary school children paid from 2.50 yen to 10 yen per year for textbooks, although children from poor families received them free of charge. Even in the light of an impoverished population these charges do not seem excessive, and the system does not appear to differ essentially from that in use in most districts of the United States and in the other Allied countries. If there was any inequality of educational opportunity it was in the fact that compulsory education was provided to too low a level, making it necessary for secondary school pupils to pay a tuition fee. Article XXVI of the new *Constitution* states that all compulsory education shall be free, and the *Educational Reform of 1947* contemplates nine years of compulsory education, achieving a level comparable to that enjoyed in the United States.

The Handicapped. Discrimination against the handicapped is more a measure of public indifference than of any positive antipathy. Official Ministry of Education statistics indicate that there were 141 schools for the handicapped (exclusive of reform schools and penal institutions) with an enrollment of 4,072 students in 1940 but this figure must be accepted with some skepticism since private records of the Tokyo School for the Deaf indicate that there were 7,647 children enrolled in schools for the deaf alone. The national government, the prefectures, and some cities, have established and maintained a few fee-free schools for the blind, deaf, and dumb, but institutions of this sort have traditionally been private or charity schools, frequently founded by some socially conscious individual who has suffered the personal tragedy of an afflicted child. The *Nihon Rōa Gakkō* (Japan School for the Deaf) in Tokyo, for example, was founded in October 1920 by Dr. A. K. REISCHAUER, President of the *Meiji Gakuin* and noted Occidental authority on Buddhism, who had a deaf daughter; and the *Shigakenritsu Rōa Gakkō* (Shiga Prefectural School for the Dumb) was founded in May 1928 at Kusatsu-machi by NISHIKAWA Kichinosuke, also the father of a daughter who was deaf-mute. The *Ōsaka Rōkōa Gakkō* (Osaka Prefectural School for the Deaf and Dumb), founded in May 1926, and recognized by the Ministry of Education on 11 January 1928, and the *Tōkyōshiritsu Rō Gakkō* (Tokyo Municipal School for the Deaf), founded in June 1926, are examples of city-sponsored institutions. The *Nagoya Mōa Gakkō* (Nagoya School for the Dumb and Blind) founded in May 1901 by NAGAOKA Shigetaka, himself born blind, and by 1912 under the direct control of the Nagoya municipality was an example of the public recognition and support of an outstanding private foundation. The most famous of the schools for the blind, *Tōkyō Mō Gakkō* (The Tokyo Government School for the Blind), was founded in March 1876 by a philanthropic society, the *Rakuzen Kai*, headed by FURUKAWA Tashiro, formerly an instructor of the blind in Kyoto, Dr. Henry FAULDS, Scotch Presbyterian missionary, and a Dr. BURCHARD [whose first name has been unrecorded in all official Japanese records, including those of the Tokyo Government School for the Blind itself], missionary of the German-American Lutheran Church. It admitted students in 1880 and on 21 November 1885 was taken over by the national government and received its present name.

These individual institutions have done much to awaken the public to the social need for such schools, and although national laws since 1923 have made it compulsory for all prefectures to establish at least one school for the blind, deaf, and dumb, the essential step of making the national compulsory education laws ap-

plicable to the handicapped has never been taken. Even Article
XXV of the new *Constitution* includes the loophole that all children shall be entitled to receive "ordinary education" and shall be
entitled to receive an equal education "correspondent to their
ability." Psychological counseling for the maladjusted, considered
a necessity in good American schools, is virtually unknown in
Japan. Special schools for the crippled, for those with health
handicaps, for those with speech defects (other than the mutes),
and for those with impaired eyesight (other than the blind), do
not exist in Japan. In the sense that a blind, deaf, or dumb child
may be admitted to a tax-supported institution without social opprobrium and there receive virtually the same course of studies as
is given in the regular schools of comparable level plus certain
specialized training designed to prepare him for one of a rather
limited number of professions—there is no discrimination. But in
the sense that other handicapped children do not receive properly
specialized education, that only about 56% of the blind, deaf, and
dumb who should be receiving education are actually enrolled in
schools, and that the graduate of such a school unless he comes
from a family of position and wealth capable of providing him
with private tutors or a foreign education, is barred from advanced study—there is discrimination.

The deaf learn arts and crafts, especially tailoring and dress-
making, cabinetmaking, shoe and *geta* (wooden clog) making,
engraving, printing, photography, and metalworking. The blind
learn Japanese massage (*amma*); acupuncture (*hari*), a Chinese
form of medical practice involving the stimulation of nerves and
muscles by a silver or gold needle; moxacautery (*kyū*), also an
ancient Chinese medical practice of burning the down made from
the leaves of plants at certain spots on the surface of the body; and
music, especially *koto*, a long horizontal harplike instrument with
13 strings, and *shamisen*, a crude three-string banjo. The technical instruction of both blind and deaf follows accepted Occidental practices. The old system of sign-communication gave way
to the oral method of instructing the deaf largely through the
efforts of Dr. Reischauer and Mr. Nishikawa Yoshinosuke during the 1920's. The system used was that developed at the Clarke
School for the Deaf at Northampton, Mass. All blind instruction
is conducted through the medium of Japanese Braille, invented in
1890 by Ishikawa Kuraji of the Tokyo Government School for

the Blind and based on the international system invented by Louis
BRAILLE in 1829.

Sex. The most obvious and pernicious form of discrimination
against students has been that directed against women. At the
elementary school level there has been segregation within the
classes if not a complete absence of coeducation. Above the level
of the elementary school there has been little or no coeducation.
The secondary schools for girls (*kōtō jogakkō*), the women's
normal schools and higher normal schools (*shihan gakkō* and *joshi
kōtō shihan gakkō*), and women's colleges (*semmon gakkō*) have
been notoriously inferior in quality. The curricula for girls'
schools have continued to follow the Confucian philosophy of the
social inferiority of women and to perpetuate the feudal ideals of
womanhood expressed in the *Onna Daigaku* ("The Greater
Learning for Women"), compiled from the *Dōshikun*, written by
KAIBARA Ekken (died 1714). A woman must "look to her husband as her lord and must serve him with all reverence and worship." A few women have in the past been admitted to the Imperial
universities in Sendai, Fukuoka, and Sapporo, but the true measure of equality, admission to the highly desirable Imperial universities in Tokyo and Kyoto, has been denied. In 1944, for
example, there were only 40 women in Imperial universities as
compared with 29,600 men, or about two tenths of 1%. Of the 12
government universities only two (*Tōkyō Bunrika* and *Hiroshima
Bunrika*) admitted women. A few private universities (notably
Waseda, Hosei, Meiji, and *Nippon*) admitted a few women students each year. But the ratio was kept very low. *Tōkyō Bunrika*,
for example, had graduated only 1 woman to 38 men. Although
women outnumber men in Japan 100 to 89, their political, legal,
economic, and intellectual influence has until recently been virtually nil. Educational discrimination has been only a small, and
relatively innocent, part of a great pattern of sex discrimination
which has reduced the Japanese woman from her pre-eminent
position in Court and public life a millennium ago to a position of
pallid subservience to her husband and indifference to the social
and political questions beyond her home. In 1011 MURASAKI
Shikibu completed *Genji Monogatari* ("Tales of the *Genji*"),
immortalizing both herself and woman's position in Japan of that
period. In 1909 the Minister of Education, Baron KIKUCHI
Dairoku, said that the purpose of education for women was to

prepare them to be "good wives and wise mothers." Silent acquiescence to the male will in the family and devotion to the
drudgery and esthetics of the home appear to have been the mark
of the "good and wise." The old Japanese expression *hakoiri
musume* (box-enclosed maiden) needs no interpretation.

The fight for equality of educational opportunity for women
has been inseparably linked with the fight for the political and
social emancipation of women. It cannot now be considered without a brief note on the larger pattern of sex discrimination and the
suffrage movement it evoked. Before the Occupation women in
Japan were not permitted to vote nor to hold public office. They
were bound to the family system and virtually were a chattel of
the head of their own or their husband's family. Except in rare
instances and with great limitations on their free control they
were not permitted to hold real property, especially real estate.
In even wealthy families, with servants in greater proportions
than in most Occidental families, the woman was expected to
perform innumerable household tasks which occupied her time
to the exclusion of outside interests. Although Occidental observers, frequently missionaries or persons from the New England
tradition, have exaggerated its extent and importance, the mores
of Japanese society permitted and encouraged the existence of a
double moral standard with its consequent humiliation and subordination of the wife. The Japanese woman traditionally had almost nothing to say about her choice of husband, frequently not
meeting her fiancé until immediately before the wedding ceremony. If widowed, divorced, or discarded after a trial marriage
(consummated by a religious ceremony but not officialized by
recording at the local government office) the woman was faced
with the choice of living on the charity of the male head of her
husband's family or of returning to her father's or, if he be dead,
to her brother's home. If such a woman had been fortunate enough
to bring forth male issue, she might expect a respected position
as the mother of her all-important son, but if not, she was a dead
and useless branch on the family tree, one that should be pruned.
Economic necessity and social custom usually demanded an immediate remarriage, almost certainly to a lower social level which
would be willing to accept such used and damaged goods in order
to have a connection with the more influential family. If she were
past the age of 26 the law permitted her the choice of her husband,

or even a single life supported by her own efforts, a choice seldom adopted by the daughter of a respectable family. The Japanese nation is founded on its family system. The family name (*sei*) was and is the most treasured possession. Families will even force a son-in-law to enter the family by adoption and assume the name if there is no legitimate male descendant, thus perpetuating this vital link with the ancestors of the past. Japan has been a feudal state and primogeniture is at the basis of its entire legal and social system. This is the greatest sex discrimination.

It would be improper to give the impression that Japan in the Occupation, or even immediately before the war, was still rigidly bound to all these old prejudices and mores. Japan was an industrial nation and the masses of people concentrated in cities and working in factories had eroded many of the traditional conventions. Young women were educated for employment, as clerks, typists, teachers, factory workers, skilled artisans, and in limited numbers as professional people. Young women in the cities frequently had all of the personal freedoms enjoyed by girls in the United States. They attended dances, saw motion pictures, read sentimental novels, attended parties, and had "dates" unchaperoned, worked in industry, traveled, and chose their husbands or lovers. At times their feverish and callow exercise of the Anglo-Saxon freedom made them both ridiculous and the target of official and conservative censure. The few leaders of the suffrage movement in Japan frequently engaged in the distasteful exhibitionism which seems to be an inevitable concomitant of any revolutionary movement. The war in Japan, as in all the nations of the world, wiped out conventions and forced a new participation in public efforts upon the women. They were evacuated, they worked in war plants, they served in auxiliaries to the armed services, they lived nervous, exhausted, disillusioning lives, they were forced by necessity to assume family responsibilities in the absence of fathers, brothers, and husbands.

The Occupation did not lessen the impact with old traditions. Japanese women for the first time came in contact with large numbers of men who were in general respectful and considerate of their sex. They were barraged with propaganda urging on them the right to vote, the right to choose their profession, the right to social equality, the right to choose their mate. They were given the right to vote, and saw it written into Article XV of the new *Constitution*. They were assured the right to hold public office by Article XLIV and saw women seated in the National Diet. They were granted absolute equality under the law by Article XIV and saw the basic institution of primogeniture outlawed. They were given the right to organize and to bargain collectively by Article XXVIII and saw women elected officials of labor unions and educational associations. They were given freedom and suddenly the equality of education which had been promised them became vitally important. Unless they were educated to use this new liberty it would be a Pyrrhic victory.

On 4 December 1945 the Ministry of Education released a document entitled, "The Women's Education Renovation Plan." That portion outlining practical measures to be taken during the following academic year is quoted:

1. (a) Regulations impeding women to enter higher educational institutes will be revised or abolished; women's universities will be newly established; and the co-educational system will be adopted in men's universities.

   (b) Graduates of women's colleges designated by the Education Minister will be made eligible for universities.

   (c) Some of the now existing women's colleges will be elevated to the status of women's universities.

2. The creation of women's higher schools will be considered later. For the time being, however, the course of study of women's colleges and the graduate course of girls' high schools will be elevated to that of men's higher schools.

3. The course of study of girls' high schools will be elevated to the standard of boys' secondary schools. Text books will be unified.

4. The subjects and the number of school-days of young women's schools will be made equal with those of young men's schools.

5. University and college courses will be open to women. To uplift the intelligence of both men and women, courses on politics and science will be enlarged. (*Mombushō* trans.)

If this program were actually carried out, the provisions of Article XXVI of the State Department (and FEC), "Policy for the Revision of the Japanese Educational System," which says, "Equal opportunity for both sexes should be provided at all levels of education—primary, secondary, and tertiary," would be implemented, and the provisions of Article XXVI of the new *Constitution* would be accomplished.

In August 1946 the first two women officials at a policy-making level in the Japanese Ministry of Education were appointed to serve in the School Education Bureau and the Social Education Bureau. When the schools opened in April 1947 all official textbooks for girls were identical with the corresponding textbooks for boys, and the number of classroom hours spent on similar courses were made identical. All tax-supported universities have become co-educational and in the first year, 1946, Tokyo Imperial University admitted 19 out of 66 applicants, Kyoto Imperial University admitted 17 out of 71 applicants, Osaka Imperial University took 3, Tohoku Imperial took 8, and Kyushu Imperial took 4. *Yamaguchi Kōtō Gakkō* was the first of the boys' higher schools to become co-educational in 1946, and all public institutions of this level will eventually be converted. By March 1946 at the time of the visit of the United States Education Mission, 23 new private women's colleges had been founded. The famous Tsuda College, Tokyo Women's University, and Tokyo Women's Christian College, all in Tokyo, Doshisha University in Kyoto, and Miyagi College in Sendai, which in the past have been outstanding in their higher education of women, are serving as models and are providing from their graduates many of the instructors. In September 1946 the Japan Association of College Alumnae, later renamed the Association of Japanese College Alumnae (*Daigaku Fujin Kyokai*), was organized "to unite college women for work on the educational and social problems of the country." This organization has undertaken the major task of nonofficial accrediting and curriculum supervision of the women's schools. The *Educational Reform of 1947* provides for co-education through the ninth grade. The former laws prohibiting co-education from the third through the sixth grades—Article LI of the Regulations Relative to the Enforcement of the Elementary School Ordinance, Ministry of Education Ordinance No. 4 of 14 March 1941—were repealed in October 1946 and co-education above that level has been made permissive.

Discrimination against women on the grounds of sex has been thoroughly legislated, and is in the process of being actively implemented, out of existence. In the law the woman student shall be granted equal educational opportunity. But discrimination is a matter of public opinion and social organization. As long as Japanese society makes the economically self-sufficient woman

the rarity—and the household drudge or carefully protected dev-
otee of the flower arrangement and the tea ceremony the usual
—discrimination will continue in spite of the law. An editorial,
"For the Emancipation of Japanese Women" in the 13 July 1946
issue of the *Nippon Times*, points to this danger:

It would be a grave mistake, however, to think that the emancipation
of women will soon be a reality. However determined the enlightened
members of the female sex may be to secure all their properly due
rights and privileges, and however willing and cooperative the sympathetic elements among the men may be to aid the women in the
attainment of their aims, for the vast majority of the rank and file of
Japanese womanhood actual emancipation will be but a futile dream
for a long time to come. The reason is that the women of Japan are
still held slaves to a binding tyranny which political and legal reforms
cannot touch.

This tyrannical force . . . is the force of an unintelligent, irra-
tional, inefficient, and archaic pattern of daily living. The prevailing
mode of living makes the Japanese woman a household drudge whose
waking hours are so full of such heavy demands that, aside from a
small minority of women in exceptional circumstances, there are few
who have the time and energy to develop any interest in political or
social activities even if the most generous political and legal conditions
are granted them.

The women of Japan have received the right to equality of educational opportunity. Now they must seek the right to use the
education they have won.

Political Belief. Discrimination on the grounds of political conviction has in the past been so common that it has hardly been
considered discrimination but merely normal control. Thus students who by speech, action, or affiliation have demonstrated
themselves to be antagonistic to the government or to an officially
accepted political philosophy such as the *kokutai* became the
object of both educational discrimination and police action.
Thought control with all its punitive ramifications and the educational lockout were the weapons of the authorities. In the early
months of the Occupation students who participated in school
strikes became the target of official disciplinary action which frequently could only be considered discrimination. It was customary to categorize any liberal in prewar Japan as a "Communist," and students who had been so stigmatized were the object of

severe discrimination. Although the Communist party was permitted to exist in the Occupation and although the USSR was nominally one of the Occupying Powers, a student who was an accused Communist was not accorded the same educational treatment as the more democratically inclined. Because the United States and Great Britain, as the dominant powers in the Occupation Forces, were actively anti-Communist and because the Japanese governments which were permitted to exist in this period were essentially conservative, there was no official pressure to enforce these student's rights to equality of educational opportunity. In somewhat the same position was the ex-military student, the boy without a school and without a friend who dared to be his advocate. Because this group of students constituted a pressing practical problem in the Occupation and provides a convenient case study of the development, detection, diagnosis, and cure of discrimination a brief summary of its history may be warranted.

The military and naval academies in Japan ceased to exist as operating institutions early in August 1945 when the dismemberment of the military forces became evident and the continuation of military training became meaningless. Classes stopped, faculty began to dissolve, and students began to return to their homes. Formal closing of all military academies was accomplished on 18 August 1945 when the Emperor, acting in his capacity as Commander in Chief of the Japanese Imperial Army issued Army Ordinance No. 116 closing all army schools in the country. This was implemented by the Ministry of War Command No. 369 of the same date. The naval academies, although they were decommissioned and their personnel was demobilized just as rapidly and with considerably better order and discipline, were not formally closed until 30 September 1945 by an unpublished order, No. 1500, of the Ministry of the Navy. By 5 November 1945 a searching investigation by Occupation Headquarters confirmed the claim that all such institutions were both legally and actually closed and that all military instruction had ceased. What had become of the students?

The Ministry of Education on 5 September 1945 issued Order No. 120 entitled "On the Admission and Transference of the Graduates and Undergraduates of Military and Naval Schools." It appears to have been a sincere attempt to make available to these boys and young men some form of civilian education which would assist in their assimilation into a peaceful economy. It provided for admission to universities (*daigaku* and *semmon gakkō*) on the basis of a physical examination and personal interview of students who were graduates or third-year students of the Military Academy, Military Aviation Academy, Military Paymasters' School, Naval Academy, Naval Engineering School, and Naval Paymasters' School. At the higher school (*kōtō gakkō*) level it provided a similar table of equivalent preparation for boys in the lower undergraduate classes of the above institutions, the Military Preparatory School, Naval Preparatory School, and for those who were graduates of a number of military and naval preparatory and practice courses. A similar table was presented for admission at various levels of the civilian secondary schools (*chu gakkō*). Provision was made for the ex-military student to indicate his first, second, and subsequent choices of institution, and the civilian schools were officially "urged" to make every effort to assimilate as many as possible, even to the extent of setting up extra classes and establishing a platoon system in the lower age groups. Special training courses were to be set up for those students who did not have an adequate preparation for the civilian course of study. Finally, in an effort to solve the problem as rapidly as possible, avowedly activated by a desire to remove this minority group from possible subversive influences and to disperse them widely in civilian institutions, provision was made for almost immediate admission: in April 1946, or the beginning of the next academic year, for universities but on 15 October 1945 for *kōtō gakkō* and 1 November 1945 for secondary schools, both in the middle of the then current academic year. It was patently evident that the Ministry of Education looked upon this group as a minority which by their prediction of probable Occupation policy and later by the actual terms of Paragraph 1, b (3) of SCAP Educational Policy Directive AG 350 (22 Oct 45) CIE, should be accorded protection from discrimination. Some of the civilian students in the schools which began to accept these ex-military students did not agree.

On 24 September 1945 the Occupation Headquarters Counter-Intelligence Corps first received reports of student resentment and in the month that followed this resentment developed into an open educational battle that could not be ignored. Although reports of student strikes, mass meetings, and newspaper editorials came from various sections of the country, the center of the trouble appeared to be in *Waseda Kōtō Gakuin*, one of the higher school preparatory departments of Waseda University in Tokyo. On 26 October 1945 there was held a mass meeting in which admission of ex-military students was condemned and an appeal was made to other schools in the Tokyo area, which contained one half the higher educational institutions of the country, to present a united front. The university authorities adopted a policy of noninterference and did nothing. On the preceding day an article, probably inspired by this group, had appeared in the *Asahi Shimbun*, leading Tokyo paper, which stated that it was undemocratic to admit ex-military students in midyear when civilian students were not allowed to enter. On the day of the mass meeting, 26 October 1945, there appeared an editorial in the *Nippon Sangyō Keizai* which attacked the policy of mixing ex-military and civilian students on the grounds that the civilian students would be indoctrinated with militarism. Delegations of students visited Occupation Headquarters and presented petitions. The movement against ex-military students was linked to the wave of school strikes which was receiving unfavorable Japanese and foreign publicity. The punitive sections of SCAP Headquarters were hot on the scent of any minority discrimination or violation of the civil liberties and educational rights which had been assured in the 4 October and 22 October 1945 SCAP Directives. A full-dress investigation was ordered.

Stripped of emotionalism, which had in all probability been deliberately injected by political organizers, the argument presented by the civilian students and their sympathizers was that the admission of former military students was unfair and discriminatory because they were permitted to enter in midterm, whereas civilian students would have to wait until the following April (1946) when the new term began; that extra classes were provided and the maximum enrollments were increased, whereas civilians had been denied admission on the grounds of lack of space; and that admission was granted without entrance examination, whereas civilian students had in the past been forced to take such examinations and had been excluded from the more desirable schools or from further education entirely on the basis of their results. They further argued that admission of ex-military students, who presumably had absorbed the philosophy of militarism during their previous training, was contrary to policy in that it would tend to develop powerful and militant minority groups in the civilian institutions, and that it would tend to indoctrinate the previously unsullied civilian students.

The ex-military students suffered badly in that they had practically no advocates. Minister of Education, MAEDA Tamon, and Chief of the Second Demobilization Ministry, ex-Rear Adm. NAKAMURA Katsuhei, were almost the only ones who cared or were brave enough to plead their case openly. The defense they presented was impressive. They pointed out that at the level of universities, colleges (*semmon gakkō*), and normal schools Order No. 120 had not permitted the ex-military students to enter before the beginning of the next academic year, at the same time that civilian students would be admitted; that Order No. 184 of 12 September 1945 on "School Education under the New Conditions," and *Mombushō* Instruction issued on 8 October 1945 on the "Reconversion of Technical to Commercial Schools," provided for immediate admission and special courses for civilian students who had been evacuated or otherwise denied the normal continuation of their education; that the civilian students in the vast majority of institutions had not been required to take entrance examinations in April 1945, the beginning of the then current academic year, and hence could not have been denied admission on that ground, and were not required to take entrance examinations for special admission during October 1945 under the provisions of the orders just mentioned; that despite Order No. 120 practically all ex-military students who were candidates for special admission had in fact been given a rigorous written examination as well as the required physical examination and personal interview, and that a high percentage (approximately 95% in the better schools) were denied admission on that ground; that those actually admitted had constituted only 5.6% of the enrollment in secondary schools and 6.5% in colleges and higher schools; that it was manifestly absurd to consider boys of 13 to 16 years of age (those seeking admission to the secondary school level) an unreclaimable militarist group or an intransigent ideological threat to the other students; that approximately 300,000 ex-military students were affected, representing the physically and mentally most able youths of their generation, and that this number was too large to be ignored; that denial of education on the grounds of their prior military indoctrination would be inconsistent with the enunciated policies of the Occupation in that it would constitute a discrimination against a minority group, that it would deny rehabilitation education to the group most needing it, and that it would turn loose in society a large group of disillusioned, desperate, and idle young men, which would "constitute a grave problem for social equilibrium."

An independent investigation by the Education Division of the Civil Information and Education Section of SCAP and by the Counter-Intelligence Corps of the USAFPAC, substantiated the factual statements of MAEDA and NAKAMURA. Although the Ministry of Education maintained that their original order of 5 September 1945 by implication included all students who had through no fault of their own been deprived of the opportunity for continuing their education, such as students who had been repatriated from foreign possessions, the Occupation Authorities insisted that a public announcement of this provision be made. On 17 November 1945 the Ministry released a press statement and on 20 November 1945 notified all schools under its jurisdiction that military and civilian students were to be treated in an identical manner. In one element, however, some Occupation officials felt that theoretical equality would have to defer to practical occupational necessity. It was feared that because of their admitted mental and physical superiority the ex-military students might in an open contest win a majority of the admissions to certain highly desirable schools, such as the so-called "numbered higher schools." The famed First Higher School in Tokyo, headed by Dr. ABE Yoshishige, later to be the second Minister of Education under the Occupation, for example, had admitted 90 ex-military students out of 1,855 ex-military applicants which constituted 12.3% of the total enrollment. With annual increments from lower schools which had also admitted ex-military students this percentage would go higher. This group of Allied officials considered such a concentration of presumably militaristically indoctrinated youth potentially dangerous and secured the establishment of a policy of not permitting more than 10% of ex-military students in any one school. No perceptible animosity has been shown by the faculties and other students against these minority groups. Discrimination, except for the temporary and relatively unimportant 10% limitation, was erased. In July 1946 even this 10% rule was modified to free all ex-military students with less than one year of military training from inclusion in the category.

The Teachers—
From Purge to Professional Preparation

On p. 62 of the little volume, *Education in Japan,* United States Bureau of Education Circular No. 2, there is an evaluation of the Japanese educational system and its problems quoted from a report of Mr. R. G. Watson, Her Britannic Majesty's Secretary of Legation at Edo, which was read in the British Parliament:

. . . the need of properly-qualified native instructors is one of the greatest, if not the greatest of the many needs of Japan. The sudden, almost violent, revolution in educational as well as political ideas, through which this country has passed, has discovered that sore need. It is quite safe to say that hitherto the western idea of a trained teacher and of a science of teaching has been unknown to the natives of this country.

*   *   *

So long as the old education of Japan consisted merely in obtaining what we consider the mere work-tools and so long as they made an end of what we count the means, it could not be expected that instructors, such as are now needed, should appear.

*   *   *

So long as education consisted in a tread-mill-round of committing to memory the Chinese classics, learning to read Japanese history and government-edicts, to write, and to reckon on the abacus, such a thing as mental development was unknown.

*   *   *

The old teacher poured in, the new teacher must draw out; the old teacher was a drill-master, the new one must be that and more; the old one stifled questioning, the new one must encourage it. We believe it to be the right of every student to drain his instructor dry; a scholar, unless manifestly endeavoring to waste the time of teacher and class, should be heard and answered. The teacher should be very careful how he calls any question foolish.

*   *   *

The native teacher of the future must depend less on traditional authority and more on the resources of a richly-furnished mind. He must be a student himself; he must be able to get out of the ruts; he must be capable of developing the minds of youths, not merely of stuffing them; he must welcome the appearance of an unusually bright and eager mind as a gem to be polished with extra care, and not as a stone to be crushed into regulation shape and size for the common turnpike-road.

Only a note need be added to this appraisal. It was written on 30 November 1873, and published in 1875. The wheel of life has turned a full cycle.

Many of the problems of the teacher in Japan are identical with those in nearly every nation of the world. The teaching profession is so grossly underpaid that it cannot attract the ablest talent the country produces but must be content with mediocrity. During the Occupation and in the face of monetary inflation teaching salaries, even when supplemented with bonuses and special subsidies, have been so inadequate that it has been financially impossible for a considerable proportion of teachers to remain in the profession. There has existed a continuing attrition due to social causes. Young women have married. Girls have attended the normal schools with no intention of ever practicing their profession but merely as a device for securing a cultural education otherwise barred to them. Young men have been inducted into the armed forces and have lost their lives or their political acceptability for teaching in the military service of their country. Teacher preparation has followed the familiar pattern of overstandardization, mechanical pedagogical techniques, and political and professional indoctrination. Supervision has been no more than a check to determine the teacher's conformity to official directions. Teachers have not only not been encouraged to think for themselves but have been prohibited from doing so. The successful teacher has been the one who has most minutely and exactly followed the prescribed pattern of thoughts, loyalties, and actions. Now that pattern has been shattered and the Japanese teacher is pathetically trying to salvage the shards.

The solutions to many of the manifold problems facing the Japanese teacher are the same as those available to the teachers of other nations. In some ways the Japanese teacher is more fortunate than others. As in other Oriental countries he holds a position of dignity and influence in the community which is in no way a reflection of his inadequate monetary recompense. *Sen-nichi no kingaku yori ichi-nichi no meishō* ("One day with a great teacher is better than a thousand of hard study") runs the Japanese proverb. His government and people have repeatedly demonstrated a willingness to make financial and personal sacrifices unsurpassed by any nation to support his educational program. Despite the thought control and censorship under which he has labored, there has been available to him most of the accumulated technical knowledge in his profession which has been available in Occidental nations, through libraries, through scholars trained in Europe and America, and through a small but important influx of foreign teachers into outstanding private schools. It is the considered opinion of members of the United States Education Mission to Japan and of officers who served on the technical staffs of Occupation Headquarters that there exists somewhere in Japan an acceptable solution to every educational problem which faces the Japanese teacher and administrator. He needs only the eyes to see, the mind to understand, and the will to emulate. But has he these indispensable minima, these eyes, this mind, and this will? This is the real problem of the teacher.

It is probable that until the last day of October 1945 the Japanese had never really scrutinized their teacher. To foreign observers he had long been a caricature, a little man in formal black, with spectacles and gold-filled teeth, pompous strut, and nervous, high-pitched laugh. To some he was pathetic, to others dangerous, to still others an enigma. But to the Japanese themselves he was an important man. He was the master, one who instructed, not one who helped the student to learn. From the village schoolmaster riding on his bicycle with his umbrella under his arm to the famous professor at the Imperial University, the Japanese teacher was accepted in his own community as a man of authority. He represented the government. But on 30 October 1945 the Imperial Japanese Government was handed SCAP Directive AG 350 (30 Oct 45) CIE, "Investigation, Screening, and Certification of Teachers and Educational Officials." This document commanded the Ministry of Education to establish suitable administrative machinery and procedures for the individual scrutiny of every teacher, present or prospective, in every school in Japan. For the first time the 506,000 licensed teachers then employed in Japan were to be questioned on their acceptability. And to ensure that there could be no misunderstanding of the thoroughness demanded of this purge, Paragraph 2, b (1) directed the

Ministry to prepare in detail and to submit to Headquarters for approval: "A precise statement of how acceptability of the individual is to be determined, together with lists of specific standards which will govern the retention, removal, appointment or re-appointment of the individual."

The Purge. The Purge in Japan was a punitive action. In its political and economic phases it was avowedly an implementation of that portion of the *Potsdam Declaration* which stated, "There must be eliminated for all time the authority and influence of those who have deceived and misled the people of Japan into embarking on world conquest." Its obvious purpose was to eliminate active exponents of militarism and ultranationalism. Its critics allege that its underlying purpose was to remove the political and economic talent from Japanese affairs and thus render impotent the nation's economy. These critics argued that it attacked success and not ideological unacceptability.

The educational phase of the Purge had in statement and in fact a rather more idealistic motive. In addition to eliminating present and future militaristic and ultranationalistic influences, it proposed to provide a demonstration of the democratic processes as applied to an educational field; to increase the individual parent's interest and participation in education; and to increase the degree of local control through the establishment of a decentralized screening machinery. But whatever laudable by-products of the process might be expected, the fundamental object of all phases of the Purge was the removal of personnel. It was a punitive action, neither greater in extent nor in importance than any of the several similar purges of Japan's intellectual class by the thought control authorities. In one element only is it worthy of extended analysis. It forced Japan to produce a concrete set of standards of acceptability. It forced a practical implementation of the lofty but nebulous concept of what constituted a "democratically inclined teacher." It produced a new criterion for teachers.

The history of the production of the Imperial Ordinance No. 263 of 7 May 1946, which officially established the procedures and standards for the investigation, screening, removal, and reinstatement of teachers, epitomizes the compromise and pragmatism which characterized the Occupation. Knowing from Paragraphs 1, b (1) and (2) of the 22 October 1945 SCAP Educational Policy Directive that a screening was demanded, and knowing unofficially the probable contents of the 30 October 1945 SCAP Educational Screening Directive, the Ministry of Education prepared and was able to submit two days after the publication of this latter directive, a proposed draft of a plan for screening. Dr. TANAKA Kōtarō, Professor of Commercial Law at Tokyo Imperial University and later the third Minister of Education under the Occupation, was then Chief of the General Education Bureau in the Ministry and was charged with preparation of the plan. On 6 November 1945 this draft was rejected on the grounds that it was entirely unworkable since it established no standards of acceptability and provided only a tiny fraction, perhaps one-thousandth part, the number of screening committees and review machinery needed. On 17 November 1945 Brig. Gen. Ken R. DYKE, Chief of the CI&E Section of GHQ, SCAP, and members of his staff met with the Minister of Education, MAEDA Tamon. Because it was evident that the Japanese officials still completely underestimated the magnitude of the task, a detailed list of minimum requirements was given Mr. MAEDA. The final item is pertinent:

The plan should include a definite set of precise standards, not a mere rewording of the general policies laid down by the Allied Powers. These standards must guide local committees in their action. They should include lists of schools and organizations as well as specific acts or experience which would bar a teacher from working in the schools. The responsibility for submitting this set of standards is the Ministry of Education's responsibility, but the Education Sub-Section Staff will cooperate in preparing the list. Each standard should be based on some fact which is demonstrable and which might be introduced in evidence. These standards would include such things as graduation from specific schools between specific dates, service in specific organizations between specific dates, membership in specific organizations, the holding of an office or position of leadership in specific organizations, the delivery of public lectures advocating specific policies, the writing of letters or publication of articles advocating specific policies, and the statement in class of views advocating specific policies—all of which are prohibited by the directives of the Allied Powers. (Official stenographic transcript.)

The promised co-operation developed into virtual authorship and on 1 December 1945, after a second Japanese draft had proved only slightly more acceptable, a third draft was completed jointly and submitted to the Allied Headquarters. It died unborn.

For weeks there had been a violent disagreement between certain sections of the Headquarters over the proposed political Purge. The Economic and Scientific Section, the Civil Intelligence Section, the Government Section which was the nominal author, and various of the Military Staff sections of Headquarters had been unable to compromise their differences of opinion and the Supreme Commander under pressure to purge Japanese militarists finally settled the matter by a command decision. Since it was mistakenly believed that the Civil Information and Education Section would have no vital interest or jurisdiction, it was not consulted in the preparation of the political directive and in fact did not know of its imminence until asked for formal concurrence immediately before its publication. By then it was too late to make any radical change and the resulting directive, AG 091.1 (4 Jan 46) GS, "Removal and Exclusion of Undesirable Personnel from Public Office," was issued. It is probably one of the most important and certainly one of the most controversial documents of the Occupation. Its effect upon the educational plan was disastrous.

AG 091.1 (4 Jan 46) GS was essentially composed of three lists: a list of positions, termed "public office," ordinarily held by persons with the civil service rank of *Chokunin* or higher; a list of positions, called "government service" from which persons would be barred, including all positions in national and prefectural governments, and their agencies, local branches, bureaus, offices, and corporations in which these governments or their agencies had financial interest or control; and a list of positions considered to be presumptive evidence of militaristic and ultranationalistic tendencies, called Appendix A. Reduced to its simplest form this directive commanded the Imperial Japanese Government to remove all people who were included in the third list (Appendix A—Removal and Exclusion Categories) from all positions included in the first list, and to bar them from future employment in any position in the second list.

In effect the removal clause proposed that virtually all persons in public office holding the *Chokunin* rank, estimated to be about 600 key officials by the Headquarters but actually considerably more, should be purged or removed from office, since almost every person of that elevated rank would at some time have been affiliated, perhaps only in a formal or perfunctory way, with one of the organizations listed in Appendix A. The limitation of *Cho-*

kunin rank or above was drawn for the acknowledged purpose of permitting the lower ranking officials to remain in office temporarily to prevent a collapse of government. Paragraph 18 of the directive warned that there would be additional restrictive measures taken against "certain classes of individuals at all levels in special fields," and subsequent action was in fact taken to extend the Purge to lower-ranking public officials, private individuals in industry, and key professional groups. The exclusion clause, however, was immediately far more drastic. It provided that no person could be employed in any government position without an investigation and clearance. In an official interpretation of this the Government Section specifically held that every teacher, every janitor, every street cleaner, every handyman who repaired a broken window in a remote schoolhouse or police box in any part of Japan would have to be investigated and cleared before employment. The principal feature of the screening process was the execution of a four-page questionnaire, in English as well as in Japanese, by every person affected.

The effect of this Purge Directive on the Educational Screening Plan was to halt all further work on the third draft. There were absurd discrepancies which when applied to education produced discrimination utterly inconsistent with the principles that the Headquarters had enunciated. Thus it barred any man who had once been a regular army officer, even if he had seen no military service since the war with China in 1894, from holding the position of teacher, janitor, or school official in the smallest rural elementary school. Yet it did not bar an admiral or a general, if he had escaped arrest as a war criminal, from holding the presidency of the largest university in Japan, since it was private. The former presidents and certain professors of Keijo Imperial University and Taihoku Imperial University would have to be purged merely because those institutions were located respectively in Korea held since 1905 and Formosa held since 1895. Both of these territories were the recognized possessions of Japan. But even more inexplicable were the provisions that persons should be dismissed on simple accusation without hearing or opportunity to present a defense and that persons removed would be denied their rights to public or private pensions, including the savings from their own prior salaries which had been paid into annuities. Some of these inconsistencies could be eliminated or lessened by the adroit drafting of the Educational Screening Plan, but no amount of patchwork or evasion could obviate the fact that any plan consistent with this Purge Directive would be an open invitation for "witch hunts," personal revenge, and discrimination and would be a denial of the civil liberties which the Occupation professed to advocate.

The Civil Information and Education Section faced a dilemma. If it wrote an equitable educational screening plan it would openly deny the principles set down in the political Purge Directive, embarrass the Headquarters, and produce so complicated a procedure the local Japanese authorities probably could not implement it successfully. If, on the other hand, it conformed to the principles of the political Purge Directive it would flagrantly deny the principles of civil liberty and democracy which for weeks it had been preaching to the Japanese. Yet by its 30 October 1945 Directive it had demanded a screening and neither the Supreme Commander nor public opinion would permit mere inaction. In the face of this dilemma it took the easier road out. It bequeathed its problem to the Japanese. On 11 February 1946 it officially informed the Ministry of Education that while "fully aware of all the difficulties in setting up standards, procedures and organizations," it had such confidence in the responsibility and sincerity of the then high officials of the Ministry that it would permit them unconditioned liberty in setting up the organization, procedures, and plan of operation and would be willing to accept any set of standards presented, provided that as a minimum they included the standards established by the 4 January 1946 Purge Directive and subsequent purge directives which might be issued by the Headquarters. The Japanese were then informed that this liberty to solve the problem by themselves was considered to be a privilege which would be removed if the screening were not conducted in good faith. On 27 April 1946 the sixth and final revision of the Plan was accepted by Headquarters and on 7 May 1946 it was officially issued as Imperial Ordinance No. 263.

Three elements of the final educational plan are worthy of note: the criterion of acceptability, the machinery for implementation, and the practical results.

The criterion of acceptability was entirely negative. Of the two obvious divisions of political and professional acceptability only the political was considered. In the political area it was assumed that any person who was not unacceptable by reason of his acts or by his prior contamination with ideologies considered presumptive evidence of his own indoctrination, was fitted to teach. No positive qualifications were demanded. The exclusion categories were based on five types of evidence: prior training or education, experience or prior employment, membership or affiliation, personal actions, and personal statements. The exclusion categories of Appendix A of the 4 January 1946 SCAP Purge Directive were taken as a basis. In addition the Ministry of Education excluded from teaching positions those persons who had previously resigned or been dismissed because of "militarism or ultranationalism" in accordance with the 22 October and 30 October 1945 SCAP Education Directives; persons who lectured or wrote in support of Nazi, Fascist, or Pan-Asian totalitarianism, racial prejudice, or Shinto ideology with the intent of inspiring racial superiority; persons who had compiled textbooks with a militaristic or ultranationalistic intent; persons who had "persecuted religion"; those who had co-operated with the Nazi or Fascist governments in carrying out their policies; those who had spoken in an attempt to discredit the policies of the Occupation or to antagonize the people against the Occupation; those who had served for ten years or more as reservists in the military service; professional Shinto priests; those who had been graduated from a list of presumably subversive schools since 7 July 1937; those who had been affiliated with a list of subversive or ultranationalistic organizations for a period of at least two years since 7 July 1937; and those who had been at any time an official or influential member of a list of more extreme organizations. The attempts to define what would constitute a positive evidence of acceptability and what would constitute professional acceptability, written into the preliminary drafts, were deleted in the final Imperial Ordinance.

It might be presumed that the list of unacceptable schools in Annex II would offer some clue as to what constituted desirable and undesirable training. But only the obvious generalities of ultranationalism, foreign imperialism, militarism, and Shintoism may be deduced. Thus, the Ritual Service Course of *Jingūkō-gakukan Daigaku*, the college attached to that university, and the Shinto Course of *Kokugakuin Daigaku*, all designed to train Shinto priests, were considered unacceptable preparation. The *Kenkoku*

Daigaku in Manchuria, the various courses of *Kōa Semmon Gakkō*, and six Colonial or Pioneering Courses in various universities and colleges (*Morioka, Mie, Miyazaki, Takushoku,* and *Fukuoka*), all designed to train overseas administrators or colonizers, were also considered unacceptable.

If the standards were less than satisfying, the provisions for implementing the educational screening were equally so. The basis of decision was not an open hearing with the submission of evidence to support formal charges and the opportunity for cross-examination, defense, and review, but merely by the execution of a questionnaire. The penalty for willfully making a false entry or deliberate omission, equivalent to perjury, was set at less than one year of penal servitude or a fine of less than 3,000 yen ($200 United States currency at the then official exchange), by Imperial Ordinance No. 542, 1945. The various exclusion categories were watered down by provisions that if there was available "no suitable replacement" the accused need not be removed. If the person excluded for reason of military service had subsequent to that service completed a civilian higher education course, or without further training possessed some technical skill, such as medicine, pharmacy, veterinary science, foreign languages, music, business management, and other "techniques, special sciences or arts," he might equally evade the Purge. A number of the exclusion categories were based on evidence of "intent," virtually an impossible thing to prove and an open invitation for the persecution of persons who might in reality be quite innocent. The questionnaire avoided some of the most glaring errors of the political document, including the requirement that every applicant for more than half a million educational jobs as well as their then present incumbents should fill out a lengthy document in English. And the machinery of committees for the scrutiny of these questionnaires and review of appealed cases, although cumbersome, was large enough to give some promise of ultimately accomplishing the work. It failed, however, to decentralize beyond the prefectural level—with the exception of the committees formed in the individual institutions of higher learning, an evidence of the powerful tradition of university autonomy—and hence missed the opportunity to give the local authorities and parents experience in self-government and control of the schools. The composition of the committees was a compromise between the centrally appointed boards of professional bureaucrats originally advocated by the Japanese authorities and the locally elected committee representative of regional economic, cultural, and political groups advocated by the educational officers in Headquarters.

The results of the educational screening procedure are difficult to assay. It was inevitable that it would not make the spectacular removals that accompanied the political and economic purges. The most obvious of the unacceptable officials and teachers had long since voluntarily resigned or been removed. By the time the Purge got into motion, a year after the Occupation began, there remained to be screened only those unacceptable persons who honestly thought they had done nothing wrong, those few who were insensitive to faculty and public censure, and that infinitesimal minority who had managed to maintain secret their prior indoctrination and sympathies and who were determined to retain their posts to seek an opportunity to subvert the Occupation policies. Neither the prestige nor the pay of a teacher during the Occupation offered any inducement for an accused person to resist removal. The Japanese authorities were under a constant pressure from the world press and from Occupation Headquarters to show "results" in their screening. There was a demand for heads to roll, and the success of the process was measured in the utterly fallacious terms of what percentage of the existing teachers were removed. The official report of the Supreme Commander for the Allied Powers on the completion of two years of the Occupation indicated that 115,778 Japanese teachers and administrators had resigned [or been removed by the Japanese authorities] prior to the issuing of the Imperial Ordinance No. 263 of 7 May 1946 which initiated the formal "Purge." In the year that followed 2,643 were removed automatically under the provisions of this ordinance, and 2,268 additional school officials and teachers were found unacceptable by the Japanese screening committees.

It was generally conceded that a strict observance of the letter of the exclusion categories would require the removal of virtually every qualified teacher in Japan, since no person who had taught at any time before the Occupation could have failed to "advocate publicly" in some degree principles of militarism, ultranationalism and National Shintoism. The Occupation Authorities would not have approved, or permitted, such an uncompromising purge, as it would have constituted in effect a general lockout of essential public employees. But no one did, or could, set what was a reasonable percentage. For despite the constant pressure to purge more teachers, the ratio of teachers purged to that retained simply was not a measure of the success of the process. The only lasting benefits which might be expected from the screening experiment were experience in the orderly procedures of democratically handling an unpleasant necessity, and a new and widespread respect for the personal liberties which are the cornerstone of the democratic method of government. As a punitive measure the Japanese learned nothing the Thought Control Police had not more thoroughly taught them. As a barrier to the possible subversive indoctrination of the pupils, it was too little and too late.

Reinstatement. Prominent in the thinking of the Occupational Authorities during the first few weeks after Surrender was the problem presented by the mass of liberal and antimilitaristic teachers presumed to have been removed, discriminated against or even imprisoned in the years before Defeat. The so-called "Japanese Bill of Rights," the SCAP Directive of 4 October 1945, had secured the release of all such persons who were imprisoned. The Educational Policy Directive, SCAP AG 350 (22 Oct 45) CIE, had directed that all such persons "be declared immediately eligible for and if properly qualified . . . be given preference in reappointment." On 1 November 1945 the Ministry of Education issued Order No. 17 in which it directed the presidents of all autonomous schools and the prefectural governors to give priority to "those teachers and educational officials who were dismissed, suspended from office, or forced to retire owing to their anti-militaristic or liberalistic tendencies or actions" in reappointment wherever they were still technically qualified to fill a position. Each of the drafts of the Educational Screening Plan carried a similar directive and Imperial Ordinance No. 263 of 7 May 1946 stated that any person who had so been discriminated against could be given preferential appointment if he presented himself within six months of the promulgation of the order.

It was one of the great disappointments of the Occupation that only a tiny proportion of the expected numbers of these persecuted persons were discovered and reinstated. On 17 November 1945 Minister of Education MAEDA Tamon in a conference with

Brig. Gen. Ken R. Dyke, Chief of ci&e, ghq, scap, and his staff, stated that many professors and teachers who were eligible were not applying for reinstatement because they were afraid or because they did not know through which channels to work. He requested permission to advertise in provincial newspapers to encourage such hesitant professors to apply, but he was denied this permission on the grounds that if he waited until the screening machinery was completed it might serve for both removal and reinstatement. Mr. Maeda was ultimately caught in the same Purge that he helped prepare and was forced to resign, the screening machinery was still inoperative a year after the Occupation began, and the appeal to this little group of people who had stood up to Japan's military might and had suffered much for democracy, was forgotten in the red tape of military administration.

The purpose of the original gesture was laudatory. Simple justice demanded that the Allied Powers recognize and aid these people who had defied the militarism of their own government. Public reinstatement would broadcast a pertinent lesson in the rights of the individual. A considerable body of able teachers which would otherwise be lost to the re-education program of the Occupation would be salvaged. And above all, a nucleus of liberal and progressive leaders might be discovered to guide in the democratization of the educational system. But achievement of these ends failed because of an unforeseen reluctance of the injured persons to reveal themselves. Why?

In part this reluctance was due to the standards which were established for their reinstatement. They had to meet three general tests: was their original expulsion or removal in fact an injustice; were they still technically qualified for the position; and did they actively desire reinstatement. Few injured persons cared to reopen the old wounds of their dismissal. A jail sentence was not proof of injustice, and the teacher had to face at least a sympathetic review of his case. In a large proportion of the cases it was obvious that the stated cause for removal and even detention, was not the real reason but only a subterfuge through which a liberal was attacked. Yet it would indeed be difficult in most cases for the liberal to prove such an evasion. Because the military clique had been in power almost without opposition from early in the 1930's, a considerable proportion of the injured persons presumably had not practiced their profession for more than a decade.

It required real courage and a new sacrifice to abandon the livelihood which they had substituted for teaching and submit themselves again for competitive employment in education. Many could not present teaching qualifications which were acceptable in the present school system. Their training was both outdated and inadequate. They were no longer temperamentally qualified for active teaching. Many were old, sick, and tired. And in the *sine qua non of* reinstatement—their indicating a desire for reinstatement—most were deeply reluctant. They feared that the Occupation would be very temporary and that upon the withdrawal of Allied troops the old militaristic element in Japan would return to power and again subject them to persecution. They feared failure or public humiliation. Many felt that they had been wronged and should be invited back to their places rather than be put in the position of a suppliant. Many felt that they would be subjected to future discrimination on the part of employers who were reluctant to hire them. Some apparently resented the fact that their reinstatement would be handled by the machinery and processes which were designed primarily to remove unacceptable personnel.

On the basis of its results the project can only be counted a failure. The numbers which were reinstated were insignificant. Few if any outstanding leaders arose in the postwar educational system from this group. The propaganda value of a public demonstration of justice was unexploited. The opportunity of publicizing what the ideals of these men had been which made them outstanding liberals and which drew the fire of the militarists was lost. No lessons of what a good teacher ought to be were learned.

Re-education. One of the more obvious necessities which faced both the Occupation Authorities and the Japanese Ministry of Education after Surrender was that of re-educating the teachers then employed in the schools. As an immediate problem some re-education was crucial. Unless a major proportion of the trained teachers were permitted to remain in their positions the school system would collapse, nearly 18 million children would be loosed on the streets, and control of the civil population would be made immeasurably more difficult. But the majority of the teachers could only be retained if they were reoriented so that their teaching itself did not constitute a perversion of Occupation policies and their leadership incite the very civil disturbances that the schools were kept open to prevent. As a long-range problem both the Foreign Powers and the responsible Japanese authorities recognized that re-education of the teachers promised one of the most potent instruments for encouraging the growth of the democratic tendencies which had been planted. The schools controlled 36% of the population—the most important 36% by far since it would constitute the next generation. The thinking of 15 years hence would be determined in a large measure by what was taught them and how it was taught. An approved textbook with approved content could be put in the child's hands, but in the countless millions of uncensored class hours which these youngsters would experience in the aggregate, it would be the teachers' attitudes which would leave the lasting impression.

Officially the re-education program is a continuing effort, but actually by its very nature it was a short-term project. It was essentially counterpropaganda directed to the teachers and through them to the students by all the available mass media. But the natural impact of the new society in which the teachers lived and taught soon surpassed in influence any of the controlled propaganda. The discard of official viewpoint for self-evaluation is perhaps one of the most encouraging evidences of growth in the educational profession. A successful teacher in a democracy cannot continue to depend upon outside "reorientation" even if that redirection of his ideas be into democratic channels. If he is to teach self-direction, he must be capable of self-direction in his teaching. Fortunately the discontinuity between the old and the new in postwar Japanese life was so inescapable that the lesson of his daily life far surpassed any counterpropaganda in potency. The endless bomb-flattened ruins which he could see through the window of his school discredited his former leaders and their mode of life more than the most persuasive argument. His ration of rice, the cold of his house, the endless ride on the dilapidated streetcar, the contrast between the courtesy of the Occupation troops and his former Japanese military forces, the protection of his shrines which he knew were an anathema to the very soldiers protecting them, the courteous indifference shown by the invader to his Emperor who now seemed shrunken to an ordinary man, these and a thousand other stimuli were daily conditioning him.

The formal reorientation started on 28 August 1945 when the

Ministry of Education issued Order No. 118 on "Reopening Schools under the New Conditions." On 12 September 1945 Order No. 184 was issued on "School Education under the New Conditions." These two basic orders, and a statement of official educational policy issued in the form of a press release on 11 September 1945 under the title, "New Education Principles and Changes Made," are the only important instructions to the teachers which the Ministry was able to make between Capitulation and the establishment of an Educational Sub-Section in the Headquarters of the Occupation Forces in Tokyo. After that time no instruction issued by the Ministry was uninspired or uncontrolled by the Occupation Authorities. Most were merely amplifications of orders received from the Headquarters. This constant stream of official orders, averaging about one important directive every three days, gradually built a pattern of the new education: the disposal of weapons in the schools, how textbooks should be taught, the removal of militarists from positions, the reorientation of youth schools, the abolition of glider training, the promotion of social education, the suppression of the military arts in physical education, the restoration of religious teaching in private schools, the abolition of Shinto in tax-supported schools, the suspension of morals, history and geography teaching, the reform of women's education—to mention only a few of the first three months. The pattern of what they were intended to believe and to teach was becoming clear to any thoughtful teacher.

But in addition to these specific and official orders there was a program of direct counterpropaganda, cloaked with the official euphemisms of "reorientation" and "civil information." In compliance with Order No. 201 of 8 October 1945 an official broadcast to teachers, known as "The Teachers' Hour," was begun on 22 October and after one or two false starts became a daily feature. The script of every lecture or demonstration-class broadcast was precensored by the Education Division of CI&E, GHQ, SCAP. The lecturers were selected from the ranks of unpurged Japanese educators and frequently were men of ability and liberal viewpoint. Their topics were chosen for them by the Ministry of Education and consisted mainly of accounts of educational experience in the United States and commentaries on official educational policy. A series of student programs was broadcast during school hours and was compulsory in schools having radio equipment. Typical of the type of counterpropaganda directed to the schools in a form designed to be used by the teacher in his classes, and incidentally to influence his personal thinking, was the dramatized history of the Pacific phase of the second World War begun on 13 December 1945 and broadcast under the title, "Now It Can Be Told." This script was written hurriedly, and with some glaring errors and omissions, by a member of the Special Projects Division of CI&E, GHQ, SCAP. Every newspaper and journal in Japan was under the direct control of Occupation Headquarters. No Japanese-inspired news could be published until officially inspired stories had been given their space. Since all were postcensored, if any educational theory were expounded which did not follow the Occupation policy line, the offending publication was subject to immediate suspension or withdrawal of vital newsprint. By April 1947 national newspaper circulation had risen to 15,935,155—every word SCAP controlled. It was not quite as efficient propaganda as the prewar Japanese military clique had directed, but considering the handicaps of war damage and language the new rulers were making a creditable showing!

The Japanese Ministry of Education conducted a systematic reorientation of the teachers through a program of lectures known as "The New Educational Policy." Key educational officials from the prefectural offices, heads of secondary and youth schools, and principals of teacher training institutes and normal schools were assembled in Tokyo in October 1945 for a series of lectures and conferences on the new education policy, as seen through Ministry of Education eyes. They then returned to their schools or prefectures and lectured to the elementary and youth school-teachers on what they had learned. On 5 February 1945 the Ministry began an extensive series of school inspection tours in which the inspectors, in addition to checking on compliance with directives, organized discussion groups on the subject matter presented in the "New Educational Policy" series. The old *Kyōiku Kenshu Sho* (Institute for Educational Research), which before Surrender had provided the Bureau of Social Education with the propaganda with which to indoctrinate teachers, was reorganized and itself "reoriented" and began to prepare new material with which to re-indoctrinate teachers. This time the indoctrination was to be along "democratic" lines. Teachers' meetings and special teachers' institutes offering short courses were set up during the winter holidays in 1945–46 by the Ministry of Education in the normal schools and teachers were offered a bonus as an inducement to attend. Streaming out from the Ministry of Education, the only Japanese organ permitted to have direct liaison at a policy level with the Occupation forces, a systematic reorientation propaganda flowed to ostensibly nonofficial organs such as the *Zen Nippon Kyōin Kumiai* (All-Japan Teachers' Union), and the *Nippon Kyōikusha Kumiai* (Japan Educators' Union).

But the most diligent effort of the Ministry of Education to redirect the thinking of the teachers was probably the production of the *Guide to New Education in Japan*, published in May 1946, which has already been considered in the section on philosophy. As evidence of the immense distance the Ministry had come in reforming its own attitudes from those which created the Thought Control Bureau and issued the *Kokutai no Hongi* as the compulsory philosophy of education to be accepted by all teachers, pertinent sections of the introduction to the *Guide* are quoted:

The purpose in compiling this book is to give educators guiding principles as to what the new education of Japan is to aim at, what points it is to place emphasis on, and how it is to be carried out.

* * *

The Education Ministry does not intend to force the contents of this book on educators. Therefore educators neither need memorize this as a textbook themselves, nor teach it as a textbook to pupils. It expects, on the contrary, that the educators will avail themselves of these hints and by free investigations and criticisms, discover the purpose of the new education for themselves, grasp the most significant points, and work out their own methods. Or otherwise, if they make a more suitable guide to education after concerted study of this book and free discussion of its contents, it will be most desirable. On such an independent and cooperative attitude of educators themselves, more than on anything else, is to be founded the democratic education of Japan. In order to help you think about educational problems, at the end of each chapter, we put several problems to be researched or discussed by educators. (*Mombushō* trans.)

What were the results of this program of re-education? Two attitudes predominated. One was complete bewilderment at the sudden responsibility for self-direction and a complete lack of understanding of the meaning of the new social and political concepts which they inherited, "democracy," "freedom," "liberty," . . . The other was an honest desire to attempt something, to make a sincere effort to comply with these new responsibilities and to experience these new freedoms. But there have been grave difficulties. One is the tradition of guidance. The teachers always have been told what to think and it is difficult now to originate their own ideas. A second is the contradiction of teaching self-direction by imposed orders or by punitive measures. The Ministry of Education denied that it intended to force its policies upon the teacher, but the teacher knew that he would not teach long if he rejected them. The Occupation Headquarters claimed that teachers would be encouraged to evaluate critically the contents and policies with which they must work, but the teacher knew that if he even protested against one of these policies he would be purged and prohibited in perpetuity from practicing his profession. A third great difficulty has been the fear of deviation from an established interpretation. When the threat of dismissal or purge is present in every class period the teacher does not dare attempt any original explanation. He seeks some established cliché which has proved to be innocuous in the past and presents that as his explanation. Finally, there is the ever-present difficulty of the language and the writing system. The teacher cannot understand the difficult official phrases. He cannot read the more difficult passages in *kanji* (Chinese characters). The authors of *Guide to New Education in Japan* recognized these barriers to understanding and reorientation, and in their writing limited the ideographs to the 1,134 most frequently used as determined by the 1942 list of the Society for the Investigation of the National Language, and rewrote all passages that were not understandable to a test group of elementary schoolteachers.

Professional Preparation. The re-education of existing teachers merges almost imperceptibly into the program of the professional preparation of future teachers. The very changes made in the normal schools as a measure of reorientation for the students who had partially completed their training became in part the curriculum for future classes. But in one important point the two differ. Re-education was admittedly counterpropaganda. But the professional preparation of a teacher for a democracy is inevitably destined to fail if it is based on a conscious and deliberate attempt to force a change in the teacher's thinking. Traditionally Japanese teachers have been well trained. A few have even been well educated. But teaching in a democracy requires far more than a mere proficiency in pedagogical techniques. It demands a peculiar attitude of mind which can come only through inner growth and not from indoctrination from without.

During the first year of the Occupation there were made a number of changes in the curricula and administration of the normal schools. In general these changes were the obvious corrections demanded by certain of the changes which had been imposed on the schools: elimination of all military training, suspension of certain courses banned by the Occupation Authorities, elimination of certain types of supervision consistent with the abrogation of thought control laws, organization of student governments, granting of greater autonomy in minor details of administration, prohibition of further training in attitudes of militarism and ultranationalism. But almost without exception these were negative. They removed some of the obstructions of the past but they did not fabricate a structure for the future. Almost the only positive contributions to the professional preparation of teachers destined to guide children in a democratic state were the creation of forums and discussion groups which considered Occupational directives and the introduction of courses in current events—one of the personal interests of the Supreme Commander.

Establishing a positive program for the preparation of teachers in a democratic society is an exceedingly difficult task. As a minimum it must embrace five interlocking but fundamentally different programs. The first is the recruitment of appropriate personnel. This involves a complex of social recognitions, financial incentives, economic commitments to the structure of the system—all those things which will attract and hold the ablest in society. The second is the recognition of what characterizes good teaching and a good teacher. This involves such diverse elements as general acceptance of a respected but unimposed philosophy of education, conformity to a widely recognized code of teaching ethics, and establishment of standards for certification. The third is an adequate system of professional education. As an irreducible minimum, in a democratic system, this must set as its goal at least three types of learning: a general education which permits the teacher to interpret his own subject field in terms of the larger social implications; a thorough knowledge of the subject matter he is to teach; and a technical training in the various aspects of his profession—child psychology, school administration, teaching methods, and theories of pedagogy. The fourth is an administrative and supervisory organization which provides a congenial setting for the type of education proposed. This, in a democracy, presupposes a considerable degree of self-direction on the part of the teachers, of opportunities for professional recognition, of adequate teaching facilities, of suitable protection from occupational jeopardy yet continued stimulation of competition. And the fifth is continued intellectual and professional growth. This program must offer facilities for in-service education, for travel, for teachers' forums and conferences, for observation of demonstration and experimental schools, for sympathetic and professionally stimulating supervision, for incentives to aspire to higher degrees, and for the wide dissemination of educational researches through professional journals.

It is perhaps surprising in view of the widespread criticism of the Japanese educational system to note that in almost every detail of this complex program Japan has traditionally been acceptable and even outstanding. Even when the educational system was operating in the chaos of the early months of the Occupation, it was difficult for the foreign observer to point to any specific omission. He knew that the end-product of the existing system was not an acceptable teacher for a democratic society, but he frequently was at a loss to assign a cause. The United States Education Mission to Japan had as one of its five major committees a "Committee on Teaching and the Education of Teachers," headed by Dr. Frank N. Freeman, Dean of the School of Education of the University of California, and Dr. George W. Diemer, President of Central Missouri State Teachers College, as co-chairmen. Without a single exception every suggestion made by this committee in its report on 30 March 1946 for the emergency re-education and later in-service education of teachers had already been put into practice at least in a limited degree. After a searching investigation and with the sincere assistance of a Japanese committee including some of the ablest liberal educators in the nation, this committee was able to offer suggestions for only two fundamental changes in the formal preparation of future teachers: to increase the requirements for certification, and simultaneously to raise the normal school to the level of a four-year college; and to permit a considerable degree of autonomy in curriculum construction in the improved normal schools. Both reforms have been frequently advocated by Japanese educators even during the period of domination by the Japanese military clique.

Wherein was the old teacher training bad? It was not bad. It was very, very good. For the preparation of teachers who were to practice their profession in the society of prewar Japan and to teach the prescribed curricula in the official schools of a totalitarian state, the Japanese teachers were eminently successful. Their job was to transmit knowledge, not to create it nor to assist in learning. Their teaching was formal and stereotyped, not free and inspiring. In memory work and manual skills their techniques were acknowledged to be without peer. But their purpose was to train standardized units for the State, not to awake the latent best in the individual. The thing which has been discredited with Defeat and Occupation is the goal of these teachers, not the methods which they used to attain that discarded goal. The *Report* of the Education Mission to Japan says on p. 34: "Democratic education can be characterized by recognition of individual differences in pupils, by an emphasis on the development of the potentialities of the individual, and by the goal of acceptable and effective participation in the social group."

Can the old methods achieve this new goal? Will the existing program of teacher preparation supply new methods?

The teachers of Japan must learn to think for themselves. They must learn to direct their own activities. Only practice and the force of necessity is likely to achieve this change. The Japanese must be prepared for many mistakes, for loss of efficiency, for poor teaching, for dismay and bewilderment. But if democratic education is to survive, the teachers must be given the chance for inner growth. The old methods will not achieve this new goal. The existing program of teacher preparation is unlikely to supply new methods which are better able to achieve it. But free competition with proper incentives and appropriate relinquishment of controls will produce leaders among the teachers who will devise the new methods. The teachers must be thrown on their own resources. They must face the alternative of thinking for themselves or of failing. The system of teacher training in Japan today is adequate in everything but the determination to be self-directing. Fortunately many gifted Japanese themselves recognize this lack and maintain a constant pressure for its correction. A quotation of a portion of an editorial, "Education for Personality" which appeared in the 4 November 1945 edition of the *Nippon Times*, is typical of this viewpoint:

The basic fault of the old educational system . . . was not that it emphasized militarism and ultra-nationalism, necessarily, but that it regimented the students and subordinated them to the immediate purposes of the State. The true aim of education, particularly in a democratic society, should have for its principal aim the development of personality.

Education for the development of individual personality, by the very nature of things, cannot be fostered by bureaucratic control. Regimented indoctrination in democracy is hardly more democratic than regimented indoctrination in totalitarianism, and is just as destructive of personality. A truly democratic education requires real freedom of learning and instruction. Where there is little freedom, there can be but little development of character and personality. And freedom cannot prevail in education as long as bureaucratic control of the schools prevails.

The educational policy of the past, which deprived the people of their freedom of judgment and which extrolled obedience as the highest virtue, was made possible by the rigid control of the schools by the State. If this old policy is to be changed, it cannot be done by mere fiat by the State; the State must withdraw from its rigid control of the schools and leave direction of the schools to the educators.

A great teacher is a rare phenomenon in any age or country, but education for democracy depends upon the creative initiative of great teachers. Everything must therefore be done to promote the emergence of such teachers in Japan at this time. If this involves the withdrawal of government control from education, as it undoubtedly does, such withdrawal should be carried out without hesitation.

Methodology, Curriculum and Textbooks— From the Authoritarian to the Democratic

It is impossible to consider traditional Japanese method, curriculum, and textbooks as anything but inseparable. In a democratic state where the curriculum is determined by the faculty of the individual school, by the desires of the parents and the individual needs of the students, and where the teacher is at liberty to select his own textbook and choose his own method of presentation, both commercial competition and professional incentives combine to present an almost limitless array of alternatives. But in totalitarian Japan where the goal of education was established by the State, where the teachers were trained and later compelled to present their material in a stereotyped and approved manner, where the content of the instruction was determined by the State, and where all textbooks and teachers' manuals were minutely censored and sanctioned and the majority, at least in the compulsory education system, were actually written by the State, the method, curriculum, and teaching matériel became an interlocking whole efficiently designed to implement the canonized educational philosophy. The purpose of education was to create a high level of utilitarian and technical attainment and to provide the State with an ample supply of efficient instruments of national policy. The foreign observer stigmatized Japanese education as formal and stereotyped. The Japanese replied that it was efficient. None denied that it was authoritarian.

These characteristics of Japanese education are not a product of the war nor of the years immediately preceding the war. They are a heritage of the great social revolution which accompanied the Meiji Restoration. They are not a product of militarist and ultranationalist manipulation, but an inherent element in the social philosophy which produced Japanese militarism and ultranationalism. These latter ideologies may be discredited and abandoned, yet the conception of the absolute subservience of the individual to the state remain. With it would remain authoritarianism in education. Five brief quotations drawn from the writings of qualified foreign observers may serve to illustrate the traditional quality of this characteristic.

In *The Educational System of Japan*, Occasional Report No. 3, to the Director General of Education in India, Dr. W. H. SHARP, Professor of Philosophy at Elphinstone College, Bombay, and an educational observer in Japan, wrote on p. 35: "But amid all the fluctuations of detail, the leaders of Japan cannot be said to have wavered in their main objects, to enable her to hold her own with the other nations of the world in peace and in war, and to instil into her children those principles of loyalty, patriotism, and self-help, to which their country owes so much today."

In 1915 the *United States Bureau of Education Report* carried a monograph entitled "System of Public Instruction in Japan," which included this passage on p. 750: "Loyalty to the Emperor, morality, industry, and thrift, the necessary qualities of good citizenship, are the purposes toward which the instruction in all schools and higher institutions is constantly directed, and this final purpose is kept steadily in view in the administration and organization of the system of education."

In 1924 J. Ingram BRYAN, for 16 years a teacher in Japan, wrote in his volume, *Japan from Within*, p. 192:

In the Japanese system all pupils are turned into the same machine, and in a prescribed time are all turned out after the same pattern, models of absolute subservience to authority, recognizing no other duty, and claiming none but conferred rights, yet grossly ignorant of the first principles of citizenship and good government, as understood in occidental countries.

In an article entitled, "Educational Trends in Japan" in *School and Society* for 8 February 1930, Ernest W. CLEMENT wrote on pp. 178–179:

One great obstacle to proper education in Japan has been, and still is, the fact that the curriculum is overcrowded. Modern Western branches of learning (which have come to be a necessity) were superimposed upon the former Sino-Japanese course of study (which cannot be eliminated). It is quite a common thing for a pupil to have about thirty hours, more or less, of work with a teacher in his regular schedule. It is true that in some cases, previous preparation is unnecessary, but, in general, the student can not make proper preparation; so that the work which should be done by the pupil in his study has to be done with the instructor in the classroom. The latter, therefore, may not be entirely to blame if he resorts to the lecture system. . . .

Another problem in connection with the rigid system and tyranny of its red tape is the tremendous emphasis placed on examinations. The proportion of candidates that can be admitted to higher schools averages about 20 per cent of the applicants who take the examinations and in the case of certain favored schools it falls as low as about 12 per cent. . . . The tyranny of the examination system puts cramming at a premium; also the memoriter methods of study that have been inherited from the old system encourage cramming.

Dr. C. Burnell OLDS in his article, "Education for Conquest: the Japanese Way," in *Foreign Affairs* for October 1942, p. 38, wrote in connection with the higher schools and universities:

Often the student is subjected to 35 hours of lectures a week; adding the hours needed for directed study, this leaves practically no time for private reading. The examination is ever in view. If the student is not prepared to express himself in that and in every other way just as officialdom requires, so much the worse for him. There is a set of approved principles and ideals, and on these he is spoon fed. Accept them, give utterance to them, think in accordance with them, and all goes well. But break away from them, repudiate the mass-production requirement, think independently, and all will go badly. Students are herded through their courses in batches. Originality of thought is not only not desired, it is not tolerated.

The Curriculum. The Japanese curriculum since 1872 has been a modified form of the French encyclopedic curriculum. Historically the two stem from similar causes, the necessity of training citizens for a highly centralized and authoritarian state. The Japanese curriculum of 1872, established by the *Educational Code* of that year, was an admitted copy of the French plan, and despite almost continuous, and minor, revisions in the courses of studies, the Japanese curriculum of the next 75 years was a direct denial of official claims of "uniqueness." So evident are the French origins of the existing curriculum that a startling parallelism exists between the Japanese and other copies of the French system—the Argentine and Turkish, for example. Three characteristics are evident: it is static, it is uniform, and it is imposed.

The curriculum has been astonishingly static. If the courses of studies in the two levels of the elementary school may be taken as a sample, and these two curricula are overwhelmingly the most important on the basis of numbers with never less than three quarters of all the students of Japan currently enrolled at that level, the changes made in 75 years appear negligible. The plan of studies which accompanied the *Educational Code of 1872* provided for an elementary school of two levels: the lower division having children of the first four grades (6 through 9 years of age); and the upper division having the next four grades (10 through 13 years of age). The curriculum included morals, Japanese language (spelling, writing, conversation, reading, grammar, and letter writing), arithmetic (as far as division in the lower grades and trigonometry and geometry in the upper), history, geography, science (including outlines of botany, chemistry, "natural philosophy," and physiology in the upper division), singing, and gymnastics. In localities where there was a need and demand for them, the following four subjects might be added: one or two foreign languages (English, French, and German), book-keeping, drawing, and political economy (civics and government)/ The Elementary School Ordinance of 1890, Imperial Ordinance No. 215, in Articles II and IV, made sewing for girls in the lower section and agriculture, geometry, and commerce in the upper division electives. The course in commerce replaced the old offering of bookkeeping. Geography was increased and divided into two courses, foreign geography and Japanese geography. The "normal year" of 1937 showed almost no changes. History in the lower division (by then six years in length) was confined to Japanese history, and handicrafts and technical studies for boys and girls had replaced the regionalized studies of agriculture and commerce in the upper (which was reduced to two or three years in length). The name arithmetic was given to the mathematical courses in the upper division, although the content was similar, involving simple algebra, elements of plane geometry, and the rudiments of trigonometry. In 1947, with the gradual readmission of the temporarily banned courses in morals, history, and geography, the general offerings were again almost identical with the exception of the prohibition of military arts and military training in the physical education program.

The amount of time devoted to each of these subjects has fluctuated constantly but always within narrow limits. Thus the basic Imperial Ordinance No. 215 on Elementary Schools, issued in 1890, set a minimum of 18 and a maximum of 30 hours per week for the lower division; and a minimum of 24 and a maximum of 36 hours per week in the upper division. The constant pressure to include more subjects so that the child would be given a "broader education" led the Japanese educational authorities to schedule very close to the maximum and the total number of hours per week did not vary more than 10% in the half century between this ordinance and the writing of the present basic curriculum. In the "normal year" of 1937 there were 21, 23, 25, 29, 30, 30, 30, and 30 hours per week, respectively, in the eight grades of elementary school.

The emphasis and orientation of the individual subjects has shown almost an equal lack of change. Such subjects as mathematics, language, and physical education might reasonably be expected to have evaded the increasing nationalization which the country was experiencing in that period. But in *Shūshin* (morals or ethics), the very heart of the nationalist propaganda, it was to be expected that wide changes would be made if the rise of ultra-nationalism was in fact a true ideological revolution and not merely the revelation of an ideology which had always been present. In the little volume, *An Outline History of Japanese Education*, prepared for the Philadelphia International Exposition and published by D. Appleton & Co. in 1876, the Japanese Department of Education on page 20 wrote that the contents of the courses on morals then included, "Doctrines to foster filial obedience; conversations on how to behave; work on virtue, written in pure Japanese; guide to the customs and manners of the world, etc." Sixty years later the purpose of the morals courses was given in Article II of the "Regulations Governing the Enforcement of the Elementary School Act," and quoted in the volume, *Education in Japan*, VII Conference of the World Federation of Education Associations (Tokyo, 1937), p. 395:

[. . . [to] help children in the practical application of filial piety, brotherly love, affection, diligence, respectfulness, modesty, fidelity, courage and other virtues. As the course gradually develops, the application should be extended to the obligations to the state and the community, and efforts should be made to implant in the minds of the pupils loyalty and patriotism, to ennoble their character, to solidify their principles of life, to promote their progressive spirit and to heighten their sense of public morality] (*Mombushō* trans.)

The explanation of this pronounced resistance to change in spite of innumerable superficial reforms lies in the Japanese belief in the desirability of uniformity. Four elements have contributed to this concept: the body-of-knowledge philosophy, the State-centered curriculum, the confusion of uniformity with efficiency, and the creation-by-authority procedure.

The Japanese adopted from their French model the conception of a curriculum as a body of knowledge. Theirs was not essentially different from the traditional American conception of the curriculum as a prescribed quantity of subject matter, which gave way to the revolutionary idea of the curriculum as a selection of activities, including, of course, the acquisition of knowledge, first dictated by the student's own capacities, interests, and needs, and more recently extended to his relationship with the community. The French, and Japanese, argued thus. There is a specific body of accumulated knowledge. A certain determinable portion of it is "necessary" if the student is to be "educated." *Ergo*, give the student the indicated dosage of each of the disciplines. Japanese education, instead of experiencing the child-centered revolt against the tradition, strengthened this philosophy by a well-developed conception of the State-centered curriculum. If a student is thought of solely as a unit in a political structure and not as an individual with personal needs and desires, it should theoretically be possible to devise the perfect list of skills and attitudes he should display. These skills could then be taught and the attitudes be induced by an efficient and standardized training program. Education would thus be reduced to exposure to a pre-determined number of hours of each of the subjects considered necessary to train the citizen for his particular predestined niche. The education program would be placed on the same impersonal level as a machinery for the buffing process in manufacture. In justification of this ruthless denial of the individual it was argued that uniformity was, or at least created, efficiency. The fallacy of this viewpoint has already been explored in the section on philosophy and need not be belabored. Uniformity does bring a shallow and superficial type of efficiency in lowering the per-unit cost of training. It fails miserably, however, in attaining the real efficiency of utilizing fully the natural abilities of the individual. But if the State-centered and uniformity-efficiency concepts are accepted, the final belief that the curriculum must be constructed by a central authority and handed down to lower educational echelons as an inviolable entity, can hardly be attacked. The State should be able to dictate the training program it requires.

Perhaps a less fundamental but equally cogent reason for the relatively small amount of change occasioned by the repeated "curriculum reforms" may be found in the character of the officials employed as curriculum experts. They have been typical bureaucrats, rather less than technically qualified, fearful of break with precedent, protecting their tenure by conformity with accepted procedures of the past. A quotation from the penetrating and prophetic report of Mr. R. G. Watson, in *Education in Japan*, United States Bureau of Education Circular No. 2, p. 58, is as pertinent today as in 1873 when it was drafted:

The native officials . . . varied their leisure by changing the course of studies and adopting new ones. It was simply a matter of mensuration and Chinese characters. So many hours per week, so many square inches of paper, fill up the squares with Chinese characters (which often mistranslate what the native official knows almost nothing about), and the new curriculum is laid down, not to be taken up again for several weeks. Having found out, however, that he had not attained to perfection in curricula-making, the official, believing that he had struck the right course this time, tried another. Having thus in a few months acquired skill in making short roads to learning, gained some routine-knowledge and a faint conception of foreign education, he was promoted to a higher office in the same or another department and a new, inexperienced, and incompetent man stepped into his place.

The curriculum is imposed by superior authority. In its simplest form it is a course of studies imposed by law or by Ministerial order. This is the curriculum of the bureaucrat who shuffles subjects and class hours. But the curriculum in its broader sense is imposed by two devices: the control of thought, and the interlocking with other elements in the educational system. This is the curriculum of the classroom, the content of teaching.

Thought control was presumed to be dead in the Occupation and Japanese and foreigner alike hoped that it would not be resurrected after the final withdrawal of direct influence by the Allied Powers. But control of thought continued. Fear of deviation from the absolute letter of the law was just as strong a deterrent to the teacher under the Occupation as it was to the teacher under Gen. ARAKI Sadao, prewar Minister of Education. He still received the detailed orders, the list of subjects, the teachers' manuals, and the official interpretations, first from Headquarters, SCAP, and then from the Ministry of Education. He still feared punitive action for any misstep, any statement which might be construed to be contrary to "occupation policy." He knew that a vigorous accusation against him, based on any deviation from the official statement might put his job or his person in jeopardy. He still taught from an official, censored textbook. He still listened to an official, censored radio. He still read an official, censored press. He was not blind to these controls from central authority. He was in fact inured to them. But while they continued to exist it was unrealistic to expect him to take the dangerous step of breaking with tradition, of evading the stultifying official curriculum, and of attempting to enrich its minimum offerings from his own resources.

The curriculum is imposed through its interlocking action with other elements of the system. The teacher-training program has been a plodding, methodical preparation to teach the official courses in the official manner. The textbooks have been supplied the teacher and with them official manuals. No other texts have been legal. If the teacher is to teach he must teach the official courses, from the official texts, according to the official methods. The school organization has been dictated. Accelerated and enriched classes are dangerous if not impossible when the most minute detail of the administration and organization of the schools is established by law. It is not possible to introduce a new course without permission from the Ministry of Education, and during the Occupation from the Allied Headquarters. The schools, the grades, the days, the hours, the lessons, the subjects, the explanations have been dictated by the central authority. Only the rare individual has broken with these controls in the past, and he almost inevitably was forced to teach in private schools. The Occupation brought lip service to a flexible curriculum, but the restrictive controls remained.

Methodology. The same criticisms which have been leveled at the stereotyped Japanese curriculum may be made of traditional Japanese methodology. It is formal, stereotyped, and authoritarian. The traditional is perpetuated by the inflexible instruction in the normal schools, by the minutely detailed teachers' manuals, by the frequent inspections of national and prefectural supervisors who check compliance but offer little inspiration for personal growth; and by the system of evaluating the success of the teacher through the results of his students in the severely competitive and formalized examinations. A method is judged by its effectiveness in inculcating the predetermined attitude or required skill, by its efficiency in accomplishing this end at a minimum of expense and time, and by its consistency with subject matter of the instruction. It is conceivable that education for citizenship in a totalitarian state might be centered in the personality of the individual child, but it is an unlikely and somewhat ludicrous possibility. The Japanese student was being trained to obey blindly, to accept anonymity, and to efface his own personality. Any method but an authoritarian one would have seemed inappropriate. Now having exchanged masters he neither expects nor receives much more liberty.

Not all of the authoritarian techniques which characterized prewar Japanese educational methodology were due to the militaristic and ultranationalistic political philosophy of the State. Many were a heritage of the remote past, when China was the only model, and Buddhist monks and impoverished *samurai* were the only teachers. Chinese education was the laborious mastery of the mechanical and artistic skills of writing, the painstaking memorization of the accumulated knowledge of ancient scholars, and the development of a reverence for antiquity. The Chinese sage and teacher transmitted knowledge, he did not stimulate the student to create knowledge. In the millennium before the Meiji Restoration during which Chinese education was modified to fit the Japanese scene, the development of a graceful calligraphy, the ability to imitate standard Chinese styles of writing, the mastery of utterly mechanical calculations with the abacus (*soroban*), the prodigious memory feat of learning to recognize and to reproduce several thousand Chinese ideographs, and a thorough indoctrination in Confucian ethics constituted the basis of education. Japanese contributions during this period included a knowledge of the formal techniques of the tea ceremony (*cha-no-yu*), an appreciation of the extremely formal and traditional drama (*Nō*), grace in the ancient Japanese dance (*odori*), deftness in flower arrangement (*ikebana*), and skill in the military arts (*budō*). These were not studies which produced originality or self-direction. They were not taught by masters who tolerated self-expression. In the schools taught by *samurai* the teacher drilled his pupils as he drilled his troops. In the *terakoya*, or temple school, the students were drilled by Buddhist monks, frequently *Zen* to whom rigid self-discipline, meditation, and denial of self were integral and indispensable parts of their philosophy. The student literally looked to his master with religious reverence. Which of the two voices was the more authoritarian, the brusque bark of command or the passive whisper of enlightenment, it is difficult to decide. Both have echoed long beyond their age.

The effects of Latin scholarship on the methods of teaching English are familiar to every student of American education. Perhaps a short description of a Japanese class in calligraphy (*shūji*) may draw the parallel and illustrate the perpetuation of the Chinese and Buddhist tradition. This is not an ordinary class in writing conducted in some rural school by an overworked elementary schoolteacher. It is not an ordinary class with a forest of children's arms moving in unison, writing in exaggerated brush strokes in the air or tracing evanescent ideographs in clear water on a flat absorbent stone. This is a class conducted by a specialist teacher in calligraphy, a model class presented to officials of the Occupation and later to the members of the United States Education Mission to Japan as the ideal to which the more progressive schools should aspire. The notes of a naval officer on the staff of CI&E, GHQ, SCAP, are quoted:

When we arrived we found the class-room to be a special one constructed to look like an ordinary room in one of the better Japanese homes. It was also used for certain of the classes in *shūshin* (Ethics) and for the tea-ceremony. The floors were covered by the traditional *tatami* or rice-straw matting. On one side were sliding doors with rice paper windows pasted on a fragile and intricate lattice of wood. On the other was the *tokonoma* or alcove, which the peasants say is reserved for the Emperor should he pay a visit, but which is actually used to display some treasured work of art. On the wall of this alcove was a single *kakemono* or wall hanging composed solely of four beautifully executed Chinese characters in *sōsho*, the cursive form known as "grass-writing." Below this on the floor was a simple piece of driftwood, weathered a beautiful silver grey. On the floor near the door was a low vase with a flower arrangement which appeared to excite the admiration of the visiting Japanese as a masterpiece of execution.

The students, perhaps a dozen girls in their early teens, were lined up in a row facing the *tokonoma*, all dressed in *kimono* and all kneeling Japanese fashion. Before each one was a neat stack of rice paper provided for this occasion though due to paper shortage old newspapers are ordinarily used. At their right knee and arranged in a rigid geometric pattern were their instruments: a flat box with a wet stone to take the India ink, a thick stick of the ink, a tiny pot of water, and the indispensable brush or *fude*. When writing ordinary lessons the students use a slender bamboo brush with a wisp of hair drawn to a fine point, and their delicate strokes make ideographs of almost microscopic lines. But in a practice class or in a formal exhibition of calligraphy, which is considered an art not a tool, a large thick brush with a bulb of ox hairs as thick as a slender wrist is used. Each of the students was silent, impassive, apparently unaware of anything but her meditation.

The teacher entered the room. He was dressed in a brown *kimono* and his head was shaven in the distinctive manner of a Buddhist priest. He walked with the gliding motion which is considered etiquette in a formal Japanese gathering. He was careful never to step on the black cloth strips which marked the joining of two mats. He made right angle turns and paralleled the walls. He buckled his knees and silently and effortlessly collapsed into the kneeling position. No word had been spoken, yet in the oppressive silence of the room the man's personality was so profound that a tension was obvious in both students and spectators. The teacher bent forward to the floor and remained a moment in silent meditation. It appeared, though it may have been an illusion, that he was in prayer. At last the man raised himself and continued to kneel in apparently sightless meditation. His face was like a mask. At last, and it must have been minutes after he had kneeled, he began to prepare his tools. Each piece was lifted with a precise and deft touch, without looking or fumbling. Each was handled in a rigid vibrating manner, almost as if the man were in a trance and his muscles were jerking through some outside force. He worked the ink stick back and forth on the stone, then took the brush and worked it back and forth on the stone until it was thoroughly saturated. All this had been done with only his right hand, but now in a highly stylized and dignified manner he grasped it first with his left, then ran his fingers along the handle and over the end to grip it tightly in his right fist, point downward.

Suddenly the man appeared to explode. He lunged forward as if stabbing the paper and smashed the brush against it to make a great smeared blot. Then with the muscles of his bared arm rigid and the hand quivering with intensity he traced the ideograph with a continuous sweep made up of jerky strokes. When he had completed two intertwining characters, vaguely resembling tigers, which are both symbolically and semantically connected with the ideographs, he sat back on his heels again, kneeling Japanese fashion, and formally put his brush away. His chest was rising and falling with the exertion, but he had not said a word nor allowed any emotion to show on his face.

Apparently without signal but at exactly the same moment each of the students began to duplicate the master's actions. Each drew two characters, the same two. Each made her bow. Each knelt in silence. When they were through, the teacher rose formally and glided along behind the rows. He spoke less than a dozen words, all too low to be heard by the spectators, but two of the students were crushed, one elated. Only their eyes betrayed them. The master left the room and the students silently followed. The class had taken forty minutes and despite the cold I was perspiring. One of the Japanese officials kept repeating "How inspiring" and "How beautiful."

Most classes, of course, have not retained the exotic quality of this class in *shūji*. At the elementary level they are rather formal lesson and recitation periods not unlike the traditional form of

American classes. At the secondary school level they are cramming sessions in the boys' schools, at least in the section leading to the university, with every effort bent on preparing the student for his competitive examinations to the higher school. In the girls' schools they are routinized instruction in the several domestic arts, in a somewhat diluted curriculum of nationalism, a simplified copy of the boys' curriculum, and in those fine arts considered essential to the cultured woman. At the university level they are lectures in which a body of knowledge is transmitted to the student, not periods of research and experiment in which the student learns. With the notable exception of some distinguished private schools, of classes in certain special skill subjects such as music and art, of the excellent kindergartens, and of classes in a small minority of technical subjects at the university level such as surveying or accounting, Japanese education may be characterized as directive rather than participatory. The teachers, instead of participating in teachers' meetings, modifying their own courses of study and teaching techniques, and working out their own instructional problems as in an American school, simply follow the explicit directions from the Ministry of Education, from the teachers' manuals, and from the supervisors. The students, instead of taking part in the selection of material, organization and preparation of the lesson, and conduct of the class merely obey, memorize, demonstrate proficiency, accept blindly what the teacher or the textbook presents.

Many Japanese teachers who remember the relative liberty they enjoyed before 1937, may protest these statements as being too sweeping and unfair. They will point out that in their own classes some of the freedoms just denied were granted the students. In the light of subsequent events, however, the ostensible freedoms appear to have been only a more adroit form of control. A trained horse is not constantly pricked with the spurs or pulled up by the bit. As long as student and teacher were doing what the *Mombushō* wanted, they were permitted to pretend to certain liberties. But the threat was always present and with the rise of the war crisis, the controls were not even camouflaged. The Occupation again adopted the stage setting of freedom but retained the controls.

It would be incorrect to say that there is apathy, for there is a spurious vitality to the class, the disciplined interest produced by the whip of the teacher's voice and by the constant pressure of conforming to the accepted pattern of class behavior. In higher levels this interest is real inasmuch as the student knows that his entire career depends upon mastering the subject material and successfully demonstrating his mastery in the annual competitive examinations. But there is nowhere the intellectual curiosity which produces living classes at the elementary level and scholarship at the higher. The child is assigned a lesson, he memorizes the content, and he repeats by rote the appropriate answers to the questions. Few schools in Japan below the higher level have libraries in the Occidental sense. Those that exist are deposits of authority, not sources for independent learning. The laboratories are for mass repetition of some classic experiment whose results are already known and memorized by the class, not for the pragmatic solution of problems arising from the individual student's interests and needs. Japan has in form every teaching technique that has been developed in the Occident. Classes of students visit every conceivable institution or locality which might serve their education, from vantage points in the mountains for "cherry blossom viewing" to massive industrial installations for the production of newsprint or the generation of electricity. They have libraries, laboratories, field trips, practice classes, seminars, colloquiums, in-service training, correspondence courses, even progressive schools, at least to the extent of modifications of the Dalton and Winnetka Plans. In some individual instances these appurtenances of the democratic methodology have been successful, usually where the faculty has the ferment of some foreign-trained instructors. But considered as a system Japanese methodology is still formal, stereotyped, and appallingly autocratic.

Textbooks and Teaching Manuals. On 20 September 1945 the Ministry of Education, independently and without the knowledge of the embryonic Educational Sub-Section in Occupation Headquarters, broadcast a set of directions to all schools in Japan entitled "Directions Concerning the Handling of Textbooks in Accordance with Postwar Conditions." Because it constitutes tangible evidence of what the Japanese themselves considered unacceptable in their texts, the opening paragraphs are quoted:

(1)   Although it will be permitted until further notice to continue to use the same text books in the primary schools, supplementary schools [youth schools], and secondary schools it is required that

all teaching materials that are not appropriate in the light of the Imperial Rescript proclaiming the end of the war be struck out either entirely or partly, or be handled with utmost care. Such materials are the following: (a) Materials that emphasize the national defence and armament. (b) Materials fostering the fighting spirit. (c) Materials that may be harmful to international goodwill. (d) Materials that have become obsolete as being entirely removed from present postwar conditions and the everyday life of the students. (e) Other materials that are not appropriate in the light of the Imperial Rescript.

(2) It is allowed to introduce new teaching materials in order to make up for the omissions provided that they are: (a) Materials concerning the maintenance of the national polity [*kokutai*] and the establishment of high moral education. (b) Materials promoting culture and moral education. (c) Materials concerning agricultural production. (d) Materials fostering the scientific spirit and its concrete application. (e) Materials on physical education and hygiene. (f) Materials on international peace. (*Mombushō* trans.)

The remaining portion of the broadcast document contained a list of lessons found in the national readers which were considered examples of the type of material to be eliminated. The lessons listed in three of these books, taken at different levels, will serve as an illustration.

In the Second Reader for the Lower Section the lessons on *The Divine Sword*, *Submarines*, *The South Seas*, *The Movie*, *The Military Flag*, *Presents for the Soldiers*, and *The Three Heroes* were considered objectionable. Thus the propaganda of militarism had been carried from the Sacred Sword of Murakumo which *Susano-o* the Storm-God, brother of *Amaterasu Ōmikami*, took from the tail of the serpent, to the three soldiers who died as a human torpedo in the China Campaign and whose statue in Shiba, Tokyo, had become a symbol of heroism and loyalty to the Emperor to every Japanese boy. The Sixth Reader of the Lower Section contained *The Mother of the Sailor*, *The Invisible Entry*, *The Country of Formosa*, *The Eighth of December* (the American December 7), *The Death of the Invincible Man of War*, *Landing in the Face of the Enemy*, and *The Hospital Ship*. The Second Reader of the Upper Section contained *A Solitary Flight*, *Driving in the Attack*, *The Transport Ships*, and *The Naval Battle of Hawaii*.

This last story will serve as an example of the perplexing inconclusiveness of even the most flagrant of the propaganda inserted in these texts. The story was that of a young naval officer in one of the one-man submarines used in an attempt to sneak past the peripheral defenses of Pearl Harbor. As presented in the story, and without the psychological context of Japanese perfidy possessed by the least informed American student but unavailable to the Japanese, the attempted entry into the harbor by this officer, his participation in the attack, and his death in the submarine, seem relatively innocuous. He was represented as having no prior knowledge of the mission, of being informed of the existence of a state of war while at sea on a secret mission, of driving into the harbor while buzzing Japanese planes were fighting with American surface defenses, and of dying at his post after the submarine was disabled. If the names and dates had been altered, thus stripping the story of its context, it would not have been unacceptable in translated form in an American reading textbook, designed for the same age level. It was the context which made the story vicious and the context was missing. The context was supplied by the teacher, and the teacher was directed by the teachers' manual. If this flagrant propaganda could present so innocent an outward appearance, might not other equally objectionable materials escape detection where the context was not so well known to the officers charged with censorship?

If at times during the subsequent censorship of the 173 official national textbooks there grew doubt as to whether the Ministry had in fact intended them to serve as propaganda, this doubt was dispelled by reference to a passage in a Ministry of Education news release (No. 11 of May 1941) on the occasion of announcing the new national textbooks. It said in part:

But even in the life of these innocent little ones there is some element of gravity and piety. On *Tenchōsetsu* (the Emperor's birthday), *Meijisetsu* (anniversary of Emperor Meiji's birthday), New Year's Day, and *Kigensetsu* (Empire Day) they attend the ceremony held at their school, when they pay respect to the Imperial Portraits and sing the national anthem. At home they lead a moral life in their way, performing their filial duties to their parents and grandparents. There are also the family Buddhist altar, the family Shinto shrine, and the Shinto shrine of their birthplaces, institutions to which they are taken by their parents to offer prayers. The environment in which these little ones live is full of things which contribute to the fostering in them of the concept of national polity (*kokutai*) and spirit of piety and of reverence toward their ancestors.

Children's songs, such as "Evening Burning, Little Burning" and "O Full Moon" are the expressions of praise of their beautiful land, and their search for cicadas and grasshoppers may be regarded as the beginning of their interest in science. Playing marbles and shop develop in the children mathematical and economic ideas. Drawing, paper-work and toy making all help to foster creativeness and inventiveness in the child's mind. Those brought up in the mountainous districts have a yearning after the sea lying beyond the hills, while the children born and bred by the sea grow up to the defense of the island country. Since the outbreak of the current hostilities, they have seen their fathers, uncles and brothers leave for the front, and have heard from those relatives about the battle fields over the sea. And not a few of the children become ambitious to go over to the Continent. They play soldiers, address soldiers in the street, take radio calisthenics, coax their parents to buy them toy tanks, pore over picture books of warships, are keenly interested in the airplane, and fly model planes. Thus we are surprised to find that so many things in the children's life are available for training them as Japanese subjects all sound and up to date. Schoolbooks for the first period (lower elementary school) are intended to draw attention to their lives which are occupied with such innocent games and lead them educationally so as to develop their spiritual lives. They embody, so to speak, the spirit of what we call the highly organized national defense structure.

Pre-Surrender control of Japanese textbooks was of three types: at the university level, where few textbooks were used, there was virtually no control except postcensorship and banning in the case of books antagonistic to the *kokutai;* at the secondary level, in some classes of the youth schools, and in virtually all technical and vocational fields, the private writing and publication of textbooks was permitted provided the manuscript had been precensored and "sanctioned" by the Ministry of Education; and at the elementary level all textbooks were written, published, and distributed by the Ministry of Education. These three basic systems constitute the full range of alternatives if the textbooks are to be controlled formally: postcensorship, precensorship, and direct official preparation.

On 27 February 1946 after an extended investigation of the continued banning of books in the libraries of Japan, the Headquarters of the Supreme Commander ordered the Imperial Japanese Gov-

ernment to remove all bans on the free circulation of books. This
directive was aimed at the abuses of Article XIX of the Publication Law (No. 15 of 14 April 1893) which authorized the
Naimushō, Minister of Home Affairs, "to prohibit the sale, and
confiscate the draft of books and other publications, the contents
of which are deemed injurious to peace and order or prejudicial
to public morals." This responsibility was delegated to the
Hoanbu, or Peace Preservation Department of the *Naimushō*,
and through it to the local police units. In 1941 this responsibility
was turned over to the Bureau of Information (*Jōhōbu*) of the
Imperial Cabinet (*Naikaku*), which in December 1945 was disbanded. The stupidity of these police officials contributed almost
as much as the fanatical nationalism of the government to an
oppressive, and ludicrous, prohibition. Books ordered banned were
of four types: books advocating political or social changes at
variance with the status quo in Japan; books attacking the mythology connected with the early history of Japan, the divine origin
of the Emperor, the people, the land, and State Shinto; books on
the Christan religion; and books of an erotic nature. Among the
foreign books banned were the Holy Bible; the *Outline of History* and *The Work, Wealth and Happiness of Mankind* by H. G.
WELLS; the collected works of Karl MARX; and the philosophical
studies of Bertrand RUSSELL, including *Education and the Social
Order, Power*, and *An Inquiry into Meaning and Truth*. Among
the Japanese volumes banned were the constitutional studies of
Dr. MINOBE Tatsukichi; the works on capitalism and materialism
by Dr. KAWAKAMI Jotaro, including *Shihonshugi Hattatsushi*
("Historic Development of Capitalism"); the studies of the social
foundations of politics by the exiled Communist, ŌYAMA Ikuo;
those on political economy by Dr. KAWAI Eijiro of Tokyo Imperial University; critical studies on ancient Japanese history, including *Jindaishi no Kenkyū* ("A History of the Mythological
Age") and *Jōdai Nihon no Shakai Oyobi Shiso* ("Thoughts and
Society of Ancient Japan"), by Dr. TSUDA Sokichi of Waseda
University; and the book, *Ikite Ita Heitai* ("Surviving Soldiers"),
by ISHIKAWA Tatsuzo, on the atrocities committed by Japanese
soldiers during the rape of Nanking. A measure of the ridiculous
implementation of this postcensorship was offered when the local
police officials, interpreting their instructions to the letter, directed
university library authorities to remove the banned books from

the stacks and to put them in a separate place under lock and key. They admitted to the librarians, however, that there was no restriction on the free access of the faculty members to the depository. As a result in every university investigated by the Occupation Headquarters, including Waseda University and Tokyo Imperial University, the restriction had the sole effect of putting the banned titles on reserve and of emphasizing their contents.

The precensorship of privately prepared textbooks through the system of Ministry of Education "sanction," is familiar to students of education in any centralized educational system. Two procedures for control are commonly used. In the first procedure, the Ministry issues a precise list of the required content of the courses in the required curriculum. Commercial competition makes any textbook which does not concur with this minutely detailed content and organization doomed to financial failure. Authors must write to fit the course, and space limitations prohibit their writing beyond the course. The other procedure is to require that each proposed text be submitted in manuscript form for exhaustive scrutiny and censorship. Any reference to unacceptable material or any interpretation or commentary antagonistic to the official view is not only censored but becomes the basis for punitive action. Japan has used both methods: the former in general for the textbooks in the social studies, and the latter for the textbooks in vocational and technical subjects. The Occupation Forces perpetuated the latter form of precensorship by its requirement that the manuscript of all books, textbooks and lay literature alike, had to be approved by CI&E, GHQ, SCAP before publication.

The most extreme form of governmental control over textbooks was that of the exclusive monopoly exercised by the Ministry of Education over the 173 national textbooks, their accompanying teachers' manuals and teaching materials, including wall charts and maps. These textbooks were required in all courses in *Shūshin* (morals or ethics), history, geography, national language, mathematics, science, drawing, and music, in the two levels of the elementary school and the youth school. Officially sanctioned texts were required in the boys' middle school, the girls' middle school (also called the girls' higher school), and the normal school. The complete procedure for producing these texts was the responsibility of the Bureau of Textbooks (*Kyōkasho Kyoku*), which was divided into three sections: the General Affairs Section, which was responsible for determining basic standards for the writing of the textbooks, and for distributing the copies after production; the First Section, formerly the Compilation Section, which was responsible for collecting the materials, writing stories, and editing; and the Second Section, formerly the Publication Section, which was concerned with the making of the books after the manuscript had been edited, and in addition with the special task of preparing the normal school textbooks.

The controls exerted over the textbooks by the Ministry of Education will be more apparent if a typical textbook is traced through the stages of its production to its use in the hands of a pupil. The content and organization of the various subjects at the various grade levels are established by the appropriate section of the Bureau of School Education (*Gakkō Kyōiku Kyoku*) of the Ministry of Education, and are given the force of law by being published as a *Mombuhōrei*, or Educational Law. The General Affairs Section of the Bureau of Textbooks (*Kyōkasho Kyoku*), of the Ministry of Education, maintains a continuing inspection of books and analysis of their suitability for the existing curricula. When it is determined that the current textbooks are outmoded, a set of standards and directions for changes to be made is drawn up and the First Section (*Dai-ichi Henshu Ka*) of the Bureau of Textbooks takes over the work of "compiling" the new manuscript. This process is exactly what the name implies. It consists of scissors-and-paste editing of materials published previously in acceptable textbooks, and in the editorial adaptation of current materials to the designated age level. Occasionally there will be included a lesson or two of original material written to meet the specific requirement of some superior authority—in pre-Surrender days usually a demand of the Ministries of War or Navy which had filtered down through the bureaucratic structure of the Ministry of Education, and during the Occupation usually some form of democratic propaganda from the Allied Headquarters. Even less frequently these original contributions exhibited real scholarship and literary ability. Once the manuscript is completed it is presented to a Board of Textbook Investigation (*Kyōkasho Chōsakai*) which before Surrender was composed of approximately 20 persons from outside the Ministry who were presumed to represent the professions, business, the Army, the

Navy, and the educational system. In a sweeping reform of this board begun on 20 November 1945 and completed by Imperial Ordinance No. 4 of 9 January 1946, the representation was extended to labor groups, the general public, and to a wide selection of professional, business, and educational groups, while it was denied to the defunct Army and Navy. After approval by this board, the manuscript is copy edited and turned over to the Second Section (*Dai-ni Henshu Ka*) for publication.

The Second Section maintains standing contracts with a number of private printing firms, eight at the time of Surrender though only one, the *Tōkyō Shoseki Kabushiki Kaisha* (Tokyo National Publishing Company) and its two subsidiaries, the *Nagai Kabushiki Kaisha* of Kyoto and *Chugtsu Kabushiki Kaisha* of Toyama Prefecture, were actually operating. Each of these printing firms is given an exclusive territory of several prefectures for the sale of the official textbooks. The copyright is retained by the Ministry of Education. After the textbook has been set in type, proofed, corrected, printed, and bound, sample copies are examined and approved by the Ministry of Education and the companies are given permission to run off additional printings, distribute the books to their local dealers, and sell to the students. The Ministry of Education instructs the individual school heads, or the prefectural educational offices in the case of elementary schools and other institutions under prefectural control, that the new textbook is official and shall be used in all appropriate classes, but the actual sale is conducted through commercial establishments. At the time of Surrender there were 36 wholesalers holding the official monopoly and 2,200 retailers. The name, the author or translator (if any), volume number, date of publication, date of printing, the schools which are to use the text, the courses which are to be taught from the book, the publisher, his address, and the legally fixed price must appear on the title page or at the end of every official textbook, and are reproduced in the official gazette, the *Kampō*. The Ministry receives 1%, the publishing house 82%, the wholesaler 4%, and the retailer 13% of the selling price of the textbook.

After Surrender the Occupation Forces were faced with a dilemma in regard to the future control of the content and method of instruction. Although in principle the problem applied equally to curriculum, teacher training, methodology, and teaching materials, it was in its application to the preparation and publication of textbooks that the problem was so pressing that a solution could not be delayed. The principal purpose of the Occupation was to transfer the power of government from a powerful oligarchy to the people and to make the choice of democracy an easy if not an inevitable one. Yet for reasons of military and political control the people could not be given complete freedom. In the content of instruction the Occupation Authorities wanted to encourage a democratic form—with a child-centered or community-centered curriculum. But at the same time they wanted to control the Japanese because they were fearful of local interpretation of and compliance with Occupation policy. In the continued use of extreme honorifics toward the Imperial Family, in the popular desire for continuation of *budō* or the warlike arts, and in the continued expression of certain of the superficial adjuncts of a military organization, such as the use of uniforms, marching, standing at attention while reciting, and class organization into platoons and squads, the Occupation Headquarters thought that it saw a perpetuation of the militaristic and ultranationalistic ideologies which it was determined to extirpate. In the preparation of textbooks this dilemma was simply the choice of a free textbook market or of a continuation of the traditional control through censorship and monopoly. Did the Occupation Authorities dare to trust so vital a propaganda instrument to the inexperienced and possibly insincere control of local authorities?

Two factors contributed to the difficulty of the problem. The Japanese educational authorities were under pressure from SCAP directives, the recommendations of the United States Education Mission to Japan, and the insistent demands of the Japanese teachers, students, and press to adopt democratic procedures. But the Ministry of Education was under equally great pressure to continue its traditional controls so that it might ensure compliance with these same SCAP directives, so that it might, in turn, utilize untrained teachers presumed to be incapable of self-direction, and so that it might salvage something of the traditions and vested interests of the official personnel. The Ministry could hardly be expected to set the pace in liquidating its own powers. The second of the two factors was the acknowledged inexperience of the Japanese teachers. They obviously wanted more self-direction and a majority probably would have made a sincere attempt to teach in a democratic manner, but it was considered very doubtful if they had the inner resources to do an adequate job. They were attracted by the novelty of democratic education. They welcomed personal freedom and the increased self-respect which accompanied their position of increased responsibility. Some recognized the incongruity of teaching democracy by force. But they had learned to teach by slavish attention to their teachers' manuals, and through long practice had come to lean on drill methods, official interpretation, and the official textbook to the exclusion of their own thought.

A continued censorship of the textbooks was assumed by the Japanese. It was not considered inevitable but completely normal. It is probable that until 22 October 1945 when the SCAP Educational Policy Directive was issued, the possibility of an uncontrolled and uncensored production of textbooks simply had never occurred to the authorities in the Ministry of Education. The 11 September 1945 press release and the 20 September 1945 Japanese Directive are evidence that a new censorship of the textbooks was considered one of the most vital reforms, so important that it should be undertaken before the Occupation Forces were fully organized, and presented as a *fait accompli* upon their arrival. It was not, however, a pre-ordained and inevitable policy, but one which was undertaken reluctantly and which in the opinion of some foreign observers may eventually prove to have been a costly choice. The educational officers in CI&E, GHQ, SCAP in effect inherited the censorship plan from the Japanese, who had produced a trial re-editing and expurgation of about one quarter of the official texts before the Allied Headquarters began actively to investigate them. These officers knew that censorship would introduce delay, would place upon them the responsibility of determining in each individual case whether a text was acceptable or not, and would bring charges of "book burning" and "totalitarian oppression" from the liberal press in the United States. All of these fears were later realized. But they were also fearful of publicly ordering the Japanese to stop the censorship they had already begun, of being confronted with apparent indifference to textbooks which contained antagonistic and subversive passages, and of causing the possible collapse of the educational system by bringing to a halt the accustomed practices for the preparation and distribution of textbooks vital to the reopened schools.

The latter set of fears won and the Occupation drifted into rather than positively embarked upon a plan of censorship. The Japanese had exchanged one master for another.

Once the policy of censorship had been adopted, officially dated 30 September 1945 when the staff study was begun but actually in a nebulous state until the publication of the SCAP Directive on "Suspension of Courses in Morals, Japanese History, and Geography," AG 000.8 (31 Dec 45) CIE, the difficulties of this responsibility mounted rapidly. In general they were of two types: those involving criteria of acceptability; and those involving procedures for censorship.

Admittedly the criteria of acceptability have fluctuated, and the set which obtained at the time of the visit of the United States Education Mission to Japan, although undated, is here presented. It was negative in character and limited to the standard for elimination of elements dealing with three unacceptable areas: ultranationalism, militarism, and National Shintoism (here called Religious Discrimination).

Ultra-nationalism: In order that the educational program will not be hampered in developing concepts and attitudes conducive to democratic tendencies and friendly international relations based upon principles of equal rights and individual responsibilities, that subject-matter shall be deleted from textbooks which is designed to promote:
1. The Greater East Asia Co-Prosperity Sphere doctrine or any other doctrine of expansion;
2. The idea that the Japanese are superior to other races and nationalities;
3. The concepts and attitudes which are contrary to the principles set forth in the Charter of the United Nations;
4. The idea that the Emperor should be obeyed with unquestioning loyalty;
5. The idea that the Emperor of Japan is superior to the heads of other states and that the Tenno system is sacred and immutable.

Militarism: In order that the educational program will not be hampered in developing concepts and attitudes which will contribute to a peaceful, non-aggressive government of Japan, that subject-matter shall be deleted from textbooks which is designed to promote the spirit of militarism and aggression through:
1. The glorification of War as a heroic and acceptable way of settling disputes;
2. The glory of dying for the Emperor with unswerving loyalty;

3. The idealization of war heroes by glorifying their military achievements;

4. The development of the idea that military service is the most patriotic manner of serving one's country;

5. The objects of military glorification: guns, warships, tanks, fortresses, soldiers, etc.

Religious Discrimination: In order to contribute toward achieving religious freedom for the Japanese people and the separation of religion and state, that subject-matter shall be deleted from textbooks which is designed to promote the doctrine, creed, or philosophy of any religion, for example, Shinto.

It is probably superfluous to point out that such a set of criteria inevitably became the source of mounting perplexity in interpretation. The extreme was reached when it was seriously proposed that the rather grandiloquent trade names of rice seed, taken from the honorific titles of the nation and the Imperial Family, should be banned.

The procedure for censoring and approving textbooks was arrived at by a process of trial and error. The 22 October 1945 SCAP Directive on Educational Policy in Paragraph 1, c (1) had ordered the Japanese Ministry of Education to examine all existing curricula, textbooks, teaching manuals, and instructional materials and to eliminate objectionable material of a militaristic or ultranationalistic nature. The Japanese proceeded independently to make a textual analysis of the current textbooks and on 28 November 1945 requested permission of CI&E, GHQ, SCAP to issue a Ministerial Order to the schools of Japan directing the teachers to make a physical deletion of those objectionable passages included on a list supplied by the Ministry, and to discontinue using the texts in morals, Japanese history, and geography. This latter step was recommended by the Ministry on the grounds that their scrutiny of the textbooks in these three subject fields had revealed that so large a portion would have to be eliminated, with a consequent physical and organizational mutilation of the existing texts, that it was considered impractical to continue using the expurgated copies. They would be in tatters, and the deleted sections would direct attention to the censored material rather than prevent its dissemination. The Education Division had meanwhile been conducting a parallel study and had come to the same conclusion, which was a major recommendation in a staff study then before the Supreme Commander. Rather than permit the Japanese to make this voluntary step, and incidentally make anti-climactic the SCAP Directive which was contemplated, the Ministry was denied permission to issue the order, the schools were required to continue teaching from the objectionable textbooks, and after completing its textbook survey and finishing the staff study, Occupation Headquarters issued SCAP Directive AG 000.8 (31 Dec 45) CIE suspending the courses in those subjects until suitable textbooks had been prepared. The implications of this remarkable concession to military bureaucracy and self-esteem were not lost on the Japanese.

Three sets of textbooks were contemplated in the textbook reform program of the Occupation: the expurgated copies of existing textbooks used as an emergency measure during the remainder of the school year during which the Occupation began, a set of interim textbooks consisting of cheaply printed copies containing a compilation of lessons taken from prewar textbooks which were considered innocuous by the standards above quoted, and an entirely new set of official textbooks carefully prepared by the Ministry to give positive aid to the program of democratization. The interim textbooks were planned for use in the first full school year under the Occupation, 1946–47, and about 190 million were actually printed and used. By December 1946 the Ministry of Education had collected and pulped 1,005,480 kan (1 kan = 8.27 lbs.) of the banned books and realized a credit of 1,601,781.74 yen from their sale. This was the sole, and somewhat feeble, reply to world charges of "book burning." The first of the entirely new textbooks were expected to be ready for the start of the second full academic year under the Occupation in April 1947 and a considerable number, though not all, did in fact appear at that time.

Each of these three types of censorship required a complicated machinery. After eliminating all existing Japanese history, geography and morals textbooks, Occupation Headquarters was content to let the Ministry of Education determine the inappropriate portions of the remaining textbooks. But in the preparation of the interim textbooks, and later the new textbooks, a system roughly analogous to the Japanese procedure for "sanctioning" a privately prepared textbook was set up in SCAP Headquarters. The Ministry of Education submitted to CI&E, GHQ, SCAP a Japanese text of the proposed manuscript together with an English summary. The Education Division of CI&E then indicated on the summary sheet those portions which it wished translated into English for censorship. To expedite the procedure the Ministry of Education was permitted to set in type and pull proofs of the complete textbook while the English text of the controversial portions was being studied. After the corrections directed by the Education Division had been made in the proof, a revised Japanese copy and a full English translation were again submitted to the Education Division and upon approval the textbook was printed and distributed.

A major difficulty in this procedure is immediately apparent. The Caucasian Occupation officials, some of whom had long prior residence in Japan and presumably an able command of the written language, were not able to censor critically the Japanese text. Even Allied nationals of Japanese ancestry were unable to sense the spirit or the psychological context of many portions of the Japanese manuscripts with sufficient accuracy to censor the nuances and implications where the most effective form of propaganda is usually found. Censorship of the English translation was at best a rather futile gesture. No portion which was so bald as to be detectable in the English translation would have appeared in the manuscript except through the sheer stupidity of one of the Japanese compilers. Recognizing the emptiness of the censorship of the translated manuscript and yet unable to secure adequate Allied personnel able to censor directly the Japanese text, the Education Division finally adopted a somewhat desperate expedient. It had civilian Japanese nationals censor the manuscripts of their own government. Stripped of the official legerdemain of the Occupation Headquarters' pretense at censorship, the censorship of textbooks in Japan from the beginning of the Occupation was done by the Ministry of Education itself and by the independent scrutiny of a handful of Japanese nationals, some employed by SCAP but the larger number serving as volunteer assistants. This latter group was composed mainly of advanced students of pedagogy at Tokyo Imperial University.

One of the most serious mistakes which Occupation Officials at times made was that of allowing their own position as political rulers to betray them into an underestimation of the sagacity of the docile and apparently naïve Japanese with whom they worked.

The Japanese were experienced bureaucrats and were quite appreciative of the mistakes the Occupation bureaucracy made. One highly placed Japanese official, whose name shall be withheld, in commenting on the Occupation's censorship of textbooks remarked that the reform had accomplished three notable ends: it had perpetuated and strengthened the Ministry's strangle hold on all textbooks, it had proven that any small minority in temporary power could rewrite the textbooks of the nation with any content it desired in a year's time, and it had blinded the people to the vital truth that it was defeat and not scissors which proved the old textbooks bad.

An Appraisal and a Solution

In an appraisal of the recent past it is readily apparent that the greatest mistake made was that of confusing punitive action with implementation of the democratic philosophy. Three questions have to be asked. Has punitive action been necessary? Has it been effective? And has it proven desirable?

There can be no question that some punitive action has been necessary both in control of personnel and in control of subject matter. It may be argued that the purge of a dissident teacher is justified on the principle of removing a rotten apple from the barrel. And some exclusion of the old traditional nationalistic propaganda seems clearly indicated. But both procedures resolve into problems of degree, and in the solution of this problem the answer is not so clear. Not all teachers were bad and not all content or teaching method was bad. Where to draw the line, who is to draw the line, and how that line is to be drawn become the vital issues.

The second question, that of whether the punitive action has proven effective, can probably never be accurately answered. It is futile to attempt to measure the detailed results. The number of persons purged, the number of schools closed and courses abandoned, the number of pages snipped from books are meaningless. Even the evidence of changed public opinion is too transitory and too easily manipulated to be trustworthy as an index. It is only the end result which gives evidence of success or failure. Over a period of 75 years the old system brought Japan to one of the most disastrous military defeats in history. If 75 years of trial of the evolving system brings Japan to some measure of eminence as a peaceful nation of the world, it will mark a successful reform.

The final question is the most important, for it provides a guide to the future independent direction of the schools by the Japanese themselves. Has punitive action proven desirable? The answer must be twofold. If the punitive action is an imposed control by a police state its desirability can be categorically denied. But if it is a self-censorship, an implementation of a self-imposed code of educational ethics, then it is both necessary and desirable.

The experience of the Occupation taught thoughtful Japanese a number of pregnant lessons. It demonstrated, for example, that punitive action could easily prove to be an unsupportable cure. In the Purge, even when considered necessary, where the procedure adopted achieved the desired results of removing tainted personnel, and where the prohibitions enunciated could be enforced, the very machinery made necessary by this policy could prove to be a greater danger than the original malady. Power would be centralized in the hands of a minority. The indispensable support of an investigation and enforcement body would make a secret or thought police almost an inevitability. The teachers and students would be subjected to the constant threat of denunciation and purge. The teachers would be educated to measure their success not in terms of professional growth but in their resistance to or evasion of police investigation and removal. The Purge, even when motivated by the most lofty ideals, degenerated into persecution and became the antithesis of democracy. In control of methodology it was clearly demonstrated that teachers could be ordered to do something but that it was futile to order them to think something. Compliance with an order to act could be enforced but a change in thought could come only from within. Censorship by its very nature was incompatible with freedom. It killed individual initiative and creation. It trained blind submission or hopeless acquiescence to central authority. It brought the stigma of "book burning" and world disapproval of thought control. In every field of control punitive action was demonstrated to be a technique of totalitarian rather than democratic government.

And the alternatives to punitive action, self-direction and professional growth, appeared terrifyingly inadequate. Laissez faire seemed only to bring bewilderment and chaos. People who had not experienced liberty were apparently incapable of assuming all its responsibilities at once. And the flexible, self-imposed yet potent control familiar in American professional groups and non-governmental associations of schools seemed the distant objective of the impractical dreamer. True implementation of the philosophy of democracy in education could only come through experience. The role of the Occupation Authorities and later of the independent Japanese Government, if they were to do more than perpetuate the evil practices of pre-Surrender Japan while momentarily diverting them to a desirable use, would have to be that of establishing the environment in which democracy could grow. Then authoritarian restraints would have to be relinquished and real liberty of action be given the teachers and the public whatever the cost of their mistakes while learning.

Perhaps no more telling appraisal of the problem of implementation could be presented than that of an editorial entitled "Why Instead of How," which appeared in the 26 October 1945 issue of the *Nippon Times*. The Japanese recognize this problem. A Japanese, within a few weeks of the Surrender, wrote this editorial. It is quoted in part:

. . . the chief fault of Japanese education in the past has been not the fact that it emphasized nationalism or militarism but the fact that, whatever it taught, it sought to indoctrinate as something authoritative which was not to be questioned. Under such a method, the students could never develop the ability to think for themselves. If now the mere outward forms of democracy should be forced upon the students in the same way, there would be a change in the content of education, to be sure, but there would be no assurance that the students would not be susceptible at some later time to still another change in the direction of indoctrination. It is not indoctrination which is needed, not even indoctrination in democracy, but the development of the ability of each student to think for himself. Only such an education is consistent with the spirit of democracy, and only such an education will be able to ensure the permanent retention of democracy by the Japanese. For only the development of the ability to think for themselves will make it possible for the Japanese to acquire as their own spontaneous conviction the appreciation of the superiority of the democratic philosophy.

The only solution which is consistent with the prior decisions outlined in this volume—with a sincere desire to reform and to

survive culturally, with a new and democratic educational philosophy, with a decentralization of educational controls, and with
a fundamental simplification of the writing system to ensure accessibility of vital knowledge—seems vaguely sterile and anti-
climactic. It is the solution of so arranging the environment of the
educational system that the people of Japan are forced to seek their
own answer to the problems. It is the solution of throwing the
people on their own resources in a situation which precludes indifference and inaction. It is the solution of making democratic
self-direction necessary and inevitable. The Japanese have available the examples of the best practices devised in those countries
of the world which have passed these initial stages of democratization. They may look and they may choose. It is the power of
choice which is essential and which till now has been denied. Any
other solution but this would be inconsistent and meaningless.

For the Allied Powers this is the solution of withdrawing the
stultifying controls over the details of education which they
established early in the Occupation, and of demonstrating openly
their real belief in the essential strengths of the democratic process
which they have avowed. The ultimate goals and the broad limits
of educational philosophy have been proposed. Now the Allies
must have faith that the superiority of the system they advocate
will make it attractive to the Japanese people. Protective pa-
ternalism and continued authoritarian control can only doom the
experiment to certain failure. Every teacher who is dismissed by
directives, every textbook which is censored, every subject which
is banned in the future can only be a public admission by the
Allied Powers of their failure to establish a democratic system and
their lack of faith in the power of democracy to compete and
survive.

For the Japanese Authorities this is the solution of abandoning
the traditional centralized and restrictive controls over every
phase of education, and of demonstrating openly their sincere
conversion to the principles of democratic control which they
have accepted under duress during the Occupation. The Japanese
have proclaimed that they accepted as fundamental human rights
the freedom to learn and the freedom to teach, the freedom to
speak and the freedom to write. If they are sincere, and without
sincerity the growth of democracy in Japan has already been
defeated, let their leaders demonstrate it by relaxing the controls

which prohibit these freedoms. Let the leaders grant these rights or let the people abandon and repudiate their leaders. Let them truly remove the barriers of discrimination on the grounds of race, sex, creed, nationality, political conviction, social position, and financial standing. Let them match the legal reforms with positive social reforms which give, for example, equal opportunities for employment to women, without which co-education is meaningless. Let these leaders grant to the teachers of the nation the right—and lend to them encouragement to use this right—to create their own teaching methods, to develop through their own joint efforts the curricula, to set their own standards for teacher preparation and certification, and to conduct their own investigation and dismissal of the unfit. Let these leaders encourage a free textbook market and demonstrate to the people their belief that competition and opportunity will produce better materials and better methods than any imposed stereotype dictated *ex cathedra* by a Ministry.

And for the Japanese people this is the solution of accepting the responsibilities of their own importance as individuals, as parents, and as citizens. Primary in importance must be their desire to direct the administration of their school system and to implement their educational policies. They must organize themselves and they must inform themselves. They must demand that the teachers of their children are the type of people they really desire and that the things which are taught their children are the things which they approve. They must rebel against bad textbooks and demonstrate their approval of good by pressure to adopt them. They must anticipate an inevitable percentage of errors in their self-direction and not become disheartened when occasional ludicrous or distressing mistakes are made. Just as there is a thin segment of the population whose remarkable gifts set them apart as leaders to guide and inspire the great mass of people, so there will be in any society another thin segment which is fanatic, stupid, or malicious. The Japanese people must have continuing faith that over any extended period of time the general mass of the people can know and will select what is best for themselves. This is the indispensable tenet in the democratic philosophy.

INDEX